INTRODUCTION
TO CARIBBEAN
POLITICS

INTRODUCTION TO CARIBBEAN POLITICS

By Cynthia Barrow-Giles

Ian Randle Publishers
Kingston

First published in Jamaica, 2002 by
Ian Randle Publishers
11 Cunningham Avenue
Box 686
Kingston 6
Website: www.ianrandlepublishers.com

ISBN 976-637-049-4 paperback

A catalogue record of this book is available from the National Library of Jamaica.

Contents

Chapter 1

Imperialism: Colonialism, Neo-colonialism and Recolonisation

Introduction 1
Sovereignty 2
Imperialism 2
Colonialism 2
Race/racism and political systems in the region up to the mid-twentieth century 3
Neo-colonialism 4
The politics of structural adjustment: the International Monetary
    Fund and structural adjustment in the region 5
The International Monetary Fund, Liberalisation and Jamaica 7
Structural adjustment: the case of Barbados 7
Structural adjustment and the trade union movement 8
The new international economic and political order: contextualising the present order 8
The North American Free Trade Agreement 9
Likely effects of the North American Free Trade Agreement on Caribbean countries 10
Globalisation and cultural imperialism 10
GATT, the WTO and the Multilateral Agreement on Investment: Recolonisation? 11
Key words and phrases 13
Questions to consider 14
Activities 14
Readings 14
Suggestions for further reading 72

Chapter 2

Struggles of the Working Class People

Introduction 74
Background to the 1930s political crisis 75
General labour conditions in the British West Indies 75
Other dynamics affecting labour conditions in the British West Indies 76
The Moyne Commission Report 78
Summary of recommendations from the Moyne Commission Report 78
A brief assessment of the Moyne Commission Report 79
The colonial and imperial design for the nationalist movement 80
Key words and phrases 81
Questions to consider 81
Activities 82
Readings 82
Suggestions for further reading 122

Chapter 3
The Politics of Constitutional Decolonisation and the Westminster Model

Introduction 123
Democracy 124
Main assumptions of liberal democracy 125
Participation or imposition? 126
Constitutional decolonisation in the Commonwealth Caribbean 127
The Westminster model in the region 127
Modifications or transformation? 128
Parliamentary vs presidential systems of government 132
Key words and phrases 136
Questions to consider. 136
Activities 136
Readings 136
Suggestions for further reading 160

Chapter 4
Party Systems and Electoral Politics in the Region

Introduction 162
What is a political party? 163
Political parties in the Commonwealth Caribbean 163
Electoral politics in the Commonwealth Caribbean 165
Summary. 169
Key words and phrases 169
Questions to consider. 169
Activities 170
Readings 170
Suggestions for further reading 192

Chapter 5
Trade unionism in the Commonwealth Caribbean

Introduction 194
Origin and development of trade unions. 194
Global changes, international restructuring and Caribbean trade unions. 195
The Caribbean state and labour 196
Key words and phrases 197
Questions to consider. 197
Activities 197
Readings 197
Suggestions for further reading 201

Chapter 6
The Politics of Change

Introduction: background to the 1960s and 1970s. 202
Theory of the non-capitalist path to development 203
Alternative development strategies in the region. 203
Guyana: cooperative socialism. 204

Jamaica: democratic socialism 1974-80 204
Is socialism a viable option for the region? 208
Key words and phrases 209
Questions to consider. 209
Activities 209
Readings 209
Suggestions for further reading 222

Chapter 7
Regional Integration: Economic and Political Aspects

Introduction 223
Definitions 224
Imperatives of regional integration 224
Early beginnings: the West Indian Federation 224
Distinctive characteristics of a federal system of government 225
CARICOM and the Treaty of Chaguaramas, 1973. 226
The Organisation of Eastern Caribbean States 227
The Grand Anse Declaration of 1989 228
The Manning Initiative of 1993 228
The CARICOM Single Market and Economy 229
Association of Caribbean States 230
The Barbados-OECS Initiative. 231
Regional security and the regional security system 232
Key words and phrases 233
Questions to Consider 233
Activities. 233
Readings 233
Suggestions for Further Reading. 268

Appendices 270
Bibliography 288

Foreword

This reader, conceptualised and compiled by Cynthia Barrow-Giles of the Department of Government at the University of the West Indies, Cave Hill Campus, provides students of Caribbean politics and those with a general interest in West Indian political experiences with an exposure to analyses on Caribbean political development.

Its publication follows a tradition started as far back as the late 1960s in the Department of Government at the University of the West Indies, Mona Campus, by Archie Singham, Trevor Munroe, Rupert Lewis and facilitated by Professor G.E.M. Mills. At the Mona Campus the early readers were put together to facilitate access to important materials by students of government. The objective is the same today.

This reader covers the politics of the Caribbean from slavery to the labour revolts and from the labour revolts to structural adjustment and globalisation. It reflects readings used in courses in government and politics in the West Indies and the introduction to Caribbean politics over the years. Now, useful selections of these have been compiled for easy access by students and researchers who need to cover or address the major themes of Caribbean political development.

These range from Benn's overarching coverage of ideologies and political development, to Arthur and Gordon Lewis and my own analysis of the birth of the modern West Indies; from Munroe and Emmannuel's elaboration on the mechanics of the politics of development, to Wickham and Boxill on the strategic concerns of integration; from political unification and the strictures of our political economy as painted by Thomas and Payne, to the contemporary phenomena which create an impact on our societies through the rise of globalisation and neo-liberalism addressed by Watson and McAfee. These scholars are among the many, representing generations, spanning the twentieth century.

I am confident that this publication represents another much needed successful collection of important Caribbean political writings, now made more readily available to enhance the political education of large numbers of Caribbean persons in the future.

George A.V. Belle
UWI, Cave Hill Campus

Acknowledgements

I owe a debt of gratitude to a number of people for their support at different stages in the development of this book, which initially derived its shape from my teaching the first year course Introduction to Caribbean Politics at the Cave Hill Campus at the University of the West Indies. The idea was to make the task of locating and procuring texts easier for students of Caribbean politics.

I wish to thank my colleagues at the Department of Government, Sociology and Social Work for their support in completing this project. Special thanks must also be given to Mr Ian Randle, Professor Wayne Hunte and Dr Alvin Thompson. Mr Randle was extremely receptive when approached in May 2000 about the possibility of a reader, specially designed for the student of Caribbean politics. Professor Wayne Hunte, Dean of Graduate Studies and Development at the Cave Hill Campus, quickly responded to my application for a small monetary donation to assist in the final tidying up of the manuscript. To Professor Thompson of the Department of History, Cave Hill Campus, I owe special gratitude. He was my mentor while I was a student and has continued to offer critical and invaluable advice in my tenure here at the Cave Hill campus.

Special thanks must also be extended to Cyrilene Walcott and Michelle Grandison, who provided useful administrative support; and Natalie Walthrust and Joan Cuffie.

Finally, special appreciation is extended to my husband Stephen Giles, who suffered terrible neglect and never complained during the preparation and completion of the manuscript.

From the Publisher

The Author and the Publisher are grateful to the authors and original publishers for permission to reproduce their work in this volume. Listed below are the original publication details.

Imperialism, Colonialism and Reconciliation

Denis Benn, "Crown Colony Government and Imperial Trusteeship. The Political Theory of Crown Colony Rule," in *Ideology and Political Development: The Growth and Development of Political Ideas in the Caribbean, 1774-1983* (Institute of Social and Economic Studies, UWI: Mona, 1987) pp. 31-56.

Hilbourne A. Watson, "Global Restructuring and the Prospects for Caribbean Competitiveness: With a Case Study from Jamaica," in *The Caribbean in the Global Economy* (Ian Randle Publishers: Kingston, 1994) pp. 67-90.

Kathy McAfee, "The IMF/World Bank Prescription," in *Storm Signals: Structural Adjustment and Development Alternatives in the Caribbean* (Zed Books: London, 1991) pp. 69-81.

McHale Andrew, "The New International Economic Environment: The WTO and Implications for the OECS," *Journal of Eastern Caribbean Studies* Vol. 24, no. 2 (1999) pp. 69-95.

Ankie Hoogvelt, "Globalisation," in *Globalisation and the Postcolonial World: The New Political Economy of Development* (Macmillan Press Ltd.: London, 1997) pp. 114-262.

Struggles of the Working Class People

George A.V. Belle, "The Struggle for Political Democracy: The 1937 Riots," in *Emancipation III: A Series of Lectures to Commemorate the 150th Anniversary of Emancipation,* edited by Woodville Marshall (Department of History, UWI, Cave Hill: Bridgetown, 1988) pp. 56-91.

George A.. Belle, "After 1937: The Politics of Wynter Crawford: 'Institutionalising' Labour and the Demise of Planter Government." Unpublished Masters Thesis.

W. Arthur Lewis, "Social Conditions," in *Labour in the West Indies: The Birth of a Workers' Movement* (New Beacon Books: London, 1977) pp. 15-43.

The Politics of Constitutional Decolonisation and the Westminster Model

Harold A. Lutchman, "The Westminster System in the Commonwealth Caribbean: Some Issues and Problems," *Transition* Issue 24 (Feb. 1995) pp. 1-26.

Arend Lijphart, "The Westminster Model of Democracy: Democratic Ideals and Realities," in *Democracies* (Yale University Press: Newhaven, 1984) pp. 1-20.

Douglas V. Verney, "Parliamentary Government and Presidential Government," in *Oxford Readings in Politics and Government. Parliamentary Versus Presidential Government* (Oxford University Press: place, date) pp.31-47.

Party Systems and Electoral Politics in the Region

Arend Lijphart, "Electoral Systems: Majority and Plurality Methods vs. Proportional Representation," in *Democracies: Patterns of Majoritarian and Consensus Government in Twenty-One Countries* (Yale University Press: New Haven, 1984) pp. 150-168.

Patrick A. Emmanuel, "The Electoral System," in *Governance and Democracy in the Commonwealth Caribbean: An Introduction* (Institute of Social and Economic Research, UWI, Cave Hill: Bridgetown, 1993) pp. 37- 57.

Patrick A.M. Emmanuel, " Parties and Party Systems," in *Elections and Party Systems in the Commonwealth Caribbean, 1944-1991* (Caribbean Development Research Services: St. Michael, 1992) pp. 77-94.

Trade Unionism in the Commonwealth Caribbean: Past and Present

Lawrence Nurse, *Trade-Union Stewardship and Workers' Interest Representation in a Changing Environment: A Brief Comment,* presented to the Fifty-sixth Annual Delegates' Conference of the Barbados Workers' Union in Barbados, August 1997.

The Politics of Change

Clive Y. Thomas, "Cooperative Socialism: Guyana," in *The Poor and the Powerless: Economic Policy and Change in the Caribbean* (Latin America Bureau: London, 1988) pp. 251-265.

Gordon K. Lewis, "1979-1983: The Revolutionary Achievement," in *Grenada: The Jewel Despoiled* (The Johns Hopkins University Press: Baltimore, 1987) pp. 25-34, 211-212.

Regional Integration: Economic and Political Aspects

Terrence Farrell and DeLisle Worrell, eds., "Monetary Union: A Guide for the Perplexed," in *Caribbean Monetary Integration* (Caribbean Information Systems and Services: Port of Spain, 1994) pp. 12-25.

Peter W. Wickham, "Factors in the Integration and Disintegration of the Caribbean," in *Issues in the Government and Politics of the West Indies,* edited by John Gaffar LaGuerre (School of Continuing Studies, UWI: St. Augustine, 1997) pp.39-74.

Ian Boxill, "The Evolution of Regionalism in the Caribbean," in *Ideology and Caribbean Integration* (The Consortium Graduate School of Social Sciences: Mona, 1993) pp. 31-48.

Earl Huntley, "Background Considerations," in *The Union of East Caribbean States: Thoughts on the Forum* (Ministry of Foreign Affairs and International Trade: Castries, St. Lucia).

one

Imperialism: Colonialism, Neo-colonialism and Recolonisation

Introduction

This chapter is concerned with the impact of imperialism on the sovereignty of Commonwealth Caribbean states and examines the infringement of Commonwealth Caribbean sovereignty by international actors, whether by governments, transnational and multinational corporations (MNCs), international financial institutions such as the International Monetary Fund (IMF) or international treaty and trading agreements. It is becoming even more pressing to re-emphasise infringements such as the intellectual New Right of the 1980s and the 1990s, which sought to thrust upon Caribbean people a so-called value-free ideology of global neo-liberalism. It seems capital and capitalism have resorted to any means necessary to prevent and subvert any nationalist attempt to block the extraction of surplus value by international capital.

Given the interdependence that increasingly characterises global politico-economic relations, it was commonplace in the 1990s to question the idea of the nation-state and by extension the notion of self-determination. However, despite the defeat of nationalism and national liberation struggles, issues of national self-determination are critical. The degree of external participation by overseas interest in the region's national decision-making processes is a cause of concern, as it will no doubt compromise the independence of Caribbean nation-states. In an era of rapidly changing global economic and political relations, such independence will be further compromised as the issue of recolonisation rears its ugly head. Nevertheless, it is critical that examinations of the mechanics of imperialism are continued and that that exposure restricts the threat to the region's independence and indeed, developmental possibilities in general.

The chapter will therefore focus on five areas: sovereignty, imperialism, colonialism, neo-colonialism and the many faces of recolonisation, all in the context of international economic and political developments.

Sovereignty

There are two dimensions to sovereignty:

(a)   The formal and legal aspect of sovereignty, which, simply defined, means the freedom of the state from outside interference, within the limits set by the international community of states.

(b)   The political aspect of sovereignty, which refers to the ability of states to take advantage of their formal independence through economic, technical, psychological, sociocultural and military means.

It is particularly the latter aspect of sovereignty that is the primary concern of this chapter.

Imperialism

Traditional discourse on imperialism has suggested various interpretations and definitions:

(a)   Classical Marxism referred to imperialism as a stage of capitalism leading to political, economic and military rivalry and conflict between the advanced capitalists.

(b)   A relationship of dependency not necessarily involving the forceful annexation of territory.

(c)   The economic exploitation of weaker nations.

(d)   Neo-colonialism and recolonisation, that is, sovereignty over formerly independent nations.

V.I. Lenin has provided quite a comprehensive analysis of imperialism, which he broadly identified as characterised by five basic features:

(i)   concentration of production and capital to create a monopoly that plays a critical role in economic life

(ii)   merging of bank capital with 'industrial capital' to form finance capital and the creation of a financial oligarchy

(iii) export of capital as distinct from the export of commodities

(iv) formation of international monopolist-capitalist combines (conglomerates) that share the world among themselves

(v)   the territorial division of the world among the biggest capitalist powers[1]

While Lenin's theory has been subjected to much criticism, his identification of the growth of conglomerates and the territorial division of the world, even if not in the old colonial sense is, however, relevant, as foreign penetration intensified with the programme of *Industrialisation by Invitation*. So much so that on the eve of independence in some Caribbean states, significant sections of the local economy were controlled by foreign multinationals in several areas such as, agriculture, banking, petroleum, bauxite, transportation, communication, trade, international financial institutions and the insurance industry.[2]

What is important about the extensive role of MNCs in the region, are the ways in which they have affected the sovereignty of Commonwealth Caribbean states by way of the influence they have exerted on taxation, monetary and economic policies. Gordon Lewis has concluded that this development, which began in the pre-independence period has resulted in a situation where:

> . . . the possession of political sovereignty (which Jamaica has, while Puerto Rico does not) is, in fact, of negligible value, since it is rendered largely nugatory by the surrender of large slices of economic sovereignty to outside forces both financial and political.[3]

Colonialism

Colonialism can be defined as the conquest and settlement of a weak or backward country for the purpose of settlement by a stronger or advanced alien nation.[4]

Kwamé Nkrumah defines colonialism as:

> The policy by which the 'mother country' the colonial power, binds her colonies to herself by political ties with the primary object of promoting her own economic advantages.[5]

The importance of understanding colonialism is evidenced by the fact that it was the prime determinant of societal relations in the British West Indies and has shaped the political economy of the region. British colonialism was characterised, among other things, by dependency and exploitation; racism; plantation economies; very rigid social structures and weak social classes.

Colonial domination in the region resulted in British business interest securing raw materials and was achieved through the policy of mercantilism, enforced by a series of Navigation Acts. Mercantilist policies had the effect of:

(i) preventing colonial peoples from establishing manufacturing industries and in so doing made them non-manufacturing dependencies

(ii) keeping colonial peoples technologically backward

(iii) maintaining colonial peoples as producers of primary raw products

(iv) keeping colonial peoples bound to the mother country through the policy of trade exclusivism

(v) limiting horizontal linkages between the colonies except through the British government

The policy of mercantilism, therefore, was not only designed to expropriate the surpluses from the region to help in the development of Britain, but it also had the effect of distorting and retarding the development of the economies of the region.

Race/Racism and political systems in the region up to the mid 20th century

Race refers to the biological attribute of people, defined by such characteristics as skin colour, hair texture etc. Racism uses race, the physical features of a person or a group of people, as a basis for the derogatory judgement of the non-physical attributes of a person. Racism is an ideology that promotes the idea that one race is superior to another.[6] In an effort to put the enslavement of a people in the context of racism, Walter Rodney writes:

> ...no people can enslave another for centuries without coming out with a notion of superiority, and when... colour and other physical traits of those peoples were quite different it was inevitable that the prejudice should take a racial form.[7]

Rodney goes on to argue that, whereas African enslavement by Europeans was motivated by economic concerns, Europeans found it necessary to rationalise their enslavement in racist terms. In his view:

> Oppression follows logically from exploitation, so as to guarantee the latter ... Oppression of African people on purely racial grounds accompanied, strengthened and became indistinguishable from oppression for economic reasons.[8]

Racism in the Caribbean permeated every aspect of social, economic and political relations, and was institutionalised by the political systems in the region.

The two dominant political systems within the Caribbean from the seventeenth and twentieth centuries were the Old Representatives System (ORS) and Crown Colony Government (CCG). Much of the debate, in the post-1865 period, on the early political systems in the region focused on the change over from the ORS to the CCG. This debate emphasises:

(i). The limited democracy that characterised the ORS when compared to a CCG that was more authoritarian and anti-democratisation.

(ii). The changing needs of Caribbean societies in the post-1838 period.

(iii). The role/impact of the Morant Bay Rebellion of 1865 in Jamaica.

Two major positions in the debate on the imposition of the CCG in the region emerged. On the one hand, it was felt that the change over was a humanitarian development and that it provided impartiality to a biased government; on the other hand, it was felt that the change was racially motivated and that the CCG reflected the institutionalised racism of the region.

Roy Augier conforms to the latter view. He contends that, although the British government argued that the CCG would serve to tidy up the public service and administration; look after the interests of blacks and provide impartial government, this new colonial

FIGURE 1: THE HIERARCHY OF THE EARLY WEST INDIAN GOVERNMENTS (BWI)

Model 1 Old Representative System (ORS)

CROWN – British Monarchy
(Colonial Office – Secretary of State for Colonial Affairs)
↓
COLONIAL GOVERNORS
↓
NOMINATED COUNCIL
↓
Bicameral Legislature
HOUSE OF ASSEMBLY

Model 2 Crown Colony Government (CCG)

CROWN – British Monarchy
(Colonial Office – Secretary of State for Colonial Affairs)
↓
COLONIAL GOVERNORS

↓
LEGISLATIVE COUNCILS (nominated)

government was less than concerned with instigating equality and fairness. As evidence, he cites the practice of the colonial government in appointing members of the plantocracy and the merchant class to the legislative council. This, he felt, compromised the ability of the government to look after the interest of blacks and to provide impartial government. This practice '... reinforced the dominance of the power of wealth and frustrated the thrust of the power of numbers.'[9]

James Millet endorses this view by asserting that, under the ORS, the numerically superior black population posed a political danger for the white economic ruling class and it was this political danger which gave way to the CCG. In his view, the CCG was ' ... in essence a racial adjustment to the ever present menace of colour in government.'[10]

As Millet points out, had the concern of the British government been to correct a partial and unjust government, then the logical step should have been to completely democratise the political system by widening the franchise to allow for participation by non-whites. Millet concludes that the imposition of CCG and the surrendering of representative institutions after 1865 was, ' ... quite clearly motivated by a desperation to keep the machinery of political control out of the hands of the rising black and coloured people.'[11]

Neo-colonialism

In the post-independence period, colonialism gave way to neo-colonialism. Neo-colonial theory refers to that body of thought which views the political independence of former colonies as a façade, behind which lurks the former mother countries, other imperialist nations and powerful Western financial and economic interests. To many third-world scholars the achievement of constitutional independence and sovereignty did not result in the freedom of the newly independent state, as the termination of colonial status did not end economic colonialism.

At the core of neo-colonial writings is the assertion that traditional discourse on developing countries made little distinction between political and economic sovereignty and as such, the failure to achieve economic independence impacts negatively on political freedom. Berman argues that:

> ... Independence for these former colonies has meant trading the direct political control of colonialism for the indirect economic, political and cultural controls of neo-colonialism.[12]

Attesting to the largely symbolic nature of independence for postcolonial states, Nkrumah argues that:

> The essence of neo-colonialism is that the state which is subject to it is, in . . . theory, independent and has all the outward trappings of international sovereignty. In reality its economic system and thus its political policy is directed from outside.[13]

He states further that, ' . . . for those who practice it, it means power without responsibility and for those who suffer from it, it means exploitation without redress'.[14]

Nkrumah suggests that neo-colonialism manifests itself in five main areas, namely the political, economic, ideological, military and cultural sectors. While the method, form and processes may vary, neo-colonialism is normally associated with the following: invasion of territory; economic or monetary control; high rates of interest; control of the world market by international capital; control of the prices of commodities; multilateral aid; trade union activity; control of shipping; military occupation; control of news and print media; religious and cultural penetration and control of terms of trade.

Largely influenced by modernisation theory, many third-world leaders sought to transform their largely backward agricultural economies to industrialised ones. For these development purposes the state had two options; it could either source foreign investment to help in the development of the economies, or undertake such developmental work itself, despite the reluctance of domestic merchant capital to undertake such activity.

Where the state opted to seek foreign investment for developmental purposes, capital continued to seep from the economy in the form of repatriated profits, wages, royalties, services interest on loans and debt repayment, which often outweighed investments in the economy. Moreover developmental aid has given foreign investors a lever to intervene in the policy-making decision of postcolonial societies, which have both domestic and international implications. Gordon Lewis contends that:

> Theoretically, independence confers sovereignty upon the new nation. But economic development of the Puerto Rican type precludes the use of sovereign police power in implementing any serious programme of social radical change, since nothing must be done, as the local planners see it, to disturb the 'confidence' of the foreign investor in the local financial 'climate'.[15]

Concrete illustrations of such strategic and diplomatic advantages in the Caribbean can be seen in the support for Japan at the Whaling Commission in return for investment in the fisheries industry in some Eastern Caribbean countries and the exclusion of Grenada and Cuba from benefiting in the Caribbean Basin Initiative (CBI) of 1981. Nkrumah describes the situation as one in which those who provide aid insist on:

> The inclusion of commerce and navigation treaties; agreements for economic co-operation; the right to meddle in internal finances, including currency and foreign exchange, to lower trade barriers in favour of the donor country's goods and capital; to protect the interests of private investments; determination of how funds are to be used; forcing the recipient to set up counterpart funds; to supply raw materials to the donor; and use of such funds – a majority of it in fact – to buy goods from the donor nation. The conditions apply to industry, commerce, agriculture, shipping and insurance, apart from others which are political and military.[16]

Recently, Commonwealth Caribbean countries signed Ship-Rider Agreements with the United States, seen by some as an infringement on their sovereignty.[17] In pursuit of its unilateral and joint countermeasures to drug trafficking, the United States government often pursues suspects into the territorial waters of Caribbean countries, arresting suspects sometimes without the formal notification of 'sovereign' Caribbean governments. Attempts to formalise these operations of the United States government in the region in the late 1990s was a source of much controversy. Barbados and Jamaica felt that in pursuit of suspected vessels, the United States should not violate the territorial air and sea space of Caribbean countries.

Countries defined as neo-colonial states, therefore, possess economies in which the global terms of trade operate to their disadvantage and to the advantage of industrial nations. The asymmetrical global economic relations result in the favouring of the export products of advanced industrialised countries at the expense of primary exports of developing countries. Nkrumah argues that:

> . . . On the economic front, a strong factor favouring Western monopolies and acting against the developing world is international capital's control of the world market, as well as of the prices of commodities bought and sold there.[18]

Such structural imbalance of the world market leads to foreign exchange crises. Billions of dollars continue to be extracted from poor countries for the benefit of rich countries. This leads to a reinforcement of the dependency of the neo-colonial state on loans and investment funds from developed countries and foreign firms. Aid donors can withdraw or withhold aid from the borrowing nation if these governments are reluctant, or fail to adopt the policies demanded by the donor. Often, foreign exchange crises are resolved by resorting to the loans from multilateral agencies such as the IMF and the World Bank (WB). Unfortunately, negotiated loan packages usually carry with them conditionalities which have severe economic, political and social consequences.

Other forms of neo-colonial penetration occur by way of military bases, foreign advisors, media propaganda, evangelism and CIA subversion. Very often, postcolonial states depend on former colonial and other imperialist nations for arms, training and military advisors. In the Commonwealth Caribbean there is a strong reliance on the United States for training of the special service units within the police force and for funds and other forms of assistance to the regional security system.

It is this extensive and persistent control which led Franz Fanon to view colonialism as insidious, extending beyond the independence period. According to Fanon:

> . . .Violence alone, violence committed by the people, violence organised and educated by its leaders, makes it possible for the masses to understand social truths and gives the key to them. Without that struggle, without that knowledge of the practice of action, there's nothing but a fancy-dress parade and the blare of trumpets. There's nothing save a minimum of re-adaptation, a few reforms at the top, a flag waving: and down there at the bottom an undivided mass, still living in the middle ages, endlessly marking time.[19]

The politics of structural adjustment: the IMF and structural adjustment in the region

The IMF was created for the purpose of providing loans to its member states which were facing payment deficits and it is worthwhile noting that its programmes have their ideological roots in western economic and political philosophy, which underscore the importance of market-based developments over state control and state intervention. The IMF and its twin sister the WB are considered to be two of the most powerful supra-national governments in the world. This is facilitated by the cross conditionality of the two institutions. Cross conditionality refers to a situation where a borrowing country is forced to accept the conditions of one institution to qualify for assistance from the other. Creditors often require, even when financial assistance from the IMF and the WB is not required or forthcoming, their 'seal of approval' before any resources are provided.

Attesting to the power of the IMF, Cheryl Payer states that,

> . . .All of the major sources of credit in the developed capitalist world, whether private lenders, governments, or multilateral institutions such as the World Bank group, will refuse to lend to a country which persists in defying IMF advice.... [20]

She goes on to add that:

> . . .Since its founding at the end of the second World War, the IMF has been the chosen instrument for imposing imperialist financial discipline upon poor countries under a facade of multi-lateralism and technical competence. In this area, the status of a country's relationship with the IMF is the most accurate guide to the fate of its aspirations to autonomous development.[21]

A critical dimension of the IMF is its specific conditions, referred to in the literature as 'conditionalities', which the Fund imposes on qualifying countries. Conditionalities are the economic policies that are typically imposed by the IMF on developing nations as conditions for accessing loans. These measures are aimed at stabilising the economies by adopting fiscal, monetary and exchange rate measures. These include reductions in public expenditure, restrictive fiscal and monetary policies, devaluation of the currency, removal of restrictions on the free flow of trade and foreign investment, removal of subsidies and price controls, privatisation of public enterprises and an open-door policy towards foreign investment. These conditionalities involve serious political, social and economic costs for developing nations.

To understand the role played by the IMF and the WB in the region, it is important to place their operations within the context of the politics of the late 1960s and 1970s. Since the decade of the 1970s, beginning with Jamaica and Guyana, the IMF has been an important participant in the decision making process in the Commonwealth Caribbean. The decade of the 1970s in particular was marked by:

(i)   increasing radicalism of economic-policy nationalisation programmes, designed to achieve some control of the economy
(ii) increasing economic role of the state with the creation of the state-owned sector
(iii) radicalism of various political parties
(iv) radicalism in foreign policy
(v)   growing indebtedness of the state

Evidence throughout the third world and specifically in the Caribbean has shown the extensive political and economic implications of the standard IMF prescriptions. The major conditionality of the IMF has typically been to devalue the local currency to achieve a reduction in the balance of payment's deficit. In this way it was expected that devaluation would reduce the demand for imports, and force local manufacturers to export. Unfortunately, the experience of most developing countries is that devaluation merely increases inflation, by raising the size of the import bill (inputs into domestic industry are primarily foreign based) without necessarily increasing the level of exports. Again, evidence suggests that most of the typical export products of developing nations are primary products, which do not necessarily fetch higher prices when demand increases. Reducing the value of the national currency will not automatically lead to a proportionate increase in trade and consequently, might lead to a worsening of the trade deficit and an increase of the balance of payment's deficit. The net effect is likely to result in political crisis and upheavals, as governments are forced to use austerity programmes.

Apart from devaluation, the IMF's Structural Adjustment Policies (SAPs) include policies aimed at increasing exports by lowering the cost of producing goods designed for the export market. These policies have emphasised wage freezes and wage ceilings and have negatively affected labour and the trade union movement. Structural adjustment policies have also emphasised reductions in government spending on public and social services that have led to serious cuts in the education and health sectors. The IMF package has also stressed the need to eliminate subsidies and price controls. The effect has been a worsening of the position of workers and those who are least able to bear the burden of government adjustment. Thus, structural adjustment policies 'punish the millions for the mischief of the few' by way of increases in the cost of living, reduction in education spending, reduction in health spending, lower wages and wage freezes, public and private sector employment cutbacks and higher personal taxes and indirect taxes

TABLE 1: 1 COST OF FEEDING A FAMILY OF FIVE/MINIMUM WAGE, 1979-91

Month	Cost of Feeding a Family of Five Weekly J$ (1)	Minimum Wage Weekly J$ (2)	(2) as a % of (1)
June 1979	24.27	26.00	107.1
December 1983	77.00	30.00	40.0
December 1989	207.04	84.0	40.5
December 1991	629.24	140.0	22.2

Source: Norman P. Girvan, 'Liberalisation and the Social Sector in Jamaica', *Journal of Caribbean Affairs*, April–June, 1992, vol. 5 no. 2.

such as value-added tax (VAT) which fall heavily on the poor. [22]

By contrast, SAPs support policies that are favourable to business and capital, including government subsidies to the private sector for construction of port facilities, roads, facilities for electricity generation, government services and factory buildings. SAPs are also favourable to foreign investors who are rewarded with lowered taxes on business, tax-holiday periods of five to 20 years, removal or reduction of tariffs and levies on exports, privatisation or de-nationalisation and the opening of the domestic market to foreign-based exporters of manufactured goods. [23]

The immediate goal of adjustment by the fund is to give indebted countries money to stave off bankruptcy, while the long-term goal is to restructure poor-country economies favourable to foreign investors. While structural adjustment has ushered in short-term improvements in the Caribbean, in the view of Kathy McAfee it has failed to produce sustainable development and equity.[24] Available evidence suggests that structural adjustment policies have questionable results. What is clear is that structural adjustments have worsened the position of the under classes vis à vis the economic ruling class and have extended the role of international capital in the region. Ultimately, this has greatly facilitated the process of recolonisation of the Caribbean state.

For the Caribbean, the IMF has assumed the role of the new resident manager of the financial and economic affairs of the individual nation-states, control of which was critical to the nationalists of the 1960s and 1970s.

The International Monetary Fund: liberalisation and Jamaica

Several Caribbean countries including Jamaica, Guyana, Barbados, Trinidad and Tobago and Dominica have carried out SAPs with the WB and the IMF. In an article entitled 'Liberalisation and the Social Sector in Jamaica', Norman P. Girvan argues that liberalisation associated with the IMF has affected the social sector in Jamaica in two major ways. On the one hand, with macro-level impact devaluation, which has reduced the standard of living, and on the other hand, with a sector-level impact, which has seen cuts in social services.

While Girvan acknowledges that liberalisation may have positive effects, he concludes that it has had a greater negative rather than positive impact, given the serious deterioration of social services in Jamaica between 1979 and 1991.

The main features of the SAP in Jamaica were: liberalisation of trade and reduction of tariffs; liberalisation of exchange rates; reform of public institutions; privatisation of development institutions and constrained fiscal policy through expenditure cuts, tax reforms and the sale of public assets.

Structural adjustment: The case of Barbados

In 1991 the government of Barbados implemented a stabilisation and structural adjustment programme, which included:

(i) an eight per cent reduction in the wages of public sector employees

(ii) a stabilisation tax of four per cent in annual income of more that B$15,000

(iii) an increase in National Insurance contribution and employment levies

(iv) a three per cent consumption tax increase

(v) an 11 per cent increase in petrol prices

(vi) a 20 per cent increase on 'luxury' imports

(vii) removal of duty free concessions to industry

(viii) a B$22 million cut in subsidies to public sector enterprises

(ix) privatisation, which included the sale of government shares in Barbados External Telecommunications (BET) and Barbados Telephone Company (BARTEL), the bus service and Heywoods Resorts

(x)   a 50 per cent increase in bus fares

(xi) a 50 per cent increase in government housing units

(xii) increased interest rates – notably the Barbados package did not include the typical devaluation condition[25]

Structural adjustment and the trade union movement

Structural adjustment programmes (SAPs) have had serious implications for labour in the Caribbean. Roodal Moonilal argues that the main targets of such programmes are trade unions.[26] Direct attempts were made to reduce the effectiveness of the labour movement through wage cuts and freezes, increase in taxes and reduction of private and public sector employment.

These direct methods have laid the groundwork for further institutional strategies, which are aimed at reducing the overall effectiveness of unions, which Moonilal defines as 'union busting'.[27]

Implemented under the guise of labour market reforms, these strategies included: deregulation, where employers are given the right to hire and fire workers at will, and to fix wages; promotion of flexibiltiy as it relates to wages, work hours and the workforce generally and the use of modern management techniques.

The new international economic and political order: contextualising the present order

It is widely accepted that the New World Order, with its most basic feature being the economic and political restructuring of the international system, has tremendous implications for developing nations like those in the Caribbean.

Foremost among the changes that have transformed the New World Order are the technological transformation and the globalisation of industry, commonly called the Second Industrial Revolution (SIR). Conventional trade theory, which emphasised comparative advantage, assumed that financial gains could be obtained from specialisation with the use of local, domestic and regional resources such as land, labour and capital. Increasingly, however, it is the international movement of these factors of production, themselves spearheaded by transnational corporations (TNCs), which are at the forefront of production and international competitiveness. A major strategy used by TNCs is the search for new areas where labour is cheap. The spread of liberalisation under which production has become globalised or internationalised, that is, the separation of labour intensive production of goods so that components of consumer products are assembled in low-wage countries and re-exported to the destination market, facilitates this process.

Moreover the globalisation of trade is underscored by the innovations which have occurred in the production process and the communications revolution. Spearheaded by Japan, Korea, Singapore and Taiwan (The Asian Tiger/Pacific-Rim Countries) is 'lean production', which emphasises economies of scope, rather than economies of scale. The hegemony of post-Fordist/Taylorist model of production or a Toyotorist Model of production includes:

• Total quality – zero production defects and continuous improvement
• Just-in-time production that reduces the need for inventories and promotes efficiency at every phase of the development of the product
• Low-cost global sourcing of inputs and components
• Lean production

These are at the core of the transformation of the technology designed to cut the production cost and consequently increase international competitiveness. The second industrial revolution has therefore transformed the way in which goods and services are produced. This has had serious repercussions for labour, as the emphasis on 'lean production' has accelerated the shift of production from labour intensity to machine intensity. 'Lean production', with its emphasis on the application of computers, robotics and related high technology-derived processes to the production process, whether of material and non-material commodities, has rapidly transformed the industrial base of developing countries. According to Hilbourne Watson:

> . . . In the process, many new commodities have appeared to replace moribund ones, the productivity of labour has increased many-fold, competition has risen to new levels, supranational finance capital has established its ascendancy in the world economy.[28]

Today comparative advantage is based increasingly on the ability of a firm or an industry to exploit the technological innovations as they relate to production, exchange and reproduction of goods and services. New technological developments have not only resulted in the phasing out of certain industries and the emergence of new industries and new products, but also in the equalisation of production prices and so on, which have almost rendered national capital advantages non-existent. The globalisation of production has made it increasingly difficult to determine the national origin of products, as international financial and trading actors have been able to successfully harness global resources, and to organise production on a world scale. These developments do not augur well for Caribbean states, which must be able to compete internationally in order to survive. It demands that Caribbean governments at a minimum level must among other things, deepen the regional economic integration process and reduce labour intensive industries to enhance international competitiveness by adopting appropriate levels of industrial and technological infrastructure.

The rapid technological advances and other innovations which are at the centre of the changing economic and political world systems have been primarily motivated by the need to maintain international competitiveness and sustainability. While globalisation of investment and trade patterns has been one tendency in this new development, integrated regional production is increasingly emphasised. Free trade areas (FTAs) will not only help regional trading but also maintain varying degrees of protection against other regions. Therefore, it is not surprising that as part of the changing global dynamics, we have witnessed increased regionalism, for example:

1. European Community (EC) – Single European Act of 1986, Maestricht Treaty of 1991
2. North American Free Trade Agreement (NAFTA) – 1994
3. Economic Developments in the Pacific Rim

The creation of the single market in Europe and the NAFTA are direct consequences of the international shift to 'lean production' which will provide the following:

*   Some protection against external investment capital
*   An enlarged market
*   Low-cost labour, especially through the utilisation of integrated regional production

The North American Free Trade Agreement

The NAFTA was formally established on January 1, 1994, as an economic arrangement between the United States, Canada and Mexico and was brought about to remove the barriers to trade between the three participating countries. The Agreement involves a market of 375 million people and a national income of more than $US6.5 trillion, and is the world's most powerful trading bloc. The NAFTA is far broader in scope than any other trade agreement ever signed; while it aims at the reciprocal liberalisation of all trade among the partners, it is not limited to a trade agreement designed to reduce and/or eliminate tariffs and non-tariff barriers. It contains an accession clause for new membership that unequivocally states its intention to achieve a larger process of hemispheric trade liberalisation. The Agreement also covers trade in services, intellectual property, trade-related investments, labour and the environment.

Such broadening infers that traditional sovereignty is eroded as domestic policy issues are now placed on the negotiating table and that rules are becoming more detailed. Also, in case of non-compliance with such rules, international actors and institutions resort to so-called impartial solutions rather than overtly political solutions.

The NAFTA represents both a geopolitical and economic response from the United States to its waning economic hegemony. Under the NAFTA, the United States has vertically integrated Mexico and to a lesser extent Canada into its economy, and has provided those countries with unrestricted access to foreign investment.

The NAFTA, is therefore one of the most comprehensive free-trade pacts negotiated between regional trading partners and provides for the following:

1. Phased elimination of tariff and most non-tariff barriers on regional trade within ten years. (Elimination of barriers to trade and the facilitation of cross border movement of goods and services between the partners).
2. Free trade in agricultural products between the United States and Mexico within 15 years.
3. National treatment for the NAFTA investors (substantial increase in investment opportunities in the countries of the trading partners).
4. Opening of the financial services market in Mexico to the United States and Canada by the year 2000.
5. Removal of all tariffs and quotas on regional trade in textiles and apparel.
6. Preferential treatment that discriminates against outside parties.
7. Provision for adequate and effective protection and enforcement of intellectual property rights in each party's territory.

Potentially, the NAFTA can pose tremendous problems to the Caribbean region, because an important component of the NAFTA is its ideological base. Any country wishing to enter the NAFTA must commit itself to adopt not only reciprocal market access but also a comprehensive package of economic policies, which includes

(i)   the adoption of a private sector-led, market-driven model of development

(ii) market liberalisation

(iii) the opening of the economy to investors and to service providers

(iv) the advancing of the privatisation programme, which was started under the IMF's SAPs in the region

(v)   instituting market-determined exchange interest rates

Likely effects of the NAFTA on Caribbean countries

One possible consequence of the NAFTA for the Commonwealth Caribbean is the further reduction of economic assistance, foreign investments and preferential trading arrangements. Mexico is likely to have a competitive advantage because of market size, low-wages and proximity to the United States. In contrast, Caribbean export products are largely uncompetitive due to comparatively higher wages, high rates of unionisation and higher transportation costs. Ultimately, as presently formulated, the NAFTA may result in a diversion of trade and investment to Mexico, as the lifting of tariff and quota restrictions on Mexican exports to the United States and Canada may cause labour-intensive industries to relocate. In all likelihood, the NAFTA will result in a reduction in trade between the United States and the Caribbean, as Latin American products are likely to capture market share in the United States given the cost factor, and a reduction in investment finance, given the larger Latin American domestic market.

The challenge of maintaining the integrity of the Caribbean Community stems from the different relationship which the individual Commonwealth Caribbean countries have with the United States. Although Caribbean countries can gain NAFTA parity separately, there are also benefits to be derived from the creation of the NAFTA and its evolution to an American Free Trade Area (AFTA) in the twenty-first century. This requires that the Caribbean position itself to take advantage of opportunities offered. Therefore, survivability for the Caribbean hinges on the ability of the region to strengthen its economic integration process, securing greater support from its Latin American neighbours and gaining NAFTA parity.

Globalisation and cultural imperialism

Both historically and in contemporary society, the mass media in the Caribbean has had significant foreign input and control. Such input has had and will continue to have implications for culture in the region, and as such, affects the way in which civil society responds to the environment. The Caribbean purchases most of its programming from the United States and this has a powerful impact on the transmission of information to the region, leading to further cultural dependency.

In terms of the importation of television programming, the third world countries are the largest importers. More specifically, in the Caribbean in the mid-1980s, Jamaica, for example, imported 76 per cent of its television programming, while Montserrat imported 95 per cent. This tendency towards foreign importation worsened in the late 1980s and early 1990s, as more individuals and firms entered the field of television programming, and Caribbean people began to consume western and North American software and hardware.

The Caribbean did attempt to moderate this cultural dependency, and to participate in the growing global culture. This was illustrated by:

- The organisation of the Miami-based, Jamaican-owned and West Indian-run Caribbean Satellite Network (CSN).
- The planned acquisition of a satellite transponder to be shared by members of the Caribbean Broadcasting Union (CBU).
- The production of popular local television programmes such as 'Gazelle', 'No Boundaries' and 'Oliver at Large'.

However, such intervention is inadequate. The Caribbean needs to focus more on its regional creative imagination, as evidenced by Derek Walcott's Nobel Prize for Literature in 1992, and its numerous musical and other literary successes. Moreover, Caribbean governments must attempt to participate more meaningfully in the explosive growth and development of the global cultural information industry by producing software in the areas that they are competent. This will not only earn revenue for the region, but will also contribute to the global culture while assuring that Caribbean cultural identity is not eliminated.

While the obstacles seem insurmountable, the failure to do the above will result in the total recolonisation of the region. Clearly cultural imperialism is helped by the failure to produce more culturally relevant media programming for consumption by the people of the region, and to participate more actively in the evolving global culture.

GATT, the WTO and the Multilateral Agreement on Investment: Recolonisation?

The eighth Uruguay round of the General Agreement on Tariffs and Trade (GATT) negotiations began in 1986 and ended in 1994 and was ratified by the United States Congress that same year. GATT provides for:

(i) greater trade liberalisation via the reduction on tariffs

(ii) reduction of subsidies to agriculture (implications for bananas in the Windward Islands)

(iii) open trade in services

(iv) focus on non-tariff barriers to trade (NTBs). NTBs have traditionally protected domestic producers by mechanisms such as government procurement practices

(v) the enforcement of intellectual property rights

An examination of GATT rules will show that a significant area is devoted to economic activity with the aim of ensuring that economies worldwide are kept open, without undue restrictive regulations. Under GATT rules, countries must put into place laws, which are designed to protect and enhance patents as well as other industrial property rights of TNCs.

GATT has also ruled in favour of developed countries, as the lowest tariffs are placed on capital goods and industrial products. Chakravarthi Raghaven contends that:

> . . .In essence, it (GATT) is an attempt to restructure and refashion the rules of the international trading system to make this even more favourable than at present to the interests and concerns of the major trading nations – the industrialised countries of the Economic North. . .a new International Economic order . . .will be more iniquitous and inimical to the development aspirations and needs of the poor developing countries than the order against which they have been protesting for so many years.[29]

The iniquitous nature of GATT and the World Trade Organisation (WTO), which epitomise the new trends in the global economy, was made clear in the recent ruling of the WTO that condemned the European Union's (EU's) preferential banana import regime. In September 1997, the Caribbean lost its appeal to the WTO to maintain the special banana regime for Caribbean banana exports to the EU. The September 1997 WTO ruling stated that the preferential treatment which the African, Caribbean and Pacific banana exports obtained from the EC market was against the tenets of world free trade, as it gave an unfair advantage to the EU's overseas territories and former colonies. The EU accepted the ruling and it was applauded by interest groups in the United States, which has large multinational banana companies in Latin America and deals with Latin America producers.

Caribbean countries supplied most of the demand for bananas in the British market and a small quantity of the Italian market, controlling only three per cent of the entire European market for the product. Latin American producers, dominated by three TNCs from the United States – namely Chiquita, Dole and Del Monte – provided more than two-thirds the European demand. In 1990, they controlled 75 per cent of the world market share for the product, much of which was directed to Germany, Belgium, Denmark, Ireland, Italy and the Netherlands. With respect to Britain, the Latin American producers provided 12 per cent of the demand of that market. The basis for the agreements which oversaw the importation of bananas to the European market is to be found in several regimes which partly stemmed from historical associations.

The decision by the European Economic Community (EEC) to establish a single European market by the end of 1992 and the rules of the GATT rendered all existing regimes problematic. The problem stemmed from the fact that under the fourth Lomé Convention, Article One clearly stated that the traditional access of African, Caribbean and Pacific (ACP) states to the European market would be guaranteed at least until the year 2000. On the other hand, GATT rules and regulations demanded the liberalisation of trade in tropical products, which would have a major impact on ACP bananas. A new banana regime was therefore proposed in 1992, which continued to provide preferential treatment to the ACP bananas.

From the outset, the new regime came under attack from within the EU itself, Latin America and the United States. The United States maintained a solid hardline position in relation to the issue and it was principally the United States which carried forward the political and economic agenda of the American corporations already in firm control of the world's trade in bananas. A three-pronged attack of the Latin American banana concerns took shape. The first strategy was to put pressure on the EU and this was done both directly and indirectly. In the first instance, formal pressure was brought on the EU through the WTO. The United States exploited differences on the issue itself within the Union by capitalising on the opposition of Germany and Italy to the regime. The United States government argued that the new banana regime was inconsistent with the obligations of GATT and therefore a discrimination against Latin American producers.

The GATT panels earlier ruled that the new banana regime was in contravention of the international agreements on tariff and trade, to which the EU countries were signatories. It also ruled that the Lomé Accord, which bound the ACP countries with the EU, was superseded by GATT. The response of the EU was to make further adjustment to the regimes. Thus, the three large Latin American TNCs had scored a political and economic victory.

Notwithstanding these adjustments, the United States government continued to protest by threatening trade sanctions against all parties concerned. Ultimately, the Dispute Settlement Board of the WTO ruled in favour of the United States and their interests, penalising the EU to the tune of US$196 million for the loss of market share due to continued protection of the ACP banana market in Europe.

The main objective of the GATT proposal is to close off development options and opportunities for third world and developing nations. GATT is therefore symbolic of economic and cultural colonialism that will further erode the independence of developing nations. Spearheaded by TNCs, GATT (now under the auspices of the WTO) can be considered as a vehicle for the recolonisation of developing nations.

The Multilateral Agreement on Investment (MAI) sponsored by the Organisation of Economic Cooperation and Development (OECD) is yet another mechanism of overseeing and managing the global market to the benefit of the Western concert of nations. If successful the new constitutionalism of the MAI will permanently paralyse the developing nation's ability to emphasise economic nationalism in their economic development strategies. Politically, the MAI will be accompanied by the increased presence of TNCs and their control of the local state.

The OECD, which spearheads the MAI, is composed of 29 of the wealthiest industrialised nations in the world. Four hundred and seventy-seven of the world's fortune five hundred companies, which are the rich-

est companies in the world, are in the OECD. The politics of the MAI is to remove virtually all barriers to investments by these corporations in the host economy. The MAI aims to:

- Eliminate existing restrictions to foreign direct investments (FDIs). This is referred to as the *Pre-establishment merit.*
- Eliminate discriminatory treatment both before and after establishment. Under the MAI proposals foreign investors should have the right to establish themselves in a host country on a basis that is no less favourable than that accorded domestic investors and will ultimately close off important developmental options of some countries. This is the *Right of Establishment* Proposals.
- These proposals will also empower transnational companies to sue a country in case of any infraction of the proposal for anticipated revenues lost. Referred to as the *Expropriation and Compensation Rules*, collectively they arm foreign investors with the power to challenge nearly any government action or policy as a potential threat to their profits. It is one-dimensional, as TNCs will have all the rights and no responsibilities.

Politically the MAI will succeed in depriving all nations of their right to differentiate between local and foreign companies. It will also allow TNCs to challenge any existing local law which they deem to be discriminatory. According to the director general of the WTO it is 'the constitution of a single global economy'.

It is this capacity of globalism, highly beneficial to the private financial and economic firms that dominate the global economy, which permits opportunities for the recolonisation of nations. These distinctive features, therefore, make the new global paradigm of development infinitely more dangerous for the postcolonial world.

Thus, while the current state of global events reduces the capacity of all states to actively intervene to improve local economic conditions, and compels all national governments to play the role of governor for 'metropolitan imperialism', possibilities for the most powerful to block, and even veto the exercise of state authority in some global aspects, exist. It is this capacity to use the objective developments of globalisation, which differentiates the more powerful states from the weaker states, allowing them the ability to maintain sovereignty and the pursuit of self-determinism. While such capabilities are critical for the realisation of the above, it also affords opportunities for the individual powerful states and the transnational global metropolitan imperialism to consciously and deliberately manipulate global developments to disadvantage and subvert the capacity of postcolonial nations to sustain self-determination. It is against this backdrop, according to George Belle, that recolonisation occurs.

It is this sinister action and capacity of powerful global actors, which has led Belle to contend that:

> .... Former paradigmatic bases, defining colonialism, anti-colonialism and anti-imperialism are in this view inadequate to assisting the addressing of resistance to C21st. Metropolitan Imperialism and recolonisation; because the category firstly, defines developments and characteristics which are not contained in the earlier designations and secondly, because taking account of the quantum leaps in the historical knowledge of mankind, during the second half of the C20th, the tools available in the former paradigms are insufficient to reverse recolonisation. 'False' decolonisation will not be the result this time around. Instead, we will simply fail to prevent recolonisation.[30]

These economic global developments, especially the transnationalisation of capital, have led to notions of the farcical nature of the nation-state. Proponents of the central role of TNCs/MNCs in the world economy contend that self-determination and the nation-state in the traditional sense no longer exist. Moreover, to survive in the new global division of labour, the nation-state is no longer a viable economic unit. For the Caribbean, the assault on the nation-state and the very concept of the nation-state posed by global market capitalism touches on very sensitive issues, in particular that of sovereignty. Nowhere more clear than this, was the response in some quarters of the Caribbean, to the 1997 signing of the Shiprider agreements.

The 1990s have thus witnessed a profound economic revolution, underscored by the increased internationalisation of production, trade and finance. It also offers tremendous challenges to all actors on the international scene. Apart from the economic developments, significant political developments have occurred. These include the end of cold war politics and the attempts to reintegrate the former communist societies with the global economic system. Between 1989 and 1990, Eastern European countries under the hegemony of the Soviet Union were 'liberated'; Germany was reunited in 1990 and the entire economic and political systems in the Soviet Union crumbled with the removal from power of Mikhail Gorbachev on August 19, 1991. Effectively then, the politics of economic transformation in Europe and the Soviet Union during the late 1980s and early 1990s saw attempts to set up a market system with considerable western encouragement and support. The above was consolidated by the IMF assistance to the East European countries of Czechoslovakia, Poland and Hungary to help in early economic reforms. Czechoslovakia's portion of that loan amounted to US$1.8 billion. These are among some of the most decisive recent developments that have implications for development alternatives and modes of doing business for Caribbean states. It is also necessary to examine the role of the IMF which has promoted the idea of liberalism at the ideological level, and the WTO, which has created the conditions for a recolonisation of developing postcolonial societies. These institutions and the developments of mega trading blocs are attempting to reshape the international trading and economic system to promote and maintain the maximum freedom of TNCs to operate worldwide.

Key words and phrases

1. Imperialism
2. Colonialism/colonisation
3. Metropole
4. Neo-colonialism
5. Cultural imperialism
6. Recolonisation
7. Globalism
8. Neo-liberalism
9. Finance capital
10. Crown Colony Government (CCG)
11. Old Representative System of Government (ORS)
12. International Monetary Fund (IMF)
13. General Agreement on Tariff and Trade (GATT)
14. World Trade Organisation (WTO)
15. The World Bank (WB)
16. Multilateral Agreement on Investments (MAI)
17. Mega trading blocs
18. North American Free Trade Agreement (NAFTA)

Questions to Consider

- Clearly distinguish between neo-colonialism and recolonisation. Is recolonisation inevitable for the Caribbean? Discuss with reference to the experiences of the Commonwealth Caribbean.
- Identify ways in which liberalism, sponsored by the GATT/WTO has affected and will continue to affect Commonwealth Caribbean countries.
- 'Global apartheid is the likely consequence of the New World Order'. Critically discuss with reference to the positioning of Commonwealth Caribbean states
- Outline the mechanisms that lead to global domination of Caribbean states. In what ways and how have these mechanisms changed and are there any substantial differences in the impact on the Commonwealth Caribbean? Discuss in relation to theory and with useful examples.
- Identify the main features of the political economies of the region at the turn of the nineteenth century. What factors best account for these features?
- Does globalism signal a further consolidation of the economic, political, social and cultural hegemony of the West over the Caribbean state?
- 'Colonial governments from the seventeenth century to the mid-twentieth century were essentially exclusive and elitist'. Critically discuss this view with reference to democracy and the nineteenth-century debate and with useful illustrations.
- Assess the historical and contemporary socio-economic, cultural, psychological and political importance of race in the Caribbean. Illustrate your answer with relevant examples from at least two Commonwealth Caribbean countries.
- Critically assess the extent to which independent Caribbean countries have failed to achieve real and effective independence. Is such a state possible? Illustrate with examples from the experiences of the English-speaking Caribbean countries.

Activities

- After reading this chapter and other related works, has your understanding of the Caribbean improved? To what extent has your view of Caribbean society, culture, economy and politics changed? List at least six ways in which your views have been transformed.
- List examples of characteristics of your own country that you have observed, which needs changing? How best do you think that such changes can occur?

- Have you ever confronted racism? Briefly explain and describe your experience.
- List ways in which you think that racism can be overcome.
- Discuss your views on the above with members of your group.
- In groups, discuss what your country's independence means to you.
- In which country, region or continent would you prefer to live? Your own country, another country in the Caribbean, the United States, Canada, Britain, a country in Latin American a country in Africa, a country in Asian or any country in Europe? Give reasons for your choice and compare your response with other members of your group.

Readings

Ideology and Political Development: The Growth and Development of Political Ideas in the Caribbean 1774-1983

Denis Benn

Chapter 2

Crown Colony Government and Imperial Trusteeship The Political Theory of Crown Colony Rule Liverpool to Moyne

Even before the final collapse of the Old Representative System in Jamaica in 1865, an alternative constitutional form was being developed and applied elsewhere in the region in the newly acquired territories such as Trinidad and St. Lucia.[1] **The new form, which became known as Crown Colony government, eliminated the elective assembly and vested executive and legislative functions in the Governor assisted by a nominated legislative council, subject to the overriding authority of the imperial government exercised through the secretary of state for the Colonies. As Martin Wight [340, p.17) has stated,**

> Crown Colony government is built on two great principles of subordination:
> (1) the legislature is subordinate to the executive; and
> (2) the colonial government is subordinate to the imperial government.

While the new system of government marked a change in constitutional form and a break in the trajectory of political development under the Old Representative System, it represented an essential continuity, and, indeed, a consolidation, of imperial control in the region.

The origin and development of Crown Colony government were partly an outcome of the constitutional struggles between the elective assemblies and the imperial government under the Old Representative System. As noted in the previous chapter, the 17th and 18th centuries had witnessed a determined attempt on the part of the Crown to assert its authority in the colonies but had found itself thwarted by the prevailing legal and constitutional theories which upheld the legislative independence of the assemblies. Lord Mansfield's judgement in the *Campbell v. Hall* case of 1774 had laid down the principle that the Crown automatically forfeited its legislative authority on the grant of a representative assembly to a colony and therefore amendments to the colonial constitution could only be made by invoking the legislative supremacy of Parliament. The corollary of Mansfield's judgement, was of course, that the power of the Crown, in the absence of a formal grant of a representative assembly, remained whole and entire and therefore could determine the form of government to be adopted in a new colony. The principle was earlier applied under the *Quebec Act* of 1774 which provided for the establishment of a constitution based on a Governor, and a nominated legislative council and therefore the Act may be said to have served, in some respects, as a constitutional precedent for the system of government eventually introduced in Trinidad in 1831.[2]

Nevertheless, legal considerations apart, there were a number of practical circumstances which influenced the decision of the British government to retain close political supervision over Trinidad. First of all, the colony represented an important strategic and economic prize. Among its principal advantages was its proximity to the Spanish American mainland and therefore its potential as a base for trade with the Spanish colonies. Moreover, it contained large tracts of fertile land suitable for cultivation. As the enclosure to the despatch from Hobart to the Commission dated October 16, 1802 stated, 'the acquisition of Trinidad has opened a fresh field for the employment of British industry and capital' [4(1)]. But there was a complicating factor in the fact that the island contained a cosmopolitan population comprising not only French and British planters, but also a free coloured group who constituted a majority of the free population.

Following its capture in 1797, the island was placed under the military governorship of Thomas Picton. However, the need to develop the resources of the colony required that its government should be established on a more settled basis. This was one of the principal reasons for the appointment in 1802 of a commission comprising Picton, William Fullarton and Samuel Hood, whose function was to prepare for consideration 'a system of Government applicable to the peculiar circumstances of the island'.[3] The principles which governed the eventual establishment of Crown Colony government in the island were embodied in a number of Colonial Office despatches and minutes in the period between 1802 and 1831. In this respect two documents are of special importance - (1) Liverpool's despatch to Hislop dated November 27, 1810 [4(1)], which outlined the reasons why a representative system along the traditional lines was considered inapplicable to the circumstances of Trinidad, and (2) Goderich's despatch to Grant dated May 25, 1831 [4(2)] which defined the constitutional features of the new government.

In the first despatch, Liverpool stated four principal objections to the establishment of an independent elective legislature, namely, the predominance of the free people of colour in relation to the rest of the free population; the presence of a foreign element among the whites; the need to ensure the effectiveness of the abolition of the slave trade; and the desirability, on general grounds, for the imperial government to retain overriding control in a new colony. With regard to the free people of colour, he argued that not only would their exclusion from a representative system of government provide grounds for legitimate grievance, but he doubted whether 'it would be consistent with the spirit of capitulation'. Moreover, he considered that a representative system based on the principles of the British constitution would be unsuited to the non-British elements among the white population. He concluded therefore that it 'is not advisable (sic) to establish within the island of Trinidad any independent internal legislature'. Adumbrating the constitutional form of the new government, he stated that the legislative power of the Crown was to be exercised through the Governor whose acts were nevertheless to be subject to revision, alteration or revocation by the Crown. Further, the Governor was to be assisted by an advisory council selected by him, subject to his power to act contrary to the opinion of that body.

Goderich's despatch attempted to give a more precise definition of the general outlines of the new system of government.[4] In relation to the nominated legislative council he raised the question of the constitutionality of conferring legislative functions on a body not established by popular elections.[5] But he raised the issue only to avoid it. Instead he proceeded to emphasise the inapplicability of a 'representative legislature' in the circumstances of Trinidad. With regard to the general powers of the new government, Goderich stated that in terms of the constitution embodied in the commission transmitted to Governor Grant,

> The Governor and Council would have power to legislate on every subject of domestic policy provided that the power be always exercised in subordination to the authority of Parliament, and of the King in Council; and, with an exact observance of all restrictions prescribed in your commission and instructions [4(2)].

He also urged that the legislative power should be exercised in such a way as to bring the laws of the colony in as much conformity to the laws of England as circumstances would allow.

Once the constitutional form had been established, the imperial government set out to elaborate a political theory to legitimate Crown Colony rule. In reply to a petition from a number of merchants and planters for a modification of the system to provide for greater local control over taxation and expenditure, Goderich pointed not only to the general inapplicability of the introduction of 'the laws, customs and privileges of Parliament' in a small colonial society such as Trinidad, given the small number of inhabitants capable of exercising the franchise and the 'antipathies' existing among the different sections of the white population, but he argued that the existence of slavery imposed special responsibilities on the imperial government to prevent the abuse 'not only of the domestic jurisdiction of the owner, but all the power with which he may be entrusted either as a magistrate or as a legislator'. As he expressed it, 'the slaves have a peculiar claim to my watchful care, from the helplessness of their condition and the want of any agent authorised to advocate their interests in this country'.[6] Goderich was in fact feeling his way towards a doctrine of trusteeship based on a humanitarian concern for the slaves to justify a system that had originally been established essentially upon a principle of expediency.

Not surprisingly the actual grant of emancipation necessitated a shift in theory to meet the needs of the new situation. In this respect Taylor's minute, which was written in 1839 at the time of the attempted sus-

pension of the Jamaica Assembly by the Melbourne government, perhaps best illustrates the arguments by which the Colonial Office sought to justify the unfettered political control of the imperial government in the post-emancipation situation.[7] Attacking the Jamaica Assembly as an irresponsible oligarchy, Taylor argued that the social changes produced by emancipation necessitated a corresponding change in the political structure of West Indian society, since he felt it would be 'in the nature of a political solecism' to leave the existing political framework intact. He firmly believed however that oligarchy would be the inevitable consequence of any attempt to establish a representative system. In any event, the position of the newly emancipated Negroes presented special difficulties for the working of a representative system on the principles envisaged by Taylor. In this respect, Taylor saw 'property' and 'knowledge' as the indispensable basis of a system of elective representation and since the Negroes possessed neither they 'cannot therefore have political power, or communicate it through any exercise of the right of a constituency', although he conceded that as a majority of the population their 'interests' ought to be represented. But more important still, Taylor believed that an extension of the principle of representation on the basis of property would also be undesirable, since

> in no long time under the operating of the existing ten pound franchise, and with the facilities which exist for creating fictitious freeholds, every white member may be turned out of the Assembly and the revolution of affairs may bring-up suddenly a coloured and black ascendancy [321, p.257],

Thus, if imperial intervention was designed to prevent the political domination of a local white oligarchy, traditionally hostile to the imperial power, it was also intended to secure the political exclusion of the coloureds and blacks.[8] In other words, Taylor was rejecting both oligarchy in the short term and democracy in the long run in favour of an indefinite autocracy. Nevertheless, in spite of its questionable foundations, by the end of the 1830s the Colonial Office had succeeded in elaborating a doctrine of imperial trusteeship, claiming descent from the humanitarian tradition associated with the emancipation issue, that was to serve as the legitimating principle of Crown Colony government for a century or more.

This is not to suggest that there was a lack of genuine concern on the part of the imperial government for the welfare of the Negroes. On the contrary, colonial policy, during the emancipation controversy and the period immediately following, exhibited a marked degree of humanitarianism which derived its stimulus from the crusading zeal of Clarkson, Buxton, Wilberforce and others associated with the abolitionist campaign. A series of despatches during the period testify to the desire of the Colonial Office to improve the condition of the Negro population and generally promote the ends of good government. In Trinidad, not only was the Governor required to give up claims to slaves 'becoming escheated to the Crown[9] but he was also instructed to secure the freedom of all Negroes brought to the colony in violation of the act abolishing the slave trade. The office of Protector of Slaves was strengthened and persons occupying public offices were required to give up property in slaves.[10] Religious instruction was emphasised as well as the need for the establishment of hospitals and other institutions for the relief of distress among the sick and poor.[11] The exercise of executive authority was also to be kept within proper bounds. For example, in the case involving a local political 'agitator', (de Ridder), Goderich warned against carrying into the administration of local affairs an arbitrary exercise of power which only the necessities of military subordination can justify'.[12]

The new mood of enlightenment was perhaps best exemplified by the humanitarian zeal of Sir James Stephen, Permanent Under Secretary at the Colonial Office between 1836 and 1847, who, according to Henry Taylor, virtually ruled the colonial empire.[13] Influenced by the humanitarian ideas of the abolitionists, with whom he was closely associated, Stephen was a stout protector of the interests of the slaves. He consistently attacked the prejudices of the West Indian slave-owning plantocracy and was determined to break the political control of this class and substitute in its place the superintending authority of the imperial government. In the period after emancipation, he continued to defend the rights of the Negroes against attempted encroachments by the plantocracy. For example, in 1834 and 1836, Stephen was instrumental in securing the disallowance of two acts of the Jamaica Assembly which were aimed at the political exclusion of the Negroes by seeking to raise the then existing £10 franchise.

But trusteeship in the context of empire has its limitations. Once the excitement over emancipation had subsided, the imperial government turned its attention to the needs of West Indian plantation production. From the 1840s the ideal of trusteeship was progressively vitiated by a narrow economic philosophy justified in terms of a misguided philanthrophy, and later, by concessions to oligarchy.

One of the major problems associated with the grant of emancipation hinged on the need to guarantee a ready and continuous supply of labour to the plantation once the Negroes were 'relieved from the fear of the driver and the whip'. To this end, Howick [5(c) p.383] had proposed in 1832 a tax on land in order to prevent the ex-slaves from abandoning the plantation. But this was rejected in favour of a system of apprenticeship which required the ex-slaves to provide wage-labour on the plantation for a fixed number of hours each week. However, the final termination of the apprenticeship system in 1838, and the subsequent movement of labour away from the plantation, reintroduced the issue of West Indian plantation production once again into the arena of imperial politics.

The problem of West Indian plantation agriculture was further complicated during the 1840s by the economic dislocations associated with the movement to free trade as Britain sought to dismantle the mercantilist props of the "Old Colonial System". The passage of the *Sugar Duties Act* of 1846 which destroyed the market monopoly of West Indian sugar, was followed in 1847 by a commercial crisis in Britain which forced into liquidation a number of financial institutions associated with the West Indian interests.[14] The labour problem against the background of economic depression in the sugar industry, therefore, raised serious questions about the survival of the West Indian plantation economy.

But it was Merivale who brought political economy to the aid of imperial policy. Between 1839 and 1841, Merivale, who was Drummond Professor of Political Economy at Oxford, delivered a series of lectures on the colonies which were subsequently published under the title of *Lectures on Colonisation and the Colonies* [233][15]. Although, like Adam Smith, he had attacked the Old Colonial System and slavery as contrary to the principles of sound political economy, he nevertheless supported the maintenance of the plantation economy as the basis of West Indian prosperity. Addressing himself to the problems of West Indian plantation agriculture in the post-emancipation period, Merivale identified the scarcity of labour as well as the level of wages as a function of the ready availability of land in colonies with an open resource base, such as Trinidad and Guyana, and therefore advocated a policy of indentured immigration as a means of adjusting the land/labour ratio and therefore creating a situation of 'fair' competition between the two factors of production.[16]

Grey's accession to office as Colonial Secretary in 1846 marked the new direction of imperial policy in its attempt to come to the aid of the West Indian plantation economy and at the same time to reconcile the imperatives of economic policy with the doctrine of trusteeship. In his despatch to Governor Harris of Trinidad in 1846, Grey expressed his complete support for the adoption of 'effectual measures for securing to the planters of Trinidad a greater command of labour' and also the need 'to relieve the colonists from some part of the expenses incident to the immigration of coolies.'[17] Applying a 'Merivalean' analysis to the case of Trinidad, he argued that the 'indisposition to regular labour' (which Harris had simplistically attributed to the 'careless and desultory habits of the African and Creole races'), was not a racial trait at all, but was due to the 'great extent of easily accessible land in proportion to the population'. In Grey's view, the solution to the problem was 'to place the labouring population in circumstances in which a greater amount of labour than at present shall be required to supply their wants.'

In addition to immigration, therefore, Grey supported measures for the more efficient management of Crown lands with a view to eliminating squatting, and also an increase in the price of land to render its acquisition by the labourers more difficult. As a further incentive to labour, the labouring population was also to be encouraged to acquire a taste for the products of European industry. Finally, with the same end in view, Grey proposed the adoption of a system of direct taxation on the whole population. Anticipating possible criticisms of the injustice of such a policy, Grey proceeded to elaborate a doctrine that was to remain a virtually unchallenged dogma of British imperial policy in the West Indies throughout the entire period of Crown Colony rule. According to Grey,

> such a change in the system of taxation though it might at first sight appear to press hardly upon the labouring population, would I believe be for their real advantage by relieving the cultivators of sugar from the difficulties which now threaten to overwhelm them and thus preventing the abandonment of the colony by many of the inhabitants of European race, without whose assistance the remainder must speedily sink into barbarism [4(4) - Grey to Harris April 15, 1848].

Here was trusteeship with a new slant. The salvation of the labouring population depended on the

prosperity of the plantation and therefore every interest of the labouring population was to be subordinated to this end for their own benefit.

Grey's humanitarianism was thereafter confined to an expression of concern for the proper treatment of the indentured immigrants lest abuse should lead to the 'obstruction' of immigration throughout all the sugar colonies.[18] However, in view of the difficulties involved in dealing with 'immigrants belonging to savage and half-civilised races whom *(sic)* unfitness for unrestrained liberty is not generally understood and acknowledged in this country', Grey proposed the adoption of a system based on the rigid control of immigrant labour, with the *proviso* that the power of enforcement be placed in the hands of the magistracy rather than the planters.

The year 1848 also witnessed Merivale's assumption of duties as Permanent Under Secretary of State for the Colonies in succession to Sir James Stephen. Merivale's influence is clearly visible in Grey's despatch to Harris dated April 28, 1849 [4(5)]. In commenting on the ordinance passed by the Trinidad legislature for the purpose of promoting the industry of immigrants brought into the colony at the public expense, Grey disagreed with the measure on the ground that its provisions would contradict the principle of free labour and would establish 'a system of mitigated slavery' which would secure the advantage of neither free labour nor slavery. Grey nevertheless supported the principle of a strict control of labour (immigrant as well as Creole) in order to prevent them 'from passing their time in idleness with only such an amount of exertion as would suffice to maintain them in the condition of untutored savages'. He therefore proposed the imposition of a stamp tax, along the lines of that in operation in Mauritius, payable initially by the employer of immigrant labour but which the labourer was required to work to repay. In other words, it was in method and not in principle, or rather, on economics and not on morality, that the measure recommended by Grey and Merivale differed from that proposed by the Trinidad legislature.

The 1840s and 1850s therefore saw an almost total capitulation to planter interests in the economic sphere. The major preoccupation of colonial policy during the period centred on the maintenance of the plantation economy and consequently the promotion of indentured immigration together with a strict subordination of the interests of labour to the needs of plantation production. Inevitably, there was a noticeable departure from the ideals of trusteeship in spite of an attempt to rationalise the new economic policy in the name of this principle. In some respects, the period, which was most closely identified with Grey and Merivale at the Colonial Office, marked a break with the earlier humanitarian tradition of trusteeship, born out of the emancipation controversy, the end of which was to some extent signified by Stephen's departure from the Colonial Office in 1848.

Newcastle's tenure as Colonial Secretary, from 1859 to 1864, witnessed an attempt to recapture the earlier spirit of trusteeship and to promote the ends of good government based on a more equitable system of taxation.[19] In this respect Newcastle deliberately set out to reverse Grey's earlier policy of imposing a general taxation in support of the sugar industry. For example, in 1859 he refused to sanction a number of ordinances passed by the Trinidad legislature aimed at the imposition of a general tax on the community in support of immigration on the ground that 'as long as any portion of the expense of immigration is borne by the general revenue, no new tax should be imposed other than a tax falling upon the employers of immigrants'. In the best spirit of trusteeship, Newcastle pointed out that taxation for the benefit of a particular industry 'is in the nature of a bounty . . . and is opposed to all received principles of commercial policy'. Moreover, he argued that while taxation, in support of the industry, was, to some extent, justified in the light of the economic difficulties caused by a change in imperial policy during the 1840s, it could not be justified now that the industry had achieved a satisfactory level of prosperity.

In 1861 Newcastle again objected to a proposal for a general tax on land in support of immigration, although he stated that he would offer no objection to a specific tax on land 'directly benefiting from immigrant labour'.[20] Newcastle was also responsible for establishing the principle that two thirds of the cost of immigration should be charged to the planters (either in the form of a direct tax on individual planters to whom immigrant labour was allocated or as a charge to 'some source of revenue, such as the export duty, paid by the planters) and the remaining one-third to the general revenue.[21]

Not only was Newcastle determined to establish an equitable system of taxation, but he was equally anxious to support an enlightened social policy. In 1862 the residents of Port-of-Spain had petitioned the Governor demanding the abandonment of the proposed underground sewerage system on the ground that it would increase the level of rates in the city. In

his reply to the petition, Newcastle stated that even assuming the general unpopularity of the scheme, in cases involving the application of scientific knowledge, the welfare of the community 'devolves in a particular degree on the Government; acting no doubt with much consideration for their wishes and desires, but at the same time with a permanent regard to their interests'.[22] Consequently, he supported the implementation of the scheme. It was clear affirmation of the ideals of trusteeship unblemished by motives of imperial self-interest and with a genuine regard for the welfare of the colony. It was one of the finer moments of 19th century colonialism and illustrates to some extent the ability of imperial statesmen to influence, in certain cases and within certain limits, the adoption of an enlightened social policy in the colonies.

Newcastle and Sir Frederic Rogers (later Lord Blachford), who served as Permanent Under Secretary in the Colonial Office between 1860 and 1871, succeeded therefore in arresting, to some extent, the decline in the standards of trusteeship that had set in under Grey and Merivale, although it is true to say that, in contrast to the economic crisis of the 1840s and the 1850s, the greater prosperity in the West Indian plantation economy during the 1860s enabled them to act with much more flexibility and with less regard to narrow economic interests. Even so, Rogers was determined not to sacrifice the general welfare of the colonies to 'a few men of superior intelligence with an Anglo-Saxon desire to make fortunes'.[23]

By 1866, the trusteeship ideology of the Colonial Office was still guided by the assumption that it was necessary to take measures to redeem the Negroes and indentured immigrants from 'idleness and barbarism' but its motives were no longer exclusively determined by the needs of the plantation. Carnarvon was willing to help the squatters to legalise their title to the lands which they occupied as well as generally to facilitate the acquisition of land by the labouring population. In fact, he attributed 'the barbarous squatting in wild situations' largely to the artificial regulation of the price of land to prevent its purchase by the labourers. While he felt that it was perhaps generally desirable not to provide incentives for labourers to move away from the plantation, he believed that, in the face of the actual movement of labour away from the plantation, the next best alternative was to provide facilities for the establishment of freeholds. In this respect he was prepared to see some merit in the establishment of freeholds in close proximity to the plantation both as an incentive for the freeholder to seek occasional employment on the plantation and also as a means of supplying the labourers on the plantations without freeholds, with agricultural products. What Carnarvon saw as the primary object of a satisfactory land policy was 'the favourable grouping of the population.'[24]

The 1860s therefore witnessed a recognisable shift from the earlier policy pursued by Grey, based on efforts to secure a rigid restriction of labour to the plantation which was justified as a means of preventing a relapse of the emancipated Negroes and the indentured immigrants into barbarism. The new policy recognised the futility, and even undesirability, of an absolute subordination of the interests of labour to the needs of the plantation and therefore sought a compromise by attempting to promote an orderly pattern of social development outside the boundaries of the plantation, while at the same continuing to emphasise the primacy of plantation production.

The original capitulation to planter interests in the economic sphere during the 1840s and the 1850s, was to some extent paralleled on the constitutional front by concessions to oligarchy. Perhaps the most important development in this regard was the principle laid down by Carnarvon in 1859 in reviewing the ordinance dealing with the appointment of an Assistant Receiver General which was passed by the Trinidad Legislature against the votes of a majority of the unofficial members. While emphasising the overall constitutional supremacy of the Crown under the Crown Colony system, Carnarvon stated, nevertheless, that

> it is the desire of the Crown to establish such local control in Financial Affairs as may be expected to be exercised for the public good by persons interested in local prosperity and commerce; and the Crown looks to the Unofficial Members of the Council for the performance of this Service. [4(7) - Carnarvon to Keate, August 10, 1859].

Carnarvon further pointed out that in pursuance of this principle great weight was to be given to the views of the unofficial members of the council on questions involving expenditure, and their views were not to be lightly overruled. He concluded therefore that the ordinance should not have been passed against the wishes of the majority of the unofficial members of the Council.[25] The ruling is significant because it established an important 'convention' in the working of the Crown Colony constitution.

The 'Carnarvon principle' was further amplified by George Cornewall Lewis in 1861 in reply to the claim of the Trinidad Legislative Council 'to receive and consider petitions for objects involving expenditure'. Lewis drew a distinction between control by opposition conceded to the unofficial members of the Council (under the 'Carnarvon principle') and the power to initiate financial measures which was vested in the Governor in terms of his instructions. He explained that the object of the latter provision was to secure the clear constitutional responsibility of the Governor to the Crown for the introduction of financial measures while at the same time permitting some local control over such measures by the unofficial members of the council. In his view therefore, the transfer of the power to initiate financial legislation to the Council would be undesirable since 'there would be neither individual responsibility on the part of the Governor nor control on the part of the Council'.

Lewis suggested nevertheless that within the general framework of this provision a more satisfactory system of control could perhaps be secured by the establishment of a 'committee system', comprising members of the legislative council with authority to examine financial measures and make recommendations to the Governor; with the *proviso* that official members of the Legislative Council appointed to such a committee should follow the directions of the Governor. He directed nevertheless that in the event that the system should prove impracticable, the Governor, rather than conceding a greater degree of financial control to the Council, should abandon the experiment and 'enforce inflexibly the rule that no question which involves, however indirectly, the expenditure of public money shall be debated in the council unless introduced by the Governor'.[26]

The 'Carnarvon principle' therefore made a clear distinction between the limited control of expenditure and the initiation of measures involving expenditure. Its practical effect was to establish a system of checks and balances between the executive and the unofficial element of the legislature without compromising the ultimate control of the executive over finance. The Colonial Office was of course conscious of the fact that effective control of the executive over the legislature (as was the theory of the Crown Colony System) could only be maintained by the denial to the legislature of the 'power of the purse'. In fact, it was the possession of this power by the assemblies under the Old Representative System which had rendered executive control ineffective and had thus produced constitutional conflict and deadlock. The Colonial Office was clearly anxious to avoid a return to the old system.

In 1862, as a result of continued pressure from the local planters and British merchants with interests in Trinidad for constitutional modification to provide for an elective element in the legislature, Newcastle, following Grey's precedent in St. Lucia in 1848, approved in lieu of election, an increase in the number of unofficial members so as to enable them to constitute a majority in the legislature.[27] Newcastle however reserved the right to restore an official majority 'if it should be found that the unofficial majority made a practice of working together habitually, and as a party so as to render the official votes in the council nugatory'. Colonial Office policy in the constitutional sphere during the period was therefore still one of holding the line against permitting absolute legislative control to the planters while making concessions, within those limits, to allow some measure of control by the unofficial element of the legislature over expenditure.

Helen Taft Manning has argued that Crown Colony government provides 'little room for the discussion of the finer points of constitutional theory' [216, p.298]. But this is not entirely true. Within the overall framework of the system there was considerable theoretical development and during the course of the evolution of the system, major constitutional principles were established. For example, in 1862 a number of important constitutional issues were raised during the debate on the proposed establishment of an underground sewerage system. The specific constitutional questions dealt with the degree of control exercisable by the legislature over executive action (in particular the obligation of the official members to support the Governor) and also the constitutional position of the Chief Justice in relation to the executive. In his ruling on the issues, Newcastle, while allowing that official members might refuse to support the Governor on specific questions from 'conscientious motives', stated that as a general rule the official members of the council were expected 'not to oppose the Governor without serious and cogent cause'.[28] He however upheld the right of the Legislative Council to discuss executive action since he saw it as 'imposing a wholesome responsibility on the government without necessarily impeding its actions'. With regard to the constitutional position of the Chief Justice, Newcastle ruled that while the Colonial Secretary, the Attorney General and other non-judicial *ex-officio* members of the Council formed part of the executive government and were therefore bound to support the Governor, the Chief Justice had no similar obligations since his of-

fice did not form part of the executive government and that he should in fact exercise his judicial functions independent of the government.

Newcastle's ruling represented a refinement and elaboration of the constitutional theory of Crown Colony government originally formulated by Liverpool[29] and Goderich[30] which dealt mainly with the overall subordination of the Governor and Council to the imperial government acting through the Secretary of State for the Colonies, without defining the precise relationships among the constituent elements of the system. Even the Governor's instructions, although embodying detailed provisions, were apparently not without some ambiguity as to the exact line to be drawn between executive, legislative and judicial functions.[31] The constitutional theory outlined by Newcastle underlined the combination of executive and legislative functions by the Governor and the non-judicial official members of the Legislative Council as well as the combination of judicial and legislative functions by the Chief Justice, while at the same time insisting on the constitutional independence of the Chief Justice acting in his judicial capacity. The practical distinction between executive and legislative functions in the constitution was in fact confined to the distinction between the Governor and the non-judicial official members of the council, on the one hand, and, on the other, the unofficial members of the council, who exercised purely legislative functions. The 'Carnarvon principle', discussed earlier, which conceded a degree of financial control to the unofficial members therefore recognised a limited 'democratic'[32] element within the constitution which was to some extent reinforced by the constitutional independence of the judiciary upheld by Newcastle.

Nevertheless, the essence of Crown Colony constitutional theory during the period remained the combination of executive and legislative functions by the Governor and non-judicial officials of the council and the subordination of the legislature to the executive under the overall supervision of the imperial government. Clearly the combination of executive and legislative functions, in the absence of a formal constraint on executive action by the legislature, would not have satisfied the liberal democratic ideals of the Lockean formula, with its emphasis on the formal separation of executive, legislative, and judicial functions. But in the context of 19th century West Indian society, Crown Colony government made no pretence of being democratic. In fact, on the contrary, the doctrine of imperial trusteeship positively affirmed the need for a benevolent autocracy as an alternative on the one hand, to oligarchy (based on a narrow elective franchise) and, on the other, to a more democratic solution, based on a wider extension of the franchise, which was dismissed as altogether impracticable.

The position of the official element (as defined by Newcastle) as well as of other categories of members of the Crown Colony legislature was further elaborated in the Duke of Buckingham's circular of 1868 and in Lord Kimberley's despatch to Governor Musgrave of Jamaica in 1882.[33] With regard to the *ex-officio* members of the Legislative Council, Buckingham held that while the duty of the *ex-officio* members to support the government was more explicit in their executive than in their legislative capacity, they nevertheless had an obligation in either capacity to support the government, failing which they should be required to tender their resignation. In like manner, he ruled that the nominated officials in the legislature also had an obligation to give 'general and effective support' to the government. Buckingham distinguished, however, between the position of nominated unofficials and elected unofficials in the legislature. While he confirmed the legislative independence of the latter and their right to appeal to the Secretary of State for the Colonies against an adverse vote, he held that the former had a duty not to oppose the government 'without strong and substantial reason'.

Kimberley's despatch of 1882, which was prompted by the resignation of the nominated unofficials in the Jamaica legislature following their refusal to support the government in the 'Florence issue', imposed an explicit obligation on all official members (both *ex-officio* and nominated) to give 'unreserved support' to the government in the legislature, or else be required to resign. In keeping with this ruling he proposed that in future official seats in the legislature should be assigned to offices rather than to the individuals holding such offices. Failure to support the government in the legislature would result in officials being deprived of their office as well as their position in the legislature. The limited discretion originally conceded to the nominated official element in the legislature by Newcastle and, to a lesser extent, by Buckingham was thus severely curtailed by the Kimberley despatch.

The principles laid down by Kimberley governed the working of the Crown Colony constitution until the early decades of the 20th century, when they were gradually relaxed and replaced by the convention that official members 'will vote freely unless required to vote with the government'.[34] Similarly, during the course of the present century the function of the nominated unofficials changed from that of supporters of the government (as defined in the Buckingham circular) to that of representatives of local interests in the colonies.

The 'Carnarvon principle', as amplified by Lewis in 1861, was to find its logical expression in the 'Finance Committee' system instituted in Trinidad in 1887.[35] The function of the 'Committee', which was composed of the unofficial members of the legislature under (non-voting) chairmanship of the Financial Secretary, was to consider financial proposals involving expenditure from public revenue before they were submitted to the legislature for approval.[36] The initiative of introducing financial measures still however remained with the Governor. In its more original form the 'Carnarvon principle' was given specific application in the Jamaica constitution of 1884 with the conferment of a financial veto on the elective element in the legislature, although the Governor retained a reserve power to override their legislative veto on financial issues which he declared to be of paramount importance to the public interest.[37]

In terms of the subsequent evolution of the Crown Colony system in Trinidad, a number of tentative attempts were made, during the latter part of the 19th century, to concede an unofficial majority in the legislature. For example, the nominated unofficial majority conceded by Newcastle in 1862, was terminated by the appointment of an additional official member in 1889, but was again restored by Knutsford in the following year with the appointment of another nominated unofficial.[38] Nevertheless, despite continuing debate during the 1880s and early 1890s on, the desirability of further reforms by way of the introduction of an elective element in the legislature and the appointment of a royal commission to consider the question, no fundamental constitutional modification of the pure Crown Colony formula occurred in the case of Trinidad during the remainder of the century.

Indeed the new imperialism during the late 19th century, following the decline of the 'imperialism of free trade'[39] aimed at consolidation rather than relaxation of imperial control and therefore made serious constitutional concessions unlikely.[40] Not among the least of the features of this development was the emergence of a new imperialist ideology which sought to transform the older doctrine of trusteeship into a more positive philosophy of mission and destiny.

During the period, Britain certainly never lacked defenders of her imperial destiny, whether in the form of the extreme pseudo-Darwinism of Froude or the philosophy of mission and duty of literary imperialists such as Dilke, Seeley, Ruskin, Tennyson, Coleridge, and Kipling, or even the 'sane and legitimate imperialism' of Hobson. Imperial proconsuls such as Curzon, Cromer, and Milner became the very embodiment of the Anglo-Saxon destiny. Nor were the statesmen far behind. Adderley, Derby, Gladstone, Disraeli, Rosebery and Chamberlain all shared an equal faith in that destiny. Lord Rosebery at the end of the century saw in the imperial mission 'a pure and splendid purpose . . . Human yet not wholly human, for the most heedless and the most cynical must see the finger of the divine.[41] His concern was that the world should receive an English speaking complexion. For Chamberlain, true to his businessman's instincts, empire was synonymous with commerce. But he too shared a belief in the white man's burden, based on a conviction that the non-white dependencies were incapable of self-government. Whatever the arguments, there was widespread consensus on the necessity of imperialism.

In the case of Trinidad, the new mood of imperialism towards the end of the century was signified by Chamberlain's refusal in 1895 to countenance any change in the Crown Colony formula by way of the introduction of an elective element as demanded by the Trinidad Reform Committee. According to Chamberlain, 'it is not desirable at the present time to make such far reaching change in the constitution of Trinidad as the introduction of a considerable elective element in the colonial legislature would involve'.[42] In defence of his decision, Chamberlain outlined the old but still serviceable trusteeship doctrine, together with the other standing objections to the grant of a system of representative government, such as heterogeneity of population, different levels of political maturity within the community, and the inevitability of oligarchy under a representative system. The most Chamberlain would recommend was that nomination to the Legislative Council should be made on a regional basis from among local residents or property owners - a surprising prescription for a society acknowledged to be divided by race and class. On the issue of constitutional reform the Colonial Office was seeing eye to eye with the large planting interests who were now equally opposed to any fundamental change in the Crown Colony system.

In fact during the period, the Trinidad legislature had come to be dominated by representatives of the planting interests who, in their legislative capacity, had demonstrated considerable zeal in seeking to protect the interests of the sugar industry and had exhibited, as a Colonial Office minute of the period observed, 'a tendency to legislate for the benefit of one class'.[43] It was this domination that was being challenged by the middle class professional elements associated with the Trinidad Reform Committee. But in the choice between a consolidation of the position of the planter element within the Legislative Council and the promotion of the political ascendancy of the emergent middle class, by way of a system of elective representation, the Colonial Office defended the *status quo* on the ground that concessions to the 'Port of Spain lawyers' would cause capitalists to 'fight shy of the colony'.[44]

However, local political considerations apart, imperial interests, fashioned by the logic of dominion, dictated resistance to changes in the Crown Colony system because of their likely implications for imperial control elsewhere. As the Earl of Selborne (Parliamentary Under-Secretary at the Colonial Office) stated in his minutes to Chamberlain in 1895 concerning the Trinidad position:

> I need not debate on any grave divergence from the pure Crown Colony principle in the case of Hong Kong, a vast depot of trade, a great naval station and a fortress, now more than ever to be regarded from the naval and military point of view since the emergency of Japan in the position of a great naval power, nor in the case of the dependency of Ceylon, which must be considered in exactly the same category as India. [see 4(12)].

Thus by the end of the century, despite protestations to the contrary, the Colonial Office had succeeded in creating within the Legislative Council, by a process of nomination, what it refused to concede by election - an 'oligarchy' representing the planting interest, and was now defending its bastard creation against the challenge of the rising brown and black middle class, in the name of the masses, but all the while with an eye to the consolidation of imperial interests.

Nevertheless, continued agitation for constitutional reform by the middle class throughout the region in the early 20th century, later joined after the First World War, by sections of the mass base, together with a changed international climate, put the imperial government on the defensive and cleared the way for limited constitutional concessions. In this period, two documents are of special significance in the constitutional evolution of Crown Colony government - the *Wood Report* [5(a)] of 1922, which conceded the general principles of elective representation, and the

Moyne Commission Report [5(b)] of 1938, which conceded the principle of universal adult suffrage as the basis of election to the Legislative Council. These two documents are important not only because they influenced the major constitutional modifications of the Crown Colony formula in the region during the 20th century, and thus prepared the way for ultimate political decolonisation, but they also highlight the development of the trusteeship ideology itself.

The *Wood Report* was a representative document of the period. Though often hailed as an enlightened statement on constitutional issues in the region, Wood applied an essentially conservative logic to the problem of early 20th century West Indian political development.[45] On the fundamental issues, the report reflected many of the assumptions and preoccupations of 19th century colonial policy and expressed an unwavering commitment to the premises of the trusteeship ideology. In this respect Wood emphasised the need for continued imperial control on the ground that the Crown, acting through the Secretary of State for the Colonies, in its capacity as 'trustee' has 'a responsibility of which it cannot divest itself until it is satisfied that it can delegate the charge to hands of no less certain impartiality or integrity than its own' [5(a), p.6]. However, in the face of local demands for representation in government, Wood admitted the need for constitutional concessions, which he saw primarily as a tactical necessity - to be conceded lest delay should rob them of their 'usefulness' and 'grace'. The question at issue, therefore, was the nature and extent of the concessions to be made, by way of constitutional modification, that were not inconsistent with the declared need to preserve imperial responsibility. Quite self-consciously, it was less an exercise in colonial self-government than a device aimed at imperial consolidation.

In order to put the constitutional issue in perspective, Wood distinguished between representative government and responsible government, but immediately ruled out the possibility of conceding the latter 'within any measurable distance of time'. In support of his position, he listed four principal objections - heterogeneity of population (in the case of Trinidad especially) and backwardness and political underdevelopment; the absence of a leisured class; the need for uniformity in colonial administration; and the small size of the electorate. On careful examination, however, it is evident that the arguments advanced by Wood are largely rationalisations of imperial rule and embody a number of criteria which are irrelevant to a determination of the capacity of self-government.

With regard to the first objection, it is clear that heterogeneity is a permanent feature of West Indian societies and therefore an irrelevant criterion on which to base considerations of constitutional development, since a consistent approach must inevitably see this as a permanent disqualification of heterogeneous societies for responsible government. Similarly, the condition of backwardness and political underdevelopment nearly 100 years after the establishment of Crown Colony government is more a comment on imperial rule than an argument in support of the denial of responsible government.

Wood's argument concerning the absence of a class who could take an active part in political life appears to contradict his own observation about the growth and development of a 'coloured and black intelligentsia' in the region 'ready to devote their time and energy to propaganda among their own people' [5(a), p.5]. It seems that Wood's stand on this point was in reality an attempt to justify the continuing role of the expatriate Crown Colony officials who in his view were 'independent of local ties' and therefore 'provided that detachment of outlook necessary for the effective conduct of the services controlled by government'.[46] But these were largely extraneous criteria that could only be applied in justification of a colonial relationship since they were quite irrelevant, and indeed highly undesirable, to the practice of government in the Mother country itself.

The third objection was a criterion determined by imperial considerations based on a prior acceptance of the need for a continued imperial presence in the region and therefore the need for uniformity in imperial administration among the various units. Strictly speaking therefore, it was not an argument against responsible government as such but an expression of the needs of imperial control following on the rejection of the applicability of responsible government. Similarly, the final argument dealing with the smallness of the electorate was hardly an objection since the limitation of the size of the electorate was largely an artificial creation (where the principle of election was not altogether denied) that could easily have been extended (as the Moyne Commission was to prove) if it was seriously intended to promote greater popular participation in government. Indeed, it is surprising that after nearly a century of Crown Colony rule such an argument could be advanced to justify the continuation of imperial rule.

Proceeding from the assumption of the need for continued imperial rule on the one hand and the desirability of a measure of representative government on the other, Wood recommended the inclusion of an elective element in the legislature (for example, in Trinidad, Grenada, St. Lucia and St. Vincent). In terms of this proposal he envisaged an extension of the representative principle in two phases - first, the reduction of the number of nominated members of the Legislative Council and their replacement by elected members while leaving the official element in the majority; and, later, an extension of the principle to provide for a joint majority of the elected and nominated members. In an attempt to liberalise the provisions of the Buckingham circular of 1868, Wood also conceded the desirability of the nominated members being granted the freedom to vote as they wished (particularly in the case of Jamaica).

With regard to the executive functions of government, Wood felt that it was desirable for the elective element in the legislature to be associated with the executive but anticipated that, in the absence of a system of responsible government with an executive directly responsible to the electorate, disagreement was likely to arise between the official members and the elected members if the latter were actually appointed to the Executive Council. He therefore recommended that 'Executive Committees' should be established to provide a link between the executive and popular opinion but that the existing Privy Council should continue as organised, with reservation of power to the Governor, in the legislative sphere, 'to carry into effect matters of first rate importance' and that such powers should be 'exercised subject to the directions and control of the Secretary of State' [5(a), p.9]. These then were Wood's constitutional proposals. In his scheme of things, this seemed to be the ultimate in constitutional modification of the Crown Colony formula and virtually a final state for a considerable period of time. As Wood stated, 'it is unwise to attempt prophecies in the still distant future' [5(a), p.9].

Wood next turned his attention to general social conditions and the overall economic needs of West Indian society. In this respect, Woods' idyllic characterisation of the social conditions of the broad mass of the population is reminiscent of the 19th century Carlylean vision of West Indian social realities. Pointing to the 'cheapness of the cost of living in the tropics' and the existence of 'little or no unemployment' in the region, Wood claimed that there was 'no general physical distress among the poorer sections of the community' [5(a), p.43]. Similarly, with regard to the overall economic needs of the region, in an uncompromising assertion of the ideals

of *laissez-faire* economics, Wood stated that the development of West Indian resources should be left to private capital and initiative. His prescription therefore was 'a conservative financial policy' and 'a balanced budget through the reduction of expenditure' [5(a), p.43].

In contrast, Wood displayed a conspicuous zeal for the interests of the sugar industry. Pointing to the economic depression in the industry, Wood claimed that there was no more urgent economic problem in the region demanding the attention of the imperial government. He therefore recommended a reduction in excess profit taxation by the imperial government on U.K. firms owning sugar estates in the West Indies and also a doubling of the rate of West Indian preference in the U.K. In this connection, Wood reminded the imperial government (if indeed it needed such a reminder) that the West Indies sugar industry was a British economic interest which paid taxes in the U.K. and consequently the abandonment of sugar production would not only involve a loss of U.K. capital, but would also result in the reduction of taxable revenue to the imperial treasury as well as create financial dislocation and unemployment in the region.

But economics apart, Wood maintained a more fundamental proposition which had long been at the heart of imperial policy in the West Indies - that West Indian prosperity and stability depended on the civilising influence of the European-owned plantation. As Wood expressed it:

> Finally, it is right to remember, that the stability and progress of the West Indies are largely dependent upon the presence of the European element .... From the political, social, commercial and imperial point of view, it is vital that this element should be maintained, and that this can only be done by preserving the sugar industry in those colonies where it exists [5(a), p.49].

Wood's response has a close historical parallel in Colonial Office policy under Grey and Merivale in the 1840s and 1850s and demonstrates the prevalence of the assumption under Crown Colony rule that once sugar was in difficulties all else in West Indian society was to be subordinated to its needs.

Wood's concern for the sugar industry and his emphasis on its relevance in the scheme of imperial control, stands in marked contrast to his attitude toward local peasant production and its associated problems. For example, he felt 'unable to give support' to local demands for the establishment of agricultural banks to provide advances in order to assist in the purchase of land for settlement of smallholders, among other things. He was prepared to recommend only that a scheme for such purposes financed by local capital might receive some assistance from the imperial government. Finally, with regard to a request by the Trinidad Agricultural Society for the introduction of a new usury law to limit to 15 per cent the rate of interest on advances, Wood, true to his *laissez-faire* ideals, expressed scepticism about the desirability of an 'artificial limitation of the rate of interest' [5(a), p.57].

This, therefore, was Wood's formula for a continued imperial presence - moderate constitutional concession to pacify local demands but with political control firmly in the hands of the Secretary of State for the Colonies and, on the economic front, consolidation of the plantation economy. The logic of Wood's position was clear. If the British presence was necessary to the sugar industry and the sugar industry was necessary to West Indian 'stability' and 'prosperity' then imperial rule was inevitable, and therefore no serious constitutional concession could be made, in response to local demands, that would endanger the political balance established under the Crown Colony system. In spite of Wood's professed reverence for the trusteeship ideology, the question may legitimately be asked whether Crown Colony government, as Wood conceived it, was really the exercise of a 'trust', or a device to safeguard imperial economic interests in the region.

Wood himself provides us with a clue to the answer to this question. In commenting on Trinidad, Wood observed that, apart from its cosmopolitan population,

> it is the only one of the West Indian islands which contain mining enterprises on a substantial scale, and considerable capital has been embarked in asphalt and oil development by outside corporations. It is accordingly important that no action should be taken which could disturb the confidence felt by such capital in the local government [5(a), p.23].

Wood's recommendations influenced the major constitutional changes in the Crown Colony system in the West Indies during the inter-war years. For example, in Trinidad an elective element was introduced in the Legislative Council in 1925, and in several of the other territories, constitutional modifications along the lines suggested by Wood were implemented. However, the labour disturbances of the late 1920s which signalled the entry of the West Indian masses on to the political stage, not only effectively repudiated Wood's idyllic description of West Indian social

conditions but also rendered his constitutional formula irrelevant to the needs of the new situation, and thus forced further imperial intervention in the form of the Moyne Commission of 1938.

The Moyne Commission not only operated in a different historical context but, its membership was also much more progressive in outlook. Moreover, it approached West Indian socio-political realities from an entirely different set of assumptions. For example, the Commission rejected the entire *laissez-faire* tradition, that had been so ardently embraced by Wood, and adopted instead a more interventionist posture. Pointing to the traditionally negative character of colonial government in terms of its confinement to law and order functions, the Commission emphasised the need for greater governmental intervention 'in most spheres of life and work' [5(b), p.301].

In keeping with this philosophical outlook, which was doubtless influenced by the assumptions of British Fabianism, the Commission recommended the establishment of a *West Indian Welfare Fund* to promote the social development of the colonies. It recommended further that the Fund should be financed by an annual grant of £1 million provided by the British government and that payment of this sum should be assured for a period of not less than 20 years.

Moreover, unlike Wood, who accepted the inevitable dependence of the West Indian economy on the sugar industry, the Moyne Commission specifically warned against the dangers of specialisation produced by an exclusive dependence on sugar. The expansion of the peasant sector was seen by the Commission as necessary not only to ensure the increased production of food for local consumption but also as a means of dealing with the problem of under-employment. In this respect, the Commission was following the earlier precedent established by the West Indies Royal Commission of 1897 (the Norman Commission) and the West Indies Royal Commission of 1929/30 (the Oliver-Semple Sugar Commission) both of which had advocated greater diversification of the West Indian economy based on the promotion of peasant production. The 1929/30 Commission had also emphasised the need for the provision of adequate credit facilities to enable peasant production to establish itself in the face of competition from the larger units of plantation production.

Although the Moyne Commission was appointed principally to investigate the 'social and economic conditions' of the colonies and matters connected therewith, following the disturbances occurring in the region in the late thirties, it did not fail to see the political implications of the incidents of social protest in the region. Consequently, the Commission sought to link the issue of social reconstruction to the question of constitutional reform. As it stated,

> It is doubtful whether any schemes of social reform, however wisely conceived and efficiently conducted, would be completely successful unless they were accompanied by the largest measure of constitutional development which is thought to be judicious in existing circumstances [5(b), p.373].

Starting from the assumption that it was more important to ensure the creation of a more representative system of government than to introduce any drastic change in its functions, the Commission recommended that efforts should be made to ensure the representation of all important sections and interests in the Executive Council and further that consideration should be given to the adoption of a Committee System to function in an advisory capacity in order to give elected representatives an insight into the practical work of government. It also recommended that the representation of officials in the legislature should be limited to the Colonial Secretary, the Treasurer and the Attorney General and that the resulting vacancies should be filled by nominated members. In addition, it urged that early consideration be given to the reduction of the margin between the qualifications for voting and those for membership of the legislature since it felt that the latter was unnecessarily high. Moreover, contrary to Wood's conservative approach to the question of franchise reform, the Commission struck a much more progressive note in recommending the introduction of adult suffrage as the basis for a more democratic system of political representation - even though some members of the Commission felt it should be introduced later rather than immediately.

Nevertheless, the Commission fell back on a conservative political principle by introducing a variant of the trusteeship ideology which linked constitutional change to financial viability and, consequently, justified on this basis continued imperial control. According to the Commission,

> control must continue to be exercised in the interests of the home taxpayer, over the finances of the colonies receiving substantial assistance from funds provided by Parliament [5(b), p.374].

Accordingly, the Commission recommended that 'the initiative in formulating policy should remain with the Governor in Executive Council' [5(b), p.514],

but felt that some provision should be made to allow popular representatives to influence executive policy-making, the absence of which the Commission saw as one of the major weaknesses of the Crown Colony system. Nevertheless, whether under the *laissez- faire* philosophy of Wood or the interventionist ideology of the Moyne Commission, the prescription was the same - continued imperial rule.

However, as far as the West Indies are concerned, the Moyne Commission Report, seen in historical perspective, was a significant document, since it provided the basis for far-reaching political changes in the region during the post-World War II period. By conceding the principle of popular representation under the Crown Colony system, in terms of a system of elective representation based on universal adult suffrage (which was subsequently introduced in Jamaica in 1944), it contributed to the development of mass-based party politics which served as a springboard for further attacks upon Crown Colony government, leading ultimately to political independence.

In assessing the character of Crown Colony government, it is evident that the system was based on the professed belief in the incapacity of the majority of the local population for self-government. This has led to much controversy and misunderstanding about the nature of imperial trusteeship. In this respect there has been a tendency to argue that Crown Colony government was evolutionary in conception, leading consciously to eventual self-government for the non-white dependencies.[47] But this is a highly debatable proposition. Clearly, acceptance of the principle of self-government for the non-white dependencies hardly predated the 1930s. In fact, throughout the 19th century it was boldly affirmed by imperial policy-makers that representative institutions were not suitable for non-white communities. The views of statesmen such as Grey and Chamberlain on the question are well-known. Lord Curzon's vision of the British Raj 'not as a passing stage and necessary preparation, but as a final state and absolute good'[48] was highly representative of the imperial temper at the end of the 19th century. Even as late as 1921, Lord Lugard, in spite of his more sophisticated interpretation of trusteeship in the form of the 'Dual Mandate' could not see independence for the dependencies on 'the horizon of time'.[49] As Charles Jeffries has remarked, the trust (exercised under Crown Colony government) 'tended to be one which could be held indefinitely' [178, p.24].

Neither were the initial concessions towards representative government necessarily intended to suggest an evolution in the direction of complete self-government. As is evident in the recommendations by Wood and the Moyne Commission, concessions towards representative government were seen as a means of accommodating local demands for a measure of representation in government rather than a surrender of the substance of imperial control. As E.W. Evans has noted,

> Representative Government in the colonial empire was never intended to foreshadow any real transfer of power from the home government to some local authority. It was never intended to be a forerunner of responsible government. It was intended to achieve both stability and finality in the constitutional development of the colonial empire [385, p.14].

It is only against the background of this statement that we can begin to appreciate the significance of Wood's distinction in 1922 between representative and responsible government in the West Indian context.

In an age of colonial independence it is perhaps difficult to understand how imperial policy-makers should have thought of empire as a final political condition. Nevertheless, it is certain that the belief in the permanence of empire was, for a long time, very real indeed. Even progressive groups in Britain found it difficult to escape this dilemma and to give unqualified support to the principle of colonial self-government. The British Labour Party, in spite of its comparatively enlightened attitude to the colonial question, still subscribed to a variant of the trusteeship ideology up to the beginning of the 1940s.[50] In fact, it was not until after the Second World War that the Party finally accepted the principle of self-government for the dependencies.

The truth is that the war itself, as well as post-war developments in the colonial world put imperialism on the defensive. In this respect, Britain's post-war involvement in colonial struggles in Malaya, placed a heavy strain on her resources,[51] which were already depleted by her war effort, and thus paved the way for a final assault upon Crown Colony government. To be sure, it was not the mere generosity of the imperial power but the efforts of the colonised, against the background of changing international power relationships, that produced the demise of the Crown Colony system, although it is true to say that once the inevitability of the process was accepted, Britain sought to conduct the liquidation of empire with a considerable degree of grace and dignity.

This is, of course, not to deny the existence of a commitment to certain humanitarian ideals in British colonial policy during the period of Crown Colony rule. Such a commitment was never entirely absent in the attitude of men such as Sir James Stephen and Sir Frederic Rogers who were directly concerned with the formulation of colonial policy during the 19th century, and the spirit was certainly fed from without by individuals such as Clarkson, Buxton, Wilberforce, Mill and other enlightened elements whose attack on the more glaring injustices of colonial rule counter-balanced the more extreme utterances of apologists of imperialism such as Carlyle, Froude and others. However, it is misleading to see humanitarianism or trusteeship[52] as the primary motivation of imperial policy (at least in the case of the West Indies) since, as Lord Olivier [254, p.6] has reminded us, 'no nation has ever colonised, annexed, or established a sphere of influence from motives of philanthropy towards the native population'. Clearly, it was never pure altruism and, moreover, varied with time and circumstances as well as with the will of individual statesmen and administrators, but, in the final analysis, was influenced primarily by the economic and political imperatives of dominion.

Nevertheless, whatever its merits or demerits, the legitimacy of Crown Colony government and its underlying ideology of trusteeship were coming under increasing challenge, both directly and indirectly, in the West Indies during the 1940s.[53] Even before that period, systematic intellectual critiques of its basic premises were being elaborated as part of a nationalist or, perhaps more accurately, a proto-nationalist consciousness. Consequently, the foregoing exposition of the origin and development of the Crown Colony system provides an indispensable background to the discussion of the intellectual content of West Indian nationalism in the next chapter.

Notes

[1]   Formally introduced in its developed form in Trinidad in 1831, the system was extended to the British Virgin Islands in 1859, Dominica in 1865, Jamaica (following the surrender of the Old Representative System), Antigua, St. Kitts and Nevis in 1866, St. Vincent in 1868 and Grenada in 1875. During the course of the 19th century it became the dominant constitutional form in the region - with only Barbados, Bermuda and the Bahamas retaining the Old Representative System. Although captured from the Dutch in 1803 and brought under control of the Crown, Guyana (or Demerara as it then was) retained its old Dutch representative institu-

tions (based on the Court of Policy and Combined Court) which differed in many respects from the classical Crown Colony model. Throughout the 19th century it remained what Clementi [63, p.371] later described as "a Crown Colony 'gone wrong' ". It was not until 1928 that its constitution was remodelled and brought into line with the other Crown Colonies in the region.

2   Apart from Quebec, other early examples of the application of the model were Martinique and St. Domingo in 1794 (both of which were subsequently relinquished), the Cape in 1796, Ceylon (as it then was) in 1801, and also St. Lucia and Mauritius - see [339, pp. 33 - 52].

3   Hobart to Commission dated October 16, 1802 see [4(1)].

4   In 1831 the original advisory council was replaced by a legislative and an executive council.

5   As indicated in the previous chapter, Long, for example, had argued against the principle of vesting legislative powers in a nominated council.

6   Goderich to Grant dated 30th January 1832 - see [4(2)].

7   See [321] in which the minute is quoted. Taylor was an important official at the Colonial Office during the period following emancipation. His autobiography is also revealing in terms of the insights it provides into his political outlook. His conservative temper and his suspicion of democratic principles were partly reflected in his attitude to such 19th century Progressives as John Stuart Mill, Charles Austin, John Romilly and Charles Villiers whom he referred to as 'radical Benthamite doctrinaires'. While conceding Mill's powerful and admirable intellect he thought that his political philosophy was 'at heart something in the nature of political fanaticism' [321, pp.77 and 79].

8   In much of the literature it is the former that is emphasised and trusteeship is interpreted to mean an almost exclusive concern on the part of the imperial government for the fate of the Negro masses both before and after emancipation. For example, Margery Perham in the Preface (p.xi) of [731] has stated that 'strong government first needed for a conquered island was prolonged, under new humanitarian influence to protect and assist the still voiceless masses.' Similarly, J.R.M. Butler [376, p.17] in commenting on the introduction of Crown Colony government in Jamaica, has remarked that 'the Jamaica rising and the surrender of the old Jamaica constitution in 1866 were landmarks, and almost created the presumption that where self-government meant the domination of a white oligarchy it must not be conceded, and where already conceded it should be withdrawn'. Clearly both of these statements involve considerable oversimplification of the motives for the introduction of Crown Colony government.

9   Goderich to Smith August 15, 1831 - see [4(2)].

10   Goderich to Grant May 27, 1831 - see [4(2)).

11   Ibid

12   Ibid

13   Stephen was in fact associated with the Colonial Office since 1813, first in the capacity of a part-time legal adviser and from 1825 on a full time basis, before assuming the office of Permanent Under-Secretary. For a fuller treatment of Stephen's role in the formulation of colonial policy, see [189].

14   According to Eisner [99, pp.189 - 199] 'in twelve months (from August 1847) 13 West Indian houses went into liquidation, while the failure of the Planters Bank added to the general confusion'.

15   It was this publication which led to Merivale's appointment in 1847 as an Assistant Under-Secretary of State in the Colo-

nial Office and Permanent Under-Secretary the following year in succession to Sir James Stephen, in which capacity he served until 1859. Merivale had a reputation as an intellectual and was a regular contributor in the Edinburgh Review. As a political economist he was a disciple of Adam Smith and a firm supporter of the principles of free trade.

16   Referring to the immigration of free labour, Merivale stated 'for Demerara and Trinidad it is the one great requisite, the *sine qua non* of their future prosperity. Its immediate effect would be to bring down the enormous rate of wages by fair competition. Its ultimate effects would be to extend production indefinitely, and convert the precarious condition of those settlements into one of unexampled prosperity' [233, p.318]. In the case of Trinidad, the possibility of introducing immigrant labour was in fact discussed as early as 1802. In his despatch dated February 16, 1802 (Hobart to Picton [4(1)], Hobart had suggested that, given the growing unpopularity of the slave trade, consideration might be given to the importation of Indian labour from the Spanish American colonies. Similarly, in the enclosure to his despatch dated October 16, 1802 (Hobard to Commission [4(1)] he had discussed the advantage of introducing Chinese labour which he added would at the same time provide 'a new market for English commodities'. The immigration of labour was therefore a subject very much under discussion but it was Merivale who justified the policy in the West Indies on the basis of economic theory.

17   Grey to Harris 24th October 1846 - see [4(4)].

18   In 1848 the House of Commons Committee on Sugar and Coffee Plantations (under the chairmanship of Lord George Bentick, who was himself connected with the West India interest) advocated immediate relief for the West Indian planters on the ground that emancipation had been carried into effect 'without sufficient provision having been made for providing many of the colonies with an adequate command of labour' see [5(c)]. In the same year Parliament guaranteed a loan of £350,000 in support of a programme of indentured immigration to Trinidad and Guyana. For further details on indentured immigration to the West Indies during the 19th century, see, for example, C.F. Carrington [58]; I.M. Cumpston [79]; and K.O. Laurence [193].

19   Before this, Newcastle had served for a shorter period (1852 - 1854) in the same capacity.

20   Newcastle to Keate, October 10, 1859 - see [4(7)].

21   Newcastle to Keate, October 15, 1861 - see [4(8)].

22   Newcastle to Walker, July 7, 1860 - see [4(8)]. The principle was re-affirmed in Fortescue to Walker, October 19, 1860.

23   Newcastle to Keate, 23rd October 1862 - see [4(8)].

24   Quoted by J.R.M. Butler [376, p.60].

25   Carnarvon to Acting Governor, August 20, 1866 - see [4(9)].

26   Newcastle subsequently allowed the ordinance to continue in force on the ground that it was in the interest of the colony - see Newcastle to Keate, October 10, 1859 [4(7)]. But this did not alter the principle laid down by Carnarvon.

27   Lewis to Walker, August 16, 1860 - see [4(8)].

28   Newcastle to Keate, September 3, 1862 - see [4(8)].

29   Newcastle to Keate, October 7, 1862 - see [4(8)].

30   Liverpool to Hislop, March 15, 1810 - see [4(1)]

31   Goderich to Grant, May 25, 1831 - see [4(2)].

32   Goderich in his despatch to Grant dated May 25, 1831, see [4(2)] had in fact urged a separation of judicial and executive functions but in a general way only.

33   The term 'democratic' in this context is used in a special sense to indicate a limitation on the autocratic powers of

the Governor. In reality it was not democratic in the wider sense of the term. Rather it may be said that the provision recognised an 'oligarchic' element (representing mainly planter interests) in the council.

34   See Martin Wight [339, pp.109 - 114].

35   See Wight [339, p.112].

36   The system was previously adopted in the straits Settlement.

37   The fact that membership of the Finance Committee was confined to unofficial members of the legislature (apart from its non-voting chairman) meant that its composition differed somewhat from the system proposed by Lewis in 1861 which envisaged the appointment of some officials to the committee, with a right to vote.

38   Under the provisions of the 1884 constitution, the legislature comprised, in addition to the Governor, nine elected members, four *ex-officio* members and two nominated members. A further three nominated seats were held in reserve, thus ensuring a provisional elective majority. Within this overall arrangement any six of the nine electives could impose a veto on financial proposals. Under the 1895 constitution, which also conceded a provisional elective majority in a legislature comprising the Governor, five *ex-officio* members, 14 electives and 10 nominated members (six of whom were appointed and four held in reserve), the votes of nine of the 14 electives were required for a financial veto.

39   With the addition in 1893 of two more members (one official and one unofficial) the Trinidad legislature comprised 10 nominated members and eight officials, excluding the Governor. For details of this later period of constitutional development in Trinidad and Tobago, see H.A. Will [444].

40   The term is borrowed from John Gallagher and Ronald Robinson [386]. The Gallagher/Robinson thesis is that Britain during the free trade era pursued a policy of informal imperial control based on trade rather than domination. The discussion is however of little direct relevance to the colonies of exploitation, such as the West Indies, producing staples for the British market, which were always under imperial political control.

41   The Colonial Office was beginning to regret the constitutional concessions made in Jamaica in 1884 after they were seen to threaten unfettered imperial control and also to bring into political prominence the 'Kingston Jews' and the coloured professional element at the expense of the traditional planting interests. In 1887 R.G. Herbert, the Permanent Under-Secretary at the Colonial Office, in commenting on Governor Norman's proposals for an increase in elective representation in the Jamaica legislature, expressed fears that further concessions would trigger off similar demands elsewhere so that 'ultimately there will hardly be a Crown Colony left', (quoted in Will [444, p.708].

42   Rosebery's Glasgow Rectorial Address in November, 1900, quoted in Gerald Graham [129, p.206].

43   Chamberlain to Broome, November 14, 1895 - see [4(12)].

44   See [4(11) - Vol II File No. 4101 (Trinidad)].

45   See [4(11) *ibid*].

46   Wood's recommendations were eagerly endorsed by Hume Wrong [354]. This was perhaps not surprising since Wrong believed that public opinion in the West Indies was 'temperamental rather than rational' and that a good governor was 'of far higher value than a good constitution' [354, p.23].

47   In pressing his argument on this point, Wood also attempted to tie the experiment in responsible government to the question of economic development which he felt was greater than the physical condition of the region seemed to allow. In this respect be also expressed the fear that responsible government might lead to the growth of a 'financial oligarchy' who would use its political power for its own selfish ends. This was perhaps Wood's most effective argument. But it should be noted that Wood's own conservative economic prescriptions were hardly designed to promote meaningful economic development in the region.

48   See Harlow [392, p.1871]. Harlow refers to Crown Colony government in the post-1838 (Durham) period as 'a form of tutelage in which static units were retained under efficient and benevolent control, and out of which progressive units of whatever nationality, could be led by ascending gradations to an ultimate self-determination.'

49   See Nicolas Mansergh [217, p.5].

50   Quoted in Kenneth Robinson [281, p. 12].

51   For confirmation of this point, see Rita Hinden [151, pp. 115-125].

52   Michael Barrat Brown [46, p. 194] states that the cost of involvement in Malaya was over £50 million a year.

53   For example, D. K. Fieldhouse [105, p.378] has stated that the common denominator of the modern empire was a humanitarian concern for the interests of subject peoples, which was expressed in the concept of 'trusteeship'.

The Caribbean in the Global Political Economy

edited by

Hilbourne A. Watson

Global Restructuring and the Prospects for Caribbean Competitiveness: With a Case Study from Jamaica

Hilbourne A. Watson

This chapter situates the Caribbean in the process of the globalization of the world economy, the restructuring of its industrial base, the international division of labor, and the international socialization of production.[1] What is distinctive about this process is that it is unfolding within the crystallization of a new industrial revolution that is driven by computer-integrated manufacturing (CIM)–the basis of flexible production systems and the driving force in the globalization of high technology production. International regionalization is intensifying with examples such as the North American Free Trade Agreement (NAFTA), the Enterprise for the Americas Initiative (EAI), and the Single European

Market (SEM). Production and trade regimes are also being restructured in a handful of Third World countries (LDCS) where certain aspects of the technology foundation and production process tend to resemble those of the industrialized economies. Concepts of national economy and comparative advantage are losing their importance in economic analysis. Industries and firms are pursuing competitive advantage on a global scale through innovation-driven technologies; comparative advantage based on simple price competitiveness and location is declining.

The garment (apparel) industry is selected for analysis with special reference to Jamaica. Recent experience and performance are analyzed against the background of the U.S. textile industry complex and trade policy. The apparel industry was chosen for several reasons: the textile industry was central to the industrialization of old and new countries in the past; it is highly internationalized and has been undergoing restructuring under computer-integrated manufacturing; it has been a growth industry for Third World exports for many years (during the 1970s, exports of garments accounted for between 22 percent and 41 percent of Third World global exports of clothing, exports that went mainly to North America and the EC); and it reveals the structural limitations of Caribbean economies relative to technological restructuring. This problem and the relationship between merchant capital, entrepreneurship, and technological innovation are explored relative to issues of export competitiveness.

Globalization and Industrial Restructuring

Globalization is an intensive process that conforms to the tendencies and laws of motion of capital. Globalization occurs in production, distribution, marketing, exchange, technology, information, telecommunications, and other aspects of economic activity. Globalization demands market liberalization and the removal of practices that restrict the "free" movement of capital; its ideological couplet is neoliberalism, which is being championed by the United States and the leading multilateral institutions.

Globalization is a quantitative and qualitative process: it undermines national economic and political borders; transforms the character of industries, production, and commodities from national to global; and is concretely expressed in international regionalization such as the European SEM and NAFTA. Globalization mirrors strategies of companies operating on a global scale with leading-edge technology and

with deep roots in local markets: global companies face new contradictions of scope (global versus local), scale (big versus small), and structure (decentralization versus centralization) (Taylor 1991: 91-95). Globalization and industrial restructuring form a couplet and reflect the new global reach of the capitalist mode of production.

Restructuring

Restructuring is more than a technical process: it is a social process that involves the shift from extensive resource-driven technologies to intensive, brainpower-driven, high-innovation technologies. It also includes privatization, debt-equity swaps, mergers, and acquisitions, and other ways of centralizing and concentrating capital. Restructuring is designed to re-equip the productive base of industry and labor by revolutionizing the instruments of production and intensifying the production process. It involves new techniques of production (Harmon and Peterson 1990); the reorganization of the labor process and management; marketing; distribution; inventory systems, and the relationship between producers and consumers.

Capital relies on restructuring, especially in moments of economic crisis, to intensify competition and restore the falling rate of profit. Under global restructuring, technology acquires a truly global character and the law of international value tends to become exclusive. As a technical process, contemporary restructuring is driven by three interrelated clusters of new technologies—microelectronics technologies, biotechnologies[2], and new-materials technologies—via the CIM medium[3]. In this process, science and knowledge have become productive forces in their own right (Schnaars 1988).

Computer-integrated Manufacturing (CIM)

CIM technologies reduce the turnover time of constant and variable capital by shortening the product development and production cycle. Flexible production–including flexible manufacturing and Just-in-Time (JIT) production–is being realized as a result of CIM. As a totally-integrated communications system, CIM uses the computer to tap the benefits of integration by means of robots and other smart tools. CIM also uses information in digital electronic form to substitute for inventory, tooling, space, material movement, human skills, vertical integration, and lead time. CIM production processes reflect certain highs and lows: high variety, speed, data content, fixed costs, and responsiveness; and low labor content, cost per unit of operation, and lead time. Mass-produced diversity is a product of CIM–one at a time, one of a kind, made to order, high-speed/short-cycle, distributed capacity, close-coupled sequences, and complex and augmented production processes–(*Wall Street Journal,* 5 September 1991: Al; *Business Week,* 23 November 1992: 90; *Wall Street Journal,* 21 December 1992: Al). Increasingly, economies of scope take precedence over economies of scale; and learning curves become less important. CIM uncouples people from machines to intensify the production process, creates new benefits such as lighter products, and eliminates waste. Demand curves become inelastic and fixed costs become more important than variable costs.

The transition from the learning-experience curve to the innovation-experience curve requires the removal of technical and organizational barriers that separate management from labor; engineering from design; and manufacturing, marketing, and R&D from the customer (Ansari and Modarres 1990). The quest for competitiveness, market dominance, and customer loyalty dictates fragmenting the market into thin slices, controlling the market, and customizing production to meet diverse needs. CIM technologies and flexible production are helping capital to transcend the structural limits of the old mass-production system while creating new contradictions.

Japanese manufacturing techniques are the most concrete expression of CIM technologies at work. They symbolize the reinvention of the factory (Harmon and Peterson 1990). The Japanese assert that economic leadership in developed countries (DCs) will rest on control of "brainpower" technologies. Japanese industrialists believe that blue-collar work, financial control, and traditional cost advantages represent a misallocation of resources and undermine company-specific and location-specific competitiveness in developed countries. Japanese producers hope to abandon their own products and move from Total Quality Management (TQM) to Zero-Defects Management (Z-DM). They are investing heavily in strategic LDCs in Southeast Asia, southern Europe, Latin America, and in the Mexican side of the U.S.-Mexico border. The main reasons for this strategic move—foreign protectionism and growing labor shortages aside—is that it is cheaper to combine advanced technology with cheap (skilled) labor in strategic LDCs to produce for those markets than it is to rely on expensive labor at home to produce for markets in LDCs *(Wall Street Journal,* 2 September 1991: A12). This strategy raises new questions about the status of underdevelopment theory under intensive global capitalism.

The global restructuring process described above depicts the global arena in which the Caribbean countries must attempt to compete in the 1990s and beyond. The message is unmistakably clear: international competitiveness can neither be achieved nor sustained by continuing to produce the same goods with traditional labor intensive technologies. The absence of a capitalist class in the Caribbean that is capable of technological innovation, the high fixed costs of developing innovation technologies, the short life cycles of new technologies and products, and the need for foreign capital to finance joint ventures in developing and/or applying new technologies, find the region a very weak participant in the globalization and restructuring process.

The Caribbean Problematic

The transition to competitive advantage refers to the ways CIM technologies are reshaping production of goods and services as varied as semi-conductors and food products. In agriculture, for example, competitive advantage in economies with a modern technological base means applying biotechnologies to the production in laboratories of food crops that used to be produced in LDCs with labor intensive technologies (see Chapter 3). Whereas comparative advantage tends to be location specific, competitive advantage tends to be industry specific and driven by high-technology production. High-technology production is altering the structural composition of world output at an unrelenting pace.

UN Global Outlook (1990: 174, 186) projects that the shares of agriculture and services in world output will decline relative to the share of manufacturing for the 1990s and beyond. Genetic engineering and the rise of chemical substitutes for many LDC primary commodities will aggravate this trend. While the newly industrializing economies (NIEs) have made progress in developing microelectronics and information technologies, developments in informatics remain quite embryonic in the LDCs (Watanabe 1988). In the world electronics industry, the cost per integrated circuit is becoming higher in the Third World manual assembly operations than in semiautomated and fully automated assembly operations in the United States (see Chapter 8). East Asian NIEs are struggling to transcend the limitations of price advantage by importing cheap labor for their labor-intensive industries and exporting some labor-intensive assembly operations to low-wage Asia and Central America and the Caribbean, while combining new technologies for investment- and innovation-driven advantage at home.

Competitive Advantage

The pressures generated by global restructuring have led Caribbean technocrats and economists to examine questions of export competitiveness. Nicholls (1989: 4-5) defines competitiveness as the "ability to produce and sell goods at prices that assure long-run viability" in a context of price efficiency and timeliness. Nicholls linked the absence of competitiveness from Caribbean economic consciousness to the fact that access to "guaranteed markets and prices including transfer prices (for sugar, bananas, some regional agroproducts, manufactures and ... bauxite and petroleum)" sheltered Caribbean exporters from the vagaries of the world market. Nicholls sees the symptoms of a lack of export competitiveness in inadequate foreign exchange, chronic balance of payments deficits, limited economic growth, high unemployment, low utilization of resources and capacity, and protectionism; but he is silent on the role of merchant capital in reproducing "technological underdevelopment."

Worrell (1991) argues that the failure to identify areas of comparative advantage to produce and export at internationally competitive prices is basic to problems of attracting capital to the Caribbean — more so than the shortage of capital. Downes et al. (1990: 72, 57) link productivity and competitiveness to adopting a "more vigorous export promotion-cum-marketing policy, technical change, and changes in real wages, organization and management" (see Unger 1990: 480-495). Pastor and Fletcher (1991: 106) call on the United States to increase Caribbean access to its market for sugar, steel, and textiles to promote competitiveness; but they are silent about the future of these industries or their ability to drive investment or innovation in the region. Pastor and Fletcher do not even mention the significance or implications of global restructuring or the new technological paradigms for their recommendations. There seems to be an element of technological voluntarism in all of these arguments, a mainstay in the neoclassical analytical structure (see Dosi and Soete 1988: 402-422). It is a simple fact that promoting competitiveness in the Caribbean — given the lack of a capitalist class rooted in modern science, industry, and technology — is highly unlikely through state promotion of areas of comparative advantage and adoption of "appropriate" export and related policies. This intellectual lacunae about competitiveness is also a function of the paucity of research into the relationship to en-

trepreneurship of innovation, technical change, and industrialization.

The Caribbean suffers from "technological underdevelopment or a weak capacity or inability to support or use effectively four elements of development including modern production facilities, useful/available knowledge, effective organization/management, and technical abilities/skills (*UN Global Outlook* 1990: 140; Unger 1988: 480-481). Caribbean governments and capitalists tend to lack mechanisms for identifying basic research with commercial potential. The state and private sector do not support highly focused applied research. Marketing techniques, appropriate for the assessment of market needs, are prescientific, and the absence of a modern industrial culture practically rules out engineering/industrial R&D and commercial technologies.

Basically, "technological underdevelopment" tends to preclude the effective transfer of modern technology (Unger 1988: 483), for there is an absence of dense technological and capital goods infrastructures and business culture in which to absorb it. Brewster (1991) argues that the requirements of "pre-competitiveness" for international competitiveness must be met in a global environment where traditional strategies of comparative advantage are being displaced. Brewster notes that export competitiveness must be seen relative to global standards rather than from the perspective of other LDCs that compete in metropolitan markets: in other words, it is the law of international value that defines the standards of global competitiveness to which Caribbean producers must conform.

While Brewster is mindful of the challenges the Caribbean will face from CIM technologies—information/telecommunications, genetic engineering/advanced materials, applied meteorology/climatic change, and new energy systems/rational energy use—he did not discuss the implications of the lack of an industrial class with a capability in technological innovation. Unger (1988: 480) anticipates these implications when he argues that "the dynamics of competition and learning in less developed countries need to be better understood before we ... model the entrepreneurial reactions and attitudes toward innovation that would be necessary to accommodate together the micro- and macro-objectives of the new industrialization strategies in those countries."

Export competitiveness in the global market is not reducible to having an export platform: it rests on factors as diverse as the quality of a country's capitalist class and its ability to employ productive capital, the quality of the productive forces and prospects for adapting new technologies, the role of government, and other factors. In the new global "quality complex," factors such as national character, geographical location, natural resources, market size, government policy, and management styles assume importance. There is nothing magical about them. Azel (1991: 23) recognized this situation when he argued that company-specific opportunities are more important than location-specific advantages for investment and innovation. Azel argued that these regimes must apply the insights of corporate decisionmaking to the process of government policymaking. While this is plausible, it does not address the contradictions that such a strategy would pose for the state in its normal decision-making activity, even if its role is restructured along market norms.

The State

Direct and indirect state participation in economic production in the Caribbean has been justified on grounds of employment creation, equitable distribution of assets, and the achievement of appropriate welfare objectives. The restructuring of welfare state policies in Europe and the United States in the 1980s led to a demand for the weakening of the state's role in productive economic activity to conserve resources, rationalize production, and improve the ratio of returns on loans to output and repayments from multilateral institutions. But the neoliberal strategy and ideology that underscore this outlook fail to explain the basic reason(s) for state participation in productive activity in the LDCS. The absence of a modern capitalist class in these countries forced the state to become a surrogate capitalist. The merchant capitalists consistently depend on a wide range of public sector supports and protectionism to stay afloat. Resources, which were nationalized in some countries like Trinidad in the 1970s, included enterprises that foreign capital had decided to divest. State participation in commercial and industrial enterprises was intended to create a productive capitalist class. This is the same class whose inefficiency and lack of familiarity with modern science and technology have been lamented by leaders from Jamaica to Trinidad and Tobago in the 1980s. The Guyanese state fared no better in the transition to state capitalism without the attributes of modern technology and entrepreneurship.

The absence of an innovative capitalist class deprives both the private and public sectors of an adequate supply of highly trained professional and technical workers with expertise in modern R&D, management, technology, and other areas. This situation is aggravated by the intellectual and social hiatus between scientific and technical (academic) labor and capitalist interests. There is scarcely any cooperative research activity to foster vital links among industry, government, and the universities, in spite of the fact that such links are important for keeping scientific, technical, and professional workers abreast of the economy's needs, and providing industry with ready access to the latest research developments to enhance competitiveness. Such links are also important at the academic level for the training and placement of highly skilled and educated college graduates.

The state consistently promotes trade and development at a major disadvantage, via the infrastructures of the nonprice determinants of competitiveness. This can be seen in the role of tourist boards, industrial development corporations, export promotion corporations, and other agencies (McIntyre 1990). These state agencies and the technocrats who run them are seldom linked to productive activity at any level. Largely, labor exists for capital under capitalism; to that extent, the requirements of merchant capital have dictated the reproduction of the forms of labor power in the Caribbean. This has become an untenable situation relative to the region's future development.

Problems with Merchant Capital

In industrialized economics merchant capital and industrial capital form a unity with the former being subjected to the norms of the law of value. In the Caribbean and other LDC regions, there is an inherent tension in the relationship between merchant capital's preoccupation with circulation (use values) and industrial capital's need to expand the sphere of production (exchange values) (Kay 1975). The scope of the former is extensive, while the latter, when it engages in productive activity, is of the intensive (enclave) type. At the global level, supranational finance capital subjects merchant capital to its sway, reproducing distortions of "technological underdevelopment" in the production structures of LDC economies.

Thus, even where merchant capital engages in production proper (e.g., sugar production) it retards the development of the productive forces by exploiting the economy without transforming the productive base of the industry (in the exampled case, sugarcane production) or creating or sustaining complex linkages with the rest of the economy. In this context, foreign commercial banks function as proxy merchant banks.

Azel (1991: 23) alludes to this situation when he says that the Caribbean does not offer opportunities for FDI firms to gain a "sustainable competitive advantage ... (and) firms in this setting have little reason to disrupt the industry's competitive equilibrium via an FDI commitment. In the absence of a competitive threat, the more likely strategy is to preserve flexibility by postponing commitment."

While the lack of a modern entrepreneurial class impedes industrial development, there is sufficient variety in the new technologies, especially the knowledge intensive ones (data processing and telecommunications), to redefine the way some technological knowledge may be transferred.[4] For example, the development of a modern telecommunications infrastructure in Barbados and Jamaica in conjunction with AT&T and Cable and Wireless is what makes these countries sites for the export of back- office white-collar jobs from the United States *(Wall Street Journal,* 14 August 1991: A1). Major technological change is taking place in switching and line capacity: fiber optic rings, digital switching, teleports, and other means of lowering costs have been built or are being constructed. New jobs for professional and technical workers and mass-production jobs in information processing and remote data entry, are exported to these countries, in spite of the absence of an innovative entrepreneurial class. However, it does not compensate for this deficiency relative to a development strategy driven by the logic of high-technology production.[5]

Part of the problem is that merchant capital, government policy, and culture tend to inhibit the process when interest rate and exchange rate policies generate negative consequences for technology development or technology transfer, and when foreign exchange controls limit access to foreign technology. The effectiveness of government agencies charged with national standards development, the promotion of industry, agriculture, tourism, export trade, and quality control depends on the quality of private sector institutions and the networks that integrate information services, and the critical mass of professional and technical expertise.

These are not the only institutional limitations associated with merchant capitalism. Race and ethnicity, which play a significant role in the Caribbean, are reflected in the relations between capitalists and professional, technical, and kindred workers (Watson 1989,1990; Lewis 1990). Economically and socially dominant racial groups in the Caribbean tend to be defensive about their position in society; it is customary for these groups to rationalize their position by noting that they provide stability in an otherwise unstable environment. For example, white Barbadian businessmen see the process of change to facilitate the development of black entrepreneurs in the core areas of the economy as "long-term and necessarily slow (because) anything done in haste could set us back in our social and economic development" (see Lewis 1990a: 36-37).

ECLAC (1990:73) links the development of the productive forces and the capacity to absorb technical progress to the concrete relationships with capital and analyzes the role of the institutional, social, and political makeup of a country. ECLAC argues that the nature of social and technical aspects of class relations among "entrepreneurs, professional, technical and kindred workers and their capacity to take concerted action to raise productivity" depends on the quality of the representative organizations for the groups whose leadership legitimacy stems precisely from their capacity to mount concerted efforts." The social distance between the races, the limited interest of merchant capital in the professional and technical development of workers, and the failure to support technical measures to advance the technological learning process reinforce limitations and constrain the development of a highly skilled labor force for international competitiveness.

CARICOM (Bourne 1988: xxxiv) argues that such structural weakness can be addressed by means of development expenditures and closer collaboration and interaction between production sectors and scientific research institutes. CARICOM emphasizes several areas that could receive attention: materials, products, and engineering design; the development of a stratum of technologists and technicians essential to technology adaptations; and development and changes in policies and conditions pertaining to the acquisition of imported technology. These objectives cannot be achieved without modern producers with appropriate global links to modern enterprises for joint ventures and subcontracting arrangements. Caribbean countries must deepen their integration into the global economy for several reasons: education for international competitiveness demands technological innovation; weak or negative domestic savings require foreign savings to finance economic growth; the widening gap between export and import earnings reinforces reliance on foreign capital; and technologies will have to be imported and adapted to enhance international competitiveness (Bourne 1988).

The record of net FDI inflows to the English-speaking Caribbean between 1974 and 1988 underscores this necessity. FDI inflows to CARICOM countries (excluding the Bahamas) and the Dominican Republic, Haiti, and Suriname were U.S.$505.1 million in 1974. FDI levels declined yearly to U.S.$176.9 million by 1979. In 1981, FDI rose to U.S.$575.9 million, due mainly to a significant increase in inflows to Trinidad and Tobago. Annual FDI inflows fell from U.S.$336 million in 1982 to $80 million in 1986, and in 1988 it was 25.3 percent of the 1981 level. As a whole, the region received 2.3 percent of the world's total FDI flows between 1974 and 1988, with half of this amount going to Trinidad and Tobago (see Table 5.1). International capital did not find the Caribbean an attractive site for productive activity between 1974 and 1988. This new pattern was reflective of the global restructuring of investment — driven by the revolution in industrial manufacturing, biotechnologies, materials sciences, and transportation— a process that has undermined traditional exports from the region. These wrenching changes reflect world market trends in consumer tastes, competition, and income elasticity of demand in importing countries for commodities like sugar and bananas *(Caribbean Business,* 29 March 1990: 21). Merchant capital has failed to anticipate and plan for these structural changes in the world economy.

Restructuring in the Caribbean Apparel Industry

CIM technologies are significantly shortening the life cycles of products and increasing competition from some developing countries in "technologically more advanced industries or higher quality segments of the traditional industries such as high-quality and fashion textiles,... (and) industrial electronics" (UN Global Outlook 1990:187). Asian producers are also investing in the U.S.-based textiles and garment industry. In 1987, FDI in the U.S. industry complex was US$1 billion compared with about $499 million in 1985. Ready access to a large pool of cheap immigrant labor from the LDCs and in the Mexican maquiladoras helps to cheapen the cost of labor and keep industry wages relatively competitive in the United States, where production is more capital intensive than in the LDCs. In spite of access to this cheap labor pool, a basic dilemma for the U.S. textile industry complex is how to overcome a comparative disadvantage in labor costs, with employment continuing to decline in response to high-technology production and industrial concentration (National Academy of Engineering 1983:41-43, 58-59).

The development of offshore garment assembly sites in the Caribbean by U.S.-based producers has been part of a strategy to address this contradiction. Prospects for the future development of this industry in the region are tied to the fortunes of the U.S. industry, and technology developments in the United States, the Far East, and Europe. CIM technologies are transforming sectors of the U.S. textile and clothing industry via the use of open-end spinning and shuttling looms, computer-aided spectrophotometers, which improve accuracy in repetitive production of particular shapes and patterns, and operator programmable multipurpose machines that significantly increase labor productivity and reduce the demand for labor in the sewing stage of garment production (UN *Global Outlook* 1990:185). NAFTA will help the United States by shifting a larger share of its textile industry complex to Mexico. The EC industry complex is also undergoing technological transformation (Pantin 1991c).

U.S. Textile Industry: The 807 and 807A Programs

Integration into the U.S. industry complex is linked to several factors. U.S. capital dominates garment (export) production in the Caribbean and the direction of investment in the industry is driven by U.S. market requirements. The U.S. market is likely to remain the primary destination of exports in view of the investment source, proximity, labor costs, and the lack of export-market diversification in the region —provided NAFTA does not neutralize the region's advantages (Watson 1992). Not only that: U.S. demand for clothing is also expected to increase. At the same time, the restrictions imposed by the United States on trade in textiles and wearing apparel from East Asia have boosted regional exports (Economist Intelligence Unit (EIU) 1988:2).

Under U.S. trade regulations, "807" is a tariff provision and "807A" is an import quota provision. Apparel assembled in Caribbean beneficiaries of the Caribbean Basin Economic Recovery Act (CBERA) from fabric cut but not formed in the United States received a duty break under 807. The United States implemented 807A in 1986 as a liberalized "Special Access Program" that gave liberal import quota treatment to U.S. companies that used U.S. formed fabric parts, knitted or woven and cut in the United States, in CBERA assembly operations. In effect, 807 and 807A strengthened the integration of Caribbean economies into the U.S. economy.

TABLE 5.1 NET FOREIGN DIRECT INVESTMENT INFLOWS (CONSTANT U.S.$ MILLIONS, 1998=100)

Region, Country	1974	1975	1976	1977	1978	1979	1980	1981	1982	1983	1984	1985	1986	1987	1988	1974-88 Total	% of World Total
Caribbean																	
Antigua	0.0	0.0	0.0	4.2	11.3	12.3	25.9	29.5	30.7	6.9	6.1	21.5	20.8	31.3	0.0	178.0	0.1
Barbados	5.6	48.3	14	9.2	14.7	7.7	3.7	11.0	6.2	5.0	0.0	6.7	9.1	7.5	0.0	148.6	0.1
Belize	0.0	0.0	0.0	0.0	0.0	0.0	0.0	0.0	0.0	0.0	-5.2	5.1	5.4	7.3	12.9	25.6	0.0
Dominica	0.0	0.0	0.0	0.0	0.0	0.0	0.0	0.0	0.3	0.3	3.2	4.1	3.2	9.2	6.9	27.2	0.0
Dominican Rep.	125.6	134.7	121.9	135.3	104.6	24.8	122.7	104.9	-1.9	66.1	95.6	50	58.8	95.5	106.1	1,344.7	0.0
Grenada	0.0	0.0	0.0	-0.2	2.3	0.0	0.8	0.0	2.5	3.4	3.9	5.7	5.9	13.6	17.0	54.2	0.0
Guyana	3.1	1.8	-53	-3.3	0.9	0.8	-2.3	5.9	6.5	6.3	2.5	0.0	0.0	0.0	0.0	-31.0	0.0
Haiti	18.6	5.5	15.7	15.2	16.8	17.4	17.2	10.7	9.3	11.5	6.1	6.9	5.8	5.2	10.2	172.2	0.1
Jamaica	71.6	-3.8	-1.2	-18.4	-43.7	-38.3	36.7	-15.1	-21.1	-25.6	17	-12.4	-5.4	57.3	-12	-14.7	0.0
St. Christopher	0.0	0.0	0.0	0.0	0.0	0.0	1.3	1.2	2.9	18.5	8.4	11.0	7.0	9.4	8.2	67.9	0.0
St. Lucia	0.0	0.0	6.1	24.6	33.9	37.8	40.9	50.3	35.4	13.7	16.7	23.5	21.8	23.6	26.0	354.2	0.2
St. Vincent	0.0	0.0	0.0	0.0	-0.8	0.9	1.5	0.7	2.0	2.9	2.0	2.5	3.5	3.9	3.6	22.5	0.0
Suriname	-0.8	0.0	0.0	-24.4	-13	-22.7	13.6	45.3	-7.9	62.2	-56.9	18.2	-38.8	-76.8	-96.1	-198.2	-0.1
Trinidad	281.5	195.9	268.5	158.1	211.9	136.2	244.3	339.8	271.7	161.4	158.0	1.6	-17.1	35.5	62.9	2,510.3	1.2
Subtotal	505.1	382.4	372	300.3	315.2	176.9	508.5	575.9	336	332.7	261.2	146.9	80.0	222.5	145.6	4,661.4	2.3
Other Caribbean																	
Bahamas	260.4	102.4	29.6	59.5	-1.1	14.0	5.1	45.3	4.0	-8.2	-6.6	-40.6	-15.0	11.3	37.9	497.8	0.2
Panama	80.9	16.1	-21.6	20.6	-4.1	72.3	-61.7	7.5	3.7	98.2	13.3	81.7	-73.2	62.1	-36.2	259.7	0.1
Subtotal	341.3	118.5	8.0	80.1	-5.2	86.3	-56.5	52.8	7.7	90.0	6.7	41.1	-88.2	73.4	1.7	757.5	0.4
Central America																	
Costa Rica	108.5	145.3	126.0	118.3	79.9	63.2	69.6	91.6	38.6	83.2	78.0	96.5	71.8	86.2	80.7	1,337.4	0.7
El Salvador	47.1	27.6	26.3	35.3	38.4	-14.5	7.8	-7.5	-1.3	38.5	17.2	17.1	28.4	-1.7	-1.8	256.8	0.1
Guatemala	111	168.6	25.4	184.4	209.5	170.0	146.5	168.0	101.9	61.6	53.1	84.0	79.3	163.0	328.1	2,054.6	0.1
Honduras	-2.7	14.8	10.7	16.8	21.6	40.9	7.7	-4.7	18.4	28.8	28.5	38.0	35.3	41.6	46.8	342.5	0.2
Nicaragua	32.4	23.0	26.3	18.9	11.5	4.1	0.0	0.0	0.0	0.0	0.0	0.0	0.0	0.0	0.0	116.2	0.1
Subtotal	296.3	379.4	214.6	373.7	361.0	263.7	231.6	247.4	157.6	212.1	176.9	235.6	214.8	289.0	453.9	4,107.5	2.0

Source: Jorge R. Calderin-Rossell, Foreign Direct Investment in Central America and the Caribbean: Policies and Strategies: A Background. FIAS-UNDP Roundtable, St. Peter, Barbados, November 14-15, 1990.

U.S. consumer spending on textiles and garments in 1986 was U.S.$75.7 billion, and it is projected to reach $101.9 billion in 1995. The value of output in the industry was $20.88 billion in 1975 and should reach $38.4 billion in 1995 (EIU 1988: 29, Table 3.8). Tax incentives under Section 936 of the U.S. Internal Revenue Code (see Chapter 12) made the "twin plant" strategy between Puerto Rico and other Caribbean sites attractive and enhanced the scope of 807 operations. The economic crisis in the Caribbean, reflected in the rapid deterioration of agricultural and industrial export staples, the high transitional cost and instability of structural adjustment programs, the decline of net FDI inflows, falling standard of living, and the need to create employment at any price, made garment production a pragmatic alternative for several countries.

U.S. textile industry complex and trade policy made it attractive for the Caribbean to do labor-intensive garment assembly operations from materials that are cut and shaped in the United States, with marketing and final product distribution left to U.S. producers. The 807 program is not intended to destroy production in the U.S.-based industry in favor of offshore production sites. On the contrary, "the USA sought to curb and ... effectively discourage the emergence in the Caribbean of more highly integrated garment enterprises capable of producing items with a higher local added value ... insofar as they were primarily oriented toward the U.S. market" (EIU 1988:4).

The U.S. industry adopted this approach for several reasons. The industry is labor intensive and highly concentrated in a small number of politically influential states, a factor that boosts the industry's clout in shaping U.S. textile trade policy (EIU 1988: 30-31). In 1987, about 44 percent of employment of approximately 1.28 million workers in the industry was concentrated in five states—New York, California, Pennsylvania, North Carolina, Georgia, and Tennessee. Imperatives of politics, employment, and competitiveness converged in the form of 807, 807A, and the CBI to boost offshore production.

The textile industry also exploits the provisions of the "Multifibre Arrangement" (MFA) that regulates international trade in textiles under the GATT; the guiding principle is "market disruption," defined in terms of damage to domestic industry with special reference to sales, market share, profits, employment, and production. In 1986, MFA IV was created to encourage orderly expansion of the textile trade with liberalization, equity, and avoidance of market disruption in mind. The MFA gives some LDCs a chance to

enter this global industry, without a guarantee of access to the markets of industrialized countries or commitment to promote industrial modernization (EIU 1988: 34-36). Stripped of its subtleties, the MFA epitomizes protectionism for the textile industry in the industrialized economies and violates the spirit of trade liberalization.

Restructuring in the U.S. textile complex has helped to overcome certain old contradictions while creating new ones. For example, JIT production was expected to eliminate overproduction; but innovation reduces the labor (value) content per unit volume and forces companies to producer larger volumes in order to increase sales to maintain or exceed revenue levels, and counteract falling profit rates. This is a contradictory process for Caribbean and American workers alike: the revolutionization of the productive forces raises the productivity of American labor: it also intensifies employment insecurity. The subtlety in this situation for U.S. workers is that it represents a profound structural shift in the technical composition of capital. It intensifies the international socialization of production, and reduces the demand for labor power in production. In part, it becomes a problem of too much productivity as opposed to too little productivity.

NAFTA apart, the extent to which Caribbean countries may continue to benefit from offshore garment production will depend on a number of factors: CIM technologies are not cost-competitive in short production runs; some areas of production are not yet sufficiently responsive to technological innovation in terms of cost and assembly; the fickleness and volatility of the fashion market make large scale, long production runs of many designs and styles unfeasible (Watson 1990: 24-25); and price support policies limit access to cheap fabrics on the world market. With respect to what may be expected under the EC single market, quantitative restrictions are likely to be built into any Uruguay Round Agreement on textiles and garments with a timetable for their reduction and eventual elimination (Pantin 1991c: 20-21).

The 807 program frees U.S. manufacturers of duty to be paid "on the value of the U.S. content of goods assembled overseas from components manufactured in the U.S. when such goods are reimported into the U.S. as finished products" (EIU 1988:48). The advantages of the 807 program are many: provision of supplies, capital, equipment, markets, marketing, and distribution arrangements by foreign producers and suppliers; exposure of workers to the discipline and other labor market requirements of low-wage (industrial) capitalism; and relatively easy access to foreign exchange. These advantages should not be dismissed out of hand. But there are no empirical studies on their impact relative to the imperatives of industrial restructuring and export competitiveness in the region.

While the 807A program is a trade-facilitating mechanism, it has obvious limitations. It does not contribute to the creation of modern industries; garment workers do not gain meaningful technical experience from sewing and packaging; managerial and technical positions in the labor process tend to be reserved for foreigners; foreign exchange benefits and profit margins are low; scarcely any funds are provided for industrial infrastructure or capital accumulation; opportunities for technology transfer at this level are nonexistent; the transitional costs of structural adjustment for wage competitiveness are extremely high; and foreign suppliers readily close operations as market conditions change (EIU 1988). As matters stand, Caribbean merchant capital is not positioned to exploit these contradictions in order to use the garment industry as a vehicle for industrialization.

When all is said, the 807A program was designed to enhance the international competitiveness of the U.S. wearing apparel industry. While the 807A arrangement offers guaranteed access levels (GALS) to eligible products for the U.S. market, it does so under protectionist constraints that limit production in offshore Asian operations in the region. Its preference for labor-intensive production limits opportunities for higher value-added based on skilled labor. NAFTA and the lack of price competitiveness with low-wage Asia will compound the problem by limiting the ability of the Caribbean with its relatively small labor force and weak mercantile bourgeoisie to develop a textile complex to become a major competitor in the U.S. market.

Jamaica in the U.S. Textile Industry Complex

Whatever degree of wage competitiveness Jamaica may have registered in apparel assembly activity, it has largely been the result of lowering the real price of labor via devaluation and other aspects of structural adjustment programs: it has not resulted from the industrial efficiency that comes from technological innovation.

Jamaica has several characteristics that made it an attractive location for 807 and 807A operations (EIU 1988: 86-95). Like the Dominican Republic and Haiti, Jamaica carried out currency devaluations during the 1970s and 1980s under structural adjustment programs

TABLE 5.2: HOURLY WAGES FOR WORKERS IN CENTRAL AMERICA AND THE CARIBBEAN – 1988 (IN U.S. DOLLARS)

Country	Wage/Hour
Virgin Islands	4.50
Puerto Rico	4.28
Barbados	2.10
Bahamas	1.80
Dutch Antilles	1.80
Trinidad and Tobago	1.80
Panama	1.77
Antigua	1.25
Honduras	1.22
St. Vincent and the Grenadines	1.15
Costa Rica	1.15
Guatemala	0.93
Montserrat	0.92
St. Kitts and Nevis	0.90
Jamaica	0.88
Mexico	0.88
Belize	0.85
Dominica	0.83
St. Lucia	0.75
Grenada	0.75
Guyana	0.70
El Salvador	0.65
Haiti	0.58
Dominican Republic	0.55

Source: Ramia 1989

designed to stabilize the economy and improve price competitiveness. The prevailing minimum wage level is extremely low by many standards (see Table 5.2), but generally higher than in several other low-wage Asia economies that dominate the U.S. wearing apparel market. Offshore producers typically employ low-tech methods. The labor pool is substantial and easy to train; and labor productivity levels are about 65 percent of comparable U.S. labor. The state offers liberal incentives that tend to benefit foreign companies, and the U.S. market is the main destination for the finished goods. Given the high cost of investment capital, stemming partly from structural adjustment, and in light of the drive by the U.S. industry for enhanced international competitiveness (Watson 1992), these conditions are predictable.

External transportation links to Jamaica are excellent but local producers concentrate mainly at the low end of the U.S. mass market. They have no real visibility at the middle or upper end of the spectrum. The work week is forty hours in Jamaica compared with forty-four hours in the Dominican Republic and forty-eight hours in Haiti. Production is concentrated in the Kingston corporate area and the Export Free Zone (EFZ). The immediate impact on the labor force and infrastructure tends to be a function of the degree of concentration of industrial location.

Participation rates for females are very high in the industry. Female workers are preferred by employers, who argue that women are more skilled and adept than men in performing sewing and related tasks (Ramia 1989). Related issues of gender, age, skill composition, and public policy in the context of the preponderance of female employment in sectors of the eastern Caribbean are detailed in this volume by Green (see Chapter 9). The concentration of women in the workforce mirrors trends in the industry worldwide. The inability of female employees in the industry to reproduce their labor power and meet social/family responsibilities intensifies poverty and social decay in these societies. Many women are single heads of households, and must rely on extended family networks and at least two jobs for survival. These problems aggravate the high dependency ratios in these households, a phenomenon that reproduces economic insecurity and poverty. The effectiveness of trade unions is compromised by government policy that restricts union activity in the Export Processing Zones (EPZs) and by the structural adjustment measures that have had the effect of reducing the real effective wage rate. Like the other apparel exporters in the region, Jamaica has failed to meet the GALS offered under 807A, which speaks to its limited production capacity. The absence of a developed textile industry complex in the region deprives Jamaica and other Caribbean countries of opportunities to rationalize garment production toward competitive advantage.

In fact, the growth of garment production is predicated on the ability of U.S. producers to obtain a steady flow of textiles to supply their Caribbean assembly operations. Many of the problems facing the U.S. industry complex may increase supply uncertainties. In addition, due in part to troubled mergers and leveraged buy outs, leading U.S. textile companies—Burlington, West Point-Pepperell, Field Crest Cannon, and J.P. Stevens Textile Group—are facing a crisis. Leading U.S. apparel makers are considering getting out of the apparel making business altogether *(Business Week,* 16 September 1991: 117). NAFTA offers a reprieve for several of them to the detriment of U.S. and Caribbean workers (Watson 1992).

Jamaica accounts for 12.5 percent of the two hundred thousand jobs in the apparel assembly industry in the CBI countries, but NAFTA could significantly reduce this number. Already a number of companies with operations in Jamaica, and/or those planning to locate there, have decided to expand, shift, or locate production in Mexico to exploit NAFTA provisions (Watson 1992). Japan and the United States are developing technologies to automate all aspects of garment production, including types of work now done in the Caribbean. These technologies are still not uniformly developed for nor applied to several processes; namely pre-production, assembly, and pro- and post-assembly (Pantin 1991c: 41-42). The textile provisions of NAFTA and the way these technical problems are resolved will concretely influence the policy options the textile lobby will employ in dealing with foreign competition via offshore assembly operations.

Although other markets, such as the EC, offer opportunities for exports from EPZs (Sengupta 1991), Caribbean producers have remained highly integrated into the U.S. market. Jamaica is the only CBI beneficiary country exporting yarn-based clothing to the EC; these exports are produced by Far East companies and shipped under preferential access provisions of the Lome Convention (EIU 1988:141-142). Jamaica would like to exploit the Canadian market with the help of locally-based Far East companies, but for several reasons there are no prospects for large-scale exports to Canada—NAFTA, market size, the limited marketing capabilities of CBI countries in isolation from foreign suppliers, the restriction imposed on textile exports from the region under CARIBCAN, and the influx into Canada of large numbers of Hong Kong Chinese immigrants with capital and expertise in apparel production.

Research findings on CARIBCAN (Institute for Research on Public Policy, 1988), and on the impacts and implications of the U.S.-Canada Free Trade Agreement for the Caribbean (Conference Board of Canada 1987; also in this book see Chapter 8) indicate that neither program offers much to the Caribbean in terms of enhancing technology for industrial development. The administrative and certification requirements of the 807A program are cumbersome and they have limited Jamaica's ability to exploit its provisions. Development and public policy issues in the Caribbean, relative to apparel and other commodities, are overshadowed by new technological processes such as conservation in raw material use; the use of advanced materials such as plastics and ceramics in production;

rising levels of efficiency in energy use; the widening gap in productivity between the North and South; and the difficulty of obtaining and mastering computer technology in most of the LDCs *(Wall Street Journal,* 15 October 1990: A-11C). Jamaica and other Caribbean economies simply lack "the evolutionary sequence of entrepreneurial build-up of technological capabilities . . . amenable to technological leapfrogging or to the sudden change to export-oriented industrialization" (Unger 1988: 480-481).

Brewster (1991: 105-106) noted that no amount of devaluation or wage restraint could make Jamaica competitive with China. Jamaica's retained value-added in manufacturing is one-fifth that of China; and its wages are five times as high. Furthermore, the structural dichotomy of Caribbean economies poses a virtually insoluble problem for exchange rate policies. Brewster also notes that for countries in the Caribbean the predicament is deepened by the difficulty of limiting the transmission of devaluation to domestic prices to the full extent, and by the widespread and enduring effects of the transitional costs from devaluation relative to their expected benefits. Jamaica's recent experience with devaluation is instructive. While the value of manufactured exports rose from $40 million in 1984 to $141 million in 1988, the indicator of relative competitiveness did not improve. And while there was a depreciation of the nominal exchange rate against the U.S. dollar by some 40 percent in this period, it was offset by a rise in domestic prices (Brewster 1991).

The wage-restraint argument — considered apart from the relationship of nominal wages, real wages, and labor productivity changes relative to technological innovation—can also be misleading (see Downes et al 1990). Wage restraint, driven by an incomes policy, will not necessarily encourage merchant capital to invest profits (occasioned by lower wages) in capital goods to enhance the technological base of enterprises. There are other unanswered questions around the impact of lower wages on savings. These relate to the movement of interest rates and merchant capital's preference for unproductive assets over productive assets; foreign assets relative to capital goods; and the impact of lower wages on the revenue base of the state. A plausible idea circulates on this issue: that the uncoupling of production from employment reinforces the need for an income policy to restrain wages and reduce the rate of substitution of capital for labor—while enabling firms to remain viable and allowing them to pursue options for economic change (Blackman 1991). But

this idea is a political statement and little more than a disguised version of the old-fashioned price-driven, appropriate technology thesis. It places job creation ahead of productivity as a short term expediency by recommending price competitiveness over technological competitiveness.

Downes et al. (1990: 52-53) argue that the relationship between nominal and real wages and labor productivity has not been adequately explored. The study by Downes et al. suggests that real wages have risen more slowly than nominal wages and that increases in real wages in Jamaica, Trinidad, and Barbados have not kept pace with labor productivity. The evidence is inconclusive that the lack of an incomes policy, including wage restraint, has eroded price competitiveness in the Caribbean. The main factors that have weakened Caribbean exports are the near hegemony of circulation over production; guaranteed markets that also distort the allocation of resources; changes in consumer tastes; net (negative) transfer of resources from the area; high energy cost, and, especially, intensive technological restructuring. If wage costs are high in the region, the way to compensate for this factor is to develop the productivity of labor via technological restructuring.

Social Consequences

In Caribbean societies, where low-technology dominates production, and most workers are unskilled, ideology and economic rationality become inseparable from those factors that shape the social reproduction cost of labor power. Rising wages become a basic incentive for capital to modernize plants and technology for competitiveness, where investment and innovation hold sway. In the technological restructuring process, economies of scope take over from economies of scale, and productivity increases faster because inputs decline as output rises; and companies will tend to invest in plant and equipment to boost productivity. Advocates of cheap labor operate under the illusion that they are doing workers and the economy a favor. What they are doing is propping up the incompetence of merchant capitalism and reinforcing poverty among the masses.

The social consequences of structural adjustment intensify unemployment in such an environment and further erode the standard of living. In the present global conjuncture—where technology and machinery, expressed in knowledge intensive production, are increasingly becoming cheaper than labor power, where skills are very flexible, and markets highly segmented and yet integrated via mass-produced diversity—it is imprudent to rely on a low-tech/cheap-labor strategy to achieve export competitiveness. Export competitiveness removed from a rising standard of living tends to keep an economy stagnant.

It already has been shown that wage restraint will not make the Caribbean competitive with low-wage Asia. Brewster (1991:105-116) and Bourne (1988: 49) reiterate the need for the Caribbean to upgrade the technology of production relative to the imperatives of local standards and global competition. In questioning the merits of the wage restraint argument (Blackman 1991), we must ask neoclassical theory to explain how Caribbean workers are to survive with cheap-labor strategies that do not develop the skills base of the labor force, at a time when restructuring is lowering the average price of labor power worldwide, even for very skilled workers. This type of wage restraint argument reflects the lag in ideological consciousness at the level of production relations.

Linkages

In noting that "capital goods production has been considered ... as one of the main vehicles for the acquisition of a technological capacity," Unger (1988: 487) stresses that "the link becomes even stronger when one considers the present surge of innovations in microelectronics, since many of [these innovations] take place as a result of matching of microelectronics applications to capital goods." While the absence of a capital goods sector limits the range and quality of options and linkages between engineering and industry for innovation, available world knowledge of genetic engineering and biotechnology makes it easier to consider limited initiatives. Caribbean governments must promote innovation and development in education at all levels *(Barbados Advocate,* 26 September 1991:14) to build links between academic and research faculties in universities. Cuba is ready to make an important contribution in this regard through its scientific, technical, and commercial achievements in biotechnology production (ECLAC 1990:110; and in this book see Chapter 7).

It is necessary to develop ties with research universities and institutions in North America, Latin America, and beyond to reduce the constraints imposed by merchant capital on the development of modern production. Such linkages are vital. As an OECD report stated it, other kinds of commercial activities "also add to the dense network of international relationships in science and technology (including) share investments in small foreign high technology firms, the commissioning of research by institutions in other countries, the extensive use of international consulting firms and the vast expansion of commercial data bases and services for scientific and technical information." (OECD 1988a: 10-11).

The Caribbean must strengthen such ties with Cuba, Mexico, Costa Rica, and other countries in Latin America where steps have been taken to promote R&D structures to link teaching, research, consulting services, contracts, and informatics to the development of new industries and products (ECLAC 1990:121). The negative implications of NAFTA for the CBI (Watson 1992) mean that the region cannot count on the CBI for sustainable investment. Azel pointed out in an article in *North-South* that from "the strategic perspective of firms, a CBI-based investment in the region does not offer a sustainable advantage. Even when firms perceive a CBI-based advantage, the advantage may be readily imitated and thus easily nullified by other firms" (Azel 1991: 23). The region is yet to investigate the nature of the official relationships between the United States and the Caribbean, with special reference to U.S. public policy- and decision-making methodologies, the conflicts and contradictions that normally surface in relations between the branches of U.S. government, and how these contradictions are mediated in the formulation and implementation of foreign policy around initiatives like the CBI, the EAI, and NAFTA relative to their implications for the Caribbean.

Immigration

Global restructuring is forcing Canada and the United States to reform their immigration policies. About three hundred thousand Chinese immigrants, including rich, skilled, and professional workers—roughly 6 percent of Hong Kong's total population—will settle in Canada by 1997 under a special immigration program for entrepreneurs. These new investor-immigrants take to Canada their business talent, about U.S.$2 billion to $4 billion per year, and close ties with leading trading houses in Asia. Canada is relying on this infusion of talent, capital, and skills to aid the modernization of its electronic technologies and garment industries *(Business Week,* 23 September 1991:50-51). If this plan succeeds, it could limit immigration to Canada from the Caribbean and erode the marginal position the region has in Canada's market for nontraditional goods (see Chapter 8).

The U.S. Immigration Act of 1990 increases the number of visas that can be allocated to skilled workers and immigrants, following the reduced demand for unskilled immigrant workers caused by the restructuring of U.S. industry *(Wall Street Journal,* 27 September 1991: B-1; and *Washington Post,* 8 November 1990). For the Caribbean, this raises the prospect of intensifying unemployment and foreign exchange problems associated with declining emigration. But neither Canada nor the United States has anything to gain from writing off the Caribbean as an economic area. The United States is becoming an increasingly trade dependent country, and whenever its exports contract the trend leads to economic contraction and rising unemployment at home. U.S. exports to, and the trade surplus it enjoys with, the Caribbean account for 110,000 U.S. jobs (Watson 1992; Graham 1991:12-14; Kishimoto 1991:17-18).

The Caribbean must develop its resources, but it must be skeptical of those who—unable to demystify the contradictory consequences of global capitalism— advocate retiring behind neo-autarkic constructs as a national or regional development strategy (Pastor and Fletcher 1991:101-103). No economy, especially those dependent on foreign capital goods and technology, can survive outside the global economy. Neo-autarky and appropriate technology (cheap-labor production) are ideological constructs that present, in the guise of scientific economic theory, moral outrage at the excesses of global capitalism. In the age of global capitalism, the future of Caribbean workers lies in intensifying the development of their productive powers in keeping with global standards.

Conclusion: The Compromising of the National Option

The contradictions of globalization and restructuring are not unique to the Caribbean. But the new competition for capital and CIM-derived technologies has weakened the economies of the region in matters of raw materials, labor, markets, and sites for productive investment capital. Even if structural adjustment offered a way out of the predicament, such measures would be compromised by the priorities of the World Bank Group, the ruling classes in the Caribbean, imperialism, and the "structural dichotomy" of Caribbean economy. The case of the apparel industry illustrates this reality as it relates to the U.S. textile industry complex and policy.

The globalization of high-technology production and the transitional costs of structural adjustment suggest that growth in the industrialized economies may not lead in the Caribbean to growth along mo-

dem technology lines. What separates the present organic and conjunctural process from the past is the unprecedented scientific and technological dynamic, which is structuring change at the global level and simultaneously compromising options available to the nation-state (shifting critical decision-making power away from its national base). The national option becomes increasingly compromised in the age of global capital, and with it the nation-state and its attributes of sovereignty and the like. While economic management styles may reflect the degree to which a regime anticipates change and exploits technological space, or other options, at any given point, it is unsatisfactory to argue that the economic crisis in the Caribbean is mainly a function of poor public economic management.

Since Caribbean countries are not likely to be on the cutting edge of R&D, technology development, and manufacturing, they must deploy their limited resources in prudent ways. They must monitor technical change and applications and pay close attention to the pursuit, where feasible, of competitive advantage, by lobbying for information, knowledge, and markets. One sound way to do this is to learn to adapt technologies in everything from information services, office automation, and education systems in management to business, teaching, and other areas. To achieve competitiveness in so-called services requires an understanding that modern services are an integral part of the new technological and industrial base of the global economy. The ability to exploit modern services will also depend on the quality of the technology foundation, education, and entrepreneurship. In the present global context, if private productive capital is left to market forces, it will not rush to the Caribbean. The weaknesses of merchant capitalism demonstrate that the extent to which an innovative capitalist class in the Caribbean may have a future will depend on the nature and quality of its global industrial and technological linkages, for it can have no viable future in national or regional economic or political space.

Notes

1. Research for this chapter was funded by grants from the Department of Political Science and the University-sponsored Research Program in the Social Sciences, Humanities, and Education at Howard University.
2. For details about the nature and number of alliances formed among U.S., European, and Japanese biotechnology companies in marketing, research, equity, and investment since 1980 see the *Washington Post* (Washington Business section), 23 September 1991.

3. My basic working concept of CIM is based on the American Society of Mechanical Engineers (ASME) CIM Systems Theory Applications Course, sponsored by the ASME and General Electric, the National Technological University, 1986 (video).

4. The new information technologies are also transforming the secretarial profession. *Sunday Sun,* (special supplement), 21 April 1991:8.

5. Intel, which closed its assembly operations in several Caribbean countries in 1986, will fabricate chips in Dublin, Ireland, at a new U.S.$500 million plant. Ireland meets the strategic requirements of such a project: large amounts of land near an international airport; capital; highly trained engineers and technicians; advanced telecommunications; electricity and clean water; very liberal tax breaks and incentives; parity in major markets to sell the products; a large labor pool from which to draw general labor supplies; a software industry; a very low 10 percent corporate tax on FDI; a 6 percent GNP growth rate; 2.7 percent inflation; the lowest average labor cost in Europe; and 20 percent unemployment (*Financial World,* 15 October 1991: 38-40).

6. CIM-derived technologies are in use in the Caribbean (see Chapter 8 for details).

7. The Barbados Mutual Life Assurance Society (BMLAS), one of the oldest mutual insurance companies in the Americas, is typical of the corporate merchant monopolies with a strong aversion to directly productive activities. For details of BMLAS' aversion see *Caribbean Week,* 24-30 November 1990:14.

8. Castro says he appreciates the experience, talent, and capacity of foreign investors and Cuba is pursuing foreign investment and joint ventures with Canadians, Europeans, and Latin Americans. Cuba has more than two hundred foreign companies operating with mixed investment projects. *Barbados Advocate,* 26 September 1991: 10; *Miami Herald,* 20 February 1991: 3A; *Washington Post,* 12 September 1991 :A-32.

9. For details of the development of graduate programs in business at the three campuses of the University of the West Indies, and of linkages with U.S. universities; see *Sunday Advocate* (Sunday Splash), 21 April 1991:15-19.

10. Caribbean countries are trying to woo Hong Kong Chinese with citizenship in return for investment in hotels, condominiums, treasury bonds, and government development funds. See *Weekend Nation,* 27 September 1991:13A; *Wall Street Journal, 29* October 1991: A-1.

Storm Signals: Structural Adjustment and Development Alternatives in the Caribbean

Kathy McAfee

The IMF/World Bank Prescription

The devastation wreaked upon the Caribbean peoples, through economic policies whose true purpose is hidden from us, is crushing our hopes for a better future. It is increasing poverty, especially among women, breaking up families, and deepening the cries and pain of our children, even those yet to be born. The dependency syndrome purposefully designed to favour US interests has tied our economies in debt that each one of us is forced to pay until we reach our deathbed. It is really a recolonisation by the North of the South.

Josephine Dublin, Caribbean Association for Feminist Research and Action

USAID's Caribbean policy, with its emphasis on privatisation and market-led growth, has failed to stimulate the increases in employment and investment promised by US policymakers. With the CBI discredited, the elusive goal of free-market development appears dim on the horizon, while the region's trade deficits and swelling debts loom large. In this context, AID has increased its emphasis on structural adjustment as a way, in the words of one AID official, 'to postpone the big crunch', of a drastic fiscal crisis for US allies in the Caribbean.

Structural adjustment is the economic strategy currently being promoted, not only in the Caribbean, but also in the majority of indebted nations in the South, by the US government, the World Bank, and the IMF. Its purpose is to improve the fiscal balance sheets of governments and stimulate economic growth, mainly by increasing exports. The idea is that impoverished countries will thus be able to dig their way out of debt and become paying customers in the global marketplace. Structural adjustment redirects resources away from consumption by the citizens of indebted countries in the South and toward debt payments to foreign lenders. It shifts capital, minerals, land and labour away from production for local needs and towards increased production for export.

Its proponents call it strong economic medicine which the ailing countries of the South must swallow for their own good. The economy doctors of the World Bank and the IMF, backing their pronouncements with computer projections, warn of dire consequences for the patients who do not swallow their medicine. The sponsors of structural adjustment also contend that it is urgent and essential to the preservation of the current global economic system. 'As the 1980s draw to a close, economic turbulence and uncertainty persist,' noted the World Bank in its 1988 World Development Report. The adoption of Bank-recommended policies by the North and the South for 'global adjustment', the report states, 'provide the best chance to avoid a worldwide economic downturn'.[1]

The Caribbean has been a structural adjustment testing ground. Jamaica was among the first countries to accept economic re-programming by the sponsors of adjustment; as of 1988, it had received more funds per capita in World Bank nations to help them cope with their balance of payments deficit. These deficits reflected the gap, which had developed during the years following the independence of most former colonies, between the borrowing countries' earnings from their exports of raw materials and their costs of importing the manufactured goods which they could not yet produce themselves. The IMF predicted that this gap would be closed gradually and that its loans could then be repaid with the proceeds of industrialisation and increased exports. The fact that prices for many commodities exported by the South were rising during the period of most active lending in the 1970s, after a long period of decline, made this scenario seem plausible to some. These raw material exports were then, and are still, the main source of income for most indebted countries.

By the end of the 1970s, however, it was apparent that the debt-paved path to prosperity was much steeper than anticipated. The prices of the mineral and agricultural commodities exported by the South resumed their decline. At the same time, the prices of manufactured imports, including those needed to build the planned roads, dams and factories continued to increase. Consequently, many of these large infrastructure projects proved too expensive to complete, while those that were completed typically failed to generate enough money to cover the cost of constructing them.

In addition, the rapid rise of interest rates saddled borrowing nations with annual debt bills that had doubled or tripled over the course of a few years. The World Bank estimated that developing countries' real interest rates rose 30 per cent in just two years (1980 to 1982).[4] Soon many debtor nations were forced to borrow immense sums merely to cover the interest payments they owed on previous loans. As the combined total of Third World debt edged towards US$1 trillion in the mid-1980s, it became obvious to borrowers and lenders alike that this tremendous debt bill could not be paid. Bankers, finance ministers and heads of state worldwide became alarmed. At stake was not only the wealth of the commercial banks and the health and prestige of the multilateral lending agencies but also the stability of the global economy and faith in

the free enterprise system as the basis for economic development in the South.

Adjustment in the 1980s: A New Level of Control

At the end of the 1970s, the economic experts of the World Bank seized upon structural adjustment as the solution to this looming crisis. Their reasoning was that underdeveloped countries that could not pay their debt and import bills were living beyond their means. The immediate causes of the borrowing countries' insolvency, falling commodity prices and rising interest rates, were outside the debtors' control. Moreover, the loans now overdue had been urged upon Southern governments by the banks and lending agencies themselves. Despite this, the World Bank and other lenders determined that impoverished debtor nations would now have to pull their belts tighter. They had to be compelled to consume less and to increase their export earnings at the same time. Structural adjustment was the tool for making sure that they did so. If indebted country governments could come up with enough revenue to make payments on some of their debts, the big lenders would then agree to roll over the remainder until some future date.

Most of the parties involved realised that the debts, especially the commercial bank loan bills now bloated by soaring interest charges, would never be repaid at their full face value; but, by refinancing their loans and by enforcing structural adjustment, the World Bank and IMF could postpone the day of reckoning. In the meantime, the commercial banks could recover as much as possible of their paper losses and the illusion of a stable international financial system could be maintained.

Structural adjustment lending had already been initiated by the IMF. During the 1970s, the IMF had devised a set of more or less standard stabilisation policies which the Fund required as a condition for refinancing past loans and extending new ones. At the core of these infamous IMF conditionalities were sweeping austerity measures intended to force borrowing countries in the Third World to spend less and earn more. (The largest debtor nation of the North, the United States, has never been subjected to similar pressure, despite the financial instability and the widely recognised danger to the global economic system created by the huge US government debt.)

By the early 1980s these austerity programmes had already provoked massive protests in some countries and contributed to the demise of a number of governments. Nevertheless, IMF austerity policies were the foundation upon which World Bank-sponsored adjustment programmes were built, and the two agencies continue to work hand-in-hand in designing and implementing those programmes. The two mega-agencies deny that they enforce cross-conditionality – the practice of requiring World Bank loan recipients to meet IMF conditionalities before Bank loans funds are released, or vice versa. However, the Bank and the Fund not only hold joint annual meetings and co-ordinate their general policies but also cooperate intimately in monitoring debtor country finances and in planning and supervising structural adjustment programmes. In the Caribbean and elsewhere, the World Bank negotiates structural adjustment loans in conjunction with IMF Structural Adjustment Facilities (SAFs), a loan category devised by the Fund in 1985. Cross-conditionality has in fact become standard practice.

From 1979 through 1987, the World Bank advanced 121 adjustment loans totalling US$15.3 billion. These include 51 structural adjustment loans and 70 sectoral adjustment loans, which are used to restructure particular sectors of the borrowing countries' economies, such as trade or agriculture. The adjustment loans ranged in size from US$500 million to Mexico to US$3 million to Dominica. The total amount of World Bank adjustment lending alone in 1987 was double the amount spent by the United States for development assistance worldwide in the same year. In 1988, World Bank adjustment lending increased further to 25 per cent of all new World Bank loans that year. The Bank is pleased with the policy clout it has achieved through its adjustment lending:

> Adjustment lending has become a major part of the Bank's development program ... It has involved the Bank, for the first time on a significant scale, in addressing short- and medium-term economic policy issues through its lending operations.[5]

The World Bank-sponsored structural adjustment programmes of the 1980s far surpassed the scope of IMF austerity policies. In addition to regulating the finances of indebted countries, the major task of the IMF, the Bank stepped in to regulate the internal economic policies, the distribution of resources and even political and social priorities within the countries undergoing adjustment. The degree of control assumed by the Bank has in many cases approached that of the former colonial powers over their subject nations.

During the 1980s, USAID became increasingly active in planning and enforcing Caribbean structural

adjustment policies, both in conjunction with the World Bank and IMF, and also independently. A 1988 AID memorandum asks:

> Is there any possibility that not only governments contemplating structural adjustment, but also the opposition parties and other interests in the societies, can be brought into the process? The important thing is not the analysis, but that the analysis convince all concerned of the costs and benefits of structural adjustment.[6]

In its Caribbean programme budget request for 1988, AID noted that, 'Although some structural adjustment measures have already been adopted, major additional adjustments are needed.' This emphasis was reiterated in AID's 1989-91 programmes.[7] AID now makes certain of its Caribbean project grants contingent on the recipient countries' compliance with IMF and World Bank conditionalities. The Agency also attaches structural adjustment requirements of its own to the budgetary support grants it gives to Caribbean governments, and even as a condition of US food aid. As shown in chapters 7 and 8, AID has taken a leading role in designing and implementing structural adjustment programmes in Dominica and Grenada.

Components of Caribbean Structural Adjustment Programmes

Structural adjustment programmes typically require the governments of indebted countries to adopt policy changes to achieve the following:

Reduced local consumption. This goal can be accomplished by various means, including currency devaluations which make imported goods more expensive. Such measures can be especially harmful to the populations of countries which depend on imported food. Another means of forcing needy people to consume less is by the reduction or removal of subsidies or price ceilings that many governments use to limit the prices of staple foods and other basic goods. Whether the means employed are currency devaluation or the removal of subsidies or price controls, the result is the same: prices rise and most people cannot afford to buy as much. The adjustment experts describe the policy goal of reduced consumption in terms such as 'tightening of domestic demand' or 'reduced local absorption'. This abstract economese obscures the fact that the direct intent of these measures is to force already-impoverished populations to get along on even less.

Higher personal taxes and other means of increasing government revenues by collecting more from the poor and middle classes. Many structural adjustment programmes include new forms of indirect taxation, such as sales or value-added taxes (VAT) that fall disproportionately on the poor. Adjustment programmes generally discourage taxation of businesses and high-income individuals. This is to encourage increased domestic savings by allowing the better-off sectors of society to retain more of their incomes. According to adjustment theory, the wealthy will then invest these savings locally in economically productive activities. In reality, however, business people and large-scale landowners frequently invest their higher incomes and profits abroad, or spend them on luxury consumption and speculation. Deregulation of the uses of foreign exchange and the *laissez-faire* thrust of structural adjustment programmes leave affected countries with few means of preventing these practices.

Government subsidies to the private sector. To qualify for most adjustment loans, governments must agree to spend a larger proportion of both local revenues and the foreign assistance they receive on projects to aid private investors, particularly foreign corporations. Such projects typically include construction of port facilities and roads to expedite the shipment of exports and the provision of water, electricity, government services and factory buildings, often at rates below their actual cost, to businesses engaged in export manufacturing. Such measures are designed to entice foreign investors to channel local land, labour and capital into export production. These policies, however, also reduce the ability of local enterprises, which often cannot compete with large foreign corporations, to provide jobs and to supply local products to meet local needs.

In structural adjustment terminology, such spending priorities make up an adjusting country's Public Sector Investment Programme (PSIP). This term refers to spending by the public sector, not primarily for public needs, but rather for the private sector. While some components of PSIP programmes, such as better roads, are undoubtedly needed by the adjusting countries, priorities within the PSIP, such as where new roads are to be built, are determined more by their potential enhancement of export profits rather than by the needs of the local population for greater economic self-reliance and food security.

Lower taxes on businesses and tax holiday periods of 5-20 years, during which time new investors are not required to pay taxes to host country governments. These and other financial incentives are designed to attract investors, especially foreign inves-

tors, by making the production of exports more convenient and profitable. The tax revenue losses to host countries, however, especially when added to the expenses incurred under PSIP programmes, often end up costing countries much more than they gain from new foreign investment. And foreign corporations frequently pocket the proceeds of government subsidised low-wage manufacturing, then move their operations elsewhere when tax holiday periods expire.

Removal or reduction of tariffs and levies on exports. Such taxes have been used by governments to tap some of the wealth generated by the exporters of agricultural and mineral commodities. Since they may, however, counteract the structural adjustment goal of maximising exports at all costs, they are discouraged or forbidden under the terms of most structural adjustment programmes.

Decreased public spending on services to local citizens, including health, education, sanitation and housing, and on other activities that do not directly enhance export earnings. In addition to, or in lieu of, structural adjustment loans, the World Bank sometimes arranges sectoral adjustment loans to be used by governments to 'rationalise' health, agricultural extension, education and other programmes.

Sectoral adjustment programmes in public service sectors attempt to reduce government spending by means such as raising school fees and the prices of books, reducing the numbers of teachers and scholarships, and charging new fees for services, such as health clinic visits and vaccinations, which were previously provided free of charge. The sponsors of adjustment tend to view these services as unaffordable luxuries, even though they address the needs of the world's poorest people and even though the governments of the South already spend a much smaller portion of their revenues on social services than do the industrialised nations.[8]

The dismantling, scaling down, or sale of government-owned enterprises, except those which directly or indirectly support the private sector, and the sale of publicly owned lands, utilities and industries at low cost to private investors. In the view of the adjustment experts, agricultural co-operatives, as well as government-owned farms, factories, power companies and marketing corporation are, by definition, inefficient. However, no standard yardstick of efficiency is used to evaluate and compare the operations of private corporations, or of aid projects or public agencies that support and subsidise private enterprise.

Reduction of the number of government employees. Like the selling of government enterprises, public sector retrenchments (lay-offs) are intended to increase efficiency, reduce public spending and balance government budgets. But since, at the same time, governments are required to provide increased services to businesses, it is those services that benefit the poor majority of citizens which typically suffer most as a consequence of reduced government payrolls.

Lower wages, especially for workers in export agriculture and manufacturing. By keeping a lid on public employees' salaries, freezing wages or failing to enforce minimum wage laws, and by doing whatever is necessary to reduce the influence of trade unions, governments are expected to improve the business climate for foreign investors.

Adjustment experts frequently blame the failure of poor country economies to grow on the high cost of doing business there and, in particular, on non-competitive wages. World Bank emissaries exhort the governments of adjusting countries to freeze real wages or to enact currency devaluations, which have the same effect of lowering workers' incomes, in order to compete in attracting investors with other poor countries which are lowering their own workers' wages in response to identical advice from the Bank.

Opening of domestic markets to foreign-based exporters of manufactured goods and food. One way of doing this is by eliminating import quotas and tariffs that are sometimes used by governments to raise the prices of imported products and thus to protect their own countries' industries from foreign competition. Such protectionist policies violate structural adjustment doctrine. The World Bank contends that, 'An outward-oriented strategy is superior to one in which trade and industrial incentives are biased in favour of production for the domestic market over the export market'.[9] This is an updated version of the time-worn economic development theory of comparative advantage. According to this theory, World Bank countries will do best by producing bananas or baseballs for export, while importing things like wheat and radios, leaving the production of these and most other goods for local consumption in the hands of the developed countries.

Foreign corporations, World Bank economists still insist, can better supply most consumer goods, machinery and even food to poor nations than can local producers. Low-income nations, they say, should confine their economic efforts to the export of what they are currently best at producing, mainly unprocessed agricultural and mineral commodities and the products of low-wage assembly industries. The outcome of such advice in case after case has been the reinforcement of dependency and of poverty-creating patterns of trade.

Expanded Tourism. The Caribbean version of structural adjustment also calls for the expansion of tourism, with few restrictions or guidelines other than the goal of bringing in foreign currency. The region's tourist industry has already despoiled the environment, contributed to increased drug abuse and prostitution, replaced farms on agricultural land with hotels, and placed many beaches and scenic areas off-limits to local people. But tourism does bring in dollars that can help pay debts, and that is the adjustors' main concern.

The Caribbean Precedent: Region-wide Orchestrated Adjustment

Oscar Allen, leader of the Rural Transformation Collective in St Vincent and the Grenadines, observed at a meeting of development organisations in the Eastern Caribbean in March 1988:

> The stranglehold on us by foreign institutions today is more total than under the colonial situation, because it is cultural and social as well as economic, and because it includes co-operation and co-ordination among Caribbean governments under terms dictated by the IMF and the World Bank.

The Caribbean is the only area of the world, thus far, where the structural adjustment programmes of an entire group of nations are being orchestrated by a region-wide organisation dominated by outside forces. This body, the Caribbean Group for Co-operation in Economic Development (CGCED), is led by the IMF and the World Bank, and includes more than 30 government and multinational agencies and 22 Caribbean states. Through the CGCED, the United States, other governments and the multilateral lending institutions co-ordinate decisions about how much and what kind of aid the indebted Caribbean countries will receive, whether countries will be allowed to postpone some debt payments and what kinds of policy changes will be required as a condition of the aid given or the debt rescheduling permitted.

AID is an active member of the CGCED and, while not bound by CGCED decisions, generally pursues policies parallel to those of the CGCED. The CGCED's resources, especially those of the World Bank and IMF, far outweigh those of AID, and the consortium has been more effective in promoting AID's privatisation and structural adjustment priorities than AID itself. This has been particularly true since 1988, when AID budget cuts reduced the Agency's influence over the details of adjustment programmes for the region. Until 1988, AID has been using ESF grants to help plug the budget gaps of the United States' Caribbean allies in return for those countries' promises to implement structural adjustment measures. The bulk of Caribbean ESF funds were, however, eliminated from the 1988 US foreign assistance budget. Zak explained that the Caribbean ESF cuts were made because, 'They're small countries, they're in our backyard, and the US has no overwhelming security interest there at present, since Grenada is no longer a problem.'

The lack of ESF funds reduced AID's bargaining power in the CGCED, 'Nobody believes them [AID] any more', remarked an official of the World Bank's Caribbean programme. AID complained to Congress that, 'In effect, the elimination of ESF in FY [financial year] 1988 to the Caribbean takes AID out of the macroeconomic policy dialogue, AID's highest priority in the Caribbean region.' The ESF cuts prompted AID to attach more stringent structural adjustment requirements to other types of aid, including PL 480 food donations and development assistance. According to David Cohen, then AID's Caribbean Programme Director, however, 'The economic issues are the same, whether the agency dealing with them is AID, the IMF, or the [World] Bank.'

The CGCED: Caribbean adjustors' club

The CGCED usually meets for one week every 18 months in Washington. The IMF and the World Bank set the group's agenda and chair its meetings. Attending the ninth CGCED meeting in Washington in June 1988 were representatives from 17 Caribbean recipient countries, 10 donor nations (Canada, France, Germany, Italy, Japan, the Netherlands, Spain, Britain, Brazil and the United States), and 9 international aid or lending institutions. More than 350 delegates and observers, the majority from the North, attended. Non-government organisations from the Caribbean member countries were not permitted to attend. Between meetings, the World Bank and IMF send monitoring missions to examine the finances and economic policies of the Caribbean member states. Recommendations resulting from these missions become the basis for discussions and decisions made at CGCED sessions and sub-committee meetings on the various member countries.

The donor governments and agencies, of course, have their own agendas. They hold bilateral negotia-

tions outside of the CGCED context, and do not always comply with CGCED recommendations. One World Bank official complained after the 1988 CGCED meeting that some member governments are giving too much aid to certain Caribbean states:

> The availability of financing by other donors inhibits countries such as Antigua and Barbados from accepting the need for structural adjustment. It allows them to postpone the inevitable. . . if a country is not ready to put structural adjustment in place, the Bank abstains from lending, or we go in with minor involvement until they accept the need to adjust, and the social costs of investment. It's not just a question of cutting public expenditures, but also of providing adequate incentives and a framework for foreign investment.[10]

In general, however, the IMF and World Bank have used the CGCED successfully as a means of getting donors to line up in support of structural adjustment in the region. According to CGCED chairman and World Bank Vice-President S. Sahid Husain, 'the Group has increasingly provided a useful forum for policy dialogue and for co-ordinating external finances for adjustment'.

Many Caribbean leaders see it differently, 'What is referred to as "policy dialogue" is a method of manipulation,' says William G. Demas, a respected Caribbean economist and former head of the CDB:

> To the extent that AID and the multilaterals veer away from project lending and into policy dialogue – in which they impose their own policies, with their lack of knowledge of the region – it doesn't work. Their simplistic structural adjustment policies, stressing growth above all else, have led to a depressing of demand and the suffering of the poor. When you make the poor suffer, you erode the human capital on which development depends.[11]

Through the CGCED, the multilateral agencies have succeeded in imposing their own policy priorities on many Caribbean governments. Ricky Singh, a Guyanese journalist and astute observer of Caribbean politics, comments that, 'The multilaterals are refining their technique, trying to get governments to institute IMF-type policies as if the governments themselves were requesting them.'[12]

According to a World Bank position paper prepared for the June 1988 CGCED meeting, 'Most of the CGCED countries are small. . . Smallness means that economic growth must inevitably be export-led, at least in the long run.' This view seems to have been accepted by nearly all the current leaders of Caribbean governments, who, in their presentations to the CGCED, stress their eagerness to comply with related adjustment criteria. World Bank economist Roger Robinson, at the time assigned to Jamaica, noted in 1988 that the 'policy dialogue' between the Bank and Caribbean governments on the issue of export-led development has been 'intense' but effective. Immediately after the June 1988 CGCED meeting, Robinson remarked with an air of satisfaction that, 'Most of the governments in the CGCED now see that the main potential for growth is external.' In this context, even countries which do not have official World Bank or IMF-sponsored structural adjustment programmes, such as St Vincent and the Grenadines, come to the CGCED donor consortium to request funds and to report on their policies.

The policies of the seven-member nations of the OECS are subject to the tight scrutiny of a CGCED sub-committee called the Tighter Consultative Group (TCG).[13] 'The TCG has Caribbean staff, including economists, but they must play by the USAID rulebook,' observed University of the West Indies political economist Dr Neville Duncan.[14] The failure of Grenada to satisfy the criteria of the TCG is the reason given by both World Bank and US officials for the lack of support for Grenada by the IMF and the Bank, and for the slashing of Grenada's USAID programme.

As part of their effort to overcome the smallness which, in the World Bank's view, sentences them to external export dependency, the OECS countries asked the CGCED in 1985 to deal with them as a group, co-ordinating funding and related adjustment measures through the OECS secretariat. The World Bank would not agree. According to the USAID official responsible for structural adjustment in the Eastern Caribbean, Robin Phillips, 'No multilateral, and probably not AID, would put money into something controlled by someone else.'

CGCED decisions are made behind closed doors. The conditions and terms on which they are based are rarely made public, even though they often have a direct impact on Caribbean taxes, wages, prices, social services and living conditions. When the World Bank commissions studies and projects in connection with structural adjustment programmes, the relevant documents are made available to consultants and bidders for the contracts, but not to the Caribbean citizens whose futures are at stake.

The arm-twisting that takes place at CGCED sessions is hidden behind a public façade of jovial diplomacy and consensus among equals. This secrecy

helps Caribbean governments to preserve the illusion that it is they, and not their creditors, who set policies for their nations. The CGCED reflects the degree to which the sovereignty of the region has become (or, more accurately, has remained) subordinate to the powers and priorities of governments and institutions outside the Caribbean. The co-ordinator of a non-governmental development agency in St Vincent and the Grenadines, Cecil Ryan, commented at a 1988 meeting on development goals:

> What we are facing is a new form of an old problem. The mechanisms to withdraw resources from our countries have become more sophisticated. Now international capital is being used to extract value from the Caribbean through regional institutions, and our own governments are co-operating more in going along with it.

In the eyes of many Caribbean observers, the extent of control by the World Bank and the IMF over the economic options of Caribbean states represents a new stage in a process of recolonisation. As such, the CGCED may be an ominous precedent for other impoverished countries, particularly those in sub-Saharan Africa whose weakened economies, high levels of non-commercial foreign debt and lack of political bargaining power may make them subject to similar mechanisms of outside control.

Adjusting to the Power of International Control

The immediate goal of adjustment is to give indebted governments quick cash to stave off bankruptcy, make payments on their debts and avert a collapse of the banking system in the North. To a limited extent, this goal has been achieved. By the World Bank's accounting, the less developed countries (LDCs) of the South paid to the banks and governments of the North US$43 billion more in 1988 than they received in aid and new loans.[15] The net flow of financial resources from South to North, out of poor countries and into wealthy nations, corporations and institutions, has accelerated yearly since 1985. This has helped ease the mood of near panic among bankers and finance ministers in the North but it has not resolved the debt crisis.

The long-term goal of adjustment lending is to restructure poor-country economies to give maximum advantage and a free hand to private investors. With the private sector at the helm, propelled by the winds of free trade, poor countries will, the adjustors contend, be able to steer a course towards rapid economic growth. Corporations and business owners, they say, are better able to take the steps, especially the wage reductions, necessary to make poor countries' exports cheaper and thus more competitive in world markets.

This international competitiveness, in the opinion of the sponsors of structural adjustment, is the key to economic growth. Economic growth, in their view, is the essence of development. Whether most of the low-income indebted countries can achieve growth, much less development, by increasing their exports is doubtful, but it is particularly unlikely in the case of the small, fragmented economies of the Caribbean. 'We're told we must have free trade,' Arnhim Eustace of the CDB told the author, 'but there's no way we can compete internationally on those terms.'

Whether viewed as stranglehold or stewardship, the imposition of structural adjustment has failed to produce sustainable development in the Caribbean. Some countries have experienced short-term improvements in balances of payments, reduced government budget deficits, and modest GDP growth, but at a terrible cost to social infrastructure, environment and prospects for longer-term or broader-based development. The pattern is not unlike that elsewhere in Latin America and in Africa. In September 1989, the UN Commission on Trade and Development (UNCTAD) added its voice to that of the UN Economic Commission on Africa (UNECA) and the growing number of international development agencies and analysts who challenge World Bank claims of structural adjustment success.[16]

The Bank itself has not yet conceded failure but it has begun to shift its emphasis from structural adjustment programmes *per se*. In March 1990, World Bank Vice-President and then chief economist Stanley Fisher announced that the Bank was planning to reduce the proportion of quick-disbursing structural adjustment loans in its portfolio while increasing the total amount of its lending for specific projects. (Part of the Bank's motive in steering away from structural adjustment loans is the realisation to that such reforms are failing, that highly indebted countries may be unable to pay these and other World Bank loans, and that this could threaten the Bank's own high credit rating.)[17] As the case of Jamaica illustrates, however, increasingly the Bank ties such project loans to the same conditionalities that are contained in structural adjustment agreements.

Adjustment-related measures, especially the rescheduling of poor-country debts, may indeed have helped to postpone a global financial catastrophe. But almost everywhere it has been attempted, structural adjustment has been accompanied by increased poverty and unemployment, declining export incomes, higher debts and political unrest. This is clearly true in the Caribbean, where the results of adjustment experiments suggest that for impoverished nations, structural adjustment medicine is likely to worsen the conditions it is intended to cure.

Notes

1. World Bank, *World Development Report*, Washington, 1988.
2. Giovanni Andrea Cornea, Richard Jolly and Francis Stewart, *Adjustment with a Human Face*, UNICEF, Clarendon Press, 1987; Susan George, *A Fate Worse than Debt*, Food First/Grove Press, 1988; 'The Berlin Statement' by NGOs to the joint annual meeting of the World Bank and the IMF in Berlin in 1988.
3. Congressional Consultation sponsored by the House of Representatives Subcommittee on Western Hemisphere Affairs and the Washington-based development advocacy agency, The Development GAP.
4. World Bank, *World Development Report*, Washington DC, 1988.
5. 'Lending for Adjustment', *World Bank News*, Special Report, Washington, April 1988.
6. USAID 'New Initiatives', unpublished memorandum.
7. USAID *Congressional Presentations*, 1988-91. According to Marilyn Zak, Acting Director of AID's Caribbean and Latin America programme: 'There's been some improvement in government policies in the region because of structural adjustment programmes worked out with the IMF and the World Bank. We see progress toward our goals in privatisation, divestment, and tax policy reform.' (Interview with the author, June 1988, Washington DC.)
8. World Bank, *World Development Report*, Washington, 1988.
9. World Bank, *World Development Report*, Washington, 1987.
10. Author interview, June 1988.
11. Author interview, December 1987.
12. Author interview, November 1987.
13. The OECS includes the independent nations of Antigua and Barbuda, St Kitts/Nevis, Dominica, St Lucia, St Vincent and the Grenadines, and Grenada, and the British crown colony, Montserrat.
14. Author interview, November 1987.
15. World Bank, *World Debt Tables*, Washington, 1989.
16. UNECA, August 1989; UNCTAD Report, 1989.
17. *Washington Post*, 15 March, 1990.

Journal of Eastern Caribbean Studies
Vol. 24 No. 2 June 1999

Commentary

The New International Economic Environment: The WTO And Implications For The OECS

McHale Andrew

Introduction

The countries which comprise the Organisation of Eastern Caribbean States[1] (OECS) have, since the post World War II period, witnessed a relatively favourable development process based, among other things, on a trading environment characterised by one way preferential access to international markets, concessional development financing and generous inflows of aid, technical assistance and investments. It is indeed estimated that official development assistance accounted for about 25% of the Gross National Product (GNP) of the sub-region during the relatively buoyant decade of the 1980s.[2]

Contemporary international economic trends, including the much vaunted process of globalisation, have however threatened to derail the development gains of these micro-states and heightened their vulnerability by exposing their economies to the full effects of reciprocal trade. As the era of special and differential considerations in international trade and economic relations races to an end, these seemingly hapless states have little choice but to develop coherent, coordinated strategies for responding to the new global economic changes.

This note traces the reshaping of the trading international economy from the immediate post war period to the establishment of the World Trade Organisation (WTO) in 1995, with a major focus on the key principles, obligations and challenges inherent in membership of that new body. The implications for the OECS and the imperatives, which the author believes must be embodied in an effective strategic response, are also highlighted.

Historical Overview of the International Economy

Nationalism and factionalism in the industrial world, particularly in the United States of America during the early part of the 20th century, hindered the world trade that was necessary for financing the war debt and reparations in the aftermath of World War I. It is believed that the protectionism which was influenced by this state of affairs may have prolonged and exacerbated the Great Depression of the 1930s. This in turn may have influenced World War II, which itself had both a disastrous and cathartic impact on world trade. By the end of the War in 1945, major improvements in transportation, as well as the astounding increase in the number of merchant ships set the stage for a new era in international trade. The United States was the only unscathed industrialized economy and in accordance with President Roosevelt's 'New Deal', the only surviving economic giant that would oversee preparations for the restoration of world trade.

In July 1944, forty-four (44) countries including Great Britain, the USA and USSR met in Bretton Woods, New Hampshire, to hammer out an agreement which saw the creation of the International Monetary Fund (IMF) and the World Bank. An International Trade Organisation (ITO) was also to have been created under the terms of the agreement, as a specialised agency of the United Nations. The ITO's draft charter extended beyond trade disciplines to include proposed rules on employment, commodity agreements, restrictive business practices, international investment and services. (Most of these ironically are now the subject of ongoing WTO negotiations). While the ITO negotiations were still taking place, 23 of the 50 participating countries decided in 1946 to accelerate the pace of trade liberalisation by agreeing to reduce customs tariffs to the tune of US$10 billion or one-fifth of total world trade. The 45,000 tariff line concessions together with some of the trade rules of the proposed ITO, which were accepted by these pioneering 'contracting parties,' became known as the General Agreement on Tariffs and Trade (GATT). The ITO however failed to materialize after the US Congress refused to ratify the charter which had been agreed at a 1948 International Trade and Employment Conference in Havana, Cuba. The GATT also served as an 'interim secretariat' for international trade negotiations.

GATT 1947

The GATT was salvaged from the stillborn ITO as an institution but GATT, the agreement, was more of a diplomatic than a legal accord. It nevertheless survived as the only multilateral mechanism for ordering international trade relations, from 1948 until the creation of the WTO in 1995. There were seven (7) 'rounds' of trade negotiations from 1947-1986, most of which concentrated on tariff reductions, but later extended into other trade disciplines such as anti-dumping and non-tariff barriers (NTB's) to trade.

The GATT however remained a voluntary agreement among the ever growing number of participating states. It was not legally enforceable and any member could veto or ignore its attempted sanctions with impunity if they felt so inclined. During its embryonic stage the GATT had a membership of 23 countries, which encompassed the majority of the world's wealth but excluded most of its population, Nevertheless from 1948 to 1994 it achieved remarkable success in increasing the volume of world trade as well as in the reduction of tariffs; world trade growth averaged 8% per annum during the 1950s and 1960s and consistently outpaced production increases throughout the GATT period. Further, from 1948-1994 average tariffs on industrial goods fell from about 40% to approximately 5%.

Globalisation Era - 1980s and 1990s

Notwithstanding the gains of GATT, it became clear by the 1980s that an overhaul of the international system was required in order to make the GATT more 'global' and more attractive to the emerging economies of the developing world.

The globalisation of the world economy was proceeding steadily along during the 1980s, ushering in unprecedented economic and trade liberalisation. That initial push gathered tremendous momentum during the early 1990s as the US became the only superpower in a unipolar world and the age of 'information technology, dawned.

But what is globalisation? It has been said that, 'Globalisation of the Caribbean economy is not a late twentieth century phenomenon; it has always been a companion of production specialisation, from the sugar plantations of the past to the tourist enclaves of today... What is different today is the increased vulnerability of the Caribbean political economy ...'.[3]

Indeed, the concept of globalisation itself is not new but when used in the analysis of contemporary international economic trends it refers to a confluence of new economic and political phenomena that have helped to shape the new international economy. These include:

i. the deeper and more widespread integration of both markets and production processes at the international level. This trend has been spurred by the increasing regionalisation of international trade through the plethora of new

regional Free Trade Areas (FTAs) and the recognition of the need for strategic global alliances in the quest to maintain competitiveness in an increasingly competing world.

ii. the increased interconnectedness of national financial markets as barriers to capital flows are dismantled at the same time as improvements in information technology. This, of course, leads to greater susceptibility to contagion effects as financial turbulence in one national market quickly spreads to another, even if the macro-economic fundamentals in the latter are strong.

iii. the increased international vulnerability of small countries in particular, as special and differential treatment based on traditional political and economic ties gives way to full reciprocity in trade, as well as greater competition for development finance on commercial terms and more intense efforts at attracting inward investment.

iv. freer, faster and more voluminous information flows across international borders. This makes the world truly a 'global village' and introduces an entirely new dimension to trade, marketing and information sharing.

Unipolarity and the era of instant information have influenced a more homogenous economic philosophy throughout the world, the fall of communism and the concomitant break-up of the Soviet Union have allowed many more countries to embrace free market disciplines, as they seek to attract greater investment flows and to satisfy the employment and welfare needs of more demanding populations.

An international trading system consequent upon the establishment of the WTO, which is more rules-based, has more effective enforcement powers, is increasingly competitive, and more global as regards the number of participating countries.

Technology development taking place in many more countries, as opposed to the traditional western powers and Japan, and *ipso facto* vastly improved access to technology in the production processes of many countries.

The concept of 'universal jurisdiction' has replaced 'absolute sovereignty' as witnessed in the recent case of former Chilean dictator Augusto Pinochet, the UN Security Council sanctions against Iraq since 1991 and the Bosnia War crimes tribunal, among others. This new concept in international political and diplomatic affairs has crept into economic accords as witnessed in the WTO, the embrace of governance issues by the IMF and World Bank, as well as in G7 communiqués.

Advent of WTO

The establishment of the WTO was a seminal achievement of the Uruguay Round of the GATT. From 1986-1994 various agreements on trade liberalisation, encompassing but not limited to tariff reductions, were concluded among the growing number of GATT member states. The Agenda, however, was very much set by the larger industrialised countries with inconsistent participation by most developing countries. Nevertheless, the WTO came into existence on 1 January 1995, marking the most comprehensive restructuring of the international trading system since 1948. It is the sole international institution with responsibility for regulating trade between nations, as well as the first legally enforceable multilateral trade agreement at that level.

The main WTO Agreement is quite brief with a mere 16 articles which provide for the establishment of the organisation, its mandate, as well as its institutional and procedural structure. This is followed by four (4) annexes; Annex 1 covers the multilateral trade agreements in the areas of goods (1A), services (1B), and intellectual property (1C); Annex 2 deals with dispute settlement procedures; Annex 3 comprises the trade policy review mechanism, and Annex 4 extends to the plurilateral agreements on government procurement, civil aircraft, dairy and meat.[4]

The three main purposes of the WTO are to:

- help international trade flow as freely as possible;
- serve as a forum for multilateral trade negotiations; and
- serve as a trade dispute settlement body.

WTO members are guided by four major principles, namely; non-discrimination, liberalisation, predictability and competitiveness.

Non discrimination

The two major aspects of the non-discrimination principle are Most Favoured Nation (MFN) and National Treatment. MFN simply means that when one country accords a special benefit or preference to one trading partner, it is obligated to extend that same 'most favoured' treatment to all other WTO Members. MFN is such a prominent feature of the WTO that it is embodied in Article 1 of the GATT (1994), Article 2 of the General Agreement on Trade in Services (GATS) and Article 4 of the Agreement on Trade Related Aspects of Intellectual Property (TRIPS). There are however some exceptions to the MFN rule, the most notable being the exemption allowed to members of a Regional Free Trade Area (RFTA).

National treatment requires that local and foreign products and services, as well as trademarks, copyrights and patents should be treated equally. In its most basic form it means that non-nationals should be given the same treatment as nationals. This principle is also an integral requirement of the GATT (1994) (Article 3), GATS (Article 17) and TRIPS (Article 3).

It must be noted that national treatment only applies *after* a product or service has entered the market. Customs duties on imports without an equivalent charge on domestically produced goods would therefore not be inconsistent with the principle of equal treatment.

Liberalisation

Given the forty-seven (47) years of steady liberalisation under the GATT, the WTO seeks to widen and deepen the trade liberalisation process through adherence to the principle of 'progressive liberalisation.' This includes reduction of tariff and non-tariff barriers, and other trade restricting practices.

While promoting the opening of markets through tariff reductions and removal of other trade restricting practices the WTO also recognises the possible adverse effect of too rapid liberalisation on the economies of developing countries and accordingly allows those countries to introduce these reforms gradually. Article XI (2) of the WTO Agreement, Article 16 (1) of Part X, and Article 27 (Part VIII) of the GATT 1994 are but a few of the codified examples of this recognition.

Predictability

In order to allow potential trading partners and investors the opportunity of knowing what trade regime, including tariff levels, obtains in any one country, WTO members 'bind' their commitments when they agree to open up their markets for goods and services. In the case of goods, 'binding' means placing ceilings on import tariff rates, and in services countries agree not to place any new restrictions on non-resident/non-national service providers. Changes in bindings usually require negotiation with affected trading partners, who would then be eligible for compensation for the loss of trade arising from the changes. In practice however, developing countries generally tend to bind tariff rates at a much higher level than the actual rates, while developed countries on the whole bind at existing tariff levels.

Binding engenders a measure of market security and predictability for traders and investors. The WTO seeks to promote such stability by also discouraging the use of quantitative restrictions on imports and by requiring a high level of transparency and clarity in each country's trade rules. This calls for full public disclosure of governments' trade related policies and practices and requires notification to the WTO as well.

The following table illustrates the percentage of bindings (by tariff lines) before and after the Uruguay Round for developed and developing countries and economies in transition (mainly Eastern European countries in transition from centrally planned to market based economies).

TABLE 1: PERCENTAGE OF TARIFFS BOUND

	Uruguay Round	
	Before (%)	After (%)
Developed Countries	78	99
Developing Countries	21	73
Transition Economies	73	98

Competitiveness

This principle underscores the WTO's mandate to promote fair competition among its members. In a world of disparate countries, as regards size, economic influence, structure and practices, it makes utmost sense for the establishment of a system of rules designed to ensure open, fair and undistorted competition. While the WTO agreements provide in large measure for such a system, the absence of a specific agreement on competition policy is cause for concern. This is particularly so when mega-mergers and other forms of production integration lead to harmful monopolistic or oligopolistic practices by multi-national corporations (MNCs). It is nevertheless expected that the European Union's (EU) competition policy regime would influence a similar agreement at the WTO level during the 'Millenium Round' negotiations which are set for 1999/2000.

As mentioned earlier, the WTO Agreement essentially comprises the GATT 1994, the GATS and the TRIPS Agreement. A glimpse into the major undertakings in these agreements may allow a deeper appreciation for the extent to which the establishment of that institution has helped reshape the international economy. It is worth noting nevertheless that the WTO is the base from which all future trade agreements would be negotiated; while Article XXIV of the GATT 1994 provides for the co-existence of customs unions and regional free trade areas with the WTO, it recognises 'that the purpose of a customs union or a free trade area should be to facilitate trade between the constituent territories and not to raise barriers to the trade. . . .' This is in keeping with the WTO requirement to progressively liberalize all trade between member countries. The WTO agreements, including GATT, GATS and TRIPS, are essentially binding contracts between WTO member governments for the regulation and conduct of international trade.

GATT 1994

The WTO charter at Article II (4) states that 'The General Agreement on Tariffs and Trade 1994 as specified in Annex 1 (A) (hereinafter referred to as 'GATT 1994') is legally distinct from the General Agreement on Tariffs and Trade, dated 30 October 1947, annexed to the Final Act adopted at the conclusion of the second session of the Preparatory Committee of the United-Nations Conference on Trade and Employment, as subsequently rectified, amended or modified'.[5]

However, though legally distinct from GATT 1947, GATT 1994 includes the substantive and legal provisions as well as the understandings of the former, as amended, rectified or modified by the terms of the legal instruments which have entered into force before the date of entry into the WTO Agreement.[6]

The effect of this is to distinguish GATT 1947 (The Agreement) from GATT 1947 (The Institution). With the advent of the WTO, GATT 1947 (The Agreement) as amended, was wholly incorporated into GATT 1994 which forms an integral part of the WTO Agreements, while GATT 1947 (The Institution) which served as an 'interim' secretariat for trade negotiations for forty-seven (47) years, was replaced by the WTO, as the sole institution for regulating multilateral trade.

The major trade liberalising achievements of the Uruguay Round as contained in GATT 1994 were as follows:

- Tariffs on industrial goods were cut by 30-35%.
- Duties on selected products e.g. medical equipment, toys, beer, furniture were scheduled for abolition.
- Subsidies on agricultural exports are to be reduced by 36% by 2001.
- The quantity of agricultural exports benefiting from subsidies are targeted for reduction by 21% during the same period.

- Quantitative restrictions (import quotas) on agricultural goods would be immediately replaced by tariff equivalents and these tariffs themselves would be reduced by 36% in six (6) years for developed countries, and 24% in ten (10) years for developing countries.
- In the sensitive area of textiles, discriminatory trade practices were agreed to be phased out by 1 January, 2000 and the multi-fiber agreements would be abolished by 2005.

GATS

The General Agreement on Trade in Services (GATS) is the first ever multilateral agreement in the area of services and, quite apart from liberalisation of services themselves, could have a profound impact on production processes, technological development and investment.

The GATS, like the agreements on goods, includes; (i) a main text containing general principles and obligations, (ii) annexes dealing with rules for specific sectors and (iii) individual countries' specific commitments to provide access to their market. GATS however, goes one step further than the goods agreement to include a fourth element, namely lists showing where countries are not applying the Most Favoured Nation principle of non-discrimination. These commitments are all an integral part of the GATS and even the withdrawal of MFN treatment can only be temporary under the rules.

Major Principles of GATS

The overall objective of GATS is to develop rules that will result in improved transparency, stability and consistency, legal certainty, and freer, less discriminatory norms and regulations. The agreement covers all internationally traded services except, for the time being, air transportation/airline services. However, publicly provided (government) services not in competition with the private sector are not under the purview of the GATS.

The *Modes of Supply* of internationally traded services are also defined in the agreement in four specific ways:-

v.   Cross Border Supply; services supplied from one country to another (e.g. international telephone calls);

vi.   Consumption Abroad; consumers or firms making use of a service in another country (e.g. tourism);

vii. Commercial Presence; a foreign company setting up subsidiaries or branches to provide services in another country (e.g. foreign banks or hotels setting-up operations in the OECS);

viii. Presence of Natural Persons; individuals travelling from their own country to supply services in another (e.g. entertainers, consultants, medical doctors).

The *MFN* principle simply means that one's trading partners must be treated equally. Under GATS, if a country allows foreign competition in a sector, equal opportunities in that sector should be given to service providers from all other WTO members, even if the country has made no specific commitment to provide foreign companies access to its markets. However some special *temporary exemptions* may be allowed.

Another key principle is *National Treatment;* this requires that once a foreign company or individual has been allowed to supply a service in one's country, there should be no discrimination between the foreign and local entity. National treatment is a general principle for goods (GATT) and in trade-related aspects of intellectual property (TRIPS) but in GATS it applies only where a country has made specific commitments.

The WTO also requires that member governments publish all relevant laws and regulations in order to satisfy the principle of *Transparency.* By the end of 1997 all WTO member countries should have set up contact or inquiry points within their bureaucracies for publishing information, standards, regulations, etc.

There is also a requirement for regulations pertinent to the provision of services to be administered *Objectively, Reasonably and Impartially.* In that regard member governments are mandated to provide impartial means, such as tribunals, for reviewing administrative actions and decisions affecting the supply of services.

The *recognition* of other countries' qualifications that affect the licensing or certification of service suppliers must not be discriminatory. Where two or more governments have such mutual recognition agreements, other WTO members must also be given a chance to negotiate similar accords.

Restrictions on international payments and transactions affecting trade in services are not allowed except where severe balance of payments difficulties are being experienced and even then can be applied only temporarily and within agreed limits and conditions.

Specific Commitments

Individual countries are required to make commitments under the four modes of supply with respect to market access and national treatment. The commitments are listed in schedules that outline the sectors being offered, the extent of market access allowed in these sectors (e.g. whether there are restrictions on foreign ownership), and any limitations on national treatment (e.g. whether foreign companies will be accorded the same rights as local ones).

These commitments are 'bound' and like tariffs they can only be modified or withdrawn after negotiations with affected countries; where injury or other adverse effects are proven then the affected country would be entitled to compensation for the loss of market access.

If a sector is not included in a country's offers then the general obligations on MFN and transparency would still apply but specific obligations/commitments would not.

TRIPS

The Agreement on Trade-Related aspects of Intellectual Property (TRIPS) Is also an integral part of the WTO Agreement and like services is included as a distinct discipline at the multi-lateral level with legally binding rules for the first time. The Uruguay Round saw wide agreement on intellectual property rights including patents, copyrights, trademarks, geographical indications, industrial designs and trade secrets. The new agreement focuses on five broad issues in intellectual property, namely: (i) how the multi-lateral trading system's principles should be applied to intellectual property rights; (ii) how best to afford protection to holders of intellectual property rights (iii) how to enforce that protection; (iv) how to settle disputes, and (v) what should happen while the system is gradually being introduced.[7]

National Treatment and Most Favoured Nation treatment are to apply in respect of all intellectual property rights covered by the agreement. It also recognizes the right to control anti-competitive practices and, to this end, provides for consultation and cooperation among members.

It must however be noted that one can only acquire intellectual property rights through the prescription of laws. If there is no law, domestic or otherwise, to confer rights on the holder of intellectual property then no legal rights exist and *ipso facto,* no protection can be entertained or enforced. The enforcement provisions of the TRIPS agreement are designed to ensure that IPRs established under the agreement can be effectively and expeditiously enforced under national law.

Developed countries had one year to implement the TRIPS agreement, that is, by 1 January 1996, while developing countries have until 1 January 2000 and least developed countries until 1 January 2006. However, the National Treatment and Most Favoured Nation commitments would apply for all countries regardless of the date of implementation.

Reshaping International Trade - GATT vs WTO

From the foregoing, it is quite clear that the Uruguay Round of multi-lateral negotiations under the auspices of the GATT, not only created the WTO, but in so doing significantly altered the rules of engagement, scope of operations and legal enforceability of trade and trade-related agreements at the international level.

When the GATT was established in 1947/48 international commerce was dominated by trade in goods and the scope of the agreement reflected primarily the interests of developed countries. Since then many more developing countries and economies in transition have undergone economic restructuring and have effectively inserted themselves into the international economy. Many goods and services which are now traded internationally were not even being produced then. Major advances in information technology, together with significant improvement in transportation have spawned a wave of trade in services such as banking, travel, insurance, and telecommunications. Thus there is a new role for services in economic development as business services, computer based services, telecommunications and information technology, among others, have radically changed the outlook of firms all over the world, leading to more efficient production in all areas. Indeed, total world trade in services now represents a 65% share of global GNP or about US$1.4 billion.[8]

Then there is also the related mushrooming of trade in ideas or intellectual property, such as designs, inventions and so on. The WTO therefore had to give due consideration to these developments if it was to gain any relevance in international trade regulation. The concept of universal jurisdiction as opposed to absolute sovereignty would also have influenced an acceptance of the overarching mandate of the WTO in 1994 as opposed to 1948.

Thus the major differences between the WTO and the GATT 1947 can be chronicled as follows:[9]

GATT was ad hoc and provisional; It was never ratified in national parliaments and contained no provisions for the creation of an institution given the demise of the ITO.

- The WTO and its agreements, on the other hand, are permanent within a sound legal framework and agreed rules on procedures, operations and dispute settlement mechanisms.
- The WTO has 'members', but GATT had 'contracting parties,' underscoring the contractual as opposed to institutional nature of the GATT.
- GATT dealt exclusively with trade in goods, whereas the WTO covers services and intellectual property as well.
- The WTO dispute settlement is faster and more automatic than the old GATT system of voluntary acceptance of sanctions arising from 'breach of contract'. Any GATT member could have simply blocked the setting up of a dispute settlement forum, but that cannot happen under WTO rules.

Despite the significant achievements under the Uruguay Round, the WTO seeks even further liberalisation through its 'Built-in-Agenda' which commits members to a programme for applying the various agreements and obligations, as well as for new negotiations in various disciplines. The Built-in-Agenda includes:

a. Unfinished business in basic telecommunications, financial services, maritime services and intellectual property as well as in the GATS generally;
b. New negotiations for progressive liberalisation in agriculture, services and Trade-Related Investment Measures (TRIMS) and government procurement; and
c. Regular review of specific disciplines such as safeguards, subsidies, rules of origin, sanitary and phyto-sanitary measures and the dispute settlement mechanism.

Additionally, a number of related issues, some of which have already been the subject of discussion, are likely to be included for consideration and possible adoption in the future. These include regional economic groupings; trade and the environment; trade and investment; competition policy; transparency in government procurement; and trade facilitation.

Impact on Developing Countries

The WTO categorises its member countries as either *Developed, Developing or Least Developed* on the basis of the United Nations (UN) classification. In general the WTO Agreement 'embodies provisions conferring differential and more favourable treatment for developing countries, including special attention to the particular situation of least developed countries.'[10] In fact, Article XI (2) of the main WTO Agreement provides that the least developed countries will only be required to undertake commitments and concessions to the extent consistent with their individual development, financial and trade needs or their administrative and institutional capabilities.

In general, developing countries are accorded special consideration only through the mechanism of longer implementation periods for their commitments and by way of technical assistance, from the WTO or its more developed members, to meet these obligations.

For many of the developing countries in Asia, Africa, Latin America and the Middle East, as well as the Eastern European countries in transition, unilateral trade liberalisation has proceeded along with economic reform efforts, in addition to the plethora of Regional Free Trade Arrangements (RFTA) that have proliferated the globe since the start of the Uruguay Round. Indeed, it is estimated that there are about one hundred (100)[11] RFTAs, excluding non-reciprocal agreements such as the General System of Preferences (GSP) and the EU/ACP Lomé Convention protocols on bananas, sugar and rum.

Much of that unilateral and regional liberalisation influenced the new multi-lateral trade negotiations during the Uruguay Round and therefore the WTO agreement generally accorded with that process. It must be borne in mind however that the WTO disciplines are typically wider in scope and the MFN principle would require extension of the unilateral preferences to all WTO members. Thus some of the regional preferences would be gradually eroded as developing countries meet their WTO commitment schedules. There was always a concern about the trade diversion possibilities of RFTAs as liberalisation is partial therein and thus discriminatory, unlike with unilateral liberalisation where there is no explicit discrimination between domestic and foreign suppliers so that there is no trade diversion. However the empirical evidence[12] suggests that RFTAs have not unduly retarded global integration or inhibited increased world trade. Indeed, it is estimated that global welfare gains consequent upon the establishment of the WTO could amount to as much as US$510 billion (although estimates of $25 billion are given at the lower end of the spectrum).[13]

RFTAs have generally developed concomitantly with the growth of trade in non-RFTA members as regional liberalisation has paralleled unilateral liberalisation while creating more intense competition at the global level. Such increased competition, other things being equal, should result in production efficiencies, welfare gains through reduction in price levels and economic growth as global income increases.

However, economies do not always operate that smoothly and there will always be winners and losers at both the international and domestic levels. Some countries will gain from greater specialisation at the expense of others and some sectors within particular countries may prosper while others would perish. Then there is the troubling issue of the dislocative impact on employment, at least in the short term, as business responds to the new challenges of global liberalisation and competition.

The more advanced developing countries would be better able to minimize the dislocative effects and to capitalize on the opportunities presented by multilateral trade liberalisation, as they have the financial, administrative, institutional and entrepreneurial capability to respond to these challenges. But not all developing countries are alike and in the case of the independent countries of the OECS[14], which are all members of WTO, these challenges may be more acute and the opportunities more difficult to grasp.

Implications for the OECS

For the micro-states of the OECS, which are among the smallest countries[15] in the membership of the WTO, the effects of globalisation and the reshaped international economy have already begun to be felt. These countries have over the last 15-20 years enjoyed fairly favourable economic circumstances, characterised by access to preferential markets (Lomé, CBI, CaribCan, GSP)[16] for most of their commodity exports; concessional development financing; and generous aid flows and non-reimbursable technical assistance. These circumstances are inexorably being reversed, as witnessed by the rapid decline in aid flows and graduation from eligibility for 'soft window'[17] financing.

In theory, the overall effect of WTO styled liberalisation should be beneficial even to the OECS countries. Classical specialisation theory suggests that it would lead to a shift of resources to more efficient uses, thereby boosting productivity and income and leading to a rise in living standards. Further, because of the narrow resource base of OECS countries and their typically higher tariffs compared to developed

countries, the differential between tradables and non-tradables would be relatively high. A lowering of tariffs as a result of WTO commitments would therefore influence efficiency and welfare gains.

The increase in global income and purchasing power that would result from an increase in global trade should also influence a greater demand by developed countries for the exports of developing countries, and vice-versa, thus reinforcing the cycle of trade and economic growth which should, other things being equal, spur increases in employment,

In reality, however the OECS countries have severely limited production possibilities arising from their extremely narrow resource and economic bases. This has in turn spawned a rigidity in economic structures that makes it difficult to respond to changing international economic circumstances and the new opportunities and challenges springing therefrom. They have difficulties in meeting even the most basic WTO obligations, as evidenced by the paucity of offers made thus far in both goods and services. Of course, the WTO has promised assistance to developing countries to facilitate meeting their technical obligations on schedule but for these tiny island states, even the ability to identify their technical assistance needs could be quite taxing given their lack of experience in such matters.

The situation is not helped by the scarcity of financial, natural, administrative, technical and institutional resources in these micro-states. Their ability to compete on the basis of technological endowment is also severely limited.

These constraints obviously impact on the ability of OECS countries to exercise market access rights that the new WTO regime would confer upon them (and all other WTO member countries). However, even if they were successful in gaining access it would require an overwhelming effort to maintain access (security and certainty), to such highly competitive markets.

Possible Effects on OECS

Some of the likely direct effects of the WTO-centered international economy on OECS economies are:

- There would be an eventual loss of preferences whether by unilateral withdrawal as a result of incompatibility with WTO rules or by implication consequent upon their relative erosion under MFN terms. Preferences are always relative and even if, for instance, the commodity (bananas, sugar and rum) preferences into the European market were kept (which is unlikely in the case of bananas and rum), they would no longer be 'preferences' as such if the EU, in accordance with WTO principles, had to eventually remove restrictions on the entry of non ACP products into its market.

It must be noted that while Article XXIV of the GATT 1994 allows MFN exemptions for RFTA's and custom unions, it also provides that countries should not raise barriers to trade with non-FTA members when entering into new FTA's or while in existing ones; FTA's should encompass substantially all trade and eliminate barriers where they exist; and interim arrangements in (i.e. phase-in time to full FTA), regional agreements should take place within ten (10) years.[18]

This obviously has implications for the OECS' participation in the Free Trade Area of the Americas (FTAA) and signals a need for them to begin the process of at least considering the prospect of surviving in a world which is increasingly intolerant of the concept of special and differential treatment for smaller countries.

- The loss of preferences may make it even more difficult for the OECS countries to attract inward investment which is so vital in the economic transformation process. A substantial proportion of the relatively low level[19] of foreign investment that comes to these countries (tourism related investment excepted), does so in order to take advantage of their access into preferential markets under the aforementioned bilateral and multi-lateral non-reciprocal duty-free access arrangements. Thus a drop in investment, particularly in the electronic assembly and garment sectors may be witnessed.
- Full reciprocity may also have a devastating effect on domestic industry and this may be even more so, where the private sector typically thrives on protection from foreign competition by way of relatively high tariff and non-tariff barriers to trade. One must, of course, balance the effects on domestic industry with the probable welfare effects of replacing inefficient with efficient enterprises, but the unemployment that may arise, given the rigidity in labour markets in the OECS, may hinder a smooth transition to efficiency.
- The inclusion of agriculture in the WTO disciplines and the liberalisation schedule thereof, particularly reduction of subsidies, could see a rise in the food import bill of OECS countries. They are also likely to witness an even more serious deterioration of their terms of trade as the price of their export

commodities fall due to the removal of preferences and more open competition on the world market.

Another possible direct effect is the net transfer of royalties from developing countries, including the OECS, to developed countries as intellectual property regimes are brought in line with the WTO TRIPS. By limit of their size, resources constraints, lack of technology, and underdevelopment, OECS countries are net consumers of intellectual property emanating more from developed countries. There should however be an absolute increase in the royalties received by OECS states, once they have implemented the regulatory and administrative requirements for establishment of an effective intellectual property rights regime.

With all member countries acceptance of the WTO strictures a loss of national sovereignty will result, but that would be even more so with the hapless, powerless OECS countries. There is also the fact of these countries being unable to effectively introduce the retaliatory measures which the WTO allows aggrieved members in a trade dispute. For retaliatory measurers to be effective the implementing country must be able to inflict some economic injury on the offending party, but given their small markets and insignificance in world trade this is unlikely to be of any use to OECS states.

A disproportionate reliance on taxes on external trade and transactions in the sub-region means that tariff reductions would result in fiscal dislocation. However, this need not be once these countries institute the necessary fiscal restructuring by introducing alternative revenue measurers such as general sales or value added taxes. This may actually rebound to their benefit as these latter taxes may serve to widen the tax base, minimise smuggling, remove the inherent bias towards inefficient production and reduce the over-generous exemptions regime.

On the positive side, notwithstanding the major administrative, financial and institutional challenges, liberalisation could result in welfare and efficiency gains and may also force policy makers to undertake the necessary policy reforms for effectively inserting the OECS sub-region into the new international economy. It could, just as well, engender better trade and economic regimes and could introduce new economic management and trade disciplines so vital for survival in this new globalised environment.

Imperatives

What then are the imperatives for mounting an effective response, despite the heightened vulnerability and relative incapacity of OECS economies?

First there must be a coherent development strategy and overall guiding philosophy which must be resolutely, consistently and judiciously implemented. Such philosophy must take into consideration the economic potential of the sub-region, its development experience, its resource endowments, the goodwill and assistance that is still available from friendly countries, the imperatives for survival in this rapidly changing economic climate, the social dimension of development and the achievements in economic and social development thus far. It must therefore be realistic but innovative, general in scope but all encompassing in its reach.

It is worthy of note that the fastest growing sectors in the OECS are tourism and telecommunications. Much of the growth of the latter however is due to that of the former. Tourism continues to grow and is the largest foreign exchange earner, as well as the largest single sectoral contributor to GDP[20] in *all* of the OECS countries. In 1996, Tourism (Hotel and Restaurants) related activities accounted for 10.07 per cent of total GDP at factor cost while other tourism related activities namely, Wholesale and Retail Trade and Transportation accounted for 12.47 per cent and 11.33 per cent, respectively. When seen within the context of the wider Caribbean,[21] the significance of this sector is even more glaring. With a population of less than 1% of the world total the region receives more than 6% of world tourist arrivals despite being the third most expensive regional destination.[22] What it offers in sea, sand and sun is not exclusive to the Caribbean. It is the exotic allure, the unique culture and warm hospitality of the Caribbean that is responsible for such success and any meaningful economic development strategy must be oriented to those attributes.

In that vein, the export of cultural services and products, diversification of the tourism product to embrace more of the cultural and exotic charms of the Caribbean and orienting even manufactured exports and agricultural marketing in that direction may, be the sub-region's best chance for survival in the increasingly competitive economic environment.

The strategy, however, needs to be executed within an appropriate enabling political/constitutional framework. The inherited constitutional/political structures largely reflect that of the former colonial power without having the benefit of her mores, conventions, development experience and institutional support mechanisms. Retention of these in the new quest for meaningful development is at best regressive.

Resource constraints and the constrictions of size, population, technology and available expertise dictate a pooling of effort, first at the sub-regional level and extending in wider concentric circles to the wider regional, hemispheric, commonwealth, and international levels. There is also the need to nurture and cement ties at the south-south level, as well as with strategically positioned bilateral partners. Regional integration, nonetheless, is a *sine qua non* for the further development of the sub-region and indeed the wider region.

The OECS has to embrace the idea of economic, if not political, union much more seriously now if it is to compete effectively, even within CARICOM. The successes which have attended the sub-region when it has integrated effectively[23] are enough to influence a reconsideration of the belief that any one country can 'go it alone'. If erstwhile world powers such as the United Kingdom, France and Germany can see fit to form an economic union to safeguard their own development, then who are we as tiny specs to believe that we have a chance as individual nation states?

Of course the aforementioned economic restructuring and adjustment must also be tackled even in the intervening period, before economic union and political reform. Investment facilitation mechanisms must be streamlined;[24] the necessary fiscal restructuring must be done; institutional reform including judicious public sector reform must be embraced and enterprise development as well as capital markets facilitation should be instituted forthwith.

All the above imperatives require a broad attitudinal change if they are to succeed. First, there must be a change on the part of both public and private sectors from dependency to self-reliance, and from *diagnosing* problems to finding and *implementing* solutions. Then, there must be a change in attitudes, particularly in public service institutions, laws and practices, from control and prevention to facilitation and promotion. The control syndrome is part of the colonial legacy which was inherently elitist in a period when knowledge was mostly 'privatised' and 'oligopolised.'

It goes without saying that a major human resource development thrust is required to sustain and fuel the reform process. Much has already been said in the region and beyond about this and it is only left to say that no matter how small a country is, its ability to interface with the world on terms favourable to its development depends very much on the quality of its human resources. Human resources, along with marine resources are the regions most abundant if most underutilised resources.

Then there is the ubiquitous Caribbean diaspora which is a ready source of expertise, investment, marketing and consumption. Israel, Cyprus, India and Egypt are among the countries which have relied heavily on their diaspora to spur their economic development. The Caribbean boasts one of the largest diasporas per capita in the world but has not been able to tap into that fountain of economic growth other than to rely on their relatively paltry remittances.

Conclusion

A new globalised and still rapidly changing international economy has emerged over the last five to ten years with the establishment of the WTO as its most prominent testimony. Much of the restructuring of the global economy has been fuelled by phenomenal technology innovations including major advances in information technology. Erstwhile isolated countries or regions now find themselves inevitably inserted into the world economy as the world becomes more homogeneous as regards economic structure.

The WTO has now succeeded the GATT as the sole multi-lateral institution with responsibility for the regulation and arbitration of world trade. It ushers in an era of rules-based trading, replete with a dispute settlement mechanism and legally binding commitments from member states. Developing countries have now embraced multi-lateral trading disciplines as more relevant sectors such as agriculture and services, as well as intellectual property rights have been included in the scope of the WTO.

For the OECS countries, which are among the smallest and most vulnerable WTO member states, globalisation brings with it countless challenges and many opportunities. Their limited resources, small size, vulnerability and incapacity make it much more difficult for them to meet these challenges and capitalize on the opportunities. These tiny countries have enjoyed relatively favourable economic circumstances, characterised by non-reciprocal preferential access to metropolitan markets for their commodity exports, generous inflows of budgetary aid and technical assistance, and concessional development financing.

Globalisation has already begun to reverse those favourable circumstances and these relatively incapacitated countries find themselves woefully underprepared for open global competition.

They are immobilised not only by their resource constraints and inexperience but also by general political fear and inertia, acute vulnerability to natural disasters and economic oscillations in traditional mar-

kets, the dependency syndrome and the overwhelming number of issues, meetings and levels of operation[25] that they must encounter.

Nevertheless they must respond effectively to these new challenges if their development is to be sustained. While the agenda is set mainly by the industrialised powers, small countries must stake a claim to the benefits of globalisation if they are not to be further marginalised.

The OECS' response would have to be within the context of a coherent and consistently applied development strategy within the framework of deeper regional integration and an appropriate political/constitutional structure.

As small, middle-income countries they cannot expect to continue to have their development underwritten by once reliable developed allies. Evidence of a new intolerance for the concept of special and differential has already been witnessed in the WTO arbitrated dispute between the EU and the US over the EU/ACP banana protocol and this trend continues even at the ongoing FTAA negotiations.

Mounting uncertainty now coincides with rising expectations from the people, institutions and business in the sub-region. The real challenge, however, is to mitigate the uncertainty while realistically and steadfastly meeting the challenges and turning them into real opportunities for balanced growth and meaningful development in the OECS.

Endnotes

1. Anguilla, Antigua & Barbuda, British Virgin Islands, Dominica, Grenada, Montserrat, St Kitts & Nevis, St Lucia, and St Vincent & The Grenadines
2. A proposed Economic Development Strategy for the OECS - (ECCB) Unpublished paper, December 1993.
3. Towards 2000: The Caribbean confronts changing trends in international trade - Anthony T Bryan, in *Caribbean Affairs* Vol. 8 No. 1 - June - March 1998.
4. The plurilateral agreements are binding only on those WTO members that have accepted them. The 'single-undertaking' approach therefore, does not apply to the plurilateral agreements.
5. Marrakesh Agreement establishing the WTO at page 7
6. See GATT 1994 text Articles 1 (A), (B) & (C)
7. See WTO website (The Agreement summary)
8. United Nations Conference on Trade and Development (UNCTAD) 1997 Report
9. WTO op. cit.
10. WTO Singapore Ministerial Declaration, 13 December 1996.
11. Kirmani, Nalteed - 'Overview of recent trade policy developments' - IMF staff mimeograph, n.d.
12. IBID.
13. Uruguay Round studies by World Bank, OECD & GATT Secretariat, among others.

14. Antigua & Barbuda, Dominica, Grenada, St Kitts-Nevis, St Lucia and St Vincent & The Grenadines.
15. The six countries have a combined land mass of about 345 km², population of about 510,000 and GDP of approximately US$1.5 billion
16. Lomé is the development cooperation convention between the European Union & sixty-nine (69) African, Caribbean and Pacific former European colonies. It includes commodity protocols on bananas, rum and sugar which are exported free of duty and under special access preferences into the EU. CBI is the one way preferential access accord between the USA and Latin American and Caribbean countries under which selected commodity exports from the latter enter into the US duty free. CARIBCAN is a similar one-way arrangement between Canada and the Commonwealth Caribbean. GSP is the general system of preferences accorded to selected developing countries by their more developed counterparts.
17. For example, the World Bank's International Development Association (IDA) and the Enhanced Structural Adjustment Facility (ESAF) at the International Monetary Fund. Graduation therefrom usually sends signals to other lenders to lend to these countries on strictly commercial terms.
18. GATT 1994 Article XXIV 5 (a), (b) & (c), 8 (a)(i) & (ii).
19. Low by International standards.
20. See *ECCB National Accounts Statistics* (1997)
21. Caribbean Tourism Organisation (CTO) member countries.
22. See CTO publications.
23. E.g. The Eastern Caribbean Central Bank, joint marketing of bananas and joint external relations.
24. See Andrew, McHale (1993), An external Economic Relations Strategy for the OECS -mimeograph OECS/ECCB.
25. Unlike larger countries OECS states operate at several levels including sub- regional, regional (CARICOM) wider regional (ACS), hemispheric (OAS, FTAA), Commonwealth and International (WTO, UN)

Bibliography

Andrew, McHale. (1993). *An External Relations Strategy for the OECS* – ECCB/OECS Mimeograph, December.
Bryan, Anthony (1998). "Towards 2000: The Caribbean Confronts Changing Trends in international Trade", *Caribbean Affairs*, Vol. 8, No. 1.
Draft Singapore Ministerial Declaration - WTO Ministerial Conference, Singapore, 9 –13 December 1996.
Eastern Caribbean Central Bank. (1993). *A Proposed Economic Development Strategy for the OECS* - ECCB. Unpublished, December 1993.
Eastern Caribbean Central Bank: National Accounts Statistics, 1997.
"Globalizing Free Trade", Vol. 75, *Foreign Affairs*, 1 May 1996.
International Monetary Fund. (1998). *Overview of Recent Trade Policy Developments*. IMF Staff Mimeograph.
Johnson, Paul (1992). *Modern Times*. Rev. Ed. - Harper Perennial,
Marrakesh Agreement - World Trade Organisation, 1994.
Minyard, Alan "The World Trade Organisation's History, Structure and Analysis", http:// www2.netdoor.com/~aminyard.
Robertson, David. "New Burdens for Trade Policy", in *American Express Bank Review Awards Essays, Bronze Award 1994*.
Schott, Jeffrey J. ed. (1989). *Free Trade Areas and US Trade Policy*. Institute of International Economics Conference Papers, 1989.
The Role of the World Trade Organisation and Post-Uruguay Round Issues, op cit., Frieder Roessler.

United Nations Conference on Trade and Development (UNCTAD) Report 1997.
World Bank. World Development Reports, 1991 - 1997.
WTO Website - www.wto.org.wto/about/facts0.htm.
"WTO Head Calls for Single Global Economy", *Trade News,* -Vol. 5, No. 16, 5 November 1996.

Globalisation and the Postcolonial World: The New Political Economy of Development

Ankie Hoogvelt

Globalisation

'Globalisation' is a term that has been fashionable since about the mid-1980s, when it began to replace terms like 'internationalisation' and 'transnationalisation' as a more suitable concept for describing the ever-intensifying networks of cross-border human interaction. The concept covers a great variety of social, economic and political change, and it is therefore not surprising that different disciplines have assigned different meanings to it and that this has led to often spurious debates between them, particularly in respect of the question of whether globalisation is or is not happening.

Much of this rather spurious debate arises from a confusion of globalisation with its precursor movements, namely internationalisation (as in the increasing interwovenness of national economies through international trade) and transnationalisation (as in the increasing organisation of production on a cross-border basis by multinational organisations). Thus, for example, economic globalisation is often perceived as a process in which distinct national economies, and therefore domestic strategies of national economic management are increasingly irrelevant.

> The world has internationalized in its basic dynamics, it is dominated by uncontrollable market forces, and it has as its principal economic actors and major agents of change truly transnational corporations that owe allegiance to no nation state and locate wherever in the globe market advantage lies.[1]

Such definitions are an open invitation to refutation. In their recent book, *Globalization in Question*, Paul Hirst and Grahame Thompson review the historical evidence of world trade and capital flows in relation to output, degrees of financial and monetary integration and the character of governance in the international economy. They come to the conclusion, much as we did in Chapter 4, that the level of integration, interdependence, and openness, of national economies in the present era is not unprecedented.

However, we must be careful not to confuse 'globalisation' with the integration of real territorial economies. As we saw in Chapter 4, the peak period of integration of real economies as measured, for example, by the amount of goods and services that cross frontiers as a percentage of all goods and services that are produced world-wide, was the year 1913 when that percentage (the export ratio of production) reached 33 per cent. Today it is about 31 per cent.[2]

As for the equation of globalisation with the growing dominance of transnational corporations in world production and trade, here too the overall picture that emerges is one of remarkable constancy, and not of dramatic change, in the long historical period. First in relation to total world output, the percentage share of world production subject to transnational corporate control has remained relatively stable[3] (see also Chapter 4); second, as Hirst and Thompson note, as far as the leading OECD economies are concerned international businesses are still largely confined to their home territory in terms of their overall business activity, that is in terms of location of sales, affiliates, declared profits, and research and finance.[4] Similar findings have been reported by others.[5]

Nor must we confuse globalisation with the integration of real territorial economies world-*wide*. While globalisation has proceeded in the last few decades, the geographical reach of world capitalism has actually receded. For example, if we take as an indicator of global reach the percentage share of all five continents in world trade, then we find that the percentage share of two continents, Latin America and Africa, in world trade has actually declined. Likewise the global reach of foreign capital flows (the percentage share of global foreign investments going to Africa and to Latin America) has declined by a wide margin since the colonial period.[6]

In fact, I have argued that the expansive phase of world capitalism is over. The expansive phase of capitalism was characterised by the *extension* of the fundamentals of economic activity, namely trade and productive investment, ever further into more and more areas of the globe; that phase has now been superseded by a phase of *deepening, but not widening capitalist integration*. I prefer to reserve the term 'globalisation' for that deepening phenomenon. To understand this 'deepening' phenomenon we have to start with the sociology of globalisation.

The Sociology of Globalisation

Even if today 'globe-babble' has penetrated the discourse of *all* social science disciplines, it is probably fair to say that sociologists have been at the forefront in efforts to give it a rigorous and consistent theoretical status.[7] In the work of prominent authors such as Roland Robertson, David Harvey and Anthony Giddens, we find distinctive formulations that may help us to overcome the limits of the globalisation discourse which has so vexed economists and international relations theorists. This is the aim of this chapter.

Roland Robertson: World Compression and Intensification of Global Consciousness

Robertson's writings are firmly welded to a conventional mainstream sociological theory of society as a social system. Social system theory is elaborated in Parsons'[8] well-known formulation in which any social system is thought to have four subsystems that are functionally related to serve the maintenance of the whole. These subsystems and their functions are:

1. The economic (adaptive function);
2. The political (mobilisation for collective purposes);
3. The social (integrative function); and
4. The cultural (providing the governing value system necessary for reproducing the system through time).

Robertson[9] argues that already for some time there has clearly been a process of social system building at the global level. In the economic sphere it predates even the rise of capitalism and the modern world because of the growing networks of international trade and production. It has also been actively fostered at the level of the political subsystem with the international cooperation between states and the emergence of international organisations. But as Malcolm Waters[10] notes in his succinct review of the evolution of Robertson's theories, in his earlier work with Nettl, in 1968,[11] Robertson had argued that the process of globalisation was still being hindered by unresolved cleavages in the cultural arena which thus far had prevented full system development. There were three such cleavages: religious (between fundamental Islam and Christianity); legal-diplomatic between democracies and absolutist states (the West versus East divide); and industrial between cultures that emphasise norms consistent with industry (rationality, individualisation, impersonal authority) and those that do not (the North-South divide).

In more recent works, however, Robertson has come around to the view that the potential for a closing of these cleavages is today greatly enhanced. Globalisation at the cultural level has begun because of two things which he now introduces into his definition of globalisation: namely 'compression of the world' and 'global consciousness'. Compression of the world is the real experience of the way that interdependencies are being created in the economies of the world to such an extent that, today, the way we live our lives on this side of the globe has immediate consequences for people on the other side of the globe. Shifts in preferences of consumption in Europe and America, for example, deeply affect jobs in the Far East. Industrial processes of development and growth in one country can have environmental and ecological impacts in neighbouring countries. Big dam projects in India cause flooding in Bangladesh; an earthquake in Kobe, Japan, causes a fall in the dollar; and the forest burning practice of the Brazilian peasant colonists in the Amazon burns holes in 'our' ozone layer. This is what is meant by 'compression' of the world.

World compression is not a terribly new idea, what makes for its novelty in Robertson's work is that he argues that world compression intensifies 'global consciousness'. Global consciousness is manifested in the way we, peoples all over the world, in a discourse unified through mass communication, speak of military-political issues in terms of 'world order' or of economic issues as in 'international recession'. We speak of 'world peace' and 'human rights', while issues of pollution and purification are talked about in terms of 'saving the planet'. Thus, although in Robertson's view globalisation has been going on for a very long time, predating even the rise of capitalism and modernity, it has accelerated only in the last decade or so because it has moved to the level of consciousness.

David Harvey: Time/Space Compression

While for Robertson the point of departure of the analysis of globalisation is a well-worn conventional sociological theory, namely social system theory, there are others who have theorised it from a completely different angle, namely the concepts of space and time, and space/time compression.

Following the works of Pierre Bourdieu, a contemporary sociologist, David Harvey,[12] who is himself a social geographer, argues that symbolic orderings of space and time provide a framework for experience through which we learn who or what we are in society. Remember the commonsense notion that 'there is a time and a place for everything'. Certain behaviour that is encouraged in the classroom, for example, is not expected around the dinner table, and vice versa. In previous years, when we did not have so many students, academic tutors would sometimes try to create the informal atmosphere of home for their tutorials by inviting students to classes held in their homes, precisely to break the habit of 'habitus'. (Note that the Latin word 'habitus' means both location and habit.) Ordered space is a signpost for expected social practices, and serves as a reminder of these social practices. Let us think about this a bit more.

The organisation of space defines relationships, not only between activities, things and concepts, but by extension between people. The organisation of space defines social relations. Harvey argues that the development of cartography in the Renaissance permitted the objectification of space and the accurate measurements of land, thus supporting the emergence of private ownership in land and the precise definition of transferable property rights, thereby replacing the confused and conflicting feudal obligations that had preceded it.

The organisation of space holds the key to power. Today, the freedom to move capital wherever it is needed world-wide gives the capital-owning international bourgeoisie a decisive advantage over the mass of workers who are restricted in their movements and migrations by the passports they carry.

Like space, time too represents a source of value and power. In capitalist enterprises the costs of production are calculated in terms of the time it takes to produce things, and labour is subjected to constant efforts by employers to reduce the time spent on a particular task. 'Economy of time', said Marx, 'to this all economy ultimately reduces itself.' The time-and-motion studies of Frederick Taylor's scientific management gave Henry Ford a decisive advantage over his competitors, and eventually ushered in the world-wide system of production called Fordism. Bitter class struggles have been fought over the length of the working day. In the competitive battle today it is not even minutes but seconds that count. In a harrowing narrative of life on the shop-floor in a flexible production plant in the UK, Rick Delbridge *et al.* report how work intensification resulted in a saving of '0.85 seconds on standard time.'![13]

Time, argues Harvey, also defines the value of money itself. In capitalist economies, accountants calculate interest rates as 'the time value of money'. The time of production together with the time of circulation of exchange are referred to as the *turnover time of capital*. The greater the speed with which the capital that is launched into circulation can be recuperated, the greater the profit will be. If an investment in this country gives me the value of my money back in five years, whereas in Singapore I can get it back in three years, then I am hardly likely to invest here, and I will prefer my money to go to Singapore.

Anthony Giddens: Time/Space Distantiation

However, the really important thing in all this discussion is the relationship between time and space. In capitalist economies, *space is expressed in time*. The distance needed to travel in order to do business or to transport commodities to their final destination, or to crosshaul intermediate products for fabrication, are all calculated in terms of the time it takes to cover the distance. Anthony Giddens, whose globalisation theory bears some resemblance to that of Harvey, calls this 'time/space distantiation', which is a measure of the degree to which the friction of space has been overcome to accommodate social interaction.

Technological progress has compressed the time-space equation enormously. Harvey has illuminated this equation in a graph that is described here. Between 1500-1840 the best average speed of horse-drawn coaches and sailing ships was 10 mph. Between 1850-1930 it was 65 mph for steam locomotives and 36 mph for steam ships. By the 1950s, propeller aircraft covered distances at 300-400 mph while today's jet passenger aircraft makes a cool 500-700 mph.[14]

All this refers to the transport and the covering of distances of material commodities and human bodies. But now think of the electronic age which we have just entered. Today's telecommunications using satellite TV and the linking of computers through cyberspace allow most 'disembodied' services, for example technological designs, managerial instructions and operational controls, as well as media images of wars and earthquakes and representations of consumer fashions, to enter the minds of people instantly anywhere in the global system. This shrinking of the world to a 'global village' amounts to a virtual *annihilation of space through time*. As Giddens sums it up:

> Globalisation can thus be defined as the intensification of world wide social relations which link distant localities in such a way that local happenings are shaped by events occurring many miles away and vice versa.[15]

Today people can have social relations and even organised community relations regardless of space; that is, regardless of the territory that they share. This has enormous consequences not only for the role of the nation-state as territorially bounded community, but also, as we shall see below, for the organisation of economic production on a cross-border basis. It permits the emergence of 'imagined' communities, cultures and even systems of authority and social control that cross borders. The other day I heard Mary Robinson, the President of the Republic of Ireland, say in a radio interview that Irishness exists not so much in blood and land but in shared culture and traditions. When the Ayatollahs in Iran decided to pronounce the Fatwa on Salman Rushdie it was not because they had stumbled across the book themselves, but because Muslims in Bradford had faxed them a copy of the offending pages. When the much maligned 'fat cats' of recently privatised British utilities are vilified for their perks and pay they can still sleep at night without undue embarrassment or shame because their peer group, their own social reference group, is a community of utility chiefs and other boardroom fat cats across the Atlantic with whom they are probably more immediately and continuously in touch through e-mail, telephone, fax and video-conferencing than the people in the street where they live.

What these examples show is that while we still have local lives as physical persons, we also now experience phenomenal worlds that are truly global. It is this globalisation as shared phenomenal worlds which today drives the processes of economic globalisation.

Such privileging of the sociological aspect of globalisation is not to deny the importance of other factors, more especially the dynamics of historical capitalism which — as Wallerstein and many others in the Marxist tradition have argued — always had a 'globalising' imperative from the beginning. The development of transnational corporations and the growth of international finance in particular, testify to a complex multi-causal logic of globalisation. Rather, what is being argued here is that, owing to the present reconstitution of the world into a single *social* space, that self-same historical process has now lifted off and moved into a new ballpark. If, previously, global integration in the sense of a growing unification and interpenetration of the human condition was driven by the economic logic of capital accumulation, today it is the unification of the human condition that drives the logic of further capital accumulation. In the next section, I shall clarify this theoretical position.

The Economics of Globalisation

I suggest that time/space compression drives the economics of globalisation in three principal ways. *First,* the 'shared phenomenal world' supports the emergence of a global market *discipline as* contrasted with the existence of a mere global market-*place. Second,* the annihilation of space through time compression re-orders the way economic activities are being conceptualised and, as a consequence, organised. Whereas, before, it was common to classify economic activities *either* into three categories: primary, secondary and tertiary (agriculture, industry and services), *or* — as in more recent works on international economics — into a chain of high value-added and low value-added activities, today it makes more sense to re-order economic activities into two: 'real-time' activities where distance and location are no longer relevant as a determinant of economic operations, and 'material' activities where there is still some 'friction of space' that limits choice of location. As we shall see below this twofold conceptualisation is beginning to inform the organisation of transnational business today, and, as a result, the global organisation of work. *Third,* money itself has become a 'real time' resource permitting a degree of international mobility that is qualitatively different from anything witnessed in previous eras. In summary, I suggest that economic globalisation has three key features:

1. A global market discipline;
2. Flexible accumulation through global webs; and
3. Financial deepening.

A Global Market Discipline

To begin with, it is important that one makes the distinction between a global market-*place* and a global market *principle. A* global market-place exists when there is an international division of labour and, consequently, an international market exchange between different goods and services that are produced in different nations. Such international trade dominated the prewar and immediate postwar period. It was essentially *complementary;* that is, countries that specialised in the export of one type of product would exchange that product for other types that they did not produce themselves. .

As a result of the growth and organisational evolution of multi-national companies, this pattern of *inter-product trade* gradually has given way to *intra-product trade.* There is no longer a neat division of labour between countries. There is now export com-petition between producers in different countries in the same product lines. Countries that are high volume exporters of cars are also high volume importers of cars. How did this situation come about?

Liberalisation and technological progress have steadily altered the way in which international production is being undertaken. At first, multinational companies adopted *simple* integration strategies where they set up foreign affiliates producing, typically with technology obtained from the parent company, the same standardised commodities that previously had been subject to cross-border trade. Second, parent companies would set up foreign affiliates engaging in a limited range of activities in order to supply their parent firms with specific inputs that they were in a more competitive position to produce.

Next, multinational companies began to adopt *complex* integration strategies where they turned their geographically dispersed affiliates and fragmented production systems into regionally or even globally integrated production and distribution networks. Thus, multinational companies (by this time, that is the 1970s, often referred to as 'transnational' companies or even 'global' companies) farmed out different parts of the production process to different affiliates in different national locations. Each subsidiary took part in the production process, but not one single affiliate produced the whole product from beginning to end. The hallmark of this global fragmentation and organic integration of the production process was an enormous increase in international trade in components and semi-processed manufactures. This began in the 1960s and soon overtook the growth in world trade itself.[16] Telling evidence of this global integration at the level of production is found in data on intra-firm trade. Whereas in the early 1970s intra-firm trade was estimated to account for around 20 per cent of world trade, by the early 1990s that share was around one-third, excluding intra-TNC transactions in services.[17]

For many observers and analysts of the world economy, this development of an integrated international production system is sufficient evidence of the emergence of a truly 'global economy'. And in some ways it is. That is to say it prepares the *structural* conditions for the emergence of a global economy. For it means that a global market *principle* (a dominant standard of price, quality and efficiency) begins to impose itself on the *domestic* supply of consumer goods, intermediate and half-processed goods, technology, and indeed the factors of production, capital, labour and raw materials. As a consequence of the shift from inter-product trade to intra-product trade, global competition has intensified. Instead of being complementary, international trade has become *predatory or* 'adversarial', as Peter Drucker puts it.[18]

The corollary of global competition is that even goods and services that are produced and exchanged *within* the national domestic sphere have to meet standards of quality and costs of production that are set globally. A good example is the United States, the country with the largest domestic market. As Stephen Cohen reminds us in a revealing statistic: whereas in the early 1960s only 4 per cent of US domestic production was subject to international competition, today over 70 per cent is.[19] The contrast between the global market-*place* and the global market *principle* can not be put more sharply, for in the 1960s the US-dominated international manufacturing trade contributed 25 per cent of all international trade flows, whereas in the 1990s its share of world manufacturing trade has dropped to just 12 per cent.[20]

However, of still greater significance is the manner in which such structural integration is becoming *internalised* in the behaviour of economic agents, be they entrepreneurs or workers, consumers or producers. If the expression 'market principle' refers to a structural constraint, I use the expression 'market discipline' to address the internalisation of this structural constraint by individual agents in their own conduct. Writers of the Regulation School which we discussed in Chapter 5 have tried to stretch their concept of 'mode of regulation' to include the internalisation of relevant social values and norms. For example, Aglietta[21] speaks of the 'socialisation of the mode of life', Boccara refers to 'anthroponomic factors',[22] while Alain Lipietz uses the term 'habitus' borrowed from Bourdieu to indicate that values and norms that might sustain a mode of regulation are internalised in individual conducts.[23] Yet, as Bob Jessop has pointed out, none of these writers have managed to pinpoint the precise process of transformation because they have failed to theorise how modes of regulation *actually become* internalised in individual conducts.[24]

Our discussion of time/space compression and the 'shared phenomenal world' clarifies this internalisation process. For, it is the *awareness* of global competition which constrains individuals and groups, and even national governments, to conform to international standards of price and quality. We are constantly reminded, in the experience of others' own daily lives, but even more so in the way that this experience is reinforced by media coverage of events occurring elsewhere, that unless we conform to these standards we

will lose the competition, lose our own jobs. Workers come to accept that it is 'proper' that jobs should be lost because their company 'has to' move elsewhere where wages and social conditions are less demanding.

In 1992, the American Hoover company was faced with pressures for higher wages from its Dijon workforce and it decided to move the plant to Glasgow. The point about the 'discipline' of the global market is that such companies do not actually have to move. It is sufficient for them to 'threaten' to move. Time/space compression has permitted us all to share in the phenomenal world of the Dijon workers (and in that of numerous other victims of company relocations elsewhere), and this has created a social discipline on workers all over Europe, indeed all over the world, that unless they toe the line, companies can move plant abroad. Because of the existence of a global market discipline, it is sufficient for a company to merely *threaten* to set up a plant abroad, for it to successfully drive down the wages to the globally competitive level. Charles Sabet reports on German plants where charts of defect rates for particular processes are displayed on videoscreens next to equivalent data for their Brazilian subsidiaries.[25]

Thus, while global competition has created the structural conditions for the emergence of a global market discipline, it is time/space compression that creates the shared phenomenal world that supports and reproduces this discipline on a daily basis. And not just on workers. Companies, too, know they to have to adopt the best quality and the most efficient costs, and engage in constant innovation, because they know that otherwise they will lose their markets and someone else will move in. The same holds true at the consumer end of the organisation of economic life. Consumers in China can see on their satellite TV screens western lifestyle products which they will want, regardless of their government's desire to limit foreign imports and give a boost to local producers. The Chinese government even tried to ban satellite television for that reason, but to no avail.

To give another example: when traders in the London or Tokyo stock market see on their screens the price of dollar interest rates move up by just one notch, they will immediately want to move out of yens and pounds and buy US dollar-denominated bonds, thus putting pressure on other governments to follow suit soon and raise interest rates too.

Flexible Accumulation Through Global Webs

As the costs of transporting standard products and of communicating information about them continue to drop (another example of time/space compression), modern factories and state-of-the-art machinery can be installed almost anywhere in the globe. Routine producers in the UK and the US therefore are in direct competition with millions of producers in other nations. In his book, *The Work of Nations,* Robert Reich, the influential Secretary of State for Labor in Clinton's administration, gives spectacular examples of the speed with which factories and productive capital investments have become footloose. For instance, until the late-1970s, the American telephone and telecommunications company AT&T had depended on routine producers in Louisiana to assemble standard telephones. It then discovered that producers in Singapore would perform the same tasks at a far lower cost. Faced with intense global competition they then had to switch to cheaper routine producers in Singapore. But already by the late 1980s they switched production again, this time to Thailand.

Routine production is no longer the preserve of deskilled jobs in industrial plants. The fusion of computer technology with telecommunications makes it possible for firms to relocate an ever-widening range of operations and functions to wherever cost-competitive labour, assets and infrastructure are available. The new technologies make it feasible to standardise, routinise and coordinate activities which previously were subject to the friction of space and therefore regarded as non-tradable. They enable such activities to be turned into 'real-time' activities. Take, for example, data-processing services of all kinds. Airlines employ data processors from Barbados to Bombay to punch in names and flight numbers into giant computer banks located in Dallas or London. Book and magazine publishers use routine operators around the world to convert manuscripts into computer readable form and send them back to the parent firm at the speed of electronic impulses. The New York Life Insurance Company was dispatching insurance claims to Castleisland, Ireland, where routine producers, guided by simple directions, entered the claims and determined the amounts due, then instantly transmitted the computations back to the United States.[26] British Telecom has all its software computer programming done by programming specialists in India.

The next evolutionary step in this process of global integration of production comes when the global market principle becomes imposed upon *production capacity* itself. In some industries production capacity is now sufficiently flexible to be viewed as a commodity, something that can be instantly bought and sold on the market. Harvard Business School researchers, Ramchandran Jaikumar and David Upton studied a number of manufacturing industries and came to the conclusion that in some cases world-wide manufacturing capacity can be allocated by competitive market forces through the use of information technology linked with cell-based manufacturing technologies.[27] They argue that in many industries, the application of CAD and CNC means that manufacturing concerns can establish small, independent cells that operate effectively and economically with only a modest capital investment. These production units can be organisationally and physically separated from design, marketing and engineering. Such independent providers of flexible capacity are next networked to the company in a kind of internal electronic market. This is now referred to as the IntraNet, as distinct from the InterNet. They compete with each other for subcontracting orders.[28]

This is what is meant here by flexible accumulation through global webs. The United Nations *World Investment Report, 1994* provides several examples of it. The NIKE footwear company with annual sales of nearly $4 billion subcontracts 100 per cent of its goods production. NIKE itself currently employs only about 9000 people, while nearly 75 000 people are employed by its independent subcontractors located in different countries mostly in the Third World. NIKE has a performance-oriented inventory control system on its computer network and it gets orders from retailers in advance in return for guaranteed delivery times and discounts, making it possible for it to organise timely production (through its computer network) from its different producers located abroad. The subcontractors are all networked to the parent company. The parent company is really no more than a marketing and research and design company. Benneton and IKEA too rely on their computer networks to receive and place orders and monitor sales.[29]

Thus, transnational enterprise is evolving from company organisation to a loosely confederated network structure (global web) in which many discrete fabrication activities and services are bought in for the short term. This relieves the buyer of the costs of accessing capacity by committing to its continued use. By organising their suppliers not as wholly-owned subsidiaries but as independent agents, the contemporary transnational is in a position to combine the advantages of market competition with all the advantages that used to be associated with 'administrative fiat'; that is, company control over productive operations by wholly-owned subsidiaries.

Economic networking has been made possible by the fusion of telecommunications with computer technology (time/space compression). But there are also important social and institutional requisites that need to be brought into place to ensure its success.

Much of the work of the Regulation School and the new 'institutional economics' addresses these social and institutional requisites (see Chapter 5). What is argued here is that these *requisites* must be regarded simultaneously as structural *consequences* of the converging logic of global competition in which system standards and economic measures take precedence over nation-state diversity. We shall return to this in Chapter 7 where we consider the consequences of globalisation.

Global Financial 'Deepening'

We have referred before to the phenomenon of 'financial deepening' which occurs when the growth of financial transactions far exceeds the growth of the underlying economic fundamentals of production and trade.

In the 1980s the growth of the financial or 'symbol' or 'balloon' economy outpaced the growth of the fundamentals of trade and investment in the OECD countries seven times, and at a conservative estimate the total annual value of transactions in the world's financial markets is now twice the total value of world production.[30] Peter Drucker, the doyen of the management community, claims that '90 percent or more of the transnational economy's financial transactions do not serve what economists would consider an economic function'.[31] As Frederic Clairmont writes in his usual, colourful language:

> Today, more than at any time in capitalism's history, the profits of finance capital are based on debt and exponential debt creation. Private, corporate, and household debt worldwide surpasses US$31 trillion, galloping at a compound rate of over 9 per cent yearly, or three times faster than that of world GDP and world trade. It is clear for whom the bells are tolling. The tocsin is heard.[32]

What this means is that, evidently, money is increasingly being made out of the circulation of money, regardless of traditional restrictions of space and time as when money transforms into bricks and mortar. The financial revolution since the 1980s has been characterised by a potent fusion of financial deregulation on the one hand with powerful advances in telecommunications and information technology on the other. The upshot of this has been a tremendous

increase in the international mobility of capital. This mobility refers not only to the speed and freedom with which money can now move across frontiers at the press of a computer button, it also, more significantly, refers to the way it is being disconnected from social relationships in which money and wealth were previously embedded. It is because of this 'disembedding' that globalisation entails a process of intensification of linkages within the core of the global system, while its counterpart 'peripheralisaton' becomes a process of marginalisation and expulsion that cuts across territories and national boundaries, rendering areas within the traditional core subject to the same processes of expulsion as large swathes of territories in Africa, Latin America and Asia. Hence the structure of core-periphery becomes a social division, rather than a geographic one.

Let us explore the meaning of this heightened international mobility of capital a bit further. In particular let us examine why this should represent a form of *imploding* capitalism rather than a further expansion of world capitalism.

When our pension funds invest in, say, the Hong Kong stock exchange, which has seen a rise of 300 per cent in 1993 alone, they can then benefit from the rising values of the stock and, if they are clever fund managers (which we certainly hope they are), switch out of that stock exchange when it goes down and invest in another rising one somewhere else. There is no need for them or us to wait and see what happens to the companies that build skyscrapers in Hong Kong or sell textiles back to Europe. But of course the connections between the world of high finance and the economic fundamentals of world trade and production are not completely severed. There is still no such thing as a free lunch. What has happened, rather, is that the integration of the world's financial markets and the development of a whole range of novel financial instruments, permitted since the deregulation of these markets, have made it possible to connect up the arteries of real production and trade, and thus squeeze the last drop of surplus out of workers and peasants all over the world, in a manner that makes there innumerable threads that lead to our pension fund invisible and therefore unchallengeable.

To stick to the same example: the rise and rise of the Hong Kong stock market owed in large measure to Chinese provincial authorities investing borrowed money in Hong Kong's stock market and real estate, with dire consequences for the Beijing government's ability to hold the value of its currency and pay the peasants in northern China for its grain procurements. The world is now like this: if our pension fund works well for us, the peasants in northern China will just have to go a bit more hungry. If we, as we did during the consumer boom of the 1980s, push up interest rates through our incautious use of credit cards, it has knock-on effects for the interest rates that Brazil pays on its loans, and this in turn prejudices the livelihood of peasants in Brazil.

The speed with which money can move across borders removes the need to anchor it firmly in (national) social relationships. Globalisation makes national social solidarity (as expressed in transfer payments to the old, the sick, the unemployed and the lower income groups) *dysfunctional* from the point of view of the rational economic interests of those who participate in the global economy. This process is being sharpened by recent deregulation in the core countries which encourages the globalisation of small private investors and undercuts the last remaining vestiges of national social solidarity. The privatisation, for example, in the area of pension schemes (a transition from 'defined benefit' or occupational and state pension schemes, to 'defined contribution' schemes or 'personal' pension schemes) is a case in point.

Thus today, in the advanced countries, the pressures for globalisation (maintaining liberal and deregulated markets for finance and trade, and resistance to policies of protection for national territorial economic activities) come not just from a tiny group of international capitalists, that is from, those dominant fractions of corporate capital that have global interests, but also from a broadly-based stratum of society, the 13 per cent of senior citizens and those with an eye to their pensionable future, whose continued survival, to put it bluntly, is better secured in the rising economies of the Far East than by reproduction of the labour power (and pension premiums paid) by the shrinking younger generation that steps into their shoes. As *The Economist* has put it:

> Ageing populations in rich countries and freer flowing capital the world over are changing the way people save and invest. American and British institutional money is flooding foreign markets.[33]

This de-territorialisation of economic rationality as it affects not just organised capital but the mass of middle-class individuals in bourgeois societies is a key consequence of globalisation.

In this chapter we have argued that globalisation today is essentially a *social* phenomenon that drives cross-border economic integration to new levels of intensity. In our discussion we have already touched on some of the consequences of this process and we shall examine these consequences more fully in the next chapter. It is worth noting two points in conclusion. One is that globalisation is a *process,* not an end-state of affairs. There is no such thing as a global economy or a global society yet! Whether the process of globalisation continues along the pathways which I have identified depends largely on whether and how national governments resist the process or go along with it. This, in turn, depends largely on a correct identification of, and policy response to, the key elements of globalisation. The sceptics in the globalisation debate make rather much of the continuing, indeed in some cases apparently enhanced, exercise of sovereignty and regulation by national governments. And yet, as we shall see in the next chapter, much of this regulation amounts in effect to no more than a regulation *for* globalisation.

Notes

1. P. Hirst and G. Thompson, *Globalization in Question?* (London: Polity Press, 1996) p. 195.
2. Cf. S. Kuznets, 'Quantitative Aspects of the Economic Growth of Nations: X-level and Structure of Foreign Trade: Long-Term Trends', *Economic Development and Cultural Change,* 15 (2) Part II (January 1967) pp. 7-8. Kuznets gave the historical figure. Today's figure is based on statistical tables in World Bank, *World Development Report* (Oxford: Oxford University Press, 1994). See also Table 4.1, p. 71 in Chapter 4 of this book. Note, however, that World Bank sources stress the tremendous growth in world trade relative to world income since 1990. See S. Otsubo, *Globalization: Accelerated Integration through World Trade* (Washington: World Bank International Economics Department, 1995) discussion paper.
3. United Nations, Conference on Trade and Development, *World Investment Report 1994: Transnational Corporations, Employment and the Workplace* (New York: United Nations, 1994) pp. 133-5.
4. P. Hirst and G. Thompson, *op. cit.,* note 1, pp. 95-7.
5. For example, A. Glyn and R. Sutcliffe, 'Global but Leaderless? The New Capitalist Order', in *Socialist Register* (London: Merlin Press, 1992), pp. 76-95; and D. M. Gordon, 'The Global Economy: New Edifice or Crumbling Foundations?', *New Left Review,* no. 168 (1988) pp. 24-64.
6. See Chapter 4 of this book, p. 77.
7. For a compact review of sociological theories of globalisation, see M. Waters, *Globalization* (London: Routledge, 1995).
8. T. Parsons, *Societies* (Englewood Cliffs: Prentice Hall, 1966); and *The System of Modern Societies* (Englewood Cliffs: Prentice Hall, 1971).
9. R. Robertson, *Globalization* (London: Sage, 1992).
10. M. Waters, *Globalization, op. cit.,* note 7, *passim,* pp. 39-46.
11. J. Nettl and R. Robertson, *International Systems and the Modernization of Societies* (London: Faber, 1968).

12. D. Harvey, *The Condition of Postmodernity* (Oxford: Basil Blackwell,1989). The summary here is based on Chapters 14,15 and 17 of his book.
13. R. Delbridge, P. Turnbull and B. Wilkinson, 'Pushing Back the Frontiers: Management Control and Work Intensification under JIT/TQM Factory Regimes', *New Technology, Work and Employment* (Autumn, 1992) pp. 97-107, p. 104.
14. D. Harvey, *op. cit.*, note 12, p. 241.
15. A. Giddens, *The Consequences of Modernity* (Cambridge: Polity Press, 1990), p. 64.
16. UNECOSOC, *Multinational Corporations in World Development* (New York: UN, 1973).
17. UNCTAD, *World Investment Report, 1993* (New York & Geneva: UN, 1994) p. 143.
18. P. Drucker, *The New Realities* (London: Heinemann, 1989) pp. 123-5. See also K. Ohmae, *Triad Power, the Coming Shape of Global Competition* (New York: Free Press, 1985); and *The Borderless World: Power and Strategy in the Interlinked Economy* (London: Collins, 1990).
19. S. S. Cohen, 'Geo-economics and America's Mistakes', in M. Carnoy et al., *The New Global Economy in the Information Age* (London: Macmillan, 1993) p. 98.
20. For the figure for 1990, see P. Dicken, *Global Shift, The Internationalization of Economic Activity* (Manchester: Paul Chapman, 1992) 2nd edition, Table 2.5, p. 30.
21. M. Aglietta, *The Theory of Capitalist Regulation* (London: Verso, 1976), p. 122.
22. P. Boccara. 'Qu'est-ce-que l'anthroponomie?', in *Cahiers du l'IRM, Individues et Société, 1,* and cited in R. Jessop, 'Regulation Theories in Retrospect and Prospect', in *Economy and Society,* 19 (2) (May 1990) pp. 153-216, p. 168.
23. A. Lipietz, *Mirages and Miracles* (London: Verso, 1987) p. 15.
24. R. Jessop, *State Theory* (Oxford: Blackwell, 1990) pp. 317-18.
25. C. Sabel, 'Experimental Regionalism and the Dilemmas of Regional Economic Policy', paper presented to the conference on 'Socio-Economic Systems of Japan, the United States, the United Kingdom, Germany, and France', Institute of Fiscal and Monetary Policy, Tokyo, Japan, 16 February 1996.
26. R. Reich, *The Work of Nations* (London: Simon & Schuster, 1991) p. 211.
27. S. A. Bradley, J. Hausman and A. Nolan, *Globalization, Technology and Competition: The Fusion of Computers and Telecommunications in the 1990s* (Cambridge, Mass.: Harvard Business School Press, 1994) p. 111.
28. R. Jaikumar and D. M. Upton in S. A. Bradley *et al.*, pp. 173-4.
29. UNCTAD, *World Investment Report, 1994, op. cit.*, note 3, p. 194.
30. Based on C. Crook, 'Global Finance', *The Economist,* 19 September 1992.
31. P. Drucker, *op. cit.*, note 18, p. 121.
32. F. F. Clairmont, *The Rise and Fall of Economic Liberalism: The Making of the Economic Gulag* (Penang: Southbound and Third World Network, 1996) p. 29.
33. *The Economist,* 27 November 1993.

Suggestions for further reading

Barry, Tom, Beth Wood and Deb Preusch, *The Other Side of Paradise: Foreign Control in the Caribbean* (New York: Grove Press Inc, 1980).
Duncan, Neville (ed.) *Mechanisms of Impoverishment in Anglophone Caribbean: The Role of the Bretton Woods Institutions and the Recommendation of Caribbean NGOs* (Kingston: FES, 1995).
Fanon, Franz, *The Wretched of the Earth* (New York: Grove Press, 1968)
LaGuerre, John (ed.) *Structural Adjustment: Public Policy and Administration in the Caribbean,* (Port of Spain: University of the West Indies, 1994).
Lenin, V.I., *Imperialism: The Highest Stage of Capitalism: A Popular Outline* (New York: International Publishers, 1939).
Lewis, G.K., *The Growth of the Modern West Indies* (London: Monthly Review Press, 1968).
McAfee, Kathy, *Storm Signals: Structural Adjustment and Development Alternatives in the Caribbean* (London: Zed Books Ltd., 1991).
Nkrumah, K., *Neo-colonialism: The Last Stage of Imperialism* (London: Nelson, 1965).
Rodney, Walter, *How Europe Underdeveloped Africa* (London: Bogle L'Ouverture Publications, 1972).
Sunshine, Catherine, *The Caribbean: Survival, Struggle and Sovereignty* (Washington: EPICA, 1980).

Notes

1. V.I. Lenin, *Imperialism: The Highest Stage of Capitalism a Popular Outline* (New York: International Publishers, 1939).
2. T. Barry, B. Wood and D. Preusch, *The Other Side of Paradise: Foreign Control in the Caribbean* (New York: The Grove Press, 1984).
3. G. K. Lewis, *The Growth of the Modern West Indies* (New York: Monthly Review Press, 1968) p. 403.
4. Ralph Gonsalves, *The Spectre of Imperialism: The Case of the Caribbean* (Mimeo).
5. K. Nkrumah, *Towards Colonial Freedom: Africa in the Struggle Against World Imperialism* (London: Panaf, 1973).
6. Linden Lewis, 'The Politics of Race in Barbados', *Bulletin of Eastern Caribbean Affairs,* 16:6 (1990).
7. Rodney, *How Europe Underdeveloped Africa,* p. 89.
8. Rodney, *How Europe Underdeveloped Africa,* p. 100.
9. Roy Augier, 'Before and After 1865', in *Caribbean Freedom: Economy and Society From Emancipation to the Present,* ed., by Hilary Beckles and Verene Shepherd (Kingston: Ian Randle Publishers, 1993) pp. 170–80; and Trevor Munroe and Rupert Lewis, *Readings in Government and Politics of the West Indies* (Kingston: Department of Government, Mona Campus, 1971) pp. 71–4.
10. James Millette, *The Genesis of Crown Colony Government in Trinidad* (Port of Spain: Moko Enterprises, 1970).
11. Millette, *The Genesis of Crown Colony Government in Trinidad.*
12. B. Berman, 'Clientelism and Neo-Colonialism: Center-Periphery Relations and Political Development in African States', *Studies in Comparative International Development,* 15:2 (1974).
13. K. Nkrumah, *Neo-Colonialism: The Last Stage of Imperialism* (London: Nelson, 1965) p. ix.
14. Nkrumah, *Neo-Colonialism: The Last Stage of Imperialism.*
15. G. K. Lewis, *The Growth of the Modern West Indies,* p. 402.

16. Nkrumah, *Neo-Colonialism: The Last Stage of Imperialism*, p. 243.
17. See Appendix 1.
18. Nkrumah, *Neo-Colonialism: The Last Stage of Imperialism*, p. 241.
19. Franz Fanon, *The Wretched of the Earth* (New York: The Grove Press, 1968).
20. C. Payer, *The Debt Trap: The International Monetary Fund and the Third World* (New York: Monthly Review Press, 1974).
21. Payer, *The Debt Trap*.
22. Ankie Hoogvelt, 'IMF Crime in Conditionality: An Open Letter to the Managing Director of the International Monetary Fund', *Monthly Review*, 39, (1987).
23. Kathy McAfee, *Storm Signals: Structural Adjustment and Development Alternatives in the Caribbean* (London: Zed Books Ltd., 1991).
24. McAfee, *Storm Signals*.
25. N.C. Duncan, 'Barbados and the IMF–A Case Study', in John LaGuerre, ed., *Structural Adjustment: Public Policy and the Administration in the Caribbean* (Port of Spain: University of the West Indies, 1994) pp. 54–87.
26. R. Moonial, 'Structural Adjustment, Union Busting and the Future of Trade Unions', in John LaGuerre, ed., *Structural Adjustment: Public Policy*, pp. 130–55.
27. Moonilal, 'Structural Adjustment, Union Busting', pp. 130–55.
28. H.A. Watson, 'The Changing Structure of World Capital and Development Options in the Caribbean', in Watson and Frobel, eds., *The Future of the Caribbean in the World System* (Kingston: University of the West Indies, 1988), p. 1.
29. Chakravarthi Raghavan, *Recolonialization: GATT, the Uruguay Round and the Third World* (London: Zed Books Ltd., 1990), p. 23.
30. George A.V. Belle, 'Against Colonialism: Political Theory and Recolonisation in the Caribbean', a paper presented at a Conference on Caribbean Culture (Mona Campus: University of the West Indies: March 3-5, 1996), p. 25.

two

Struggles of the Working Class People

Introduction

The decade of the 1930s served to highlight the limited accomplishments of CCG in the region. Indeed, the prospects of CCG held out by the British government were actualised in the failed promises of the 1930s. The results of that failed reformist agenda were therefore predictable in the widespread outbreaks of violence of that decade. However, the central thesis of this chapter is that although the revolts which took place in the Caribbean in the 1930s represented a revolutionary period, the political and economic policies in the post-1930s period can be considered as a victory for the economic ruling class in the region. The end of the revolutionary period left intact the economic power base of the ruling planter-merchant oligarchy, and thus their political power also remained virtually untouched. The social, economic and political gains of the working masses, can be viewed as the politics of appeasement and consequently, containment of the masses. One strategy used by both the colonial and imperial ruling classes was the legalisation of trade unions and the organisation of political parties. Gordon K. Lewis has declared that:

> . . .after 1938 the potentially revolutionary *Elan Vital* of the masses was anesthetized by being canalised into institutions – trade unions, political parties, co-operatives – controlled by the bourgeoisie groups. . .[1]

While no attempt is being made to belittle the role of the trade unions in Caribbean societies or to underestimate the contributions made by these early organisations from the 1930s to the 1960s, it is being suggested that the 1930s represented much more than what was actually achieved by the working class.

Ken Post argues that the events of the 1930s and the constant slave rebellions in the Caribbean reflected the revolutionary potential of black West Indians. However, the leadership of the movement was passed to the middle class, whose interests were different from those of the workers.[2] Post asserts that if the workers were marked by a relatively high level of class consciousness, not only would their revolutionary potential be utilised, but the leadership would have passed into the hands of the grassroot leaders. Such a development may well have resulted in greater gains for the nationalist movement. Post also contends that the imperial government was more predisposed to negotiating with the middle class than with the under classes. With reference to the 1938 Royal Commission, Post concludes that:

> . . . The purpose of the Commission had not merely been to collect information; . . . but also by giving a group of businessmen, academics and politicians, who were not going to challenge the colonial system as such, the chance to propose remedial policies.[3]

This chapter is divided into three main sections. The first deals with the background to the decade of the 1930s; section two identifies the main recommendations of the Moyne Commission Report and section three will briefly assess these recommendations.

Background to the 1930s political crisis

The decade of the 1930s can be regarded as a watershed in the history of the British West Indies. Not only did the events of the 1930s and their aftermath accelerate the pace of constitutional and socio-economic developments but they also signaled the attack on the entire structure of colonial administration and society. The 1930s was therefore the period that saw the emergence of the modern West Indies and witnessed a structural crisis of the old order. The old order was characterised by a lack of a democratic culture in the Caribbean, the absence of legitimate channels through which the people could express their grievances and frustrations and the skewed nature of the ownership of resources in the region.

The events of the period were therefore the reaction and the response of the socially, politically and economically-dominated working class and the peasantry (the under classes) to their position in society. This reaction took the form of riots, strikes and demonstrations and represented an attack on the existing power relationships.

In the post-emancipation period, the colonial ruling class throughout the Caribbean enacted legislation designed to limit the mobility of the workers and to maintain the existing socio-economic and political relations in the colonies. The failure to reform the socio-political and economic systems revealed not only general insensitivity to the plight of the people in the region by the colonial authorities, but also the bankruptcy of CCG. The coincidence of interests between the state and the propertied classes throughout the region was apparent not only prior to the 1930s but also in their combined response to the unfolding crisis.

General labour conditions in the British West Indies

In the view of Gordon K. Lewis, the raw material conditions of the working class struggle in the 1930s can be found in the general labour conditions of the time. Unemployment and underemployment continued to prevail in the British West Indian colonies. However, not only were unemployment and underemployment widespread, but also, labour was poorly paid and working hours excessively long. A prime example of this situation was evidenced by the conditions of dock workers and women in the domestic service.[4] With reference to the specific labour conditions of workers in Jamaica, Lewis wrote:

> . . . The Kingston dock workers providing the worst example of that evil system; the exploitation of a surplus labour economy by the socially unconscionable employer, the plight of women workers in the urban establishment and in domestic service being grim evidence of that situation, the evil of rotational employment system which simply served to exacerbate the real problem of intermittent employment.[5]

In Barbados, the Deane Commission Report of 1937[6] also painted a disturbing picture of labour conditions in that island. Wages were below subsistence levels, particularly among the agricultural workers and did not exceed 18 cents a day. So appalled was the Deane Commission at the working conditions in Barbados that it stated that nothing short of a bankruptcy of trade and industry should cause such low wages.

In Trinidad and Tobago, the working conditions of petroleum and dockworkers were so deplorable that the then Secretary of State, W. Ormsby-Gore was moved to comment on the Harbour Scheme:

> . . . The labour conditions on this scheme are scandalous . . . The Harbour Scheme authorities are out to suck the labour orange dry and throw the rind on the dung heap.[7]

West Indian labourers were therefore in need of relief, but none was in fact forthcoming. These labour practices were imposed on the already bad social conditions in the British West Indies. Susan Craig, Gordon K. Lewis and Ken Post hold the view that the existing social conditions in the West Indies showed the inadequacy of the colonial governments. They all observed that one hundred years after the emancipation of slaves, 'every testimony about living conditions bore witness to a serious crisis'.[8]

In commenting on the social conditions in the British West Indies, the Moyne Commission showed the extent of the deplorable housing conditions in the region. Apart from the poor construction, the conspicuous absence of proper sanitation and an adequate water supply, the Commission pointed out that as a rule throughout the Caribbean, whole families consisting of a mother, father and numerous children, had their meals and slept in one small room.[9] In Trinidad and Tobago, social conditions were no better than that which prevailed in Guyana, Jamaica and the rest of the Caribbean. Reports of various commissions on the living conditions of workers in Trinidad and Tobago in the 1930s testify to the distressing conditions. John Jagger described the living conditions to the Commission as '. . .The vilest thing in housing accommodation that man can ever have seen . . . The sanitary arrangements were primitive in the extreme.'[10] He continued:

> . . .perhaps most dreadful of all were the round iron cisterns at each door containing drinking water for the residents, in which every creeping and crawling thing imaginable, plus endless masses of mosquito larvae.[11]

As to the dietary conditions in the 1930s, the Orde-Brown Report identified many deficiencies. According to the report, the typical diet of the West Indian labourer was:

> . . .decidedly deficient in animal protein and certain vitamins, with an excessive proportion of carbohydrate. Fish and diary produce (sic) milk is largely used.[12]

The nationalist and political activist in Barbados, W. Algernon Crawford in a memorandum to the Moyne Commission, in reference to the colonial situation which had produced the 1937 Riots in Barbados, vehemently stated that:

> . . . It is high time, that this infamous tyranny, this system of fascism, better known as colonial imperialism, should be completely destroyed. There is no name too evil to be applied to a system which keeps thousands of workers in semi-starvation, denies them all

human rights, and crushes with brutal military force any effort on their part to lift their standards of living.[13]

Other dynamics affecting labour conditions in the British West Indies

A variety of other factors also influenced events in the 1930s. These include:

A lack of constitutional and adequate labour relations machinery for redressing grievances.[14]

Selwyn Ryan notes that the unrepresentative nature of the colonial political system was a major factor underlying the labour rebellions in the 1930s.[15] While Arthur Lewis' view, that had a constitutional machinery been put in place there might well have been no upheavals, is debatable – as its mere existence does not suggest willingness and thus capacity to undertake change – his view is extremely relevant.[16] The hostility of the propertied class and the colonial government to the workers was reflected in their failure to institutionalise collective bargaining procedures. Ryan argues that in Trinidad and Tobago this was perhaps the most immediate of the forces provoking the disturbances.[17] The absence of this vital machinery left the workers frustrated and isolated and gave them only one real political alternative, which was amply demonstrated by the social upheavals that marked the 1930s.

The effects of the Great Depression of 1929–1930

Whatever the precise origins of the 'Great Depression', the crash of the American Stock Market and the resultant international industrial depression had a severe impact on the economic and social landscape of the British West Indies. In the late 1920s and the early 1930s, as Western powers combated economic recession, the main approach to resolving the issue was to implement currency depreciation and to build high tariff walls in an attempt to protect domestic industries from competition and to defend their share of international trade. The decade of the 1930s began with the passing of the protectionist Hawley-Smoot Tariff Act by the United States in 1930, which increased the duties on imported sugar, thereby affording protection to domestic sugar producers. This was followed by a spate of similar new tariffs or increases in existing tariff levels, as other countries began to feel the impact of the Great Depression. By 1931, the second aspect of the international response to the crisis began with the depreciation of the British currency in 1931, followed by the United States in 1934. The cumulative effect of the individual state action only served to further shrink the total quantity of international trade and intensify international economic recession. Not only were salaries and wages reduced, factories and businesses closed, but also profits plummeted and unemployment increased, further deepening the international crisis. It is in this context that the state undertook a third response to the crisis. Most European, Latin and North American countries as well as Caribbean countries, including Cuba, placed restrictions on immigration as local populations came under pressure from the devastation caused by the global recession.

The most notable impact of the Great Depression on the British West Indian colonies was the collapse of the economies at the outset of the depression, which resulted in difficulty in marketing products and a rise in unemployment. Secondly, the international recession also impacted directly on the remittances which emigrants had sent home to their families. Thirdly, the closing off of immigration channels contributed to population pressure in the Caribbean, while the economic recession abroad forced many migrants to return home.

Many British West Indians traditionally found outlets for their economic, social and political frustrations by migrating to a foreign metropolis. However, from the 1920s, the immigration outlets were virtually closed to West Indians as the effects of the 'Great Depression' became internationalised. While emigration had partially relieved the growth of the population in the British West Indian colonies, the virtual closure of Cuba, Panama, the United States, Britain and other countries to immigrants, further worsened the escalating socio-economic and political problems in the colonies. Cuba for example, had been an important outlet for many British West Indians who had found employment on the sugar plantations. The imposition of the Hawley-Smoot Tariff Act by the United States on imported sugar, had deleterious effects for the Cuban sugar industry and the economic environment in general as sugar formed the base of the economy. Not surprisingly, in the immediate aftermath of the Hawley-Smoot Act, unemployment and underemployment increased in Cuba. The effect of these developments, coupled with the return of many West Indians who had previously migrated only served to exacerbate an already explosive situation. The Moyne Commission Report noted that this was particularly true of Barbados, where the return of migrants in the early 1930s

contributed even more to the growth of population than the excess of births over deaths.[18] Moreover, the expectations of the returning migrants from abroad, given the socio-economic conditions in the British West Indies could not be fulfilled. It is not surprising that many of these migrants formed part of the leadership of the nationalist movement, as the evolving movement drew heavily from that sector of the population.

Over population in the West Indies

The Moyne Commission Report noted that the population in all the British West Indian colonies was increasing with great rapidity. According to the Report, by the 1930s the rate of natural increase of the population was higher than it had been in the previous 25 years. The number of births in Jamaica and the Leeward and Windward Islands in 1937 were more than double the number of deaths.[19] The Report noted that the 1.5 to two per cent population growth in the British West Indian colonies in the context of an absence of important mineral resources and the limited supplies of fertile land, would have detrimental socio-economic impact which the region could ill-afford. Indeed, the commission noted that:

> Behind the various economic and social defects. . . the rapid increase in population is to be found, sometimes as a major cause, and almost always as an aggravating factor. It has contributed more than any other single influence to the formidable increase of intermittent employment in the country, and has thus gone far to nullify the effects of wage advances in improving the standard of living. It has led in areas where an independent peasantry proprietorship had previously been established to the sub-division of holdings into plots so small that their owners are compelled to rely largely on wage-work for a livelihood. It has contributed. . . to the difficulty of providing adequate housing accommodation. . . again the difficulties of providing adequate school accommodation are greatly aggravated by the large annual increase in the number of school-age; for in many colonies it is difficult to find money for school-building on a scale sufficient to keep pace with this increase.[20]

The Italian invasion of Ethiopia

The overthrow of Haile Selaisse also sparked off concerns particularly among the Rastafarian community in Jamaica and the increased activity of the core organisation of the Ethiopian Salvation Society in the country. The fall of Ethiopia, which was the last remaining resistance to colonialism on the African continent, contributed to black nationalism in the British West Indies.

The impact of local nationalist agitators

In all Caribbean colonies, individual leaders were critical to the development of the 1930s and post 1930s period. In Trinidad and Tobago the activity of Uriah Butler was a major factor in the occurrence of social disturbances. In Barbados it was Clement Payne.[21] In fact, Ryan notes that in Trinidad and Tobago, given Butler's popularity with the workers, he was responsible for the events of 1937. The attempts by the British to arrest him only served to heighten the unfolding crisis in the colony. According to Ryan:

> . . . By moving against Butler, the authorities had in fact co-operated in his 'martyrdom'. Butler's historical role was thus to provide the catalyst, to crystallize and articulate the grievances that people had long nursed, and to offer them an 'acceptable' outlet for aggressive dispositions which Cipriani had held in check.[22]

Race

This was also a critical determinant of the disturbances. Many of those who suffered in the 1930s were the non-whites.

The role of Garveyism

Garveyism had tremendous philosophical importance in the 1930s. The central theme of Garvey's teachings was black nationalism and the need for blacks to get political power. He argued that the lack of political power had created a situation of social, economic and cultural deprivation in the black diaspora. Garvey's emphasis on race in the context of the 1920s can be viewed as an important philosophical and intellectual input into the 1930s movement. An important component of the demands of the Nationalist movement was the liberation of the West Indian masses, which owed much to the teachings of Marcus Garvey. It is important to note however, that though the Moyne Commission attempted to marginalise the race question, race and racism was a fundamental cause of the disturbances.

These other dynamics affecting labour conditions in the British West Indies, that is, the emergence of Black Nationalism and the onset of the Great depression of 1929 among other factors, spawned numerous political parties and trade unions.

The Moyne Commission Report

Colonial and imperial government reaction to the unfolding crisis was mixed. It represented a blend of ideological rigidity and pragmatism. The major official response of the British government to the potentially revolutionary situation in the Caribbean was to appoint a Royal Commission empowered in August 1938 to '. . . Investigate social and economic conditions in Barbados, British Guiana, British Honduras, Jamaica, the Leeward Islands, Trinidad and Tobago and the Windward Islands'.[23] It therefore sought to 'remedy' grievances of two local populations that had caused the events of the 1930s.

The Report of the West India Royal Commission, or The Moyne Commission as it came to be known, recommended several policies that held promise for most classes in the British West Indies. According to Post, the proposals made by the Royal Commission in no way represented radical departures from lines of policy already firmly established.[24] Post contends that the only novel aspects of the Royal Commission's report were the allocation of large amounts of money for social welfare services and the creation of an overarching organisation to take control. In a strong condemnation of the Royal Commission's report, G.K. Lewis contends that:

> . . . the report of the Royal Commission. . .was nothing more. . . than a futile proposal to make charitable social services do duty for economic, social and political reform.[25]

Summary of Recommendations from the Moyne Commission

1. The establishment of a West Indian Welfare Fund of $1,000,000 annually for 20 years to be administered by a special Comptroller of Welfare Services. Such funding to be provided by the British government was to be allotted for the improvement of the social sector, that is, education, health, housing and so on.
2. Social services recommendations:
   a. Education
      · Establishment of teacher training colleges
      · Establishment of more schools
      · Additional equipment to be provided for schools
      · Adult education to be encouraged
      · Vocational education for girls
      · Girls to be encouraged to compete for scholarships on the same basis as boys
      · Free school meals and clothes for poor children

b. Public Health
- Appointment of a medical advisor
- Centralisation of certain medical facilities
- Creation of one school of hygiene for research and teaching in preventive medicine
- Preventive medicine to be encouraged
- Training of nurses

c. Housing
- Clearing of slums
- Rural housing to be provided and financed by government
- Land to be provided by estate-owners

d. Labour and Trade Unions
- Laws to protect trade unions especially against Law of Tort
- Legislation for peaceful picketing
- Labour departments to be created where they did not exist
- Wage boards to be created where they did not exist
- Scheme of workmen's compensation to be enacted
- Unemployment insurance to be enacte

3. Economic
- Intensification of agriculture through mixed farming
- Britain to increase sugar quota by 120,000 tons
- Improved imperial preferences
- Little industrial development
- Develop peasant agriculture
- Land settlement schemes provided with credit facilities for support

4. Communication
- Britain to provide two small ships for trade between the islands
- Regular air service to be provided
- Wireless service to be provided

5. Political
- Universal adult suffrage
- Greater elected representation in government
- Support for political federation of the Windwards
- Power to remain in the hands of the Governor

A brief assessment of the Moyne Commission Report

There are varying views on the political significance of the Royal Commission report. Ken Post holds that politically, the recommendations were modest, while Arthur Lewis argues that on the political front, nothing short of a revolution had occurred.[26] For Arthur Lewis, the social changes which the Commission introduced were not as important as the fact that the working classes became politically organised, and their interests forced into the foreground. G. K. Lewis contends that the encouragement of political parties served to split the nationalist movement and weakened its potential. It also served to halt the mass mobilisation which had occurred, thereby facilitating the further exploitation of the West Indian under classes.[27]

The Royal Commission came under great pressure from the region's middle class representatives for the kind of constitutional reform that would satisfy their class designs for social and political mobility. The Commission did not recommend responsible government but recommended more representative government for the colonies. While the Commission recommended the extension of the franchise based on adult suffrage, it nevertheless failed to reduce the power of the local governors who controlled the executive in the colonies. Trusteeship was therefore the prevailing British attitude.

The political recommendation of adult suffrage was extremely significant because for the first time, the underclass could now be included in the decision-making process. Moreover, the extension of political democracy through the vote was the springboard for the development of mass-based, rather than the elitist political parties that had dominated the period preceding the 1930s. It therefore represented a means of accommodating the demands of a segment of the population for greater representation. The development of mass-based political parties, which served as a platform for further attacks on CCG.[28]

From the late 1930s to 1950s, the number of political parties in the region expanded rapidly, mobilising more working- and middle-class West Indians into the political arena. However, despite any impression of an overwhelming victory for the under classes, power remained vested in the hands of the imperial administration.

In the short-term, the political recommendations served to appease local demand without relinquishing imperial domination of the political system. The concessions granted to labour in connection with the specific trade union legislation were important and represented gains of the under classes, albeit under middle-class leadership. However, the legalisation of trade unions served to facilitate collective bargaining. It also served to allay the fear of the planter/merchant oligarchy in the region of the disruption to the accumulation of capital by that class. George Belle also contends that the above strategy was part of a wider imperial design to contain and control developments and conflict in the region by institutionalising the conflicts.[29]

Economically, the Moyne Commission's report did not usher in any revolutionary changes. In no way were the existing economic patterns of relationships challenged, so that in effect, the economic recommendations, in terms of social relations, represented victory for the national and imperial bourgeoisie. The ruling class in the region consolidated its position by appeasing and containing the workers.

According to Susan Craig the recommended social reforms brought few tangible benefits to the workers in the short-run, as they continued to suffer from low wages and poor living conditions.[30] The implementation of various forms of social welfare immediately after 1939 did not significantly remedy the basic problems of social and economic inequality in the region. While the 1930s was a formative period in the shaping of the modern West Indies, Susan Craig is of the view that with hindsight, the changes were mere shadows rather than substance. The 1930s, given the co-optation of the nationalist movement and the desire of the imperial and colonial states to maintain an economic and political system beneficial to the continued accumulation of capital by international capital, did not usher in deep-seated socio-political and economic changes.

The recommendations of the Royal Commission report fell far short of the demands of the nascent nationalist movement in the 1930s. The most authoritative position of the demands can be found in the resolutions put before the Moyne Commission by the leaders of the British Guiana and West Indies Labour Congress in November 1938.[31]

The colonial and imperial design for the nationalist movement

To understand the development of the early nationalist phase in the Commonwealth Caribbean, it is critical that an examination of the role of the imperial and colonial ruling class in shaping the movement be undertaken. Overall, the British colonial ruling class adopted two strategies.

Flexible strategy: appeasing and containing the workers and their leadership. This was a deliberate strategy designed to manipulate the nationalist movement in order to secure power in the long run.

Rigid strategy: a policy of constitutionalism, which envisaged gradual constitutional advancement to independence under the tutelage of the British government.

The legitimisation of trade unions and the granting of universal adult suffrage were two of the most important concessions of the British and the colonial ruling class to the workers. However, these two institutional forms of the nationalist movement also reflected the political presence of the ruling class. Both these organisations served to effect the control and supervision of the ruling classes over the under classes through the policy of containment. The ultimate objective of the ruling class was the containment of social conflict and its survival. It was in the political interest of the ruling class to recognise the political organisations of the subordinate classes and to widen the franchise to give the political parties greater mass appeal. In this they showed their flexibility, which is also evident in the ways in which they manipulated the weaknesses in the political alliance of the classes which confronted them in the 1930s. A divide and rule strategy was the first tool used to effect their political objective through the establishment of separate organisations in several British West Indian colonies.

In Jamaica, a combination of the two most powerful leaders, Norman Manley and Alexander Bustamante would have been extremely helpful to the nationalist platform. However, not only did the colonial authorities fail to ensure unity among the two leaders, but also the ruling class policy was to effect the division of the labour leaders.[32] Bustamante was highly ambitious, a maverick with substantial popularity among the poorest sections of the population and was building a formidable labour movement through the Bustamante Industrial Trade Union (BITU), which was the largest labour organisation in Jamaica. Manley was of socialist orientation and had an important base among the middle class. He was building a social democratic organisation, which had the potential for raising the consciousness and political sophistication of the workers and presenting an effective challenge to colonialism. One primary goal of Manley's People's National Party (PNP) was to mount an effective campaign for self-government. However, this required mass support and therefore effective linkages with the labour movement, which could be provided by the BITU. According to Ken Post at the start of the campaign the PNP organisation was:

> . . . a very imperfect instrument for such an enterprise . . . its potential for reaching the peasants was on the decline, while its financial position was shaky . . .'[33]

Post notes that despite the limitations of Bustamante's overall style of leadership and the poor financial position of the trade union, politically, the Jamaican labour movement meant the existence of the BITU.[34] It was therefore critical at this juncture that the BITU and the PNP forge a strong alliance. Post further notes that Governor Arthur Richards recognised and appreciated the political significance of the growing alliance between Bustamante's trade union and the PNP. The destruction of this alliance was critical in the context of the PNP's political platform of self-government and socialism, which was regarded as disadvantageous to the British government. The statement of Governor Richards on the growing strength of the PNP and its alliance with the BITU is instructive. According to Governor Richards:

> . . . It is difficult to assess the progress being made by the People's National Party. It is certainly not very rapid or spectacular at present, but it is making slow progress and it now has working groups organised in every parish. Its unstable alliance with the Bustamante Union would give it great strength in any universal suffrage election, but of course it is not in the nature of Bustamante to allow any rival near the throne. He regards the limelight as his own special prerogative and he cannot therefore be relied upon to support for long any cause but his own . . .[35]

There is no doubt that notwithstanding the concern which Bustamante generated in 1940s Jamaica, he was regarded as a more acceptable political opponent than Norman Manley of the PNP. Of Manley, Governor Richards wrote:

> . . .I regard him as a political dreamer whose success as a b arrister and whose   unquestioned intellectual ability and culture have obscured his lack of political ability. I think he sincerely desires to build a better Jamaica and is passionately determined to inspire others with that ideal, but he refuses to see how imperfect are the tools with which he must fashion his New Jerusalem and how sordid are the motives which actuate most of his followers . . .[36]

The ruling class led by Governor Richards worked to split the embryonic nationalist movement into two rival political and trade union arms, thereby weakening the anti-systemic movement aligned against them.

The ruling class also manipulated the ideological weaknesses of individuals and groups which confronted them in the 1930s. They nurtured the same anti-socialism as Bustamante, which gave rise to an anti-ideological and anti-intellectual leadership. This facilitated the persistence of an ideology already in place, and permitted opportunistic rather than philosophical stances to be taken by the leadership of the movement. A similar divide and rule policy was also affected in Trinidad and Tobago.[37] George Belle traces the post-1937 developments in Barbados arguing that the British government aided in containing and limiting the impact of the nationalist struggle in the country on behalf of the ruling economic and political elite,[38] which had negative implications for the overall development of the nationalist movement in that country.

Key words and phrases

1	Appeasement
2	Labour unrest
3	Rebellion
4	Containment
5	Revolution
6	Moyne Commission
7	Deane Commission
8	Co-optation
9	Legislation
10	Concession
11	Trade unions
12	Mass-based political parties
13	Mass mobilisation
14	The Nationalist Movement

Questions to Consider

- Assess the socio-economic and political recommendations of the Moyne Commission and consider the ways in which they ushered in a 'modern West Indies'. Illustrate with examples.
- Critically assess the view that 'the recommendations of the Moyne Commission Report were mere shadows than substance'.
- Assess the role of the British government in containing the labour rebellions of the 1930s.

Activities

* Seek out one member of the West Indian community who lived through the experiences of the 1937 riots and discuss with them their experiences.
* In groups, discuss your findings.
* Do you believe that changes to the conditions of Blacks in the Caribbean would have taken place without their active participation?
* In what ways can Caribbean societies, economies and politics benefit from further change? In group discussion identify ways and strategies for promoting change.

Readings

The Struggle for Political Democracy: The 1937 Riots

George A.V. Belle

Method of Analysis

I do not intend to describe the events of 1937; the story is essentially known already. My task, as I see it, is rather to advance explanation and understanding of the political significance of the revolt, and place it in the context of the struggle for political democracy in Barbados.

I will pursue this task in the following way. I will first briefly outline my method of analysis; secondly, 1 will give a synopsis of the disturbances; thirdly, I will analyse the causes of the revolt: fourthly, I will analyse the rebellion itself; fifthly, I will examine the outcome, what developed immediately as a consequence of the disturbances; and, sixthly, 1 will suggest some parallels between the 1937 period and the contemporary situation and make some final conclusions.

With respect to my method, I bring to this lecture the orientation of my training as a political scientist. As a political scientist, I am less concerned with painting a detailed description of the "'disturbances" and more with increasing an understanding and explanation of what happened in terms of its political significance. I think it is necessary to say this because at this point in this lecture series on post-emancipation Barbados, I believe there is a break from the line of lecturers that have gone before. I believe that every lecturer so far has been a historian. The last three in the series this year will be all political scientists, and I am the first one.

Our discipline's orientation is different from that of a historian's and so our concerns, our research, etc. are different from that of the historian. In fact, I began my research on this period back in 1973 as a post-graduate student, and the research involved building and identifying a theory of development for Barbados and in testing various developmental theories. So, I looked at the 'disturbances' with this concern in mind rather than as a task in historical investigation. Therefore, my concern is less to give you more details about what happened and more to seek to increase your perception of what happened.

My method is also intended to demonstrate not just the uniqueness of the event, for that in my view would distort its reality by isolating it, but to identify the parameters of causation and the interrelatedness of the event with wider happenings regionally and internationally and the place of the event in terms of process, both in terms of the social development of mankind generally and the historical process within Barbados itself. My method also seeks to identify and relate the impact of many actors, individual and mass, on the event and its outcome; and not to build analysis around any one personality. I will show the inter-connectedness and interactions of these actors one upon another and the implications of their collective input upon the developments. Further, my method involves identification of the qualitative features of the rebellion through subjecting the revolt to analysis informed by political theory in order that our comprehension and knowledge concerning its significance may be heightened. Finally, my method is also to empirically illustrate significant features relevant to the nature of the disturbances.

Description of Disturbances

I move now to a synopsis of the disturbances. This is intended to remind you of what happened. W. Arthur Lewis gives a brief but, I think, accurate description of the events. He was commissioned by the Fabian Society as a research student at the London School of Economics to do this, after the revolts.

He first of all starts off by saying that Barbados is "a tiny island". Its plantations were almost entirely in European hands, and its government at the time was one of the most reactionary in the West Indies. Then, in March I 937, one Clement Payne arrived in Barbados. He was a friend of Uriah Butler, the man who later was to lead the oil-field workers' strike: he came from Trinidad, this Clement Payne, to urge upon the working classes of Barbados the virtues of organisation. He held a number of meetings and got a good hearing and the government therefore looked around for some reason to suppress him. They found it in the formalities associated with his entry into the colony. For Payne was the son of Barbadian parents and had grown up in Barbados, but had been born while his mother was in Trinidad, and on entering the colony, he had stated that he was born in Barbados. So the police changed him before a magistrate with wilfully making a false statement as to his place of birth. This happened, Lewis says, soon after the disturbances in Trinidad which clearly affected his consciousness of the Barbadian people. Huge crowds followed Payne to and from the trial and when, on 22 July, he was convicted and fined $48.00, he appealed and announced his intention of leading a procession to the Governor's residence, to protest against his conviction. Lewis tells us, the police refused to let him see the Governor, and, as he persisted, he and a number of his followers were arrested and an order issued for his deportation. On 26 July, the Court of Appeal quashed his conviction on the grounds that he might not have known that he was born in Trinidad.

However, the efforts by counsel to rescind the deportation order were unsuccessful and on the same day he was deported. His supporters were furious at this treatment. Lewis says, and a large crowd assembled on the wharf where Payne was expected to embark, but the police sent him off at another point. When the people learned of this, they became very excitable and out of control, a coronet was sounded, they assembled in the Lower Green and Golden Square where they were "harangued", as the official report says. The mob then spread through the city in bands smashing motor cars and electric street lamps, and when the police tried to stop these outrages, the mob rained showers of stones and bottles upon them in a fray in which Sgt. Elias had two fingers fractured and three other police constables received injuries. The official report says that the police, only armed with batons, succeeded with the greatest difficulty in restoring some sort of order, but they were unable to make a single arrest. Lewis points out that, on the following morning, the orgy continued with smashing of shop windows and cars, and that the disturbances spread quickly, by groups of people commandeering cars and buses which carried the news throughout the country where looting started in shops and raiding in the potato fields. The official report states that lawless acts committed in the country were "more purposive" than those committed in Bridgetown and it would appear that hunger or the fear of hunger coupled with the news of the disturbances in Bridgetown were chief causes of the outbreak in the country districts. In attempting to restore order, the police were forced to fire, killing 14 and wounding 47, and over 400 arrests were made and many persons imprisoned for sedition.

Causes of the Disturbances

What were the causes of these disturbances? Some of them have been touched on in preceding lectures. I wish to start by identifying the fact, mentioned by Lewis, that there was a most reactionary regime in place in Barbados in terms of its politics. We were under what is called the "Old Representative System", but it really had little about it that was representative. If you look for instance at the individuals who were present in the Assembly and the Legislative Council and on the Executive Committee and the Executive Council, you would see many names associated with Barbados Shipping and Trading. You would see names like Leacock, Manning, Pile and Gardiner Austin. So, the economic elite of Barbados also controlled its parliament. They had significant influence and power over the Governor. In fact, the class had always been a quite strong class; they in a sense kept the British colonial power very often at bay.

Indeed, the preservation of the "Old Representative System" in Barbados came out of a struggle between the British attempt to impose Crown Colony Government at the end of the 19th Century and the successful resistance to it by the Barbadian plantocracy. So, they remained very much in command of Barbados even to a greater extent than most of the other similar classes in the rest of the Caribbean.

This was the political system which dominated us. It excluded the majority of the people on the basis of a restricted franchise. Some Black people had penetrated the Assembly by the beginning of the 20th Century. Of course we had Samuel Jackman Prescod from soon after Emancipation of the slaves. But this system excluded; it could therefore hardly represent. This was one of the major causes of dissatisfaction in the society, not only among the working class, but also among the middle class. These felt they should have more say in the direction of policy.

The Old Representative System was at the same time an example of similar forms of colonial government throughout the Caribbean. So when we say we had the Old Representative System in Barbados and there was Crown Colony Government in Jamaica or Trinidad, you are very much dealing with an elite dominating a local parliament; and it is an instrument and extension of the colonial government in the metropole, Britain; and politically it is one of the serious causes of resistance throughout the region.

There are a number of persons who, very early on, demonstrated their ideas on what should be done about the conditions political, social and economic, prevailing in the West Indies at the beginning of the 20th century. I wish to illustrate the influence of some of these individuals.

If we start at the lower qualitative level, but nonetheless an important level, with Cipriani in Trinidad, you have Captain Cipriani who is in fact a white man in Trinidad, coming back from the War and from the effects of the War, seeing what West Indians did, seeing what they were required to do in the 1st World War as soldiers for the Imperial armies. He feels something should be done about the desperate conditions within the West Indies. Cipriani becomes known as "the Champion of the Bare-foot man" in the West Indies. His movement eventually develops into the one which Butler leads and he recedes into the background: but he early on demonstrates a consciousness of the conditions and what should be done about them.

He is an early contributor to provision of organisational skills in leadership for the working people, something they hardly had an opportunity to experience before because of the absence of political parties, a consequence of the rstriction on the franchise and the exclusion of the masses from politics. So, even though the franchise is still affecting his party's capacity to influence politics, he nonetheless, by having a presence, passes on these experiences to people who are participating with him.

He also develops a programme which it is possible to use to identify some of the problems which existed and some of the suggestions that were being made on how to overcome them. We will find that, later on, some of his positions are retained in the British Guiana and West Indies Labour Congress which carries the programmes of the wide labour leadership of the Caribbean before the Moyne Commission of 1938-9.

Cipriani is saying in the early part of the 20th century that he wants to have Workmen's Compensation; he wants to have a minimum wage; he wants the eight-hour day; he wants statutory restrictions against the use of child labour. (Now if you want statutory restrictions against the use of child labour, it means that child labour was a feature of the conditions of the 1930s in the West Indies). You want compulsory education; you want priority of appointment of local men in the public service, rather than expatriates. You want the democratic control of native economic resources and heavier taxation against foreign corporations exploiting national resources. He wants a social welfare policy and universal suffrage. These things, these ideas, these expressions, these programmes, they filter into the consciousness of the people naturally, having been expressed organisationally. So they become a part of the building up of feelings, of critique, of a direction to go, in the early years of the 20th century.

There are other people paralleling him in these early years of the century. Another notable figure is Marcus Mosiah Garvey, the Jamaican. One is a Trinidadian, the other a Jamaican; you cannot isolate the Barbadian rebellion from these people. It is not just created in Barbados. Barbadians are hearing about Cipriani and they most certainly are also hearing about Garvey; and Garvey is indeed very significant. Garvey is one of the most significant West Indians in the history of the West Indies.

Garvey, a West Indian, is able to organise, to set up an organisation that becomes international, that affects continents. It is affecting Africa, it is affecting Central America, it is affecting the United States of America. Between 1916 and 1922, Garvey built an organisation with a membership of several million in the United States, Latin America and Africa. The character and intensity of his organising, his attempt to prepare people to carry out functions in every part of society, in terms of his conception of what would have to be done in the rebuilding of Africa and the rebuilding of her people as a great people, that is reflected in his organisation. If you look at the way he organised the Universal Negro Improvement Association (UNIA), you see that he has to deal with religion, the African Orthodox Church; for people with that aptitude, they have something to work through. He has the Universal African Legion. It is paramilitary. He has the Universal Black Cross Nurses. He has the Universal African Motor Corps and the Black Flying Eagles; and in 1924 he had established the Negro Political Union, the political arm of the UNIA. He also has a weekly newspaper, the *Negro World*, which is carried around the world by seamen, in particular, distributed in Africa, Central America, South America, the West Indies and Barbados. He has a commercial arm of the UNIA, the Black Star Line, the Black Star Steamship Company and he has the Negro Factory Corporation.

At its first Congress in 1920, the UNIA get delegates from twenty-five countries and twenty-five thousand people attend the opening ceremonies. So you are dealing with a formidable organisation and a formidable political programme produced by the activity of Marcus Mosiah Garvey; and you are going to find that many of the grass-root leadership of the revolt throughout the West Indies are ex-Garveyites or active Garveyites. They are bringing a consciousness of Pan-Africanism, a consciousness of pride in black history and in black civilisation and they are also getting skills in leadership and organisation and practice in politics. In the West Indies this is important for people who are excluded from the political process, excluded from leadership positions. Garvey organisations would otherwise be labourers in the oppressive system under which they lived. They could not express their talents or their intelligence; but Garvey is giving them the opportunity to develop these skills, and put them to good use in the revolt that develops. So, Garvey makes a qualitative and significant contribution to the rising of the resistance of the West Indian people. So we have to remember Garvey, and what he has done.

The Commissions which inquired into the revolts of the 1930s did not stress the national and racial question as a cause. The main cause was identified as the economic depression and material deprivation. Revolutionary theory and the experiences of people as they have struggled to change their society support a recognition that there is no direct correlation between the impoverishment of people and social rebellion, in fact, sometimes with increased impoverishment and material deprivation, the confidence, the ability to resist is diminished; these can create dependency and prostitution of people and very often revolt and resistance happen on the up-take, when an economy is on the up-take, when things are improving. People get back some pride and some confidence and a material base on which they can fight.

But the Commissions wanted to obscure the race factor. Some questions were asked about what was the effect of Abyssinia on the West Indies. They were attempts to diminish the impact of Abyssinia, i.e., the invasion by Mussolini and his Fascists of independent, sovereign Ethiopia. In Jamaica, for instance, a whole "Ethiopianism," the pride and resistance of the black-mail developed around the observation of what had gone on in Ethiopia. It fitted in with Garvey's work. So we have to examine very carefully if in fact there was not this sharp race consciousness in the revolt as well; if in fact it was not something embarrassing and even dangerous to be recognised by the Commissions. Certainly some people (e.g. Walter Rodney), have described the West Indies as "the laboratory of racism".

So it is difficult to see, if that is said even today, why it was not true at the beginning of the 20th century when the racial situation would have been far more serious.

Likewise, I wish to say that the question of the role and influence of significant revolutionary events at the beginning of the century have to be recognised. What was the impact of the Soviet revolution and the rise of the Soviet Union? Now, in my view, an important event like that could not have but reached the ears of working people. It is like when the discussion on the abolition of slavery was going on in circles in Europe, the slaves got to hear about it and they started saying that there are some people up there saying that we should be free. Likewise, if an event like a set of workers and peasants overthrowing their king and then saying they are establishing workers' power, if an event like that happened, I am sure that working people were going to be listening.

But we can go beyond that because there is evidence in the security files of the time, evidence of conscious attempts by black communists, black Marxists, to reach their black fellow workers in the West Indies in the 1930s. The West Indies was identified by them as "a region in problems", "Trouble in the West Indies".

There are pamphlets that were coming out of Hamburg in Germany, where George Padmore, a black Trinidadian, with international prestige in the Marxist movement, internationally recognised as a outstanding communist, was consciously sending information to the workers of the Caribbean on how to organise, and how to throw off colonialism and establish democracy. Likewise, the Communist Party of the United States in which there was a high proportion of black people, was also sending out information to the working people of the Caribbean, to agitate for the end of colonial domination and for democracy.

So, when you examine those files, you find pamphlets like "The West Indian Organiser" published by the West Indian Workers' Progressive Society on "How to organise the Struggle"; pamphlets addressed to "the workers and oppressed peoples of the West Indies", by the West Indian American sub-committee of the International Trade Union Committee of Negro Workers, and you have the "Negro Worker" coming out of Hamburg, Germany with articles in it such as "Trouble in the West Indies", requesting the establishment of an anti-imperialist movement.

There are instructions in some of these pamphlets which the Governor knew were reaching the working people of Barbados; some of them directly spoke to the Barbadian working people. They told them tasks and aims: how to "agitate", organise and educate the working masses; how to "build revolutionary unions"; how to "link the struggle of the workers in Panama, Honduras, Guatemala and other Latin American countries with the islands"; how to "expose reformist misleaders like Cipriani" in Trinidad; how to popularise the work of the Latin American Confederation of Labour and of the International Trade Union Committee of Negro Workers of Hamburg, Germany; how to fight against: "Imperialist War", because they were predicting that another World War would come; how to "defend the Soviet Union" and the "Chinese masses" who were "up in revolution".

These pamphlets were being read. The Governor was very nervous about it. He was sending telegrams down to the Governor of the Leeward Islands to tell him that ships were coming down and that they were distributing pamphlets which he called "these inflammable seditious rags".

Therefore, at a concrete agitational level, the methods of Marxist revolutionaries were reaching the working people. But this does not mean you had Marxists in Barbados, leading the revolt. In fact, in looking at the period we can only identify explicit Marxists in the movement in Jamaica, in the cases of Hugh Buchanan and Richard Hart. Internationally you would have had Padmore, but he is away; you have C.L.R. James, but he is also away.

You can have, on the other hand, Marxist-inspired leaders, and these Marxist-inspired leaders are inspired by the agitation and by the literature which they can read; by the fact that what is suggested relates to what they are experiencing and can be put into action. And I think what we find as a synthesis in the leadership of the revolt is a combination of Garveyism AND Marxist agitational methods. You see this, not in the higher intellectual or Fabian socialist leadership, but in the "grassroots" leadership which in fact was the most outstanding leadership and which was suppressed and was removed and was pushed into the background after the revolt. You see it in Clement Payne. You see it in Butler. You see it in Hugh Buchanan in Jamaica. These people do not lead the process after the revolt. A lot of then are in jail for sedition, and then techniques are used to see that they do not re-emerge. But we do have that evidence of that linkage

We can come more local and recognise our own Barbadian, Charles Duncan O'Neal. He is doing locally for us what Garvey was doing internationally. He is bringing organisation to the island, which must im-

pact on the political culture, because it is something different. You don't have it before; the only thing coming close to a party in Barbados before Charles Duncan O'Neal's is the attempt by Samuel Jackman Prescod in the 1840s to establish the "Colonial Union of the Coloured People" and that is mainly at the level of an idea he attempts to carry forward. He is operating in far more difficult conditions than would O'Neal be in the early 20th century.

So O'Neal gets the chance to be the first one to actually establish an organisation. Much of Prescod's work had to be underground. Prescod went into Trade Unionism, but he had to be very secret about it. He couldn't demonstrate that at all. But, nonetheless, he was organising strikes in the cane fields when the Masters and Servants Act was being brought in soon after the end of Apprenticeship. But O'Neal is bringing organisation, giving people the chance to develop leadership skills and he is putting out a programme which can identify with the conditions they are living under.

He is making a linkage, also, with the development of socialisrn as expressed in Britain, the socialism of the Independent Labour Party, Fabian socialism. But it is an alternative to anything that had gone on in Barbados before. The presence of the organisation is restricted by the franchise. It is restricted by the fact that most of his supporters are not going to be able to demonstrably support him. They cannot vote. But, just by being present, that changes the culture; it qualitatively impacts on the political culture. It is different. It has to be recognised and it goes into the consciousness of the people; that is a reality of human social develop merit. You see something for the first time, you experience it, and people are participating in it; and they grow in relation to their interaction with and reaction to it. They carry that on as an experience. It never disappears again. It is something they have gone through. it becomes a part of them and it becomes a part of the people they come into contact with. It becomes a part of the culture. The culture qualitatively changes because of the presence of this new feature. That is the contribution of O'Neal, even if he never got his party to last, even if he never got his party to actually win power in Barbados, which he hardly could. The point is that he made that qualitative impact on the political culture of Barbados; so that it never changes back to what it had been before he came on the scene.

At the intellectual level, at the level of arguing the positions, we have the case of the outstanding Clennel

Wickham, a hero of Barbados. When I mention Wickham, it leads me to say that any time we consider putting up a statue of anybody, we must remember to recognise three personalities representing different levels of struggle; but no one personality can be said to be more important than the other. Though my party did not agree with me in proposing to re-name Trafalgar Square, Golden Square (they said that it should be 26th July Square), I feel that it should be called Golden Square. They said that if you mention Golden Square, that Golden Square has to be out by the Fire Station; so re-name the Empire Cinema, Golden Square Cinema. But I would call Trafalgar Square, Golden Square and I would put Wickham, O'Neal and Clement Payne up in Trafalgar Square. And the moment that you call Trafalgar Square, Golden Square, Admiral Lord Nelson would have to get down, because he could not take it. He would turn in his grave if he were standing in the square of the insurrectionary working class of Barbados. He was the hero of the slave masters, and the hero of the slave masters could not live comfortably with the heroes of the insurrectionary working class.

Wickham is very important, and Wickham is tragic in terms of what happened to him. He was destroyed by the planter class and he was destroyed by, at the time, the misguided Grantley Adams. So, in Barbados, we have people building up the struggle as well. We have the international impact, the international intervention, and you have people who are here locally active. You have O'Neal, you have Wickham, you have Payne. You have people that are Garveyites, who are organising; you have Israel Lovell and Ulric Grant; they are paralleling those people who are active in the other islands. They are acting in Barbados too.

It is because Barbados is not that unique. Every country has its unique features, but there are certain objective structures that make countries similar, and people act then in relation to those similarities in similar ways. This is why things are happening all over the place. It is not because of any plan, any master plan. It is the "feeling that making people move" like that. They are feeling the same thing they are responding in the same way. They are getting similar responses, and they are growing in the same way. And you get the revolt coming through from 1935, every island, coming right down into Guyana as well. Barbados is not left out. If it were so unique there would have been no 1937 in Barbados.

These are some of the causes. The most outstanding feature of cause officially identified, as I have mentioned, related to the Great Depression and the serious economic conditions that were present in the island at the time. Indeed, I am saying that this condition was identified comfortably by the Commissions of Inquiry to be the main cause. But we have seen all these other things that were acting there, until we get the culmination of the revolt.

The British policy at the time did nothing to ease those conditions, particularly economic conditions, which were aggravated by the Great Depression. In fact, British policy was that "the colonial government should not embark upon any undertakings" that are not "absolutely essential"; "for the present it is imperative that every colonial government should if possible balance its budget by reducing expenditure"; and "a conservative financing policy is dictated by necessity of the times". So that, at the very time when things are getting harder, the British government's instructions are that you should restrict ameliorative reforms in relation to the economy or support-activity to help people out of their suffering.

Some features of the economic conditions in Barbados can be noted so that you can get a picture of the situation. The Deane Commission, which was set up after the 1937 revolt as our local Commission before the Royal Commission comes out under Lord Moyne demonstrated that it was not possible to have a "living wage" in Barbados. They tried to work out a working man's weekly budget. They said (it would sound low for you, but it was a serious thing at the time) that food would work out at 51.09c, clothing at 44 .64c, medicines at 8.30c, washing at 24c, fuel and light at 17.05c, house rent at 39c, subvention to a Friendly Society at 12c. These are things they assumed that working people would spend money on. And it all came out to 396.53c per week. And when they calculated the best worker's wage on a plantation, they came to the conclusion that the wage would reach $1.78c. So that it was not possible, for even the best paid worker, to maintain what they felt was a reasonable budget for a working man. While the Commissioners were identifying the working man's budget, they were able to state that the sugar factories were still profitable operations and could have paid better wages.

We can look to other examples of working class conditions in 1937, as identified by the Deane Commission. There was the case of the Central Foundry where before the Commission it came to light, that the Manager was using his apprentices to do contract work. In some cases, they had been working for a long time, but were still paid the wages of apprentices. Some had served five years, others, four years. They were receiving three cents an hour, others two cents an hour, etc. The manager, on the other hand, was saying that he was doing a favour for these people; for, if they didn't get this kind of work, they would not have any work. A kind of paternalism on his part therefore surfaced. He was also very angry at what had happened in revolt. He said it was because of certain communistic ideas which had taken root in the minds of some; and also because of the utterances of cheap political orators, who said things that excited the minds of working men.

Some of the relationships between employers and workers suggest almost pre-capitalist relations; a working class person is not supposed to function like that under capitalism. It is really a trailing over from slavery; a slave form of domination continuing under new economic relations, which are not quite able to develop because of the restricted political system which holds down economic activity. The whole attitude of the employer class is one of either paternalism or total containment of workers. Of course, you don't have any trade unions. It is illegal in Barbados to have a trade union at this time. The stevedores are identified in the Deane Commission Report as having made, between January to August 1937, some one thousand pounds in profit.

There is the case too of the bakers which is a good illustration of these backward relations. Some of these bakers were asked to work 11 to 18 hours per day, and sometimes as much as 22 hours. The economic conditions are affecting the middle class as well. Some of the persons giving evidence before the Commission indicate that the middle class is having a hard time. Mr. E.D. Mottley, who later became Mayor of the City and was a politician in the City, said that he had found that conditions were very desperate among the middle class, and he is supported in this by others.

Comments in the legislature by Grantley Adams in the 1930s relate to his observation of the slum conditions in the city. We have the benefit of an investigation which possibly responded to the bad conditions after the revolt and to the reports of the Commissions. It gives us something of a picture of what these conditions were like. In places like Chapman's Lane, Cats Castle and Suttle Street, you had a very desperate situation. The survey recorded that in Chapman Lane there were 345 houses in which 360 families lived or the equivalent of 1,161 people; 53% of these houses were owner-occupied while 47% were rented. Ninety-one of the families in Chapman's Lane were seen as being in an overcrowded situation.

Some 173 houses were deemed unfit for habitation. In Suttle Street, you had a situation where there were 76 families or 140 people occupying one acre of land. There were 21 houses in Suttle Street, 14 of which were rented. Fourteen out of the twenty-one houses were condemned as unfit for habitation. The rents in Suttle Street were $3.75 per month for "flats", $2.60 per month for rooms. This is a brief illustration of the harsh conditions at the time.

The Disturbances: riot, revolt or revolution?

I wish to move now into the rebellion itself and an analysis of the rebellion. I wish to look at this through the concepts of "riot", "revolt", and "revolution", since I hear these terms being thrown around a lot today. The traditional description is of course "riot". Even the topic as presented to me for discussion to tonight specified "riots". Some other people are telling you that it was a revolution. So, to the extent that it was a "revolution", then I hope everybody here knows that we are all revolutionaries! that we have a revolution in Barbados which is being built on now; that, starting in 1937, we have "revolutionary Barbados". I have not, however, heard about its recognition internationally. So I don't know if all of the people who go into these things and identify revolutions, I don't know if, because of the "uniqueness" of Barbados, they cannot identify "revolutionary Barbados". But there is supposed to be "a revolution" that was "started in 1937". I suspect that the same people who were calling it "riot" are calling it "revolution" now; for the same reason, to ensure political obfuscation.

What is a riot? A riot is like when, some years ago, a man who was not black, kicked a man who was black in Swan Street, and the people spontaneously reacted against that; because it is very insulting to kick somebody, and with our social history of racism and the feeling and emotion on race, they responded instinctively. To say: they are going to do something about it, and they are not caring about any policeman telling them anything; that is a condition of a riot. You can quickly identify a condition of riot when you personalise it between a policeman, the main representative of authority in a situation of breakdown of order, on the one hand, and the people, on the other. A policeman usually gives instructions and, resting on the whole socialisation process and the acceptance of the authority of the system, he is expected to be obeyed. He says "move and keep moving" and you move and keep moving. In a condition of riot, when he says move and keep moving, you don't move. And when he moves at you,

you move at him. That is a condition of riot, and it is a very strange condition for a policeman. He meets those conditions not when dealing with normal citizens, but with criminals. Usually, then, all the same, the criminal will run. But, in a condition of riot, the people often will move at the police. But it is an isolated event, as we saw in Swan Street.

We saw it also in Independence Square in 1966. I was very young then, but I saw it because I was there. So I know how it happened: because the people wanted to hear and they could not hear, and they wanted to see better, but they could not see. There was something blocking them. So, a very limited programme was developed. A riot has a limited programme. It doesn't have any big programme. In thee case of Swan Street, it was "we going to get the man that kicked that man". In the case of Independence Square, it is "we want to hear and we are going to see that we hear". So you move forward. You start to walk forward. There were chairs between the people and what they wanted to see and hear. So they moved the chairs. And people who were on the stage had to get off the stage and go into fishing boats and go down the careenage. And the police who were there, who were the representatives of law and order and the state, they put up a white flag; and at that point they obviously said that they had to get help. So it is at that point that I observed for the first time, some other policemen coming across the Swing Bridge, with big hats and big basket-like things on their arms and long sticks. And I went home.

But a lot of free bread was shared out that night in Fairchild Street. Bread carts were overturned. And there were people walking up and down saying, "we free now, we free now"! But that was not a programme. There wasn't any build-up like what we were seeing before. There wasn't any Duncan O'Neal, any Clennell Wickham, there was no Garvey to make that thing happen in Independence Square. It was simply that the people could not hear and they could not see and they wanted to hear and they wanted to see and chairs were blocking them. Simple programme. Move forward, push everything down. Simple programme, isolated, unique in itself.

But the 1937 revolt in Barbados is not unique. There are riots right through the Caribbean. There is a programme that is built up over time. There is a consciousness that has developed. The people have an idea of where they want to go. They are not too clear on it, but they have an idea and people have worked out programmes, suggested programmes of ways to go forward. So, you have to put it in the context of all of that which is going on: strikes, industrial unrest, riots not only here but elsewhere, the international influences, the rising of the consciousness. It is a revolt. It is a part of a rebellion that is taking place.

It is not any revolution either. I am going to the experts on revolution who are, in this 20th century, Marxist revolutionaries. I am going to the leader of the Bolshevik revolution, and he is an authority on revolution. I don't think you can say otherwise. His name is Lenin. And Lenin is identifying what is a "revolutionary situation", not just a "revolutionary condition". For a Marxist, "a revolutionary condition was in place from the end of the 19th century. But because you have "a revolutionary condition" it does not mean you have "a revolutionary situation". "A revolutionary situation" is a very special thing for the people who are really serious about revolution. You have to identify it and you don't deal with that in a dogmatic way. If some critical features are not present, then you know that really it is not possible to accomplish certain things, or that certain things will not likely happen. But Lenin tells you most of what should be there and we can examine these to see whether some of these things were present in 1937.

Lenin is saying:

> For a revolution to take place it is not enough for the exploited and oppressed masses to realize the impossibility of living in the old way. For a revolution to take place it is essential that the exploiters should not be able to live and rule in the old ways. It is only when the lower classes do not want to live in the old way, and the upper classes cannot carry on in the old way that the revolution can triumph.

This, he says, can be expressed in other words:

> ... revolution is impossible without a nation-wide crisis, affecting both the exploited and the exploiters. It follows that for a revolution to take place it is essential first that a majority of the class conscious, thinking and politically active workers should fully realise that revolution is necessary and that they should be prepared to die for it. Second, that the ruling classes should be going through a governmental crisis which draws even the most backward masses into politics.
>
> Symptomatic of any genuine revolution is a rapid ten fold and even hundred fold increase in the size of the working and oppressed masses, hitherto apathetic, who are capable of waging the political struggle, weakens the government and makes it possible for the revolutionaries to rapidly overthrow it.

You must clearly study this thing, because some people read a few books on Marxism and then start to criticise Marxism. Many more don't even read. But if you are a revolutionary and a Marxist revolutionary you study Marxism as a science.

There were conditions present in 1937 in Barbados which suggested a developing "revolutionary situation", but there were many critical qualitative features which demonstrated otherwise. One of the very important features identified in a "revolutionary situation" as outlined by Lenin is the "division in the ruling class"; and that cannot be observed in terms of a "governmental crisis" in 1937; because again you can't isolate Barbados. The government of Barbados is also the government of the United Kingdom. It is the colonial government. So there had to be a crisis up there too. When the Haitians made their revolution, France was in revolution.

So any time you made a revolution in Barbados in 1937, you had to take on the British military forces. That is what you would have to take on; or their ruling class would have to be in crisis. But, even locally, you can't really identify any serious crisis in the local ruling class, if you go back to 1876, to the Confederation Revolt (which is erroneously described as the "Confederation Riots") there was a condition of civil war. You can identify a crisis in the government of Barbados at that time. There were other conditions which made a revolution not possible at that time too. But, in 1937, there is no crisis in the ruling class and in the colonial government on the scene.

We are going to find that there are a few people in the grassroots leadership whose consciousness is very high; and who are "prepared to die". There is certainly an "increase in the political activity of the masses". A lot of people are active who would not normally be active. But when Lenin talks about "a majority of the class conscious thinking and politically active workers should fully realise that revolution is necessary", he is talking about the consciously organised workers, those who are leading the struggle; and we are not going to identify that either in 1937.

We are going to identify embryonic organisation. In fact, it would seem that the analysis of many of the "Marxists"' to whom earlier I referred, their view of what happened in the 1930s in the West Indies is that the insurrection broke out too early, before the movement had matured, before the leadership could have consolidated its relationship with the masses and their political education, and before the development of instruments to carry forward the struggle. And, in any

event, they were not aiming at revolution. For the Caribbean Marxist in the 1930s the programme is not revolution in any event. This is another confusion that many people have; in applying Marxism you identify programmes in relation to the stage of struggle.

The programme of a Marxist at that time is the programme of Garvey. It is anti-colonial, and democratic. It is support for trade union organisation to build up the organisational experience of the working class and to build up an instrument of defense; organisationally, these are not offensive tactics. But, again, it must be emphasised that insurrection is not created by the revolutionaries. The people make the insurrection. They decide when they are going to rise up. If you understand the social laws of society, you prepare for the insurrection. But you also carry out a whole lot of programmes before that. But nobody is going to be able to get up and tell anybody "rise up now". You can go off shouting all over the place "rise up now", and the people are not going to rise up until they are ready to rise up. And then they rise up when you don't expect them to rise up, as they rose up in 1937. A lot of people thought that the revolt would not reach Barbados. But the revolt did not demonstrate any organised political leadership sufficient to suggest "a revolutionary situation". We cannot find that organisation, we cannot find the division in the ruling class, we do not find other features. But those are important, and we have the colonial state.

I will quickly also refer to another authority on insurrection. I refer to him as an authority in this specific context only. He is Leon Trotsky, a renegade from Bolshevism. But he was an excellent insurrectionist in the Russian Revolution. In this instance he is grounding his position on the work of Lenin himself. So he is seeing it as a Leninist position.

He repeats what I have just been saying to you briefly. He says that people do not make revolution easily any more than they do war, with the difference, however, that in war compulsion plays the decisive role. In revolution there is no compulsion except that of circumstances. A revolution takes place only when there is no other way out, and the insurrection, which rises above a revolution like a peak in the mountain chain of its events, can no more be evoked at will than the revolution as whole. The masses, advance and retreat several times before they make up their minds for the final assault.

He next considers the question of "conspiracy and planning" an insurrection. He says that the feature of "a plan", a "conspiracy", is often associated with revolutionary action. But the conspiracy and the plan which are isolated from the mass movement are not what he is speaking of. Such a form of conspiracy can take place in, for instance, "coup d'etat", and this can take place in almost any country given certain circumstances. But that will be some thing completely different from a popular insurrection. However, he points out, even though insurrection emerges out of the people, it is possible to prepare for it, to plan for it. It is possible to work out some ways of seeing what is coming, and developing it in this way serves to smooth the path and hasten the victory of the insurrection.

But, it is also possible for an insurrection to be successful to the extent of overthrowing the "old power" even without what he refers to as the conspiracy and the plan. You can have spontaneous strikes and demonstrations and then an outbreak and the overthrow of the old power. But the question of holding the power is another problem. Trotsky says that in most cases where there is just an insurrection, without this compensating organisational feature, that the power is transferred to other parties, even those who might have been opposed to the insurrection in the first place. For instance, in the context of an anti-feudal revolution where there also happens to be a competition between a working class and what he would call the bourgeoisie i.e., the capitalist class, the bourgeoisie may win the power in such a situation not because it is revolutionary, hut because it is bourgeois. It has in its possession, property, education, the press, a network of strategic positions.

I want you to remember this in the context of the West Indian revolt in terms of what the middle class did. Our middle class is not the bourgeoisie, but in our context the middle class has skills, it had culture, cultural development. It had the capacity to deal with the British when they brought their "plan", the constitutional tutelage. They could say that the thing was too complicated for the working man to understand, and the working class itself was dependent on them because of its lack of experience in certain political activity. So, in a way, this is analogous to the feature Trotsky is speaking of in the context of the bourgeoisie and proletariat:

> The bourgeoisie may win the power in a revolution not because it is revolutionary, hut because it is bourgeois; because it has possession of property, because it has education; it has the press, a network of strategic positions, a hierarchy of institutions. But, unlike them,

the working class is deprived, in the nature of these things, of all social advantages. An insurrectionary proletariat can count only on its numbers, its solidarity, its cadres, its official staff, that is to say, its organisation and its party.

To win, to get victory, you need this feature of organisation. This is being suggested by people who made these things possible.

So, in summary, Trotsky is saying: "in order to conquer the power, the proletariat needs more than a spontaneous insurrection; it needs a suitable organisation, it needs a plan, it needs a conspiracy, such is the Leninist view of this question." The plan and the insurrection have to come together. The organisation and the insurrection have to come together; and the plan does not have any final control over the insurrection; but the plan has to be around by the time the insurrection comes. So you have to be working on that plan, on that organisation long before there is much probability of any insurrection.

The work by Communist and Marxist agitators in the Caribbean had started up at the beginning of the 1930s. Garvey had been active before that and into the 1930s. The results in some way were showing by the mid 1930s. But I said earlier that the Marxist view of the revolt was that in a sense it had come before the movement had consolidated. But there is another reason too, and from the theory on "a revolutionary situation" and the "art of insurrection". We raise the question: What was the nature of our society both before and after 1937?

If you look at the economy, the relationship to "monopoly capitalism" and the planter-merchant domination of the economy. the relationship of domination is in place before and after 1937. It is even in place now; that domination is the profoundly significant, qualitatively significant feature of 1937. The planter-merchant domination is not defeated. A whole set of forces come into play at the time including the British government. The British government helps to defeat the domination, politically, because it tells the plantocracy to get out of the way, that they must learn to concede in order to survive; in order that planter-merchant capitalism can survive, in order that monopoly capitalism can survive, you have to give up office. And the British, they know their own experience with their own working class from the 19th century. They have their own philosophers of liberal democracy such as John Stuart Mill writing in the 19th century and advising them what to do with their working class, how to make concessions, how to make reforms, how to give everybody, eventually, the right to vote, in order to survive the pressure coming from below, as the consciousness and sophistication of the workers and the culture of the society increase.

You have some "hard headed" people in Barbados, but they are told that they have to learn, and some of their own class then start to teach them, like the Attorney-General, E.K.Walcott. You see him lecturing them in the House of Assembly: they have to let trade unions come in; they have to allow reforms; they have to let the vote be given to the people. Do it gradually, but do it, that is the way you will save yourselves. The British can tell them that, because the British know about it from before. In 1946, in Barbados, the Governor is ahead of even the leader of the labour movement. The Governor is ready to give adult suffrage, and the leader of the labour movement is saying: "we not ready yet".

So you have a significant victory. But because you have a significant victory, because you have a profound victory, it doesn't mean you have a revolution. A revolution is something much more than that. And if you tell people you have a revolution, you are only trying to fool people. Because the revolution is yet to come! In terms of social change in the 20th century, the transfer of social power suggests the transfer of power to the working people and the working class. There is no transfer of this social power in the context of Barbados. The middle class wins through, in terms of a state office, in terms of their promotion in the bureaucracy, in terms of professional expression. Some of them think they have won the power, but they gain authority, they win "the shadow for the substance", but they go around boasting that they have power. But if they had power, in the last elections nobody would have to talk about "White Shadows", which is not to belittle what they had attained by that date.

But when it comes to critical things, as is exemplified by the case of Michael Manley in Jamaica, when you are suggesting, even if you are not too serious, but suggesting that you want to carry out certain radical changes, and the other side they feel they are going to be affected and get nervous, you then see what real power is. So, in Manley's case, he then found himself without power. By the time he faced the electorate in Jamaica, he was powerless. He had authority but didn't have power. That is when the real thing comes to the fore, in periods of conflict. This is why it is useful to study periods of conflict, because they reveal the true nature of relationships. This is perhaps contrary to what most people will tell you. They will tell you, when

it is stable you will see the real thing. But, when there is equilibrium, things are very often hidden, submerged, and component parts not sharply discernible. When disequilibrium and conflict emerge, the reality of the whole shows forth. And if a ruling class is very nervous, then they allow these features to be revealed even when you are only saying and not even doing.

Now, just to illustrate quickly some of the features of militancy and consciousness among the Caribbean working class and the Barbadian working class, I want to go first to Jamaica as a means of illustration, for these Caribbean events are clearly inter-connected.

I want to deal with the question of the perceptions of the leadership and the state of consciousness of some of the people. One of the features we saw in the "revolutionary situation" is the willingness of the revolutionaries to die. Ken Post, who has done the most extensive analysis of a revolt in the West Indies in the period, *"Arise Ye Starvelings"*, on the 1938 Jamaican revolt, isolated one member of the Jamaican working class to demonstrate this point. He is a man called Daley. Post is using a situation similar to one I made reference to earlier, i.e., where a policeman in the execution of his duty says to you "move and keep moving"'. In this case, however, Daley and his gang are moving with sticks, and the police are moving with rifles. So, the police come up to Daley and tell Daley, "we want your stick", and Daley tells them: "No not a rass! You have your gun and I have my stick". Now if you tell a policeman with a gun "No", you must be prepared to die; and he died. Daley died. So he was prepared to die; and Daley died. The policeman with the gun killed Daley.

In Barbados, we have Israel Lovell, Garveyite, lieutenant of Clement Payne, leader of the revolt. The police are monitoring Lovell, and they are listening to the speeches in Golden Square. He is making these speeches after the case is brought against Payne, and Payne is threatened with deportation. Lovell is responding to that by speaking to the people. The police take down notes of thiss speech and use it as evidence against Lovell and he ends up in Glendairy on a charge of sedition.

Lovell is telling the people:

> They can't deport me. . .!

This is a seditious statement. If I were saying this in 1937, I would be quickly arrested.

> They can't deport me, they can only send me to jail. If you people had retaliated, the town would still be smoking and some of the policemen would be in the

cemetery. If the people had used force, what the hell would this little island be tonight...

This is Barbados he is talking about and he is a Barbadian.

> So, if the government lets loose with ruthlessness, what the hell they leave the people to do! I know what is going to take place. I can die now.

He was prepared "to die" or he is saying so any how!

> Payne was brutalised this morning, but don't let us be afraid of what is happening. Let us organise and withstand violence. If we were organised. . .

He is suggesting that they were not organised sufficiently. He is making the point I made earlier. If they had the "organisation", they could deal with the "organisation" of the other side. The other side is organised. They are organised through the state. The "instrument of the state" that faces the people is the police. They are employed to do so, some are the brothers of the workers. In 1876, they joined the rebels; they put sugar into the ammunition. But they didn't do that in 1937. They killed fourteen Barbadians in one day.

If we were organised, Goddard [the Deputy Commissioner of Police]

> would have thought a thousand times before he touched Payne. There is no justice in Coleridge Street, for judges sit down and misjudge us. . .

So he deals now with the judiciary which also came up for examination in the Commission of Inquiry. He is saying that the judiciary is prejudiced against the working people, that it is not an impartial judiciary.

> Payne is no criminal. . .

There is a question of who is calling whom criminal.

> Payne is no criminal, we cannot steal from the white man. . .

This is some of Garvey coming through, I suppose.

> We cannot, steal from the white man because, if we take anything, it would be only some of what they have stolen from our fore-parents for the past two hundred and fifty years. But Christ has been crucified today. Awake friends, this is the beginning. Inspector Plunkett kicked a policeman's son; policemen have the wealth of this country in their hands and yet they are starving, if you want to see one negro beat another negro, give him a bunch of keys, a stick or make him a policeman. Let all the Goddards know, we are not tak-

> ing things as before, and we want bread and butter just like Bowring and Darnley Dacosta. . . I am fighting this cause until death. Trinidad police is responsible for the violence in their strike. Goddard has given us a mission to do and we are going to do it.

That is the first speech for which Lovell was charged for sedition. In the second speech, he says:

> The situation in Barbados is a funny one. We make the wealth of this country and get nothing in return. Our slave fathers were in a better condition than we are today. The world is against us, so let us unite in mass formation and stand up like men. Dickens the [Commissioner of Police] has a bunch of slaves under his command. Of course some of them were cowboys and they should know that they are servants. All of them are public servants. All of them from the highest to the lowest are rogues and vagabonds and if you people yesterday had a different temperament, by now Barbados would have gone up to heaven. Instead of Payne being in jail it should be Goddard. . .

So he had "a programme", to put the Commissioner of Police in jail!

> If we were organised, before Goddard handled Payne yesterday, he would have bitten his fingernails. Or even if he had six-men-of war. . .

He is conscious of the British Imperial army and navy; they came sailing into the harbour. This might be a little bit of emotionalism and adventurism, but he is saying it nonetheless.

> even if he had six-men-of war in the bay and all the policemen and volunteers with rifles, he could not be saved, if this thing ever happens again, don't run, for they don't have jails sufficient to hold all of us.

Which is a real point.

Now it is significant that, in the Jamaican rebellion, which lasted almost two and a half weeks, only eight people were killed. In the case of Barbados, where the disturbances lasted effectively two days and a bit, the official report says that, on 27 July, fourteen people were killed. This reminds us of some of the points that were made in previous series of these lectures about the nature of the Barbadian state under pressure. So, I think that this is an indication of the intensity of the violence that came down from the state on little, conservative, docile Barbados. More people were killed in Barbados, with a smaller population, in a shorter time, than in Jamaica, which is supposed to be so "dread".

The outcome of the revolt can be examined through the programme of the British Guiana and West Indies Labour Congress of 1938 and the response to that by the Moyne Commission of 1938-39. What happened was that, on the one side, the labour leadership which had emerged put their position together in Trinidad and then went with a common programme before the Moyne Commission. On the other, the Commissioners in their report responded to their investigation of the disturbances. So, if you examine those two documents, you get a picture of what the interaction was like between the colonial power and the labour leadership which had emerged. But this was a leadership, however, which was not exactly the leadership that had led the revolt.

Arthur Lewis has conveniently enclosed in his pamphlet the resolutions of the British Guiana and West Indies Labour Congress, the programme of the labour leadership. This programme reflects reforms ranging across simple democratic reforms to revolutionary democratic reform, suggesting structural adjustments which, by extension, had sociopolitical implications for the ruling classes of the Caribbean at the time. So there is a mix in the propositions.

We have proposals such as that on constitutional reform. We have a request for extension of the franchise over time. Although it is not explicit in Resolution No. 2, they are asking for a movement in that direction. They are asking also for a Federation which is the mechanism through which they feel the West Indies can move to self-government. There is a significant Resolution No. 3, which is asking for the nationalisation of the sugar industry and which, if it were accepted, would have implications for the survival of the plantocracy, and which is objectively a revolutionary demand. There is a demand for co-operative marketing and the development of co-operatives in the economy. There is a call for the nationalisation of public utilities. Then there is a section of the programme dealing with social welfare and social reform, requesting old age pensions, national health insurance, unemployment benefits. It asks for a forty-four hour week without reduction in pay; for minimum wages for all workers; workmen's compensation; for a trade union law.

There is a resolution asking for reform of the courts; for relaxation of political offences dealing with the interpretation of sedition. At that time, many people were in jail on sedition charges, which this leadership would have felt ought not to have been. There is a call for reform in the police force, especially in relation to the racial exclusiveness in the higher ranks.

There is a call for reform in relation to education and health services, for the development of diversification of the economy to remove dependency on sugar. There is a call for facility in emigration, which is seen as a natural part of the programme of labour at that period in time. There is a demand for a scientific investigation of the population, the precise nature of it, that is to say, a census. All this comes out of the revolt.

So, when I say there are some revolutionary demands in the programme, this is to recognise, in a sense, a response to that aspect of the revolt, which reflected either the rise of revolutionary consciousness and the militant pressures of the workers on this leadership, or/and, as Ken Post also says in his analysis on Jamaica, that in many ways the working people of the West Indies, the working class and the peasantry, were "revolutionary in spite of themselves." So, I have made the point that we do not see a revolution; but he is saying they were "revolutionary in spite of themselves" in relation to the demands they were making, such as the demands for "higher wages", "more land" and "more work". Because Post is saying that while the system could respond to the demand for "higher wages", it could not respond positively to the demand for "more work" and "more land" without structural adjustment and transformation.

Some of the demands were therefore objectively revolutionary because of what would be required in terms of structural adjustment in the society were they to be implemented. These demands do not then emerge because of a revolutionary consciousness of the people. They emerge out of their natural experience, which is the way revolt builds. It is not built solely by the preaching of Marxism-Leninism or Garveyism. That is important, and that is going on and is helping the protest to develop, as I have already pointed out. But the people are responding to what they are experiencing in general. They are saying: "we want to live better". It is that which motivates the resistance. They want to live in peace.

Containment of the Revolt

Now, as I was suggesting, the British are also recognising the nature of the problem. And they have time to sit down and work it out. So, they respond through the Moyne Commission. This is an illustration of their response. They recommend the establishment of a West Indian Welfare Fund to be financed by an annual grant from the British government of one million pounds and to the administered by a special organisation independent of the local governments, which suggests the suspicion the British had of the local administrations. The money was to be used for schemes to improve education, public health services, housing, and social welfare facilities. You see the reaction of the British to the demands. In addition, the Commissioners recommended that steps be taken to encourage trade unionism. So that they recognise the need to make that concession to the working class. They recommended the promotion of agriculture and the settlement of people on the land as small holders. They are doing these things to appease the militancy, to cool the situation. They are recognising the need to give something in order to gain something else.

The trade union has a two-fold role. It is a defensive organisation for the workers, but it is also an institution for containment of the workers by the ruling class. Once a ruling class has reached the point of self-confidence and sophistication, which some of them in Barbados had not reached, they can make such a reform, grant that reform. The British already knew that. They had to teach it to the ones down here, and they then learned it with the help of E.K. Walcott.

You promote agriculture and the settlement of land by peasantry. This is seen also to be helpful in cooling down things. As a matter of fact, the Jamaican rebellion was significantly affected, with respect to its cessation, by the Governor coming out and saying that he would give land to the Jamaican peasantry. And while the agricultural labourers had been uncontrollable before that, the moment land reform was mentioned the revolt cooled down. So, the significance of that reform was known. Give the people some land. But, of course, there is going to be a problem in implementing the reform, because if you are going to give land (in Jamaica it is easier than Barbados) certainly if you are going to give land in Barbados, somebody is going to have to give up their land!

Dealing with the political aspect, the Commissioners say that: "Rightly or wrongly a substantial body of public opinion in the West Indies is convinced that far-reaching measures of social reconstruction depend both for their initiation and their effective administration upon greater participation of the people in the business of government". So, they are recognising the need to concede the right of participation. Moreover, they say:

> We are satisfied that the claims so often put before us that the people should have a larger voice in the management of their affairs represents a genuine sentiment and reflects a growing political consciousness which

is sufficiently wide-spread to make it doubtful whether any scheme of social reforms, however wisely conceived and efficiently conducted would be completely successful, unless they were accompanied by the largest measure of constitutional development which is thought to be judicious in existing circumstances.

Now, they say a lot there that is really a reflection of the seriousness that they perceive in the nature of the revolt. They have observed the political linkage of the middle class, the working class and the peasantry; which is something that didn't happen in the 19th century. It happened in 1937. It is a political force the British cannot deal with easily. It is too costly if they try to deal with it in the wrong way. The British are saying that you have to reform, otherwise there will be problems for the Empire and they are not prepared to pay for that.

So you see clearly the response of the British. They then set out on a path of constitutional tutelage, which leads us up to the present and which we have ourselves experienced (or at least the older ones among us), and which leads to the development of the present liberal democratic system, with the right to vote, trade union rights, rights protecting the individual, rights protecting property, etc., and the assertion of liberty. These rights become a part of the growth of a political system and culture which we call today the Westminister model. The process reaches maturation with constitutional independence. Of course, with its own peculiar features, our state form is a frozen model of the British system which is itself a flexible system even if very stable.

This strategy of constitutional tutelage which led to the adoption of a frozen version of the Westminister model was a part of a wider imperial strategy, which was being implemented throughout the Empire, and it was a policy not perceived by all to be the most positive for a process of decolonisation. For example, C.L.R. James viewed this constitutional tutelage as a process of miseducation. For the British, it was a means by which they could contain and control developments and conflict in the West Indies by a strategy of institutionalisation of the conflict. In this way, development could proceed on their terms and could be channelled in conformity with British interests, so that local and British ruling class interests would not have much to fear from the West Indian labour movement. James states:

> By delaying the achievement of self-government, having to appoint a Royal Commission after the upheavals of 1937-1938 and by the mean and grudging granting so many the vote, so many to become ministers and all

the palaver and so-called education by which the British government claimed that it trained the West Indian population for self-government, a terrible damage was inflicted upon us. In reality our people were miseducated, our political consciousness was twisted and broken. Far from being guided to Independence by the 1960s . . . the Imperial government poisoned and corrupted that sense of self-confidence and political dynamic needed for any people about to embark on the uncharted seas of independence and nationhood.

But this is what the British wanted and this is what they knew that they would get if they could win the loyalty of the middle class, if they could "tutor" the West Indian people in "the art of government"' and give them "the shadow for the substance". Without elaborating then, that is more or less the rise of institutional features, rights, political system and culture out of the 1930s revolt". This process represents victories and defeats. We do not see at the end many of those lenders who were present at the beginning. Many of the programmes that were suggested are still to be implemented and in fact have reemerged in the radical politics of the late 1960s, the 1970s and the present period. Some of those very programmes of the British Guiana and West Indies Labour Congress are part of the programme of what are called the "subversive groups" today. These things were not implemented and the struggle continues.

But we have also to preserve those rights that were won by the blood of the working class in 1937. The issue is not to turn back those rights, but to build on them. We are not in a frozen situation. In 1937, the people at that time did not see the "Old Representative System" as something that could not be changed. It was "representative" the planters said. The working people at that time wanted it to be democratic and liberal. They gave their lives and their blood. They liberalised it and democratised it. This was allowed because it served the ruling class at the time to do so.

In these days we need more effective instruments to carry forward the needs of society and people living in it. We need to democratise further. Democracy is not a frozen thing. Democracy changes over time; it relates to the political culture; it relates to what become basic needs at one period in time as against another. The basic needs of 1937 are not the basic needs of 1987. Because somebody could accept a crocus bag or coal-pot in 1937 does not make it a basic need today. We need to recognise that the culture has changed, the basic minimum standard expected has changed, and the relative difference between that minimum

standard and the riches obtaining in the country remains important. So that is why you still have people militant about "living better". So it is not a matter of saying whether "you living better than in 1937". We hope so. The issue is where you have to go now; and what is your minimum standard now; and what can you see being produced as surplus from the surplus of your labour, and your recognition that you should have a greater part of it.

Lessons of the Past

Finally, I wish to stimulate some perspective on the way my method of analysis was used, since that method is also intended to help us analyse the contemporary situation. I am not saying that these points are particularly definitive positions in terms of commentary on development.

We could very well be living through a period of parallel accumulation of political energy, as was the case in the early 20th century. Such periods are recognised as features of social development. That is to say, society builds up in terms of inputs and then, like a kettle boiling, it then blows. You get hotter and hotter and then you boil. The boiling is the revolution or the insurrection. Suppose we ask, where is Garvey today? Does Jamaica have the influence it had in the 1930s? And we might well answer: there was a Jamaican called Bob Marley and there is Reggae and there is Rastafari, although Rastafari was around in the late 1930s in Jamaica as well. We might ask, where is the communist agitation and the Marxist inspired leadership? And we might answer: look at the so-called left-wing parties and at the Marxist-Leninist parties, which are present in the region at the present time, and at the impact of them on the political culture. You might ask: where are the riots?

But we must not look at this thing in a cyclical way all the same. I said that a part of my analysis is its recognition of process. So, I know that when you start doing this thing, some people say: "it is happening all over again". *It is not happening all over again.* Bob Marley is not Garvey and the Rastafari of 1987 is not the Rastafari of 1937. And the communist agitators of 1937 are not being repeated in 1987. Different people, different experience, even if younger, more experienced!

If you ask, where are the riots? Don't look for the little riots. Look for the 1970 rebellion in Trinidad, the rise and fall of Michael Manley, the Grenada revolution. It you ask, where is the Democratic League? Look at what became of it. It is the Democratic Labour Party and Errol Walton Barrow. You might find another parallel for that! Where is "the Great Depression"? It is all around us! Where are the debilitating diseases? You can check out AIDS and the illegal drugs. And where are the international influences that are telling us about the struggles of others as well as giving us colonialist ideology? We can watch CNN on mornings. We see both South Africa and Reagan. South Africa in revolt, in revolution, and Reagan in counter-revolution! And where is the Barbadian insurrection? Well, we are celebrating the 50th anniversary of 1937 in 1987 and if you check the arithmetic between 1816, 1876 and 1937, you will see when the next one is due. For some reason, the accumulation periods are almost exactly sixty years minus one or plus one, since 1816. Every sixty years in Barbados since 1816 you have had an insurrection. We are now in the fiftieth year!

Finally, I am saying that it is good for us to examine an event as significant as the 1937 revolt because in doing this, and doing it in the way that I hope I have done it, we look to the past to see the future in the present. So, if this is a lesson for all in methodology, then the lesson for the working class is that, if it is to ensure a positive future, both for itself and for its children, it must learn to put its organisation in place well before the class rises in majority to decisively challenge the system.

"Persecution we shall face. Tribulations and trials we shall bear, but the longer the battle, the sweeter the victory"!

Suggestions For Further Reading

George Belle, *The Political Economy of Barbados.* M.Sc. Dissertation. U.W.I. 1974

George Belle, *The Politics of Development: A study of the Political Economy of Barbados.* Ph.D. Dissertation. University of Manchester. 1977

R.P. Dutt. *The crisis of Britain and the British Empire.* 1953

C.L.R. James, *Party Politics in the West Indies.* 1962.

V.I. Lenin, *Marxism and Insurrection,* Selected works. 1971

W.A. Lewis. *Labour in the West Indies.* 1938. 1977

Tony Martin, *Race First, the Ideological and Organisational Struggles of Marcus Garvey and the UNIA.* 1976

Ken Post. *Arise ye starveling.* 1978

Report of the Commission to enquire into the Disturbances (The Deane Commission). 1937

Report of the West Indies Royal Commission. 1938-39 (The Moyne Commission). 1945

After 1937: The Politics of Wynter Crawford: 'Institutionalising' Labour and the Demise of Planter Government

by   George. A.V. Belle

Introduction

The main body of this extract is taken from seminal research undertaken on this subject almost thirty years ago. Although accepted for publication almost twenty five years ago this Reader will actually provide for its publication for the first time. Editing of the original has been kept to a minimum, so as to retain as far as possible the required focus, emphasis and intensity of the analysis at the time, because of its seminal nature. The article captures a significant range of politics engaged in after the 1937 labour revolt in Barbados, and the initiation of political reforms as a response to that revolt. It first describes concretely, the completion of the institutionalisation of the Barbados labour movement, which had involved significant political intrigue and political infighting within the Barbados Progressive League during 1939. Of note it records the Barbados version of the British manipulation of the reforms which followed the region wide labour rebellions of the 1930's decade. The article further displays the Barbados case of intense rivalry for leadership within the labour movement. Significantly the Barbados version of all this is encapsulated in the much celebrated 'Bushe Experiment'. This constitutional experiment by the British colonial authorities introduced the movement to embryonic democratic self - government in Barbados. The character of the politics surrounding it set in place the plane of Barbadian politics at least up to independence, some twenty years later. It launched a political cascade which flows even into the contemporary period.

Institutionalising Labour.

Having survived the rebellion of 1937, and negotiated accommodation in 1939, colonial authority and the local ruling class then proceeded with the granting of concessions to the underclasses. This could now be done under the tight control of a compromised labour leadership, combined with the continued ruling class dominance over state power. By mid 1939, this was further assisted by the outbreak of World War II, which facilitated the opportune use of the Defense Regulations as a controlling constraint over the struggling masses. For it was just six weeks after Adams won the presidency of the Barbados Progressive league that World War II broke out in Europe and there is little doubt that this occurrence also severely restricted the chances for a successful counter attack to be launched against his opportunism of 1939, by the 'left' wing of labour. For the colonial authority was unlikely to allow high-handed labour activity to raise the possibility of internal unrest and instability in one of its colonies during a period of war.

Despite all the events between 1937-1939, the granting of concessions which started during and continued after that period, opened up the basis for the strengthening of the labour movement, in terms of extension of democracy to the underclasses. A Minimum Wages Bill passed its second reading in the House in April 1938, introduced at the instigation of colonial authority, it met with 'Caustic' if not determined resistance from the planter interests.[1] The Governor in Executive Committee was given the power to order a minimum rate of wages in any industry or occupation in which the Governor in Executive Committee and his advisors were satisfied that wages were too low.

A court order could be made for outstanding wages to be paid where the minimum had been too low; all wages below the declared minimum became void; and the law could be enforced by fines against offenders.

On June 12th 1938, the Labour Officer Bill passed its second reading and the duties of this officer as stipulated by the Acting Colonial Secretary were:

i) to receive and investigate complaints of employers or of workers with a view to the settlement of disputes and grievances and to conciliation, especially with regard to hours and conditions of work and regulation of wages and to report on these to the Governor in Executive Committee;

ii) to prepare cost of living indices, statistics of earnings and unemployment returns;

iii) to foster the formation of trade unions, trades boards and collective bargaining subject to the law in force in these matters;

iv) to advise regarding the setting up of Industrial Courts and Workmen's Compensation, including agricultural workers;

v) to be liaison officer between Government's Labour and Health services;

vi) to be registrar of trade unions and trade boards;

vii) to carry out such other duties as the Governor in Executive Committee may from time to time prescribe.[2]

There was again planter resistance to this legislation and although serious enough to bring about deletion of the proposed functions of the Labour Officer "to foster trade unions, trade boards and collective bargaining, and to act as liaison between the labour and health services" and to cause the omission of the provisions in respect to workman's compensation,[3] it was nonetheless passed by the planter government if only because as C. L. Elder, the representative for St. George stated, "... to keep in good graces of the British Government if we want them to help us to get out of our difficulties..."[4]

The Trade Disputes (Arbitration and Enquiry) Act was passed on June 12th, 1939. It established arbitration machinery and boards of inquiry to deal with disputes between workers and employers. With the agreement of the parties to the dispute, either a single arbitrator, or an arbitrator advised by assessors, nominated in equal numbers by both parties could be appointed by the Governor; or both parties could nominate equal arbitrators with the Governor's nominee acting as chairman. Where arbitration was not agreed to, a Board of Enquiry could be appointed by the Governor to assess the dispute. The findings both of arbitrators or Boards of Enquiry were not legally binding upon the disputes.

Other notable concessions granted during this period were the enactment of a Workmen's Compensation Act and a Wages Board Act which gave legal sanction to agreements between representatives of labour and capital. To further assist the working class, the reliance on mainly indirect taxation for government revenue through customs duties (which affected the working people the most) was shifted more to the increasing of income tax on the more wealthy. Subsidisation of foodstuffs was also introduced and old age pension increased from 1/6 to 2/ and the age of pensioners was reduced from seventy to sixty-five. It was also at the start of the 1942-44 session that Grantley Adams was appointed to the Executive Council as the representative of labour.

The last of the more important pieces of labour legislation which came as a concession to compromise was the Trade Union Act which had its second reading on August 2nd, 1938. It was then revised and reintroduced in March 1939 and conveniently passed finally on December 27th, 1939 by which time, social democratic opportunism had been safely entrenched over the labour movement and World War II with its Defense Regulations was opportunely present. The Bill only became officially effective on August 1st, 1940.[5]

The Trade Union Bill, after having its first reading on June 28th, 1938, and a second reading on August 30th, was referred to select committee and was subject to what would appear to be deliberate cold storage, to the extent that the Speaker of the lower House complained on November 29th, 1938 (some three months after), on the lack of progress by the Committee. The Bill did not make its appearance in the House until March 14th, 1939 [6] just a week after the acceptance of Herbert Seale's resignation. It seemed to have benefited however, in appearing after the sitting of the Moyne Commission in January 1939, as Francis Mark states:

> There was little discussion and no opposition to the Bill in the House and this may be attributed to the strong support which the Commissioners had expressed for trade unionism and collective bargaining.[7]

It could also be explained by the perception by the planter class representatives in the elected House that a section of Labour could be handled and the legislation would be a more efficient means of controlling labour; rather than to have to face a threat of another wild-cat General Strike such as occurred in February. Consequently, the Bill was read a third time and passed on August 29th, 1939.

However the right wing of the planter class, nominated to the legislative council, demonstrated the essence of the reaction of their class, by scorning the tactics of control and opting to resist outright the Bill. This section of the ruling class aimed their attack at the presence of two clauses which had been added to the Bill after its reintroduction In March 1939. These provisions provided (a) for the absence of liability for torts on the part of trade unions; and b) provisions for peaceful picketing the Legislative Council duly after reference to a select committee amended the Bill on December 5th, deleting section 9, the peaceful picketing provisions, and returned the amended Bill to the lower House on December 19th, 1939.[8]

In the Lower House, Grantley Adams, speaking for the B. P. L. wing of the labour leadership, was nonetheless forced to answer this attack by extreme reaction in the Legislative Council. But he found that planter interest in the Lower House bolstered by its right wing was now prepared to pressure reformist labour into conceding to plantocracy even more than it had planned to.

> I view any suggestion to take peaceful picketing out of the scope of the Trade Union Bill in two ways. In the first place, it is undoubtedly a symptom of the desire to yield to public opinion as regards the necessity for

social reform, the necessity for getting some sort of machinery for the settlement of trade union disputes while preserving your real feelings perhaps or your real prejudice towards combinations of working men.... [9]

E. K Walcott, Attorney-General, the man who had introduced the original Bill, as a spokesman to the supposedly more liberal planter interest of the lower House and of colonial authority - now cut the ground from under his supposed colleague at the 'conference table', Adams, by upbraiding him for his unrealistic arguments, and suggesting that Adams should accept as preferable half-a-loaf, rather than no bread. Compromised labour not for the first or last time lost out before the solidarity of reaction; an early lesson in politics which Adams never learned; (even to his final fiasco of West Indian Federation, when on its collapse, he ran to the Colonial Office to save their creation only to be scoffed at, by Reginald Maulding).[10] On this occasion, Keith Walcott pulled up Adams as though he were disciplining a school boy, and the Trade Union Bill was passed without the picketing clause.[11]

> Sometimes one finds oneself in the position of asking people to get away from the theory and get down to practice. The point of difficulty of persuading honourable members as to the value of having peaceful picketing in the Bill has long passed. Honourable members are still agreed on it. We all passed it and it is no use our talking in the air or beating the air. Let us now come down to the practical position in which we find ourselves and deal with it as practical politicians. If we refuse the amendment of the Other Place today, have we bettered our position in any way? I think a clear answer is no. If examined in the theory of trade unions, it may be a necessary one. It may be that time has proved especially in the shape it is now to be in this Act, that this is the right way of putting in picketing. But the deletion of it does not destroy the value of the Bill and I think the Honourable members would agree with me that if the Other Place had taken out that section relating to exemption from liability of torts... they would have removed a very necessary part of the Bill.... Trade Unionism had been functioning for years before these two important sections were added to the Bill. If Honourable members will examine the Bill they will see that a trade union can function and function effectively.... If we thought they could not function without Section 9, I would agree that it would be no value in having something that is useless. But the Bill is almost perfect without it, why then should we destroy the whole ground on which we will

build our trade unions? It is not as though we might get a trade union to grow in a day and bear fruit. It has to develop. The time is near at hand when we should consider the question of starting it again. Why then deprive ourselves of nine-tenths of a loaf of bread because someone has denied us the other one-tenth?[12]

Despite the fact, however, that the working people through the weakened politics of Adams and the Progressive League, lost one of the main weapons in their fight against the capitalist class, that is the right to picket; nonetheless, the passage of the Trade Union Act represented a major victory for the working class against the employers in the struggle for democratic rights. And this Bill probably more than any other laid the foundation organisationally[13] for the political struggle which was to end in the demise of planter government in 1946.

Political Reform

Similarly and logically the struggle for democratic rights for the underclasses in the society extended itself to the political arena in the battle for further extension of the franchise and the attainment of Adult Suffrage. Within the constraints of the limited franchise, the Progressive League's winning of the five seats in the House in the 1940 election had to be described as a 'magnificent achievement' and a 'major victory',[14] but planter government remained and in 1942 the reality of the situation was made clear, when rather than gaining more seats, the League won only four.

One of the main interests of the Barbadian middle class politicians in their allied struggle with the working class against plantocracy was the attainment of political office, and thus one of their more genuine resolves was the need to defeat planter government. Indeed, the need to capture political office and then legislate change was one of the means by which the B.P.L. leadership kept more radical demands at bay. In the words of Grantley Adams, "... the remedy is like the evil, primarily political. When the political fight is won, economic ills will disappear".[15] It is with this understanding that the intensity of the 1943 struggle over extension of the franchise must be understood: despite the fact that the labour leadership had made their peace with plantocracy. It is useful to understand that the League's leadership must have reasoned that a compromise with the planters should mean that while the planters kept the power based on the economic control of the society; they, the labour

leaders should be conceded the political authority. As usual as is repeatedly seen in this arrangement, the labour leaders had to even beat the concessions out of the liberal section of the planter class whose 'good faith' they believed in.

The debate in the House, on the Representation of the People Bill was initiated as a further fulfillment of the recommendations of the Moyne Commission and took place in April and May of 1943. Wynter Crawford, the new spokesman for an increasingly radical wing of the labour movement, outside of the Progressive League set the tone by making it clear to the planter interests, that he had no illusions about why the Bill was before the House:- "... the present Bill before us today is not the result of any desire on the part of this small ruling section to extend the franchise; it is the result of the prodding on the one hand, by the Colonial Office, and on the other hand, by the last commission that visited this island.[16] If it had not been for these two factors instead of lowering the franchise there might be an attempt to raise it..."

But the initial bitterness in the debate, resulted from the Progressive League (for the reasons already mentioned), moving an amendment to the Bill as introduced by the Attorney General which had simply asked for an increase in the franchise. The League demanded Adult Suffrage. Through Grantley Adams its position was stated:-

> "... the senior member for St. James will be putting forward the suggestion that the income qualification should be reduced to £30. Nothing could be more ridiculous than that, it brings in nobody as a class ... unless honourable members vote for adult suffrage, they are, in my submission definitely excluding the vast numbers of agricultural labourers in this island who are the back-bone of the island who produce our wealth ...[17]

The Attorney General in reply contradicted the case of Adams in terms of the class of people who would be included and went on to make a case for gradualism in a move to adult suffrage. It was yet another instance of Adams being beaten again at his own game of compromise and consequently while the other larger British colonies in the West Indies were moving towards adult suffrage, the right of the vote for the masses of the working people in Barbados was forfeited for another seven years, through the B.P.L. leaders' trust in the ruling class of Barbados. E. K. Walcott put the position of the liberal wing of the plantocracy with firmness and subtlety:

... The Government Bill was introduced with the £30 qualification but as far as I am concerned I am willing to accept the £25 qualification which is recommended by the Select Committee. That represents an average of 9/8 per week and I am surprised to hear anybody say that that is not likely to include a very much larger number of voters ... particularly as it will include woman suffrage. If you look through the returns from plantations you will see that the regular agricultural labourer's pay for a year maintains an average in the vicinity of 10/- a week or more. That is a fact. We will have to consider as a matter of reasoning what is the qualification for voting and to say that merely the attainment of the age of 21 is a reasonable method of arriving at who is entitled to vote seems to me to be rather strange ... I say that anybody who has done canvassing will know that the ordinary man, although he has reached the age of 21 does not appreciate what he is voting for ... there are some who believe we are fit and ripe for Adult suffrage and there are some ...who on the contrary believe we have to work towards Adult Suffrage and it is safer and better that it should be reached by gradual stages.[18]

It was left to the growing radicalism of Wynter Crawford to expose some of the 'crooked' reasoning of the Attorney General, but even then the Adult Suffrage amendment was defeated on May 4th, 1943 and the amendment to further reduce the income qualification to £25.00 carried.

Crawford wanted to know why a great deal had been made by the attorney general of the recommendations by the Moyne Commission that adult suffrage should be granted by 'gradual steps' and at the same time ignored completely the sentence coming after that in the commission's recommendations which requested the setting up of committees in all the colonies to consider the extension of the franchise. Crawford went on, "...in Trinidad, British Guiana, Jamaica and other places where there is not adult suffrage, immediately after this recommendation was known, proceeded to set up committees to consider this question ... I take it that if a local committee had been set up, this Government would not have had the effrontery to send down a Bill of this sort. The expressions of public opinion would have been so universal, that no government, not even the government of this colony, would have dared to take such a stand in front of public opinion. It is for this reason and no other that no committee was set up here ..."[19]

The Representation of the People (Amendment) Act 1943, despite the fact that it did not introduce Adult Suffrage to Barbados, was nonetheless critical to the political development of the island, since it did still provide the means to sufficiently broad numbers of the middle and working classes to facilitate their voting planter representation out of the House of Assembly or at least to facilitate labour representation attaining a majority in the House, as the 1944 and 1946 General Elections were to demonstrate.

In a despatch[20] to the Secretary of State for the Colonies the Attorney General reported that the 1943 Act, amended the Representation of the People Act of 1901 (Act No. 2 of 1901) in several particulars. The most important of these were that it made women eligible for membership of the House of Assembly on the same qualifications as had previously existed for men. The Act also extended the franchise by conferring the right to vote on women, by removing the incapacity of domestic or other menial servants to vote and by reducing the various incomes and property qualifications which conferred on their holders the right to vote.

The qualification in respect of the annual value of lands or the profits and rent from such was reduced from £5 to £2. The qualification in respect of payment of taxes assessed by the vestry in respect of the city of Bridgetown was reduced from £2 to £1. The income from pension, occupation office or trade qualification was reduced from £50 to £20. The qualification relating to the value of lands or tenements held by joint tenants or tenants in common or the rents of such were reduced from £5 to £2. per annum for each of such tenants and the qualification in respect of the payment by co-partners in trade or businesses of taxes for the city of Bridgetown was reduced from £2 to £1.

The qualification of £4.3. 4- per month in respect of employment for twelve months by any private person which was previously contained in paragraph (5) of section 3 of the Representation of the People Act 1901 (Act. No. 2 of 1901) was deleted. It was further stated that the 1945 Act made provision for the use of rooms in public elementary schools by candidates for the purpose of holding public meetings. Provision was also made for the making of a deposit by candidates and for the forfeiture of the deposit all the event of the candidates' failure to secure more than one-sixth of the votes polled.

Despite the compromised framework in which they were granted, the concessions made to the underclasses between 1937-1944, but particularly between 1942-1944 were significant, even critical to the strengthening politically of these classes and it needs to be understood that while at least the more liberal sector of the plantocracy understood that if open rebellion was to be kept in check, it was necessary for those concessions to be made, it was never with the intention of removing themselves as a class from political government; but rather it was to postpone, if not prevent this development that they undertook this policy, prodded on by the Colonial Office. The overall strategy was thus always one of control. To control and institutionalise the threatening struggles of the working people. They had already partially succeeded in doing this by getting the type of labour leadership they desired in 1939. But if this capturing of the labour leadership, put off the immediate possibility of a transformation both political and economic, it became increasingly clear to plantocracy, definitely by 1944, that the implication and the inevitable progression from the concessions they were making was heralding the end of their occupation of the political government. Thus, the manifestation, of resistance and qualification, in the passage of the reformist legislation, wherever it seemed to be setting up the progression, to go beyond the intention of control, and institutionalisation, of the working class struggle. This two-faced resistance was clearly manifested in the debating and legislative maneuvering which was encountered in the process of the reformist legislation of 1937-1944, in the Lower House, and in the outright resistance and reaction from the nominated vested interest in the Upper Chamber.

It is therefore not an accident that a showdown came, and that it came just prior to and during the 1944 elections, which were to take place with an increased franchise and a legally organised trade union and developing labour party in the fray.

Crawford

There was one other factor, however, which induced the showdown and this was the new development in the left wing of the labour movement. The left wing was increasingly once again becoming a new challenge to the leadership of the B. P. L. It now stood under the banner of the Congress Party led by Wynter Crawford. This new militancy from the left put pressure on the Adams leadership in respect to it remaining at the head of the labour movement.

The showdown with plantocracy, and the B.P. L.'s attempts to head-off the new challenge from the left of the labour movement, first became manifest in the bitter and long strike at the Barbados Foundry which broke out in October 1944. Mark described it as the 'major rallying point in the history of the Barbados Workers Union',[21] and Hoyos reported, "In due course, the crisis arrived with the Engineers' strike in 1944. It was the first real showdown between capital and organised labour in the island as the employers marshaled their forces in the sure and certain expectation that they would root out the new organisation".[22]

The strike went on for eight weeks and became an integral part of the 1944 election campaign. One reason for it being so drawn out was the refusal by the workers to seek arbitration and it is clear that a newspaper like the Advocate was not grasping the full implications of the strike, when in an editorial "a Sorry Plight" it upbraided the B. P. L. leadership for continuing to sponsor 'the impetuosity of a few hot-heads'[23] who had shut the door on arbitration and taken the law into their own hands. The Advocate said:

> "... We would be doing less than justice to the reputation of men like Mr. G. H. Adams, President of the Workers Union and Mr. Hugh Springer, its Secretary, if we did not assume that they as lawyers and men in public life, did not advise the engineers that as soon as an arbitration tribunal was set up, it was their duty to go back to work and await the decision of the arbitrator. Assuming that this was done, we fail to see how the executives of the Union could justifiably give relief to men who had flouted this decision".[24]

But Grantley Adams and the B. P. L. not only had to give relief, but organised relief for 97 men who were not even in good financial standing with the Union when the strike was called.[25] The politics of the moment demanded it.

It is noteworthy that the strikes started for as seemingly fickle a reason, as the dismissal of a turner at the Foundry who was found to be 'working too slowly' and who also happened to be Divisional Secretary at the Foundry, i.e. one of the most influential union workers at the factory. After eight weeks the strike only ended with the intervention of the Governor and as Mark states, Brathwaite, the dismissed turner accepted gratuity in lieu of re-employment and became employed by the B.W.U. and the settlement gave the workers substantial wage increases, incremental scales of wages and increased war bonus and was set to be for three years duration.[26] The strike added significantly to the momentum of organisation for the B. W. U. as is reflected in growth of membership at the time with obvious implications for plantocracy and for the success of the B. P. L.

Crawford and the W.I. Congress Party:

The 1944 elections was the arena for the combatants in this struggle for political government, in which for the first time in the political history of Barbados, the survival of planter government seemed to be at stake. On the side of labour was the B. P. L. led by Grantley Adams and the militant Congress Party led by Wynter Crawford, for the planter government came the Electors Association.

In opening its campaign through its newspaper organ the Barbados Observer - the Congress Party-made clear to the people the importance of the moment in the political development of the island and identified the foe against whom they should struggle. Although Hoyos in *The Rise of W. I. Democracy* - can only concede that the Congress Party supported much the same programme of reforms as the League,[27] there seems to be a lot to make the case that the Congress Party, during the election campaign took over the leadership of labour from the B. P. L., and to further demonstrate their superiority over the League, defeated them at the polls by winning eight seats to the B. P. L's seven, although Hoyos again strangely states that the Congress only won 'an equally substantial victory'[28] as the League.

Commenting on the approaching elections and setting the tone for its campaign, the Barbados Observer, organ of the Congress had this to say:

"...Throughout the history of this island, it has been dominated by a small and selfish clique and it is indeed remarkable that now, this clan senses that it has reached a crisis, it has actually had the shamelessness and the temerity to publicly appeal to the people of this island and ask them to help them consolidate their weakening position ... for sheer presumptuous impudence it is unparalleled. It is an absolute insult to the intelligence of the people. Only the congenital idiots among the masses will vote for the candidates of the Electors Association on November 27th".[29]

The Observer went further and described Barbados as being 'in revolt':

"Barbados is in revolt against the status quo. Throughout the country thousands of middle and working class men and women are voicing the most determined protests against poverty and unemployment. These thousands are resolved to put more of the wealth in the colony at the service of the people; these thousands are in deadly earnest, this spirit may well be called the NEW DEMOCRACY... on every hand, the indications are that the people have resolved that the old order

should pass away ... No longer are the people of this island prepared to entrust their destinies to the representatives of big business".[30]

In introducing its manifesto[31] the Congress, through the Observer, made the call to 'vote for a new Barbados' - 'Forward to a People's Victory' - and 'Bring Socialism to Barbados'. The Manifesto was not revolutionary, at most militant social democrat, the Congress supposedly accepting that change would for the time being be under the constraint of colonial authority. It nonetheless seemed to head-off the B.P. L., who despite its social democratic programme had had the opportunity to suggest initiatives before the rise of the Congress Party, but had chosen accommodation and had been forced to accept the concessions with compromise of 1939-1944. Of course, the Congress policy could have been rooted in demagogic opportunism. But this was not demonstrated by the Congress Party's actions in Parliament, during the 1944-1946 session; nor even in its actions after the 1946 election set back.

The more important calls by the Congress which it consistently stuck to were land settlement and collective farming in agriculture; compulsory education; books and hot lunches for school children; national health, unemployment insurance and pension scheme; excess profits tax; super tax on large incomes; and tax on unimproved land; Adult Suffrage; and the House of Assembly to elect its representatives on the Executive Committee;[32] abolition of Special Juries; Government ownership of Barbados Telephone Co., the Barbados Gas Co., and the Barbados Electric Supply Corporation; Rent Restriction Act; an early census; and Disestablishment of the Anglican Church.

The November 27th elections saw the first electoral victory for the labour movement in Barbados, the West Indian National Congress Party won the elections with eight seats and defeated the B.P.L. with seven; the combination of labour seats, Congress eight and B. P. L., seven, defeated the Electors Association eight and thus defeated planter government for the first time. But the election did not remove planter government. The Observer nonetheless, hailing the victory for the working people, stated:

"Disaster has descended like Vesuvius on Pompeii and Herculean upon the Electors Association. Monday, November 27th will henceforth be remembered as ushering in a new era in the political life of the island. On that day, the candidates put up for election by the reactionary association which regarded itself as omnipotent, bit the dust and went down to crushing defeat. Out of a total of 18 candidates only 8 secured election and of these, only 2 were returned as senior members.[33] Many of its candidates, notable Messrs. D. S. Payne of St. Philip (President of the Electors Association and Chairman of Committees in the House) and Michael Greaves of St. Joseph (son of a former Chief Justice) forfeited their deposits of £30. The Electors Association met its Waterloo on Monday".[34]

The Barbados Advocate, conceding defeat for the establishment was more dour in its comment on the election results, which it saw as a swing to extremism:

"In a world in which so many changes have been instituted and in which the doctrine of reform has been so continuously preached, Barbados could have hardly have avoided this wholesome reaction ...But ... the true analysis of this somewhat disturbing situation is that the pendulum must reach the extreme before its return and in this case it has now reached the left. There is however, no need for alarm, before the days of normalcy return and with them easier feeling in political relationships..."[35]

The Demise of Planter Government

Despite the continued resistance to the growing reality, by the plantocracy, the implications of the 1944 elections were clear to the Colonial Office. The political development of Barbados had reached the stage of the demise of planter government. The major concern of the colonial authorities became the need to ensure that the demise of planter government remained just that; the planter-merchant ruling class was not to be destroyed, but made to see the need to concede the holding of political office, particularly to a labour leadership which had struck a compromise with plantocracy and was prepared to practice accommodation. Fabricano Hoyos, in an attempt to justify Colonial Office policy, adequately expressed the dilemma that arose before the colonial authorities after the 1944 election, and the victory of the Congress Party over the B. P. L. Hoyos wrote, "During the years of social upheaval and war, Sir Grattan Bushe[36] tried, with unfaltering courage, to steer a course between reaction and revolution. To attain the end, which he kept constantly in mind, he was ever ready to accept any means by which progress could be achieved in a gradual and constitutional manner".[37] What that in essence meant was that the Governor was prepared to go to any end to see that the change over from a planter

leadership, to a labour leadership, in government would be done under an accommodationist labour leadership which intended to contain and institutionalize the working class movement.

It is not surprising consequently that when after the 1944 election, the Governor had to make the choice of labour appointees to the Executive Council, that he arbitrarily ignored the labour party which had won most seats in the election i.e. the Congress Party and preferred to appoint G. H. Adams, and Hugh Springer, the President and Secretary, respectively of the B. P. L. On this arbitrary and undemocratic action by the Governor, Hoyos, the historian of *The Rise of W. I. Democracy* was only prepared to state, "The Congress Party, which had won eight seats in the House, looked forward to having one of their members appointed on the Executive. But Sir Grattan decided instead, to give the seat on the Executive Committee to Hugh Springer".[38] Hoyos continued that the Governor's choice was based on his judgment of Springer's qualities, which Hoyos described as "his debating powers", "his moderation", "his practical wisdom".[39] With the delicate question of the 'right' leadership settled, the demise of planter government could now be the grand concession, in fulfillment of the grand design of Imperialism. Governor Bushe could now proceed to outline operation change-over, better known as the "Bushe Experiment".

"The Barbados constitution as it works at present appears to be incapable of coping with modern conditions. The defect of the constitution lies in the imperfect distribution of Power and Responsibility. The Governor has the whole responsibility of Government, but he is given no power. The House of Assembly possesses the power but has no responsibility. Throughout the history of British Parliamentary institutions, it has been realised that the great evil which must be avoided is Power without Responsibility and in order to avoid it, it has been the custom to entrust the executive power to a cabinet and not a chamber, that is, to a small body of persons upon whom responsibility can be fixed and not to a large body of persons who can avoid personal responsibility. But although cabinets wield large executive power, they must not be without control. That is where Parliament comes into the picture.... On the assembling of the new House, therefore, the officer administering the Government will send for the person who appears to him to be best able to command a majority in the House of assembly and will ask him to submit to him names from the House for membership to the Executive Committee and members of the Ex-ecutive Committee will be asked respectively to take charge of the general policy relating to particular de-partments of government for the purpose of dealing with the affairs of these departments in Executive Com-mittee and in the House of assembly. The Executive Committee will then in practice cease to be merely a collection of individuals nominated by the Governor for the purpose of advising him, and will become an effective organ of government accepting collective re-sponsibility for policy, though the Governor must under the constitution as at present existing, retain ultimate responsibility. Such an alteration in constitu-tional procedure will also bring, I trust a new sense of responsibility to the House of assembly.... I have tried to steer a course between reaction and revolution and to indicate the means by which progress can be at-tained in a gradual and constitutional manner...[40]

With the design of the change-over from planter government outlined, the 1946 elections became the climax of the struggle that had started in 1944 for suc-cession on the part of the B.P.L. and the more radical Congress Party, and survival for planter government. The significance of the struggle was not lost on any section of the society which had a political interest; Hoyos claimed,"the General Elections at the end of 1946 were fought with more than usual intensity",[41] and the establishment newspaper the Barbados Advo-cate, said that the elections were without precedent, both from the number of candidates and from the intensity of the campaigning and that further the re-sults were also likely to be history making.[42]

The bitter struggle which had been going on be-tween the two wings of the labour movement became very manifest during the campaign and reflected itself in the initial comments on the instrument of 'change-over' and the role and significance of the designer of the instrument, Governor Bushe. The Beacon,[43] the newspaper organ of the B. P. L. had nothing but praise for the role of Bushe, whom it saw as a "historic fig-ure" in originating the experiment in "ministerial responsibility on the part of members of the Execu-tive Committee"; in the paper's opinion, Governor Bushe would be "considered in the first rank of im-partial and courageous administrators" throughout the island's history.[44]

The Congress Party newspaper organ, the Observer, on the other hand, had a totally opposed view of the role and significance of the departing Governor. In its view, Bushe had consistently refused to implement any

of the major recommendations of the Royal Commis-sion of 1938-1939; and while the Congress Party's leader Wynter Crawford, it claimed, had been struggling for acquisition of land to carry out the recommendation of the Commission for land settlement, Bushe had sim-ply ignored such submissions and the Party could only conclude that Bushe was 'strongly opposed to offend-ing the ruling classes in Barbados'. Bushe, it continued, also ignored imposition of an Excess Profits Tax and the enactment of Legislation to restrict house rental changes (these recommendations had been contained in the Congress' 1944 Manifesto); and in the Observer's opinion, the Governor did not try sufficiently to fulfill the Moyne Commission's recommendations in respect to franchise reform, so that the franchise reforms had still only gone so far as the £20 franchise and women suffrage which had been passed in 1943. The paper took issue also with the continued existence of the "Special Jury System" although as it said, the Governor had seen "at first hand, its 'viciousness'"; and while accepting a salary increase for himself, the paper said the governor had resisted increase in wages for workers at the pump-ing stations and the road labourers.[45]

These criticisms of the Governor and the reforms of the so-called years of change while being taken in the context of an electoral campaign, nonetheless should add to the perception of the reality that the 'Bushe Ex-periment' in removing planter government was not designed to facilitate a victory of the labour movement, but simply tied in with the stratagem of fostering social democratic opportunism and the creation of a com-promised and accommodationist labour leadership, which would lead to the control and institutionalisation of the working class rebellion generated in 1937. This was what the Congress Party meant, when in an Edito-rial in the Observer on November 16th, it declared, that what distinguished it as a party, was that it "does not want to be 'masters' but servants of the country".

The Congress in a November 2nd Observer article also referred to the 1945 struggle with the plantocracy and the B. P. L. It stated that at that time it had organised a trade union among the sugar workers and "endeavoured to get a substantial increase in the price paid for the reaping of the cane crop". The Party claimed that that struggle was protracted and described it as the "greatest fight between industrialists and workers over wages in the island"; it went further to claim that the victory which the workers won in that struggle led by the Congress Party "aroused the undy-ing enmity of the planter class". In demonstrating what it called the "coalition" of the B. P. L., and the

Electors Association, the Congress Party in the Editorial of the same November 2nd issue of the Observer stated:

> "We are engaged in a life and death struggle between the haves and the have nots. The primary and ultimate aim of government should be the welfare of the people. For the last session, 15 members were returned to the Assembly on a labour ticket, 8 of the Congress Party, 7 of the Progressive League. Throughout the session, both on the Executive where the League had 2 seats and in the Assembly, the coalition comprised of the Electors' Association - the party of wealth and influence and the League, concerned itself with safeguarding the interests of reaction and buttressing the bulwarks of the ruling classes. The coalition protected the wealthy from increased taxation, refused to render adequate relief to the poor and needy, placed obstacles in the way of educational advancement for the masses of the people and strenuously resisted efforts aimed, at the abolition of monopolies, at land reform, for increases in the salaries of deserving public servants, even at general implementation of the more outstanding recommendations of the Royal Commission. It took two years of questions and addresses in the Assembly, of speeches and pressure exerted on every possible occasion for our public works and road board workers to receive the princely wage of £1.12 per day. People who hardly get more than six months work in every twelve. The same coalition fought severely against the Congress and successfully used its weight of members to hand out increases of seven dollars per day to officials already working for twenty, thirty and even forty dollars a day."

The accusations of the Congress against the B.P. L., are largely substantiated, on examination of the Debates of the House of Assembly for the 1944-1946 session. It can definitely be perceived, particularly in the case of Adams and Springer, that as members of the Executive Committee they increasingly defended government positions against other labour members, particularly the Congress Party members. Even to the extent that when a Bill was introduced, seeking to amend the Representation of the People Act 1901 as amended by the Representation of the People Act 1943-41 and 1944-53, which was seeking to introduce Adult Suffrage, it was opposed by Grantley Adams on the grounds that it did not cover the area of removing income qualifications for membership of the House and that the Bill should be sent to Select Committee so that all additions could be added which would make the democratic process totally so.

Edwy Talma, (Adams' trusted lieutenant of the 1939 affair) led the opposition to this position taken by Adams, accusing Adams of "filibustering" and delaying tactics, and went on to say that the Bill should go through as it then was and additions could be dealt with later, particularly because an important election was soon due and select committees took considerable time in their deliberations.

Nonetheless, the B. P. L. countered by accusing the Congress of being responsible "for every defect" in the legislation of the 1944-1946 session; and of being opposed to the "Bush Experiment". On the latter question, the B. P. L. through the Beacon continues, "Those who are opposed to this offer and shrink from gasping this supreme opportunity of their political lives have an overwhelming fear - the fear of exposure. The very intensity of their infantile vituperations is the clearest symptom of a political inferiority complex. They know that they lack the capacity, the administrative ability to govern Barbados. They cannot govern themselves. They have no desire to be exposed. Put in the seats of government, all men will see them for what they really are - pygmies in giant places, swamped and overwhelmed by the robes and cares of office, valiant in opposition, impotent in active administration... " [46]

The Barbados Progressive League with an image of "responsible leadership" behind it, nurtured by the Colonial Office and its local representative, Governor Bushe; with its claim of leadership experience in administration on the Executive Committee; and with a growing trade union organisation behind it, won nine of the 24 seats in the elections; the Congress Party won seven; the Electors Association seven; and one Independent was returned. Planter government had been overturned, but if anybody had won the election, it was the Colonial Office, for a labour coalition was formed by the B. P. L., as the majority party. Grantley Adams was sent for by the Acting governor as the person "best able to command a majority in the House of Assembly". From the rationale of the Congress party, the politics of the moment, necessitated the coalition[47] and in any event they were in a minority situation: the weak position of both labour parties necessarily strengthened the position of the planters. In comments in the Observer on the 28th and 23rd of November respectively, the Congress stated: "Quite contrary to the expectations of both labour parties, neither side was returned with a working majority. The final count showed an unexpected triumph for the conservatives who managed to secure as many as eight of the twenty four seats". And on the 23rd in respect to the question of unity, it stated: "The great opportunity now before the people of Barbados emphasizes the importance of strengthening the unity of the labour movement in every possible way and of carrying forward this unity into the battles which lie.

Notes

1. See debates in the House of Assembly and the Legislative Council, April 1938.
2. F. Mark, *History of the B.W.U*, op. cit., p. 64.
3. F. Mark, *History of the B.W.U.*, op. cit p.66.
4. Debates on Labour Officer Bill - House of Assembly, June 1938.
5. In contrast with the larger British territories in the Caribbean, this was rather late - legal recognition of trade unions being granted in Jamaica in 1919, British Guiana 1921, Trinidad in 1932.
6. See House of Assembly debates of June 1938; August 1938; November 1938; March 1939.
7. F. Mark, History of the B.W.U., op. cit., p. 66
8. See Legislative Council Debates - December 1939.
9. Grantley Adams speaking to the House of Assembly Debates re amendment to the Trade Union Bill, December 19th, 1939.
10. Reference is made to the "Save the nation delegation" of March 1962 to the Colonial Office on the collapse of the West Indian Federation.
11. Even when the amendments were passed re the Trade Union Act in 1943 - the clause on picketing was not included and G. H. Adams declared then that he supported that passage, because he did not want the contention around the picketing clause to arise again and prevent passage. He had come full circle and was speaking the language of E. K. Walcott. It is useful to further note that the picketing clause was not passed until the 1960s under the D. L. P. Government.
12. E. K. Walcott, Attorney General, speaking in the House of Assembly re: amendment to the Trade Union Bill, December 19th, 1939.
13. For the early organisation and development of the B. W. U., see Francis Mark, *History of the B. W. U.*, p. 98-104.
14. F. Mark, History of the B.W.U., op. cit., p. 9
15. G. H. Adams in Hoyos, *The Rise of W. I. Democracy*, op. cit., p. 61.
16. These of course, did their prodding - because of the pressure from the working people.
17. Grantley Adams in House of Assembly Debate re the Representation of the People in (Amendment) Bill 1943 - May 4th 1943.
18. The Attorney General, E. K. Walcott in House of Assembly Debates re the representation of the People (Amendment) Bill, May 4th, 1943.
19. Wynter Crawford in House of Assembly Debates re the Representation of People (Amendment) Bill, May 4th, 1943.
20. Despatch No. 6 of 8th January 1944. Enclosure 2. Legal Report by the Attorney General.
21. F. Mark, *History of the B. W. U.*, op. cit., p. 117
22. F. Mark, *History of the B. W. U.*, op. cit., p. 117.
23. F. A. B. Hoyos, *The Rise of W. I. Democracy*, op. cit., p. 94.
24. Ibid.
25. F. Mark reports that "of the 121 men out on strike, only 24 had been in good standing in the Union, when they answered the strike summons", in *History of B. W. U.*, op. cit., p. 118.
26. F. Mark, *History of the B. W. U.*, op. cit., p. 117.

27. Hoyos, *The Rise of W. I. Democracy*, op. cit., p. 105.
28. Ibid.
29. Barbados Observer of Saturday 4th November, 1944.
30. Barbados Observer of Saturday 4th November, 1944.
31. Barbados Observer of Saturday 18th November, 1944.
32. This was to be important to Congress, since after winning a majority in the 1944 election it still was not given a representative on the Executive Committee by the Governor.
33. Barbados had a system of double member constituency representation with a senior and junior member for each constituency. This system remained in force up until the 1971 General Elections.
34. Article in Barbados Observer of Saturday, December 2nd, 1944.
35. Barbados Advocate - Editorial "The Elections" of 28th Nov., 1944.
36. Sir Grattan Bushe, Governor of Barbados.
37. F. A. B. Hoyos, *The Rise of W. I. Democracy*, op. cit., p. 106.
38. Ibid.
39. Ibid.
40. Extract from speech to the House of Assembly, October 1st 1946, by Sir Grattan Bushe, Governor of Barbados.
41. F. A. B. Hoyos, *The Rise of W. I. Democracy*, op. cit., p.109.
42. Barbados Advocate of Tuesday, November, 1946.
43. The Beacon was started in September, 1946.
44. The Beacon of October 19th, 1946.
45. See the Observer of October 26th 1946, Editorial: "End of an Administration".
46. Editorial "The Choice" in the Beacon of November 2nd, 1946.
47. It says something of the differences between the parties that in the first session after the elections the coalition broke down; but labour government by the B. P. L., nonetheless held on.

Labour in the West Indies: The Birth of a Workers' Movement

by W. Arthur Lewis

Social Conditions

So much has been written on this subject in recent months that it is hardly necessary to go into it in great detail. We shall therefore content ourselves with a summary of the position.

Wages

Wages and the cost of living vary from island to island. Wages of agricultural labourers range from 1/3 a day in the smaller islands to 2 /-* a day in Jamaica. Receipts other than wages also vary. In some places the labourer is given a plot of land on which to grow food; in others this can only be obtained at a fairly high rental. Similarly housing is provided at a low rental in barracks on some plantations. The money level of wages thus tells us very little. But in every island where official committees have investigated the earnings of labourers it has been found that they are so low as just to permit subsistence at a deplorably low level. And evidence of this jumps to the eye in the ragged clothing, dilapidated housing, and undernourished condition of the masses and their children.

Housing

'In no aspect of our inquiry,' wrote the official Commission on the Disturbances in Trinid0ad in 1937,

> 'have we been more impressed by the evidence placed before us and by our own investigations than as regards the conditions in which large numbers of the working population, both urban and rural, are housed.'

A good proportion of the agricultural labourers — as much — as 50% in some places — lives on the plantations in 'barracks', constructed on the same principle as stables. To quote the same report, they consist for the most part

> 'of a long wooden building roofed with galvanised iron, divided from end to end by a partition and subdivided on both sides into a series of single rooms.'

each of which would be occupied by a labourer and his family. A relic of slavery and indentured labour, they are almost always old, battered, and much too small for their inhabitants. The labourers' own huts vary from mud or coconut branches to unpainted wood, but are also too small.

Urban workers usually live in houses on the average somewhat better than the rural hut, though there are some terrible patches of slums.

Disrepair, absence of sanitary arrangements, high rents and overcrowding are the four main evils. An official Barbados report states that two-thirds of the population live in dwellings of two rooms or less. Indeed the typical case is to find the family living in a single room.

Recently some plantations have started to improve their housing conditions, and municipalities are launching out on slum clearance. But progress is slow, and in the absence of legislation, depends mainly on public opinion for its driving force.

Health

Malnutrition plays havoc with productive efficiency and resistance to disease. There are thousands of people too poor to eat as much as is necessary, and any teacher can give cases of children coming to school on a breakfast of sugar and water, with no prospect of lunch. But far greater numbers eat enough and are yet malnourished because their diet is unbalanced. There is an abundance of starchy foods, but milk, meat and other fats are so expensive as to be beyond the reach of the working classes, except as Sunday luxuries.

Consequently West Indians are prey to a number of diseases which weaken but do not kill, especially malaria, yaws, hookworm and venereal diseases. These could all be eradicated fairly easily by expenditure on drainage, injections and clinics, by propaganda and by improved nutrition. To the powers that be this presents a vicious circle; they claim that productive efficiency cannot increase until health improves; health cannot improve until more money is spent on medical services; and money cannot be found for medical services until productive efficiency increases. But there is no vicious circle for men of determination.

Social Legislation

There is practically no legislation concerning housing or working conditions, and no unemployment or health insurance. Old age pensions are only just beginning to make their appearance, so are minimum wage machinery and a wholly inadequate system of workmen's compensation, which does not apply to agricultural workers. Truck Acts exist, but there is no one to enforce them, and they are consistently ignored. West Indian Governments have been wholly identified with planter interests, and have hitherto not been much concerned about these matters.

Education

An official Education Commission in 1932 began its report as follows:

> 'An experienced observer of education in several parts of the world, after a recent visit to the West Indies, informed us that, in his opinion, primary education in the West Indies was the least progressive of any which he had encountered in the British Empire. In forming this impression, he had taken specially into account the money which was being spent, facilities for the training of teachers, and contact with modern educational thought. He noted also that the school buildings were the worst which he had ever seen. We, too, have had opportunities of studying education in other parts of the Empire. Our general impressions, as a result of our tour, are not unlike those of the observer whom we have quoted.'

This statement is certainly a gross exaggeration, but it is unfortunate that so much of it should be almost true. There is more primary education in these islands than in any other British colony, and yet the number of children in school is only somewhere between 50% and 70% of the children of school age. In most of the islands there is a compulsory education ordinance, but as there are not enough schools, no attempt is made to enforce it. The result is that more than half the children get some sort of primary education, but as the Report quite rightly points out, it is given in unfortunate conditions.

Conclusion

Professor Macmillan has written two sentences which in a nutshell describe West Indian conditions.[1]

> 'A great many of the people everywhere show independence on a modest competence; but the masses are poor or very poor, with a standard of living reminding one of the native and coloured communities of the Union of South Africa even more than of the peasants of West Africa ... A social and economic study of the West Indies is therefore necessarily a study of poverty.'

This low standard of living is the background of recent political activity and we must keep it in mind.

The Labour Movement

We can now go forward with our main task of examining the reactions of the working classes to these conditions. Even before the Emancipation the slaves rebelled frequently, and throughout the last hundred years there have been isolated strikes, riots, political organisations, and even trade unions. But not until recent years has there been anything that could be called a movement.

We propose to take the year 1935 as our starting point because it is the first year of the more recent series of upheavals. Early in that year there was a general strike of agricultural labourer in St. Kitts, out of which serious trouble developed. It was followed, in February, by a strike in the oilfields of Trinidad and subsequent hunger march, and later in the year by strikes in British Guiana, a serious disturbance in St. Vincent and a coal strike in St. Lucia.

After all this activity 1936 was a fairly quiet year, but there was widespread trouble in 1937. The strikes in Trinidad in June were followed almost immediately by an upheaval in Barbados and by strikes in British Guiana, St. Lucia and Jamaica. This series of protests first brought West Indian conditions to the eye of the British public.

But it was the general strike in Jamaica in the following year, immediately succeeded by further strikes in British Guiana, which really roused the public mind. By that time at least 46 persons had been killed in the course of suppressing these upheavals, 429 injured, and thousands arrested and prosecuted.

What accounts for this sudden burst of activity? Undoubtedly each occasion has had its own special features acting as the immediate spur to activity. But underlying it all have been certain factors common to all the islands.

In the first place it is generally agreed that the specially bad conditions which have ruled in recent years are a major predisposing factor. The prices of the principal West Indian exports were on the average halved between 1928 and 1933, and workers were forced to submit to drastic wage cuts, increased taxation, and unemployment.

A second factor has been the steady drift of unemployed workers from the plantations to the towns. There their numbers have been reinforced by labourers repatriated from Cuba and Santo Domingo. Long unemployment without any dole has made these workers very bitter and militant, and they have sometimes used periods of emergency for looting and demonstrations. The official reports are usually content to describe such people as 'hooligans', but more often than not they are genuinely unemployed workers who have drifted into the towns and have no means of support.

Again, a number of factors have combined to increase the political consciousness of the workers. Foremost is the Italian conquest of Abyssinia. West Indians felt that in that issue the British Government betrayed a nation because it was black, and this has tended to destroy their faith in white government, and to make them more willing to take their fate in their own hands. News of sit-down strikes in France and America was also followed with the greatest interest.

Had there existed constitutional machinery for the redress of grievances, there might well have been no upheavals. But Government and employers have always been hostile to collective bargaining, and the political constitution is deliberately framed to exclude the workers from any control ever the legislature. Consequently the general strike and the riot have been the worker's only weapons for calling attention to his conditions.

In the following pages we shall trace these upheavals island by island, paying particular attention to the trade union and political organisations to which they have given birth.

St. Kitts

This island, which experienced the first of the recent series of explosions, is a tiny member of the Leeward group with a population of less than 20,000. It consists almost wholly of plantations owned by Europeans; there are hardly any peasants; and the general atmosphere is most reactionary. In the twenties and early thirties there was a fairly militant *Representative Government Association* led by some members of the middle classes, but this was mainly concerned with political questions. There have also been a number of working class societies, of which the *Workers' League* and the *Universal Benevolent Association* are the most notable, but they have not had a large membership.

Social conditions in this colony are so much worse than elsewhere that in 1929 a West Indian Commission made them the subject of a special report, but no action was taken on this.

In the year 1935 the beginning of the sugar cane reaping season was set for 28 January, and throughout the preceding weeks labourers were discussing between themselves the necessity for wage increases. Some workers felt that no increase could be expected at the ruling price of sugar, while others thought that an increase was justifiable. However, when the 28th arrived it turned out that the employers did not intend to grant any increase.

The Governor states in his official report that the strike movement was started by some of the unemployed labourers in the capital. A group of these started to march round the island persuading the workers on the plantations to strike for an increase of wages. Their numbers grew steadily; the news flashed round the island, and by next morning there was practically a general strike.

Trouble arose when a crowd invaded an estate to demand higher wages from its proprietor. He fired upon them, wounding three. The crowd determined to beat him up, and when the police arrived they were unable to disperse the people until they had opened fire, killing three and wounding eight. With this the spirit of the strikers was broken. The police arrested large numbers, a warship arrived, and in a few days everyone was back at work — except the many who were consigned to prison on various charges and others whom the employers refused to take back. Wages were not increased.

This sporadic upheaval left hardly any permanent mark. It was not led by any organisation, and with its collapse the workers were left merely with the discouragement of failure.

St. Vincent

Not so in St. Vincent, which exploded later in the year. With the death in the early thirties of the *Representative Government Association,* political conditions in this island of 50,000 had long been fairly quiet, until the October events came to ginger them up.

What precisely happened is still uncertain, as the Government imposed a strict censorship on the press, and no official report was ever published. It appears however that the trouble was due to the decision of the Government to increase the Customs duties. The public was strongly opposed to this measure, and on 21 October while it was being debated in the Legislative Council a crowd demanded to see the Governor and present a petition. The Governor would not yield, and the crowd appears to have got somewhat out of hand, breaking some of the windows of the Chamber. Some of the unemployed started looting, and in the course of the subsequent disturbances 3 were killed and 26 injured. The Governor declared a state of emergency, instituted a strict censorship of the press, and summoned a warship; and in a few days all was quiet. Then began a series of prosecutions culminating in a trial for treason so ridiculous that at the preliminary hearing the magistrate threw out the case without calling on the defence.

The reaction of the general public throughout the West Indies, even as far as Jamaica, was amazement and deep resentment against the repressive measures adopted. In St. Vincent it resulted in the formation of a *Workingman's Association* with a radical programme, in the forefront of which stand land settlement and constitutional reform.

In three short years the Association has become the focus of radical opinion in St. Vincent, and a body of great political influence. It is not registered as a trade union, but represents the workers in all negotiations. It has also attracted wide middle class support, and its candidates were enthusiastically returned at the last General Election. It is one of the new organisations which is changing the orientation of West Indian politics.

St. Lucia

Some 60,000 people live in St. Lucia, and although the principal occupation is wage labour on plantations, there is also an important trade in supplying ships with coal. This trade was at its best in pre-war days, providing employment for large numbers in the neighbourhood of Port Castries, and contributing largely to the colony's revenues, but it has now largely declined owing to the increasing use of oil.

Politically St. Lucia is one of the quietest islands, its *Representative Government Association* having died some years ago. There have been working class societies from time to time, but they have never taken root. The most militant workers have been those engaged in coaling ships, and there is a long record of sporadic strikes among them in the last fifty years.

One such strike occurred at the end of 1935. It was quite free from violence, but the Governor, with the events of St. Vincent on his mind, decided on a demonstration. He mobilised the Volunteer force, summoned a warship, had marines patrolling the streets, and at night played the ship's searchlights upon the town, dazzling the inhabitants and disturbing their sleep. Well accustomed to coal strikes, the peaceful inhabitants of Castries deeply resented this show of force.

On the Governor setting up a committee to investigate the coal trade, the strikers returned to work, and in due course the committee reported, on the basis of evidence taken *in camera* from the firms concerned, that no wage increase was possible. There was much dissatisfaction but the matter rested there.

In August 1937 the agricultural labourers on the sugar plantations struck for higher wages. This most unusual action followed close upon the news of strikes in Trinidad, Barbados, Jamaica and British Guiana, and was largely inspired by it. Again there was no violence, but again the Government was moved to demonstrations of force, this time being severely criticised by its own nominees in the Legislature for what they regarded as the waste of public funds entailed by unnecessary mobilisation. A committee was set up to investigate agricultural wages, and it recommended slight increases subsequently embodied in a minimum wage order.

No new organisation emerged in the succeeding months, but the evidence given before the committee and news of movements elsewhere created a profound impression, especially upon the minds of the younger members of the middle classes. The outcome of all this has been the formation in January 1939 of the first St. Lucian trade union, which proposes to function as a general union of agricultural and urban workers. It is as yet too early to say anything about its progress.

Barbados

This is a tiny island, with a population of over 1,000 per square mile depending for its existence on plantations almost entirely in European hands. Its Government is one of the most reactionary in the West Indies, and though in recent years a number of middle class leaders have appeared, until 1937 they had made little impression on either the Government or the masses.

In March 1937 one Clement Payne arrived in Barbados. He was a friend of Uriah Butler, the man who was later to lead the oilfield workers' strike, and came from Trinidad to urge upon the working classes of Barbados the virtues of organisation. He held a number of meetings and got so good a hearing that the Government looked around for some means of suppressing him.

They found it in the formalities associated with his entry into the colony. Payne was the son of Barbadian parents and had grown up in Barbados, but had been born while his mother was in Trinidad. On entering the colony, however, he had stated that he was born in Barbados, and the police charged him before a magistrate with wilfully making a false statement as to his place of birth. This happened just after the disturbances in Trinidad, and the Barbados masses, already excited by the news from the sister colony, realised at once its purport. Huge crowds followed him to and from the trial, and when on 22 July he was convicted and fined £10, he appealed and announced his intention of leading a procession to the Governor's residence to protest against the conviction. The police refused to let him see the Governor and as he persisted, he and a number of his followers were arrested and an order issued immediately for his deportation to Trinidad.

On 26 July the Court of Appeal quashed his conviction on the ground that having been brought to Barbados very young he might not have known that he was born in Trinidad. Efforts by counsel to have the deportation order rescinded were, however, unsuccessful, and the same day he was deported.

His supporters were furious at this treatment. A large crowd assembled on the wharf where Payne was expected to embark, but the police secretly sent him off from another point. To quote the official report,

> 'when they learnt that Payne was already on board the steamer and that the possibility of preventing his deportation was gone, the passions of the crowd, which had been excited by the events of the day, became uncontrollable. A cornet sounded the assembly and the crowd marched to meetings in the Lower Green and Golden Square where they were again harangued. The mob then spread through the city in bands smashing motor cars and electric street lamps. When the police tried to stop these outrages the mob rained showers of

stones and bottles upon them in a fray in which Sergeant Elias had two fingers fractured and three other police constables received injuries. The police, who were armed only with batons, succeeded with the greatest difficulty in restoring some sort of order; but it is noteworthy that in the face of the considerable disorder and damage to property they were unable to make a single arrest.'

Next morning large crowds again collected and once more began an orgy of smashing shop windows and cars. The disturbances spread quickly. Groups of unemployed commandeered cars and buses and spread the news, and soon the country people were busily engaged in looting the shops and raiding potato fields. To quote again,

> 'The lawless acts committed in the country were more purposive than those committed in Bridgetown; and it would appear that hunger or the fear of hunger coupled with the news of the disturbances in Bridgetown were the chief causes of the outbreaks in the country districts.'

In attempting to restore order the police were forced to fire, killing 14 and wounding 47. Over 400 arrests were made, and many persons imprisoned for sedition, including a young man who was given ten years for a speech which 'tended to raise discontent or disaffection amongst His Majesty's subjects or to promote feelings of ill-will and hostility between different classes of such subjects' by urging workers to organise in trade unions.

These disturbances suddenly opened the eyes of Barbadians of all classes to the existence of poverty in their midst, an impression confirmed by the official Commission who attributed the trouble mainly to unemployment and poverty, and almost for the first time in Barbadian history directed attention to the conditions of the masses. Government, pushed by the Colonial Office, immediately began plans for old age pensions and legislation governing workmen's compensation, trade unions and minimum wage machinery.

Out of the succeeding middle and working class ferment the *Barbados Progressive League* was born in August 1938. Its main purpose is on the one hand to organise trade unions and on the other to run candidates for election in an attempt to force the Government to provide adequate social services, to assist emigration, and to promote land settlement. Led by a prominent lawyer it has attracted widespread middle class sympathy, and is encouraged by the workers' response to hope that it will soon be able to sponsor trade unions for agricultural labourers, shop and clerical assistants, and waterfront workers; but it is handicapped by the continuous fear of victimisation which keeps away many who would otherwise support it. The views of the League are expressed through the *Barbados Observer,* a radical paper of many years standing.

British Guiana

This colony, of which only a coastal strip has so far been developed, consists of a large portion of South America. Nearly half of its population are East Indians brought over as indentured labourers to work on plantations, and their descendants. There is also some Negro agricultural labour, but the bulk of the Negro element is to be found in the towns, in transport, or in the relatively small mining industry, extracting gold, diamonds and aluminium.

In 1919 the *British Guiana Labour Union* was formed, and its membership rose rapidly to 12,000. But with the general decline of economic activity which followed the slump of 1920 the union declined. It never ceased to exist, however, and its Secretary, Mr. Hubert Critchlow, is still active in preaching the virtues of organisation, though with most success among the urban workers.

Until 1932 the East Indian agricultural workers had their interests supervised by an official 'Protector of Immigrants' whose duty it was to enforce the elaborate legislation governing the employment of indentured labourers. This post was, however, abolished in 1932, and though the legislation remains, its enforcement is not very rigorous. Conditions on the plantations have always been very bad, since it has been regarded as axiomatic that the 'coolie' worker has the minimum of needs. Consequently there is a long record of strikes, dating from the nineteenth century.

In September 1935 a further serious outburst of strikes occurred. There was no violence, and the main demand was for increased wages in view of the record crop. The Labour Union was associated with the strikes, though it cannot be said to have organised them. The strikes were spontaneous, widespread and determined, and lasted off and on throughout September and October. A subsequent Commission of Enquiry stressed the need for setting up machinery through which the workers might represent their grievances to their employers.

Towards the end of 1936 the *Manpower and Citizens' Association* was formed, and it was registered as a trade union in September 1937. It has had remarkable success, especially in organising the agricultural workers. East Indian agricultural labourers have proved easier to organise than Negro workers. They have a greater sense of national solidarity, being bound together by their own languages, religions and social customs. The principal leaders of the union are themselves East Indian, and there has been some fear that this may become a cause of friction with Negroes. This, however, is strongly denied by the leaders. They point out that the union is open to all, irrespective of race, and that all their propaganda is on class rather than racial lines. They point out, too, that there are a fair number of Negroes in the union, and that many of them occupy important administrative posts, especially in the country branches where the standard of literacy amongst the East Indians is not very high.

Within two years the Association attained a membership of 10,000, and though it has attracted the bitter hostility of the employers, the Government has been forced to recognise it as the body with which to negotiate in case of dispute.

Since September 1935 there has been a series of further strikes on the plantations. None of these has been called by the union, which exercises all its influence in favour of collective bargaining. Thus in June 1938 when serious and wide-spread strikes occurred in one county, the union advised the workers to return to the plantations, and succeeded by negotiation in securing wage increases for them.[2]

The Association publishes the only labour paper in the colony, the *Guiana Review*, which campaigns for constitutional reform, an eight-hour day, a minimum wage, and reform of the trade union and workmen's compensation laws, the former to allow peaceful picketing and the latter to include agricultural workers. At present it seems likely to capture the bulk of the agricultural workers.

Apart from this Association, there are several other small unions in the colony. Workers engaged in the mining industries (bauxite, diamonds and gold are organised in the *B.G. Miners' Association*. There are also two general unions, the *B.G. Labour Union*, already mentioned, and the *B.G. Workers' League*. Waterfront workers are catered for by the *Seamen's Union*, and Government workers by the *Transport Workers' Union* (railway and inland waterways), the *Post Office Workers' Union*, the *Subordinate Government Workers' Union*, and smaller unions such as the *Medical Subordinates' Union*, the *Hospital Attendants' Union* and the *Government Messengers' Union*. Most of these unions are represented on the *British Guiana Trade Union Assembly*, a coordinating body consisting of members of the Executive Committees of the several unions, which meets fairly often. Thus since July 1938 the transport and postal workers have been negotiating with the Government, and when in December the negotiation appeared to be breaking down, the *Trade Union Assembly* arranged for a general strike of all government employees in its constituent unions. The strike was, however, averted, and the negotiations are still in progress.

The British Guiana Unions are represented on the *B.G. and West India Labour Congress*, a body coordinating labour activities in all the colonies, of which more will be said later.

Trinidad

Trinidad is the only West Indian colony whose exports are not predominantly agricultural. An important extractive and refining oil industry has developed steadily in the southern part of the island since 1908, and today oil accounts for 60% of the value of the island's exports. Nevertheless the number of workers in the industry is relatively small, sugar and cocoa between them employing seven times as many people as oil. From the labour point of view, therefore, Trinidad must be regarded with the other colonies as being predominantly agricultural. A small peasantry has emerged, but the large plantation with its dependence on large supplies of cheap landless labour continues to be the basis of the system.

Working class activity in this colony has a long history. The Trinidad Workingmen's Association was formed in the early nineties of the last century, and its radical programme attracted much attention. It declined, however, after the serious disturbances of 1903 (the 'Water Riots') when the police seized the opportunity of prosecuting some of its most prominent members, and it was not revived until 1919.

Under the leadership of Captain Cipriani, a European born in Trinidad, who had learnt in the war the worth of the 'barefooted West Indian', the Association grew steadily throughout the twenties, and was able in the early thirties to claim a membership of 120,000, out of a total population of 450,000. It never functioned as a union, but devoted its attention to legislative reforms. As an opposition party much of its work consisted in useful amendments to bills proposed by the Government; but it also consistently agitated for proper trade union legislation, factory legislation, social insurance schemes, minimum wage legislation, land settlement, constitutional reform, etc., and was responsible for forcing the Government to introduce workmen's compensation. Of the 26 members of the Legislative Council only seven are elected, but for years the Association has been well represented among the seven. It has also controlled the City Council of Port of Spain for many years, and used its power to improve the working conditions of municipal employees, to initiate slum clearance and other improvements which make Port-of-Spain one of the finest cities in the Caribbean area, and to acquire the tramway system for municipal ownership, after a long legal battle. The Association is affiliated to the British Labour Party, and fraternal delegations have been exchanged. When in 1932 the Government passed trade union legislation which did not permit peaceful picketing or project against actions in tort the Association decided on the advice of the TUC not to register as a union, and changed its name to *The Trinidad Labour Party*.

The weakness of the party was that it had no trade union basis. In 1929 the *Trinidad and Tobago Trade Union Centre* was formed as a rival organisation, and by 1930 had some 2,000 members, mainly engaged in transport. But it was in the South, among the oilfield workers, that the party's influence declined most rapidly, the workers there being prepared for more radical action than the party was capable of leading. The short oilfield strike of February 1935 and succeeding hunger march to Port-of-Spain were engineered by Uriah Butler, a man whom the party had expelled, and when in 1937 workers all over the island were coming out on strike the party was so out of touch that it could neither lead nor restrain.

The events of June 1937, destined to be a landmark in the history of Trinidad, started in the oilfields, and it is perhaps as well to start with a short description of the industry. Most of the twenty-two companies engaged in it are quite small, and in 1936 five companies produced 88% of the total output. The industry is pretty well organised as a monopoly, wages being fixed by the 'Petroleum Association' to which all the principal companies belong.

While some of the smaller companies are not faring very well, the major ones are prospering exceedingly. Profits of four of them in the year 1936-37 amounted to £1,540,000 on a total capitalisation (including all reserves and premiums) of £6,770,000. As the profits of these four companies were more than three times the total sum paid in wages by the whole industry (£473,000) it is not surprising that one company was able to declare a dividend of 30% and

another a dividend of 45%. It has been argued for many years that the income tax is too light at 2/6 in the £, but so powerful are the oil interests and so closely have they the ear of the Government, that no attempt has been made to increase taxation. It is often said that the real rulers of Trinidad are not the Governor or his Legislative Council, but the representatives of the oil industry.

The specific grievances which led to the strike of June 1937 were first the rise in the cost of living, officially estimated at 17%, and secondly the 'Red Book', a system for identifying the workers which they felt was being used to facilitate victimisation.

To focus these grievances came Uriah Butler, already mentioned as organiser of a strike and hunger march in 1935. He formed in August 1936 the *British Empire Workers and Citizens Home Rule Party*. Butler was not a man of great education, and not always wise in his choice of language, but he impressed the Governor with his sincerity, and though practically unknown elsewhere in the island, had a sizeable following on the oilfields.

The strike was no sudden storm. Negotiations had been pending for some time, and according to the official Report the police had expected it on 7 June, almost a fortnight before it actually occurred. On 19 June every single worker on the oilfields laid down his tools, and it is a measure of the general unrest and dissatisfaction in the colony that the oilworkers were soon followed by agricultural workers, and even by some of the workers in Port-of-Spain.

This strike might have remained a peaceful industrial dispute like its predecessors but for an unfortunate incident which turned it into a riot. The turning point occurred when the police attempted to arrest Butler while he was addressing a meeting on the first evening of the strike. The crowd succeeded in routing the police, and thus gave the signal for a general uprising. Responsible opinion in Trinidad has urged that there would have been no uprising if the police had had the sense to wait until Butler had finished his meeting before attempting to arrest him, but tact has never characterised the attitude of West Indian officialdom to labour leaders.

The Governor summoned the Navy from Bermuda, and with its help the disturbances were quelled, but not until 14 had been killed, 59 wounded, and hundreds arrested. The Government appointed a committee to mediate, and by 5 July most of the workers had returned to work. Subsequent history is best described under five heads (1) the oil industry; (2) the sugar industry; (3) urban unions; (4) the Labour Party; and (5) the general situation.

The Oil Industry

On the appointment of the Mediation Committee and the return of the strikers to work events moved fairly quickly. On 10 July the employers announced that the pay of the lowest workers would be increased to a minimum of nine cents per hour (three shillings a day). They also invited the workers to elect delegates for further negotiations. A meeting was held on 14 July at which the employers offered various concessions, notably an all round increase of one penny per hour, a pension scheme, one week's holiday with pay, and the replacement of the Red Book by a different system of identification. The offer was rejected by the delegates as inadequate.

On Sunday, 25 July, the *Oilworkers' Trade Union* was formed, and proceeded immediately to formulate its demands, the most important being an all round increase of threepence per hour and two weeks' holiday with pay. Almost immediately the Governor announced that the Secretary of State for the Colonies had appointed a Commission to investigate the entire situation in Trinidad. Negotiations were therefore suspended pending the arrival of the Commission, which was expected to act as a sort of mediator, and in the meantime the companies' increase of one penny per hour was accepted provisionally, and the Red Book suspended.

The Union set about the task of increasing the membership and has been so successful that it has now over 8,000 members in an industry employing 9,000, and fairly substantial cash reserves. Its power in the oilfields is unquestionable.

When the Commission presented its Report in February 1938 it was found that it had dodged the wage issue. The Union therefore immediately recommenced negotiations, on the basis of the demands put before the Petroleum Association in July. At first the Association refused to discuss the issue at all, but through the intervention of the Government's Industrial Adviser, and in face of the serious threat of strike action, it finally agreed to negotiations, and eventually to arbitration. Accordingly a special arbitration tribunal of five members sailed from England for Trinidad in November, two members being appointed by each side, with an independent chairman appointed by the Government. The tribunal took evidence throughout December, and after brilliant performances by both the union and the employers, failed to agree. The award

was therefore made by the Chairman, using his special powers, and resulted in a victory for the union, which was granted 50% of its demands, i.e., an extra penny per hour beyond the penny already granted in July 1937, instead of the extra twopence which it was claiming. Both sides have agreed to respect this finding for a year.

The Sugar Industry

The leaders of the oilworkers' union also devoted their attention to organising the workers in the sugar industry, the south being also the most important sugar area. The *All-Trinidad Sugar Estates* and *Factory Workers' Union* was founded soon after the oilworkers' union, and started a membership campaign. It was more successful in recruiting sugar factory workers than field workers, though it had a fair following among the latter, especially in the south.

In January 1938 the union formulated its demands, notably an all-round increase of ten cents per day for field workers, and an increase for factory workers of 20% for those earning less than 4/- a day and 15% for those earning more. The companies, through their union, the 'Sugar Manufacturers' Association', rejected these demands, but owing to the intervention of the Industrial Adviser and the threat of strike action a conference was arranged for 31 March 1938. This conference resulted in a deadlock, and was adjourned to consider the possibility of arbitration by the Government.

But the members of the Union's strongest branch, the employees of the largest company, were determined on a test of strength, and forced the leaders to declare a strike. The Union's leaders have been bitterly criticised for calling this strike, but reply that though they realised its inadvisability they could not but associate themselves with it in view of the determination of their strongest branch. The strike was a complete failure. Practically all factory workers went on strike and a considerable proportion of field workers. But the strike was broken by the 'cane farmers'. In Trinidad nearly half the total output of cane is grown by small peasants who own land or rent it from the sugar companies and sell them the cane to grind; these are called 'cane farmers'. When the strike broke out the companies cleverly used such labour as they could get to grind their own canes, leaving the cane farmers' canes to rot. These in turn proceeded to break the strike. Some offered their labour to the factories, while others called upon the union pointing out the hardships they were suffering and demanding that the strike should be called off. Thereupon the workers started returning to work by the end of the first week, and eventually the union fixed 16 April for the termination of the strike.

The consequences of failure were terrible for the union. Hundreds of workers were victimised, and this served only to frighten other workers away from the union. The employers took the line that the strike was a breach of faith in view of pending negotiations, and adopted an attitude tantamount to refusing to recognise the union. It will take much patient work before the union is able once more to gather enough strength to force the reopening of negotiations. A source of strength is its close association with the oilworkers' union, enabling it to bask in the reflected glory of the latter's successes.

Urban Unions
The events of June 1937 produced a great ferment in Port-of-Spain, especially under the leadership of the *Negro Welfare and Cultural Association.* With its more or less Marxist philosophy and purely working class leadership this body was probably the most radical in the island. It had existed for many years, issuing leaflets, organising street meetings and demonstrations, etc., and it seized on the general ferment left by the disturbances to organise new unions. Its project for a domestic servants' union fizzled out after a number of meetings which struck terror into the hearts of Trinidad's housewives, but it met with permanent success in organizing *a Seamen and Waterfront Workers' Union* and a *Public Works Workers' Union.* The former, after a successful strike in July 1937, was recognised by the seafront employers early in 1938; it includes about 30% of the eligible workers. The latter has a membership of 800 amongst employees of the Public Works Department, and has also succeeded in gaining wage concessions.

The leaders of the oilworkers and sugar unions have also founded a *Transport and General Workers' Union,* and a *Federated Workers' Union.* The latter operates mainly among railway and constructional workers; registered in September 1937 it entered into negotiations in January 1938 for shorter railway hours. Other unions are the *Amalgamated Building and Woodworkers' Union,* established in 1936 for building workers, and the *Printers' Industrial Union.*

In 1933 the Trinidad Labour Party founded the *Clerks' Union,* a section for shop assistants and clerical workers, which attained a membership of 500 but, in accordance with the general policy of the party, never

registered as a trade union. Since 1937, however, a rival association, the *Trinidad and Tobago Union of Shop Assistants and Clerks* has been formed, with the intention of registering as a union, and seems likely to supplant the former organisation.

Another branch of the Labour Party which must be mentioned here is the *Shipwrights' Union,* also unregistered, which is particularly notable in that it has started a cooperative section offering to build and repair boats for the public.

The Labour Party
All this trade union activity, proceeding independently of the Labour Party, has tended to cut the ground from under its feet, especially as the TUC has now written reversing its earlier opinion, and commending the formation and registration of unions. There has been a remarkable decline in the influence and activity of the party, and a tendency to forget its long record of service. It is still, however, very strong in Port-of-Spain, where it continues to control the City Council.

The General Situation
Some friction arose in the early days of the new movement through the difference in outlook between the various sections. The leaders of the south are essentially trade unionists; they are not wholly in sympathy with the leaders of the *Negro Welfare Association,* and are themselves regarded with suspicion by the leaders of the Labour Party, who are not quite reconciled to the rise of powerful new organisations outside their control. Fortunately the early mutual suspicion is disappearing, especially as cooperation in the *B.G. and West India Labour Congress* (of which more later) is proving that there is little essential difference of opinion.

Three labour papers are now published regularly in Trinidad, *the Socialist* by the Labour Party, the *Pilot* by the *Seamen and Waterfront Workers' Union,* representing in general the views of the *Negro Welfare and Cultural Association,* and the *People,* an independent paper, giving full publicity to union activities.

Conditions are now fairly quiet. All the unions are busily engaged in increasing and consolidating their membership, and it is conceivable that the success of the oilworkers' union should lead to an increased demand for arbitration proceedings.

Jamaica
Jamaica, with its population of 1,150,000, is the largest of the islands. It is also from the agricultural point of

view the most fortunate; for whereas the other islands depend upon sugar, cocoa, coconuts, citrus or cotton, products whose prices have all been very low, the prosperity of Jamaica is bound up with the banana. In 1937 bananas accounted for 55% of the value of domestic exports while sugar accounted for 18%. Recently banana diseases have been making serious inroads, but the relatively high prices secured have saved the colony from the fate of most of the others. But though as a whole the colony has been able to withstand the effects of the decline in the price of sugar, those large areas dependent upon sugar production have suffered severe depression and unemployment.

Jamaica is fortunate in possessing a relatively large peasant population, estimated variously at between 100,000 and 150,000 holdings. Their conditions are doubtless deplorable; they have not enough land-most holdings are of less than two acres; they have suffered from banana diseases; and the decline of the sugar industry has diminished the demand for their food products. But the existence of such a large peasantry has prevented unemployment and starvation from being as great as it might otherwise have been.

For the last few years there has been growing unrest associated with the decline of the sugar industry and distress amongst the peasantry. Adding to it has been the repatriation of labourers from Cuba, who have tended to remain in the towns, and with minds widened by travel, to be quicker to protest against bad conditions. Kingston has been particularly sensitive to the general unrest, and a Parliamentary reply by the Secretary of State for the Colonies on 9th February 1938, indicates something of this:

> 'There was also a demonstration by unemployed and ex-servicemen at Kingston in Jamaica in August 1937, when it became necessary for the police to disperse the crowd with batons. A number of small strikes also occurred during the year in various parts of the Colony, but as I stated in reply to a question on 1 December, agreement was reached between the employers and the labourers, and increased wages have now been given in the case of the banana labourers who were those principally concerned. There was no disorder.'

Until 1938 trade unionism in Jamaica made little progress, though various attempts were being made to organise labour. A survey in June 1938 revealed that there were then in existence twelve unions, mainly very small organisations on a craft basis. Only two were of any significant size, the *Jamaica Workers' and Tradesmen's Union* and the *Jamaica United Clerks' As-*

sociation. The former claimed to have a membership of 5,000 and was organised so as to embrace every class of labour, but the majority of its members were agricultural labourers and waterfront workers. The *United Clerks' Asso*ciation catered for shop assistants, and was very strong in Kingston.

Alexander Bustamante, who has recently sprung into prominence, was formerly a member of the *Jamaica Workers' and Tradesmen's Union,* but left it in 1937 and in the early months of 1938 conducted a strenuous campaign of meetings throughout the island, and especially in Kingston. Associated with him is William Grant, who had previously been a labour leader on his own. Both men have remarkable speaking powers and have stirred the imagination and won the loyalty of the working classes throughout the island.

In 1938 matters came to a head. One can do no better than quote the official Report:

> 'On 5 January this year a strike, which may be regarded as the forerunner of the recent disturbances, occurred on the sugar estate of 'Serge Island' in (the parish of) St. Thomas. This necessitated the despatch of reserves of Police from Kingston and a number of arrests. It was settled by wage concessions.
>
> On 29 March the Governor announced in the Legislative Council that he had decided to appoint a Commission to enquire into and report upon the rates of wages and conditions of employment of field and day labour in receipt of not more than thirty shillings a week, and the first sitting of this Commission was held in Kingston on 11 April. As a result of representations made by members of the Commission, the Governor gave instructions for acceleration of the programme of the Public Works Department in order to relieve unemployment.
>
> A serious disturbance occurred on 2 May 1938 at Frome in Westmoreland, where a strike, principally affecting labourers constructing a new factory for Messrs. Tate and Lyle (the West Indies Sugar Co.) resulted in a clash between strikers and police, four of the former being killed and nine wounded. This disturbance necessitated the despatch of the greater part of the Kingston police reserve, a part of which was still absent when the disorders under review occurred.
>
> Between 11 and 20 May, a series of small strikes by wharf labourers occurred in Kingston, but these were quickly settled; there was no general demand then for higher wages, the stoppages being due to a variety of causes. During the same period, however, a series of meetings was held in and around Kingston at which speeches of an inflammatory nature were

delivered, and workers of all classes were urged to unite together so as to be in a position to enforce their demands for higher wages. The principal speakers at these meetings were Alexander Bustamante and William Grant.

On 16 May a contractor engaged by the Kingston and St. Andrew Corporation on road construction in the Trench Pen area of St. Andrew attempted to engage labour, but the workers refused to work for him alleging that he cheated them when it came to payment of their wages. Nevertheless, he succeeded in engaging 45 men to begin work the following day. The next morning, however, a large crowd arrived at Trench Pen armed with sticks, pieces of iron, etc., and prevented any work being done. The police arrived on the scene and prevented any violence. In the result the contractor was induced to surrender his contract and the Corporation carried out the work by direct labour. This incident was not without its effect upon the labouring population of Kingston and St. Andrew.'

This then was the chain of events which led up to the explosion of May and June. As we shall see the trouble began with a general strike on the waterfront on the 21st, followed by a general strike of street cleaners on the 23rd, and immediately by an upheaval which spread rapidly throughout the island.

'On Saturday 21 May there was a general strike on the waterfront for higher wages, but a few ships were loaded and unloaded with labour procured from elsewhere; this strike continued without disorder or violence that day and the next. Crowds and strikers loitered on the waterfront until midnight on Sunday and then dispersed peacefully.

On Monday the street cleaners employed by the Kingston and St. Andrew Corporation failed to go to work with the consequence that dust bins filled with refuse remained unemptied in the streets. From an early hour mobs began to collect and parade the streets of Kingston. They rapidly became mischievous. Dust bins were overturned and their contents scattered on the streets; some Chinese shops and bakeries were attacked and goods and money stolen. . .

Between the hours of 6 a.m. and 8 a.m. the Police were able to control the situation by despatching parties of 10 to 20 men to different points where disorder was reported. They succeeded in dispersing mobs without the use of force and without incurring the hostility of the crowd.

However, as time passed the mobs were much increased by men and women who might have gone to work if left to themselves, but who were either intimidated from doing so by the mob or were unable to withstand the attraction of having a day out. They continued to parade the streets and began to threaten shopkeepers with violence unless they closed their shops and released their assistants; as a result all shops in the centre of the city had to close.

Disorder then became general and the police were insufficient in numbers to control the situation. Persons of all classes going to business were set upon, public property was destroyed, streets blocked and tramcars attacked.'

Thereafter disorder ruled for several days, despite the use of soldiers, the navy, and special constables. Moreover it spread rapidly throughout the island, and for the next fortnight soldiers and police were having to be rushed from one part of the island to another to suppress uprisings. It was clear that the unrest was not confined to Kingston; the whole island was seething with discontent. In the course of restoring order 8 persons were killed, 171 wounded, and over 700 arrested and prosecuted.

By about 10 June the island had more or less settled down to normal conditions. There were, however, further flare-ups during the rest of the year, which continued into 1939.

The events of May and June threw two men principally into relief, Bustamante, and Norman Manley, KC, Jamaica's leading barrister. Arrested on 24 May, Bustamante became the hero of Jamaican labour, and after his release on the 28th devoted his energies to restoring order. Manley had not previously been associated with labour, but on the outbreak of the disturbances he came forward and put himself unreservedly at the disposal of the working classes, offering to negotiate on their behalf with Government and the employers. He quickly won the confidence of the masses, and his negotiations played no small part in the settlement of outstanding grievances. In the past few months Bustamante has concentrated on organising trade unions, while Manley has devoted himself to political organisation. After some initial friction, both men now work in close association.

The Bustamante Trade Unions, as they are called, date from July 1938, and already claim a membership of 50,000. The organisation takes the form of one general union with a central executive and seven divisions. The divisions are Transport, General Workers, Maritime Workers (including seamen and dockers), Municipal Workers (including workers employed by Government or municipal bodies on road or other constructional work), Factory Workers, Artisans of every description, and Commercial Clerks (including clerical workers but not shop assistants). It is expected that a new division will soon be formed for Hotel Employees. Bustamante is President of the whole organisation, and it is believed that the constitution reserves wide powers to him, including the right of declaring strikes. The Central Executive consists of the President, the General Secretary of the whole Organisation, and the Vice-Presidents, who are the heads of the seven divisions.

The division of General Workers has the largest membership, and includes agricultural labour. The most completely organised division is that of the Maritime Workers, which must include well over 90% of the dock workers and seamen in the colony.

As is to be expected of a movement in its infancy, the unions are faced with difficult problems of organisation and discipline. Unauthorised strikes occur frequently, and in many cases the union heads are placed in a position of great difficulty because the strike may be about some very trivial matter or about some issue on which the leaders find themselves unable to support the men's contentions. This has thrown a great strain on the time and energies of officers, who have more than enough to do at present in trying to cope with the job of organisation. At the moment hardly anyone but Bustamante himself has any influence over the workers, and as we have seen his constitutional powers are very wide. As with Trinidad, however, where there was exactly the same sort of situation in the months immediately following the disturbances of June 1937, the passage of time, education in trade unionism, and experience, will bring home to the workers the need for union discipline and the true nature of trade union functions.

In September 1938 Manley launched the *People's National Party* at a meeting at which Sir Stafford Cripps was present. The party has had an enthusiastic reception, and proposes to affiliate with the trade unions. Its programme is Labour — land settlement, adult suffrage, social legislation, etc. The past few months have been spent in enrolling thousands of new members all over the island and there is no doubt that its formation has profoundly altered the structure of Jamaican politics.[3]

Summary

It is now possible to ask what has emerged from these years of working class upheaval, with their tale of strike and riot, death and victimisation. Two things: the rise of trade unions, and the entry of the working classes into West Indian politics.

Trade Unionism

As we have seen, new unions have sprung up in the bigger colonies for all the principal types of labour, while in the smaller colonies there are either new unions, or other organisations which though not registered as unions, perform the same sort of function. The sections which have proved easiest to organise have been oilfield workers, and people engaged on the waterfront, in inland transport, on public works, and in shops. In most areas their unions have already secured important wage concessions. Agricultural workers, however, have proved exceedingly difficult to organise, and it is only in British Guiana, where special circumstances prevail, that there can be said to be a flourishing agricultural union.

The legal obstacles to the growth of trade unionism have frequently been pointed out. The unions have not the right of peaceful picketing or protection against actions in tort, two rights conferred in Great Britain by the Act of 1906. The Government of Trinidad has also on more than one occasion exercised its right of withholding registration from unions of which it disapproves. But it is not so much legal obstacles which have restrained the growth of trade unionism as the attitude of the Government and employers. The Secretary of State for the Colonies has announced his desire to foster the growth of trade unionism and collective bargaining, and has appointed Labour Advisers in each colony to assist in bringing unions and employers together. But the colonial administrations have not yet rid themselves of the notion that trade unionism is treasonable. Union leaders are in some places continuously shadowed by the police, and the mildest utterance may provoke a prosecution for sedition. The Government of Trinidad has frequently exercised its right of prohibiting street processions in order to prevent labour demonstrations from taking place. Again, trade unionists are often prohibited from travelling from one colony to another on temporary fraternal visits. This is not the sort of atmosphere in which the object to which the Secretary of State has committed himself is likely to be achieved.

As for the employers, in general they detest the unions and their leaders. They withhold recognition as long as possible, and only the threat of strike action is able to wring concessions from them. The Labour Advisers are supposed to be of assistance in this connection, but whether because of their own lack of interest, or the obstinacy of the employers, the general rule is that they are never successful unless the union is already sufficiently powerful to be able to threaten the employers with strike action. The employers' principal weapon in fighting the unions is victimisation, and they use it mercilessly. In a small community where everybody knows what everybody else is doing and saying, it is easy for employers to keep each other informed of the names of 'troublesome' workers. Many discharged workers have found themselves not only unable to get work with any other employer, but also forced to give up at short notice the house or land which they may have been renting. It is this easy victimisation which is the main obstacle to the growth of the unions.

In view of all this it is surprising that the unions have met with such response from the workers. Indeed in many of the newer unions the leaders are faced with the problem that their members, with a bitter sense of generations of injustice, are over-militant, and anxious to strike on the flimsiest pretext. In the absence of trade union traditions it is a slow and difficult task to inculcate the subtleties of trade union strategy, and it will take some time before the workers have grasped the nature of trade union functions and methods, and grown to accept trade union discipline. That is why some leaders are tending to discourage strike action at present, and devoting themselves to consolidating and instructing their membership. In the task of education they are helped by the labour press which has been started in the larger colonies, by issuing pamphlets, and by regular meetings. There is also a great demand for literature on trade unionism, and any person or organisation in Great Britain who desired to help the movement would probably serve it best by sending out such literature, and by endowing club rooms where libraries may be kept and where workers may gather after work for social intercourse and for educational meetings.

As for the leaders, it must be admitted that one or two are irresponsible extremists brought into prominence by their genius for agitation in a period of unrest and upheaval. But such men are a tiny minority. Indeed one interesting feature of the last few years has been the way in which the agitator who led a major upheaval has given way after the upheaval to sober responsible men who set themselves the task of building up trade unions. The vast majority of the new leaders are extraordinarily capable and intelligent; a few are lawyers or other members of the educated middle classes, but most of them are just workers with a genius for organisation and a capacity for sacrifice.

They are very conscious of their responsibility, and though the difficulties in their path are many, they are confident of eventual success.

Politics

Important as have been the results on the trade union front, on the political front nothing short of a revolution has occurred. It is not merely that the British Government has been forced to appoint a strong Royal Commission specifically to investigate social conditions. Nor is it even the fact that Governments have already been forced to adopt all sorts of measures to meet the grievances of the workers — land settlement, fixing minimum wages, expenditure on public works and slum clearance, old age pensions, enactment of workmen's compensation, etc. This is indeed a revolution, for hitherto West Indian Governments have not regarded measures of this sort as of primary importance. But even more important than all this is the fact that the working classes have become organised politically, and that their interests have been forced into the foreground.

To understand the full significance of this revolution, we must take a glance at the history of West Indian politics. In our introductory chapter we described the political attitude of the educated coloured elements, pointing out that while some sought to identify themselves with the ruling oligarchy others rebelled and sought through political action to secure for the Negro a higher status in society. This has always been true of West Indian politics; even before the emancipation of slavery the free coloured people were in constant conflict with the plantocracy, and throughout the nineteenth century that conflict continued. It came to a head after the Great War with the formation of *Representative Government Associations* throughout the Lesser Antilles. These associations were narrowly middle class in their aims; they wished particularly to see more middle class representation on the legislative councils, and to increase the number of posts in the civil service to which educated Negroes might be appointed. Mass support was easily obtainable for such liberal ends, the urban workers willingly associating themselves in meetings, demonstrations and petitions with the demand for constitutional reform and racial equality in the civil service. But there was hardly anything in the programmes of these associations of direct working class interest, only the associations of Trinidad and Grenada (significantly *called Workingmen's Associations)* including in their programmes such things as slum clearance and workmen's compensation.

Agitation for constitutional reform was intense just after the war, and as a result the Colonial Office sent Major Wood (now Lord Halifax) to visit the colonies in 1921. His recommendations were followed by constitutional changes in Trinidad, the Windward Islands and Dominica in 1924, providing for the election of a minority of middle class members to the Legislative Councils on a very restricted franchise. This was a victory for the movement, but it was felt that the numbers to be elected were far too small, and agitation continued. At the same time the Associations became convinced that the colonies could not achieve much if they acted separately, and federation sprang to the forefront of their programmes.

This further agitation led the Colonial Office to appoint in 1932 a commission to consider the possibility of closer union between Trinidad and the Windward and Leeward Islands. So soon as the announcement was made representatives from these colonies and one from Barbados met in conference at Dominica in November 1932.

The main task which the Dominica Conference set itself was the elaboration of a West Indian constitution, on the two major foundations of federation and full elective control. All went well until the question of the franchise was raised, the representative of Trinidad leading the demand for adult suffrage. On this there was no agreement, and eventually the conference adopted a compromise solution permitting each colony within the federation to settle its own franchise qualifications. It was clear that many of the leaders of West Indian politics were unsympathetic to the aspirations of the working classes.

The real significance of the revolution of 1935-38 is that such narrow political thought has faded into insignificance. The major issues discussed today no longer revolve round the aspirations of the middle classes, but are set by working class demands. Federation and elective control are still in the forefront, but they are now desired in the interest of the masses, and side by side with them are new issues — industrial legislation, slum clearance, social services, land settlement, extension of the franchise and others — which were seldom discussed before. Initiative has passed into the hands of trade union leaders and new working class bodies like the *Progressive League* of Barbados, the *Workingmen's Association* of St. Vincent, and the *People's National Party* of Jamaica. These also have much middle class support, and many have strong middle class leadership, but their programmes are much wider than their predecessors.

Focusing all this new spirit is the *British Guiana and West India Labour Congress,* newly established as a clearing house for labour opinion. Its inaugural meeting was held in British Guiana in June 1938, and was attended by delegates of trade unions and labour organisations from British Guiana, Dutch Guiana, Trinidad, Barbados and Jamaica. The first meeting merely set up machinery and expressed solidarity, but on the announcement of the appointment of a Royal Commission a second meeting was summoned for November 1938 in Trinidad, and delegates invited from labour organisations in every colony.

It is a far cry from the Dominican Conference of 1932 to the Trinidad Congress of 1938. As will be seen from the Report quoted in the Appendix, federation and full elective control figured prominently in the resolutions, but even more attention was devoted to the demands for adult suffrage, dismemberment of plantations and creation of a cooperative peasant community, nationalisation of the sugar factories and public utilities, provision of old age pensions, health and unemployment insurance, and reformed industrial legislation. This was essentially a Labour Congress. It is mainly on the development of this united labour movement that future progress in the West Indies depends.

Notes

*　1/3 and 2/- are equivalent to 6p & 10p UK respectively today. The equivalents in the Caribbean currency of the time would have been 30 cents and 48 cents.

1　*Warning from the West Indies,* p. 44 (Penguin Edition).
2　On 2 March 1999 the employers' association signed an agreement with the union recognising it for purposes of collective bargaining, giving it the right to negotiate in any case of dispute, and to hold meetings on the plantations.
3　Since the above paragraphs were written, there have been important developments. Friction between the Bustamante unions and the older *Jamaica Workers' and Tradesmen's Union* led Mr. Bustamante early in February 1939 to declare a general strike. This action was very unpopular; the Governor declared a state of emergency; and after much high feeling the strike was eventually called off.

As a result of the general situation produced by Mr. Bustamante's action, Mr Manley, after consultation with him and with the Governor, announced the formation on 22 February of a small 'Industrial Advisory Council' to advise the trade union movement. Its members are prominent in the People's National Party, and are mainly of professional and middle class status.

The Council's first action was to take steps to heal differences between conflicting unions. On 25 February the *Jamaica Trades Union Council* was formed, and it has been successful in bringing the principal unions together. Its first meeting was attended by representatives of the Bustamante unions, the *Workers' and Tradesmen's Union,* the *Montego Bay Clerks' Association,* the *Builders' and Allied Trades' Union,* and the *Jamaica United Clerks' Association.* A constitution was adopted giving the *TUC* important advisory powers.

It is expected that the Council will soon urge that the constitutions of the Bustamante unions should be revised so as to make them more democratic, in view of continuous complaints of the autocratic position of the President.

Suggestions for further reading

Bolland, O. Nigel, *On the March: Labour Rebellions in the British Caribbean, 1934-1939* (Kingston: Ian Randle Publishers, 1995).

Bolland, O. Nigel, *The Politics of Labour in the British Caribbean* (Kingston: Ian Randle Publishers, 2001).

Craig, Susan, *Smiles and Blood: The Ruling Class Response to the Workers Rebellion in Trinidad and Tobago* (London: New Beacon Books, 1988).

Lewis, Arthur, 'The 1930s Social Revolution', in Beckles and Shepherd, eds., *Caribbean Freedom: Economy and Society from Emancipation to the Present*, pp. 376-92.

Lewis, Gordon K., *The Growth of the Modern West Indies* (London: Monthly Review Press, 1968).

Post, Ken, *Strike the Iron: A Colony at War, Jamaica 1939-1945*, vols. 1 and 2 (New Jersey: Humanities Press Inc., 1981).

Ryan, Selwyn, *Race and Nationalism in Trinidad and Tobago: A Study of Decolonisation in a Multiracial Society* (Toronto: Toronto University Press, 1972).

Report of the Commission to Enquire into the Disturbances (The Deane Commission Report, 1937).

Report of the West Indies Royal Commission, 1938-1939 (The Royal Commission Report).

Notes

1. Gordon K. Lewis, *The Growth of the Modern West Indies*, p. 397.
2. See Ken Post, *Strike the Iron: A Colony at War Jamaica 1939-1945*, 2 vols. (New Jersey: Humanities Press Inc., 1981).
3. Post, *Strike the Iron*, p.85.
4. Lewis, *The Growth of the Modern West Indies*.
5. Lewis, *The Growth of the Modern West Indies*, pp. 179-80.
6. See the report of the Commission appointed to enquire into the disturbances which took place in Barbados on July 27, 1937 and subsequent days (The Deane Commission Report).
7. Quoted in Susan Craig, *Smiles and Blood: The Ruling Class Response to the Workers Rebellion in Trinidad and Tobago* (London: New Beacon Books, 1988) p. 21.
8. Craig, *Smiles and Blood*, p. 21.
9. Arthur Lewis, *Labour in the West Indies: The Birth of Workers Movement*, (London: New Beacon Books, 1977) for a general discussion on social conditions in the West Indies in the 1930s.
10. John Jagger, a member of the 1938-1939 Arbitration Tribunal quoted by Craig, *Smiles and Blood*, p. 21.
11. Craig, *Smiles and Blood*, p. 21.
12. Craig, *Smiles and Blood*, p. 22.
13. See *The Royal Commission Report*, (The Moyne Commission) pp.177-8.
14. In chapter one, I discussed the nature of political participation under colonial government.
15. Selwyn Ryan, *Race and Nationalism in Trinidad and Tobago: A Study of Decolonisation in a Multiracial Society* (Toronto: University of Toronto Press, 1972) chapter 3.
16. Arthur Lewis, 'The 1930s Social Revolution', in Beckles and Shepherd, eds., *Caribbean Freedom: Economy and Society from Emancipation to the Present* (Kingston: Ian Randle Publishers, 1993) p. 376.
17. Ryan, *Race and Nationalism*, chapter 3.
18. The Report of the West India Royal Commission (The Moyne Commission), (London: His Majesty's Stationary Office, 1945) p. 11.
19. The Report of the West India Royal Commission, p. 12.
20. The Report of the West India Royal Commission, p. 243.
21. George Belle, 'The Struggle for Political Democracy in Barbados: The 1937 Riots', in Woodville Marshall, ed., *Emancipation II* (Bridgetown: University of the West Indies, 1988).
22. Ryan, *Race and Nationalism*, p. 56.
23. See *The Moyne Commission Report*.
24. Post, *Strike the Iron*, pp. 90-3.
25. Lewis, *The Growth of the Modern West Indies*, p. 181.
26. See Post, *Strike the Iron* and Lewis, *Labour in the West Indies*.
27. Lewis, *The Growth of the Modern West Indies*.
28. Denis Benn, *The Growth and Development of Political Ideas in the Caribbean* (Kingston: University of the West Indies, 1987) p. 51.
29. Belle, 'The Struggle for Political Democracy in Barbados', p. 87.
30. Craig, *Smiles and Blood*.
31. See Appendix 2.
32. Post, *Strike the Iron*
33. Post, *Strike the Iron*, see p. 124.
34. Post, *Strike the Iron*, see chapter vi.
35. Post, *Strike the Iron*, see p. 134.
36. Post, *Strike the Iron*, see p. 134.
37. Ryan, *Race and Nationalism*.
38. See George Belle, 'After 1937: The Politics of Wynter Crawford: "Institutionalising Labour and the Demise of Planter Government"', in the readings which accompany this chapter.

three

The Politics of Constitutional Decolonisation and the Westminster Model

Introduction

In political science, public participation in the decision-making process is considered to be an important indication of political development and a basic requirement of democracy. If it is to be accepted that public participation is a basic prerequisite for democracy to exist, then on the eve of independence, notwithstanding the existence of universal adult suffrage since 1951, Commonwealth Caribbean countries were for all intents and purposes both politically undeveloped and lacking in meaningful democracy.

The basis of this argument stems from the fact that the drafting and ratifying of the various independence constitutions, was marked by the absence of participation by all sectors of civil society. This has led Ann Spackman to describe Caribbean constitutions as mere Orders in Council of the British government.[1] While Commonwealth Caribbean constitutions have been severely criticised, it is important to note that the supreme law of the land that defines our political systems enjoys great legitimacy. Such legitimacy is reflected in the fact that political systems are generally acceptable and that Commonwealth Caribbean countries with few exceptions (Grenada in 1979, Trinidad and Tobago 1970 and between the 1990s and 2002), experience basic stability in their political affairs. This general stability differentiates them from other parts of the developing world. This chapter will focus on: the assumptions of democracy and liberal democracy; the process of drafting and ratifying West Indian independence constitutions; the Westminster model in the region and basic modifications of West Indian Independence constitutions.

Democracy

Joseph Schumpeter defined democracy as a system 'for arriving at political decisions in which individuals acquire the power to decide by means of a competitive struggle for the people's vote'.[2]

Robert A. Dahl contends that while in practice democracy has always fallen short of its ideals and suffers from many defeats, 'In spite of all its flaws, however, we must never lose sight of the benefits that make democracy more desirable than any feasible alternative to it. . .'[3]

For democracy to exist ten conditions must generally be satisfied:

(i) elected officials control the state and make key decisions

(ii) constitutionally elected officials are accountable to the people

(iii) the existence of constitutional, legal and practical constraints on executive power by the presence of independent institutions, such as the judiciary, parliament and other mechanisms of horizontal accountability. This refers to the notion of the separation of power, which liberal philosophers contend would limit arbitrary control, and the development and persistence of 'cruel and vicious autocrats'

(iv) the legal right of groups of people to form a political party and to contest elections. In effect, good governance demands that government not only be freely elected but that elected officials will be subjected to periodic review by the electorate. This infers that they can be replaced through free and fair elections

(v) the freedom of citizens, with different loyalties to have access to multiple channels for expression and representation of their interests. This includes different and competing independent associations and movements. Democracy therefore guarantees persons in civil society the maximum opportunity to protect their interests and freedoms

(vi) a guarantee to civil society of several fundamental rights that are absent in non-democratic political systems. Citizens have substantial freedom of belief, opinion, speech, publication, assembly, demonstration and petition. These freedoms in combination with the above are critical as they make electoral competition and political participation meaningful

(vii) individual and group liberties which are laid out under a constitution (written or unwritten) and which are effectively protected by an independent, non-discriminatory judiciary

(viii) the rule of law which protects citizens from unjustified detention, exile, terror, torture, and undue interference in their personal lives. In a democratic state, when infringements on individual freedom occurs, the impartial judiciary can adjudicate such matters.

(ix) the existence of alternative sources of information, including an independent media to which citizens have unrestricted access. A relatively unrestricted press is a major defining condition of a democracy and any attempt to stifle or fetter such freedom amounts to political censorship. The mass media in the Caribbean has been subjected to repeated and blatant attempts to muzzle its activity. While almost every single Commonwealth Caribbean country is guilty of some form of muzzling, events in St Lucia in the late 1990s under the United Workers Party (UWP) administration, Grenada before and during the period 1979–1983, Guyana, Antigua and Barbuda and Trinidad and Tobago, bear testimony to the attempted erosion of this vital democratic institution

Of interest is the *Green Paper on Media Law* in Trinidad and Tobago which provided for:
The introduction of a comprehensive press and broadcasting Act which sought to redefine the law of libel, defamation, contempt of parliament or of court and refusal to disclose sources of information. The Act also sought to give power to the government to punish or stop media behaviour that imperils national security or undermine its democratic fabric.
Journals and newspapers to avoid publication of reports which tend to promote tensions likely to lead to civil disorder, meeting or rebellion. They are required to support only articles which would promote national unity and economic and social progress; promote responsible journalism, police the press and become an organ of government.

(x) the subordination of the military and the police to constitutionally elected civilian officials.

Liberal political theorists also contend that democracy is the only system of government that can foster a high degree of political stability and equality. Moreover, they view the economic performance of democratic governments as superior to that of countries with non-democratic governments.[4] For Dahl, these advantages make democracy 'a better gamble than any attainable alternative to it.'[5]

Proponents of democracy claim that it causes equity and enhances reform and that other advantages of democracy include political freedom and political equality. In their view, such democratic features provide a favourable environment for the poor, in which they are able to advance their political and economic interests through collective action. To prevent such mass mobilisation which could provide the fillip for political instability, elected officials will enact measures aimed at reducing inequality and poverty. On the question of economic performance of democratic governments, critics claim that democratic governments have a poor record of achieving equality. This is particularly pertinent to countries that attempted to make the democratic transition and consolidation in the second half of the twentieth century. Using Latin America as a case in point, critics point to the growing concentration of economic resources as well as the coexistence of widespread and acute poverty with representative democracy. In Brazil for instance, between 1960 and 1990 (for the period 1964 and 1985, Brazil had a military authoritarian political regime but achieved remarkable economic transformation, leading most observers to describe its economic successes as an economic miracle), the share of the poorest 50 per cent of the population of national income declined from 17.7 per cent to 15 per cent in 1970, 14.2 per cent in 1980 and to 10.4 per cent in 1990. It was during the democratic transition in Brazil that the socio-economic position of the poorest 50 per cent of the population underwent its most dramatic decline.[6] Thus, the period associated with democratic developments in Latin America realised major redistribution problems; not only was there more inequality but it increasingly took on different dimensions. Thus to critics (specifically of liberal democracy), democracy is incomplete without equity enhancing mechanisms.

Main assumptions of liberal democracy

According to S.E. Finer, many presuppositions or basic assumptions underlie liberal democracy.[7] For him, liberal democracy, which in a very real sense is a qualified democracy, is identified by the following characteristics:

1. Government which is not only derived from public opinion, but is accountable to it. In effect, liberal democracy infers not only a government chosen by the people in an electoral system marked by fairness and freedom, but one which allows for opportunities by which government must continue to test its legitimacy.

2. A majority rule, but one which permits opportunities by which the minority opinion can become the majority.

3. Limited government, that is, the authority of government is limited and there is no muzzling of interest groups by the state.

4. Liberal democratic states are pluralist in nature, that is, the existence of a variety of groups which operate without unnecessary governmental interference, but must do so within the legal framework of the state. Moreover, government under this political system is supposed to legislate in the interest of all groups. The assumption is that government sets out to rule, not in the interest of any one group, but in the common interest of all groups.

With respect to this critical assumption of liberal democratic theory, Ralph Miliband, Michael Parenti and G. William Domhoff, among others, have concluded that this assumption is extremely flawed.[8] Pluralists argue that power in liberal democratic societies is competitive, fragmented and diffused; everybody, directly or through organised interests, has some power and nobody has or can have too much power. Accordingly, in liberal democratic societies, citizens enjoy universal suffrage, free and regular elections, representative institutions, effective citizens' rights, an independent judiciary and a free political culture. Given this central claim of liberal democracy, the view is that no government acting on behalf of the state can fail in the long-run to respond to the wishes and demands of competing interest. As the state is subjected to a multitude of conflicting pressures from organised groups and interests, it cannot show any marked bias towards some and against others.

Marxist political analysis, however, rejects this view. It contends that the state is a special institution whose main role is to protect the interest of the dominant economic group in society. Ownership of economic resources in this view gives political power to the owning class, which is used to manipulate and control the state as its instrument for the domination of society. Lenin saw the state in capitalist societies as the instrument of the ruling class used to carry out the agendas of that class in society.

Ralph Miliband therefore refutes the dominant pluralist view of the state and contends that:

> ...In the light of the strategic positions which capitalist enterprise enjoys in its dealings with Governments, simply by virtue of its control of economic resources, the notion, which is basic to pluralist theory, that here is but one of the many 'veto groups' in capitalist society on a par with other 'veto groups', must appear as a resolute escape from reality.[9]

Michael Parenti points out that given the institutional, financial and social ties which link government and business in society, the primary focus should be on not only who governs, but rather, it should focus on whose interests and agendas are served by those who govern. A policy output assessment can illuminate this. Parenti concludes that:

> ...Those who control the wealth...have an influence over its political life far in excess of their numbers...The owning class has the power to influence policy decisions through the control of jobs and the withholding of investments. In addition...the capitalists use some portion of their vast wealth to finance or exercise trusteeship over social and educational institutions, foundations, think tanks, publications, and mass media, thereby greatly influencing society's ideological output, its values and its information flow.[10]

Nevertheless the preconditions or assumptions of liberal democracy have given effect to three major characteristics of liberal democratic societies. These are:

- Representative organs – which must be elected under set conditions.
- An executive body which undertakes the task of implementing decisions reached by government and advising policy-makers on policy.
- Systems of social and economic checks and balances which are effected through the 'separation of powers', with government being organised into three branches, namely the judiciary, the executive and the legislature. Theoretically, the notion of the separation of powers is marked by the division of power. This is to ensure that there is an effective separation of power, that is to say that membership varies and none of the three branches should in any form be united under the same man or body of men, with none of the branches being able to coerce or override each other.

Britain and the Commonwealth Caribbean territories adopted a weak version of this model. Under the Westminster model, power is fused not divided, though the judiciary is not marked by the fusion which characterises the legislative and executive arms of government.

Participation or imposition?

Samuel P. Huntington has identified three main waves of democratisation,[11] namely:

1. The first long wave of democratisation, 1828–1926.
2. The second short wave of democratisation, 1943–1962 .
3. The third wave of democratisation, 1974–1990s.

In between, there were two reverse waves of democratisation, the first between 1922–1942 and the second between 1958–1975

During the closing years of the second short wave of democratisation and the beginning of the second reverse wave of democracy, the first group of British West Indian colonies were granted constitutional independence. While the global swing away from democratisation during the second reverse wave was particularly acute in Latin America, Asia and Africa, several Caribbean countries achieved constitutional independence and began the process of consolidating democracy.[12] The process began with Trinidad and Tobago and Jamaica in August 1962, followed by Guyana and Barbados in 1966 and several Eastern Caribbean countries in the 1970s and early 1980s. By the mid-1980s only Montserrat, the British Virgin Islands, Anguilla, the Cayman Islands and the Turks and Caicos Islands survived the third wave of democratisation.

G.K. Lewis argues that constitutional independence merely represented a redefinition of the legal status of society without bringing in its wake a profound social metamorphosis. Lewis further contends that independence terminated the official political control of the former colonies, which had been given expression through the appointment of a Colonial Secretary based in London. For Lewis:

> ...Independence puts an end at least to that particular absurdity in a society that has been full of absurdities, of ossified institutions existing like so many Egyptian-style mummies in the hospitable colonial climate of opinion...[13]

Nonetheless two important features of the politics of constitutional decolonisation left their indelible mark on Commonwealth Caribbean countries. A notable feature of the independence constitutions of Commonwealth Caribbean countries is the extensive input of British civil servants, which resulted in an unquestionable acceptance of the Westminster model as appropriate for the region. In effect, Caribbean independence constitutions were partly borrowed, and partly written by British civil servants. Secondly the process of drafting the constitution itself was severely limited in the narrowness of the representative interest which composed the constitution committees. Trevor Munroe has shown that in the case of Jamaica, of the two committees which were established (the Upper and Lower House), both were representative only in the most formalistic sense, as their social base and their political origin reflected little mass or public support. The narrowness and thereby the interest of the constitution drafters is thus explicit. In commenting on the composition of the independence committee Munroe asserts that:

> . . .Whereas ordinary law was debated in public, the fundamental law was drafted by a few men in secret conclave, presented to parliament and passed as the basic law of the land.[14]

In Trinidad and Tobago, the independence constitution was largely the work of one man – Sir Ellis Clarke.

The exclusion of many sectors from the drafting committee was exacerbated by the speed with which the constitutions were drafted. In Jamaica's case Norman Manley was prepared to give the public only two weeks to respond, via memoranda, to the committee. The people of Trinidad and Tobago were given six weeks, while Errol Barrow, in keeping with his counterpart in Jamaica, who had vehemently stated that the independence committee of which he was Chairman, did not 'have much time to fool around',[15] categorically stated that '. . .I do not propose to discuss or debate this for a period of four weeks'.[16]

The quality and the lack of participation in the drafting of West Indian constitutions are also reflected in the fact that several opposition political parties boycotted discussions on the draft constitutions. In St Lucia for example, the opposition St Lucia Labour Party (SLP) held the view that independence should be preceded by a referendum or early elections as they claimed that the UWP government had mishandled domestic political matters. While the UWP countered in its white paper that independence had always been on its political agenda, thereby rendering a referendum and early elections unnecessary, the SLP's position was legitimate, given the spate of civil unrest in the country on the eve of independence. This in-

cluded the bombing of some public sector establishments, political protest against the British government in early 1979 and a strike against the government by the Teachers and Civil Service Association for pay increases.

The circumstances under which Caribbean independence constitutions were drafted and ratified, make questionable their indigenous nature. And it is important to note that the elitist nature of the process lends itself to the criticism that, despite the psychological importance of the independence 'grant' from Britain, the democratic principles exhibited by Commonwealth Caribbean constitutions emerged out of an undemocratic process controlled by imperialist influences.

Constitutional decolonisation in the Commonwealth Caribbean

The process of constitutional decolonisation must be distinguished from true or full decolonisation. In the main, it is argued that a process of false decolonisation characterised the constitutional progression of the British West Indies from colony to nationhood. This position is based largely on the grounds that there were no genuine attempts to formalise a political system different to that of the former colonial master. Undoubtedly, notions of false decolonisation also pervade the existing literature on Caribbean political systems because the model of economic development pursued in the region served to reinforce the traditional dependency of the region.

The process of constitutional decolonisation involves the transfer of control over the domestic political systems to the nationalist leaders. As such, it refers to the relinquishing of power and control over the dominated state's constitution by the imperial or the dominant state.

The Westminster model in the region

K.C. Wheare defines a constitution in two ways. In a wide sense, the word constitution describes the collection of rules, which establish and regulate government.[17] In a narrower sense, the word constitution denotes the selection of legal rules which regulate the government of a country. Thus, constitutions can be either written or unwritten. An unwritten constitution comprises well established institutions and practices. Only three older democracies, namely Britain, Israel and New Zealand have unwritten constitutions.

Unlike the American political system, the Westminster model is defined by the fusion of power and the nature of its differentiated bicameral legislature. In contrast to the separation of the legislative and executive arms of government, which is found in the American political system, the Westminster model combines these powers in one body. This is regarded as a 'striking denial of the idea of the separation of power'.[18] In effect then, the executive arm of government led by the prime minister who presides over his cabinet of ministers, exercises executive power while simultaneously commanding legislative power. The cabinet or the executive arm of government is dependent on the confidence of the legislative arm of government. The model is also marked by the notion of collective responsibility, which means that every member of the cabinet must accept and if necessary defend the decisions of government, unless he or she chooses to resign.

Under the political arrangements of the Westminster system, the prime minister has extensive power. Among these powers are the appointment and dismissal of ministers, and the dissolution of parliament and the calling of an election. These powers give the prime minister tremendous opportunity for influencing and controlling the decisions of government. It is these opportunities for controlling and influencing the collective and individual decisions of his colleagues that have contributed to the notion of 'prime ministerial government'.

Commonwealth Caribbean constitutions have produced a political system that comprises all the main features of the British constitution as well as a system in which the head of state is not the effective head of government.

However, the independence constitutions did witness minor modifications in their transfer to the West Indies. Among these were:

1. A written constitution whose most important provisions can only be altered by a special procedure. This refers to the entrenchment provision.
2. Provision for judicial review. The judiciary under the constitution has the sole authority to decide the constitutionality of legislation passed by parliament. Judicial review is therefore a means of exercising restraint to the legislature and is a standard practice of democratic countries.
3. A written constitution giving minority groups reassurances which are not expressly given in the British system.
4. Provision for the appointment of an ombudsman. However, in some countries the ombudsman is not a constitutional feature and is very often a post-independence development.

Because the political order which has emerged in Commonwealth Caribbean countries has its origin in the British Westminster system, it has all and more of the defects which are apparent in the British system. The essential feature of the model is majority rule, leading to its descriptive label, the majoritarian system.

Modifications or transformation?

Many changes have taken place in the Commonwealth Caribbean constitutions. Some of these changes were designed to augment the rights of citizens, but several have increased executive power at the expense of the governed, as in the case of the 1980 constitutional change in Guyana,[19] which provided for a presidential executive system. However, while the power of the new presidential executive was increased under the new arrangement, the essential parliamentary nature of the system remained unchanged. Under the new arrangement, the political accountability of the president to the national assembly is virtually removed. Under article 89 of the new constitution, he can veto all acts of parliament which can only be overridden by a special majority, which requires not only two-thirds of the members of the National Assembly present and voting but all the elected members of the Guyanese National Assembly.[20] Francis Alexis argues that under article 170 (the loophole provision) the constitution further empowers the president by giving him the authority to assent or dissolve the national assembly within 21 days after the conditions of article 89 are satisfied.[21] This therefore gives the president a powerful weapon which he can use to effectively stifle any controversial piece of legislation and to control the parliament. James and Lutchman also contend that in relation to the exercise and control of the presidential veto the balance is 'undoubtedly weighted heavily in favour of the executive president'. The 1980 constitutional modifications in Guyana are also significant given the provisions relating to the removal of the executive president from office and the immunities which he enjoys under the constitution. Under article 180 of the constitution only two grounds for the removal of the president exist:

(i) Incapacity: that is the lack of mental or physical capacity of the office holder to discharge the functions of his office. Here the motion seeking an investigation into the mental or physical capacity of the president must be supported by all the members of National Assembly whose names appeared as candidates on the same list as that of the president at the time of the last election (Guyana operates under a party list system based on proportional representation). Ultimately, however, the entire process is controlled by the executive president himself, as he not only appoints members to the cabinet of ministers but he also appoints the chancellor of the judiciary who is responsible for a board to investigate the allegations.[22]

2. Violation of the constitution or gross misconduct: James and Lutchman view the procedures required to remove the president under this heading as more rigorous than the first. Here a written motion signed by not less than half of all the elected members of the National Assembly must be given to the speaker of the National Assembly alleging misconduct and supported by not less than two-thirds of members of the legislature. The next step is the appointment of a tribunal by the chancellor of the judiciary to investigate the charges. Even in a context where the charges are deemed to be true, the support of three-quarters of all members of the legislature is required to remove the president from office.

However, in both instances, the president under the constitution can dissolve parliament within three days of the successful passing of a motion. James and Lutchman argue that:

> The power of dissolution in the circumstances must surely be regarded as an indication of the extent to which provisions in the new Constitution have been designed to protect the position and powers of the Head of Government. It is difficult to envisage a Prime Minister under the old constitution, losing support to the extent of 75% of the membership of Parliament and remaining in office, or being granted a dissolution of Parliament by the ceremonial President . . .It would require a great deal of effort to come up with a more insidious scheme to make it more difficult to remove a President from office constitutionally than that contained in the new Guyanese constitution.[23]

The 1980 constitution also provided for important immunities for the executive president. A review of article 182 of the 1980 constitution, shows that the president enjoys substantial immunities against impeachment. Under article 182 of the constitution, the president is not personally answerable to any court for the performance of the functions of his office or for any act performed during the execution of those functions. Furthermore, no proceedings, whether criminal or civil can be made against him in his personal capacity either during his term of office or thereafter. Additionally, while he holds the office of

the presidency, no criminal proceedings can be made or continued against him in respect of anything done or omitted to be done by him in his private capacity and no civil proceedings shall be made or continued against him with respect of which relief is claimed against him for anything done or omitted to be done in his private capacity. James and Lutchman contend that the net effect of this article is:

> . . .evidently to put the President above the ordinary law of the land in respect of things done in his official capacity that is as President. In this respect therefore, he is accorded total immunity.[24]

The increase in the powers of the heads of government creates a fertile ground for allegations, that the already overblown powers of the heads of government lead to dictatorial politics in the region. Against the backdrop of limited public participation in constitutional changes, it is not surprising that Commonwealth Caribbean constitutional changes appear to work against the interests of the governed. As Ann Spackman observed of the early post-independence changes, given the context within which independence constitutions were drafted:

> Not only did most West Indian leaders not really try after they took office to get mass involvement in the process of changing the constitution, but they even lost interest.[25]

Concerns over the powers of the heads of government reverberate across the region. Most of the concerns revolve around the power of dissolution of the leader of government which is regarded as an 'awesome power' used 'to cow or frighten recalcitrant elected representatives'.[26] The superordinate constitutional authority of the prime minister lends itself to autocratic decision-making similar to that which obtained under colonial government with powerful colonial governors. In Barbados, Prime Minister Tom Adams and opposition member of parliament, Erskine Sandiford agreed that the prime ministers were extremely powerful. Sandiford argued that:

> When I hear the definition of the office of Prime Minister as being *primus inter pares,* first among equals, there is no way in this country that the Prime Minister is any *primus inter pares,* any first among equals. That must have been so when the office just emerged, but today the Prime Minister is so far ahead for the other ministers of the Cabinet . . .that old Latin phrase . . .is not really applicable today. He is more than No. 1, He is it; so much so that what we have in this country, I

am positive about it, is not Cabinet Government. We have Prime Ministerial Government in this country, and we had better understand it, and what we are trying to do is ensure that prime ministerial government in this country does not run riot, that it has to be controlled by different centres of government.[27]

Prime Minster Adams acknowledged that the Barbados constitution was:

> . . .unduly generous to Prime Ministers. In effect in Barbados, any Prime Minister can play the part of Samson and drag the temple down with him, since even if he loses a vote of confidence, the Prime Minister is not obliged to resign and be replaced by another member who can command a majority. He may, if he chooses, dissolve the House of Assembly and therefore place the seat of every member of Parliament at risk. This is a very powerful power to give to a Prime Minister, and left to myself, it is not a power which I think it is always in the best interest of Parliament in small countries to have.[28]

However, the powers of the regional prime ministers remain sacrosanct as the constitutional review exercises in the region have shown. The latest of which was the Barbados Constitutional Review Commission headed by Sir Henry Forde which did not recommend any significant diminution of the role, function and power of the prime minister.[29] The Jamaican exercise of the early 1990s under the chairmanship of Carl Stone also highlights a reluctance to tamper with the power of the prime minister and his cabinet despite the view that the Jamaican legislature merely rubber stamps executive decisions.

Changes that have occurred in the constitutional arrangement of the Commonwealth Caribbean can be regarded as mere modifications of the basic Westminster model, for in combination they have not altered the primary nature of the British Westminster system. Some of these changes are:

1. *Republicanism in some territories, namely Trinidad and Tobago, Guyana and Dominica.* Here, the substitution of president as the local head of state for the governor general did not result in any substantial institutional modification of the system nor in the position, powers and role of the new president, who mirrored the former governor as ceremonial head of state.
2. *Creation of Integrity Commissions beginning with Trinidad and Tobago in 1976.* The commission is appointed by parliament to monitor the liabilities

and income of members of the house of representatives, parliamentary secretaries and chief technical officers. Its function, however, is circumscribed by government. Alexis described the commission of Trinidad as a toothless watchdog, as its only real power is that which is delegated to it by parliament. The Barbados Constitutional Review Commission Report recommended the establishment of an integrity commission and calls for the commission to receive powers if necessary (which would include the power to subpoena persons to testify before it and to subpoena documents to be produced), to investigate any declaration of members of parliament and generally to perform such duties as may be described by parliament. They are to be appointed by the president after consultation with the prime minister and the leader of the opposition. The Integrity Commission Act of 1997 of St Lucia went further by providing for the establishment of an integrity commission appointed by the governor general acting on the advice of the prime minister, who is enjoined to consult with the leader of the opposition. Under the Act, the commission is empowered to:

(a) receive, examine and retain all declarations of all persons in public life filed under this Act (this would include all assets held in St Lucia or elsewhere)
(b) make any enquiry that it considers necessary to verify or determine the accuracy of the declaration filed under the act
(c) receive and investigate complaints regarding non-compliance with or breach of this Act. The failure to comply with the provisions of the Integrity Act could result in prosecution. However, to investigate the truthfulness of the declarations, the Commission has to advise the governor general to appoint a tribunal to investigate. Under section 26 (1) of the Act a false declaration can lead to a fine of $50,000 or a term of imprisonment not exceeding five years or both. Furthermore, the property which was not declared could be forfeited to the courts. As far as property outside St Lucia is concerned, an amount equivalent to the value of the property is to be paid to the state. Again the director of public prosecution is empowered to make any decision pertaining to the imposed penalty.
(d) the commission is also empowered to decide whether gifts are personal or belong to the

state. All public officers must report gifts whose estimated value exceeds $5000 to the commission within 30 days. The commission is empowered to decide whether the gift was trivial and was not intended as a reward for doing or abstaining from doing anything in the performance of his official function. Failure to comply is liable to the payment of a fine, which will not be less than the value of the gift involved in the commission of the offence and to imprisonment for three months.

3. *Local government in some territories, for example Guyana and the devolution of a measure of self-government to Tobago.* Some form of local government exists in most Commonwealth Caribbean countries. However, thus far local government authorities are subordinate to the national political institutions. Three modalities of local government arrangements can be found in the Commonwealth Caribbean:

1. An entire island is a local government system. This can be found in Tobago and Nevis.
2. Informal local government system, as can be identified in St Lucia and St Vincent and the Grenadines.
3. A constitutionally legal local government system, the best examples being Guyana, Jamaica and Trinidad and Tobago.

The most articulated of the models is that which obtains in Guyana where the local government system has a National Congress of Local Democratic Organs (NCLDO) provided for under the 1980 constitution and the 1980 Local Democratic Organs Act and is entrenched under the constitution. This was the first time in the Commonwealth Caribbean that local government was given such prominence. Under article 74 of the 1980 constitution, 12 members of the local government sit in the National Assembly. For local government, Guyana is divided into ten regions headed by a regional chairman. All local communities are administered by elected village or city councils and each of the ten regions are governed by elected regional democratic councils. Unfortunately these councils are subordinated to the executive president and the national government, as they must seek approval for their actions from the central government. The executive president can dissolve the organs of local government at his own discretion. Each council elects a representative to sit on the National Assembly with the two remaining members elected from the

NCLDO. The Supreme Congress of the people of Guyana is comprised of all members of the NCLDO and the National Assembly. This is the central state organ of the republic of Guyana.

4. People's power in Jamaica in the 1970s and Grenada between 1979–1983 under the People's Revolutionary Government (PRG).
5. The abolition of Westminster system in Grenada 1979–1983 and the establishment of revolutionary government.
6. Promulgation of a new socialist constitution in Guyana in 1980, with the emphasis on paramountcy of the party and the executive presidency.
7. Privy Council in Guyana which was replaced by a local Court of Appeal.
8. Overseas voting in Guyana in 1968.
9. Extension of elections in Guyana from five to seven years, three months in 1979 – limited only to the 1973 Parliament. It was a deliberate strategy to obtain adequate time to pass the 1980 constitution, which gave effect to vanguardism and the executive presidency.
10. The 1974 Amendment in Barbados which gave the attorney general the power to direct or control the Director of Public Prosecution over certain areas, and so infringes on the independence of the Director of Public Prosecutions.
11. Changes in Barbados to the appointment of judges. All judges, not only the Chief Justice, under the 1974 Act would be appointed by the prime minister after consultation with the leader of the opposition.
12. The establishment of Independent Service Commissions.
13. 1980 Tenantries Freehold Purchase Act in Barbados.
14. The appointment of the ombudsman. The Ombudsman is supposed to act as a buffer between the citizen and the state and gives the citizen an institution to which, besides the law court, he or she can seek redress if he or she considers that there is a denial of their rights.
15. The creation of the office of the Contractor General through the Contractor General Act of 1983 in Jamaica. This is considered as a best practice designed to facilitate greater accountability and transparency in the political system. The contractor general is supposed to investigate government contracts on an ongoing basis to ensure that they are awarded on

merit. The office operates on a similar basis as the office of the ombudsman.

According to Francis Alexis, Commonwealth Caribbean constitutions still require further modifications to eliminate corruption, greater political accountability of elected and non-elected officials and to promote greater efficiency and democratic participation.[30] These changes should be designed to give expression to the needs and aspirations of Caribbean people. In as much as Caribbean constitutions are sadly lacking in mechanisms (except elections) which enforce accountability and responsibility of the government to the governed, Alexis recommends:

- Parliamentarians' accountability to his/her constituents at least annually through a report on activities during the year. This was also recommended by the Carl Stone Constitutional Review Committee, which called for parliamentary representatives to report to their constituencies and for the right of constituencies to recall their representatives prior to the end of their term of office.
- Recall of parliamentarian by his constituents.
- Strengthening existing channels of local government and implementing local government where it is not already in existence.

Alexis also proposes:

- The removal of the ceremonial head of state which he viewed as a:

  > . . .tradition that weighs us down with the albatross of a costly and essentially supererogatory ceremonial office, if not a sinecure. . .which we would do well to rid ourselves.[31]

The Barbados Constitutional Review Task Force of 1998 headed by Henry Forde recommended republicanism for the country.[32] Of notable interest, was the attempt by the SLP government, elected May 1997, to amend the constitution with respect to the ability of elected members crossing the floor. Such a provision already exists in Trinidad and Tobago but has proved extremely difficult to carry out. A test of the provision by the opposition PNM since the 1995 general elections which brought the United National Congress (UNC) Party to office, proved fruitless as the speaker of the House of Assembly rejected the claims of the opposition party.

'Crossing of the floor' or the defection from the ranks of a parliamentary party to join forces with another party has recently come under scrutiny in the Commonwealth Caribbean. In 1986, four members of

the Barbados Democratic Labour (BLP) Party defected and created another political party, the National Democratic Party (NDP) under the leadership of Richie Haynes. In late 1997, member of parliament Wendell Callender, quit the ruling BLP to join forces with the parliamentary wing of the DLP.

A similar situation occurred in Belize in the wake of the 1989 elections; the People's United Party (PUP) won 15 seats to the United Democratic Party's (UDP) 13 seats. The PUP succeeded in convincing one member of the UDP to join forces with it. Likewise in St Lucia, following two close consecutive general elections in 1987 (three weeks apart), Neville Cenac defected from the SLP to join forces with the UWP. Advocates for a constitutional amendment to prevent such activities argue that it is unfair to the electorate for a person seeking support based on one party platform, to defect to the party of his or her opponent, following his or her opponent's success in elections.

The Constitutional Review Task Force in Barbados also recommended:

(i)   modification of the Senate to provide for greater representation for those who do not support the government and to provide for representation of third and minor parties

(ii)   retention of the first past the post system

(iii) establishment of an Integrity Commission

(iv)   enactment of legislation creating a system of 'People's Initiatives'

(v)   renaming of the Privy Council to the Presidential Council

(vi)   amendment of sections 81 and 89 of the Independence Constitution to permit the appointment of the chief justice by the president on the joint recommendation of the prime minister and the leader of the opposition after consultation with the Judicial and Legal Service Commission. Other judges of the Supreme Court are to be appointed by the president acting on the recommendations of the Judicial and Legal Service Commission

(vii) discretion to the president to refuse to dissolve parliament on the advice of the prime minister.

Parliamentary vs presidential systems of government

There are two types of political systems in all democracies, namely presidential and parliamentary systems. Several modalities of presidentialism exist. Giovanni Sartori[34] and Juan D. Lintz identify a set of conditions, which must simultaneously exist to define a system as a pure presidential republican system:

1. The head of state and government (president) is popularly elected.
2. The inability of parliament to remove the president during his or her term of office, that is, the president enjoys a fixed time span in office.
3. The president heads or otherwise directs the government that he or she appoints and is both head of government and head of state. Additionally, the government or the executive cannot be dismissed by a parliamentary vote of no confidence.

A presidential system is therefore one in which the chief executive is elected independently of the legislature, serves a fixed term of office and is constitutionally vested with important powers. Thus, unlike his Westminster counterpart, the chief executive cannot be removed on a vote of no confidence. The classic example of a pure presidential government is the United States.

In a parliamentary system, the voters do not directly elect the executive head of government. Instead, they elect only the members of the legislative body called the parliament. The head of government, usually a prime minister, is then chosen based on the distribution of political party strength in the parliament. The prime minister is the leader of the party with the most seats in parliament or the person who can pull a coalition together. A parliamentary regime is one in which the only democratically legitimate institution is parliament. Consequently, the authority of government is based on the confidence of parliament. Members of government must vote in support of government policy, or the cabinet falls and an election is called prior to the constitutional limit. The tenure of the prime minister, his cabinet and the other members of parliament depend on the ability of the prime minister and his or her cabinet to retain the voting support (confidence) of a majority of parliament. Thus, a vote of no confidence or non-confidence in parliament against a prime minister and his cabinet introduced by the opposition, which is supported by a sufficient number of government parliamentarians, can lead to the collapse of the government and the dissolution of parliament. If they do not lose the majority, then they may remain in office until elections are constitutionally due or at the discretion of the prime minister. The capacity of the chief executive under parliamentary Westminster systems to dissolve parliaments is a distinguishing feature of the

model. The ability of members of parliament to determine the life-span of a prime minister or parliament is yet another outstanding feature of the flexible nature of the system. Opposition parliamentarians, though free to criticise, or vote against the policies set by the executive, can rarely affect them except in such situations where the legislature is fragmented and where there are many relevant political parties. The classic example of the parliamentary system is Great Britain.

The third model is the hybrid model typical of the French system, which has evolved since the inauguration of the Fifth Republic in 1958. Under this system, a combination of the United States' presidential and British constitutional systems obtains. The voters elect both the Lower House of parliament and the head of state (the president). Like the monarch in the British parliamentary system, the French president appoints a prime minister, whose role is to preside over parliament. The French president like the British prime minister and unlike his American counterpart, can dissolve the National Assembly. Thus, some hybrid systems are characterised by a divided executive with a dual authority structure in which the president shares power with a prime minister whose position is based on the support of parliament in keeping with parliamentary systems. The dual executive system, which is a characteristic feature of parliamentary systems, becomes semi-presidential when the head of government is not appointed by the head of state and where the president is directly or indirectly elected by civil society. Ultimate power depends on who controls the majority in parliament.

In the Commonwealth Caribbean no pure presidential systems exists. Instead, there exist parliamentary republics. In Trinidad and Tobago, the largely ceremonial president is elected by an Electoral College, which consists of both houses of parliament. In Guyana the executive president is elected directly at the same time as National Assembly elections on the plurality basis, which Hamid Ghany[34] describes as a most curious mixture of party list system of proportional representation and the first past the post system. This avoids the potential for gridlock which separate elections would encourage. Guyana, while not satisfying the criteria for a presidential model of government, can be described as a hybrid political form standing at the crossroads of presidentialism and parliamentarism. In Dominica, the ceremonial president is selected by the prime minister and the leader of the opposition, only standing for indirect elections by the House of Assembly if the prime minster and the leader of the opposition cannot in fact concur.

Lacking some critical defining conditions of presidentialism, Commonwealth Caribbean republics are not presidential types and are appropriately grouped under the banner of parliamentary republics. However, such distinctions may not be understood by social commentators in the region judging by the collapsing of categories, which pervade the debate on republicanism. The debate seems to suggest that only one condition is necessary to satisfy a definition of a presidential republican system of government. The idea that the only qualifying criterion for a presidential model is a system exercising considerable authority is unsatisfactory. It does not fully explain the nature of the executive legislative relation, which differentiates the two models, nor does it adequately deal with the rigidity of one model compared with the flexibility of the other.

Generally speaking each of the prototype models have their merits and demerits. The rigidity of the presidential model allows for a greater level of political stability than does the parliamentary system, which is dependent on the confidence of the legislature. However, in the Commonwealth Caribbean under the Westminster parliamentary arrangements, there are few instances of this instability stemming from the flexible nature of the constitutional provisions governing dissolution of parliament. This is partly because of the association of parliamentary democracy with an electoral system based on the plurality vote, which permits big party biases with the resultant majoritarian orientation of the system. The result is a two-party system which tends to produce strong governments.

Only in rare instances have the parliamentary systems in the region produced unstable parliaments in the form of minority governments and hung parliaments.[35] A case in point is the successful no-confidence motion against Prime Minister Winston Cenac of St Lucia in 1981.[36] This followed the development of party schisms within the SLP, which came to power in 1979 on a massive mandate, having defeated the politically dominant UWP government led by John Compton.[37]

The political stability which generally obtains under a pure presidential model is achieved at a tremendous cost. The rigidity of the pure presidential model can permit a constitutional crisis, which can be easily resolved under the parliamentary system by the simple act of dissolving parliament before its constitutional term of office expires. An excellent example of the above, was the decision of the prime minister of St Vincent and the Grenadines to cut short the NDP's constitutional term of office. Under the Grand Beach Accord signed in Grenada on May 4, 2000, by Prime Minister James Mitchell, Leader of the Opposition Ralph Gonsalves, members of the Organisation in Defence of Democracy, the Chamber of Commerce, Employer's Federation, the National Youth Council and OECS leaders, the prime minister agreed to limit the government's term of office from June 1998 to March 31, 2001. This followed protest over the government's introduction of a Pension and Gratuity Bill which was passed in the islands' parliament on April 26, 2000.[38] In contrast, under the American political arrangement an unpopular president can linger ineffectually in government until the expiration of his term of office.

The presidential model in practice in the United States pursues the doctrines of the separation of powers and division of powers to its fullest extent. The nature of executive legislative relationship backed by the undifferentiated nature of the two chamber legislative arm of government is supposed to encourage democratisation. This is in contrast to the parliamentary system where power is not only fused but the legislative arm of government is differentiated (asymmetrical) and the executive arm of government dominates the legislative chamber. Advocates of the presidential system maintain that such a division prevents dictatorship and arbitrary government. However, the downside to this is the tendency towards paralysis, filibustering, gridlock and deadlock, which small states can ill-afford. Thus, the differentiated nature of the parliament under parliamentary systems, the domination of the executive in the Commonwealth Caribbean, and the built-in mechanism of control provided to the government by a Senate which is dominated by the ruling party, ensures effective and stable government.

The direct election of a president is also seen as promoting democratisation. However, in practice, in the Commonwealth Caribbean, the dominant two party system compared with the multi-party system which prevails in many developing countries, parliamentary democracies in all but rare instances, permit the election of the head of government who can be said to be popularly elected. The choice of a governing party during a general election also determines the electorate's choice of a prime minister.

Table 3:1 highlights some crucial differences between parliamentary and presidential systems of governments. The key elements are based primarily on American and British prototypes.

Commonwealth Caribbean constitutions, including the post-independence constitutions, lack some crucial democratic elements. Such critical absence may lay the foundation for instability, especially against the backdrop of economic crisis. Notwithstanding the success of the constitutional model in the region, grave reservations remain. With the exception of Guyana and Grenada, Commonwealth Caribbean countries which have adopted the Westminster parliamentary systems have passed the test. They have remained rela-

TABLE 3:1 COMPARISON OF PARLIAMENTARY AND PRESIDENTIAL SYSTEMS

Systems of Government	Parliamentary	Presidential
Head of state and government	Separate	Unified
Nature of legislature	Differentiated/asymmetrical	Undifferentiated/symmetrical
Tenure of office of head of government	Flexible – unlimited	Rigid – maximum two terms
Removal of head of government	Vote of no confidence by legislature	Rigid (except for impeachment) – not dependent on legislative confidence
Dissolution of the legislature	Discretion of the head of government or legislative confidence	Constitutionally fixed
Termination of government	Discretion of the head of government or legislative confidence	Constitutionally fixed
Election of head of government	Selected by the legislature	Directly or direct like elections
Appointment of cabinet/executive	Head of government	Head of government and state and confirmation by the Senate (US)
Dismissal of members of the executive	Head of government	Head of government and state

Key words and phrases

1	Constitution.
2	Constitutional decolonisation
3	Democracy
4	Liberal democracy
5	Separation of Power
6	Executive President
7	Checks and balances
8	Fusion of power
9	Whitehall model
10	Westminster model
11	Crossing the floor
12	Prime Minister
13	Accountability
14	Republicanism
15	Governor General
16	Ceremonial President
17	Parliamentary system
18	Presidential system
19	Majoritarian system
20	Differentiated bicameralism
21	Undifferentiated bicameralism
22	Constitutional rigidity
23	Constitutional flexibility
24	Fusion of power
25	Dual executive
26	Collective responsibility
27	Local government
28	Contractor General
29	Ombudsman
30	Integrity Commission
31	Constitutional modifications
32	Hybrid models
33	Presidents

Questions to Consider

tively stable parliamentary democracies with political parties and elections as the lifeblood of the system.

- Isolate and examine the main political assumptions of liberal democracy and consider the extent to which post independence constitutional amendments have sought to give concrete expression and effect to these assumptions. Have such modifications improved the quality of governance? Illustrate with useful examples.
- To what extent has the Commonwealth Caribbean practice of liberal democracy undermined or extended democracy? Discuss, in relation to the cabinet, the prime minister, the executive presidency of Guyana and electoral practices in the Commonwealth Caribbean.
- 'The Henry Forde Constitutional Review report does not go far enough to deal with Prime Minis-

terial government'. Discuss with useful illustrations and with relevant examples.
- Differentiate between presidential and parliamentary systems of government. What are the main defects and strengths of the Westminster System of government?
- Outline the main elements of the Westminster Model as practiced in the region and assess the main strengths of the model. To what extent do you believe, based on the operation of the model in any single Commonwealth Caribbean country, that governance would be promoted by fundamental adjustments to the model? What kind of adjustment would be required?
- In what ways can good governance be further promoted in the Commonwealth Caribbean?

Activities

* After reading this chapter, identify the main challenges that confront Caribbean political systems. List four of them and compare them with those which the other members of your group have identified.
* Discuss with your family their views on the need for a constitutional amendment to prevent elected members of Parliament 'crossing the floor'. Discuss your findings with the class.
* In what ways do you think that Commonwealth Caribbean constitutions should be changed?
* Carefully study the recent recommendations coming from the 1998 Constitutional Review Committee and assess the extent to which they promote better governance.
* Consider the virtues of parliamentary and presidential systems and assess the strength of the present system in Barbados or any English-speaking Caribbean country.

Readings

The Westminster System in the Commonwealth Caribbean: Some Issues and Problems

Harold A. Lutchman

Introduction

Although there are conceptual difficulties in treating the Westminster system of government as a single type[1], the states of the Commonwealth Caribbean are generally numbered among the most successful in achieving satisfactory results with its characteristic institutions. In practice, these states have fashioned the Westminster system to suit their peculiar needs and circumstances. The holding of regular free and fair elections, which enjoy the confidence of the populace and the contestants for political power, is certainly regarded as among the important elements of this system of government in the Commonwealth Caribbean. Related to this is the expectation that both governing and opposition parties would, on some future occasion, exchange places and functions in response to the popular will.

Despite its apparent efficacy, elements of the Westminster system have come under critical scrutiny regarding their suitability for some of the states of the Commonwealth Caribbean. For example, Sir Probyn Innis, former Governor of St. Christopher-Nevis, has identified a number of dysfunctional aspects of the system in its application to the small states of the region in particular. Relying on his personal experience, he has argued for a review of the system, with emphasis on the functions of the judiciary and the executive arm of government. His concern is that in the absence of such review, and possible reform, there is a danger of the Westminster system wilting in the Commonwealth Caribbean.[2]

Even before Sir Probyn had spoken, action had been taken in some states to address perceived weaknesses in, or unsuitable aspects of, the system. A series of constitutional changes introduced in Guyana since its independence in 1966, are at times interpreted in this light.[3] The twin-island state of Trinidad and Tobago, too, changed its constitution in 1976 with this objective in mind. Further, a constitutional commission was subsequently appointed in 1987 to conduct a thorough review of that state's constitution and to make recommendations for its improvement.[4]

It is clear that, in many instances, the framers of the constitutions of the region had not anticipated a number of problems which became manifest after their independence. Even if they had, such was their confidence in the viability of the Westminster system that they thought that any emerging problems could be solved by resort to United Kingdom practices and precedents. It is, however, becoming increasingly apparent that there may be problems that UK experiences and practices cannot help to resolve. Even where relevant precedents exist in the UK or in other parts of the Commonwealth, practitioners in the Commonwealth Caribbean do not necessarily feel bound by them. Thus, by way of illustration, while in the United King-

dom a dismissed government minister would probably not challenge his loss of office before the courts, there is at least one case in the region where a minister did just that.[5]

Increasingly, there is a tendency to question both the wisdom of excluding certain matters from the purview of the courts, and to argue for a more inclusive approach. There is danger, however, in drawing the courts into political controversy to an extent previously regarded as inconsistent with their non-political status.

This essay considers a number of constitutional issues which would appear, by their very nature, not likely to have been anticipated at the time Commonwealth Caribbean states embarked on the experience of independence and opted for a Westminster form of government. Arguably, these issues need to be resolved if these states are generally to continue to be regarded as constitutional successes, and to enjoy the peace and tranquillity with which they are usually associated.

The One Party Monopoly Phenomenon

The existence of two parties of more or less equal strength is one of the features generally associated with the Westminster form of government. One party forms Her Majesty's Government, and the other functions as Her Majesty's Opposition. The latter should be willing and able to take over the government on defeating its rival at an election, or on securing majority support in the legislature. There is little doubt that constitutions of the Commonwealth Caribbean were, for the most part, drafted with this model in mind. This is epitomised in the number of provisions which cast on the Leader of the Opposition a consultative role in the making of certain appointments, and before certain courses of action are initiated by the government of the day.[6]

This requirement of consultation is not normally problematic in the United Kingdom and, indeed, in many other Commonwealth countries. Both the Prime Minister and the Leader of the Opposition are usually clearly identifiable and appointable persons. However, problems have arisen in the Commonwealth Caribbean in consequence of the tendency of one party to either win all of the seats at an election, or an overwhelming number thereof. Trinidad and Tobago, and Jamaica experienced this phenomenon in 1971 and 1983, respectively, when, because of disagreement between the government and opposition, the latter decided not to nominate candidates for the election. In consequence, all of the candidates nominated by the governing party were declared elected as, under existing rules, no actual voting by the electorate was necessary.

At a later date, the governing party in St. Vincent and the Grenadines also won all of the seats in the legislature. As a result, as in the previous cases, no one was available to be appointed to the constitutional position of Leader of the Opposition.[7] The question which then arose for consideration was: what should be the status of provisions of the constitution which required an input from this functionary, and how legal would be any act done without such input? Additionally, what provisions or authority, if any, could be invoked to appoint such a functionary and remedy what was seen in some quarters as a serious problem?

Answers to these questions would appear to depend on the meaning and effect of the relevant constitutional provisions in a given state. In Jamaica, it is provided that the Leader of the Opposition shall be appointed by the Governor-General. In doing so, the latter is to "appoint the member of the House of Representatives who, in his judgment, is best able to command the support of a majority of those members who do not support the government." Where there is no such person, he is to appoint "the member of the House who, in his judgment commands the support of the largest single group of such members who are prepared to support one leader."[8] In the circumstances in which one party wins all of the seats, therefore, there is evidently no way in which the relevant constitutional provisions may be activated in appointing a Leader of the Opposition.

Other provisions of the constitution, such as those relating to the bicameral system of the legislature, are likely to be affected by this problem. In Jamaica, for example, 13 "Senators shall be appointed by the Governor-General acting in accordance with the advice of the Prime Minister." The remaining eight "Senators shall be appointed by the Governor-General acting in accordance with the advice of the Leader of the Opposition."[9]

Where, therefore, only one party is represented in the lower house (House of Representatives), there would also be only one party represented in the upper house (the Senate). Were the situation, whereby only one party wins all the seats in the lower house, to occur in Barbados, the result in respect to the composition of the upper house may well be different, given the different constitutional provisions. Of the 21 members of the Senate, 12 are to be appointed by the Governor-General acting in accordance with the advice of the Prime Minister, two on the advice of the

Leader of the Opposition, and seven by the Governor-General, acting in his discretion, to represent religious, economic and social interests, or such other interests as he considers right to be represented. In this connection, the Governor-General "shall consult such persons as, in his discretion, he considers can speak for those interests and ought to be consulted".[10]

In the absence of opposition representation in the lower house, the situation then, would appear to be that the Governor-General could at least ensure that seven nominees face the 12 Government nominees in the Senate which is, *inter alia*, intended to perform important functions, including revising and improving bills on their way through the legislature.

A related issue is whether, under existing provisions, a Governor-General could, or should, use his powers to create the post of, and appoint to it, a Leader of the Opposition. Might it not be possible, for example, as was suggested in the case of Barbados, to appoint a Senator, not appointed on the advice of the Prime Minister, to that office? As attractive as this suggestion would appear to be, it is not without difficulty. Short of a constitutional amendment to this effect, there would be problems in the way of doing so. Existing constitutional provisions are clear in requiring that the Leader of the Opposition be drawn from the ranks of the lower house and not from those of the upper house.

Similar issues have arisen in the state of St. Vincent and the Grenadines where the party forming the government won all 15 parliamentary seats at an election held in May 1989.[11] The Prime Minister then advised the Governor-General to appoint four of the total of six members of the Senate, which left unappointed the remaining two "in accordance with the advice of the Leader of the Opposition."[12] The result was challenged by two citizens of St. Vincent and the Grenadines in court proceedings to test the constitutionality of the composition of the House of Assembly. The basis of the challenge was that "under section 55 of the Constitution the Governor-General acting in his own deliberate judgment, after considering that it is not practicable for him to obtain the advice of a leader of the opposition, can act without that advice and in his (the Governor-General's) deliberate judgment can appoint two senators." Further, since only four of the six senators had been appointed, the House of Assembly was not properly constituted, which rendered all tax measures and laws passed by the Assembly illegal.[13] This was regarded as an unsatisfactory state of affairs by certain sections of the population. On the other hand, one authority had succinctly commented as follows:

> "Rather than demonstrating respect for the judgment of the electorate, harsh as it was against them, and, perhaps, not justified, the opposition parties and other elements in the society have chosen to dissipate their energies and limited resources in waging a campaign for the Governor-General to appoint two senators who do not support the...Government."[14]

The problem is that there is apparently no constitutional or legal authority for the Governor-General in St. Vincent and the Grenadines to accede to such a request in the absence of a leader of the opposition. This difficulty exists in spite of existing constitutional provisions precluding the courts from enquiring whether, in making such appointments, the Governor-General in fact consulted with those prescribed in the constitution. The importance of finding a solution to this problem throughout the region lies in the clear indication that it is likely to recur in other states.

In the view of one observer, political groups in St. Vincent and the Grenadines could as a solution to this problem use their time beneficially by campaigning "for substantial constitutional changes, including a change in the electoral system..." It was further argued that the populace needed to be educated about desirable changes in the constitution to make it more relevant to the needs of the country and the wish to have a properly functioning multi-party democracy.[15]

It is unlikely that the foregoing difficulties will arise in the country from which Commonwealth Caribbean states have mainly culled their constitutional practices. For one thing, given the size and complexity of the United Kingdom, it is inconceivable that any single party could ever win all the seats in its Parliament. In addition, some of the disputes which have led parties to boycott elections in the region, thereby paving the way for only one party to be returned to Parliament, have not occurred in the UK. It should at the same time be borne in mind that the British Constitution does not suffer from some of the rigidities generally associated with the constitutions of Commonwealth Caribbean states.

Rigidities, though, are not generally the problem in effecting constitutional changes. A government with control over all of the seats in the legislature would be ideally placed to change the constitution in any chosen direction. However, one of the marked features of governments so placed in the Commonwealth Caribbean is the restraint which they have generally exercised in matters of constitutional change and amendment. Arguably, the question of constitutional change should best be raised and discussed when no party is in such a dominant position, since to encourage a government in such circumstances to tamper with the constitution is likely to lead to unintended and unfortunate consequences. It is remarkable that, notwithstanding past experience with this state of affairs (and here the cases of Jamaica and Trinidad and Tobago would appear to be particularly relevant), no formal amendments to the constitutions have been proposed to prevent, as it were, the suspension of certain provisions of the constitutions because of the dominance of one party. It may well be that this has not been done in the two states under reference for the simple reason that the phenomenon had arisen because of decisions by the respective oppositions to boycott elections. At any rate, in both cases, this did not prevent opposition parties from winning at subsequent elections. And, it is remarkable how parties tend to drop or forget issues, previously represented as involving matters of high principle, once they have triumphed at the polls.

In every Commonwealth Caribbean state in which a single party has won all of the seats in the legislature, elections were held under the first-past-the-post system which, with the notable exception of Guyana, is the existing electoral system in the region. Proportional representation (PR) has been canvassed as a means of preventing this result.[16] Thus, in the case of St. Vincent and the Grenadines, were PR the electoral system, the governing party, with approximately 66% of the votes, would have won approximately 66% of the seats, that is, approximately 10 seats. Opposition parties, with approximately 33% of the votes, would have won approximately 33% of the seats, that is, the remaining five seats.

Although PR may prove, for a number of reasons (including ensuring a better match between votes received and seats allocated), a more efficient electoral system, it has generally not been widely demanded in the region. Losing parties appear to tolerate the first-past-the-post system where they feel they have an equal and fair chance of winning a future election under it, but raise objections where they believe the system is permanently stacked against them. It would, therefore, seem a fair conclusion that PR is unlikely to be introduced to combat the phenomenon of one party monopoly in the Commonwealth Caribbean.

In circumstances in which one party wins all of the seats at an election, Dr Patrick Emmanuel has pointed to the tendency for divisions to occur within the ranks of the ruling party to the point where there is, in due course, a group or individuals constituting itself or themselves as an opposition. An extension of this would appear to be the possibility of the ruling party encouraging such a development.[17]

There are ample precedents for Emmanuel's claim. For example, after the PNM won every seat in Parliament in 1971 in Trinidad and Tobago, by June 1972 "an Opposition appeared in the form of two PNM members who had ceased to belong to the party. One of them hastily formed a new political party...thus qualifying for appointment as Leader of the Opposition with all the powers belonging to the office including that of appointing four persons to the Senate and removing any or all of them at will . . ."[18] Ultimately, the other member of the newly created party announced that he was sitting as an independent in Parliament. As a result, the Leader of the Opposition sat "in the House of Representatives leading himself as the only member of his party in the House." The absurdity inherent in this situation is readily apparent. As one writer has commented, "If the intention had been deliberately to parody the British institution we had set out to copy, the result could hardly have been more successful."[19]

Defection from the ranks of a party for the purpose of strengthening another party, or creating another party or group in the legislature, has been roundly condemned. The reasons include the belief that it is manifestly unfair to the electorate (some would regard it as a fraud against the electorate) for a person seeking its support on one basis (whether it be the efficacy of the programme of a given party or otherwise) and, after being elected, distancing himself from that basis. Such a development could also impact inequitably on existing parties and undermine their status.

Developments in Belize subsequent to the election of 1989 are instructive on these points.[20] In the wake of that election, the incumbent ruling United Democratic Party (UDP) won 13 seats as compared to 15 seats by the then opposition People's United Party (PUP). Both parties then attempted to strengthen their positions in the legislature. While it was clear that the PUP was entitled to a mandate to form the next government, it was not satisfied with its small majority of two over the UDP. On the other hand, the leadership of the latter was keen to induce a sufficient number of PUP members to cross over the floor and place it in a position to form the government. The PUP ultimately succeeded in getting a member of the UDP to join its

ranks, the defecting member arguing that he was going to be in a better position to serve his constituents. He also claimed that he was very much "independent" in his thinking, and had no strong loyalties to any party.[21] In the result, he was criticised as selfish and unprincipled, and condemned for undermining the possibility of forging "a new political culture" in the Caribbean region.[22]

A case of crossing the floor (described as one of the more well-known and distasteful examples in the Eastern Caribbean) had previously occurred in St. Lucia. The facts in connection therewith were succinctly stated as follows:

> . . . Neville Cenac . . . bolted from the St. Lucia Labour Party in May 1987 to give Prime Minister John Compton's United Worker's Party what it had failed to achieve at two national elections within one month: an effective parliamentary majority.
>
> Describing himself at the time as a "professional politician" (sic), Cenac's crossing of the floor transformed Compton's one seat majority in Parliament to the current 10-7 position leaving his former Labour Party colleagues to bitterly denounce "subversion of the democratic process" and Compton to smile all the way back to the Prime Minister's Office.[23]

Developments in Barbados in 1989 are instructive on how the defection of members could operate to the detriment of existing parties and their status in Parliament. This happened when four members of the Democratic Labour Party (DLP), which had overwhelmingly won the election of 1986, deserted their party and constituted themselves the National Democratic Party (NDP) under the leadership of a former DLP minister. According to one source, the DLP and NDP seemed "to be jostling to prove which is more dedicated to the policies and manifesto promises of the party that won the 1986 general elections when they were all together as DLPites."[24]

As a result of the defections, the leader of the newly constituted NDP was able to supplant the leader of the BLP as Leader of the Opposition and to succeed to all the rights and privileges appertaining to that office. This transpired notwithstanding that at the previously held election the BLP had won 42% of the votes cast. What brought about the displacement of the previous Leader of the Opposition was the effect of the constitutional provision stipulating the number of seats held in Parliament, as distinct from the number of votes received, as the basis for his appointment as Leader of the Opposition.[25]

In light of these examples, the need for constitutional change to provide for a system of recall of those who defect following elections has been canvassed. This has been linked to the need for a critical appraisal of the electoral systems to make them more relevant to the needs of post-colonial Caribbean societies. The requirement of greater accountability by elected representatives has been emphasised.

The state of Trinidad and Tobago stands out in the Commonwealth Caribbean in having constitutional sanctions against members crossing the floor, or defecting to other parties.[26] This, to some extent, explains why, initially, although a number of members of the NAR (which had also overwhelmingly won the 1986 elections) subsequently left that party and formed another of their own, the impact on the previously existing PNM opposition was different. The new grouping was apparently satisfied to function as the *de facto* opposition, leaving the PNM as the official or *de jure* opposition.[27] There is no indication that other states in the region are keen to provide in their constitutions for similar sanctions against members switching loyalties after an election.

Clearly, the problems which may arise when a party wins all the seats at an election could be complex, and intractable. And although constitutional amendment is frequently urged as one solution it is not at all certain what form this should take, or whether some of the implications of such changes are always fully appreciated. There are those who believe that the emergence of such a situation should not necessarily be cause for concern in as much as it is usually reflective of the democratic wish of the electorate. In other words, if the electorate at freely and fairly conducted elections vote to, in effect, exclude the opposition from the governmental processes, their wishes should be respected. The contrary view is that, given the operation of the electoral system, the winning of all the seats by a government is not always to be interpreted as a mandate to exclude the opposition as the latter can often demonstrate substantial support among the electorate. The problem then is to devise a satisfactory formula whereby that support could be reflected in representation in Parliament and other governmental forums, where the electoral system fails to meet this objective.

At times the situation is reversed, and the dominant party criticises those who are unsuccessful in securing seats in the legislature for advocating solutions described as essentially undemocratic. At the base of such criticism is the belief that the solutions tend to cut across certain fundamental constitutional principles, especially in the light of historical developments. There is frequently a great deal of substance to such criticisms. For example, among the solutions proffered in St. Vincent and the Grenadines was vesting the Governor-General with the power of nominating persons to the lower house of the legislature to serve as an opposition to the Government, or to constitute a group who did not support the Government. One of these persons could then have been designated Leader of the Opposition.[28]

There is little doubt that the constitutions may be amended to make this possible. But it would be open to the objection that it is against the grain of the pattern of constitutional development which has been in the general direction of shifting the balance of power to the political head, away from the ceremonial head, of state. One clear implication of the suggestion under reference would be to cast the Governor-General in a more active political role which could render his position untenable.

While it is arguable that constitutional provisions empower the Governor-General to appoint a certain number of persons as senators, and that in exercising this function, he is cast in an active political role, one could discern fundamental points of difference between the two sets of circumstances. The Governor-General, in the normal sense, exercises his power where both the governing party and the opposition are already represented in the lower chamber. He would then nominate members of the upper chamber on the respective advice of the Prime Minister and Leader of the Opposition. He then has a residual power to nominate persons judged competent to speak for other important interests or groups. This residual role is likely to be far more acceptable than where the Governor-General may be required to, in effect, "create" an opposition group against the Government.

The Governor-General's exercise of such power may also be interpreted as passing judgement on the behaviour of the electorate. The basic question which may be posed is: Why should a Governor-General be in a superior position to that of the electorate to decide who should or should not be represented in the legislature?

It has already been contended above that a system of PR would seem well designed to avoid the circumstances that lead to such criticisms. It is not envisaged that under PR any single party could ever win all of the seats. Therefore, some of the difficulties discussed above would be avoided. The Constitution Commission of Trinidad and Tobago, which reported in January 1974, had persuasively argued that such an electoral system was likely to prove superior to the first-past-the-post system in reconciling the conflict which frequently arises between votes cast and seats received. Further, it need not be associated with some of the negatives at times identified with it, such as weak governments and fragmentation within the political system.[29] Nor need PR be identified with the allegations of fraud which characterised the conduct of elections under this system in Guyana prior to the reform of the administration of elections there.[30]

However, it is not anticipated that PR will be a popular option until it is properly understood. Additionally, one of its likely handicaps is that it is not the electoral system of preference in the UK, which invariably serves as the model for constitutional developments in the region. In this respect, Commonwealth Caribbean states have to appreciate that institutions have to be fashioned to serve the environment for which they are designed. The difficulties experienced with the monopoly of single parties are in part the result of adopting constitutional arrangements with no record of dealing with such problems. This poses a challenge to the states to be creative in doing so.

At the same time, there has not been an absence of creativity in addressing this problem as experience in Jamaica has demonstrated. When, in the circumstances described above, the PNP found itself without seats in the legislature, and, therefore, effectively excluded from constitutional participation in the process of government, its leadership set out to organise extraconstitutionally by establishing "people's forums" at which the activities and policies of the JLP government were debated outside the parliamentary framework.[31] Although such activities were, by their very nature, different from what they would have been inside Parliament, they evidently went some way in compensating for existing deficiencies. In the result, perhaps in part due to their effectiveness at such forums, the PNP was able to overwhelmingly defeat the JLP at the following election.

There is also some indication that in the prevailing circumstances the JLP government was prepared to compromise on some of the strict rules on which it could have insisted. Thus, members of that party were permitted greater freedom to speak against, and criticise, the policies of their government than would have been the case if there had been an opposition in Parliament.

Such development may be regarded as healthy in that they conduce to the emergence of practices which are direct responses to existing problems. They may even be regarded as possessing the potential of eventually developing into conventions. However, as matters now stand, they are a long way from having the qualities of certainty and being acted on out of a sense of obligation. In this sense, they cannot be regarded as adequate substitute for constitutional amendments.

The Power of Dissolution and Prorogation

The dissolution and prorogation of Parliament in Britain are among the important functions falling within the scope of prerogative power. The general pattern is that the legal power of dissolution and prorogation resides in the Queen who, in this exercise, is obliged to act on the advice of the Prime Minister. The latter rule, as indeed is the case with many others regulating the exercise of prerogative powers, is governed by convention.[32]

More specifically, a Parliament (which in this context means the House of Commons since the House of Lords is not similarly elected or subjected to a fixed term) is elected for a period of five years. But, it is within the competence of the Prime Minister to, at any time within that period, advise the Queen to dissolve Parliament and call a general election. It is well known that in doing so the Prime Minister may be motivated primarily by political considerations. He may, for example, judge the moment to be the one best calculated to yield maximum political advantage to his party. There is nothing, for example, to prevent a Prime Minister from advising the Queen to dissolve Parliament, and pave the way for the holding of an election, after a Parliament has been in existence for, say, only two and a half years because, in his judgement, the general political climate favours the re-election of his party. Indeed, a Prime Minister need give no reason for advising a dissolution of Parliament. This principle is so well established that it does not normally feature as an issue of controversy. It is, no doubt, accepted because political parties and their leadership generally know that they could, some time in the future, equally be in a position to make use of this power to their advantage.

Yet, the ability of a Prime Minister to request a dissolution and to obligate the Queen to act in accordance with such advice, may be conditioned by a number of factors, such as, for example, the extent of the support which the government has in Parliament.

Thus, it is frequently argued that the Queen may not be obliged to grant a dissolution where the government has suffered a defeat in Parliament on a matter of importance. But she must be in a position to find someone else with majority support in Parliament able and willing to form a new government. However, it is only in exceptional circumstances that a request by a Prime Minister for a dissolution is likely to be refused on such grounds. As in other areas of British constitutional law and practice, the operative rules are regarded as well settled, and do not frequently feature as matters of political controversy.

In accordance with their usual approach to constitutional forms, arrangements in the Commonwealth Caribbean have sought to capture in written form British constitutional rules pertaining to the dissolution and prorogation of Parliament. There are, however, significant differences in how these rules work out in practice in the Commonwealth Caribbean as compared with the UK.

The constitutions of all of the states of the region provide that the legal power of dissolution and prorogation resides in the Governor-General or the President, as the case may be.[33] In exercising the power of dissolution, however, save in the case of Guyana, this functionary is to act on the advice of the Prime Minister. The constitution of St Christopher and Nevis is typical in this respect. It states: "In the exercise of his power to dissolve Parliament the Governor-General shall act in accordance with the advice of the Prime Minister."[34] In Guyana, the relevant provisions authorise the President to "at any time by proclamation dissolve Parliament."[35] This is the result of Guyana having an executive presidency whereunder formal, as well as informal, powers reside in the President. It is unlike the situation in all of the other Commonwealth Caribbean states where legal powers generally reside in the ceremonial head of state but are, in their exercise, subject to the advice of the Prime Minister.

The power to prorogue Parliament does not receive identical treatment in all of the constitutions of the region. Whereas some constitutions require that this power also be exercised in accordance with the advice of the Prime Minister, others are silent on this point.[36] One possible interpretation of this is that, in the latter cases, the power of the head of state to prorogue Parliament is unfettered. It is, however, difficult to accept this statement without qualification since there are constitutional provisions capable of being construed as limitations on this power. At any rate, the general constitutional scheme is towards reducing the involvement of the head of state in controversial political issues, and, as will be seen below, the legal power of prorogation is capable of generating serious political controversy.

Although it would appear as if the ascendancy of the Prime Minister is unquestioned where the dissolution of Parliament is concerned, there may in fact be a number of limitations on this right. These are mainly regulated by convention. However, the constitution of St Vincent and the Grenadines enumerates circumstances in which the head of state need not act on the advice of the Prime Minister in dissolving Parliament. These are as follows:

> (a) if the Prime Minister advises a dissolution and the Governor-General . . . considers that the government . . . can be carried out without a dissolution and that a dissolution would not be in the interests of St Vincent;

> (b) if a resolution of no-confidence in the Government is passed and the Prime Minister does not within three days either resign or advise a dissolution, the Governor-General . . . may dissolve Parliament.

> (c) if the Office of Prime Minister is vacant and the Governor-General . . . considers that there is no prospect of his being able within a reasonable time to appoint to that office a Representative who can command the support of the majority of the Representatives, the Governor-General shall dissolve Parliament.[37]

Although other constitutions do not specify the rules and circumstances under which the head of state is not obliged to act in accordance with the advice of the Prime Minister, there is little doubt that, in all of the states, they substantially embody practice intended to be operative. There is evidently the feeling that grounding the operation of the rules in convention is likely to provide a greater measure of flexibility in dealing with such problems in the future.

Some of the constitutions additionally describe circumstances in which, regardless of action by the head of state and/or the Prime Minister, Parliament may be dissolved. Thus, the constitution of St Christopher and Nevis provides that ". . . Parliament, unless sooner dissolved, shall continue for five years from the date of the first sitting of the National Assembly after any dissolution and shall then stand dissolved."[38] The interpretation to be applied here would appear to be that, at the end of five years (as described), regardless of whether or not Parliament is formally dissolved by the head of state, it is to be considered as dissolved.

This would seem to be reinforced by provisions addressing the extension of the life of Parliament beyond the five-year period; for example, when the state is at war. Then, the life of Parliament may be extended, twelve months at a time, for not more than five years in total.[39]

The constitution of Trinidad and Tobago also provides as follows:

> Where, between a dissolution of parliament and the next ensuing general election of members to the House of Representatives, an emergency arises of such a nature that in the opinion of the Prime Minister it is necessary for the two houses to be summoned before that general election can be held, the President, acting in accordance with the advice of the Prime Minister, may summon the two Houses of the preceding Parliament but the election of members of the House of Representatives shall proceed and the Parliament that has been summoned shall, if not sooner dissolved, again stand dissolved on the day on which the general election is held.[40]

These provisions are designed to deal with problems (which may require inputs from Parliament), arising after Parliament has been dissolved but before a new election is held. But, at the same time, there is appreciation of the need to ensure that any reactivation of a previously dissolved Parliament is a temporary measure and does not disrupt plans for the already scheduled election. On the day fixed for the holding of the election, Parliament, without further act by the head of state and the Prime Minister, is automatically dissolved. There is therefore, in such circumstances, no question of the Prime Minister having to advise the head of state to dissolve Parliament, or the head of state acting on such advice.

These rules would not appear to be controversial. Yet time and again the exercise of the power of dissolution and prorogation of Parliament has led to disagreement in some of the states of the Commonwealth Caribbean to the point where there have been calls for constitutional reform.

A notable case in point occurred in Jamaica in the wake of the military intervention in Grenada in 1983 by a joint American/Caribbean force. Jamaican military personnel were active in this force. Evidently, in the judgement of the then Prime Minister of Jamaica, Mr. Edward Seaga, there was popular support for both the intervention and Jamaican participation in it. As a consequence, (no doubt also influenced by the precedent of British Prime Minister Margaret Thatcher calling an election long before it was due in light of the popular public support for the Falklands War with Argentina) Prime Minister Seaga advised the Governor-General to dissolve Parliament. New elections were then scheduled. This in effect meant that the Parliament had only been in existence for approximately half the period of its normal life of five years before its successor was to be elected. This was seriously criticised on a number of grounds. These included, *inter alia*, the claim by the opposition that there had been an understanding between the Government and themselves that a new voters list and new voters identification were to be in place prior to the holding of new elections. Additionally, it was felt that the Prime Minister, by requesting a dissolution in such circumstances, was acting in an overtly politically partisan manner.[41]

The opposition boycotted the election and all of the seats in Parliament were won by the incumbent government. In consequence, whether a dissolution of Parliament was justified in such circumstances, and whether the Governor-General would have been justified, had he thought it right to do so, to refuse such a dissolution, became matters of public discussion. Specifically, it was questioned whether the Governor-General was not under a duty to protect the public interest from politicians who clearly intended to extract political advantage from the circumstances. Arguably, the Governor-General would only have been justified in refusing a dissolution if he were satisfied that popular sentiments were against the Prime Minister.

Controversy has also arisen over the exercise of the power of prorogation of Parliament as exemplified in Grenada, which case may be regarded as important in providing opportunity for the examination of a number of potentially far-reaching constitutional and political issues. The relevant circumstances occurred as one of the results of the splintering of the party then forming the Government.[42] As a result, the Government lost its majority in Parliament. A number of groups hostile to the then Prime Minister and his Government ultimately resolved to defeat the Government by having a vote of no-confidence passed against it in Parliament. In order to forestall this eventuality, the Prime Minister advised the Governor-General to prorogue Parliament indefinitely which advice was adhered to by the Governor-General.[43]

The forces lined up against the Government naturally disagreed with the prorogation and questioned the need for it especially as the maximum period for which Parliament was elected, was fast approaching. They contended that the dissolution of Parliament was, in the circumstances, preferable to its prorogation. A dissolution would have provided opportunity to test the popular will and ensure that no single group was able to exploit the situation to its political advantage. On the contrary, the prorogation enabled a minority party in Parliament to remain indefinitely in control of the government until it chose to advise the Governor-General to dissolve Parliament and fix the date for a new election.[44]

In the event, the incumbent Prime Minister died and a member of his party was appointed in succession to him. The apparent understanding was that the new appointee was to serve mainly on a caretaker basis and advise the Governor-General to dissolve Parliament at an early date. However, the fact remained that a party, which had clearly lost its majority in Parliament, was able to remain in office because, in part, of the power of its leader to advise the Governor-General on the prorogation of Parliament, or on when Parliament should be dissolved. This situation arose because the Governor-General chose to grant the Prime Minister a prorogation rather than dissolve Parliament, dismiss the Prime Minister and force a general election to be called.

It is because of events such as these that there has been advocacy of new rules (addressed to both the dissolution and prorogation of Parliament) likely to operate more equitably on all contestants for political power. Any rules should, in particular, not confer a lopsided advantage on an incumbent government, but should be capable of safeguarding the public interest.

One suggested solution to such problems is that Parliament should be elected for a fixed period (of say five years) with no power in the Governor-General and/or the Prime Minister to put an end to its life by dissolution or otherwise. Those favouring this change are generally attracted by the American system of government whereunder the chief executive can do nothing to cause elections to be held at a time favourable to his party. Rather, he has to take the political circumstances as he finds them and the political fortunes as allocated through the wishes of the electorate.

The issue of "fixed terms" has also been discussed in a slightly different context, that is, relative to the tenure of office of a Prime Minister. The belief is that there should be limits on the number of terms served by such a functionary, regardless of the strength of his support among the electorate or his party in Parliament.[45] The concern is that long and indefinite tenure, whether as legislator or Prime Minister, tends to lead to insensitivity, unresponsiveness and reduced effectiveness in dealing with public problems.

The arguments against fixed terms are, however, weighty in both cases. The power to, at any time, have Parliament dissolved and a new election called, is credited with providing the electorate with opportunity to vote an unpopular government from office. Thus, the electorate need not endure such a government for the full life of a Parliament. This can be achieved, for example, by the dismissal of the Prime Minister by the Governor-General where he is convinced that the former no longer enjoys popular support. He may also, in such circumstances, refuse the Prime Minister a dissolution of Parliament and/or appoint someone else as Prime Minister. But any Governor-General intending to follow this path had better be accurate in his reading of the political climate, or he may in the end find that it is his tenure that is terminated.

The electorate can force the Governor-General to act by registering serious dissatisfaction with the government's performance in many ways, including at by-elections. A Prime Minister may also become so unpopular with his supporters in Parliament that he is forced to resign office. In this, the supporters may be responding to their interpretation of public feeling and their calculation of their chances at any future election under the Prime Minister's leadership, as happened with Mrs. Margaret Thatcher in the United Kingdom. Were Mrs. Thatcher operating under an American-type situation, say as President, it would not have been possible for members of her party in similar manner to put a premature end to her tenure by indicating their unwillingness to continue to support her as leader of their party.

Placing a maximum limit on the length of time which a person may serve as Prime Minister is also regarded as unnecessary as well as associated with a number of disadvantages. Firstly, under existing arrangements, it is always open to the electorate to end the tenure of an ineffective Prime Minister and the government he leads, by depriving them of their majority in Parliament. This is seen as preferable to, and as rendering unnecessary the establishment of, constitutional provision under which even a popular and productive government may find that it can no longer be of service to its populace.

Secondly, it would appear to make little sense to effect the removal of a Prime Minister and his government under a constitutional provision where they, for example, are in the midst of implementing a successful long-term strategy of development which is yielding beneficial returns to the country.

At any rate, there are bound to be serious conceptual problems in operationalising such a system. For example, what should be an adequate tenure for a given person occupying the post of Prime Minister? And how is this to be judged by a concept such as "not more than two five year terms" neutral in its application without regard to the performance of those to whom it is applicable? It would appear as if the better approach is not to stipulate for any fixed term for such a functionary and the government he leads, but to permit the electorate and their political right to support or not support a government at subsequently held elections.

Is the Westminster System Wilting?

The system of government in the Commonwealth Caribbean is put under tremendous strain from time to time. However, there is no indication that it is wilting as a consequence. It is to be expected that any system of government would undergo adjustment and adaptation when operating in an environment with the range of challenges confronting the states of the Commonwealth Caribbean. In this respect, the small size of the states under consideration undoubtedly contributes to the difficulties at times experienced in the working of the system in the region.

Distortions may readily be identified in the working of the Westminster system in the Commonwealth Caribbean if practice in the UK is treated as the basis of comparison. But just as the Westminster system in India, Australia and Canada, is different from the Westminster system in the UK so, too, it is in many respects different in the states of the Commonwealth Caribbean.

Especially after a hotly contested election, there may be calls for change in the system. There is, however, never any serious demand for its total reform or rejection. At any rate, such demands tend fairly quickly to abate and resume their accustomed place of dormancy. The basic satisfaction of contestants for political power with the rules under which the game is played seems to be a key factor in this attitude. The fundamental point would appear to be that the contestants for political power do not necessarily see the rules as permanently favouring any group, or operating to their disadvantage. Rather, there is a general understanding and expectation that those who criticise the operation and effect of certain rules today, may well tomorrow find themselves the beneficiaries of a change and role reversal.

However, this should not be interpreted to mean that complacency should be allowed to take the place

of creative adjustments where such a need may be indicated, which is one way of preventing any wilting in the system. No system of government is ever so perfect as to be above change. Change, though, need not mean the disappearance of the essence of the system. Undoubtedly, this is the dominant sentiment in regard to the Westminster System in the Commonwealth Caribbean.

References and Notes

1. See, for example, Gregory S. Mahler, "The Westminster model away from Westminster: Is it the only way?": *The Parliamentarian*, Vol. LXVII, July 1986, pp. 106-110.
2. See "Westminster Transplant 'Wilting'": *Weekend EC News* (The Nation Publishing Co. Ltd., Barbados), September 9, 1989, p. 20.
3. Rudolph James and Harold Lutchman, *Law and the Political Environment in Guyana* (Institute of Development Studies, University of Guyana, 1985), pp. 54, et seq.
4. In the case of Trinidad and Tobago, a new constitution was promulgated in 1976. One of the main features of this constitution was the introduction of a republic form of government – See The Constitution of Trinidad and Tobago (Enacted as the Schedule to the Constitution of the Republic of Trinidad and Tobago Act (Ch 1:2.01); also *Thinking Things Over* by The Constitution Commission (1987) of the Republic of Trinidad and Tobago (Government Printery, Trinidad and Tobago, 1988).
5. See Harold Lutchman, *The Appointment Removal And Dismissal of Political Office-holders in the Commonwealth Caribbean* (University of the Virgin Islands, 1990).
6. Ibid., p. 21, et seq.
7. See Rickey Singh, "Mitchell's clean sweep: NDP victory sparks accusations",: *Weekend EC News*, May 26, 1989, p. 8. One other consequence of this overwhelming victory was that only two of the 15 members of Parliament were not assigned portfolios or to cabinet posts – *Weekend EC News*, May 26, 1989, p. 9.
8. The Constitution of Jamaica, Section 80(2).
9. *Ibid.*, S. 35 (1).
10. The Constitution of Barbados, Section 36(1). (4).
11. See, for example, Rickey Singh, *op. cit.*
12. *The St Vincent Constitution Order 1979*, S. 28. See also Rickey Singh, "Strange fight in St Vincent – Political Jiving: from Grenada to Jamaica": *Weekend EC News*, September 8, 1989, p. 8.
13. See from Our Correspondent, "Parliament Challenged": *Caribbean Contact*, December 1989, p. 7. At the time of writing this issue has not been resolved by the courts.
14. *Ibid.*
15. *Ibid.*
16. See, for example, *Report of the Constitution Commission of Trinidad and Tobago* (Presented to His Excellency the Governor-General on January 22, 1974), p. 47, et seq.
17. See "One Party Anxiety" by EC News Writers: *EC News*, May 19-20, 1989.
18. *Report of the Constitution Commission of Trinidad and Tobago*, op. cit., p. 40.
19. *Ibid.*
20. For an account of these events see Rickey Singh, "After the Belize election: Defection stench in regional politics": *Weekend EC News*, September 15, 1989.

21. *Ibid.*
22. *Ibid.*
23. *Ibid.*
24. *Ibid.* See also Lutchman, *op. cit.*, pp. 24, et seq.
25. The Constitution of Barbados, *op. cit.*, s. 74(2).
26. The Constitution of Trinidad and Tobago, *op. cit.*, ss 49 & 49A.
27. The latter later initiated the process of converting its status to that of the de jure opposition – See Wesley Gibbings, "Panday Leads the Opposition": *Caribbean Contact*, September/October, 1990, p. 10.
28. See, for example, "Great Victory; great responsibility" (Letter from Kingston by Nora Peacocke): *Weekend EC News*, September 15, 1989, p. 61.
29. See *Report of the Constitution Commission of Trinidad and Tobago, op. cit.*, pp. 54, et seq.
30. See, for example, *Something to Remember* (The Report of the International Team of Observers at the Elections in Guyana, December 1980 – Parliamentary Human Rights Group, House of Commons, London, 1980); *Political Freedom in Guyana* (Americas Watch, New York – Parliamentary Human Rights Group, London, November, 1985); Harold A. Lutchman, *The Reform of an Irregular Electoral System: Issues and Problems in the Case of Guyana* (mimeo 1993).
31. See Carl Wint, "A Testing Time for Jamaica Democracy": *Caribbean* Contact, January/February, 1984, p. 2.
32. See, for example, Wade, ECS and Phillips, G, *Constitutional and Administrative Law* (ELBS and Longman Group Ltd., 9 ed.), pp. 16-26 and pp. 162-163.
33. There are three independent states in the Commonwealth Caribbean where the head of state is not a Governor-General, viz. Guyana, Trinidad and Tobago, and Dominica.
34. The Constitution of Saint Christopher and Nevis (1983), Section 47(4).
35. The Constitution of the Cooperative Republic of Guyana (1980), Article 99(1).
36. Among the states with constitutions falling within the former category are Jamaica (The Constitution of Jamaica, Section 64(5)) and Antigua and Barbuda (Constitution of Antigua and Barbuda, Section 60(1)), St Vincent and the Grenadines (The Constitution of St Vincent and the Grenadines, Section 48) and St Christopher and Nevis (The Constitution of St Christopher and Nevis, Section 47(4)) are examples of states falling under the second category.
37. The Constitution of St Vincent and the Grenadines, Section 48(5).
38. The Constitution of St Christopher and Nevis, Section 47(2).
39. Ibid., Section 47(3). In Barbados such extension may be for two years – vide Section 61(4) of the Constitution thereof.
40. The Constitution of Trinidad and Tobago, Section 68(4).
41. See Carl Wint, op. cit.; "Selfish Ambition Served by Snap Elections: Jamaica Church Leader" (letter by Rev. Edmund Davis, General Secretary Jamaica Council of Churches): Caribbean Contact, January/February, 1984, p. 2.
42. See, for example, "Grenada guessing game: when will elections be held?": The Daily News (United States Virgin Islands) October 18, 1988.
43. Rickey Singh, "Grenada and a letter to Kingston": Caribbean Contact, September, 1989.
44. See '"Blaize To Stifle Motion"': EC News, August 18-19, 1989. It was not only Grenadian politicians who were critical of the Prime Minister's behaviour. Thus, Prime Minister Eugenia Charles of Dominica was reported as saying that "if she had been faced with the political situation that confronted Blaize she would not have prorogued parliament like he did but would have dissolved and give voters a chance to select a government to run their affairs" – vide "Call Elections Now, Mr. Blaize": That's what Charles would do": EC News, September 8-9, 1990. See also "Blaize stands alone as CDU throws weight behind Mitchell": EC News, September 15-16, 1989 where the Prime Ministers of St Lucia, and St Vincent and the Grenadines also criticised Blaize.
45. See Devonson La Mothe, "Grenadians Await Elections Date": Caribbean Contact, February, 1990, p. 7; Devonson La Mothe, "Will Gairy Win Again?": *Caribbean Contact,* March, 1990, p. 1.

Democracies: Patterns of Majoritarian and Concensus Government in Twenty-one Countries

The Westminster Model of Democracy
Arerid Lijphart

Democratic Ideals and Realities

The literal meaning of democracy—government by the people—is probably also the most basic and most widely used definition. The one major amendment that is necessary when we speak of democracy at the national level in modern large-scale nation-states is that the acts of government are usually performed not directly by the citizens but indirectly by representatives whom they elect on a free and equal basis. Although elements of direct democracy can be found even in some large democratic states (as we shall see in chapter 12), democracy is usually representative democracy: government by the freely elected representatives of the people.

Democracy may be defined not only as government by the people but also, in President Abraham Lincoln's famous formulation, as government for the people—that is, government in accordance with the people's preferences. An ideal democratic government would be one whose actions were always in perfect correspondence with the preferences of all its citizens. Such complete responsiveness in government has never existed and may never be achieved, but it can serve as an ideal to which democratic regimes should aspire. It can also be regarded as the end of a scale on which the degree of democratic responsiveness of different regimes may be measured. The subject of this book is not the ideal of democracy but the operation of actual democracies that approximate the ideal relatively closely—and that Robert Dahl calls "polyarchies" in order to distinguish them from ideal democracy.[1] These democratic regimes are characterized not by perfect responsiveness but by a high degree of it; their actions have been in relatively close correspondence with the wishes of relatively many of their citizens for a long period of time. Both definitions of democracy will also be used later to distinguish the two basic types of democracy

As Dahl has shown, a reasonably responsive democracy can exist only if at least eight institutional guarantees are present:

1. Freedom to form and join organisations;
2. Freedom of expression;
3. The right to vote;
4. Eligibility for public office;
5. The right of political leaders to compete for support and vote;
6. Alternative sources of information;
7. Free and fair elections;
8. Institutions for making government policies depend on votes and other expressions of preference.[2]

The first six of these embody the classic democratic right of liberty, especially the freedoms of speech and assembly, and they also imply the second classic democratic value of equality. In the democracies treated in this book, these rights are securely guaranteed without major variations between different countries. Guarantees 7 and 8 are also provided, but substantial differences occur in the way elections and other institutions and practices are organized to insure [SIC] responsive government. This book will focus on the variety of formal and informal institutions and practices that are used to translate citizen preferences into public policies. While recognizing and describing these differences, I will also try to discover patterns and regularities, and I will argue that both the variations and the regularities can be interpreted in terms of two diametrically opposite models of democracy: the majoritarian model (or the Westminster model) and the consensus model.

The majoritarian and consensus models of democracy differ on eight dimensions. These will be discussed in a preliminary fashion in the remainder of this chapter and in chapter 2, and they will be analyzed in greater depth in the nine chapters that comprise the bulk of the book (chapters 4 to 12). The twenty-two empirical cases of democratic regimes that will be compared— mainly the democracies of the North Atlantic area but also including Israel, Japan, Australia, and New Zealand—will be introduced in chapter 3. There are twenty-one countries but twenty-two democratic re-

gimes because the French Fourth and Fifth Republics will be treated as separate cases. The concluding chapter (chapter 13) will summarize the overall patterns of democracy that we find in our set of democracies and consider the question: to what extent are the two contrasting models of democracy not only logically coherent but also empirical models?

The principal emphasis throughout the book will be on the interrelationships among the different majoritarian and consensual characteristics. In the concluding chapter, I shall also try to explain the differential incidence of majoritarian and consensual patterns in the twenty-two democratic regimes in terms of the countries' cultural and structural characteristics: the degree to which they are plural (divided) societies, the sizes of their populations, and Anglo-American versus other cultural influences. An additional question worth asking is: how does the type of democratic regime, majoritarian or consensual, affect its performance? My analysis will suggest that majoritarian democracy is especially appropriate for, and works best in, homogeneous societies, whereas consensus democracy is more suitable for plural societies. Otherwise, there is relatively little variation in how well the democracies analyzed in this book perform. As chapter 3 will show, my cases of democracy were chosen according to exacting standards: they are all democracies of long standing and must also be judged as basically successful. Indeed, one of the principal messages of this book is that there are many different ways of successfully running a democracy. [3]

The Westminster Model: Nine Majoritarian Elements

The essence of the Westminster model is majority rule. The model can be seen as the most obvious solution to the dilemma of what is meant by "the people" in our definition of democracy. Who will do the governing and to whose interests should the government be responsive when the people are in disagreement and have divergent preferences? One answer is: the majority of the people. Its great merit is that any other answer, such as the requirement of unanimity or a qualified majority, entails minority rule—or at least a minority veto—and that government by the majority and in accordance with the majority's wishes comes closer to the democratic ideal than government by and responsive to a minority. The alternative answer to the dilemma is: as many people as possible. This is the essence of the consensus model: as we shall see in more detail in the next chapter, its rules and institutions aim at broad participation in government and broad agreement on the policies that the government should pursue.

In this book the term Westminster model will be used inter-changeably with majoritarian model to refer to a general model of democracy. It may also be used more narrowly to denote the main characteristics of British parliamentary and governmental institutions; Great Britain's Parliament meets in the Palace of Westminster in London. The British version of the Westminster model is both the original and the best-known example of this model. It is also widely admired. Richard Rose points out that, "with confidence born of continental isolation, Americans have come to assume that their institutions—the Presidency, Congress and the Supreme Court—are the prototype of what should be adopted elsewhere."[4] But American political scientists, especially those in the field of comparative politics, have tended to hold the British system of government in at least equally high esteem.[5]

One famous political scientist who fervently admired the Westminster model was President Woodrow Wilson. In his early writings he went so far as to urge the abolition of presidential government and the adoption of British-style parliamentary government in the United States. Such views have also been held by many other non-British observers of British politics, and many features of the Westminster model have been exported to other countries: Canada, Australia, New Zealand, and most of Britain's colonies in Asia and Africa at the moment of their independence. Wilson referred to parliamentary government in accordance with the Westminster model as "the world's fashion."[6]

The Westminster model consists of the following nine inter-related elements, which will be illustrated by features of the British political system—deliberately described in rather stark terms, the necessary nuances to be added later—particularly as it operated in the period from 1945 to 1970:

1.   Concentration of executive power: one-party and bare-majority cabinets. The most powerful organ of British government is the cabinet. It is usually composed of members of the party that has the majority of seats in the House of Commons, and the minority is not included. Coalition cabinets are rare. Because in the British two-party system the two principal parties are of approximately equal strength, the party that wins the elections usually represents no more than a narrow majority, and the minority is relatively large. Hence the British one-party and bare-majority cabinet is the perfect embodiment of the principle of majority rule: it wields vast amounts of political power to rule as the representative of and in the interest of a majority that is not of overwhelming proportions. A large minority is excluded from power and condemned to the role of opposition.

2.   Fusion of power and cabinet dominance. In his enduring classic, *The English Constitution,* first published in 1867, Walter Bagehot states that "the close union, the nearly complete fusion of the executive and legislative powers" is the key explanation of the efficient operation of the British government.[7] Britain has a parliamentary system of government, which means that the cabinet is dependent on the confidence of Parliament—in contrast with a presidential system of government, exemplified by the United States, in which the presidential executive cannot normally be removed by the legislature (except by impeachment). In theory, because the House of Commons can vote a cabinet out of office, it "controls" the cabinet. In reality, however, the relationship is reversed. Because the cabinet is composed of the leaders of a cohesive majority party in the House of Commons, it is normally backed by the majority in the House of Commons, and it can confidently count on staying in office and getting its legislative proposals approved. The cabinet is clearly dominant vis-à-vis Parliament.

3.   Asymmetric bicameralism. The British parliament consists of two chambers: the House of Commons, which is popularly elected, and the House of Lords, which consists mainly of members of the hereditary nobility. Their relationship is an asymmetric one: almost all legislative power belongs to the House of Commons. The only power that the House of Lords retains is the power to delay legislation: money bills can be delayed for one month and all other bills for one year. It may be argued that a purer version of the Westminster model would be characterised by unicameralism, because a single chamber dominated by a majority party and by a one-party cabinet would be a more perfect manifestation of majority rule. Britain comes very close to this ideal: in everyday discussion, "Parliament" refers almost exclusively to the House of Commons, British asymmetric bicameralism may also be called near unicameralism.

4.   Two-party system. British politics is dominated by two large parties: the Conservative party and the Labour party. There are other parties, in particular the Liberals, that contest elections and win seals in the House of Commons, but they are not large enough to be the overall victors. The bulk of the seats are captured by the two major parties, and they form the cabinets: the Labour party from 1945 to 1951, 1964 to

1970, and 1974 to 1979, and the Conservatives from 1951 to 1964, 1970 to 1974, and from 1979 on.

5. *One-dimensional party system.* The principal politically significant difference that divides the British and their main parties is disagreement about socioeconomic policies: on the left-right spectrum, Labour represents the left-of-center and the Conservative party the right-of-center preferences. This difference is also reflected in the pattern of voters' support for the parties in elections to the House of Commons; working-class voters tend to cast their ballots for Labour candidates and middle-class voters tend to support Conservative candidates. There are other differences, of course, but these do not have a major effect on the composition of the House of Commons and the cabinet. For instance, religious differences between Protestants and Catholics are no longer politically salient. Regional and ethnic difference, particularly Scottish national sentiments, arc of greater importance, but they do not present a grave threat to the hegemony of the Conservative and Labour parties. British society is highly homogeneous, and the socioeconomic issue dimension is the only dimension on which the main parties clearly and consistently diverge.

6. *Plurality system of elections.* The 650 members of the House of Commons are elected in single-member districts according to the plurality method, which in Britain is often referred to as the "first past the post" system: the candidate with the majority vote or, if there is no majority, with the largest minority vote wins.

7. *Unitary and centralized government.* Local governments in Britain perform a series of important functions, but they are the creatures of the central government and their powers are not constitutionally guaranteed (as in a federal system). Moreover, they are financially dependent on the central government. This unitary and centralized system means that there are no clearly designated geographical and functional areas from which the parliamentary majority and the cabinet are barred.

8. *Unwritten constitution and parliamentary sovereignty.* Britain has a constitution that is "unwritten" in the sense that there is not a single written document that specifies the composition and powers of the governmental institutions and the rights of citizens. These are defined instead in a number of basic laws, customs, and conventions. Parliament will normally obey these constitutional rules, but it is not formally bound by them. Even the basic laws have no special status, and they can be changed by Parliament in the same way as any other laws. The courts do not have the power of judicial review. Parliament is the ultimate, or sovereign, authority. Parliamentary sovereignty is a vital ingredient of the majoritarianism of the Westminster model, because it means that there are no formal restrictions on the power of the majority of the House of Commons.

9. *Exclusively representative democracy.* Parliamentary sovereignty also means that, because all power is concentrated in the House of Commons acting as the people's representative, there is no room for any element of direct democracy such as the referendum. In the words of one constitutional expert, "referenda are foreign to British constitutional practice."[8] Parliamentary sovereignty and popular sovereignty are incompatible, and British democracy is therefore an exclusively representative democracy.

British Deviations from the Westminster Model

The nine characteristics of the Westminster model together make the model thoroughly majoritarian. But the power of the majority should not be exaggerated. In Britain, majority rule does not entail majority tyranny. Although there are no formal limitations on parliamentary power — and hence no formal limits to what the majority of the House of Commons can do — strong informal customs do restrain the majority. The rights and freedoms of the people are not violated, and minorities are not suppressed. In the House of Commons, the minority is treated with respect, and it is also customary that the leader of the opposition be consulted by the cabinet on questions that are especially important or sensitive. British democracy, although majoritarian, is tolerant and civil.

It should also be emphasized that British politics was in close conformity with the Westminster model only in the twenty-five years from 1945 to 1970. From 1918, when the admission of women to the suffrage (although still not on the same basis as men) marked the beginning of a fully democratic system, until 1945 and again in the period since 1970, there have been significant deviations from the Westminster model of majoritarian democracy with regard to almost all of the model's nine characteristics.

1. *Concentration of executive power: one-party and bare-majority cabinets.* As David Butler writes, "single-party government is the British norm. Politicians and writers on politics assume that, in all but exceptional circumstances, one party will have a Parliamentary majority and will conduct the nation's

affairs." But he continues, "clear-cut single-party government has been much less prevalent than many would suppose."[9] In fact, one-party majority cabinets have held office for only about 60 percent of the years between 1918 and 1980. Most of the deviations from the norm—coalitions of two or more parties and minority cabinets—occurred from 1918 to 1945. The most recent instance of a clear and explicit coalition cabinet was the 1940-45 wartime coalition formed by the Conservatives, who had a parliamentary majority, with the Labour and Liberal parties, under Conservative Prime Minister Winston Churchill. There were two minority Labour cabinets in the 1970s. In the parliamentary election of March 1974, the Labour party won a plurality but not a majority of the seats and formed a minority government dependent on all other parties not uniting to defeat it. New elections were held in October of the same year in which Labour won an outright, albeit narrow, majority of the seats; but this majority was eroded by defections and by-election defeats, and the Labour cabinet again became a minority cabinet in 1976. The 1970s also provide an example of a two-party coalition. In 1977, the minority Labour cabinet negotiated a formal pact with the thirteen Liberals in the House of Commons in order to regain a parliamentary majority: the Liberals agreed to support the cabinet in exchange for consultation on legislative proposals prior to their submission to Parliament, but no Liberals entered the cabinet. This so-called Lab-Lib pact lasted until 1978.

2.   *Fusion of power and cabinet dominance.* Strong cabinet leadership depends on majority support in the House of Commons and on the cohesiveness of the majority party. When either or both of these conditions are absent, cabinets lose much of their predominant position. Since 1970 there has been a significant increase in the frequency of parliamentary defeats of important proposals introduced by both majority and minority cabinets. This has even caused a change in the traditional view that cabinets must resign or dissolve the House of Commons and call for new elections if they suffer a defeat on either a parliamentary vote of no confidence or a major bill of central importance to the cabinet. After the frequent cabinet defeats of the 1970s, the new unwritten rule is that only an explicit vote of no confidence necessitates resignation or new elections.[10] After suffering but surviving many legislative defeats, Prime Minister James Callaghan's minority Labour cabinet was finally brought down by such a no confidence vote in 1979.

3.   *Asymmetric bicameralism.* The one-year limit on the power of the House of Lords to delay the passage of ordinary non-money bills was established in 1949. Between the major reform of 1911 and 1949 the Lords' delaying power was about two years, but in the entire period since 1911 they have usually refrained from imposing long delays. No changes have taken place in recent years, although the overwhelmingly Conservative House of Lords became somewhat more assertive during the periods of weak Labour cabinets in the 1970s. This has also increased the sentiments in the Labour party to abolish the House of Lords altogether – and thus to change near-unicameralism into pure and complete unicameralism

4.   *Two-party system.* The interwar years were a transitional period during which the Labour party replaced the Liberals as one of the two big parties. In the 1945 election, the Labour and Conservative parties together won about 85 percent of the votes and 92.5 percent of the seats in the House of Commons. The hegemony of these two parties was even clearer in the seven elections from 1950 to 1970: jointly they never won less than 87.5 percent of the votes and 98 percent of the seats. But their support declined considerably in the 1970s; although they managed to win roughly 95 percent of the parliamentary seats in the three elections held after 1970, their joint share of the popular vote was only about 75 percent in the two elections in 1974 and about 81 percent in the 1979 election. The Liberals were the main beneficiaries. Although they succeeded in winning only a disappointing number of seats (14, 13, and 11 respectively in the three elections), they captured about 19 percent of the votes in the two elections of 1974 and about 14 percent in 1979. In the early 1980s, a graver threat to the two-party system appeared in the form of the Social Democratic party, mainly consisting of defectors from Labour. Only about half a year after the new party's launching in 1981, the London Economist wrote: "Its alliance with the Liberals will give the two parties at least a sporting chance of being Britain's biggest political entity in Westminster after the next general election."[11]

5.   *One-dimensional party system.* From about 1970 on, it has become increasingly clear that it is a mistake to regard British society as basically homogeneous. Especially Scotland, Wales, and Northern Ireland—the non-English regions of what is officially called the United Kingdom of Great Britain and Northern Ireland—contribute considerable diversity in political attitudes and preferences. In 1964, Rose was the spokesman of the majority of scholarly observers of British politics when he wrote: "Today politics in the United Kingdom is greatly simplified by the absence of major cleavages along the lines of ethnic groups, language, or religion." But six years later he described the United Kingdom more accurately as "a multi-national state."[12] For the party system this means that social class is not the only, although still the most important, dimension of differentiation. The ethnic factor has become especially strong in Scotland: in the October 1974 elections, the Scottish National party received more than 30 percent of the votes cast in Scotland and 11 House of Commons seats, almost as many as the Liberals. Its fortunes have somewhat declined since then, but in 1979 it still won two parliamentary seats, the same number that was won by the Welsh nationalists. Religion has not entirely disappeared as a determinant of voting behavior either: in fact, the Protestant-Catholic difference in Northern Ireland is the overwhelmingly dominant division separating the parties and their supporters in that part of the United Kingdom.

6. *Plurality system of elections.* No changes have been made in the plurality single-member district method of electing the House of Commons, but this electoral system has come under increasing criticism, mainly because of the disproportional results it produced in the 1970s.[13] For instance, the Labour party won an absolute parliamentary majority of 319 out of 635 seats with only 39.3 percent of the total vote in the October 1974 elections, while the Liberals won only 13 seats with 18.6 percent of the vote – almost half of the Labour vote. The Liberals are understandably eager to introduce some form of proportional representation, but the Conservative and Labour parties remain committed to the plurality method. It should be pointed out, however, that proportional representation was adopted for Northern Ireland elections after the outbreak of Protestant-Catholic strife by a Conservative cabinet in the early 1970s, and that the subsequent Labour cabinets continued this policy. The principle of proportionality is no longer anathema.

7. *Unitary and centralized government.* The United Kingdom remains a unitary state, but can it also be described as a highly centralized state? Two exceptions should be noted. One is that Northern Ireland was ruled by its own parliament and cabinet with a very high degree of autonomy—more than what most states in federal systems have—from 1921, when the Republic of Ireland became independent, until the imposition of direct rule from London in 1972. The second exception is the gradual movement toward greater autonomy for Scotland and Wales—"devolution," in British parlance.

8. *Unwritten constitution and parliamentary sovereignty.* Britain's entry into the European Economic Community (Common Market), which is a supranational instead of merely an international organization, in 1973 entailed the acceptance of the European Community's laws and institutions as higher authorities than the national parliament with regard to several areas of policy. Because sovereignty means supreme and ultimate authority, the British Parliament can therefore no longer be regarded as fully sovereign. Britain's membership in the European Community has also introduced a potential right of judicial review both for the Community's Court of Justice and for British courts: "Parliament's supremacy is challenged by the right of the Community institutions to legislate for the United Kingdom (without the prior consent of Parliament) and by the right of the courts to rule on the admissibility (in terms of Community law) of future acts of Parliament."[14]

9. *Exclusively representative democracy.* The rule that the referendum is incompatible with the Westminster model was also broken in the 1970s, when Parliament voted to let the people decide the controversial issue of Britain's membership in the European Community. In a unique referendum in 1975—the only national referendum ever held in the United Kingdom—the British electorate voted to keep Britain in the Community.

In one final respect, the simple picture of an omnipotent one-party cabinet using its parliamentary majority to carry out the mandate it has received from the voters is, and has always been, false and misleading. It implies that the cabinet can formulate and execute its policies without the aid of other forces in society and without encountering any significant resistance from these forces. In fact, it has long been recognized that in Britain and other democracies many organized groups compete for influence, and that they tend to check and balance not only each other but also the political parties and the government. This pluralist view of the political process has been strengthened in recent years by the "corporate pluralists," who have called attention to the fact that especially the major economic interest groups have become closely and continually involved in decision-making, and that governments have become extremely dependent on these new partners. Although the Conservative cabinet still had a comfortable parliamentary majority in early 1974, the striking mine-workers successfully defied it and forced it to call an election—which it lost. The misleading image of cabinet omnipotence has been replaced by the new image—probably also somewhat exaggerated—of "the illusion of governmental authority."[15]

Notes

1. Robert A. Dahl, *Polyarch: Participation and Opposition* (New Haven: Yale University Press, 1971). See also John D. May, "Defining Democracy: A Bid for Coherence and Consensus," *Political Studies 26*, no. 1, (March 1978): 1-14
2. Dahl, *Polyarchy*, p. 3.
3. Democratic performance has also been stubbornly resistant to meaningful and precise measurement. In the strongest attempt so far to measure how well democracies perform, G. Bingham Powell uses three indicators: executive stability or durability, voting turnout, and the absence of large-scale violence. Chapters 5 and 7 will show, however, that executive durability is not a good measure of democratic performance at all; it merely indicates the strength of the executive in realtion to the legislature. Voting turnout is a weak and peripheral aspect of performance. And large-scale violence is fortunately a rare occurrence in all of our democracies. See G. Bingham Powell, Jr., *Contemporary Democracies: Participation, Stability, and Violence* (Cambridge, Mass.: Harvard University Press, 1982).
4. Richard Rose, " A Model Democracy?", in Richard Rose, ed., *Lessons from America: An Exploration* (New York: Wiley, 1974), p.131.
5. Dennis Kavannagh, "An American Science of British Politics," *Political Studies 22*, no.3 (September 1974): 251-70.
6. Woodrow Wilson, "Committee or Cabinet Government," *Overland Monthly*, January 1884, quoted by Walter Lippmann in his introduction to Woodrow Wilson, *Congressional Government: A Study in American Politics* (New York: Meridian Books, 1956), p. 13.
7. Walter Baghot, *The English Constitution* (London: World's Classics, 1995), p. 9.
8. D.C.M. Yardley, "The Effectiveness of the Westminster Model of Constitution," in George W. Kenton and Georg Schwarzenberger, eds., *Year Book of World Affairs 1977* (London: Stevens and Sons, 1977), p. 348.
9. David Butler, "Conclusions," in David Butler, ed., *Coalitiions in British Politics* (New York: St. Martin's Press, 1978), p.112.
10. Leon D. Epstein, "What Happened to the British Party Model?", *American Political Science Review 74* no. 1 (March 1980): pp. 9-22; Philip Norton, "The Changing Face of the British House of Commons in the 1970s," *Legislative Studies Quarterly 5*, no. 3 (August 1980): 333-57.
11. *The Economist*, December 5, 1981, p. 69.
12. Richard Rose, *Politics in England: An Interpretation* (Boston: Little Brown, 1964), p. 10; Richard Rose, *The United Kingdom as a Multi-National State*, Occasional Paper Number 6 (Glasgow: Survey Research Centre, University of Strathclyde, 1970).
13. S.E. Finer, "Introduction: Adversary Politics and Electoral Reform," in S.E. Finer, ed., *Adversary Politics and Electoral Reform* (London: Anthony Wigram, 1975) pp. 6-12.
14. David Coombs, "British Government and the European Community," in Dennis Kavanagh and Richard Rose, eds., *New Trends in British Politics: Issues for Research* (London: Sage, 1977), p. 88.
15. Norman H. Keehn, "Great Britain: The Illusion of Government Authority," *World Politics 30*, no. 4 (July 1978): 538-62 (italics added).

Parliamentary Versus Presidential Government

Edited By Arend Lijphart

Parliamentary Government And Presidential Government

Douglas V. Verney

Parliamentarism is the most widely adopted system of government, and it seems appropriate to refer to British parliamentary experience in particular because it is the British system which has provided an example for a great many other countries. Nowadays when it is fashionable to speak of political systems and theories as 'not for export' it is worth bearing in mind the success with which a system adopted piecemeal to suit British constitutional developments has proved feasible in different situations abroad. This is not to imply that the British parliamentary system should be taken as the model and that others are, as it were, deviations from the norm, although generations of Englishmen have been tempted to make this assumption....

Indeed an examination of parliamentarism in various countries indicates that there are two main types of parliamentary procedure, the British and the continental....

This analysis of parliamentarism is concerned less with distinguishing the various forms of parliamentarism than with establishing the highest common factors in different parliamentary systems.... It may surprise those who have tended to regard British government as the model as well as the Mother of Parliaments to know that the United Kingdom could abolish the monarchy, adopt a single code of constitutional laws on the pattern of the French or American constitutions, transform the House of Lords into a senate (or even do away with it), introduce a multiparty system based on proportional representation, institute a number of parliamentary committees to deal with specific topics such as finance and foreign affairs, and still possess a parliamentary system.

There would seem to be a number of basic principles applicable to both of the chief varieties of parliamentary government....

1

The Assembly Becomes A Parliament

Where parliamentary government has evolved rather than been the product of revolution there have often been three phases, though the transition from one to the other has not always been perceptible at the time. First there has been government by a monarch who has been responsible for the whole political system. Then there has arisen an assembly of members who have challenged the hegemony of the king. Finally the assembly has taken over responsibility for government, acting as a parliament, the monarch being deprived of most of his traditional powers.

This has certainly been the pattern in Britain. As late as the seventeenth century King James I could still preach the doctrine of the Divine Right of Kings....

However, by establishing their power over the purse, assemblies were ultimately able to claim their own area of jurisdiction. Henceforth the monarch's role was increasingly that of an executive dependent ultimately on the goodwill of the legislature. Constitutional development entered a second phase in which the term 'legislative power' was given to assemblies to distinguish them from the 'executive power' of the king....

But even as the theory of the separation of powers was coming into vogue the transition to the third and present phase was under way in Britain. In the eighteenth century the king was already losing his executive power to ministers who came to regard the assembly, not the monarch, as the sovereign to whom they were really responsible. Ministers were increasingly chosen from among members of the assembly and resigned when the assembly withdrew its confidence from them....

In parliamentary monarchies such as Britain, Belgium and Sweden, the monarch has ceased in practice (though not in form) to exercise even the executive power. Government has passed to 'his' ministers who are responsible to the legislature. Parliamentary government implies a certain fusion of the executive and legislative functions, the body which has been merely an assembly of representatives being transformed into a parliament....

It is true that for the most part the use of the term 'parliament' at one time to include the government and at others to exclude it seems to cause little difficulty, provided some knowledge of the parliamentary system is assumed. In a comparative study of political systems, however, such ambiguity presents certain problems if like is to be compared with like. It therefore becomes necessary to insist on a more precise usage. 'Parliament' will at all times signify a body which includes the government. When it is necessary to refer to the legislature excluding members of the government the term 'assembly' will be used....

The first characteristic of parliamentarism may now be summarized. It is a political system where the executive, once separate, has been challenged by the assembly which is then transformed into a parliament comprising both government and assembly.

2
The Executive Is Divided Into Two Parts

One important consequence of the transformation of the assembly into a parliament is that the executive is now split in two, a prime minister or chancellor becoming head of the government and the monarch or president acting as head of state. Usually the monarch occupies his throne by hereditary title (though elected monarchies, e.g. in Malaya, are not unknown), while a president is elected by parliament....

3
The Head Of State Appoints the Head Of Government

The value of a divided executive in constitutional monarchies is fairly obvious. For one thing, the proper business of state can be carried on by a government responsible to the legislature while the mystique of monarchy is preserved. There seems no apparent reason, at first glance, for dividing it in republics. Admittedly it is useful to have someone above the day-to-day political warfare to receive ambassadors and to decorate ceremonial occasions, but this hardly seems to justify the expense of such an office. After all, the president of the United States, who as head of the American government bears the greatest responsibilities of any statesman in the world, manages to combine with his high and lonely eminence the even higher office of head of state.

However, it is in the very nature of the parliamentary system that there shall be two distinct offices, and that the head of the government shall be appointed by the head of state. Were the electorate itself to perform this task, directly or through a special college of electors as in the United States or Finland, the system would become, in this respect at least, presidential in character....

4
The Head of the Government Appoints The Ministry

An interesting feature of parliamentarisrn is the distinction made between the prime minister and other ministers. The former is appointed by the head of state;

the latter are nominated by the prime minister after his appointment. Usually the selection of various ministers allows a certain amount of personal choice to a head of government, which cannot usually be said of the appointment of a prime minister by the head of state. Ministers are formally appointed by the head of state, who may often no doubt exert an informal influence upon appointments—but so may the state of party alignments and factions in the assembly....

5
The Ministry (Or Government) Is a Collective Body

The transfer from the monarchical executive to a council of ministers has meant that a single person has been replaced by a collective body. Whereas under *anciens régimes* it was the king's pleasure *(le Roi le veult)*, under parliamentarism the prime minister is merely first among equals *(primus inter pares)*, though no doubt some prime ministers are more forceful than others....

6
Ministers Are Usually Members of Parliament

Members of the government have a double role to play in the parliamentary system. They are not only ministers but are at the same time members of parliament, elected (unless they are members of the British House of Lords) like the members of the assembly and equally dependent upon the goodwill of their constituents....

Since, according to the usage adopted in this chapter, parliament comprises both government and assembly, a member of the government is *ipso facto* a member of parliament, but by definition he cannot be a member of the assembly. In fully parliamentary countries such as the United Kingdom where ministers are members of parliament it is difficult to make the distinction between government, parliament and assembly clear. Indeed the attempt to make one seems artificial.

However, not all parliamentary countries have accepted the necessity for ministers to be members of one of the houses of parliament. In Sweden up to a third of the ministry of fifteen members have on occasion in recent years not been members of parliament. In The Netherlands, Norway and Luxembourg ministers are actually forbidden to be members of parliament after their appointment. Here there is a relic of the old doctrine of the separation of powers when ministers were responsible to the monarch....

Generally speaking, nevertheless, it is usual for most if not all ministers to be members of parliament. Where they are not, the system may still be said to be of the parliamentary type if they can take part in parliamentary debates and are truly responsible to the assembly for the conduct of the executive. In Norway, Sweden, The Netherlands and Luxembourg, all parliamentary monarchies, these conditions are fulfilled. In the French Fifth Republic, where the government is not responsible to parliament for the conduct of the president, they are not.

7
The Government Is Politically Responsible To The Assembly

In parliamentary systems the government is responsible to the assembly which may, if it thinks that the government is acting unwisely or unconstitutionally, refuse to give it support. By a formal vote of censure or by simply not assenting to an important government proposal the assembly can force the government to resign and cause the head of state to appoint a new government....

8
The Head Of Government May Advise The Head Of State To Dissolve Parliament

In the pre-parliamentary monarchies of Europe the monarch could, if dissatisfied with his assembly, dissolve one or more houses in the hope of securing a more amenable selection of representatives after a new election. Today, when the executive is divided, it is still the head of state who dissolves parliament, but he does so on the request, and only on the request, of the head of government....

Certain states generally regarded as parliamentary severely restrict the right of the executive to dissolve the assembly. In Norway the Storting dissolves itself, the head of state being allowed to dissolve only special sessions, but this is a departure from parliamentarism inspired by the convention theory of the French Revolution ....

9
Parliament As A Whole Is Supreme Over Its Constituent Parts, Government And Assembly, Neither Of Which May Dominate The Other

The notion of the supremacy of parliament as a whole over its parts is a distinctive characteristic of parliamentary systems. This may seem a glimpse of the obvious to those accustomed to parliamentary government, but it is in fact an important principle, all too often forgotten, that neither of the constituent elements of parliament may completely dominate the other. The government depends upon the support of the assembly if it is to continue in office, but the assembly is not supreme because the government can, if it chooses, dissolve parliament and appeal to the electorate at the polls. Many parliamentary systems have failed because one or other of them has claimed supremacy, and parliament as a whole has not been supreme over both government and assembly.

In practice the nature of parliamentary supremacy varies from country to country. In the United Kingdom and Scandinavia the emphasis is on the government's role in parliament and in Britain the system is actually called 'cabinet government'. In others, notably the French Third and Fourth Republics, the dominant role in parliament was played by the assembly....

10
The Government As A Whole Is Only Indirectly Responsible To The Electorate

A parliamentary government, though directly responsible to the assembly, is only indirectly responsible to the electorate. The government as a whole is not directly elected by the voters but is appointed indirectly from amongst the representatives whom they elect to the assembly. The earlier direct relationship of monarch and people whereby persons could petition their sovereign disappeared as parliamentarism was introduced. Today the route to the government lies through elected representatives though in Britain, for example, one may still formally petition the monarch. It is true that members of the government, like other members of parliament, must (unless they are peers) stand before their constituents for election. However, they do so not as members of the government but as candidates for the assembly in the ordinary way. The responsibility for transforming them, once elected, into ministers rests with the prime minister alone (and of course with the monarch in the case of the prime minister)....

11
Parliament Is The Focus Of Power In The Political System

The fusion of the executive and legislative powers in parliament is responsible for the overriding ascendancy

of parliament in the political order. It is the stage on which the drama of politics is played out; it is the forum of the nation's ideas; and it is the school where future political leaders are trained. For parliamentarism to succeed, the government must not fret at the constant challenge which the Assembly offers to its programme, nor wince at the criticism made of its administration. The Assembly in turn must resist the temptation to usurp the functions of Government. Here is a delicate balance of powers which check each other without the benefit of separate institutions....

Presidential government is often associated with the theory of the separation of powers which was popular in the eighteenth century when the American constitution was framed. Two writers in particular drew attention to this notion. John Locke, writing at the end of the seventeenth century, suggested that the long conflict between the British monarch and the houses of parliament would best be resolved by the separation of the king as executive from the two houses as legislature, each body having its own sphere. In the mid-eighteenth century a French observer of the British political scene, Montesquieu, pronounced himself in favour of the British system of government as one which embodied, in contrast to the despotism of the Bourbons, the separation of the executive, legislative, and judicial powers. Historically the theory as expounded by Locke and more especially Montesquieu is important for an understanding of the climate of opinion in which the American constitution was framed.

However, it is one thing to study this celebrated theory for historical purposes but quite another to trace its contemporary significance for an understanding of presidential government. It was, after all, based on the assumption that a monarch would act as executive and an assembly as legislature. The theory was considered to be an improvement on the absolute monarchies of the continent, which it undoubtedly was, and was praised with them in mind. There was as yet no experience of parliamentarism. Today such constitutional monarchies as still survive are based on the parliamentary principle.

Another offspring and successor of the theory is presidential government, but the substitution of an elected president for a hereditary monarch has, as we have seen, created a system hardly comparable with pre-parliamentary limited monarchies. If presidential government is regarded simply as a direct form or expression of the eighteenth-century doctrine of the separation of powers then (as indeed many people have thought) the Americans may, by adopting their rigid constitution, have artificially prevented their political system from developing into parliamentarism. But if, as it is argued here, the system is a successor to that doctrine then it is not like limited monarchy, the precursor of parliamentary government, but one of its two offsprings, the other being parliamentarism....

It seemed appropriate to begin an analysis of parliamentary government by reference to British political institutions. It is equally valuable to study presidentialism by first examining the American political system. The United States was the first important country to break with the European monarchical tradition and to shake off colonial rule. The break occurred in the eighteenth century when Britain was still a limited monarchy and the theory of the separation of powers was in vogue. The American constitution bears witness to these influences and to the colonial government of governor and legislature, an elected president replacing the king or governor as the executive power. A number of countries—all twenty American republics, Liberia, the Philippines, South Korea and South Vietnam—have followed the example of the United States, though rarely with comparable success. The American political system is therefore the model and prototype of presidential government. Yet the United States, like the United Kingdom, could aboli5h or transform many of its institutions and remain based on the same theory of government. For example, the framers of the 1787 constitution could have proposed an elective monarch instead of a president, a house of lords rather than a senate, and a unitary political system instead of a federal union of states without destroying the presidential principle—though the name 'presidential' would hardly be suitable for a system where the executive was an elective monarch. Presidential, like parliamentary, theory has certain basic characteristics irrespective of any particular political system.

The nature of presidential theory can best be understood by re-stating the eleven propositions [concerning parliamentary government—Ed.] as they apply to presidential government.

1

The Assembly Remains An Assembly Only

Parliamentary theory implies that the second phase of constitutional development, in which the assembly

and judiciary claim their own areas of jurisdiction alongside the executive, shall give way to a third in which assembly and government are fused in a parliament. Presidential theory on the other hand requires the assembly to remain separate as in the second phase. The American Revolution led to a transfer from colonial rule to the second stage of separate jurisdiction, and there have been some observers who have thought that the rigid constitution has prevented the 'natural' development of the American political system towards parliamentarism. This is not so. By abolishing the monarchy and substituting a president for the king and his government, the Americans showed themselves to be truly revolutionary in outlook. The presidential system as established in the USA made parliamentarism both unnecessary and impracticable in that country. The assembly (Congress in the United States) remains an assembly.

2

The Executive Is Not Divided But Is A President Elected By The People For A Definite Term At The Time Of Assembly Elections

The retention of a separate executive in the United States was made feasible because the executive remained undivided. It was not, of course, the same institution as the pre-parliamentary monarchical executive. Such a monarch governed by virtue of an ancient tradition into which he was born, and with all the strength and potential weaknesses that this implied. The presidential executive is elected by the people. In an era when governments have had to rely not on some mystique but on popular support the Americans have found a solution which has enabled their separate single executive to withstand criticism. The suggestions that the United States should adopt parliamentarism have proved abortive largely because it cannot be said of the presidency, as it could of hereditary monarchy, that the institution lacked democratic roots....

The president is elected for a definite term of office. This prevents the assembly from forcing his resignation (except by impeachment for a serious misdemeanour) and at the same time requires the president to stand for re-election if he wishes to continue in office. It seems desirable that the chief executive's tenure should be limited to a certain number of terms.... Equally important for the proper operation of the presidential system is the election of the presi-

dent at the time of the assembly elections. This associates the two branches of government, encourages
party unity, and clarifies the issues. Admittedly in the
United States simultaneous elections do not prevent
the return of a Republican President and a Democratic
Congress, but the tensions would be even greater if
the president was elected for a seven-year term as in
France....

3
The Head Of The Government Is Head Of State

Whereas in pre-parliamentary monarchies the head of
state was also the head of the government, in the presidential system it is the head of the government who
becomes at the same time head of state. This is an
important distinction because it draws attention to
the limited pomp and circumstance surrounding the
presidential office. The president is of little consequence until he is elected as political head by the
electorate and he ceases to have any powers once his
term of office has expired. The ceremonial aspect of
his position is but a reflection of his political prestige....

4
The President Appoints Heads Of Depart-ments Who Are His Subordinates

In parliamentarism the prime minister appoints his
colleagues who together with him form the government. In presidential systems the president appoints
secretaries (sometimes called ministers) who are heads
of his executive departments. Formally, owing to the
rule whereby appointments are subject to the confirmation of the assembly or one of its organs (in the
United States the Senate, in the Philippines the Commission on Appointments) his choice may be restricted
to persons of whom that body approves. In practice
the president has a very wide choice....

5
The President Is Sole Executive

In contrast to parliamentary government, which is
collective, the prime minister being first among equals,
presidential government tends to be individual. Admittedly the term 'cabinet' is used in the United States
to describe the meetings of the president with his secretaries, but it is not a cabinet or ministry in the
parliamentary sense....

6
Members Of The Assembly Are Not Eli-gible For Office In The Administration And Vice Versa

Instead of the parliamentary convention or law
whereby the same persons may be part of both the
executive and legislative branches of government, it is
customary in presidential states for the personnel to
be separate. Neither the President nor his aides may sit
in the US Congress. Few of the other American republics have copied the complete separation practised in
the United States. While ministers may not be members of the assembly (except in Cuba and Peru) they
are usually entitled to attend and take part in debates....

7
The Executive Is Responsible To The Constitution

The president is not, like parliamentary governments,
responsible to the assembly. Instead he is, like pre-parliamentary monarchs, responsible to the constitution.
But whereas in the *anciens régimes* this was but a vague
notion, in presidential systems it is usually laid down
with some precision in a constitutional document....

It is usually the assembly which holds the president ultimately responsible to the constitution by the
Impeachment process. This does not imply that he is
responsible to that body in the parliamentary sense of
depending on its confidence in any political capacity.
Impeachment enforces juridical compliance with the
(constitutional) letter of the law and is quite different
from the exercise of political control over the
president's ordinary conduct of his office. Political
responsibility implies a day-to-day relationship between government and assembly; impeachment is the
grave and ultimate penalty (only one American President, Andrew Johnson, was impeached, unsuccessfully)
necessary where ordinarily the executive and assembly are not mutually dependent...

8
The President Cannot Dissolve Or Coerce The Assembly

The assembly, as we have just seen, cannot dismiss
the president. Likewise, the president may not dissolve
the assembly. Neither, therefore, is in a position to
coerce the other, and it is not surprising that this system is, *par excellence,* one of checks and balances. In
countless ways almost incomprehensible to those accustomed to parliamentarism the presidential system

exhibits this mutual independence of the executive and legislative branches of government....

9

The Assembly Is Ultimately Supreme Over The Other Branches Of Government And There Is No Fusion Of The Executive And Legislative Branches As In A Parliament

It was remarked of parliamentary systems that neither the government nor the assembly is supreme because both are subordinate parts of the parliamentary institutions. In presidential systems such fusion of the executive and legislative powers is replaced by separation, each having its own sphere. As we have just observed, constitutionally the executive cannot interfere in the proceedings of the assembly, still less dissolve it, and the assembly for its part cannot invade the province of the executive....

Since there is no parliament there can be no parliamentary supremacy. Where, then, does supreme power lie in the event of a serious controversy? It has been demonstrated that the assembly cannot force the resignation of the president any more than he can dissolve the assembly. Moreover, both branches of government may find that their actions are declared unconstitutional by yet a third power, the judiciary. In a sense the constitution is supreme. The short answer is that it is intended in presidential government that the different branches shall check and balance one another and that none shall predominate.

Yet in a very real sense it is the assembly which is ultimately supreme. The president may have considerable authority allocated to him in the constitution but he may be powerless unless the assembly grants him the necessary appropriations. If he acts unconstitutionally the assembly may impeach him. In the event of a serious conflict even the judiciary must bow to the will of the assembly because this body has the right to amend the constitution. The American constitution is not, as is sometimes asserted, simply 'what the judges say it is'.

It may be suggested that the position does not appear to be altogether different from that in parliamentary states where ultimately the legislature may amend the constitution. This is not so. In parliamentary states the constitution has to be amended by both government and assembly acting as parliament, whereas in presidential systems the assembly may amend the constitution without regard to the president. For example, the American Congress has limited the presidential tenure of office to two terms....

10

The Executive Is Directly Responsible To The Electorate

Governments in parliamentary countries are appointed by the head of state; they are not elected. By contrast the presidential executive is dependent on a popular vote and the president alone (and vice-president if there is one), of all the persons in the political system, is elected by the whole body of electors. Whereas the pre-parliamentary monarchies could not in the end withstand the pressure of the people's representatives upon their control of government, a president can say to members of the assembly: 'You represent your constituency: I represent the whole people.' There is no reply to this argument, and it is perhaps not surprising that in many South American countries and in France at various times the president has been able to go one step further and to assert that he *alone* represented the people ....

11

There Is No Focus Of Power In The Political System

The political activities of parliamentary systems have their focal point in parliament. Heads of state, governments, elected representatives, political parties, interest groups, and electorates all acknowledge its supremacy..

It is tempting to assume that there must be a similar focal point in presidential systems. This is not so. Instead of concentration there is division; instead of unity, fragmentation. In the design of Washington DC the President's home, the White House, is at the opposite end of Pennsylvania Avenue to the Capitol, where Congress meets. Geographical dispersion symbolizes their political separation....

Those who admire efficient government may be inclined towards the cabinet government form of parliamentarism. Those who prefer more limited government may turn towards presidentialism. It should not be assumed, however, that the presidential form, because it is divided, is necessarily one of weak government. Admittedly, where presidential leadership is lacking the system may even appear to be on the verge of breaking down. But where there is a vigorous executive he may in fact dominate the assembly, as several American Presidents (notably Franklin D. Roosevelt) have succeeded in doing.

Miraculously, in the United States this domination has never gone too far. In much of Central and South America, where there is the form of presidential government but not the substance, the presidential system has been distorted by dictatorship.

It is difficult to explain the failure of presidential government in so many parts of South America and it is perilous to confine such explanation to purely political factors. Historically and culturally South and Central America are utterly different from the United States. However, there are a number of particular political features of these countries' systems which deserve note, not least of which is the multi-party system which characterizes several of them. Where a president is elected by what is in effect a minority vote instead of by the clear majority customary in the United States he lacks that sense of being the people's representative which is so marked a feature of the American presidency. At the very least it adds a complicating factor to the relations of president, assembly, and people, and in all probability contributes to political instability.

Where there is a multi-party system there is the temptation to add to the president's status and independence by giving him a longer term of office than the assembly. Not surprisingly the French Fifth Republic's constitution gives the president a term of seven years compared to the assembly's [five]. Such a long term, while of small moment in a parliamentary system, may make a president in a non-parliamentary system a powerful figure.

Finally, it may be observed that few countries have been able to enjoy the clear distinction between president and assembly so characteristic of the United States. There has been an attempt to introduce something of the 'responsibility' common to parliamentary systems. Thus there is a separate 'government' in the new French constitution, and this 'government' (but not the president) is responsible to the assembly and may be dismissed by it. Yet the history of the Weimar Republic, to say nothing of Latin America, has shown that in practice (as if to confirm political theory) the president (i.e. the real government) may be unaffected by such a procedure and it then becomes an ineffective weapon in the hands of the assembly. If he *is* affected, then the system becomes parliamentary and the attempt to create a separate executive has failed.

For there should be either a separation as in the United States and *no* focus of the political system; or a fusion with parliament as the focus.

Douglas V. Verney, excerpted from *The Analysis of Political Systems* (London: Routledge & Kegan Paul, 1979), chs. 2 and 3. Copyright Douglas V. Verney 1959. Reprinted by permission of Routledge.

Suggestions for further reading

Alexis, Francis, *Changing Caribbean Constitutions* (Bridgetown: Carib Research and Publications Inc., 1995).

Finer, S.E., *Comparative Government: An Introduction to the Study of Politics* (London: Penguin Books Press, 1970).

Payne, Anthony, 'Westminster Adapted: The Political Order of the Commonwealth Caribbean', in Jorge I. Dominguez, Robert A. Pastor and R. Deslisle Worrell, eds., *Democracy in the Caribbean: Political, Economic and Social Perspectives* (London: The Johns Hopkins University Press, 1993), pp. 57–73.

Miliband, Ralph, *The State in Capitalist Society: An Analysis of the Western System of Power* (London: Quartet, 1973).

Munroe, Trevor, *Renewing Democracy into the Millennium: The Jamaican Experience in Perspective* (Kingston: The University of the West Indies Press, 1999).

Ryan, Selwyn, *Winner Takes All: The Westminster Experience in the Caribbean* (St Augustine: Institute of Social and Economic Research, 1999).

Spackman, Ann, *Constitutional Development of the West Indies 1922–1968, A Selection from the Major Documents* (Bridgetown: Caribbean University Press, 1975).

Notes

1. Ann Spackman, *Constitutional Development of the West Indies 1922–1968: A Selection from the Major Documents* (Bridgetown: Caribbean University Press, 1975).

2. Joseph Schumpeter, *Capitalism, Socialism and Democracy* (New York: Harper, 1947) p. 269.

3. Robert A. Dahl, *On Democracy* (London: Yale University Press, 1998) p. 60.

4. Dahl, *On Democracy.*

5. Dahl, *On Democracy,* p. 61.

6. See for instance, Jorge G. Castaneda, 'Democracy and Inequality in Latin America: A Tension of the Times', in Jorge I. Dominguez and Abraham F. Lowenthal, eds., *Constructing Democratic Governance: Latin America and the Caribbean in the 1990s: Themes and Issues* (London: The John Hopkins University Press, 1996) pp. 42–63.

7. S.E. Finer, *Comparative Government: An Introduction to the Study of Politics* (London: Penguin Books Press, 1970) chapter 2.

8. Ralph Miliband, *The State in Capitalist Society: An Analysis of the Western System of Power* (London: Quartet, 1973) Michael Parenti, *Democracy For The Few* (New York: St Martin's Press Inc., 1988) and G. William Domhoff, *Who Rules America?* (New Jersey: Prentice Hall Inc., 1967).

9. See Ralph Miliband, *The State in Capitalist Society*, p. 139.

10. Parenti, *Democracy For The Few*, p. 196.

11. Samuel P. Huntington, *The Third Wave: Democratisation in the Late Twentieth Century* (Oklahoma: University of Oklahoma press, 1974), p. 15. He defines a wave as '. . . a group of transitions from non-democratic to democratic regimes that occur within a specified period of time and that significantly outnumber transitions in the opposite direction. A wave usually involves liberalisation or partial democratisation in political systems that do not become fully democratic'.

12. Jorge I. Dominguez, 'The Caribbean Question: Why has Liberal Democracy (Surprisingly) Flourished?', in Jorge I. Dominguez, Roberta A. Pastor and R. Delisle Worrell, eds., *Democracy in the Caribbean: Political, Economic and Social Perspectives* (London: The Johns Hopkins University Press, 1993), pp. 1–28. Offers a number of possible explanations for the successful consolidation of democracy in the Caribbean.

13. Lewis, *The Growth of the Modern West Indies*, p. 388.

14. Trevor Munroe, *The Politics of Constitutional Decolonization, Jamaica 1944-62*, (Kingston: Institute of Social and Economic Research, 1983), p. 140.

15. Munroe, *The Politics of Constitutional Decolonization*, p. 141.

16. *Barbados Hansard of 1966*, (Bridgetown: Government of Barbados).

17. K.C. Wheare, *Modern Constitutions* (New York: Oxford University Press, 1951).

18. Michael Cutis, Jean Blondel et. al., *Introduction to Comparative Government: A Reader* (New York: Harper Collins Publishers Inc., 1990) 2nd edition, p. 70.

19. Rudolph James and Harold Lutchman, *Law and the Political Environment in Guyana* (Georgetown: Institute of Development Studies, 1984).

20. James and Lutchman, *Law and the Political Environment in Guyana*.

21. Francis Alexis, *Changing Caribbean Constitutions* (Bridgetown: Carib Research Publishers Inc., 1995).

22. James and Lutchman, *Law and the Political Environment in Guyana*.

23. James and Lutchman, *Law and the Political Environment in Guyana*, pp. 103–4.

24. James and Lutchman, *Law and the Political Environment in Guyana*, p. 105.

25. Ann Spackman, *Constitutional Development*, p. 37.

26. Ralph E. Gonsalves, *History and the Future: A Caribbean Perspective* (Kingstown: Quick-Print, 1994) p. 53.

27. Gonsalves, *History and the Future*, p. 52.

28. Gonsalves, *History and the Future*, pp. 52–3.

29. See Appendix 3 for a summary of the Constitutional Review Report.

30. Francis Alexis, *Changing Caribbean Constitution* (Bridgetown: Carib Research Publishers Inc., 1995).

31. Alexis, *Changing Caribbean Constitutions*, p. 266.

32. See *Report of the Constitution Review Commission*. The summary of the Report can be seen in Appendix 3.

33. Giovanni Sartori, *Comparing Constitutional Engineering: An Inquiry into Structures, Incentives and Outcomes*, 2nd edition (Macmillan Press Ltd., 1997).

34. Ghany Hamid, 'Commonwealth Caribbean Presidencies: New Directions in the Exercise of State Power', in John La Guerre, ed., Issues *in the Government and Politics in the West Indies: A Reader* (St Augustine: School of Continuing Studies: UWI, 1997) pp. 142–62.

35. See the next chapter for further details.

36. Cynthia Barrow, *Political Developments and Foreign Affairs of a Mini-State, a Case Study of St Lucia, 1979–1987* (Unpublished master's thesis, Consortium Graduate School of Social Sciences, Mona Campus, Jamaica, 1993).

37. Barrow, *Political Developments and Foreign Affairs of a Mini-State*.

38. See 'Kingstown Shuts Down', *The Search Light of St Vincent and the Grenadines,* April 28, 2000; 'Government Gets Ultimatum: Resign', The News, April 28, 2000, p. 1; and 'General Elections by March 2001', *The News,* May 12, 2000, p. 1.

four

Party Systems and Electoral Politics in the Region

Introduction

Parties, party and electoral systems are important dimensions of political systems, and are central to the effective functioning of liberal democratic countries. According to Robert Dahl '. . . no political institutions shape the political landscape of a democratic country more than its electoral system and its political parties'.[1] These two institutions form the bedrock of democratic principles. With respect to the Westminster system in the region, it is highly dependent on the existence of regular, competitive elections and freely competing political parties.

Carl Stone has identified six typologies of political systems with different party systems that are to be found in developing nations and by extension the Caribbean. These political systems include: monarchical; competitive party system; one-party dominant system: (predominant or hegemonic party systems); military systems; non-communist single party systems and communist single-party systems. Generally speaking, party systems have been differentiated on three criteria:

(i) the amount of fragmentation that is exhibited by the system, which relates to the number of parties within the system and the strengths of the parties.

(ii) the distribution of strength across the left-right ideological spectrum.

(iii) coalition patterns which occur in party systems. This is particularly critical in a context where there is no single party strong enough to command a majority in the legislative body.[2]

Scott P. Mainwairing argues that a fourth criterion must be added in the analysis of party systems in countries embarking upon democracy during the third wave of democratisation. In his view, the under-institutionalisation of political parties makes it difficult for democracy to function effectively.[3]

Two main types of party systems have historically existed in the Commonwealth Caribbean, competitive and one-party dominant systems. Competitive party systems are distinguished by the role of the electorate in selecting the political leadership. In contrast, one-party dominant systems are characterised by the existence of political parties which are fundamentally weak and function under the constant threat of exclusion from the political system once they pose a threat to the dominant party. Carl Stone suggests that in essence, one-party dominant systems are effectively controlled by a single party, which permits other political parties to exist to satisfy certain constitutional criteria for legitimacy purposes. A one-party dominant system is therefore 'one-party dictatorship dressed up in constitutional trappings'. [4]

What is a political party?

According to Patrick Emmanuel a political party, refers to, '. . . an association of people under a specific name whose primary purposes are the achievement and exercise of governmental power'.[5]
Sigmund Neumann defines a political party as:

> . . . the articulate organisation of society's active political agents, those who are concerned with the control of governmental power and who compete for popular support with another group or groups holding divergent views. As such, it is the great intermediary which limits social forces and ideologies to official governmental institutions and relates them to political action within the larger political community.[6]

Given the above definitions, political parties must be characterised by the following features: electoral participation; a structure; an ideology, which would define its programmes; leadership and a life span.

Political parties therefore serve as channels through which ordinary citizens can express their political preferences and contribute to political mobilisation.

Political parties in the Commonwealth Caribbean

Samuel Huntington has argued that political development can be measured by the level of institutionalisation of the political organisation. He sees institutionalisation as incorporating four processes. They are: the institution's ability to adapt,

the coherence of the organisation, its level of autonomy and its level of differentiation. The more adaptable an institution is, the more institutionalised the organisation. Adaptability in his view can be measured by the age of the organisation and its ability to meet challenges in its environment. If the organisation still has its first set of leaders, and the procedures are still carried out by those who first performed them, its adaptability is in doubt. The greater the frequency with which the organisation surmounted the problem of peaceful succession and replaced one generation of leaders by another, the more highly institutionalised and developed it is.[7]

Early 'political parties' were described as 'personalised political parties'. This was largely owing to the over-centralised and hierarchical nature of the decision-making process, which did not permit a democratic culture and provided little facilitation for broad-based participation. For the most part, the early political parties had the following characteristics: a proneness to autocracy; minimal involvement of party members and constituencies in decision-making processes; minimal levels of communication between the different levels of the organisation; groups and branches operating in a vacuum; no education of members in the programmes and plans of the organisation; infrequent contact with the leader; absence of leaders at meetings; small membership and a sense of continuity, which satisfies a major criterion of a political party.

A combination of trade unions and political parties was the organisational form which developed in the Commonwealth Caribbean. This pattern emerged specifically after the failure of Arthur Cipriani's Trinidad Labour Party which had not been engaged in trade unionism and consequently lost its mass membership. In all Commonwealth Caribbean countries, except Trinidad and Tobago and Dominica, unions were important affiliates to or bases of political parties, leading to political unionism in the region. Two specific models of the party union affiliation emerged:

1. The Jamaican model: the dominant party/union model in which a trade union supported a political party.
2. The Antiguan model: this was the dominant form in the Leeward Islands and appeared to be a genuine union party system.

    In Antigua, the union party went by the name of the Antigua Trades and Labour Union until election time, when it was renamed the Antigua Labour Party (ALP). It was in this role of being the political arm of the union that the ALP was born.

It was not until the decades of the 1960s and 1970s that substantial reform of the early political parties was instituted. This restructuring phase took place against the backdrop of protest against the system and was fuelled by the birth of the Black Power Movement, the growth and maturation of the Rastafarian movement, the rebirth of leftist socialist-democratic and Marxist movements – with the New World Group at the forefront and the rise of militant independent unionism among the working class.

The rise of these anti-systemic movements and groups forced a critical focus on the inadequacies of the political and economic systems, which had developed in the post-1930s period. A critical focus on the institutions which developed during this period was the persistence of poverty and racial oppression. For instance, the Rastafarian movement considered the two party system as no more and no less than 'politricks'. They saw political parties as instruments which led to the manipulation of the electorate and facilitated the creation of despotic self-seeking Caribbean political leaders. The existing party organisation was increasingly viewed as stumbling blocks to change rather than machines to better enable the operation of a process of change and development.

Joseph Edwards labelled the political parties as 'Babylonian institutions' which had simply functioned to attempt to 'try and fool and soften the wrath of the working class people against the whole society.' Their main purpose according to Edwards 'is to confuse the working class'.[8]

The underlying reason for the criticism of political parties lies in the seeming absence of any real link between the party and the people. It is questionable whether the parties have attempted to effect adequate democratic functioning, for too much emphasis is placed on a small circle of influential individuals. In a context of limited upward flow from the organisational base of the party to the summit, exchange within the party is limited in several ways to a small number of involved individuals who are primarily members of the party apparatus.

Such a situation leads to the development of personality politics and the domination of the political system by a charismatic leader. This invariably lends itself to a stifling of the political system as party organs are generally composed of unconditionally loyal members or persons who are totally dependent on the leader of the party. Moreover, the personification of power often leads to a problem of succession. The conclusion therefore is that despite years of existence many political parties in the region are underdeveloped political institutions.

A good example is the leadership problem which developed within St Lucia's UWP, when Dr Vaughan Lewis was elected as party leader. The SLP also grappled with its own leadership problem, eventually leading to the selection of Dr Kenny Anthony to the party leadership.

C.L.R. James was also extremely critical of the political party as an instrument to be utilised to carry forward the interests of the working class. He located that inability in the structure, and functioning of the institution. According to James:

> The modern political party whatever its policy or program, the moment it takes hold of any Government, whatever its democratic intentions, becomes a system and a method and an organisation which is opposed to the masses of the people.[9]

James in his critique of party politics in the West Indies argued that the problem with West Indian political parties was their inadequacy of organisation which led to political misdirection. Based on an assessment of the People's National Movement (PNM) led by Dr Eric Williams in Trinidad and Tobago, James felt that the early political parties in the region were not sufficiently involved in the education of the people. He argued further that the party tended to be organised around a personality. In his view:

> at a certain stage. . .with the increase of the responsibilities placed upon the leading personalities and the increasing needs of the Party, this can become its opposite, a handicap. The Party then can expand only to the degree that the leading personality can give it time and energy.[10]

To limit what he felt to be the most negative aspects of the development of the post-1930s political parties, James suggested that:

(i) the role of the general secretary be widened

(ii) political parties should have a daily paper which would undertake the political education of the membership of the party. He felt the political leader was unable to effectively undertake this task on his own. He therefore saw an important role for the managing editor of the paper whose primary responsibility would be to build the paper into a powerful organisation

(iii) that a mass party as against the 'personal parties' was critical. In this regard, James argued that 'the organisation of a mass party is a matter of life and death for an emerging West Indian society'.[11] In his view, a mass-based political party would limit the possibilities of petty dictators, while simultaneously promoting a democratic culture. A mass-based political party, he argued, would move beyond the limited confines of the political viewpoint of the West Indian political class which saw the masses as necessary only to the extent that they gave the leaders authority and power. According to him, a mass-based political party was:

. . . the only organisation by which the people can make up for the centuries of democratic experience they never had. . . it is cruel to presume that they must be left as they are, that nothing can be done.[12]

Neville Duncan argues that political parties require significant democratisation. His main criticism centres on the role of the political leader who dominates the nomination process, the production of the party manifesto, normally written by a handful of party notables and thirdly, the lack of a properly headed and qualified staff secretariat which he claims is characterised by:

- inadequate researched information, shockingly poor intra-party communication
- weak and dependent financial bases
- untrained organisers, campaigners and candidates
- peripherialisation of young 'stars' in political parties
- aloof, autocratic leadership.[13]

Added to this are other representational gaps which are apparent in the political parties. Foremost among these is the gender gap.

Few women have been selected as party candidates and even fewer have won parliamentary seats with electoral candidacy in the region which remains male-dominated.[14] Three broad themes have emerged in the literature seeking to explain the gender gap in politics.

1. Sex-role socialisation; the social learning by women results in political passivity and the avoidance of the public arena
2. Structural factors; levels of education and employment are critical indicators of involvement in politics. As women become more educated, secure higher paying jobs and increasingly become independent, the more likely it is that they will seek political office

3. Gender-based prejudicial factors; hostility of the party apparatus and leadership to would-be female candidates.

Commonwealth Caribbean countries do not suffer from extensive proliferation of political parties and Caribbean political systems commonly fall within the ambit of competitive and single party dominant systems. The dominant party system in the region is the two-party system.

While Guyana is noted for its subversion of elections, it too, in a context of proportional representation, has shown the remarkable resilience of the two-party system. In the 1992 elections, the People's Progressive Party (PPP) with its civic component took 36 seats to the People's National Congress' (PNC) 26 seats. Eleven political parties contested the elections for the 52 available National Assembly seats, while 23 political parties registered to contest the December 15 1997, general elections.

Political parties remain critical to the functioning of Caribbean democracies. First, it is the political party which manages and legitimises elections as an orderly means of transition in society and in spite of challenges from other institutions such as trade unions, mass social movements and non-governmental organisations, they retain their uniqueness. They continue to perform the following useful functions:

- Adopting statements of public policy, primarily in an election platform. It is helpful in shaping the orientation of party candidates, directing the expectations of the electorate and giving civil society the opportunity of assessing the performance and effectiveness of competing political parties.
- Mobilising support for public policy. All modern political parties must be concerned with building a broad coalition of voters to improve their chances of being elected into office.
- Nominating candidates for public office. With the decline of independent candidates, the political party remains the only institution which provides credible candidates for political office. The modern political party should therefore provide a major training ground and launching pad for leadership.

Electoral politics in the Commonwealth Caribbean

The nature of the electoral system partly determines the number of political parties in a country. According to Arend Lijphart, electoral systems may be described in terms of five dimensions: electoral formulae; district magnitudes; provisions for supplementary seats; electoral thresholds and ballot structures. An electoral system determines how votes are translated into seats and therefore affects the behaviour of the voter. It also determines whether the electorate votes for a party or an individual. In the translation of votes into seats, the criterion is whether the translation of votes into seats is in proportion or not. The major distinction between electoral systems is between proportionality and majoritarian. In majoritarian systems such as the plurality system, the winner takes all. This system does not seek a parliament that reflects the voting distribution in a country. Instead, it seeks a clear winner. Proportional representation stands in sharp contrast to majoritarian electoral systems. The basic aim of proportional representation is to represent both majorities and minorities and instead of overrepresenting or underrepresenting any party, to translate votes into seats proportionally.

Three main groups of electoral systems or electoral formulae exist:

1. Plurality-majority systems. Four types of majoritarian electoral systems are commonly identified, namely: First Past the Post (FPTP), the Alternate Vote (AV) system, the Preferential Voting System and the Two-Round System.
2. Proportional Representation
3. Semi-proportional Systems

The party system in the region is supported by an electoral system which, with the exception of Guyana, is based on the system of FPTP method. Under this electoral system, the country is divided into several constituencies and electors cast one vote each for one of a slate of candidates. The winner is the candidate who receives the largest number, or plurality of the votes cast. This representational distortion may also produce a situation where a party wins control of the government while finishing second in the vote count. The disproportionality and big party or two-party bias, which Maurice Duverger associates with the plurality electoral system, suggests that it confers partisan advantages.

Giovanni Sartori concludes that the problem with majoritarian systems based on a plurality vote is that they are too manipulative.[16] This is primarily because the system tends to sacrifice the representation of parliament. However, such sacrifice is obtained in the interest of efficient, if not effective government. The model almost inevitably results in the election of a governing majority. Secondly the plurality system creates a more direct relationship between voters and candidates than the proportional representation system.

Proportional representation is concerned with one issue, that is, the equal allocation in proportion of votes into seats. However, while it tends to more adequately represent the distribution of popular support in a country, its one major fault is that it produces party fragmentation and copes badly with what is described as 'governability requirement'. Thus, Sartori concludes that the primary flaw of proportional representation is that the model produces too many parties.[17]

In the nearly five decades of universal adult suffrage spanning more than 130 general elections, only occasionally has one political party secured all seats in parliamentary elections. Prior to 1989, this feature was limited to six countries and was most dominant in Antigua and Barbuda and Montserrat. Since 1989, two political parties have swept the polls securing electoral victories in all the national constituencies. The tendency to exaggerate the popularity of the winning party under the plurality system casts serious doubt on the efficacy of the system. The 1989 and 1998 election results in St Vincent and the Grenadines, St Lucia in 1997 and Barbados and Grenada in 1999 are examples (not exhaustive) of the weaknesses of the system. Like St Vincent and the Grenadines in 1989, the New National Party (NNP) in January 1999 secured a clean sweep at the polls.

A long-standing feature of electoral and thus party politics, is the domination of the political system by two political parties. The election results of the region are testimony to this outstanding feature. As shown in table 4:2 below, the classic example in the region is Jamaica, where the cyclical pattern is consolidated.

TABLE 4:1 ST VINCENT AND THE GRENADINES: DISTRIBUTION OF VOTES AND SEATS: 1989 AND 1998

Election Year 1989	SVLP	NDP	Other Parties
No. of votes	13,290	29,079	1,498
No. of seats	0.0	15	0.0
% votes	30.3	66.3	3.4
% seats	0.0	100.0	0.0

Election Year 1998	ULP	NDP	Other parties
No. of seats	7	8	-
% votes	54.2	53.3	-
% seats	46.6	53.4	-

Three countries displayed dissimilarities namely, Dominica since 1980, Grenada and St Kitts/Nevis, post-1984. In the period after 1984, Grenada, with as many as five political parties contesting general elections, showed prominence in this regard, and its party system has apparently become more fragmented. The 1990 general elections resulted in a minority National Democratic Congress (NDC) government in parliament. Though the NDC was able to secure seven of the 15 parliamentary seats with 34.6 per cent of the popular vote and as such represented the largest single bloc of seats in parliament, it was without an overall majority. To ensure a level of political stability, critical alliances with opposition groups or forces were required. The defection of one of the four successful Grenada United Labour Party (GULP) parliamentarians to the NDC provided that measure of fragile stability and parliamentary majority.

The 1993 election results in St Kitts/Nevis also highlighted this discrepancy in the system of FPTP. A minority party in terms of national votes held the reigns of government in collaboration with a minority political party (People's Action Movement [PAM] under Kennedy Symmonds). The November 6, 1995 elections in Trinidad and Tobago apart from reflecting problems associated with ethnically divided societies, also resulted in a hung parliament. The PNM and the United National Congress (UNC) both secured 17 seats, with the National Alliance for Reconstruction (NAR) securing the two Tobago seats. This necessitated some form of coalition government comprising the UNC and the two Tobago seats won by the NAR headed by former Prime Minister A.N.R. Robinson.[18]

Because the system distorts the result of general elections, it cannot adequately represent the people and the wishes of the people.[19] In a parliamentary democracy, an electoral system should create a parliament which reflects the main trends of opinion within the electorate. However, as Peter A. Jamadar points out, the most serious and fundamental defect in the FPTP electoral system is that:

> . . . it regularly and repeatedly fails to create a parliament in which the image of the feelings of the nation are truly reflected. There is the general tendency to exaggerate the representativeness of the largest party and to reduce that of the smaller ones.[20]

The Government of Trinidad and Tobago Report of the Constitution Commission, 1974 otherwise known as The Wooding Commission Report of 1974, stated

that the '. . . disadvantages of the first past the post system outweigh its advantages'.[21]

TABLE 4:2 JAMAICA: DISTRIBUTION OF VOTES AND SEATS BY GOVERNING PARTY IN SUCCESSIVE GENERAL ELECTIONS, 1944–1997

Election Year	Winning Party	% votes	No. of seats
1944	JLP	41.4	22
1949	JLP	42.7	17
1955	PNP	50.5	18
1959	PNP	54.8	29
1962	JLP	50.0	26
1967	JLP	50.6	33
1972	PNP	56.4	37
1976	PNP	56.8	47
1980	JLP	58.9	51
1983*	JLP	89.7 *	6 *
1989	PNP	56.6	45
1993	PNP	60.0	52
1997	PNP	55.0	50

* The 1983 elections were boycotted by the opposition PNP, with only six seats contested by independents and marginal political groups.

TABLE 4:3 GENERAL ELECTIONS IN ST LUCIA: DISTRIBUTION OF VOTES AND SEATS 1997

Party	SVLP	UWP	Independent
No. of votes	44,062	26,325	1494
Percentage votes cast	60.01	35.8	2.03
No. of seats	16	1	0
Percentage seats	94.11	5.88	0

TABLE 4:4 GENERAL ELECTIONS: RESULT IN
BARBADOS 1999

Party	DLP	BLP
Percentage votes cast	34.6	65.4
No. of seats	2	26
Percentage seats	7.1	92.8

As the winning candidate is the individual who polls a plurality of the votes cast, a significant number of votes cast are not reflected in the seats won. Furthermore, the real support of a party is logically underestimated or alternatively overestimated, given this tendency to distort. The single-member constituency system under the system of the FPTP, tends to magnify the strength of the major parties and the weakness of the smaller ones. Moreover, the winner-takes-all system deprives third parties not only of representation after a general election but also has complications for the survivability of the party. Over time, the electorate may become disillusioned and change their political alliance as the third party under this system seems incapable of achieving a legislative presence.

The unquestionable success of the model in the region is no doubt partly responsible for more recent endorsement of the model by Constitution Commissions. In the 1998 report to the Government of Barbados, the Constitution Review Commission noted that while Barbadian civil society felt that the constitution of Barbados contained certain anti-democratic provisions, it rejected the view that the electoral system contributed to poor governance. In keeping with the above philosophical orientation, the Commission recommended the retention of the plurality system and expressly rejected the adoption of the system of proportionality as practised in Guyana. The Commission reported that:

> . . . the existing electoral system has worked well and has provided Barbados with stable government throughout its history. Examples of experiments in proportional representation have tended to lead to instability and weakness in governments in many countries.[22]

Based on the above discussion, it can be said that the plurality system helps to elect a governing majority and so promote effective government, and also reduces party fragmentation by discouraging third parties.

The other system operating in the region is proportional representation, which is the electoral choice of Guyana. Proportional representation as an electoral system requires that the distribution of seats be proportionate to the distribution of the popular vote among competing political parties. Proportional representation systems fall into three main categories:

1. List system; the open list system is characterised by an unordered list of candidates, so that it is the voters choice on election day that determine which party candidates are elected and which are not. This open list system promotes enormous uncertainty among the various candidates and encourages dangerous intra-party competition. This system results in a fragmented vote and may result in an even worse situation than the plurality vote. The closed list system adopted by Guyana is more predictable and stable
2. The mixed member proportional system
3. Single transferable vote

An electoral system that rests on proportionality is based on the proportion of votes to seats. As an electoral system it is designed to produce a close relationship between the proportion of the total votes cast for a party in general elections and the proportion of seats which the party gains in the legislature. In this way it will theoretically remove the defects of the FPTP system typified by exclusion, distortion and exaggeration and can result in an improvement of the quality of democracy. A parliament elected on the basis of proportionality increases the opportunity of third parties by providing the party with legislative seats roughly in accordance with the percentage of votes it wins. It would also create a representative body which mirrors the distribution of opinion within the electorate. For example, in the 1992 general elections in Guyana, the PPP took 53.4 per cent of the national vote and 36 seats, while the PNC got 42.3 per cent of the vote and a corresponding 26 seats.

Unfortunately, proportional representation as an electoral system has been subjected to much subversion in Guyana and so has militated against the benefits of such an electoral system. Proportional representation can also produce coalition governments which are inherently unstable. However, such a situation can also occur under a system of FPTP, which was exhibited by the experiences of St Kitts/Nevis in 1993. Patrick Emmanuel shows that five Commonwealth Caribbean countries operating under a system of FPTP were forced to adopt some form of post-election coalition.[23] This has occurred in St Vincent, Trinidad and Tobago, St Kitts/Nevis, Grenada and Dominica. While proportional representation is regarded as a better system than FPTP in fairly representing groups, the Guyana experience highlighted some of its negative aspects when the Jagan administration was prevented from assuming office in 1964 and its overt manipulation by the PNC. The need to form coalition governments also results in paralysing political action. In addition, resistance to the system by politicians who have benefited from it have militated against its extension in the Commonwealth Caribbean.

While advocates for the more extensive adoption of the proportional representation system argue that it is only fair to allow a party the parliamentary representation it has earned, the possibility of party fragmentation leading to 'stalemated coalition governments' and the promotion of poor governance are a major disadvantage.

Moreover, democracy cannot merely be equated with the exercise of the right to vote, as voters must also be in a position to choose freely. The significance of an election depends largely on conditions under which candidates are chosen prior to an election. It also depends on the conditions under which the electors express their wishes in any electoral system.

Elections in the Commonwealth Caribbean have also witnessed subversion in other ways, the most notable among these being:

(a) redistricting, that is, the changing of boundaries of a constituency to guarantee a preferred political outcome. The most commonly used form of redistricting is *gerrymandering,* which results in the contortion of district lines to maximise the strength of the party in power

(b) overseas voting

(c) over-registration and under-registration

(d) proxy voting

(e) multiple registration

(f) stuffing ballot boxes with illegitimate votes and

(g) unequal size of constituency boundaries.

Most constitutions require that countries operating under the FPTP electoral system have constituencies of equal size, to ensure that as far as possible an equal weight is given to each ballot. It is expected that no constituency be less than 90 per cent, nor more than 110 per cent of the average size of the constituencies. In the 1997 general elections in St Lucia, wide disparities in constituencies prevailed. For instance, the electoral population size of the smallest constituency was 2,322 with the largest constituency containing 12,189 registered voters, five times the size of the smallest constituency.

Summary

While the dominant electoral system in the region has tended to exaggerate the support of the winning party in parliament, it has been validated by regular constitutional changes of government. It therefore enjoys ideological legitimacy in the region. However, governments under the Westminster system operating under the plurality system have:

> . . .been the more easily turned into forms of 'elective dictatorships' between elections, with worrying implications for the preservation of civil and political rights.[24]

Key words and phrases

1	A political party
2	Representational gap
3	Political unionism
4	Party system
5	Two-party system
6	Mass-based political party
7	Electoral systems
8	Plurality system
9	Proportional representation
10	First past the post
11	Disproportionality
12	Elective dictatorship
13	Subversion
14	Distortion
15	Gerrymandering
16	Plurality vote
17	Redistricting
18	Hung Parliament
19	Competitive party systems

Questions to Consider

- Comment critically on party and electoral systems in the Commonwealth Caribbean. Are political parties in crisis?
- Consider the results of general elections in the Caribbean in the last 20 years, what are the main trends?
- What are the main strengths of the electoral formula used in the Commonwealth Caribbean? Discuss with relevant illustrations.

- Identify the main purposes of elections and party systems.
- How do elections and parties promote democratisation?

- * After reading chapters three and four, consider the effects on Barbados or any other Commonwealth Caribbean country should proportional representation be implemented. List some major features that mark Parliament and governance.
- * Consider the primary role of political parties in Barbados or your own country.
- * Identify and critically assess recent developments in electoral politics and party systems in your country. What do they portend for governance?

Democracies: Patterns of Majoritarian and Consensus Government in Twenty-one Countries

Arend Lijphart

Electoral Systems: Majority and Plurality Methods vs. Proportional Representation

The sixth dimension on which the majoritarian and consensus models differ is a clear-cut one. The typical electoral system of majoritarian democracy is the single-member district plurality or majority system; consensus democracy typically uses proportional representation. The plurality and majority single-member district methods are a perfect reflection of majoritarian philosophy: the candidate supported by the largest number of voters wins, and all other voters remain unrepresented. Moreover, the party gaining a nation-wide majority or plurality of the votes will tend to be overrepresented in terms of parliamentary seats. In sharp contrast, the basic aim of proportional representation is to represent both majorities and minorities and, instead of over-representing or underrepresenting any parties, to translate votes into seats proportionally.

This chapter will first present a more detailed classification of the electoral systems used in our

twenty-two democracies. It will then discuss the major theories concerning the relationship between electoral systems and party systems, and present the findings on the relationship in our set of countries between the electoral system and the effective number of parties. Finally, the different electoral systems will be compared with regard to their tendency to yield proportional or disproportional results, to reduce the effective number of parties in parliament, and to translate electoral pluralities into parliamentary majorities.

Electoral Formulas

Although the dichotomy of proportional representatives vs. single-member district plurality and majority systems is indeed the most fundamental dividing line in the classification of electoral systems, we must make some additional important distinctions and develop a more refined typology.[1] Electoral systems may be described in terms of five dimensions: electoral formulas, district magnitudes, provisions for supplementary seats, electoral thresholds, and ballot structures.

Figure 9.1 presents a classification according to the first of these dimensions, the electoral formula. The classification is limited to the formulas used for the election of the first or only chambers in the twenty-two democracies in the 1945-80 period, and it is therefore not an exhaustive classification of all possible electoral formulas—or even of all formulas that have actually been used somewhere in the world. The first category of plurality and majority formulas can be subdivided into three more specific classes. The plurality formula is by far the simplest one: the candidate who receives the most votes, whether a majority or a plurality, is elected. Majority formulas require an absolute majority for election. One way to fulfill this requirement is to conduct a run-off second ballot between the top two candidates if none of the candidates in the first round of voting has received a majority of the votes. An example is the method used for the election of the president in the Fifth French Republic, but it is not used for legislative elections. The National Assembly in the Fifth Republic is elected by a mixed majority-plurality formula in single-member districts: on the first ballot an absolute majority is required for election, but if no candidate wins a majority, a plurality suffices on the second ballot. Candidates failing to win a minimum percentage of the vote on the first ballot—12.5 percent since 1976—are barred from participating on the second ballot.

FIGURE 9.1 A CLASSIFICATION OF THE ELECTORAL FOR-
MULAS FOR THE ELECTION OF THE FIRST OR ONLY
CHAMBERS IN 22 DEMOCRACIES, 1945-1980

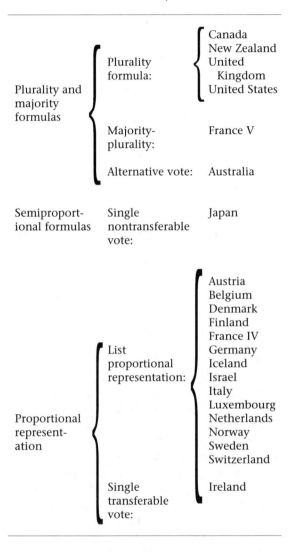

The alternative vote, used in Australia, is a true majority formula. The voters are asked to indicate their first preference, second preference, and so on among the candidates. If a candidate receives an absolute majority of the first preferences, he or she is elected. If there is no such majority the candidate with the lowest number of first preferences is dropped, and the ballots with this candidate as the first preference are transferred to the second preferences. This procedure is repeated by excluding the weakest candidate and redistributing the ballots in question to the next highest preferences in each stage of the counting, until a majority winner emerges.

Two main types of proportional representation must be distinguished. The most common form is the list system, used in a majority—14 out of 22—of our democratic regimes. There are minor variations in list formulas, but they all basically entail that the parties nominate lists of candidates in multimember districts, that the voters cast their ballots for one party list or the other, and that the seats are allocated to the party lists in proportion to the numbers of votes they have collected. List P.R. systems may be subdivided further according to the mathematical formula used to translate votes into seats. The most frequently applied method is the d'Hondt formula, which has a slight bias in favor of large parties as against small parties. The Sainte-Laguë method, used in Scandinavia, and the largest remainders method, used in Italy, in Israel for the 1951 through 1969 elections, and in some of the districts in the French Fourth Republic, are somewhat more favorable to the smaller parties.[2]

The other principal form of proportional representation is the single transferable vote. It differs from list P.R. in that the voters vote for individual candidates instead of for party lists. The ballot is similar to that of the alternative vote system: it contains the names of the candidates, and the voters are asked to rank-order those. The procedure for determining the winning candidates is slightly more complicated than in the alternative vote method. Two kinds of vote transfers take place: first, any surplus votes not needed by candidates who already have the minimum quota of votes required for election are transferred to the next highest candidates; second, the weakest candidate is eliminated and his or her votes are transferred in the same way. If necessary, these steps are repeated until all of the available seats are filled. The single transferable vote is often praised because it combines the advantages of permitting votes for individual candidates and of yielding proportional results, but it is not used very frequently. The only instance in figure 9.1 is Ireland. The other major examples of its application are the Australian Senate and the unicameral legislature of Malta.

Most electoral formulas fit the two large categories of proportional representation and plurality-majority, but there are a few that fall in between. These semiproportional systems are used rarely, and the only example in our set of countries is Japan's single nontransferable vote. Each voter has one vote to be cast for a single candidate in a multimember district, and the candidates with the most votes are elected. The single nontransferable vote makes minority representation possible—in a five-member district, for instance, about one-fifth of the votes cast for one minority candidate guarantees election—but it does not guarantee overall proportional or close to proportional results.

Other Dimensions of Electoral Systems

In addition to the electoral formula, there are four other dimensions along which electoral systems may differ:

1. District magnitude. The magnitude of an electoral district denotes the number of candidates to be elected in the district. It should not be confused with the geographical size of the district or with the number of voters in it. Plurality and majority formulas may be applied in both single-member and multi-member districts, but single-member districts have become the rule for national legislative elections. Proportional and semiproportional formulas require multimember districts, ranging from two-member districts to a single nation-wide district from which all members of parliament are elected. District magnitude has a very strong impact on the degree of proportionality that P.R. systems can attain. For instance, a party representing a 10 percent minority is unlikely to win a seat in a five-member district but will be successful in a ten-member district. Two-member districts can therefore hardly be regarded as compatible with the principle of proportionality; conversely, a nation-wide district is, all other factors being equal, optimal for a proportional translation of votes into seats. The magnitude of districts is much more important in this respect than the specific P.R. formula—D'Hondt, Sainte-Laguë or largest remainders—that is applied in each district.

Among the sixteen proportional and semi-proportional systems, there are three examples of nation-wide districts; Israel, the Netherlands, and Germany since 1957. The German electoral system is often described as a mixed plurality-proportional one, but is an unbalanced mixture that is almost entirely proportional as far as the overall allocation of seats is concerned. Three countries—Italy, Finland, and Luxembourg—have large average district magnitudes of more than ten members per district. The remaining countries have smaller districts.

2. Supplementary seats. In order to correct the deviations from proportionality caused by small district magnitudes, a number of seats may be reserved in a national pool (or in a few large-area pools) and allocated to the underrepresented parties. Especially if relatively many seats are awarded on this basis, proportionality can be closely approximated. Electoral systems with such provisions for supplementary seats are those of Austria, Denmark, Iceland, and Sweden since 1970.

3. Electoral thresholds. Nation-wide districts and supplementary seats tend to maximize proportionality and to facilitate the representation of even very small parties. In order not to make it too easy for small parties to win election, all countries with nation-wide districts or supplementary seats have instituted minimum thresholds for representation, defined in terms of a minimum number of seats won at the district level and/or a minimum percentage of the total national vote. These percentages may be relatively low and hence innocuous, as the 1 percent threshold in Israel and the .67 percent threshold in the Netherlands. But when they reach 4 or 5 percent, as in Sweden and Germany respectively, they constitute formidable barriers to small minorities.

4. Ballot structure. Douglas W. Rae suggests a final dimension of electoral systems which he calls the "ballot structure." Ballots can be categorical or ordinal. Categorical ballots "require that the voter give his mandate to [one or more candidates of] a single party," while ordinal ballots allow the voter to "divide his mandate among parties or among candidates of different parties."[3] This dimension overlaps the electoral formula and district magnitude dimensions to a large extent. Single-member district plurality systems and the single nontransferable vote have, by definition, categorical ballot structures. The alternative vote and the single transferable vote are ordinal, and so is the French majority-plurality system whenever a second ballot is required, which tends to be the case in most districts. The only electoral system that can belong to either type is list P.R., but it is rarely ordinal. Only in Switzerland and Luxembourg can the voter divide his or her vote among more than one list. In the other list P.R. systems, the voters are sometimes allowed to express preferences among candidates of the same list but they cannot vote for more than one party list or for candidates of different parties.

Electoral Systems and Party Systems

A well-known proposition in comparative politics is that single-member district plurality systems favor two-party systems, as indicated in figure 7.1 above; Maurice Duverger, writing in 1951, calls this proposition one that approximates "a true sociological law." Conversely, proportional representation and two-ballot systems encourage multipartism. Duverger explains the differential effects of the electoral system in terms of "mechanical" and "psychological" factors. The mechanical effect of the single-member district plurality system is that all but the two strongest parties are severely underrepresented, since they tend to lose in each district; the British Liberals, continually the disadvantaged third party in the postwar era, are a good example. The psychological factor reinforces the mechanical one: "the electors soon realize that their votes are wasted if they continue to give them to the third party: whence their natural tendency to transfer their vote to the less evil of its two adversaries."[4] Proportional representation does not have such a restraining influence on third and other weak parties and hence it freely allows the emergence and persistence of multiparty systems.

Several political scientists have gone further and have argued that proportional representation, as a result of its encouragement of the proliferation of parties, is a grave danger to the survival of democracy—in line with the second majoritarian proposition shown in figure 7.1. In his famous book *Democracy or Anarchy?*, first published in 1941, Ferdinand A. Hermens held proportional representation responsible for the failure of the Weimar Republic and the rise of Hilter: "P.R. was an essential factor in the breakdown of German democracy."[5] This explanation may have some validity for the case of Weimar, but it does not stand up as a general proposition. As discussed in chapter 7, in our set of countries with long records of reasonably stable democracy, the majority have multiparty systems. Similarly, most of these countries have used proportional representation for a long time. Hermens's dire warning about P.R. is obviously exaggerated.

Nevertheless, the link between electoral and party systems—Duverger's "true sociological law"—is indeed a strong one. Its rationale is reinforced by the fact that, as Duverger recognized, the relationship is mutual. Single-member district plurality systems favor the persistence of two dominant parties, but, conversely, two-party systems are also favorable to the retention of the plurality method: it gives the two major parties the great advantage of protecting their dominance against attacks by third parties. For the same reason, proportional representation is likely to be retained by multiparty systems, because for most of the parties a switch to the plurality method would be extremely hazardous.

Of our twenty-two democratic regimes, only two deviate from Duverger's law. Duverger would have predicted that the four single-member district plurality systems—Canada, New Zealand, the United Kingdom, and the United States—would produce two-party systems. Canada with its two-and-a-half party system is the only exception. For all fifteen P.R. systems and for the French Fifth Republic, he would have predicted multipartism. Duverger did not include the Japanese semiproportional system and the Australian alternative vote in his analysis, but the logic of his law leads to a prediction of multipartism, since neither contains a strong deterrent to relatively weak parties. All eighteen non-plurality systems should therefore have multiparty systems; in fact, seventeen of them do, and Austria is the only deviant case. The Austrian two-party system reflects a plural society which happens to consist of two large subsocieties, Catholic and Socialist. This case shows that proportional representation should not be said to *cause*, but only to *allow* multipartism. The exceptional Canadian case is usually explained in terms of Canada's cultural and regional diversity, which is sufficiently strong to overcome the deterrent effect of the plurality system.

Rae has contributed a number of significant refinements to the study of the links between electoral and party systems. Different electoral systems have different impacts on party systems but, Rae emphasizes, they also have important effects in common.[6] In particular, all electoral systems, not just the plurality and majority systems, tend to overrepresent the larger parties and underrepresent the smaller ones. Three important aspects of this tendency must be distinguished: (1) All electoral systems tend to yield disproportional results. (2) All electoral systems tend to reduce the effective number of parliamentary parties compared with the effective number of electoral parties. (3) All electoral systems can, to use Rae's term, "manufacture" a parliamentary majority for parties that have not received majority support from the voters. On the other hand, all three tendencies are considerably stronger in plurality and majority than in proportional representation systems. These relationships, as well as the link between electoral systems and the effective number of parties, will be discussed in greater detail in the remainder of this chapter.

Electoral Systems and the Effective Number of Parties

Duverger's law distinguishes merely between two-party and multiparty systems, but its logic allows a more refined formulation: the more "permissive" an electoral system is, the larger one can expect the effective number of parties to be. The effective number of parties should therefore be low in plurality systems, somewhat higher in majority systems, higher still in semiproportional systems, and highest under proportional representation. The first column of table 9.1 repeats the information on the effective number of parliamentary parties contained in table 7.3 above, but it arranges the countries according to their electoral systems.

Within the general category of plurality and majority systems, the four plurality regimes are listed first; among the fifteen P.R. systems, the one single transferable vote system (Ireland) is at the bottom of the table.

The evidence generally supports the refined form of Duverger's law. The greatest contrast is between plurality and P.R. systems: the average effective number of parties in the former is 2.1 and in the latter 3.8—almost twice as many. The number of parties in the French Fifth Republic, in Australia, and in the Japanese semiproportional system—3.3, 2.5, and 3.1, respectively—fall in between the two extremes. It should be noted, however, that, contrary to our expectations, the number is actually a bit lower in the semiproportional Japanese system than in the majoritarian French one.

We might also expect that within the general class of P.R. systems, the more permissive forms that is, those

TABLE 9.1. EFFECTIVE NUMBERS OF PARLIAMENTARY AND ELECTORAL PARTIES, REDUCTIONS IN THE EFFECTIVE NUMBERS OF PARTIES, AND DEVIATIONS FROM PROPORTIONALITY IN 22 DEMOCRACIES, CLASSIFIED BY ELECTORAL SYSTEM, 1945-1980

	Effective number of parliamentary parties	Effective number of electoral parties	Reduction in number of parties (%)	Index of disproportionality (%)
Plurality and majority:				
Canada	2.4	3.1	20.6	8.1
New Zealand	2.0	2.4	167	6.3
United Kingdom	2.1	2.6	17.4	6.2
United States	1.9	2.1	6.3	5.6
France V	3.3	4.8	30.7	12.3
Australia	2.5	2.8	7.2	5.6
Single nontransferable vote:				
Japan	3.1	3.8	18.7	4.2
Proportional representation:				
Austria	2.2	2.4	7.5	2.0
Belgium	3.7	4.1	10.0	2.2
Denmark	4.3	4.5	4.5	0.9
Finland	5.0	5.4	7.5	1.6
France IV	4.9	5.1	4.1	2.8
Germany	2.6	2.9	9.3	2.1
Iceland	3.5	3.7	5.2	3.0
Israel	4.7	5.0	6.6	1.1
Italy	3.5	3.9	11.1	2.2
Luxembourg	3.3	3.6	9.4	3.2
Netherlands	4.9	5.2	6.7	1.1
Norway	3.2	3.9	16.9	3.1
Sweden	3.2	3.4	5.5	1.2
Switzerland	5.0	5.4	7.4	1.5
Ireland	2.8	3.1	9.6	2.4

Source: Based on data in Thomas T. Mackie and Richard Rose, *The International Almanac of Electoral History* (London: Macmillan, 1974); *European Journal of Political Research,* vols. 2-9, no. 3 (September 1974-81); and John F. Bibby, Thomas E. Mann, and Norman J. Arnstein, Vital Statistics on Congress, 1980 (Washington, D.C.: American Enterprise Institute, 1980), pp. 6-7.

with nation-wide districts or supplementary seats—would have more parties than the less permissive systems. This hypothesis must be rejected. There is virtually no difference between the two. As we shall see shortly, the former do yield more proportional results than the latter, but this difference does not affect the number of parties.

Manufactured Majorities

The tendency of electoral systems to yield disproportional results favoring the large parties becomes especially important when parties that fail to get a majority of the votes are awarded a majority of the seats. This makes it possible to form single-party majority cabinets—one of the hallmarks of majoritarian democracy. Rae calls such majorities "manufactured," that is, artificially created by the electoral system. Manufactured majorities may be contrasted with earned majorities, when a party wins majorities of both votes and seats, and natural minorities, when no party wins a majority of either votes or seats.[7] An extremely rare fourth possibility, artificial minorities, when there is a majority vote winner that does not obtain a seat majority, occurred only once in the 239 elections in our countries between 1945 and 1980: in the 1954 Australian election, the Labor party was defeated even though it won 50.1 percent of the popular vote. (This one exceptional case will be included in our category of natural minorities.) Majorities were manufactured in as many as 50 elections, and were earned in only

28 elections. The remaining 161 elections produced natural minorities.

Table 9.2 presents the average incidence of manufactured and earned majorities and of natural minorities in the three main types of electoral systems. All three are capable of creating majorities where none are created by the voters, but this capacity is especially strong in the plurality and majority systems—closely followed by the Japanese semiproportional system, which has frequently manufactured majorities for the Liberal Democrats. The clearest cases are Great Britain and New Zealand, our principal examples of Westminster democracy. In the 1945-80 period, ten out of eleven British elections (91 percent) manufactured single-party majorities—and made single-party majority cabinets possible. One election, held in February 1974, did not produce a majority. In postwar Britain, therefore, not one parliamentary majority was actually earned. All twelve elections in New Zealand produced majority winners: 9 of the 12 majorities (75 percent) were manufactured, and only 3 were earned. In the other four plurality and majority systems, manufactured majorities have also occurred, but less frequently: in 46 percent of the elections in Canada, 33 percent in Australia, 17 percent in the United States, and 17 percent in the French Fifth Republic. The average for the six countries is 46 percent.

In contrast, proportional representation very rarely produces manufactured majorities. They have occurred

TABLE 9.2: MANUFACTURED MAJORITIES, EARNED MAJORITIES, AND NATURAL MINORITIES IN THREE TYPES OF ELECTORAL SYSTEMS, 1945-1980

	Manuf. maj. (%)	Earned maj. (%)	Natural min. (%)	Totals (%)
Plurality and majority Systems (6 countries)	45	25	29	100 (75)
Single nontransferable vote (Japan)	40	20	40	100 (15)
Proportional Representation (15 countries)	7	4	89	100 (149)
All elections in 22 democracies	21	12	67	100 (239)

Source: Based on data in Thomas T. Mackie and Richard Rose, *The International Almanac of Electoral History* (London: Macmillan, 1974); *European Journal of Political Research*, vols. 2-9, no. 3 (September 1974-81); and John F. Bibby, Thomas E. Mann, and Norman J. Arnstein, *Vital Statistics on Congress, 1980* (Washington, D.C.: American Enterprise Institute, 1980), pp. 6-7

in only five of the fifteen P.R. systems—Austria, Belgium, Ireland, Italy, and Norway—and the average incidence in the fifteen countries is only 7 percent. It is especially in this respect that proportional representation is a vital element of consensus democracy, and plurality and majority systems, particularly the single-member district plurality system, of majoritarian democracy.

Notes

1. Thorough treatments of electoral systems are W.J.M. Mackenzie, *Free Elections: An Elementary* Textbook (London: Allen and Unwin, 1958); Enid Lakeman, *How Democracies Vote: A Study of Electoral Systems,* 4th ed. (London: Faber and Faber, 1974); and Dieter Nohlen, *Wahlsysteme der Welt: Daten und Analysen* (Munich: Piper, 1978).
2. The complex French electoral law of 1951 also contained some majoritarian elements.
3. Douglas W Rae, *The Political Consequences of Electoral Laws,* rev. ed. (New Haven, Conn.: Yale University Press, 1971), pp. 17,126.
4. Maurice Duverger, *Political Parties: Their Organization and Activity in the Modern State,* trans. Barbara and Robert North (New York: Wiley, 1963), pp.217,226.
5. F. A. Hermens, *Democracy or Anarchy? A Study of Proportional Representation* (New York: Johnson Reprint Corporation, 1972), p. 293.
6. Rae, *The Political Consequences of Electoral Laws,* pp. 67-129.
7. Rae, *The Political Consequences of Electoral Laws,* pp. 74-77.

Governance and Democracy in the Commonwealth Caribbean: An Introduction

Patrick A.M. Emmanuel

The Electoral System

In the Commonwealth Caribbean, problems have arisen both over the nature of the electoral systems in principle and with regard to the practical administration of various parts of them, in particular over such matters as relative constituency size, the setting of constituency boundaries, voter registration and balloting. General elections, even by-elections, have been marked by serious conflict, including violence. The boycotting of elections by major parties in Trinidad and Tobago (1971) and Jamaica (1983) stemmed from major disagreements over the use of voting machines, and charges of corrupt registration practices, respectively.

Except in Guyana, all the countries practice the first-past-the post (FPP) electoral system, their Constitutions and electoral laws generally providing for the division of national space into constituencies, from which a single representative, gaining the highest number of votes, or being the sole candidate, is elected. In all these cases, except Jamaica, there are no constitutional limits on the (maximum) number of constituencies, which as shown, is alterable by the elected Houses of Parliament. In Jamaica, however, section 67 (subsection 1) of the Constitution places an upper limit of sixty on the number of elected members.

In Guyana, under a list system of proportional representation, the Constitution provides for the election of fifty-three representatives on the basis of each elector being entitled to cast a single vote in favour of any one of the party lists of candidates. The fifty-three seats are allocated among the parties "in such a manner that the proportion that the number of such seats allocated to each list bears to the number of votes cast in favour of the list is nearly as may be the same for each list" (S. 160:1c). Parliament is empowered to provide, inter alia, for the manner in which lists of candidates are prepared, including additional names to fill casual vacancies in lieu of by-elections; for the precise manner in which the number of seats to be allocated to each list is calculated; and for the extraction from the lists and declaration of the names of candidates elected (S. 160:3). Incidentally, Parliament may also provide that party lists of candidates may be combined for the purpose of allocation of seats, but not for the purpose of voting (S. 160:3d).

The election of the President is simultaneous with the Parliament. Each list of candidates is required to designate a candidate for the Presidency and, unless there is only one such candidate, the candidate on the list which receives the largest number of votes becomes President. In the event of a tie between two or more lists the Chairman of the Elections Commission shall publicly choose one of the candidates "by lot", and that person is declared President (S. 177).

When compared with PR methods, the FPP electoral method has the major systemic defect of disproportionality between proportions of seats won and votes received. This is a world-wide experience rather than a merely Caribbean one. The Caribbean experience in this regard is illustrated by looking at the proportions of seats and votes received by competing parties in samples of elections in several of the FPP countries (Table 3).

The table shows an almost unbroken pattern of disproportionality in the relationship between seats and votes won, always in favour of the winning party. Losing parties (and independents) relatedly are disadvantaged as they routinely receive shares of seats significantly lower than their shares of votes. During the period covered there were six occasions on which the winning party received less than 50 per cent of the votes.

But when data for specific losing parties are examined, the level of disadvantage is even more disturbing.

In recent times there have been three instances (Antigua 1984, St. Vincent 1989 and Trinidad 1981)

TABLE 3: FPP ELECTORAL METHOD: PROPORTIONATE DISTRIBUTION OF SEATS AND VOTES

Country	Election	Winning Party		Opposition Parties/Inds	
		% Seats	% Votes	% Seats	% Votes
		(A)	(B)	(C)	(D)
Antigua	1980	77	58	23	42
	1984	94	68	6	32
	1989	88	64	6	31
Montserrat	1983	71	55	29	35
	1987	57	45	43	55
	1991	57	43	43	57
St. Kitts-Nevis	1980	56	56	44	50
	1984	55	48	45	52
	1989	55	44	45	56
Dominica	1980	81	51	19	49
	1985	71	57	29	43
	1990	52	49	48	52
Grenada	1976	60	52	40	48
	1984	93	58	7	36
	1990	(47)	(35)	(53)	(65)
St. Lucia	1979	71	56	29	44
	1982	88	57	12	44
	1987	53	53	47	47
	1987	53	53	47	47
St. Vincent	1979	85	54	15	46
	1984	69	51	31	49
	1989	100	66	0	34
Barbados	1981	62	53	38	47
	1986	89	59	11	41
	1991	64	50	36	50
Jamaica	1976	78	57	22	43
	1980	85	59	15	41
	1989	75	57	25	43
Trinidad	1981	72	53	28	47
	1986	92	66	8	34
	1991	58	45	42	55

Source: *Compiled from Election Reports*

TABLE 4: SELECTED CASES OF DISPROPORTIONALITY (LOSING PARTIES)

Country	Election	Party	No. of Seats (%)		% Votes
Antigua	1980	PLM	3	(18)	39
	1984	UPM	0		23
	1989	UNDP	1	(6)	31
St. Kitts	1984	SKLP	2	(18)	41
	1989	SKLP	2	(18)	38
Grenada	1984	GULP	1	(7)	36
St. Vincent	1989	SVLP	0		30
Trinidad	1981	ONR	0		22

Source: *Election Reports*

where a party won no seats but polled vote shares of 23%, 30% and 22% respectively. A party, also won one seat while receiving 31% of total votes (Antigua 1989) and one seat with a national vote share of 36% (Grenada 1984).

In the remaining cases, vote shares of 39%, 41% and 38% realised three or two seats.

Yet the manifest unevenness of the FPP method has not engendered any very strong and persistent demands for the introduction of the PR system throughout the region. Supporters of the FPP method argue, in effect, that what its opponents see as its major defect, its disproportionality, is indeed its major advantage, as the consequence of disproportionality is effective governing majorities. The record in fact shows that ruling parties have had quite comfortable parliamentary majorities obtained in Dominica 1990, Montserrat 1991 and St. Lucia 1987, being quite exceptional.

It has been only in Trinidad and Tobago that the case for electoral reform, involving the introduction of PR, has had widespread advocacy. So much so that the 1972 Constitution Commission balancing the merits of both FPP and PR methods actually recommended the adoption of a mixed system by which one-half the seats in (a unicameral Parliament) would be chosen by the FPP method and the other one-half would be allocated on the basis of proportions of votes parties received in the FPP voting.

In this regard it is of considerable interest to note that Guyana's Constitution provides for the introduction of just such a mixed FPP-PR system if Parliament so decides:

Parliament may make provision for the division of Guyana into such number of electoral areas, not being more than half the number of the said fifty-three elected members of the Assembly, as Parliament may prescribe and for the election in each such area of one member of the Assembly, each elector having for this purpose one vote in addition to the vote which he may cast in favour of a list of candidates ... (Art. 160:2).

Thus far, however, the Guyanese Parliament has not opted to introduce the mixed system and elections and seat allocation there have continued to be under the PR system only.

In Trinidad and Tobago, the proposal of the first Constitution Commission for the introduction of a mixed FPP and PR system was strongly rejected by the then PNM Government and the new republican Constitution of 1976 contains a clause (section 73:1) which provides that: "The election of members of the House or Representatives shall be by secret ballot and in accordance with the first-past-the post system". The 1987 Commission fully supported retention of the FPP system for elections to the House.

This Commission however advanced a quite novel proposal that in an enlarged Senate, the quota of 12 opposition senators should be allocated "in proportion to the votes cast at the general election for those parties not forming the Government ..." with provisions for the minimum number of seats contested and votes received by such parties (pp. 81-82). But in a minority statement, three of the Commissioners rejected proportionality, arguing that "any differences and divisions that exist in our society today will only be exacerbated by the introduction of any type of proportional representation, however diluted or disguised" (p. 96).

Oddly, the minority statement also observed that "proportionality, i.e., the relationship between seats obtained and votes cast, does not vary substantially between the first-past-the-post and proportional representation system" (p. 96). However, a study of the outcomes of 101 general elections in ten Caribbean states (see Tables 3 and 4) categorically refutes this assertion (Emmanuel, 1992). Indeed, in the 1991 general elections in Trinidad and Tobago, the distribution of votes and seats amongst the three major parties was as follows:

TABLE 5: TRINIDAD AND TOBAGO: ELECTION RESULTS 1991

Party	% Vote	Seats Won (%)
PNM	45.1	21 (58.3)
UNC	29.1	13 (36.1)
NAR	24.0	2 (5.6)

Source: Elections and Boundaries Commission

PNM won a comfortable seat majority with only 45.1 per cent of the vote, while NAR with almost one-quarter of the vote won only 2 seats. UNC, like PNM, also took a greater share of seats (36.1 per cent) than its share of total votes (29.1 per cent). It will be recalled, as shown in Table 4, that in 1981 ONR received 22 per cent of the votes but no seats. At the same time ULF with 15.2 per cent votes, won 8 seats (22.2 percent).

If the 1991 elections in Trinidad and Tobago were held along the lines of mixed FPP and PR proposed by the 1972 Commission, seats in a House of 72 members would have been allocated as follows:

TABLE 6: TRINIDAD AND TOBAGO: SEAT ALLOCATION BY FPP & PR SYSTEM (1991 VOTING)

Party (% Vote)	FPP Seats	PR Seats	Total
PNM (45.1)	21	16	37
UNC (29.1)	13	11	24
NAR (24.0)	2	9	11
	36	36	72

Under this mixed system, the 36 additional seats are allocated in direct proportion to votes cast for the parties by the FPP voting. The mixed system would preserve a majority for PNM, i.e. 37 of 72 seats, but this is reduced from the margin, 21 of 36, afforded by the FPP system only. On the other hand, a pure PR system alone could have resulted in a distribution of PNM 16, UNC 11 and NAR 9 (assuming of course that in a pure PR election, the party vote shares would have been the same as occurred in the actual FPP election). Thus the PR system alone would have denied any party majority and called for the very coalition-based government which is regarded as a major defect of PR.

Elsewhere in the region, notwithstanding the long experience of FPP disproportionality, PR has had few advocates. The Constitution Commission in Barbados briefly considered the issue and concluded that "the introduction of such a system [of PR] could create other problems which did not seem to justify a recommendation for such a system" (p. 28). However, in a minority report, one Commissioner argued for a system of "Fixed Proportional Representation" designed to "produce a viable government and a strong opposition and discourage nuisance parties". Under this system, in a House of 30 members, a minimum of 18 seats would be allocated to the party gaining the most votes and a minimum of 9 to the next best supported party, with the remaining 3 seats allocated "in accordance with the results of the election provided that in no event the Government party will hold seats in excess of two-thirds [i.e 20] of the total number of seats" (p. 194).

A key proviso is that a party must receive at least 4 per cent of the votes to qualify for seat allocation. However, as described, the system anticipates only two qualifying parties and does not explicitly provide for sub-division of opposition seats where as in 1991, two opposition parties (BLP and NDP) would be eligible for seats.

But the major problem with this proposal is in fixing a minimum number of seats allocated to the winning party, irrespective of the vote share gained vis-a-vis all other parties. This defect results from a preoccupation with securing comfortable majorities rather than democratic proportionality, which would allow a wider variety of party interests a chance to be represented in Parliament.

Constituency Size and Boundaries

As already shown, there are constitutional requirements in the countries practising the FPP electoral system, that all constituencies be as nearly as practicable of equal size, having regard to the influence o such factors as population density, geographical bar-riers and administrative boundaries. Approximate equality of constituency size is essential for satisfy-ing the important principle of equal weight of each ballot. Wide differences in size may also exacerbate the already inherent disproportionality between shares of votes and seats seen to characterise the FPP system.

The following Table (7) applies the yardstick adopted in Trinidad and Tobago and Barbados, that no constituency should be less than 90 per cent nor more than 110 per cent of the average size of constituen-cies, to illustrate the pattern of inequality existent in several countries in recent elections.

The table shows, by country (and election year), the number of constituencies, or seats (Column A), the total electoral registration (B), average constitu-

ency size (C), the numbers of constituencies that were more than 110% of the average (D), and less than 90% of the average (E), and the totals for (D) and (E).

Separate data are provided for the smaller territo-ries in the five cases where constituencies exist on more than one land mass. In these instances, populations are small and average constituency size is less than on the main land mass.

Trinidad and Tobago is the only case in which all constituencies fell within the set range. Barbados and mainland St. Vincent are the other noteworthy cases, with only a few constituencies, i.e., four out of twenty-eight and two out of thirteen respectively, slightly outside the limits.

In all other cases, however, there are considerable disparities, as reflected in the Column (F) totals, rela-

TABLE 7: VARIATIONS IN CONSTITUENCY SIZE

Country			(Election)	Seats	Registration	Av. Size	No. Above 110%	No. Below 90%	Total D + E
				(A)	(B)	(C)	(D)	(E)	(F)
1	(a)	Antigua	(1989)	16	36,145	2,259	7	6	13
	(b)	Barbuda	(")	1	731	731	-	-	-
				17					13
2		Barbados	(1991)	28	191,000	6,821	3	1	4
3		Belize	(1989)	28	82,556	2,948	8	6	14
4		Dominica	(1990)	21	50,558	2,408	7	11	18
5	(a)	Grenada	(1984)	14	45,715	3,265	5	7	12
	(b)	Cariacou	(")	1	2,443	2,443	-	-	-
				15	48,158				12
6		Jamaica	(1989)	60	1,078,760	17,979	16	14	30
7		Montserrat	(1991)	7	7,828	1,118	1	3	4
8	(a)	St. Kitts	(1989)	8	21,224	2,653	3	5	8
	(b)	Nevis	(")	3	5,257	1,752	1	1	2
				11	26,481				10
9		St. Lucia	(1987)	17	83,257	4,897	4	8	12
10	(a)	St. Vincent	(1989)	13	56,638	4,357	1	1	2
	(b)	Grenadines	(")	2	4,453	2,227	1	1	2
				15	61,091				4
11	(a)	Trinidad	(1986)	34	850,936	25,028	0	0	0
	(b)	Tobago	(")	2	31,093	15,546	0	0	0
				36	882,029				

Source: Compiled from Election Reports

tive to Column (A), total seats. All constituencies in St. Kitts fell outside the 90-110 percentage range. In other territories, the proportions (of constituencies) falling outside this range are Dominica and Grenada - 86 per cent, Antigua - 81 per cent, St. Lucia - 71 per cent, Belize and Jamaica - 50 per cent, and Montserrat - 43 per cent. Contrastingly, in Barbados the proportion is 14 per cent and in St. Vincent - 15 per cent.

The data show a disconcerting disparity of constituency size, with exceptions of course. The extent of disparity varies within countries, some constituencies being only slightly larger or smaller than the outer limits, while others are considerably larger or smaller. Table 8 provides data for the largest and smallest constituencies in each **main island** and Belize for the election years being used.

The ratios of smallest and largest constituencies are lowest in the cases of Trinidad, Barbados and St. Vincent, but are quite high in St. Kitts, Grenada, Antigua, Montserrat, Dominica and St. Lucia. Jamaica and Belize are intermediate cases.

It has of course been pointed that in all the cases the constitutional stipulation regarding equality of constituency size is qualified by the need to have re-gard for geographical, population, communication and administrative factors. These qualifications, reasonably applied, will help explain the various levels of disparity found in some cases.

Unfortunately, reports of Boundaries Commissions have not been available for consultation, and therefore it is not possible to show their recommendations and the parliamentary responses to them, in terms of acceptance, amendment or rejection. Perusal of these Reports and the subsequent parliamentary debates and Boundaries Orders, is a task whose urgency commends itself.

Equality of the franchise, as far as is practicable, is one of the fundamentals of a truly democratic system. While there can be some real barriers to full (exact) equality, the barriers should be reasonably interpreted and applied, so that the principle of equality in most cases, overrides the inequalities derived from unreasonable use of barriers. The letter and spirit of the constitutional requirements most certainly could not permit the excesses of disparity that exist in some cases.

In terms of constituency numbers, as shown previously, except for Jamaica, there are no upper limits set for total numbers; but in a few cases, there is men-

TABLE 8: SMALLEST AND LARGEST CONSTITUENCIES (MAIN ISLANDS AND BELIZE)

Country	(Election Year)	Av. Size	Smallest	Largest	Ratio B to C
		(A)	(B)	(C)	(D)
Antigua	(1989)	2,259	1,077	3,714	1:3.4
Barbados	(1991)	6,821	6,009	7,568	1:1.3
Belize	(1984)	2,948	2,286	3,751	1:1.6
Dominica	(1990)	2,408	1,200	4,790	1:4.0
Grenada	(1984)	3,265	2,085	5,357	1:2.6
Jamaica	(1989)	17,979	13,054	25,047	1:1.9
Montserrat	(1991)	1,118	605	2,286	1:3.8
St. Kitts	(1989)	2,653	1,785	4,237	1:2.4
St. Lucia	(1987)	4,897	2,499	10,012	1:4.0
St. Vincent	(1989)	4,357	3,621	4,821	1:1.3
Trinidad	(1986)	25,028	22,755	27,157	1:1.2

Source: Compiled from Election Reports

tion of minimum numbers. In the case of multi-island states, there are special provisions in three cases to ensure separate constituencies in the smaller territories: Antigua and Barbuda provides for at least one in Barbuda, St. Kitts-Nevis for one-third of the total to be in Nevis, and there must be at least two constituencies in Tobago. At present there are two seats in the Grenadines, (of St. Vincent) and one in Carriacou/Petit Martinique (Grenada). There are also several constituencies in the Out Islands of the Bahamas.

Constituency boundaries necessarily need to be adjusted whenever there is a change in the numbers of constituencies, although boundaries can also be adjusted without such alterations in seat numbers. Since independence, seven of the relevant eleven states have increased the numbers of their constituencies, viz Bahamas, Barbados, Belize, Jamaica, St. Kitts-Nevis, St. Vincent and the Grenadines and Trinidad and Tobago.

Changes in boundaries whether or not due to increases in seat numbers, have from time to time generated accusations of "gerrymandering", i.e. manipulation of boundaries essentially for partisan benefit. However, the demonstrated inequalities in constituency size throughout the region should give rise to well-founded calls for boundary adjustments so as to bring all constituencies into the level of approximate similarity of size that the region's Constitutions and the interests of democratic integrity warrant.

Registration and Voting

Matters related to the registration of voters and the conduct of elections have been surrounded with much greater conflict in the region than constituency issues. A useful description of difficulties regularly encountered with such matters throughout the region is the following commentary, made about the Jamaican case:

> Criticisms and strictures have been directed generally against breaches provided through loopholes inherent in the system and abuses perpetuated by corrupt election officials. These have focused more specifically on charges such as 'bogus voting' that is, impersonation (voting in a fictitious name, in the name of a deceased person, etc.), multiple voting by an individual, the deliberate omission of qualified persons from the electoral list, the "padding" of the list, and the stuffing of ballot boxes. (Gladstone Mills, "Electoral Reform in Jamaica", *Parliamentarian*, LXII:2, April 1981, p. 7).

Mills' identification of problems with registration is amplified by comments made by some chief election officials in their election reports. Consider the following candid submission by Antigua and Barbuda's Supervisor of Elections:

> There are still the names of many dead persons on the list, many persons living overseas and names of persons who have registered in other constituencies. Duplication of names has caused the Electoral List to be inflated and not showing a true picture of the total number of voters. This has caused me some great concern and I wish to recommend that machinery be set up to hold complete voter registration of the nation ... Government ought to heed this suggestion in order to correct the present situation. (Report on the General Elections...1989. Supervisor of Elections, Antigua and Barbuda, p. 3).

Reports in other territories have also cited problems posed by electors such as refusal to register for religious or socio-economic reasons, or failure to submit changes of address after enumeration.

In Guyana serious socio-political concern has been long expressed particularly with overseas registration and voting, proxy voting and the transfer of ballot boxes to the capital before a preliminary count is done at polling stations. However, in a series of amendments to electoral law, these sources of abuse have been eliminated.

Elsewhere there have been many instances of protest with regard to voting and vote counting, including allegations of treated ballot paper and unfair rejection of ballots. As a result, there have been several cases of election petitions seeking judicial redress of alleged electoral wrong-doing. But no general election *in toto* has been ruled invalid in consequence of judicial examination.

Quite apart from the problems and conflicts which arise with corruption, or laxity in administering unobjectionable existing laws and regulations, there are aspects of the electoral systems themselves which seem to be inherently defective and in need of reform. In his above-cited article on Jamaica. Mills observed that there were demands "to establish an impartial body to remove the conduct of election from within the influence of an elected Minister", and that it was in response to this crisis that the Electoral Advisory Committee and Office of Director of Elections were created. (Ibid.) As has been shown, all countries now have formal arrangements in place for the independent supervision of elections, though these arrangements are not uniform throughout. Most of them have Commissions in charge while a few have Supervisors of Elections only (viz. Antigua and Barbuda, Grenada and St. Vincent and the Grenadines).

It is noteworthy that in Antigua *Parliament* is involved in the recruitment of the Supervisor. According to section 67:1 of the Constitution, "The Governor General shall by notice published in the Gazette appoint a Supervisor of Elections on resolutions to that effect of both Houses of Parliament specifying the person nominated for appointment". Parliamentary selection in fact means selection by the majority party, i.e. the Government.

The desirability of this exceptional provision merits some considerable reflection.

In this regard it is appropriate to recall that the Constitution Commission of Grenada reviewed arrangements for electoral administration there and commented that:

> Although there was no evidence before the Commission signifying widespread dissatisfaction with the manner in which the Supervisor carried out his functions, we recommend that the function of the Constituency Boundaries Commission ... be extended to include the conduct and supervision of the elections... as is the case in some other member states of the Caribbean Community...The Supervisor of Elections could become the chief administrative officer of the Commission and be subject to the direction and control only of the Commission in the exercise of his functions. His appointment could be made by the Commission or, alternatively, by the Governor-General acting after consultation with the Chairman of the Commission. (p. 22).

In Grenada, the Supervisor currently, is "the person holding or acting in such public office as may for the time being be designated in that behalf by the Governor-General acting in his own deliberate judgement". (Sec. 35:1, Constitution). In St. Vincent, the office whose holder becomes Supervisor is designated by "the Public Service Commission, or, if the Commission so decides, by such other person who is not a public officer as may for the time being be so designated, but before exercising its powers under this subsection the Commission shall consult with the Prime Minister" (Sec. 34:2, the Constitution).

In St. Vincent then, the Prime Minister may be involved in the process of appointing a Supervisor of Elections, depending on whether the PSC decides to recruit one from inside or outside the Service.

There is also room for reflection on the principle of choosing the senior election officials from within the ranks of the civil service, having regard inter alia, to the powers Prime Ministers have over senior appointments therein. Furthermore, the engagement of the Prime Minister in the process in St. Vincent is exceptional, like the engagement of Parliament in the case of Antigua. Although there is also prime ministerial involvement in the appointment of chief election officials in Barbados, Belize and Trinidad and Tobago, these cases of course differ from St. Vincent in that their officials are under the control of Elections and Boundaries Commissions. In St. Vincent however, the official is the sole authority over the conduct of elections. In Antigua too.

Another concern is the recruitment of staff of Elections Offices from within the ranks of the public service. Grenada's Constitution Commission advised that it "would be unwise for the [proposed] Electoral Commission to have to depend on the staff of another Department or Ministry of the Government under the control and direction of a Minister of Government to carry out its functions". Thus it should be made a requirement in the Constitution that the Commission "must be provided with the requisite staff and funds to enable it to perform its functions properly". (p. 22).

However, it must be recognised that in small communities, with limited numbers of requisite skills, the scope for recruitment of the very many persons needed to conduct registration and elections, totally outside the ranks of public employees, will be quite constricted. Governments employ, as teachers and civil servants, a large proportion of the requisite talent, and selection of electoral staff from these categories is a practical necessity. What matters at the least, is that by secondment from the public service to the Electoral Offices, the supervision of their electoral functions comes under Electoral Commissions rather than of Ministers.

In any event, the integrity required for carrying out electoral duties is a function of individual character, and not of employment in the public service or elsewhere. Any employee may be corrupt or corruptible. Actual experience and the safeguards in place to weed out corruption are critical factors.

One further matter that is worthy of consideration is the scope for co-operation among countries in helping each other to improve tile machinery of electoral administration. Examples exist, for instance in the case of Grenada in 1983-84 where the electoral system needed to be substantially overhauled, following its suspension after 1979. Commendable assistance was forthcoming from within the region in revising laws and regulations, instituting a system of voter identification and conducting a whole new process of enumeration and registration.

The level of expertise and experience varies from country to country and even from individual to individual. It should presumably be quite feasible to devise a system, within the framework of the Caricom Treaty, to institutionalise mechanisms for moving expertise to points where it is most needed, such as in the demonstrated cases of registration in Antigua, or Guyana. In this regard a Conference of Election Officials, under appropriate auspices, could be a useful starter. Greater attention to the subject of Electoral Administration in University courses can be helpful.

Parties and Party Systems

Patrick A.M. Emmanuel

The data presented on the distribution of votes and seats over time in the several countries constitute the basis on which an effort can be made to identify 'systemic' characteristics of the structure and dynamics of electoral competition. This effort requires some elaboration of notions of 'party' and 'system' as they are applied here.

The term 'party' refers to an association of people under a specific name whose primary purposes are the achievement and exercise of governmental power. In the Commonwealth Caribbean the established means for achieving power are success in regularly held elections. Typically, a political party is characterised by:

(a) Leadership, of an individual or collective kind;
(b) Structure or organisation, which may combine features of charisma or rational-legality;
(c) Ideology and programmes as espoused from time to time;
(d) Life-span or durability, in terms of the capacity to subsist or alternatively, to disappear or be absorbed into a new or other existing organism;
(e) Electoral performance, as measured by the numbers of elections contested, the numbers of candidates nominated, votes received and seats won.

As the record shows, the Caribbean experience encompasses stable macro-parties of long life and electoral success; defection, merger and alliance, as well as a plethora of micro-parties of short duration and no success. Caribbean parties have also varied considerably with respect to the possession of personal and institutional charisma, levels of formal and informal

organisation and the ideological bent of policies proclaimed and actualised.

In its stricter sense, the term 'system' has been applied to refer to a stable pattern of interacting parts. More usually, however, its political science usage has taken in any set of actors and activities, stable or unstable, manifesting themselves in the political arena. In this study, our application of the term raises the following empirical questions:

(a) At any point in time, how many competing actors (parties and independent candidates) are engaged?
(b) Over time, are there changes in the (major) actors, e.g., by way of the demise of old parties and/or the formation of new ones?
(c) Is there *alternation* in office among parties, i.e., a pattern of success and defeat for specific major parties, or does change take place in an unpatterned fashion?

The following paragraphs analyse the data on the basis of these relevant specifications and queries. Given the focus of the study, no attention will be paid to quality of leadership or to organisation, ideology and programme.

The data concern 101 general elections in 10 countries, contested by 133 parties and 2,911 candidates, including independents.

The record shows that all the countries have had the experience of large, successful parties and of small, transient unsuccessful groupings (micro-parties). The total number of parties, large and small, that have contested in general elections in all the countries to date is as follows:

TABLE 29: NUMBER OF POLITICAL PARTIES CONTESTING GENERAL ELECTIONS

Country		No. of Large and Small Parties
Antigua and Barbuda	(1951-89)	13
Montserrat	(1952-91)	9
St. Kitts-Nevis	(1952-89)	10
Dominica	(1951-90)	12
Grenada	(1951-90)	8
St. Lucia	(1951-87)	4
St. Vincent and the Grenadines	(1951-89)	11
Barbados	(1951-91)	8
Jamaica	(1944-89)	22
Trinidad and Tobago	(1946-91)	36
		133

TABLE 30: COMMONWEALTH CARIBBEAN: SEQUENCE OF WINNING PARTIES

Election	Jamaica	Barbados	St. Lucia	Dominica	St. Kitts-Nevis	Antigua-Barbuda	Trinidad & Tobago	St. Vincent & the Grenadines	Grenada	Montserrat
1st	JLP	BLP	SLP	Inds.	SKLP	ALP	Coalition	Eighth Army	GULP	MLP
2nd	JLP	BLP	SLP	Inds.	SKLP	ALP	Coalition	Inds.	GULP	MLP
3rd	PNP	DLP	SLP	Inds.	SKLP	ALP	PNM	PPP	Coalition	MLP
4th	PNP	DLP	SLP	DLP	SKLP	ALP	PNM	PPP	GULP	MLP
5th	JLP	DLP	UWP	DLP	SKLP	PLM	PNM	PPP	GNP	MLP
6th	JLP	BLP	UWP	DLP	SKLP	ALP	PNM	SVLP	GULP	PDP
7th	PNP	BLP	UWP	DLP	Coalition	ALP	PNM	Coalition	GULP	PDP
8th	PNP	DLP	SLP	DFP	PAM	ALP	PNM	SVLP	GULP	PLM
9th	JLP	DLP	UWP	DFP	PAM	ALP	NAR	SVLP	GULP	PLM
10th	JLP		UWP	DFP			PNM	NDP	NNP	PLM
11th	PNP		UWP					NDP	Coalition	NPP
No. of Parties	2	2	2	2	2	2	2	3	3	4

TABLE 31: FREQUENCY OF PARTY VICTORIES: COUNTRIES IN WHICH PARTIES HAVE WON ALL ELECTIONS

Country	Party	No. of Wins
Jamaica	JLP	6
	PNP	5
Barbados	BLP	4
	DLP	5
St. Lucia	SLP	5
	UWP	6
Antigua & Barbuda	ALP	8
	PLM	1
Montserrat	MLP	5
	PDP	2
	PLM	3
	NPP	1

Most of these parties as has been shown, have really been tiny cliques which have put forward small numbers of candidates at one general election and disappeared shortly afterward. A few small parties lasted longer and were able to win seats and influence for a time.

Most of the elections, in fact 91 of the 101 were won by political parties, while in the remainder no party won a majority and post-election coalitions and realignments ensued.

In all there are 24 successful parties, i.e., parties which won elections and formed governments on one or more occasions. Table 30 shows comparatively the sequence of party victories and coalitions for all ten countries and 101 elections.

Based on this table and data presented before, it is possible to classify countries in a variety of ways.

There are five countries in which elections have been won only by political parties, i.e., where there was no need for coalitions involving parties and/or independents. These are Jamaica, Barbados, St. Lucia, Antigua and Barbuda and Montserrat.

Of these five there are four in which only two parties have won, the exception being Montserrat, in which four parties have been victorious.

Then there are three other countries in which only two parties have been successful but in which on a few occasions no party had won and some form of post-election coalition was required:

TABLE 32: FREQUENCY OF PARTY VICTORIES AND COALITIONS (TRINIDAD AND TOBAGO, ST. KITTS-NEVIS AND DOMINICA)

Country	No. of Party	No. of Victories	Coalitions
Trinidad and Tobago	PNM	7	2
	NAR	1	
St. Kitts-Nevis	SKLP	6	1
	PAM	2	
Dominica	DLP	4	3
	DFP	3	

Thirdly, in the two remaining cases, Grenada, and St. Vincent and the Grenadines, three parties have won elections but there have also experienced coalition arrangements.

TABLE 33: FREQUENCY OF PARTY VICTORIES AND COALITIONS (GRENADA, ST. VINCENT AND THE GRENADINES)

Country	Party	No. of Victories	No. of Coalitions
Grenada	GULP	6	2
	GNP	1	
	NNP	1	
St. Vincent	PPP	3	2
	SVLP	3	
	NDP	2	

Origins of Major Parties

The ten cases can also be distributed in terms of the origins in time, of major-party formation and competition.

Jamaica is a unique case in that at the time of its elections (in 1944) both its major parties already existed and commenced a period of electoral competition broken only once, in 1983, when the PNP boycotted the elections.

In **Barbados**, the BLP first faced minor challenge from two small parties, the Electors' Association and Congress Party, until the formation of the DLP in time to enter the fray in 1956.

The GULP of **Grenada** faced no organised opposition until the GNP began contesting elections in 1957. But GNP has been relatively unsuccessful with only

one victory, in 1962, followed by participation in a post-election coalition (1957–61) and a successful pre-election merger (NNP 1984–89). Since the break-up of the original NNP, GNP has been renamed The National Party (TNP).

In **St. Lucia**, the People's Progressive Party provided the Labour Party with fairly strong but unsuccessful opposition, as Labour won the first four elections. Major two-party competition really began in 1964 with the formation of the United Workers Party (UWP).

In **St. Kitts-Nevis**, the Labour Party held sway from the beginning, against ineffective challenges from micro-parties and independents. But with the first challenge of the People's Action Movement (PAM) in 1966, the tide began a slow turn which brought about first a coalition defeat of Labour by PAM and the Nevis Reformation Party (NRP) in 1980, and subsequently PAM majorities in 1984 and 1989.

Effective alternative party challenge came to **Montserrat** in 1970 after the Labour Party had won all five previous elections. The new Progressive Democratic Party (PDP) defeated MLP in 1970, after which the old victor became defunct. The resulting party void was filled by the People's Liberation Movement (PLM) which was successful in the three elections held between 1978 and 1987, but was defeated by NPP in 1991.

Antigua and Barbuda's turn to experience a major challenge to the historically supreme Labour Party also took some time in coming. It was not realised until 1971, when the Progressive Labour Movement (PLM), formed in 1968, was able to mete out the first and so far only general election defeat suffered by the Labour Party. PLM, however, has since withered and a new challenger has appeared at the most recent elections in the form of the United National Democratic Party (UNDP).

In the above seven cases, there was at least one major party (in Jamaica, two) in place at the first general elections. All of these except the Montserrat Labour Party (MLP) continue to exist although at this time only two, Antigua's Labour Party, and Jamaica's PNP are in office.

In our remaining three cases, none of the parties which were to become successful, existed on the occasion of the first general elections held.

In the case of **St. Vincent and the Grenadines** the first elections were won by a loose and short-lived grouping styled the Eighth Army of Liberation. However, by the second elections, in 1953, the People's Political Party (PPP) was formed and won against independents. Then, by the third elections in 1957, the St. Vincent Labour Party (SVLP) entered. Elections between 1957 and 1972 were marked by competition between these two major parties, following which PPP went into decline and has not contested since 1979. The new dominant party in St. Vincent and the Grenadines became the New Democratic Party (NDP) which first contested in 1979, and defeated the Labour Party in 1984 and 1989.

St. Vincent and the Grenadines and Montserrat, then, are the two countries in which former successful labour-based parties, PPP and MLP, have become defunct.

Trinidad and Tobago experienced its first major-party formation in 1955 when the People's National Movement (PNM) was created. Previously, several factions contended, with the Butler Party being the most successful. PNM won all six elections between 1956 and 1981, gaining majority Afro-Trinidadian and Tobagonian support in a context of Afro-Indian pluralism. It was not until 1986 when efforts to forge an Afro-Indian alternative were successful, that the National Alliance for Reconstruction (NAR) dealt PNM its first and so far only electoral defeat. Since then, however, a section of the NAR led by Basdeo Panday, the former ULF leader, has broken away from NAR and formed the United National Congress (UNC). With NAR being defeated in 1991 at the hands of both PNM and UNC, the structure of party politics has reverted to the pattern of the 1970s.

Finally, at the other end of the scale of party formation, Dominica stands apart in that at the first elections there were no organised political groups in place. Thus independent candidates held sway not only in 1951 but in the second and third elections, in 1954 and 1957 respectively.

Efforts at party organisation bore fruit after 1957 when the Dominica Labour Party came into being. The DLP won its first four contests, between 1961 and 1975, its principal opponents being first the Dominica United Peoples Party (DUPP) in 1961 and 1966 and then the Dominica Freedom Party (DFP) which began its electoral challenge in 1970. After two unsuccessful efforts, the DFP defeated DLP in the last three elections: 1980, 1985, 1990.

In the 1990 elections however, there was a factor at work which portends the reorganisation of Dominica's party system. The new United Workers' Party replaced DLP as the major parliamentary opposition force, winning six seats to DLP's four. At present then there are three major players in Dominica's electoral arena, viz., DFP, UWP and DLP.

The Degree of Alternation

The data show that in the ten states there have been variable sequences of alternation in office among the successful political parties. 'Alternation' is typically used to denote a regularity of replacement in office among parties, moreso two specific parties.

The record indicates that 24 parties have won elections, with another, Grenada's NDC, just short of success but able subsequently to form a government. The patterns of alternation and in several cases the absence of it are as follows:

(a) **Jamaica**: Jamaica evinces a regular pattern of alternation with each of its two major parties, from the inception, enjoying two terms and then losing out to the other.

(b) **Barbados**: Alternation in the case of Barbados is evident, but not as neatly as is the case in Jamaica. The DLP won three terms (1961–71) successively after the BLP's two at the beginning. Then, however, BLP won two (1976–81) followed by two more to the DLP (1986–91).

(c) **St. Lucia**: Regularity of alternation begins to weaken with the experience of St. Lucia, where four SLP victories were followed by three UWP, then one SLP and recently, three UWP. Of course SLP-UWP rivalry began at the fifth general elections, held in 1964.

(d) **Grenada**: There were two occasions on which GULP was unsuccessful in the eight elections between 1951 and 1976, i.e., in 1957 and 1962. Since then the NNP party-alliance as well as NDC have both triumphed over Labour.

(e) **Antigua and Barbuda**: Here the pendulum has swung only once against the ALP, with the lone victory of PLM in 1971. For most of the time opposition parties in Antigua and Barbuda have varied, with PLM contesting only three elections with full slates of candidates in Antigua.

(f) Four states, **Montserrat, St. Vincent and the Grenadines, St. Kitts-Nevis** and **Dominica**, are cases where instead of alternation strictly speaking, there has been a succession of winning parties, with previous incumbents unable thus far to regain office.

In **Montserrat**, five terms of the MLP were followed by two terms of PDP, and then three terms of PLM which has recently been defeated by the new NPP. Similarly, **in St. Vincent and the Grenadines**, except for the PPP-Mitchell coalition of 1972–74, the sequence has been PPP three terms, SVLP three terms and NDP two terms.

These are multi-party sequences, whereas **St. Kitts-Nevis** and **Dominica** are two-party affairs. In the former case, six terms of SKLP was followed by a PAM-NRP coalition and then two PAM victories. (The maintenance of PAM-NRP coalition is necessitated by PAM's one seat majority in both of the last two elections as well as political requirements of a fragile federalist compact). **Dominica**'s patterns is one in which four DLP terms have been followed by three DFP successes.

(g) **Trinidad and Tobago** manifests a slightly different course of party success. there, following initial coalitions, six straight PNM victories were followed by success by the NAR party-alliance, and then a return of PNM.

The Distribution of Voting Loyalties and Seats

An important feature of the political system in general and the party system in particular, is the distribution of votes and seats going to parties and independents, over time. Rae [1971] distinguished an electoral party system in terms of the distribution of votes and a parliamentary party system as indicated by the distribution of seats won. Because of the absence of proportional representation, winning parties in the Caribbean have, except in a few cases, received higher percentages of seats than of votes. In some instances a party has won all the seats, but the losing groups have captured an appreciable share of the popular vote. Generally, the distribution of votes evidences a political pluralism which is not reflected in the allocation of seats. This structural characteristic has often led to calls for the introduction of some system of proportionality in Caribbean elections.

The following tables show how votes and seats have actually been spread in the outcomes of the elections under scrutiny.

The dominance of the ALP in the early period is shown in the very high share of the votes it received. However, by the fifth elections, won by PLM, the win-

TABLE 34: ANTIGUA – BARBUDA: PROPORTIONATE DISTRIBUTION OF VOTES AND SEATS IN GENERAL ELECTIONS

Election	Winning Party	% Votes	% Seats	Other Parties/Inds. % Votes	% Votes
1951	ALP	87	100	13	0
1956	ALP	87	100	13	0
1961	ALP	85	100	15	0
1965	ALP	n.a	100	n.a.	0
1971	PLM	58	77	42	23
1976	ALP	49	65	51	35
1980	ALP	58	77	42	23
1984	ALP	68	94	32	6
1989	ALP	64	88	36	12

TABLE 35: MONTSERRAT: PROPORTIONATE DISTRIBUTION OF VOTES AND SEATS IN GENERAL ELECTIONS

Election	Winning Party	% Votes	% Seats	Other Parties/Inds. % Votes	% Seats
1952	MLP	70	100	30	0
1955	MLP	47	60	53	40
1958	MLP	56	60	44	40
1961	MLP	58	71	42	29
1966	MLP	61	71	39	29
1970	PDP	65	100	35	0
1973	PDP	65	71	35	29
1978	PLM	62	100	38	0
1983	PLM	55	71	45	29
1987	PLM	45	57	55	43
1991	NPP	43	57	57	43

ning-party share declined and then rose again but not to the levels of the 1950s and 1960s. The strength of opposing parties has built up over the entire period.

There were four occasions on which the winning party won all the seats, but there was also one, the sixth, in which the winner received less votes than the opposition combined (but mainly PLM).

Montserrat shows greater balance in the division of voting loyalties. Opposition candidates received a low of 30 per cent, in the first elections, and on three occasions, in 1955, 1987 and 1991, have received more votes than the winning party. Winning party support was highest in the first elections, and since then has fluctuated between 43–65 per cent.

There have been three occasions in which a party won all the seats, with opposition voting at 30, 35 and 38 per cent successively.

The Labour Party's greatest triumph came in the first election when it received 85 per cent of the votes. But its support fell sharply afterwards although 1961 and 1975 were good years. In the seventh election

(1980) when Labour first lost, PAM and NRP together polled 56 per cent of the votes with Labour receiving the remainder (44%).

There were three occasions on which the winning party polled less than 50 per cent of the votes. Labour once and PAM twice. In the cases of PAM, the party, in an understanding with NRP, did not sponsor candidates in Nevis. And at the time of the coalition, the distribution of seats was PAM three, NRP two and Labour four.

Except for 1966 and 1985, winning-party vote share has never been particularly high in Dominica, and there have been three instances of winning parties receiving less votes than the combined opposition. In step with this, opposition strength has always been high, the lowest standing at 35 per cent and surpassing 50 per cent on three occasions.

The usual disproportionality of vote and seat shares obtains. In cases where more than one opposition group contests, the disproportion tends to be widest. But at no time have all seats in Dominica gone to one party.

TABLE 36: ST. KITTS-NEVIS: PROPORTIONATE DISTRIBUTION OF VOTES AND SEATS IN GENERAL ELECTIONS

Election	Winning Party	% Votes	% Seats	Other Parties/Inds. % Votes	% Seats
1952	SKLP	85	100	15	0
1957	SKLP	54	63	46	27
1961	SKLP	65	70	35	30
1966	SKLP	44	70	56	30
1971	SKLP	51	78	49	22
1975	SKLP	60	78	40	22
1980	(PAM & NRP)	56	56	44	44
1984	PAM	48	55	52	45
1989	PAM	44	55	56	45

TABLE 37: DOMINICA: PROPORTIONATE DISTRIBUTION OF VOTES AND SEATS IN GENERAL ELECTIONS

Election	Winning Party	% Votes	% Seats	Other Parties/Inds. % Votes	% Seats
1951		-	-	-	-
1954		-	-	-	-
1957		-	-	-	-
1961	DLP	48	64	52	36
1966	DLP	65	90	35	10
1970	DLP	50	73	50	27
1975	DLP	49	76	51	24
1980	DFP	51	81	49	19
1985	DFP	57	71	43	29
1990	DFP	49	52	51	48

TABLE 38: GRENADA: PROPORTIONATE DISTRIBUTION OF VOTES AND SEATS IN GENERAL ELECTIONS

Election	Winning Party	% Votes	% Seats	Other Parties/Inds. % Votes	% Seats
1951	GULP	64	75	36	25
1954	GULP	46	75	54	25
1957	-	-	-	-	-
1961	GULP	53	80	47	20
1962	GNP	54	60	46	40
1967	GULP	55	70	45	30
1972	GULP	59	87	41	13
1976	GULP	52	60	48	40
1984	NNP	58	93	42	7
1990	(NDC)	(35)	(47)	(65)	(53)

TABLE 39: ST. LUCIA: PROPORTIONATE DISTRIBUTION OF VOTES AND SEATS IN GENERAL ELECTIONS

Election	Winning Party	% Votes	% Seats	Other Parties/Inds. % Votes	% Seats
1951	SLP	50	63	50	37
1954	SLP	47	63	53	37
1957	SLP	66	88	34	12
1961	SLP	62	90	38	10
1964	UWP	52	60	48	40
1969	UWP	58	60	42	40
1974	UWP	54	59	46	41
1979	SLP	56	71	44	29
1982	UWP	56	88	44	12
1987	UWP	53	53	47	47
1987	UWP	56	53	47	47

In Grenada shares of votes going to winning parties have been over 50 per cent on all but one occasion: 1954. In 1957 three parties, GULP, GNP and PDM, won two seats each and independents won the other two. Then, in 1990, NDC won seven of the 15 seats with 35 per cent of the vote, while GULP won four, NNP two and TNP two.

Combined opposition voting has been high, with a low of 36 per cent in 1951 and a high of 54 per cent in 1954, the 1990 outcome being exceptional in that no party won a majority of seats. There was no instance in which a party won all the seats.

St. Lucia's record is one of strong popular support for losing parties. Labour improved its standing in 1957 and 1961, after modest showings in the first two elections. But when serious two-party competition began with the entry of UWP from 1964, winning party shares fluctuated between 52 and 58 per cent.

As is usually the case, there was the element of disproportionality in seats won, except for the results in 1987 when on both occasions there was exact correspondence of shares of votes and seats. An outstanding instance of disproportionality occurred in 1982 when PLP and SLP won one seat each with 27.0 per cent and 17.0 per cent of the vote respectively.

The Eighth Army of 1951 was not a really coherent party association on any reasonable minimal standard. The PPP was the first such party but fell just short of a majority of the vote on the three occasions on which it won seat majorities. In 1972, when both PPP and SVLP won six seats each and a lone independent, James Mitchell won the thirteenth one, a coalition was formed between PPP and Mitchell. In five of the six elections since 1967, winning parties have won vote majorities, varying from 51 to 69 per cent. Votes cast for other parties (and independents) have been at a high level in St. Vincent and the Grenadines.

In two elections, when opposition vote share was 30 per cent (1951) and more recently, 34 per cent (1989), the winning party won all the seats.

TABLE 40: St. Vincent & the Grenadines: Proportionate Distribution of Votes and Seats in General Elections

| Election | Winning Party | % Votes | % Seats | Other Parties/Inds. | |
				% Votes	% Seats
1951	8th Army	70	100	30	0
1954	--	--	--	--	--
1957	PPP	49	63	51	37
1961	PPP	49	67	61	33
1966	PPP	49	56	51	44
1967	SVLP	54	67	46	33
1972	--	--	--	--	--
1974	SVLP	69	77	31	23
1979	SVLP	54	85	46	15
1984	NDP	51	69	49	31
1989	NDP	66	100	34	0

TABLE 41: Barbados: Proportionate Distribution of Votes and Seats in General Elections

| Election | Winning Party | % Votes | % Seats | Other Parties/Inds. | |
				% Votes	% Seats
1951	BLP	55	63	45	37
1956	BLP	49	63	51	37
1961	DLP	56	58	64	42
1966	DLP	50	58	50	42
1971	DLP	57	75	43	25
1976	BLP	53	71	47	29
1981	BLP	52	63	48	37
1986	DLP	59	89	41	11
1991	DLP	50	64	50	36

TABLE 42: Jamaica: Proportionate Distribution of Votes and Seats in General Elections

| Election | Winning Party | % Votes | % Seats | Other Parties/Inds. | |
				% Votes	% Seats
1944	JLP	41	69	59	31
1949	JLP	43	53	57	47
1955	PNP	51	56	49	44
1959	PNP	55	63	45	37
1962	JLP	50	58	50	42
1967	JLP	51	62	49	38
1972	PNP	56	70	44	30
1976	PNP	57	78	43	22
1980	JLP	59	85	41	15
1983	JLP	(90)	(100)	(10)	0
1989	PNP	57	75	43	25

The experience in Barbados has been one in which winning party support has been fluctuating over the forty-year period. The shares dropped after 1951, rose after 1961, declined again from 1976, then rose in 1986 and further declined in 1991. Between 1951 and 1966, it must be remembered, the electoral system involved dual membership and dual voting; but from 1971 it has been a system of single membership and single voting in each

TABLE 43: TRINIDAD & TOBAGO: PROPORTIONATE DISTRIBUTION

Election	Winning Party	% Votes	% Seats	Other Parties/Inds. % Votes	% Seats
1946	--	--	--	--	--
1950	--	--	--	--	--
1956	PNM	40	54	60	46
1961	PNM	57	67	43	33
1966	PNM	52	67	48	33
1971	PNM	(84)	(100)	(16)	(0)
1976	PNM	54	67	46	33
1981	PNM	53	72	47	28
1986	NAR	66	92	34	8
1991	PNM	45	58	55	42

constituency. There have been three instances in which winning party support has been at 50 per cent or less.

Opposition vote support has been high and so has been the share of seats, except in 1986.

In Jamaica, the winning party's vote share has been in the majority in all but three cases, i.e., 1944, 1949 and 1962. In 1983, the elections were boycotted by the People's National Party whereupon JLP won all the seats, (54 seats unopposed and the remaining six in contests against minor interests), receiving 90 per cent of the votes cast. Opposition strength has always been considerable, 1983 of course, excepted.

But in elections of 1976, 1980 and 1989, the share of opposition seats has tended to be lower than previously.

Between 1956 and 1991 when parties won seat majorities in Trinidad and Tobago, there were two occasions (1956 and 1991) in which the victor's support was below 50 per cent of the votes cast. The case of 1971, like Jamaica's 1983 elections, was one in which other major parties boycotted. PNM won eight seats unopposed and twenty-eight against minor competition.

With the exception of 1971, opposition voting has been considerable, and so have been opposition seat victories, with the additional exception of 1986.

The Regional Picture

When the data are looked at regionally the following features are discovered.

There are 12 occasions on which a party won all the seats, this outcome occurring in six of the ten countries. It has happened four times in Antigua and Barbuda, three times in Montserrat, twice in St. Vincent and the Grenadines and once each in St. Kitts-Nevis, Jamaica and Trinidad and Tobago.

Second, the factor of disproportionality between vote and seat shares was most acutely manifested on 25 occasions when the party winning a majority of the seats received 50 per cent or less of the total votes. This represents 25 per cent of the 101 general elections.

The apparent unfairness of this disproportionality must be considered in the light of the fact that winning parties, and losing ones as well, did not always contest all seats in general elections. Since party percentage of vote is calculated on the basis of total votes in *all* constituencies instead of votes cast in contested constituencies, it follows that percentage shares are lower.

Consider recent experience in St. Kitts-Nevis. The People's Action Movement won six of the eleven seats, in both 1984 and 1989, and its shares of total votes are recorded as 48 per cent and 44 per cent respectively. However PAM on both occasions did not contest the seats in Nevis and its share of votes cast in St. Kitts only is 53 per cent in both 1984 and 1989.

Other factors which may also feature in these situations are variations in the sizes of constituencies, and the presence of effective third parties as occurred in Dominica and Grenada in 1990.

Suggestions for further reading

Emmanuel, Patrick A.M., *Elections and Party Systems in the Commonwealth Caribbean 1944–1991* (Bridgetown: Caribbean Development Research Services, 1992).

Emmanuel, Patrick A.M., *Governance and Democracy in the Commonwealth Caribbean: An Introduction* (Bridgetown: Institute of Social and Economic Research, 1993).

Jamadar, Peter A., *The Mechanics of Democracy: Proportional Representation vs First Past the Post* (Port of Spain: Inprint Caribbean Ltd., 1989).

C.L.R. James, *Party Politics in the West Indies* (Port of Spain: Inprint Caribbean Ltd., 1984).

Notes

1. Dahl, *On Democracy*, p. 130.
2. Gary K. Bertsch et. al., *Comparing Political Systems: Power and Policy in Three Worlds* (New York: Macmillan Press, 1999), pp.127–9.
3. Scott Mainwaring, *Rethinking Party Systems in the Third Wave of Democratisation: The Case of Brazil* (Stanford: Stanford University Press, 1999).
4. Stone, *Understanding Third World Politics and Economics,* p. 3.
5. Patrick Emmanuel, *Elections and Party Systems in the Commonwealth Caribbean 1944-1991* (Bridgetown: Caribbean Development Research Services, 1992).
6. Sigmund Newman, 'Towards a Comparative Study of Political Parties', in Jean Blondel, ed., *Comparative Government*, p. 71.
7. Samuel Huntington, *Political Order in changing Societies* (London: Yale University Press, 1968).
8. Joseph Edwards, *Readings in Government and Politics of the West Indies*, Monroe and Lewis, eds., (Kingston: Department of Government, UWI, 1971), pp. 156–61.
9. C.L.R. James, *Party Politics in the West Indies* (Port of Spain: Inprint Caribbean Ltd., 1984).
10. James, *Party Politics in the West Indies*, p. 86.
11. James, *Party Politics in the West Indies*, p. 110.
12. James, *Party Politics in the West Indies*, p. 117.
13. Neville C. Duncan, 'Barbados: Democracy at the Crossroads', in Carlene J. Edie, ed., *Democracy in the Caribbean: Myths and Realities* (London: Praeger, 1994), pp. 75–92.
14. See Emmanuel, *Elections and Party Systems in the Commonwealth Caribbean 1944-1991* and Cynthia Barrow-Giles, 'The 1997 Vote in St Lucia: The Beginning of a New Era?', *Journal of Caribbean History*, 32:1 and 2 (1998), pp. 145–60, for an elaboration of female candidates in the region generally and in St Lucia respectively.
15. Arend Lijphart, *Democracies: Patterns of Majoritarian and Consensus Government in Twenty-One Countries* (New Haven: Yale University Press, 1984), p. 151.
16. Giovanni Sartori, *Competitive Constitutional Engineering: An Inquiry into Structures, Incentives and Outcomes*, 2nd edition (London: Macmillian Press Ltd., 1997).
17. Sartori, *Competitive Constitutional Engineering.*
18. It was a national front formed in 1985 comprising the UNC and the NAR which had brought to an end the long dominance of the PNM in the 1986 general elections. In that election the national front won 33 of the 36 parliamentary seats. In the 1995 deadlocked electoral results, President Hassanali met with Basdeo Panday, leader of the UNC and A.N.R. Robinson, leader of the NAR, and on the basis of the discussions and agreements, invited Basdeo Panday to form the new government. For details on the 1995 general election in Trinidad and Tobago see, John Gaffar LaGuerre, *The General Elections of 1995 in Trinidad and Tobago* (St Augustine: School of Continuing Studies, 1997).
19. See Appendix 4.
20. Peter A. Jamadhar, *The Mechanics of Democracy: Proportional Representation vs First Past the Post* (Port of Spain: Inprint Caribbean Ltd., 1989), p. 16.
21. See the *Wooding Commission Report 1974-Trinidad and Tobago*. Also quoted in Jamadhar, *The Mechanics of Democracy.*
22. *Report of the Constitution Review Commission (1998),* sections 9.16–9.18, pp. 49–50.
23. Emmanuel, *Elections and Party Systems*, pp. 81–2.
24. Anthony Payne, 'Westminster Adapted: The Political Order of the Commonwealth Caribbean', in Dominguez et. al., eds., *Democracy in the Caribbean* (London: The Johns Hopkins University Press, 1993), pp. 57–73.

five

Trade Unionism in the Commonwealth Caribbean: Past and Present

Introduction

This chapter will attempt to provide a brief description of the trade union movement in the Caribbean, its origin and development. It will also assess the impact of recent global changes on these organisations. However, before such an examination can be done, defining a trade union is necessary. Ralph Gonsalves has described a trade union as a 'continuous association made up primarily of wage earners who use their collective labour power mainly to improve their wages and working conditions'.[1]

Gonsalves also notes that trade unions and the trade union movement cannot be seen in isolation. They are inextricably linked to capitalism and as such the fortunes and pitfalls of the movement and the institutions must inevitably reflect the changes occurring within capitalism. For Gonsalves:

> ... a trade union is a component of capitalism to the extent that it grew out of it, but at the same time the trade union is in opposition to capitalism to the extent that it represents labour which is objectively opposed to capital. Thus a trade union is in a structurally ambivalent position and must struggle either to straddle the pull of conflicting forces or to break out of them.[2]

Origin and development of trade unions

Trade unions in the Commonwealth Caribbean developed during the 1930s, amidst a period of labour unrest and a groundswell of labour activity.[3] Although there was an embryonic movement prior to the 1930s, a restrictive political environment enforced by repressive legislation did not facilitate the more rapid development of labour organisations. The small size of the working class population in the early years of capitalist development in the region, and the political opposition to such organisations by the planter-merchant oligarchy, the local state and the imperial state, which was reflected in the restrictive labour laws, did not favour the development of an effectively functioning labour movement out of which could emerge trade unions.[4] It was not until the early twentieth century that there was some slight relaxation which allowed for the establishment of trade unions. These replaced the workers associations which were established by early militants such as Cipriani and Critchlow. The 1930s thus represents an important milestone in the development of trade unions in the Commonwealth Caribbean. It was the labour militancy of this period which provided the vital basis for organising pressure upon the colonial administrators for political change and were therefore critical in the democratisation process of the Commonwealth Caribbean. In the period following the 1930s, trade unions became a permanent feature in the industrial and political environment of the region, making the issue of the political incorporation of labour a critical consideration of competing political groups in the Commonwealth Caribbean.

From the inception, trade unions were closely tied to political parties and the most important and successful political parties were either born of trade unions or alternatively established trade unions, which were important for political success in national elections. They were critical to the establishment and consolidation of credible political alternatives through participation in or by supporting new political parties, and in the process guaranteeing them significant popular support. Trade unions benefited from this association by ensuring that union issues were on the political agenda of political parties. This marriage of convenience worked successfully for a time but in the last two decades, political unionism has come under increasing attack as trade unions have come to be viewed as having a subordinate position to political parties. The result being that the unions have sacrificed some of their objectives in the interest of the political party.

In 1968, G.K. Lewis writing in the *Growth of the Modern West Indies,* contended that the development of political parties and trade unions in the region was nothing short of a concession from capital to labour. He further contended that the concession was rigidly controlled through the process of selective leadership, a leadership which would be willing to concede to capital. For Lewis, this development led to the suffo-

cating of a revolutionary movement which had taken shape in the 1930s. According to him:

> . . .after 1938 the potentially revolutionary *elan Vital* of the masses was anaesthetized by being canalised into institutions – trade unions, political parties, co-operative societies – controlled by the bourgeois groups. The leadership elements that resisted that process. . .were either pushed aside or purged by the dominant right-wing forces.[5]

Nevertheless, trade unions remain one of the most important pressure groups despite the explosion of non-governmental organisations (NGOs) such as youth, women, environmental and community groups, which civil society employs in its negotiations with government and significantly influences the national decision-making process. In more recent times, however, the extent of the trade unions' political and social influence is questionable and has led to the conclusion that they are no longer viable entities.

Global changes, international restructuring and Caribbean trade unions

In the last decade, the global economy has experienced a multiplicity of changes that can be considered revolutionary.[6] Such revolutionary changes are reflected in the creation of mega trading blocs, such as NAFTA and the EU, as well as substantial trade reforms with an emphasis on liberalisation and the general globalisation of markets and trade. The changing patterns of industrial organisation and the accompanying changing labour market conditions pose serious problems for labour unions including those in the Caribbean.

The growth in research development and technological innovation fuels the second and third technological revolutions. In the process, globalisation of technology led by TNCs has important repercussions for third world developing nations. The global division of labour, characteristic of the capitalist world economy is integrating these nations, not at the core of these developments but at the periphery. In the wake of these technological changes, Caribbean raw materials, critical to the economic survival of regional nation-states are becoming of less value to the global economy. One high point of these global developments is the ability of TNCs to globally source not only materials but also labour. Advanced manufacturing technology (AMT), which includes computer controlled to micro-electronic based equipment such as machine tools, robots and just-in-time manufacturing, all have implications for labour internationally and for the Caribbean by extension. The attempt to compete on the global scene is forcing many industries in the region into technological upgrading. This has implications for labour intensive industries and ultimately Caribbean labour. Hilbourne Watson points out that:

> Incessant innovation accelerates the transfer of productive activity from human hands and mind to machines, so as to harness human energy and skills more effectively and intensify the production of labour in production.[7]

Trade unions therefore have a major battle in confronting these developments which lead to the erosion of labour protection. Increasingly, unions find themselves in a hostile global environment, as capital perceives labour and its representatives as obstacles to the further accumulation of profit. Unions are seen as vehicles dramatically pushing up wages and generally creating conditions for industrial unrest which are not in the interests of TNCs. Therefore, we need to address the challenges posed by globalisation to Caribbean trade unions by focusing on the impact of :

(i)   greater liberalisation on unions
(ii) the development of export processing zones (EPZs) which are part of the restructuring process. Trade unions are generally restricted from operating in EPZs, placing them under the protection of the Caribbean state, a situation which will inevitably lead to a confrontation between state and unions.
(iii) downsizing and streamlining.
(iv) IMF/WB sponsored SAPs which call for a host of labour/union restrictive legislation.[8]
(v)   application of new technology in the workplace and the resultant impact on labour management of schemes like Full Time Equivalents (FTEs), Flextime and Telework.

These developments do not augur well for trade unions. In the view of Linden Lewis and Lawrence Nurse, for trade unions to survive they must attempt to form alliances with other groups and organisations in their plans for meeting the challenges.[9] The also need to mount intensive educational campaigns to sensitise the workforce and develop research departments.

The Caribbean state and labour

The strong connection between the state and labour unions in the region and how that relationship is an extension of the natural alliance of political parties and trade unions is a historical fact, one that has its advantages and disadvantages.

Advantages of political unionism

- Positively brought organised labour into the political forefront
- Provided the frontal attack against colonialism and the decolonisation struggle
- Permitted the successful institutionalisation of liberal democracy in the region by contributing to competitive party politics. Disadvantages of political unionism
- Fragmented the union movement so that labour disputes often became highly politicised with union activity used to embarrass political parties and the government
- Subordination of unions by political parties in the interest of national unity
- Frustration of democracy within the union as it became difficult to oust union bosses who were politically connected.

In more recent times, however, as the state has been forced to accommodate the demands arising out of global developments, particularly neo-liberalism, the trade union arm has been increasingly pressured to work under the control of the political arm of their respective governments. The subordination of labour and its increasing marginalisation by the state is symbolised by actions taken by the state to limit the trade union's power to undertake industrial action. The October 2000 dispute between the labour unions and the government of Grenada brings to the fore the increasingly intolerant atmosphere in which trade unions must operate.[10]

While government legislation underscored the gains made by labour in the post-1945 period, legislation also had the effect of channeling and containing the power of labour to disrupt the economy. The state, increasingly under pressure from non-state actors, has had a strong controlling effect on labour and the labour movement.

Caribbean trade unions insist that the collective bargaining process can still work. Recent changes have significantly reduced the influence of unions on the national decision making process. Nonetheless, trade unions are neither as impotent nor as wobbly as suggested in some quarters. The August-December 1997 dispute between the Barbados Workers' Union (BWU) and the offshore sector over the refusal of three companies to recognise the rights of the union to represent workers employed in that sector is instructive.

While the marketplace in this global dispensation is hostile to trade unions, they have shown a remarkable resilience. In that 1997 dispute, the Barbados Workers Union (BWU) received support from local as well as regional and international unions. In the event, one company formally recognised the rights of the BWU.[11]

Key words and phrases

1	Trade unionism
2	Trade union
3	Marriage of convenience
4	Export processing zones
5	Restructuring
6	Global division of labour
7	Liberalisation
8	Human resource management
9	Human resource development
10	Offshore sector
11	Political unionism
12	Accommodationist
13	Advanced manufacturing technology
14	Nanotechnology
15	Globalisation
16	Collective bargaining

Questions to Consider

- Are trade unions in crisis? Critically discuss with useful illustrations.
- Compare and contrast the early trade union movement with the contemporary movement and assess their varying strengths and weaknesses.
- Identify the various ways in which political unionism benefited the labour movement and trade unionism.
- Critically assess the historical significance of trade unions in the Commonwealth Caribbean. To what extent has the role of trade unions declined and why? Discuss with the relevant illustrations.

Activities

- * Based on your readings of chapters two and five, are trade unions critical to civil society?
- * List six contributions you think that trade unions have made to Caribbean society.
- * Interview members of a trade union and then compare their attitude to that of their union leadership,

the private sector and the state. Discuss your findings with other members of your group.
- * Consider any current industrial relations dispute in your own country and consider the strengths and weaknesses of the stake-holders. In your view who are the prime beneficiaries and losers?

Readings

Trade-union Stewardship And Workers' Interest Representation In A Changing Economic Environment: A Brief Comment

by Lawrence Nurse, Ph.D.
Senior Lecturer
Department of Management Studies
University of the West Indies
Cave Hill Campus

Introduction

It is by now the classic understatement that the international economy has been the stage for the unfolding of many profound changes that have been transforming the international system and reshaping its political geography. Those changes have resulted, too, in the emergence of new trading blocs and the restructuring of trading patterns and relationships. We have witnessed the increasing tendency toward the globalisation of markets and production systems, the relentless search on the part of international finance capital for profitable investments worldwide, rapid advances in and the application of new technologies in the global economy, the revolution in information technology and the high level of interdependence in the global village. Nor can we ignore the breakup of the Union of Soviet Socialist Republics and the emergence of the Single European Market as we survey the changing economic and political landscape.

The above-mentioned developments hold tremendous implications and meaning for us in the Caribbean region. In 1986, I presented a paper entitled *New Directions in Industrial Relations in the English-Speaking Caribbean* to a Technical Meeting on Industrial Relations and Development, organised by the Department of Management Studies of the Cave Hill campus of the University of the West Indies and the Friedrich Ebert Foundation. At that time I speculated, albeit tentatively, about some of the implications for trade unionism and industrial relations practice that I thought would result from the "negative influences generated from the operation of international capitalism". As the crisis in international capitalism deepened, thereby intensifying the pace of globalisation, a colleague and I made a closer examination of the "clear and present danger" that stared the Caribbean region and its peoples in the face. This paper reflects some of my views on these developments.

Knee-Jerk Responses to Globalisation

We no longer have to speculate about the meaning of globalisation for small countries like the Caribbean. We are still dealing with the trauma of structural adjustment, privatisation, organisational restructuring, or more to the point, "downsizing", since I do not believe that many serious efforts have been made to restructure Caribbean organisations, but simply to relieve organisations of labour without necessarily reducing the amount of labour power required for effective production. I am suggesting that after we have reduced our workforce in the different organisations, we expect the survivors to maintain production and performance levels. Somehow, too, and this is strange, we expect morale, commitment and trust levels to be high in the now "downsized" organisation!

And if we believe that the survivors cannot maintain current production and performance levels, we turn to alternative forms of employment – job sharing, part-time work and contract labour, for example. Even though managers might have "downsized" their organisation, it seems clear that they have not "rightsized" them since they then grope for alternative approaches for maintaining a given level of labour power in the service of capitalist accumulation! The irony of it all, it seems is that in the process, management has relieved the organisation of some of its store of wisdom. There is a "loss of community" and an obvious threat to security. In his book, **Reclaiming Higher Ground: Creating Organisations that Inspire the Soul**, Lance Secretan makes the telling point that "the employees who have survived and remain after downsizing and restructuring of the last fifteen years simply cannot dance any faster". Employers and trade-union leaders alike must take note of such a concern as employers search for ways of maximising the performance and production goals of their organisations. Through their efforts to restructure, management is in fact attempting to redefine the nature of the rela-

tionship between the forces of production and the relations of production (Lewis and Nurse, 1991)[2]. Capital is taking advantage of opportunities to reshape the workplace and workplace relations in its own image. It is therefore within such a context that we understand the so-called neutrality of the State and the preference of some employers for a union-free environment.

I believe that we may even be forced to deal with the phenomenon of people being "tired of bringing their exhausted minds to work but leaving their hearts at home" (Secretan, 1997: 6). And we still have not found durable answers for addressing the plight of those affected by downsizing. I do not believe that we have done an effective job of helping them deal with the trauma of separation caused by the "violence" that downsizing represents. Trade-union initiative, however, in providing short-term counseling services and attempts to save employment and jobs through bold, non-traditional approaches must therefore be commended. These types of initiatives are a tangible expression of and give real meaning to the theme "Standing in the Gap". They also represent alternative forms of workers' interest representation.

The Caribbean does not have to speculate any more about the meaning of globalisation for countries such as ours in the region because we are still living the results of structural adjustment programmes. Structural adjustment, privatisation and the policies emanating from the adoption of a free-market ideology have been the characteristic responses of Caribbean governments to the crisis in international capitalism. Such responses, as we understand them, have been for the most part dictated by international capital and its agencies such as the World Bank and the International Monetary Fund. These responses virtually threw the social economy of Caribbean people in shambles. Devaluation stared us in the face, especially since we are said not to be internationally competitive and we are yet supposed to maintain a meaningful presence within the international system. There was therefore no doubt about the deepening crisis that beset the region when the assault was unleashed on our living standard. Structural adjustment threw the region into a tailspin. The trade union movement was under heavy pressure to deliver, to demonstrate its relevance. Uncertainty, instability and even confusion – the result of structural adjustment – threatened the very base of unionism and challenged the industrial democratic process. The sceptics had a field day wondering whether the trade union had not outlived its usefulness, whether it had not become an anachronism.

The Challenge Ahead: Responding to the Call for Relevance

In the public's frantic search for solutions, perhaps any solution to ease the problems of the day, we forgot something. We forgot that the trade union is a creature of capitalism, and accordingly, its fortunes would in some respects reflect the crisis in peripheral capitalism that structural adjustment represented. However, trade-union viability and the integrity of the union project would still depend on the space trade-union leaders created or sought to create for dealing with the changing social dimensions at the workplace.

In attempting to create that space for meaningful involvement and for relevance, trade unions in Barbados joined with government and the private sector to offset the real possibility of the devaluation of our currency. Whatever else it might have been, the Prices and Incomes Protocol must be considered an important piece of social and institutional engineering that has made a real difference to national economic recovery in Barbados. It is a good demonstration of industrial statesmanship as the different interest groups collaborated in offering Barbados an opportunity for recovery.

As trade unions "stand in the gap", not simply looking at the balance sheet, so to speak, but reflecting on the bridges that still need to be built or repaired, the challenges to be confronted and the strategies that may be more effective in helping them shape social economy of workers as well as the future of the region, it is important for them to reflect on some issues that I believe deserve their careful consideration, along with that of other important interest groups and stakeholders in this country.

My first general point is that we in the Caribbean must endeavour to craft local solutions that reflect our experiences, without necessarily ignoring lessons from other countries. Those solutions must also reflect our vision of the paths toward development that we believe will improve the lives of Caribbean people. Yet these solutions must result in a preservation of political democracy and the forging of relations that usher in a regime of industrial democracy. These solutions must reject aspects of traditional workplace relations culture and practice that stifle individual creativity and deny the worker a voice in the determination of those issues that affect his or her interests at the workplace.

Those solutions must also reject the assumptions that support managerial domination and contemporary practice that excludes the union from participation in decision-making about issues such as production planning, productivity improvement and quality, investment and technological change and general enterprise management. In this latter connection, I wonder whether it is asking too much to have the question of productivity improvement occupy the type of central importance that it did under the Protocol!

In a related connection, I raise questions about the nature of workers' interest representation as we approach the Twenty-first Century, with management yet insisting on its "right to manage", regardless of whether such insistence has resulted in business losses or contraction, redundancies or layoffs, poor investment decisions and production scheduling, inappropriate work methods, ineffective communication practice or the demise of the business itself.

As long as trade unions endorse the management's rights clause currently enshrined in the typical collective agreement, they will not be able to create the space for the type of penetration that the above entails. How can we seriously talk about being involved in the productivity improvement process if traditional management thought, structures, practices and processes remain intact? Management jealously guards its "prerogative" to manage. I doubt whether the practice of management has resulted in the types of business outcomes that have provided the required leverage for international competitiveness or strategic human resources management in today's demanding business environment. It has not generally produced the organisational culture and climate that breed high levels of worker commitment and involvement, as well as high-trust.

New forms of worker and trade-union inclusion and involvement are required if management is to be denied total leverage in shaping the workplace of the future in its own image. They are also required simultaneously to broaden the base of democratic participation, to release the creative energies of Caribbean workers and to assist in the exploration of avenues for improving quality and productivity. These departures are possible only if there is a change in the culture of unionism and in enterprise culture. Such a change is not required for its own sake. It is required to reverse the process of trade-union entrapment, to enable trade-union leaders to formulate an effective strategy for inclusion and relevance, to facilitate the application of progressive managerial policies to the world of work and to enable labour-management relations to play a new role in the development and restructuring process in a rapidly changing economic environment.

The call for the evolution of a new workplace relations culture does not translate into a loss of trade-union independence. Trade unions must continue to develop and strengthen their independent bases of power in dealing with management. Indeed, the type of collaboration that is envisaged for making a real difference to the quality of labour-management relations in the region must be built on the foundation of a strong and vibrant unionism!

Simply put, trade-union policy and strategy must evolve into a pattern that still allows unions to exercise some political options in dealing with management and workplace issues. Unions must still be strong enough to champion the interests of workers through the medium that they have relied on traditionally for this purpose – collective bargaining. They must also, through collaborative arrangements with management, involve themselves in non-traditional areas of activity that affect the welfare of workers as well as the future of the businesses and organisations where they work. Trade unions must therefore be able strategically to combine the practice of adversarial politics with the politics of collaboration, and as far as circumstances permit, dovetail their partisan objectives with those for national development. This last-mentioned desideratum makes sense and can only be realised if trade unions become a real part of the process of planning for national development. New institutional practice in the form of collaboration does not therefore signal any tendency toward the "whittling away of the strike" or other forms of job action.

If we expect the trade union to continue to make an important contribution to national and regional development, something must be done to avoid the unnecessary threats to its existence as a vital worker's institution in our region. I must express concern about the trend that seems to be setting in with respect to the issue of recognition. While I am not that naïve to expect every employer to readily agree to a request for recognition, it boggles the mind to understand the distance some employers are prepared to travel to maintain a union-free environment.

The new orientation to workplace relations must rest on a new foundation of values that reject as unsuitable to the present era managerial insistence on its prerogative as expressed through traditional "management's rights" clauses. It must question the union-avoidance strategies of those employers who, through their practice, express a preference for a union-free environment. The readiness with which organised labour will be prepared to embrace collaboration with a given employer may to a large extent depend on how other employers continue to build a non-union wall around their workplace.

Within a democracy, the right to dissent must be preserved. That right is not to be abandoned, compromised or jettisoned. However, our point of departure is that if Caribbean countries wish to improve their industrial and organisational productivity as an important first step toward strengthening their national economies and developing or maintaining a niche in the global marketplace, the domestic rules of the game must change. If they wish to participate effectively in the changing international division of labour by improving their international competitiveness, particular attention must be paid to the types of institutions that evolve within our society, especially those in the political and workplace relations arena, the processes that are employed for managing workplace relations and the outcomes of that practice.

In *Democracy at Work: Changing World Markets and the Future of Labour Unions,* Turner adroitly observes that

> The effects of market forces and institutional arrangements at work in the contemporary politics of work organisation have profound implications for broader interest group representation, for national politics, for the success of industrial adjustment, and for the prospects of economic and political democracy (1991: 4 & 5).

The implications that we draw from this statement apply equally to the Caribbean as they do to the countries that constitute the object of Turner's study. They are that globalisation, corporate restructuring and the nature of the international economic system demand important if not revolutionary changes in the way we manage work-place relations.

Institutions will no doubt play a critical role in any attempt to reshape the practice of workplace relations in the region. Transforming workplace relations, however, involves much more than the design of a different set of institutions. We must also take into account the problematic character of labour process control and the management of work and work relations under capitalism, as well as the peculiar class interests that any set of institutions may express. We need to bear in mind, too, that workplace relations are essentially the simultaneous expression of both market and political relations.

We must not lose sight of the important connections between the strategic changes adopted by management and capital's interest in accumulation. We argue that unions have a critical role to play in shaping the management of the workplace in the future so as to offset the real possibility that capital will shape it in its own image. However, our lenses for understanding and interpreting the results of a deeper level of union involvement in the transformation project must not be so blurred as to encourage a misreading of the configuration of social and political relations that emerge in the new era. Micro-social and micro-political change at the organisational level that is effected through the adoption of new managerial strategies geared toward viability might very well be alternative methods of legitimating the practice of management and maintaining its grip on control over the management of workplace relations.

References

B. Bluestone and I. Blueston, **Negotiating the Future:** *A Perspective on American Business,* Basic Books, New York, 1992

L. Lewis and L. Nurse, "The Challenge to Commonwealth Caribbean Trade Unionism in an Age of Restructuring", A Discussion Paper, Institute of Social and Economic Research/ Department of Management Studies Jointly Sponsored Seminar, Cave Hill Campus, Barbados, Feb. 1991

_____, "Caribbean Trade Unionism and Global Restructuring" in H. A. Watson, (ed.), T*he Caribbean in the Global Political Economy,* Lynne Rienner Publishers, Boulder and London; and Ian Randle, Kingston, 1994, pp. 191 – 206.

L. Nurse, "New Directions in Industrial Relations in the English-Speaking Caribbean", A paper presented to a *Technical Meeting on Industrial Relations and Development in the English-Speaking Caribbean,* co-sponsored by Friedrich Ebert Foundation and the University of the West Indies, Cave Hill Campus, Barbados, November 1986.

L. Secretan, *Reclaiming Higher Ground: Creating Organisations that Inspire the Soul,* McGraw Hill, New York, 1997.

Turner, L. *Democracy at Work: Changing World Markets and the Future of Labour Unions,* Cornell University Press, Ithaca and London, 1991

Notes

1 This paper is a revised version of the Feature Address presented to the Fifty-Sixth Annual Delegates' Conference of the Barbados Workers' Union, August 1997. Some of the ideas expressed are part of a larger work in progress by the author that looks at the management of workplace relations under a changing economic environment. No part of this paper should be reproduced without the author's permission.

2 L. Lewis and L. Nurse, "The Challenge to Commonwealth Caribbean Trade Unionism in an Age of Restructuring", A Discussion Paper, Institute of Social and Economic Research/ Department of Management Studies Jointly Sponsored Seminar, Cave Hill Campus, Barbados, Feb. 1991

Suggestions for further reading

Bolland, O. Nigel, *The Politics of Labour in the British Caribbean* (Kingston: Ian Randle Publishers, 2001)

Gonsalves, Ralph, 'The Trade Union Movement in Jamaica: Its growth and some Resultant Problems', in Carl Stone and Aggrey Brown, eds., *Essays on Power and Change in Jamaica,* pp. 89–105.

Lewis, G. K., *The Growth of the Modern West Indies* (New York: Monthly Review Press, 1968).

Moonilal, Roodal, 'Structural Adjustment, Union Busting and the Future of the Trade Unions', in John La Guerre, ed., *Structural Adjustment: Public Policy and Administration in the Caribbean* (St Augustine: School of Continuing Studies, 1994).

Hilbourne Watson, *The Caribbean in the Global Political Economy* (Kingston: Ian Randle Publishers, 1994).

Notes

1. Ralph Gonsalves, 'The Trade Union Movement in Jamaica: Its Growth and Some Resultant Problems', in Stone and Brown, eds., *Essays on Power and Change in Jamaica* (Kingston: Jamaica Publishing House, 1977) p. 89.

2. Gonsalves, 'The Trade Union Movement in Jamaica', p. 89.

3. See Chapter 2 for more details.

4. Gonsalves, 'The Trade Union Movement in Jamaica'.

5. Lewis, *The Growth of the Modern West Indies,* p. 397.

6. A discussion of some of these developments can be found in chapter one.

7. Hilbourne A. Watson, 'Global Neo-Liberalism, The Third Technological Revolution and Global 2000: A Perspective on Issues Affecting the Caribbean on the Eve of the Twenty-First Century', in Kenneth Hall and Denis Benn, eds., *Contending With Destiny: The Caribbean in the 21st Century* (Kingston: Ian Randle Publishers, 2000), pp. 382–446.

8. For an excellent discussion of this see, McAfee, *Storm Signals.*

9. Lynden Lewis and Lawrence Nurse, 'Caribbean Trade Unionism and Global Restructuring', in Hilbourne A. Watson, ed., *The Caribbean in the Global Political Economy* (Kingston: Ian Randle Publishers, 1994), pp. 191–206.

10. The Grenada government threatened to enact legislation, which will punish trade unions in a context of increasing work stoppages and industrial disputes.

11. For more details see 'No Headway : PM Intervenes but Crisis at Offshore Companies goes on', *The Sunday Advocate,* August 24, 1997, pp. 1 and 3, 'Leave Now: PM Should ask Battling Duo to go', *The Barbados Advocate,* August 28, 1997, 'Break for BWU: Offshore Keyboarding likely to Recognise Union', *The Nation Newspaper,* August 26, 1997, pp.1 and 4, and 'Offshore Sector Wants Protocol', *The Nation Newspaper,* September 18, 1997, pp. 1 and 32a.

six

The Politics of Change

Introduction: Background to the 1960s and 1970s

For several decades, two competing paradigms dominated the analysis of the political and economic development of the developing world. Modernisation theory, which emerged in the early 1960s, concerned itself with the transformation of traditional society to a developed/modern one. The core of modernisation theory was that third world nations could effect the transition by following a parallel course to political and economic development traversed in the first world. To effect this transition, modernisation theory emphasised the diffusion of modern ideas from the developed nations to third world nations.

By the late 1960s and early 1970s, modernisation theory came under attack from dependency theory, which challenged its primary assumptions. Not only did dependency theory challenge the assumption that third world states could duplicate the path of development pursued by Western industrialised countries, but it also viewed western influence as largely detrimental to the development of the third world.

The late 1960s and the decade of the 1970s in the Commonwealth Caribbean were characterised by economic and social failure. Sir Arthur Lewis' developmental strategy for the region, *Industrialisation by invitation,* pursued by Caribbean governments, was seen as a means by which the continued reliance on the export of agricultural products could be overcome and create employment while reducing poverty levels.

The relative failure of that strategy of development led to a sustained attack by the New World Group (NWG), which argued that such a strategy merely served to reinforce the traditional economic structures of the region.[1] This rethinking of traditional economic theory and practice in the region was acompanied by an increasing political radicalism. The demand for localisation of the economy in the context of nationalism was given an added impetus with the rebirth of black consciousness by the late 1960s and early 1970s, which saw open political protests in Jamaica and Trinidad and Tobago. The Black Power protest in these two countries was directed at the external capitalist domination of the local economy and the continuing condition of economic depression and persistent poverty among the predominantly black population.

These developments led to a re-examination of existing political and economic practice in the region resulting in Socialist experimentation in Jamaica, Guyana and Grenada in the 1970s. Part of this chapter will therefore undertake a largely retrospective discussion of alternative development strategies in the Commonwealth Caribbean beginning with the theory of the non- capitalist path to development and its application to the Caribbean with specific reference to Jamaica, Guyana and Grenada.

The theory of the non-capitalist path to development

The theory of the non-capitalist path to development is an attempt to adapt orthodox Marxism to the objective conditions which exist in developing nations such as the Caribbean. Classical Marxism, which emerged from and addressed the realities of nineteenth-century European society, emphasised the role of the industrial urban working class in the transition to socialism and communism. In the Caribbean the working class is comprised of a small industrial urban proletariat and a predominant peasant class. When applied to the Caribbean, the theory emphasised the importance of the formation of a broad alliance of class forces, which in the absence of a strong industrial working class, should include not only the industrial proletariat, but also the progressive section of the petty and national bourgeoisie and the peasantry. This means that the transition to socialism in developing primarily agricultural nations is assumed to be a gradual and cautious process.

Representing a response of radical and progressive leaders to the failure of modernisation efforts, the new national alternative development models pursued in various parts of the region in the decades of the 1970s and 1980s, were viewed as opposed to the hegemony of the United States, peripheral capitalism and continued domination.

Critical to the transition to socialism under the non-capitalist path is the need for countries to adopt an anti-imperialist stance in their foreign policy and to eliminate as much as possible, foreign control and influence over the economy. To achieve this, such a goal requires a nationalisation policy, which among other things would result in the creation of a state-owned sector. It would also result in the creation of a mixed economy, comprising a public or state sector, a corporate sector and a private sector. Other goals would involve the creation of a more egalitarian society and a raising of the standard of living for the mass of the population; democratising the society politically by increasing the participation of civil society into the economic and political decision-making processes, through the formation of institutions of people's power and emphasising educational upliftment of civil society, which would engender new work attitudes and the formation of a political culture geared towards socialist values.[2]

The theory of the non-capitalist path to development in contrast to the path of socialist reconstruction, is a transitory stage to socialism. According to Carl Stone this ". . . intermediary position has structural features that combine capitalist elements with initiatives towards a state-managed socialist economy."[3]

Stone further contends that the litmus test of the non-capitalist path to development in the Caribbean, rests on its ability to offer solutions to the three basic structural problems in the region namely

   (i)   the over-dependence on mineral and primary exports
   (ii) high dependence on imports
   (iii) technological dependence, which when combined, promotes continued dependence on foreign investment, loans, credit and aid for developmental purposes. This itself makes the Caribbean a group of captured and penetrated societies, which further constrain the political directorate in terms of domestic and international policies. Such functional and structural dependency therefore impedes policies that would serve to improve the relative economic position of the working class as well as political democracy and correct the structural economic problems in the region.

Alternative development strategies in the region

The non-capitalist path to development was attempted in three Commonwealth Caribbean territories: Guyana in the 1970s and early 1980s under the banner of co-operative socialism; Jamaica from 1974–1980, with a

TABLE 6.1 POLITICAL PROFILES OF REGIMES IN THE THREE COUNTRIES

Political Feature	Grenada	Jamaica	Guyana
Ideology	Marxist	Social Democracy	Marxist
Big Power Alignment	Aligned with East	Non-aligned	Non-aligned
Base of Support	Youth	Class	Racial
Power Structure	Party State	Liberal Democracy	Party State
Political State	Participatory	Participatory	Authoritarian
Individual Freedom	Low	Medium	Low

Carl Stone, 'Wither Caribbean Socialism' op. cit. p. 296

TABLE 6:2 ECONOMIC PROFILES OF GRENADA, JAMAICA AND GUYANA

Economic Features	Grenada	Jamaica	Guyana
State Ownership	Low	Medium	High
Economic System	Market Economy	Market Economy	Market Economy
Socialist Policy Priority	Redistribution	Redistribution	State Ownership
External Economic Ties	Core Capitalist	Core Capitalist	Core Capitalist

Carl Stone: Ibid. p. 299

state philosophy of democratic socialism and Grenada between 1979–83, embracing the philosophy of democratic centralism or revolutionary democracy. Of the three cases, Grenada has been the most controversial and also constitutes the single most advanced effort to bring socialism to the English-speaking Caribbean.

With respect to these experimentations, while there were major similarities, significant variations in the approaches were also clear. Table 6:1 and 6:2 show the political and economic approaches adopted by the three countries.

Guyana: cooperative socialism

Guyana's experimentation with cooperative socialism began in 1970, under the administration of Forbes Burnham and the People's National Congress (PNC). The programme of alternative development consisted of four stated principles:

1. The establishment of a tri-sector economy under private, state and cooperative control with the cooperative sector becoming the dominant partner by 1980.
2. A programme to feed, clothe and house the nation (FCH).
3. An expansion of state (public) ownership through the nationalisation of foreign assets. The bauxite company was the first nationalised company in

1972 and was followed by the nationalisation of the sugar industry in 1976.
4. The elevation of the PNC as the vanguard party with ultimate political authority in the country.

Jamaica: Democratic Socialism 1974–1980

According to Michael Manley, democratic socialism as a developmental strategy would undertake complete social, economic and political transformation of Jamaica in keeping with the need to obtain social justice.[4] It was premised on the need to:

1. Reduce the dependence of the economy. In Manley's view, the historical domination of foreign capital in Jamaica resulted in the export of a substantial proportion of profits. Secondly, it placed the control of economic decisions in foreign boardrooms which were not particularly sensitive to the needs of the Jamaican people.[5] At the heart of democratic socialism's economic strategy was the need to exercise control over the strategic sectors of the economy.
2. Create a mixed economy with the commanding heights under state control.
3. Deepen political democracy based on Manley's view that traditional practice of democracy in Jamaica had become too remote and facilitated isolationism and authoritarianism. Accordingly,

Manley advocated the 'politics of participation' which he described as the antithesis of remoteness.[6] The 'politics of participation' would involve the Jamaican people in the decision-making process of government, in a way that was previously absent from the Jamaican political system. According to Manley, one main cornerstone of the 'politics of participation' would be the creation of mechanisms and operational methods through which institutional leadership would be constructively involved in the decision-making process. Secondly, to assist in the implementation of the politics of change, Manley advocated the complete restructuring of the Jamaican local government in a direction that could respond to the needs of the Jamaican people.[7]

4. Forge an independent foreign policy. Manley not only saw the need to extend and deepen the relationship with its traditional trading partners but also to reduce such dependency. Continued dependency was seen as inimical to the long-term interest of Jamaica.[8] For Manley, a relevant foreign policy for Jamaica was one which would involve a commitment to Caribbean economic regionalism, the search for a common third-world strategy, continuing support from the United Nations, the right to self-determinism for small countries and diversification of its international relations.[9]

5. Reduce social inequalities and in the process achieve greater economic democracy.[10]

According to Manley, the provision of food, clothing and shelter were to be the cornerstones upon which the new Jamaican economy was to be constructed.[11]

With respect to the goal of reducing the dependency of the economy, the PNP under Michael Manley undertook four major policies:

1. Selective nationalisation which saw public utilities, the sugar industry, textile operations, flour refining industry, some financial institutions and hotels coming under state control. The following enterprises were nationalised thereby creating a significant state factor: the Jamaica Public Service (JPS), the Jamaica Telephone Company (JTC), Jamaica Omnibus Service (JOS), Barclays Bank, Radio Jamaica (RJR) and majority shares were purchased in the Cement Industry.

2. The creation of a national Bauxite Commission and the establishment of the Jamaica Bauxite Institute (JBI), the International Bauxite Association (IBA) and the appropriation of lands owned by the bauxite companies and the acquisition of 51 per cent shares in the bauxite mining operation. One of the most controversial and opposed measures taken by the PNP, was the imposition of the production levy of 72 per cent on the price of aluminum ingot. In their response, the foreign-owned bauxite companies filed suit with the WB's International Centre for the Settlement of Investment Disputes and transferred bauxite and alumina production reducing Jamaica's output by almost 50 per cent.

3. A restrictive import policy, which targeted luxury goods; and the implementation of import licensing and the establishment of the State Trading Corporation (STC) to coordinate the import trade.

4. Diversification of trade with several Latin American, European and Asian countries.

In Manley's view, while economic growth was critical to achieve the new Jamaica, such growth would be:

> . . . meaningless in terms of a just society if the distribution of wealth is not equitable. A common feature of societies embarking upon the post-colonial adventure has been the gross maldistribution of wealth. Obviously, then, equitable distribution of wealth is a precondition of social justice in any country and takes on a peculiar urgency in most post-colonial societies and certainly Jamaica.[12]

With respect to its goal of creating an egalitarian society, the PNP administration introduced a land lease programme which was designed to put 'idle land into idle hands' and established a number of cooperatives as the institution suited to the projected economic and social tasks during transformation.[13] Unfortunately only 14 per cent of idle land was redistributed so that the pattern of ownership in Jamaica saw little fundamental change.

In the social sector, the Manley Government undertook measures designed to:

(i) make secondary and university education free, while also paying particular attention to primary education

(ii) provide free school uniforms for primary school children

(iii) set up nutrition programmes and provide lunches for students

(iv) increase teacher training

(v) reform school curricula

(vi) increase vocational training

(vii) improve adult literacy

(viii) improve the quality of housing through the establishment of the National Housing Trust (NHT)

(ix) reduce the cost of food to the poor, through subsidies on basic food items

(x) make housing more accessible through a policy of rent and price controls

(xi) reduce unemployment through unemployment relief programmes

(xii) improved labour legislation regarding issues such as minimum wages, maternity leave and sickness benefits and unfair dismissal was introduced. Overall, while they were successful, the ameliorative policies suffered from the lack of funding, poor application, limited administrative resources and political patronage.[14]

In terms of the political programme, apart from the increase in the influence of leftist intellectuals in the administration of the government and the retention of the political structures of liberal democracy, the Manley administration supported the creation of a number of mass organisations. Democratic socialism also focused on increasing the autonomy of the local government machinery allowing them to develop and implement plans and programmes for the community and to act as mobilising vehicles. This was designed to give real effect to the PNP's political objectives of improving political participation in the country.

The flight of capital from Jamaica, the decline of export production, the reduction in international capital assistance, improper administration and the rapid development of the state sector, all created serious financial difficulties for Jamaica. This financial crisis led to Jamaica's involvement with the IMF. Under the IMF there was a systematic undermining of the policy objectives of the PNP's democratic socialist experiment, leading to the party's removal from power in 1980.

Grenada: revolutionary democracy and democratic centralism

The fours years of revolution were, quite simply, a heroic effort in social and economic reconstruction and, at times, transformation.

G.K. Lewis, *Grenada:*
The Jewel Despoiled

. . .The real enemies (to the success of the Grenadian revolution) were, first, the outside Caribbean bourgeoisie. . .and, second, the US imperialists, who were determined to destroy the revolution from, the very beginning.

G.K. Lewis, Ibid.

. . . A cross section of the social and economic indicators as well as any evaluation of the political situation in Grenada in the summer of 1983 show a revolution about to consolidate itself. If. . . the PRG's application of the non-capitalist path would have to be considered as quite successful, only having been derailed by the failure of political leadership of the highest order.

Jorge Heine, *Introduction: A Revolution Aborted*

Revolutionary democracy in Grenada was without doubt dramatic and ushered in several changes. Grenada represented the first unconstitutional change of government in the Commonwealth Caribbean in the post-independence period. The People's Revolutionary Government (PRG) seized power and abolished the Westminster style of liberal democracy at the political level[15] and introduced mechanisms of popular participation at the village and parish levels. People's power in Grenada was designed to deepen the process of political democracy in a country that was historically marked by political corruption and authoritarianism. Several mass organisations, including zonal parish councils, were established to facilitate mass mobilisation. These organisations included: the National Women's Organisation (NWO), the National Youth Organisation (NYO), Progressive Farmers Unions and a trade unions council.

The creation of a ministry of mass mobilisation was designed to coordinate the support of civil society for the new revolutionary government, led by the New JEWEL Movement. The resulting increase in mobilisation of previously immobilised groups and individuals led to greater political participation in the system.

The quality and success of the people's power programme in Genada is a controversial subject because of the overriding influence and control of the New JEWEL Movement in the mass organisations. People's power in Grenada has been criticised on the grounds that while many parish councils, zonal councils and mass organisations were created, they had no power and no direct role in the decision-making system.[16] Moreover the failure of the organisations, parish and zonal councils to meet more regularly and to discuss national issues, detracted from the ideological objectives of People's power. Tony Thorndike argues that People's power was instructive in its attempt to mobilise and politicise Grenadian society. However, in his view, 'At no point could, or was policy challenged, let alone changed; neither could council delegate to higher organs debate priorities'.[17]

Another important feature of the political developments which defined the new political order in Grenada during this period was the creation of the vanguard party. Vanguardism meant that power was to be firmly located in the hands of the central committee as well as a strict selectivity of membership.

In the economic sphere, revolutionary democracy envisaged a tri-sectoral economy. The PRG embarked upon economic reconstruction based on the creation of a mixed economy, comprising a state sector, a corporate sector and a private sector, with the state sector playing the leading role. It also showed the importance

of the tourism and agricultural sectors and the need to diversify overseas trade and sources of investment capital. This programme was accompanied by some nationalisation and the effective diversification of external linkages. Foreign assistance also came from the former Soviet Union and Latin America. Cuba offered US$30 million worth of labour and machinery towards the construction of the airport, provided US$6.3 million for other projects and also helped in the educational training and health programmes.

Table 6.3 shows Grenada's sources of external financial assistance from 1979–83.

Important to the experimentation was land reform, which, like the situation in Jamaica was moderate. Under the Land Utilisation Act of 1982, Grenada's PRG could compulsorily acquire ten-year leases on property of more than 100 acres.

While there was moderate nationalisation, the government continued to stress the importance of the

TABLE 6:3: MAJOR GRANTS AND LOANS TO THE PRG 1979–1983 (IN $US MILLIONS)

Source	Economic Grant	Military Grant	Loans
Cuba	36.6	3.1	
Czechoslovakia		0.7	
German Democratic Republic	1.5	0.1	2.1
North Korea		1.3	
USSR	2.6	10.4	
Algeria	2.3		
Iraq	7.2		
Libya	0.3		10.4
Syria	2.4		
Canada	2.9		
Finland			7.3
Nigeria	0.1		
United Kingdom	0.4		1.9
Venezuela	0.6		
International Organisations			
CDB	1.1		7.4
ECCA			1.9
EDF	2.7		2.1
EECEF	0.3		
IMF			6.6
OAS	0.4		
OPEC			2.0

Source: Frederic L. Pryor, 'Socialism via Foreign Aid: The PRG's Economic Policies with the Soviet Bloc', in Jorge Heine, ed., *A Revolution Aborted*.

private sector, which adopted a basic cooperative posture towards the government. The new government guaranteed the private sector's role in the service industries and the industrial sector.

It was in the social sector that the PRG recorded the most impressive results. With the establishment of organisations such as the Centre for Popular Education, The National In- Service Teacher Education Programme and the Community School Day Programme, the government was able to implement an adult literacy programme, increase opportunities at the secondary and tertiary levels and generally improve the performance of the educational system. In the health sector, there was also dramatic improvement, with the establishments of medical, dental, prenatal and postnatal clinics.

Is socialism a viable option for the region?

Quite apart from the success and failures of the non-capitalist path of development in the region, there is the need to seriously consider the following:

1. The role of the United States in the region and how that country showed open hostility to all three regimes; in the case of Grenada and Jamaica there was open hostility. In Guyana, given the character of the opposition political parties a 'hands off' policy was adopted. The United States' position on Grenada served to consolidate Grenada's relationship with the Soviet Union and Eastern Europe. This subsequently led to the intensification of the United States' opposition to the regime, and to the invasion of Grenada in 1983. For Jamaica, the United States in various ways sought to undermine the regime of Michael Manley in support of the Seaga-led Jamaica Labour Party (JLP). Thus, in considering the future of socialism in the region we must bear in mind the historic role of the United States in shaping Caribbean history. Thus, the 'Imperialist Ideology and Mentality' as stated by G.K. Lewis, is critical to the analysis of the region's socio-political and economic progress.[18]
2. The role of the Caribbean itself and the effect of what Lewis has dubbed 'the dependent colonial Ideology and Mentality', must also be placed at the centre of the analysis.[19] This mentality has its roots in colonialism and as Lewis contends, led to a situation where the political leadership and civil society remain:

    > . . . loyal members of the Commonwealth, and Britain is still regarded with affection. But British Governments

are seen as being too weak or unwilling to play the old protective role. It is in that sense that the old British colonial loyalty is replaced by the new American neo-colonial loyalty. . .The Grenada action is thus important because, in geopolitical terms, it is the leading example of that switch.[20]

Lewis points to:

a. The OECS-Jamaican-Barbadian decision to invite the United States to lead the invasion of Grenada.
b. Prime Minister Eugenia Charles fielding questions for President Reagan.
c. Dean Harold Critchlow's statement that the invasion was given Jesus' support and that 'there is no doubt that our destinies lies with America. . .' [sic].
d. West Indians who wrote 'God Bless America' – so dubbed by Lewis as 'Mimic Men'.
e. The role of Tom Adams – as 'the voice of his master' – the USA.
f. The role of Seaga – 'the West Indian colonial collaborator'.

3. The role of the national and regional bourgeoisie that opposed the Grenadian and Jamaican experimentations – most notable was their opposition to the Grenadian experimentation.
4. The reaction of the region to the experimentation clearly revealing the link between economic and psychological dependency, which would have implications, as it did in Grenada's case, for the future of socialism in the region.
5. The tendency of socialist/non-capitalist experimentations to counterpose socialism and democracy, which according to C.Y. Thomas produced in Grenada a crippling limitation which had a rippling effect ultimately leading to the tragic events of October 1986.[21]
6. The vast economic and political changes which have occurred in the Soviet Union and Eastern Europe since the late 1980s and how those changes have serious implications for the ability of the Caribbean mini-states to rid themselves of the three basic structural limitations which have seriously affected their ability to meet the basic needs of the non-capitalist path to development. According to Stone, without that Eastern bloc connection which Grenada placed a high premium upon, there is little prospect for mini-states in the Commonwealth Caribbean surviving the transition stage.[22] This scenario is compounded given the changes wrought by the end of the cold war, globalism and the hegemony of the

United States in the capitalist world economy. As socio-economic transformations occur, the aftermath of the cold war poses serious problems for the Caribbean mini-state.

7. Limited administrative resources being a major constraining factor. In this respect, Lewis argues that a regional approach has a better chance of succeeding than an individual approach.[23] While the experimentations of the 1970s to the 1980s have all since collapsed, they represented an important challenge to the traditional political economy approach towards development in the region. To varying degrees they represented a challenge to the historical external control of the local economies and sought to increase local control of the decision-making process, greater civil participation in decision making, acquire increase local control of the economy and obtain greater self reliance.

8. The hegemony of global neo-liberalism and the incompatibility of many of the prerequisites of the path with the imperatives of neo-liberalism.

Key words and phrases

1	Non-capitalist path to development
2	Democratic socialism
3	Democratic centralism
4	Revolutionary democracy
5	People's power
6	Vanguardism
7	Cooperative socialism
8	Dependency
9	Modernisation theory
10	Dependency theory

Questions to Consider

• Is it fair to say that the experiments of the 1970s and 1980s were clearer expressions of the early nationalist movement than what occurred in the immediate post-independence period? Critically discuss with reference to any two Commonwealth Caribbean countries and consider the extent to which such experimentations are feasible in the context of the 1990s.

• Critically examine developments taking place in the Caribbean in the last twenty years. Does this mean that realisation of the aspirations of the 1930s and 1970s are unattainable? Critically discuss with relevant examples.

• Differentiate clearly between the paths of socialist experimentation and traditional political economy approaches in the region.

Activities

* Having read chapters two and six, list some of most important contributions of the non-capitalist path to development to the region.

* Ideologically and philosophically what were the most important differences between countries pursuing the non-capitalist path to development and the regional hegemon? Draw up a table to depict those differences.

Readings

The Poor And The Powerless: Economic Policy And Change In The Caribbean

Clive Y. Thomas

III: Cooperative Socialism: Guyana[38]

Policy

While the social experiments in Jamaica under Manley and in Grenada under Bishop attracted considerable international and regional attention, they lacked the flavour of notoriety which surrounded the People's National Congress (PNC) in Guyana under Forbes Burnham and, since August 1985, under Desmond Hoyte. The reason for this notoriety was that few accepted the regime's claim to be motivated by concern for the poor and powerless as genuine, particularly since there was increasing evidence to support the widely-accepted view that the regime existed only through the combination of force and fraud it employed to rig the national elections of 1973, 1980 and 1985, and the national referendum in 1978, which led to changes in the constitution and the postponement, until 1980, of the elections due in that year.

On independence in 1966, the dominant structural relations of the Guyanese economy and the social form through which they were systematically reproduced, ggeugg.etee..

portrayed many of the classic features of underdevelopment/dependency relations. The principal products produced were sugar, bauxite-alumina and rice. Except for a small fraction of sugarcane cultivation (less than 10 per cent), sugar was grown and processed by two foreign-owned plantations. Sugar was the dominant crop, accounting for the largest share of value added, employment, foreign-exchange earnings, capital accumulation, crop land and agricultural infrastructural resources. Rice, initially cultivated as a domestic staple, had grown into a significant export cash crop, with most of the sales to the Caribbean market. Bauxite-alumina production took place in two enclave mining areas under the control of two aluminum-producing TNCs – Alcan (based in Canada) and Reynolds (based in the US). The bulk of the production was under the control of the Canadian company. Export specialisation was complemented by extensive dependence on imported foodstuffs, manufactures, intermediate goods (particularly fuels and fertilisers) and capital equipment. Unemployment was estimated at nearly 20 per cent of the labour force, while the largest source of employed labour (sugar) operated on a seasonal basis.

In 1970, four years after independence, the ruling party declared Guyana a Cooperative (socialist) Republic. A number of factors promoted this particular development. To begin with, as in other territories in the region, while impressive rates of growth in per capita product were recorded in the 1960s, most of the acute problems of poverty and dispossession were still very much in evidence. Second, the broad mass of the population had had a particularly militant anti-colonial tradition. This militancy is reflected in the early maturing of relatively highly-developed trade-union structures in the country. Third, the tradition of militant anti-colonialism and the trade unionism was both product and producer of a situation in which large sections of the work force were influenced by Marxist ideas and functioned within organisations with Marxist-Leninist leaders. This is seen in the history and development of the People's Progressive Party (PPP) (the first Marxist party to win free and fair elections In the hemisphere) and of its associated trade union, the largest in the country and the one to have organised labour on the sugar plantations since the 1940s. Fourth, because the left of the political spectrum effectively opposed the PNC state, in order to use the state to transform itself into a national bourgeois class, the PNC had to adopt a popular socialist rhetoric acceptable to the masses.

The declaration of a cooperative socialist republic implied four major policy initiatives by the state. The first was to nationalise foreign property so that the government could assert more control over its own economy. By the mid-1970s, both the main producing sectors (sugar and bauxite-alumina), the import trade, public transport, alcohol and drug manufacturing, TNC-operated foundries and shipyards and significant sections of distribution and communications, had all been taken over by the state. With the nationalisation of sugar in 1976, the government boasted that it now 'owned and controlled 80 per cent of the economy of Guyana'. These nationalisations followed the usual pattern, namely they gave fair and adequate compensation, they took the initiative to nationalise when companies were in difficulties or threatened with closure and they provided post-nationalisation contracts to cover management, technology and licensing fees.

The second was an undertaking by the government to carry out a programme to feed, clothe and house the nation. Its aim was to substitute the private profit motive with the social goal of making 'the small man a real man'. This programme was embodied in the 1972-76 development programme and was, from the outset, heavily propagandistic. The development programme first appeared as a public document in draft form in July 1973. Since then it has never been revised or presented for public scrutiny. Moreover, the actual course of production bore little relationship to the programme's stated objective of 'feeding, clothing and housing the nation by 1976'.

The third was to ensure the cooperative sector's dominance, given the existence of a tri-sectoral (private, state and cooperative) national economic structure, for it was through cooperative ownership and control that the socialist foundations of the society were to be laid. As it turned out, Guyana's cooperative sector remained a miniscule part of the national economy. Institutions especially set up by the state as cooperatives, such as the Guyana National Cooperative Bank, did not operate on cooperative principles, whatever formal cooperative ownership structures they might have had. Many economically important cooperatives which had been set up by private initiative also operated along capitalist lines, often employing exploited wage labour. In fact enterprises frequently formed themselves into cooperatives to take advantage of tax concessions or to carry out limited objectives (such as acquiring a plot of land) and then dissolving the cooperative once it had served its purpose.

The fourth was the claim that the ruling party, the PNC, stood over all other parties and over the state itself. Since the government did not come to power either through free and fair elections or as the result of a popular social revolution, this was in effect a thinly-disguised proclamation of a dictatorship. The PNC's paramountcy was enshrined in the creation (in 1973/74) of a new government department, the Ministry of National Development and Office of the General Secretary of the PNC. As the name suggests, the PNC party office was merged into a department of the state and financed through public funds. The state thereafter rapidly proceeded to make it clear that there could be no legal or constitutional change of government. The rigged elections in 1973, the postponement of elections due in 1978 and the rigged elections in 1980, were indications of the extent to which state authoritarianism had become entrenched in Guyana.

These features of cooperative socialism were combined with certain foreign-policy initiatives by the state, which included recognition of Cuba, support for the Popular Movement for the Liberation of Angola (MPLA), militant anti-apartheid rhetoric, support for the Arab cause, support for a New International Economic Order and visits to and contacts with Eastern Europe and China. On close examination, however, it becomes evident that many of these were purely for the purposes of propaganda. For example, the Guyanese government only gave its support to the MPLA during the final stages of the war, having all along been behind the CIA-backed group, UNITA (the National Union for the Total Independence of Angola). Recognition of Cuba was also only undertaken as part of a broad-based Caribbean initiative to unite governments of differing outlooks in the interests of asserting an independent and separate identity for the region.

Despite such reservations, however, in 1975 a number of theorists[39] joined with the PPP (which after the 1973 elections had launched a programme of passive resistance and civil disobedience) in adopting a policy of critical support for the government because of the radical turn it was taking.

The PPP's new position reflected its formal acceptance of the Havana Declaration of 1975, in which communist and workers' parties agreed to support the application of the non-capitalist thesis' of revolutionary democracy to the region.[40] An important point about this is that the so-called radicalisation of the state in Guyana was accompanied by such anti-democratic measures as rigged elections, the denial of basic human and trade-union rights and the suppression of

the rule of law and the traditional independence of the judiciary. The theorists supporting the regime clearly did not associate radicalisation with increased opportunities for the working classes and peasants to develop their own democratic organisations through which to exercise their power. On the contrary, they saw radicalisation as consistent with reducing mass access to these rights and therefore directly opposed to democratic development. Another important point is that the Havana Declaration ignored the importance of the points discussed in Chapter 9 concerning internal class struggle and the role a state in the capitalist periphery must necessarily play in consolidating a hegemonic class.

As events have shown, nationalisation in Guyana aided the expansion of the state bureaucratically, ideologically and militarily and in so doing, increased the capacity of the ruling PNC to assert its various forms of authoritarian control over civil society. This process, however, required other accompanying developments however, and it is to these that we now turn.

Degeneration and Social Decay

Guyana has been in a state of continuous crisis since 1975. The numerous manifestations of this include a negative rate of growth of real product since 1975, with the result that per capita real income at the end of 1986 was less than that of 1970 and more than one-third below that of 1975; dramatic increases in malnutrition and deaths from deficient nutrition related illnesses, particularly in public institutions (hospitals, prisons and homes for the aged and disabled); widespread and endemic shortages of foods as well as other basic items of consumption; shortages of raw materials so severe that for the past decade industry has been utilising only 30 to 40 per cent of rated capacity. In addition, electricity cuts are common, with scheduled cuts in March 1986 averaging 36 hours per week for all districts in the country. Unscheduled interruptions also occurred; double figure inflation rates (between 1975 and 1985 the consumer price index had more than quadrupled); over half the labour force unemployed following large-scale public sector retrenchments; the virtual collapse of all public utilities to the point of constituting a major obstacle to production; the dramatic deterioration of social services; drastic increases in crime, corruption, clientelism, graft and nepotism in public and private life; a massive external debt in excess of US$700 million or three-and-a-half times the value of GDP, a rapidly deteriorating balance-of- payments deficit (in excess of one-quarter of GDP for the period 1976-84) and a deteriorating exchange rate; the growth of a huge black market for all items in the wake of acute foreign-exchange shortages and bureaucratic restraints on activity; and a migration rate conservatively estimated at over three-quarters the rate of natural increase of the population. Less conservatively, estimates indicate an absolute decline in the population since 1975.

An important feature of the crisis was the way in which the economic dislocation affected other areas of social life. For example, although the post-independence period witnessed a rapid expansion of state property and state intervention in economic life, the government that promoted these developments was brought to power through an Anglo-American manoeuvre in the 1960s and since then has held onto its power without holding proper elections. As a consequence, the regime has always lacked legitimacy. It is important to recognise that Guyana did not conform to the typical export-oriented Third World model, that the economic crisis was not caused predominantly by the world economic crisis and that the crisis in its export sector was not directly produced by shrinking export markets and failing prices. As the selected data in Tables 11.5 to 11.7 show, levels of output in the agricultural sector have been substantially below both rated capacity levels for these industries and peak output levels achieved many years earlier. Thus, while current annual output of sugar is under 250,000 tons, at the time of nationalisation the government placed the TNC's capacity at 450,000 tons. The peak output level of 374,000 tons was achieved as long ago as 1971. In the rice sector, annual output in 1986 was 180,000 tons, whereas the capacity of the industry was estimated at 250,000 tons with a peak output of 212,000 tons being achieved in 1977. In both these industries preferential contractual export markets paying premium prices have not been satisfied. Sugar obtains a quota and a premium price under the EEC-ACP Protocol, as well as for sales to the USA. In the case of rice, export markets in the CARICOM region are not ser-

viced, although the industry receives a premium price currently in excess of two-thirds above the world level. In the bauxite industry, Guyana enjoyed a virtual monopoly in world sales of high-grade calcined ore. In the 1960s and early 1970s, output accounted for 90 per cent of the world market. By the mid-1980s, however, the industry could only supply between 40 and 50 per cent of the world demand; the output for 1986 (at 441,000 tonnes) being approximately 55 per cent of the peak level attained in 1975. Although the Guyanese product is superior to that of the Chinese with which it has been replaced, it has lost its position on the world market because of the unreliability of its supply. It should be noted that since 1983 the alumina plant has been closed down, while dried bauxite output is currently less than half that attained in the early 1970s. In the absence of any significant diversification in Guyana's production structure the decline in the basic industries has negatively influenced economic growth. For the period between 1970 and 1975, the real growth of GDP averaged 3.9 per cent, between 1975 and 1980 it averaged -0.7 per cent and for the years 1981 to 1986 the growth rates were -0.3, -10.4, -9.6, +2.5, +1.0 and +0.3. The data on growth of GDP are shown in Table 11.5.

The decline in the export sector has also been the main cause of the country's acute foreign-exchange and balance-of-payments difficulties. While other factors, such as reduced inflows of private investment capital (through lack of confidence in the economy) and compensation payments for nationalised enterprises are important, they are not decisive. The crisis is basically a *production crisis* in that output and productivity declines are directly linked to basic deficiencies in the structure of production and not to fewer opportunities for profitable external sales. The selected monetary and price data shown in Table 11.7 reveal a per capita external debt of about US$900; per capita external arrears in excess of US$1,000; a current-account balance-of-payments deficit in excess of one-quarter of GDP for the years 1983 through 1986;

TABLE 11.5: GUYANA: REAL GROWTH OF GDP (COMPOUND % PER ANNUM

	1970-1975	1975-1980	1981	1982	1983	1984	1985	1986
Total GDP	3.9	-0.7	-0.3	-10.4	-9.6	2.5	1.0	0.3
Sugar	0.9	-1.3	10.9	-3.8	-12.6	-3.6	-	-
Rice	2.4	0.9	-2.2	15.6	-19.2	23.8	-	-
Mining	-2.3	-5.3	11.4	-31.5	-22.4	47.0	-	-
Government	10.5	1.9	1.0	-7.7	-1.9	0	-	-

large annual increases in money supply and a price level in 1985 about four-and-a-half times higher than that of a decade earlier and 145 per cent above that of 1980. A similarly rapid expansion of the internal debt can be noted, with a cumulative current-account balance-of-payments deficit resulting in net international reserves (which peaked in 1975) standing at minus US$554 million in September 1986.

Among the many causes of these basic differences are (i) an unplanned, uncoordinated expansion of the state sector (principally through nationalisation) between 1970 and 1976; (ii) the operation of political diktats in the state sector (in the narrow sense of state property being used to serve the interests of the ruling elites) which reduced efficiency and led to the nepotism, corruption and alienation mentioned earlier; (iii) the rapid emigration of skilled personnel at all levels leading to exceptionally high turnover rates; (iv) poor industrial relations with increasing numbers of employer/employee and government/worker conflicts; (v) acute foreign-exchange shortages which affected maintenance and delayed production; and (vi) inadequate monitoring of projects resulting in huge cost overruns and long delays in completing projects.

Although the tables show that production began to deteriorate with the expansion of the state sector in the early 1970s, this should not be taken to mean that state control *per se* is necessarily inefficient, but rather that the *specific* nature of the state and political configuration in Guyana since independence has been problematic.

For a start, the terms under which the regime came to power were based on the general exclusion of the then dominant PPP, which is important given the militant tradition of anti-colonialism among the Guyanese people and the PPP's Marxist-Leninist leadership.

In light of the above and also because the political opposition was left-wing, the regime sought legitimacy by presenting itself as a radical, progressive, third world socialist regime. The high point of this propaganda was the formal declaration in 1970 of Guyana's intention to become a cooperative socialist republic.

The deteriorating productive system and severe decline in living standards accompanying nationalisation ruled out the possibility of achieving any basic needs goals and undermined the propaganda appeal of cooperative socialism. As a result, the regime had to resort to the systematic use of force and fraud to maintain its rule.

There are two other important aspects of the processes indicated above. One is that political power was used to convert the petty bourgeoisie (who wielded the power) into a big indigenous bourgeoisie. This occurred despite deteriorating living standards, prin-

TABLE 11.6: GUYANA: PHYSICAL OUTPUT – MAJOR SECTORS 1970-86

Year	Population (Beginning of Year) (In Thousands)	Output (in Thousands of Tons)				
		Sugar	Rice	Dried Bauxite	Calcined Bauxite	Alumina
1970	699	311	142	2,290	699	312
1971	704	369	120	2,108	700	305
1972	710	315	94	1,652	690	257
1973	716	266	110	1,665	637	234
1974	721	341	153	1,383	726	311
1975	727	300	175	1,350	778	294
1976	733	333	110	969	729	265
1977	739	242	212	879	709	273
1978	745	325	182	1,021	590	276
1979	750	298	142	1,059	589	171
1980	751	270	166	1,005	598	215
1981	763	301	163	982	513	170
1982	769	287	182	958	392	73
1983	777	252	149	761	315	nil
1984	782	238	181	823	517	nil
1985	788	243	154	1,096	478	nil
1986	793	245	180	1,036	441	nil

Source: Government of Guyana

TABLE 11.7: GUYANA: MONETARY INDICATORS 1975-86

	Net International Reserves	National Debt		External Arrears	Balance of Payments	Government Finances (G$ million)			Money Supply	Consumer Price Index (Urban)
	US$ million	External US$ million Disbursed. (end of year)	Internal G$ million (end of year)	US$ million	Current a/c G$ million	Total Revenue	Total Expenditure	Surplus (+) Deficit (-)	(G$ million)	1970=100 (Average)
1975	+77.4	295.5	399.2	n.a	-35.2	497.7	638.8	-141.1	449.3	145
1976	-12.3	363.8	657.9	n.a	-350.8	389.9	803.0	-413.0	491.5	158
1977	-39.3	404.3	853.9	n.a	-251.1	355.1	543.6	-188.5	603.0	171
1978	-42.9	438.8	1035.2	n.a	-72.3	365.8	542.2	-176.4	667.2	197
1979	-98.5	507.1	1312.5	n.a	-208.1	412.2	690.7	-278.5	713.3	231
1980	-206.5	566.3	1650.8	45.4	-300.4	455.1	935.2	-480.1	850.4	264
1981	-267.4	660.0	1089.1	136.4	-475.8	578.9	1205.7	-626.8	997.1	323
1982	-362.2	681.3	2775.7	249.5	-426.0	550.6	1570.9	-1020.3	1269.3	390
1983	-552.4	692.6	3820.8	450.6	-468.0	568.2	1291.0	-722.8	1533.7	449
1984	-663.4	682.5	4544.0	595.5	-434.0	651.4	1830.2	-1178.8	1814.9	562
1985	-526.9	691.0	5425.7	771.9	-426.0	1200.2	1562.8	-362.6	2169.7	646
1986	-553.5 (Sept.)	707.0	(Sept.) 5399.3	897.5	-497.0	1618.1	2858.4	-1240.3	2691.7	n.a

Source: Government of Guyana

cipally through the appropriation of the relatively large amounts of monopoly rent present in a situation of such widespread shortages and scarcities of virtually all commodities. A substantial proportion of this wealth was converted into foreign assets as political uncertainty grew. The second aspect of this process was that the large state sector expanded the government's potential for nepotism as well as the scope for the intimidatory use of economic processes. Thus, not only are the faithful rewarded, but (and equally important) a host of administrative and economic mechanisms have been made available to control dissenters.

The expansion of state property was accompanied by increasing bureaucratisation of economic and civil life. In keeping with its claims, the party turned everything into ideology. For example, nationalisation of the public media was used to promote state ideology, to impose administrative restraints and to restrict publication of opposing or independent views. Another feature has been the rapid expansion of the country's security services, which on a per capita basis, became the largest in the hemisphere. There was also an increase in the number of armed groups attached to members of the party leadership, military training for young party activists and the training and arming of religious cults associated with the ruling party.

This preoccupation with security and increasingly partisan politicisation of economic functions meant that when the economic crisis first manifested itself in a major balance- of-payments crisis in the mid-1970s, the government lightly brushed it aside as opposition propaganda and proceeded to print money and expand state credit as if this were a temporary phenomenon. It also took the government many years to admit that its major propaganda plank of 'feeding, clothing and housing the nation by 1976' had been a failure.

The society seemed to contain within it a response/reaction mechanism (which I have described elsewhere as a *repressive escalator*) through which the ruling regime sought to solve its crises by repressing or rejecting political democracy. As a result, the economic/production crisis became generalised into a social and political crisis, thus calling into question the very character of the state. And since there was no legal or constitutional means of changing the government, the society was faced with a fundamental and inescapable dilemma.

There have been three main phases in the development of the state's 'repressive escalator', each of which has sharpened the divide between state oppression on the one hand and popular resistance and

deteriorating living conditions on the other. In *Stage 1* the government's attempts between 1977 and 1979 to bring down real wages so as to reduce the demand for imports, to halt domestic inflation and to overcome the country's foreign-exchange and balance-of-payments difficulties in an effort to solve the production crisis were resisted by the workers and their organisations. This resistance was directed against the state which had become the major employer of wage labour. In turn, the state responded by trying to repress the discontent and to contain the rights workers had inherited under the prevailing system of industrial relations. During this stage, there were three main forms of repressive intervention. First, the *right to* work was undermined through political dismissals and victimisation of agitating workers. Second, the *right to strike* was undermined through invoking the notion of a political strike whereby any strike the government did not consider 'Industrial' was deemed 'political' and, as such, treated as a 'subversive' activity. Third, the *corporatist* solution pursued in Latin America was adopted whereby the state, reinforced by its dominant employer status, intervened in selecting the executive and membership of the trade unions to determine the eventual composition of the national Trades Union Congress and other central decision-making bodies. As the centre trade union council fell under state direction it was made more and more responsible for individual unions which were less amenable to corporatist solutions.

In *Stage 2* all citizens had their legal and human rights curtailed simply because it became impossible to separate trade union rights from the rights of any other citizens within a framework of justice. During this stage, the struggle was centred mainly in the courts and in various church, human rights and independent social organisations associated with workers' struggles. An important by-product of this stage was the blurring of traditional racial boundaries within the work force and a rise of worker solidarity, as revealed in several major industrial actions in 1977, 1978 and 1983.

In *Stage 3,* which began in the early 1980s, trade union, human rights and legal attacks became highly politicised as economic disintegration continued and the government grew increasingly unpopular. Repression was extended to all opposition, including independent social and political groups. To maintain its control, the state rapidly consolidated its authoritarianism and, in 1978, (instead of an election) held a referendum to decide whether or not to adopt a new constitution. This was 'approved' and the new constitution promulgated in 1980, thus giving legality to an even more dictatorial form of government.[41] During this stage, political assassinations and direct repression of any form of popular expression were routine and the security apparatuses almost totally politicised.

Paralleling this 'repressive escalator' have been a number of vicious circles operating both within and outside the sphere of production which have inhibited the restructuring of the country's productive base. Principal among these are (i) the decision to build up the security apparatuses when the state is least able to afford it, resulting in funds being diverted from the productive and social sectors; (ii) shortages of consumer goods through import restrictions, increasing inflationary pressure, reducing real wages and generally destabilising the structure of employment and industrial relations. Malnutrition, poor health care and inadequate public transport have in turn affected work force morale and productivity; (iii) restrictions on public sector borrowing (necessary for obtaining IMF/World Bank credit) intensified relations between the government and the IMF/World Bank Group between 1978 and 1981. The government's inability to meet the IMF/World Bank targets has subsequently resulted in the suspension of all these agreements. The consequent failure to obtain balance-of-payments support funds operates as a serious constraint on the flexibility of the state; (iv) as external indebtedness grows and arrears accumulate the government's ability to borrow from abroad is further reduced. Crisis conditions at home are then worsened because the government cannot call on foreign savings to cushion declining domestic incomes. This then intensifies the external debt problems and reinforces the vicious circle; and (v) because sources of government revenue dwindle when GDP falls, tax increases are imposed in an attempt to improve yields. This, however, further depresses economic activity and increases the tendency towards price inflation. The government is then forced to reduce its outlays and this in turn negatively affects output and incomes.

Vicious circles such as these show how the production crisis literally feeds on itself and in the process reinforces the 'repressive escalator' which, in turn, generalises the crisis. At this point also, instead of taking steps to solve the crisis, the government becomes a part of it and a major contributory factor in its continuation and worsening in the society.

The concept of a 'repressive escalator' should not be construed too mechanically. The link between one stage and another, which reflects the unfolding dynamic of repression-resistance-repression, is a dialectical relationship and should not be seen as marking an automatic advance from one stage to another. Those who repress do not do so in anticipation of even more resistance: on the contrary they expect less. Similarly, those who resist are not trying to invite more repression. If indeed these things do occur, the determinants lie in the social relations prevailing at a particular juncture and not in the intentions of the various actors. The stages outlined are therefore not self-contained entities.

Neither can one presume an automatic link between the continuing impoverishment of the population and failure to overcome the economic crisis on the one hand and the willingness of the masses to revolt on the other. It would be disastrous for the organisers of resistance to make such an assumption, for the society's disintegration has inevitably affected the social psychology of the masses who already show a growing sense of resignation, helplessness, indifference (if not cynicism) to political struggle and extraordinarily high levels of migration.

The final conclusion to draw here is that, although wrapped in socialist/progressive rhetoric, by its systematic repression and denial of rights to the broad mass of the population, the Guyanese government has created a state that is antithetical to the interests of the poor and powerless. In this respect it differs from Grenada and Jamaica. Events in Guyana have shown the West Indian people that despite the widespread ideological acceptance of 'Westminster parliamentarianisim', the potential for authoritarian and fascist degeneration of the body politic clearly exists. When Grenada's experiences are also taken into account, it becomes obvious how important it is for the people in the region to lay singular emphasis on deepening the democratic political forms for which they fought in the past if they are to prevent future social experiments degenerating into dictatorship, whether of the right or the left. As the descendants of slaves and indentured servants, as a group they are as well placed as any other people on earth to appreciate the value of personal freedom. Their commitment to democracy can be second to none.[43]

Notes

38. Thomas 1983; 1984b; 1984c; 1984d; Committee of Concerned Citizens 1978; International Team of Observers at the Elections in Guyana 1980; Parliamentary Human Rights Group,

London and Americas Watch 1985; 1985a; Guyana Human Rights Association, n.d.

39. Mandle 1976: 37-50; Mars 1978: 71-106.
40. Thomas 1976: Struggle for Socialism in Guyana, *Monthly Review* 23-5.
41. James and Lutchman 1985.
42. Interested readers may follow the further analysis of the themes in this chapter in Thomas 1987a.

Grenada
The Jewel Despoiled

Gordon K. Lewis

1979–1983: The Revolutionary Achievement

As the People's Revolutionary Government (PRG) set up shop after coming to power it is important to appreciate the shambles they inherited from Gairyism. For Gairyite populism was not what one West Indian scholar has called the "Marxist populism" of C.L.R. James.[1] It was, rather – as already noted – a bogus radicalism geared to the private interest of the dictator and his small clique of friends, completely uninterested in any fundamental reconstruction of the society or the economy. It was "one-man, High Priest politics," as the Grenadian street parlance described it. It meant that independent Grenada in 1979 was in no better shape than colonial Grenada in 1973.

It is not too much to say that Grenada, both as an economy and a society, was in a generally disastrous condition in 1979. It was, to begin with, a stagnant economy, characterised by negative real growth rates, double-digit inflation, high levels of unemployment, and continuing deficits in the balance of payments. It was a typical raw-product export economy, selling its agricultural products – spice, nutmeg, bananas and cocoa – for low revenue to export markets whose price levels it could not control, and importing everything else at inflated prices. In more general societal terms, social services typically identified with the modern welfare state were – where they existed – backward, inefficient, and operating with a dilapidated infrastructure. One-third of the population was afflicted with functional illiteracy. For some reason Grenadians have always suffered from eye problems leading to widespread blindness, but there existed no programme to tackle the problem. Middle class people regularly travelled to Barbados or Trinidad for medical and dental care; for the majority there was no serious remedial

system. The average rural school was a large, wooden, zinc-roofed building with classes divided by movable partitions; students were taught by ill-trained teachers, some 40 per cent of whom, according to the Brizan report of 1981, entered the "profession" for pecuniary reasons only.[2] Nor did there exist any professionally competent institutional structure to meet any of these problems; in 1979 there was not even a Ministry of Trade to deal with, among other things, the crucial problems of an import-export economy. Limited employment opportunities meant that many more professional Grenadians were working abroad than in the island itself, while escape for lower-class Grenadians meant emigration, notably to Trinidad, many of them entering illegally through the so-called rat passage of the inter-island schooners.

All in all, social and economic Grenada was trapped within a global capitalist system rooted in inequity, so that, to take a single telling example, a woman worker at home cracking nutmegs for a small wage of $7.10 a day, 150 pounds a day, would finally see the finished product sold abroad at the rate of $1.00 per single ounce: the real wage of her labour thus in effect constituting some 300 times her daily wage rate.[3]

The four years of the revolution were, quite simply, a heroic effort in social and economic reconstruction and, at times, transformation. All of the available sources – the innumerable official pronouncements of the PRG state agencies, Prime Minister Maurice Bishop's published speeches, the carefully documented David Lewis thesis – testify to the personal dedication and the collective enthusiasm that went into that effort, now only too easily forgotten by all of the counterrevolutionary, reactionary forces only concerned, after October 1983, to vilify and denigrate the revolution, lock, stock, and barrel. There was, to begin with, the urgent task of modernising the capital infrastructure of the economy. That meant long-term integrated planning, with an adequate institutional framework and proper collection of statistical data on all aspects of the national economy. As early as 1981, the government carried out both a population census and an agricultural census, both hitherto uncharted areas. They became the basis for infrastructural development. Within three years the regime could report, among other things, completion of the first phase in road development, especially the Eastern Main road; the establishment of the Central Water Commission, with a much improved water supply system; a new telephone system; a new generator for electricity supply; a new radio transmitter; more than sixty-seven new feeder roads to facilitate transport of agricultural products to the port areas, always a headache for the small West Indian peasant farmer; a new stone-crusher and asphalt complex; the Cuban gift of a new prefabricated concrete-unit and block-making plant; construction of warehouses for the Marketing and National Importing Board; construction of eight fish-selling centres with deep-freeze facilities aimed at encouraging local fish consumption; new factories to produce jellies and jams from local fruits, to offset the traditional taste patterns that have always preferred imported canned foods and disdained local products; and the planned dredging of the St. George's harbour to accommodate larger ships for trade and tourism.[4]

All this, of course, necessitated a new organisational structure in the area of statistical and financial planning. The regime had to teach its electorate that everything had to be paid for. This became the responsibility of the revamped public sector. New state agencies were set up to plan and administer, among other things, the thirty state farms inherited from the Gairy regime, new agro-industrial processing plants, and the new fishing and fish-processing industry. The new Grenada Development Bank, with funds being lent at easy repayment terms to small and medium farmers and business-people with the aim of financing any project, however small, was designed to increase production and employment, while the new publicly owned National Commercial Bank established a general policy of lending half of its funds to development projects and half to the established commercial sector. The new Marketing and National Importing Board, in turn, was set up to establish import and distribution rights over products such as cement, rice, and sugar, away from the old system of private commercial wholesale and retail monopoly, thus guaranteeing fairer prices for the consumer. The success of the new public financing structure is evident from the fact that donor aid was obtained not only from friendly revolutionary Third World governments ranging from Algeria to Tanzania but also from such orthodox lending agencies as the World Bank and the International Monetary Fund.[5]

Notice must be taken of the social-welfare aspects of the revolutionary achievement as well. The effort, especially, was to increase the social wage of the Grenadian worker and farmer. The two crucial areas in this respect were, of course, education and health, both of them in almost primitive condition in 1979. Their planned reconstruction was started in 1980. In education, three phases were conducted, respectively, by the Centre for Popular Education (CPE), the Na-

tional In-Service Teacher Education Programme (NISTEP), and the Community-School Day Programme (CSDP). The CPE programme included the planned abolition of functional illiteracy, the development of technical skills, the reshaping of the school curricula, and much else, some of it accomplished with the expert aid of Paul Freire, head of the World Council of Churches literacy programme. NISTEP, in its turn, tackled the problem of a school system in which two-thirds of the country's primary school teachers were seriously under-trained. It introduced a popular-based and accelerated training programme, avoiding the costly and elitist sort of programme traditionally sponsored by the University of the West Indies, as well as laying the foundations for new free secondary education for all children. Finally, CSDP initiated the practice of bringing into the schools skilled persons, from civil servants to musicians and persons skilled in the crafts, to bridge the gulf, so typical of the old conventional West Indian school system, between the world of work and the world of learning. How successful all of these programs were can be gauged from the fact that whereas under twenty-nine years of Gairyite rule only a single secondary school was built out of public funds, a second such school had been built just one year after 1979. Moreover, whereas in the last year of the Gairyite regime only three persons had obtained university scholarships to study abroad, in the first year of the revolution the total had risen to 109.[6]

The results in health were no less impressive. Prime Minister Bishop was able to announce on the secondary anniversary of the revolution that government had instituted, among other things, an eye hospital, an intensive care unit, a maternity clinic, X-ray facilities, and a [sic] operating theater; in addition, the number of resident dentists had tripled – from one dental clinic in 1979 there were now seven. The dentistry statistics are especially interesting in light of the particular fact that before 1979 one of the very few dentists in the island, Dr. John Watts, had been better known for his political ambitions than for his professional practice, and of the general fact that adequate dental service, not only in Grenada but in the West Indies as a whole, had been nonoperative because of the peculiar white myth, going back to slavery, that black people somehow did not suffer from dental problems.[7]

The ideological aspect of the revolutionary achievement has particularly to be noted. How much of all this was "socialism," in the generally accepted sense? Further, how much of it was radical "communism," as claimed by its enemies?

Looked at in comparative terms – that is, within the general framework of British, Scandinavian, Eastern European, and Caribbean economies – it would seem to any serious observer that the Grenadian model, as far as it went in four brief years, would have to be placed more in the British-Scandinavian camp than any other. Its main programs were those of the "moderate" social-welfare economies, where the modern state has increasingly taken over responsibility for all those services vital to the public welfare. In the Caribbean alone, all of the "more developed" countries have instituted state health housing programs. All of them, likewise, even the more conservative like Barbados, are marked by extensive state planning administrative structures in areas such as tourism and developmental capital investment, including central or national banks that seek to control the twin Caribbean problems of a business sector that has always been reluctant to plough back its profits into local capital ventures geared to creating new wealth and an affluent middle class making the external balance-of-payments problem worse by its habit of irresponsible spending abroad. Even the Grenadian policy of putting the people to work through mass mobilisation institutions was not too different, in principle, from the U.S. Civilian Conservation Corps of the old Rooseveltian New Deal; and even its military mobilisation of the people, "the Revolution armed," was again not too different in principle from the state policy of limited and obligatory armed service for young males as in, to take only one example, Sweden. In this sense, the Grenada model was more "social welfarism" than socialism proper, not unlike the policies of the left-wing Michael Manley government in Jamaica in 1972-80.

Even more. The PRG government in 1979, for all of its official rhetoric, faced not a theory but a condition. Low productivity, economic backwardness, a peasantry fiercely independent and, like peasantries everywhere, imbued with the property instinct a truly appalling scarcity of available managerial and technical skills, an antiquated infrastructure: all of that meant that a giant leap forward immediately into a full-blown socialism, not even to speak of communism, would have been at once romantic and impractical. The PRG, following the early NJM policy statements, elected to follow a tripartite developmental programme based on an enlarged public sector, private sector, and a new co-operative sector. The local business groups, after all, had been an integral element of the NJM; their reward was a recognised role in the new economic regime. Both government and the local Chamber of Commerce thus worked together, with remarkable harmony when all is considered, especially in the area of tourism, centred around the construction of the planned international airport at Point Salines. The concept of the "popular front" in the anti-Gairy period was thereby carried over into the new system.

It is thus difficult to accept the curious argument of a critic like Sebastian Clark, that the "mixed economy" policy was in reality a disguise under which the new regime was really conducting a programme of genuine socialism.[8] It is equally difficult to accept the argument of critics like Fitzroy Ambursley – arguing the exact contrary – that the PRG regime was really a petit-bourgeois reformist government not seriously interested in moving forward to the necessary stage of radical socialism.[9] It is difficult to accept the Clark argument because it assumes that the PRG leaders were living a deceitful Jekyll and Hyde political existence, hardly believable to anyone who knew them personally. It is difficult, again, to accept the Ambursley argument because it runs counter to all of the known environmental factors of the Grenadian situation at that time. As already noted, this was a society in which all groups, from a Marxist-Leninist viewpoint, were ideologically backward, each suffering from its own "false consciousness." In such an environment a purely Marxist proletarian revolution was clearly out of the question. So also was a spontaneous rising of the masses along the lines advanced by Rosa Luxemburg in her debate with Lenin. The Jacobs brothers had seen that clearly when discussing the tactics and strategy adopted during the Gairyite period. "The idea," they wrote, "of a whole class of people rising up on one sunny day and overthrowing the oppressor class is idealist, romantic, and obviously impractical."[10] By the same token, the idea that later on, as Ambursley puts it, the PRG government should have undertaken immediately a proletarian offensive against the dominant class as a whole, must be seen as equally romantic, an exercise, indeed, in left-wing infantilism. For, in the circumstances of the moment, the new regime needed all the support that it would garner. A proletarian offensive would have needlessly alienated all of the groups who had already given as much as could be expected of them during the long period of opposition to Gairyism.

The point is worth further emphasis. The first obligation of every revolution is to survive. It cannot afford revolutionary heroics. That is why, after 1924 in the young Soviet Russia, Stalin insisted upon the policy of "socialism in one country" as against Trotsky's advocacy of "world revolution." That is why, too, in the Cuban case, Castro played down the policy of exporting the revolution to Latin America once Ché Guevara's ill-fated adventure in Ecuador showed that the necessary mass support for such a policy was not present in the Latin American peasant masses. Ambursley's argument, then, that the PRG regime was simply a "petit-bourgeois workers' state" misses the point. It was not genuinely socialist, according to his argument, because government ministers like Lloyd Noel, Kendrick Radix, Norris Bain, and Bernard Gittens came from the Grenadian middle- and upper-class "old families";[11] this is like saying that Engels could never be a communist because he was a wealthy Victorian industrialist. It further was argued that because so many party and government members were university graduates, that too must have contributed to a petit-bourgeois atmosphere, which is like saying that because men like C. Wright Mills, in the United States or R.H. Tawney in Britain were university professors they could never be socialists. Even to think of the Jamaican Richard Hart, who later became the PRG attorney general, in petit-bourgeois terms is at once absurd and insulting, for he had been known throughout the Caribbean for some thirty years as a dedicated Marxist who, since his expulsion from the Jamaican Peoples National Party in 1954 had suffered much for his beliefs.

Yet the anti-intellectual tone of this line of argument is not its worst feature. More damaging, altogether, was its temptation to see the local property-owning class as the leading enemy of the revolution. As far as we know that was not the case. There is no evidence to show that they at any time undertook any serious counterrevolutionary activity; many of them co-operated readily with the new government; the episode of the so-called Gang of 26, who attempted to publish an independent newspaper, hardly showed that they were a dangerous element; and in any case the same episode showed that they were easily contained. In sum, this line of criticism was even dangerous, for it assumed that the local Grenadian bourgeoisie was the leading threat to the survival of the revolution whereas, in fact, the real enemies were, first, the outside Caribbean bourgeoisie (who had had no Gairyite experience to educate them) and, second, the U.S. imperialists, who were determined to destroy the revolution from the very beginning.

Be that as it may, it is certain that, even if only out of prudence, the revolution maintained throughout its reliance on the "mixed economy" model. Whatever differences emerged later, there is no evidence that the policy was not supported throughout by all PRG elements, including Coard who, as a trained economist and minister of finance, knew better than anyone else the harsh constraints under which the economy laboured. David Lewis, writing in early 1983, saw the implications of this clearly and concluded:

> At this early stage of the revolutionary process in Grenada the issue of a Marxist-Leninist orientation within the leadership, as well as that of the possibilities for a socialist transformation of the society are, for the Grenadian masses, unreal and academic problems. That is, whereas the future of the Revolution in Grenada, and of its achievements, depend greatly on the radical nature of the process as a whole, the essence of the Revolution at this point is to effectively mobilize the Grenadian masses, to educate them, and to improve their standard of living within the process of revolutionary change. This has meant that the process of change, given the massive underdevelopment of the country's political economy, is presently restricted to what the PRG has referred to as the "national democratic state."[12]

A somewhat different way of looking at the PRG economic track record has been suggested by another Canadian observer, Anthony Maingot. There is, argues Maingot, a significant difference between the NJM 1973 manifesto and the later post-1979 PRG pronouncements. The first is a utopian declaration based on the old hope of an active peasantry producing surplus, combined with the modern idea of small-island agro-industry, as well as a nostalgic return to a simpler and more honest past; the second postulated, quite differently, the development of a modern state with a modern administrative apparatus, and now embracing a modern airport as support for tourism, which had earlier been rejected as encouraging "national-cultural prostitution." Implicit in this, although not openly stated, is the charge that the earlier utopian dream had been betrayed to an administrative statecraft based on a centralised hierarchy of command led by the organised vanguard party. Indeed, as Maingot's article is titled, Maingot's argument becomes a requiem for a West Indian utopia.[13]

It is tempting to say that this sort of criticism is in itself utopian. It cavalierly overlooks at least three crucial aspects of the case. In the first place, it neglects to note that all revolutionary change, as indeed all revolutions show, whether bourgeois or socialist, is a matter of dynamics, not of statics. Programmes inevitably change in response to fresh circumstances. Next, it fails to understand that to oppose the state is one thing, to administer it is another. Every revolutionary group discovers pretty rapidly that, once in power, it must learn to accept the pressing constraints of administrative realities; the blueprints must be adjusted to what is possible. Finally, Maingot's argument almost seems to be saying that the PRG should have remained faithful to what he calls the earlier "revolutionary aspiration and conservative nostalgia." But is that practical or feasible? It assumes a sort of pastoral socialism that has never existed in the Caribbean, nor is likely to in the future. It caters to the sort of romanticism that persuaded Albizu Campos and the Puerto Rican Nationalist party in the 1930s and 1940s to believe that before the Americans came in 1898 there existed an idyllic Puerto Rico of seigneurial coffee *hacienderos* and contented *jibaros*, which in fact never existed at all. The Grenada policies shifted from 1973 to 1980 for the simple reason that, being a Westernised society, it came to see that progress meant modernisation; the only real debate was whether modernisation should take a socialist or a capitalist direction. Grenada is not Shangri-la; nor should it be. To argue otherwise is to come perilously near to saying that these small Caribbean islands should resign themselves to becoming isolated and charming idyllic spots for the delight of the tourists.

In retrospect, the major achievements of the revolution, apart from its social experiments, were two. The first was to undertake, with some success, an economics and a politics of "breaking away," that is to say, of challenging the assumption – which had been treated almost as natural law – that independent Grenada, like everybody else, should remain within the economic and geopolitical orbit of the "Western world," which really meant the United States. That, of course, was not a Grenadian initiative. The pioneering thrust was that of Cuba after 1959, followed by the diplomatic recognition of Cuba by the Commonwealth Caribbean in the 1960s. In the economic field, it meant replacing the old neo-colonial enforced bilateralism with a new multilateralism, forging trade and commercial ties with Latin America and Eastern European countries, as well as with Arab and African countries. In part, this was hard trade bargaining (selling nutmeg to Venezuela rather than just Britain or the United States). In part, it was international left-wing solidarity (although at times the solidarity was more verbal than material). In the realm of foreign policy it meant forging new friendships and diplomatic relationships with the Third World

as a whole, while at the same time remaining a loyal member of the Caribbean Economic Community (CARICOM), the Organisation of Eastern Caribbean States (OECS), and the larger Commonwealth. As Bishop put it in his speech of April 13, 1979, Grenada was a free and independent country, not in anybody's backyard, and definitely not for sale.[14] Like Manley before him in Jamaica, Bishop became a frequent speaker on the international radical circuit (which may have contributed to his final downfall, for, as the record shows, it is always dangerous for Third World leaders to leave their home base unattended for too long). The new foreign policy, of course, made its mistakes, giving support, for example, to the repressive regimes of Libya and Syria, and voting against the United National General Assembly's condemnatory vote on the Soviet action in Afghanistan (while Nicaragua abstained). Yet it is at least arguable that the pro-Soviet tilt was in part encouraged by the relentless hostility of the United States to the new regime. Grenada rapidly discovered, like other small, weak states in the international anarchy, that beggars cannot be choosers.

The second lasting achievement of the revolution, this time internally, was to show that a Caribbean revolutionary government, with enough idealism and enthusiasm, can effectively mobilise its people in the task of national reconstruction. Few of its critics have been prepared to concede this, if only because few, if any, of them took the trouble to visit the island and take a hard, close look at what it was doing. Most West Indian island peoples have about them a general spirit of rambunctious, almost antisocial individualism which sometimes makes them antipathetic to organised discipline and hard work. Yet no one who spent any time in Grenada during those years could fail to have been impressed by their tremendous response to the revolutionary challenge. As David Lewis points out, it was not so much structure as spirit that made the revolution. Whether it was high-school students helping to educate their elders in the mass literacy drive, or young unemployed males accepting hard camp training in the army and the militia, or volunteer workers helping to build a community centre in their spare time, or village women, after a hard day, attending an evening session on women's rights in the revolution put on by volunteer speakers of the National Organisation of Women (Bishop's speech of June 15, 1979, is in a way a splendid confessional apologising on behalf of all West Indian men for the suffering imposed on women by West Indian machismo).[15] Far from being just the orchestrated acclamation of the Saturday afternoon mass rally, these activities demonstrated that whole population was serving the common cause with zeal and dedication, unaided by the material luxuries – good roads, the family car, labour-saving household appliances, television, the office electric typewriter and photocopier, air conditioning, even the functioning telephone – that all Americans take for granted. Their zeal flagged only toward the very end.

Notes

1. Peter Gomes, *The Marxist Populism of C.L.R. James* (Mona, Jamaica: Institute of Social and Economic Research, University of the West Indies, 1979).
2. George Brizan, *The Education Reform Process in Grenada, 1979–1981* (Ottawa: International Development Research Centre, 1982); and Brizan, "Conspiracy of Genuine Critique: A Response to Monica Payne's Review Article," *Bulletin of Eastern Caribbean Affairs* (Cave Hill, Barbados) (May–June 1983): 17–20.
3. *Maurice Bishop Speaks: The Grenada Revolution, 1979–1983* (New York: Pathfinder Press, 1983), p. 257.
4. "Three Years of the Grenada Revolution," ibid., see especially speech of March 13, 1982, pp. 255–72.
5. David E. Lewis, *Reform and Revolution in Grenada, ch. 7.*
6. "Education in Grenada, July 2, 1979," speech of July 2, 1979, in *Maurice Bishop Speaks*, pp. 42–47.
7. "Two Years of the Grenada Revolution, March 13, 1981," speech of March 13, 1981, ibid., pp. 128–42.
8. Sebastian Clark, *Grenada: A Workers' and Farmers' Government with Revolutionary Proletarian Leadership* (New York: Pathfinder Press, 1980). See also M. Martin, *Volcanoes and Hurricanes: Revolution in Central America and the Caribbean* (London: Socialist Challenge, 1982).
9. Ambursley, "Grenada: The New Jewel Revolution."
10. Jacobs and Jacobs, *Grenada: The Route to Revolution,* p. 123.
11. Ambursley, "Grenada: The New Jewel Revolution," p. 203.
12. David E. Lewis, *Reform and Revolution in Grenada*, pp. 206–7; see also *In the Mainstream of the Revolution* (St. George's, Grenada: Fédon Publishers, 1982).
13. Anthony P. Maingot, "Requiem for a Utopia," *Miami Herald*, October 30, 1983, pp. 10–60.
14. "In Nobody's Backyard, April 13, 1979," speech of April 13, 1979, in *Maurice Bishop Speaks*, pp. 26–31.
15. "Women Step Forward, June 13, 1979," speech of June 13, 1979, ibid., pp. 32–41. For further discussion of the economic track record of the revolution see Wallace Joefield-Napier, "Macroeconomic Growth During the PRG Regime: An Assessment," Conference on Grenada cosponsored by Caribbean Institute and Study Center for Latin America, Inter-American University, San Germán, Puerto Rico, October 17–19, 1985; and Jay Mandle, *Big Revolution, Small Country* (Lanham, Md.: North-South Publishing, 1985).

Suggestions for further reading

Ralph Gonsalves, *The Non-capitalist Path to Development: Africa and the Caribbean* (Mimeo).
Michael Kaufman, *Jamaica Under Manley: Dilemmas*

of Socialism and Democracy (London: Zed Books Ltd., 1985).
G.K. Lewis, *Grenada: The Jewel Despoiled* (Baltimore: The Johns Hopkins University Press, 1987).
Michael Manley, *The Politics of Change: A Jamaican Testament* (London: Andre Deutsch Ltd., 1974).
David Panton, *Jamaica's Michael Manley: The Great Transformation (1972–1992)* (Kingston: Kingston Publishers, 1993).
Huber Evelyne Stephens and John Stephens, *Democratic Socialism in Jamaica: The Political Movement and Social Transformation in Dependent capitalism* (London: Macmillan Press, 1986).
C.Y. Thomas, *The Poor and the Powerless: Economic Policy and Change in the Caribbean* (London: Latin America Bureau, 1988).

Notes

1. See Benn, *Ideology and Political Development* for a discussion of the New World Group and its critique of traditional political economy in the region.
2. See Ralph Gonsalves, *The Non-Capitalist Path to Development: Africa and the Caribbean* (Mimeo).
3. Carl Stone, 'Wither Caribbean Socialism? Grenada, Jamaica and Guyana in Perspective', in Jorge Heine, ed., *A Revolution Aborted: The Lessons of Grenada* (Pittsburgh: The University of Pittsburgh Press, 1990), pp. 291–308.
4. Michael Manley, *The Politics of Change: A Jamaican Testimony* (London: Andre Deutsch Ltd., 1974).
5. Manley, *The Politics of Change,* chapter 2.
6. Manley, *The Politics of Change,* p. 67.
7. Manley, *The Politics of Change,* pp.71–5.
8. Manley, *The Politics of Change,* chapter 3.
9. Manley, *The Politics of Change,* chapter 3.
10. Michael Manley, Jamaica: Struggle in the Periphery (Oxford: Third World Ltd., 1982).
11. Manley, *The Politics of Change,* chapter 2.
12. Manley, *The Politics of Change,* p. 77.
13. Manley, *The Politics of Change,* chapter 2.
14. Carlene Edie, *Democracy By Default: Dependency and Clientelism in Jamaica* (Boulder: Lynne Rienner Publishers, 1991) for the effect of patronage on Manley's redistribution programmes.
15. See Francis Alexis, *Changing Caribbean Constitutions* for a discussion of revolutionary government in Grenada and Tony Thorndike, 'People's Power in Theory and Practice', in Jorge Heine, ed., *A Revolution Aborted: The Lessons of Grenada* (Pittsburgh: The University of Pittsburgh Press, 1990).
16. *Tony Thorndike, 'People's Power in Theory and Practice', p. 41.*
17. *Thorndike, 'People's Power', p. 44.*
18. See Lewis, *Grenada: The Jewel Despoiled,* chapter 13.
19. See Lewis, *Grenada: The Jewel Despoiled,* chapter 4.
20. See Lewis, *Grenada: The Jewel Despoiled,* p. 138.
21. C.Y. Thomas, *The Poor and the Powerless: Economic Policy and Change in the Caribbean* (London: Latin American Bureau, 1988), p. 246.
22. Stone, 'Wither Caribbean Socialism?'
23. Lewis, *Grenada: The Jewel Despoiled.*

seven

Regional Integration:
Economic and Political Aspects

Introduction

The objective of this chapter is to review the regional integration movement with a focus on

(a) the economic and political imperatives for regional integration

(b) economic and political developments as they relate to the regional integration movement in the post-independence period.

(c) weaknesses and strengths of the regional integration movement.

Historically, the integration movement in the Commonwealth Caribbean has involved both regional and sub-regional approaches with an emphasis on economic integration. However, there have also been political, military, social and cultural dimensions to the movement. Two distinct features have predominated: gradualism and incrementalism. The roots of gradualism rest on the belief that a regional integration movement should proceed in a slow but steady evolutionary manner, that is, rather than in sudden, revolutionary movements. Countries with greater homogeneity should proceed within the framework of a sub-regional grouping within the overall CARICOM guidelines.

The rationale for the gradual approach is that a sub-regional grouping can be far more cohesive and viable than a wider regional grouping. This approach would not necessarily conflict with a regional approach, as the sub-region can later merge with the larger regional grouping. Alternatively, the process can, and has been marked by a policy of incrementalism. Caribbean nation-states have therefore pursued integration with respect to cooperation in specific areas. Both approaches have focused primarily on the functional path towards regional integration.

Definitions

Regional integration is usually perceived as a response to external and local challenges and can be defined as a process or a series of actions, whose main aim is to join together independent nations for the purpose of creating a new national entity. Historically, regional integration was motivated by a variety of forces, namely: political; economic; cultural; technical; security and social. Regional integration has been therefore designed to provide a recognised framework for harmonisation among member-states that share a geographical identity on a variety of issues.

Integration must be clearly distinguished from any 'interdependence', which refers to the degree to which events occurring in any unit of the world system may have impact on events taking place in other parts of the system. A regional integration movement therefore embraces formal organisations of cooperation with formal membership and formal decision making structures as the basis for such cooperation.

As regional integration refers to the process of voluntary decisions taken by independent nations to obtain greater levels of cooperation and reciprocity, it is first and foremost a political act. The regional integration movement in the Caribbean therefore requires political will to facilitate the implementation of regional decisions at the national level.

To be effective, the regional integration movement must have as its overall objectives:

   (i) promotion of developmental strategies designed to encourage regional and domestic developments particularly in the economic sphere
   (ii) reduction of geographical and commodity concentration of trade
   (iii) creation of larger markets and joint economic endeavours
   (iv) achievement of collective self-reliance
   (v) achievement of greater independence in the international arena
   (vi) strengthening of capacities for international negotiations, or the enhancement of bargaining capacity.
   (vii) Free mobility of the factors of production.

Imperatives of regional integration

A number of domestic, regional and international structural conditions are identified as imperatives of regional integration. With respect to the international dimensions for the Caribbean small states, the changing face of the world system is a major motivating force. The world system is increasingly characterised by greater prominence of international financial institutions, interdependence, the globalisation of production, the strengthening of regionalism with the emergence of mega blocs such as The Asian Pact, The NAFTA and the European Union.

These critical realignments of global economic relations present Commonwealth Caribbean countries with important policy options. They may choose between either a policy of unilateral liberalisation in a context of protectionism within regional blocs, which gives preferences to countries within that economic grouping, or an intensified regional, sub-regional economic approach designed to improve the possibility of Commonwealth Caribbean countries actively and even decisively participating in the international arena.

The refashioning of global economic relations coincided with the fall of communism in the former Soviet Union and throughout Eastern Europe, and has in turn resulted in the diversion of development aid and investment capital[1] towards those economies to assist in their transition to become 'free market' economies. These developments require a proactive approach by Caribbean nations, which in part involves renewed efforts at regional integration.

There are positive incentives for regional economic integration. It has been argued by proponents like W. Arthur Lewis and William Demas that a coordinated regional approach would remove some of the major constraints on industrialisation, thereby reducing a dependency on external investments. It has also been argued that regional integration would result in greater economies of scale in both administration and infrastructure. This would expand the region's increasing bargaining strength with respect to extra regional actors, enabling countries to obtain better prices for export products and to access concessional funding on better terms. It would also open up larger markets for the region's exports.

Early beginnings: the West Indian Federation

Three established modalities of political integration are identified in the literature, namely: a confederation, a unitary state and a federation. A federation is a form of political association in which two or more states constitute a political unity with a common government, but in which the individual member states retain a measure of domestic autonomy. Federalism means a constitutionally guaranteed division of power between the central governments and the governments of the member units or the component units of the federation. A federation may be distinguished from other forms of political associations given the coordinate relationship which exists among the units within a single country. The fundamental and most distinguishing feature of a federal system of government is the lack of subordination of the constituent units of the federation. Both the national and the central governments must therefore act directly upon the people of the federation. The basic principle of federalism is therefore the division of power between the central and national governments. The commitments to these conditions must be embedded in a written constitution and serve as protection for the national government (units), as it ensures that their rule-making prerogatives are in fact respected. As such, the autonomy of national governments must be constitutionally protected against interference by the central government. Unless participating units feel that their sovereignty is protected or guaranteed, they have little reason to support political federalism.

In contrast, a confederation is defined by the subordination of the central governments to the national governments. It is therefore not a state, but a political system in which the power of the central government machinery is derived from a treaty. In a unitary form of political integration, the national governments would be subordinate to the central governments. The critical condition of a unitary form of government is the vesting of control of internal and external affairs in a single central government. Secondly, all powers are constitutionally vested in a single central parliament, although devolution of some power to local government machinery is acceptable.

Distinctive characteristics of a federal system of government

Six distinct features of a federal system of government can be identified:

(i)   guaranteed division of power between the central and the national governments

(ii) a written constitution firmly guaranteeing that the powers of the constituent units will not be taken away

(iii) bicameralism: typically the legislatures consist of two chambers, one representing the people at large and the other representing the component units of the federation.

(iv) acknowledgement of the right of the component units to be involved in the amending of

federal constitution, while retaining the right to change their own constitutions unilaterally.

(v)   equal or disproportionately strong representation of smaller units in the federal chamber. Their share of the legislative seats exceed their share of the population. There must be parity in representation and the best-represented people are therefore those in the smaller components.

(vi) decentralised government.

What drives people toward federating?

K.C. Wheare points to several factors which he argues create a favourable climate for the success of a federation.[2] They include:

1. The political will and desire of both civil society and political leadership. While the support of civil society is critical perhaps even more crucial is the political leadership, which has the potential to bring energy to the process.

2. A desire to be united under a single government for certain purposes and to be organised under independent regional governments

3. A desire for political independence

4. A desire and scope for economic gains

5. The need for administrative efficiency, especially where critical mass is in short supply

6. A commonality of history, race, ethnicity and language

7. A commonality of political and cultural institutions

8. Geographical proximity and geographical neighbourhood. In the West Indies geographic separation was and continues to be decisive in fostering regional separatism. In the case of the 1958–1962 federation, the remoteness of Jamaica from the other islands contributed to its feeling of isolation

9. A sense of military insecurity

In 1958, ten British West Indian territories formed the West Indian Federation. British Honduras, British Guiana (present day Guyana) and the British Virgin Islands were the three territories that did not seek membership. Under the West Indian Federal Constitution there was an executive council, two houses of parliament, a governor general who was given wide powers and a weak federal premier. (Grantley Adams became the first and only federal premier). Financial control resided in the hands of the British government. In 1962, the Federation came to an end with the secession of Jamaica.

The Federation failed for a number of reasons:

1. The central government was virtually powerless.[3] The chief characteristic of the Federation was the small list of legislative and executive powers assigned to the central government, and its lack of financial resources which made it dependent on the unit governments. It only had one-tenth of the revenue of either Jamaica or Trinidad and Tobago and so could not achieve the economic transformation for which it hoped. The scope of the federal government was limited, its functions limited and its budget small.

2. The leadership was too timid. The reluctance of the leadership to enter regional politics weakened the support of civil society for unity and the effectiveness of the federal administration.

3. There were differences between the leadership of the region, particularly between Jamaica and Trinidad and Tobago on the structure and future direction of the Federation. Mordecai and Lewis contend that the conflict of interest between the leaders was the fundamental cause of the failure of the Federation.

4. There was reluctance on the part of the mainland territories to join the Federation.

5. The absence of a unifying force prompted by external danger and the want of a common struggle against a reluctant coloniser. This prevented the growth of an integrating sense of community.

6. Parochialism, which was grounded in generations of isolated history and the absence of a sense of a common identity and insular pride amounting to parochialism. Arthur Lewis, for instance, in relation to Barbados argued that: 'Three hundred years of strongly insular pride made its people somewhat indifferent to what happens outside their tiny paradise'.[4]

7. Trade and communications between the islands was sporadic.

8. Infrequent personal contact between the inhabitants of the region. Separate development and limited contact with each other, again a legacy bequeathed by colonialism, as well as a lack of effective communication: a structural and functional limitation of the early Federation.

9. Differences in levels of development, as the then increasing prosperity of Jamaica and Trinidad and Tobago was viewed as a critical determinant in the failure to generate the will and desire to integrate.

10. Delays and manipulation on the part of the government of the United Kingdom.

11. A complicating factor was the rapid constitutional progress after 1944, which made local political leaders eager to consolidate their local political gains, and fearful that they may lose them in a Federation.

12. The West Indian Federation according to Watts was also unusual among modern federations, in that it did not begin with a customs union or a common currency.[5]

Ian Boxill contends that:

> Overall, there are two major issues which would account for the failure of the federation. First, there is the historically insular development of the territories which militated against the creation of a common identity and, by implication, an ideology of regionalism; secondly, there is the conceptual framework of a federation – the idea of federation being used as a means of attaining constitutional self-government – which was not concerned with the reproduction of federation as an end in itself.[6]

CARICOM and the treaty of Chaguaramas of 1973

The formation of the Caribbean Common Market in 1974 (CARICOM) marked a decisive break with past attempts that had tended to focus on political and administrative integration.[7] This new approach towards integration tried to provide a regional approach towards the problems of economic development and to deepen the process of integration. CARICOM was preceded by CARIFTA (The Caribbean Free Trade Association Agreement 1968) which provided for a free trade area among the English-speaking Caribbean territories. CARICOM was meant to represent an attempt at closer cooperation, economic integration and foreign and external trade policy coordination.

The Treaty of Chaguaramas (4 July 1973) provided specifically for:

1. Coordination of the foreign policies of member states and achievement of a significant level of success. Notable instances of dispute and thus failure to harmonise can be seen in:
   a. Pre-1990s position on Cuba (isolation/integration)
   b. The Grenada revolution in 1979 and military invasion of Grenada in 1983
   c. Regional carrying trade, that is, disputes over transit and landing points, Leeward Island Air Transport, Carib Express, British West Indian Airways[8]
   d. The case of Haiti

2. Corporation (functional corporation) and the establishment of common services in non-economic areas. CARICOM's common services and functional cooperation are primarily manifested in non-economic fields, such as education, health, culture, sea and air transportation and information. The most notable achievements in the area of common services are: the University of the West Indies (UWI); the West Indian cricket Team; CARIFESTA; the Caribbean Examination Council (CXC); the Regional Security System (RSS); the CBU and the Caribbean News Agency (CANA).

Functional cooperation and common services therefore represent the most visible and successful aspects of the regional integration movement.

3. Economic integration, which required the establishment of a common external tariff (Customs Union) and the creation of a free trade area.

The Treaty recognised that it was important to grant concessions to the less developed countries within CARICOM and thus provided for two phases of operation, the first from 1974–1984 and the second from 1984 onwards. The lesser-developed territories entered into their own sub-regional grouping with the formation of the Eastern Caribbean Common Market (EECM), which coincided with the establishment of CARIFTA in 1968. It was felt that the ECCM could improve the bargaining power of the lesser-developed territories within CARIFTA, and increase the attractiveness of the sub-region to external investment.

The Treaty of Chaguaramas was certainly a step in the right direction, but its structure and the need for unanimity within CARICOM at the conference of Heads of Government, the principal organ along with the Common Market Council, have severely limited the ability of CARICOM to arrive at decisions and to undertake speedy implementation.

Although the Treaty of Chaguaramas gave birth to CARICOM, it was itself flawed as it did not visualise the free movement of people and capital nor the creation of a monetary union. A number of obstacles to the realisation of the stated principles of the treaty remain and these have prompted a review of the treaty and the adoption of a number of protocols which are still under discussion by the Heads of Government.

The Organisation of Eastern Caribbean States

The Organisation of Eastern Caribbean States was established by treaty and comprises seven full member-states and one associated state. In 1986, the British Virgin Islands became an associated member. In addition to the Treaty of Basseterre of 1981, the OECS functions through two other agreements, namely The Eastern Caribbean Central Bank Agreement of 1983 and The Supreme Court Act of 1967.

The OECS Treaty of 1981 is based on the joint and cooperative action of the member-states in a number of areas. Its establishment took place within a political framework of independence for a number of Eastern Caribbean states, which rendered the existing structure of the West Indian Associated States'(WISA) Council inadequate. The OECS is conceived of as an institution that would provide the legal framework for collective action at the international level, while consolidating the continuing processes of cooperation in common services and economic integration. This had begun with the establishment of the ECCM and WISA. The objective factors that had earlier motivated the formation of the ECCM were at work and underscored the need for the new organisation. The OECS went a step further than the ECCM by calling for the creation of a Foreign Affairs Committee that would meet biannually and would be responsible for taking appropriate action on matters that had been referred to it by the Authority of the OECS. This meant that there was structural transformation at the organisational levels within the Eastern Caribbean.

The Authority comprises Heads of Government of the member-states, and is the supreme policy- making institution of the OECS. Through its Foreign Affairs Committee and the Authority of the Heads of Government, the OECS attempts to achieve a greater degree of coherence of policy at both the regional and international bodies, than that which is generally achieved by CARICOM. This structure has greatly facilitated the 'unanimity' rule under the CARICOM framework, as the OECS has invariably been able to speak with one voice at the Heads of Government meetings of CARICOM.

Unfortunately, however, decisions taken by the Authority that are supposed to be binding on member governments, have suffered from the same difficulties that have faced CARICOM. The OECS is not a political unit, and as such, implementation requires political will on the part of the leadership of the sub-region. Moreover, when an examination of the role of the Central Secretariat of the OECS is made, it is clear that under the OECS framework, the director general of the OECS has at best a communicating and not an enforcement role. Lacking any enforcement mechanism, the OECS secretariat and indeed its administrative head, the director general must rely upon his persuasive powers to gain compliance of decisions. He cannot force or threaten any of the constituent parts of the OECS.

Member countries of the OECS achieved a remarkable degree of joint representation overseas and an unparalleled level of foreign policy harmonisation as compared with the rest of the Caribbean community notwithstanding the Grenada debacle. Specifically, the OECS governments have been able to utilise the cost-saving devices of multi-accreditation and joint representation with respect to overseas missions. The missions to Britain and Canada were both joint endeavours and recent developments have seen the establishment of separate missions to Britain by a number of OECS states.

The OECS and Barbados also entered into a memorandum of understanding in 1982, which outlined a number of areas of cooperation for member countries. While much controversy surrounded its establishment and indeed the need for its existence, the regional security system is another indication of joint enterprise aimed at reducing the cost of the defence function of the individual island-nations. The regional security system, in conjunction with the coast guard units, are integral parts of the regional integration movement and indeed the sub-regional grouping. In 1996 Barbados and the OECS also agreed to strengthen their economic ties and to reduce trade disputes which have clouded the regional movement.

The Grand Anse and Kingston Declarations

Although the Treaty of Chaguaramas called for the creation of a free trade area, CARICOM remains plagued by a number of quantitative as well as qualitative restrictions. The Grand Anse Declaration of 1989 sought to address obstacles to the creation of a free trade area and the achievement of a common market.

The Grand Anse Declaration proposed eleven major actions:

1. Appointment of an independent West Indian Commission
2. The establishment of a common market and economy by July 1993
3. The CARICOM Industrialisation Programming Scheme (CIPS) be established by September 30, 1989, as well as the CARICOM Enterprise Regime
4. The movement of capital

5. Removal of all remaining barriers to trade by July 1991, giving effect to the free trade area
6. The multilateral clearing facility to be re-established by 1990
7. Free movement of skilled and professional people and contract workers on a seasonal or project basis
8. To develop by July 4, 1992, a regional system of air and sea transportation
9. Joint representation in international economic negotiations and the sharing of offices and facilities
10. Establishment of an assembly of Caribbean Community parliamentarians
11. Abolition of passports for intra-regional travel by 1990

To date only a few of these recommendations have been implemented.

The *Kingston Declaration* of 1990 called for the common market to be transformed into a monetary union and represents a progressive step in the momentum towards greater regional economic integration.

The Manning Initiative 1993

The Manning Initiative represented both a gradualist and incremental approach to regional integration. It called for greater functional cooperation among three member-states of the Caribbean community, that is, Guyana, Trinidad and Tobago and Barbados. It represents a similar course taken by the OECS, but was criticised on the grounds that its realisation would lead to further fragmentation of the region. The main contention was that it merely represents a horizontal development within the region, when vertical development was required.

The Manning Initiative identified five areas in which functional cooperation could be enhanced:

1. The Caribbean Assembly of Parliamentarians (addressed in the Grand Anse Declaration)
2. Greater collaboration and cooperation in diplomatic missions, including joint missions overseas
3. Increased cooperation in sports development
4. Double taxation treaties among the three territories
5. Increased cooperation in dealing with anti-drug activity.

The response of the region to the Manning Initiative was lukewarm. The 1995 elected UNC/NAR Government under the leadership of Basdeo Panday, dismissed the proposal as contributing nothing positive to the further harmonious development of CARICOM.

The CARICOM single market and economy

The starting point for any discussion on the CARICOM single market and economy, is to clearly distinguish between the single-market concept and that of the single economy. The achievement of the single economy is plagued with far more difficulties than the former. Given that the achievement of the CARICOM economy requires a monetary union, which would necessitate a re-examination of the currency requirements in the region, the more pragmatic and politically feasible approach would be to focus on the achievement of the CARICOM Single Market.

The economies of the Commonwealth Caribbean are marked by a bewildering number of currencies and it is the one factor that has frustrated the regional economic integration process. The multiple-currency situation has had the effect of creating dependency on 'hard currency', usually the American dollar, to pay for intra- and extra-regional goods and services. This is made worse given the collapse of the CARICOM Multilateral Clearing Facility and has placed additional pressure on the foreign exchange reserves of individual Caribbean governments, further exacerbating intra-regional trade, as the ability to use national currencies to pay for regional goods and services is limited by the currency situation in the region.

Jamaica's economic difficulties in the 1980s resulted in the creation of a parallel market, which had the net effect of introducing three exchange rates in that country and also resulted in the devaluation of the Jamaican dollar against the other currencies of CARICOM. Ultimately, the impact on intra-regional trade was extremely harmful, as CARICOM goods became uncompetitive on the Jamaican market.[9]

Three types of currency regimes exist in the region:

1. A Fixed Exchange Rate in Barbados
2. A Floating Exchange Rate in Guyana, Jamaica and Trinidad and Tobago
3. A Common currency or Monetary Union in the countries of the OECS

These differing regimes have not benefitted regional trade and have made it difficult for the Commonwealth Caribbean to realise the goals of a common market and economy. However, a rationalisation of the currency regime is potentially explosive for the member-states of the Caribbean community and has militated against the willingness of regional governments to fully implement the provisions of the common market and economy. The common market and economy would require:

(i) capital mobility, necessitating not only the removal of existing legal barriers to foreign investment but equally important, the removal of foreign exchange controls
(ii) full convertibility of currencies
(iii) exchange rates bearing permanently fixed relationships to each other

The concept of the single market within the CARICOM framework implies three related sets of action.

1. The creation of a free trade area (FTA), that is, the removal of barriers to the exchange of goods.
2. It involves the creation of a customs union with a common external tariff (CET).
3. The establishment of a common market requiring the removal of all existing barriers to the freedom of movement of all factors of production including services, capital and labour. It also requires the adoption of collective trade policy *vis-à-vis* third countries.

The idea of a regional single market is as old as CARICOM itself but there has been considerable resistance to its full implementation. While the hard currency issue has proven a deterrent to greater interregional trade, the effective realisation of the single market is also hampered by a number of factors ranging from licensing systems that have been imposed by a number of CARICOM countries, differing standards, administrative procedures, the transportation system and protectionist policies designed to protect local industries. Some of the benefits to be gained from the CARICOM Single Market and Economy are:

(i) increased bargaining power in the international arena by reducing 'cut throat' competition and in so doing present a united front to foreign investors
(ii) the creation of strong regional companies to compete internationally as capital is able to travel freely within the region
(iii) an increase of the market size available to CARICOM firms
(iv) the elimination of competing and contradicting development policies
(v) regional firms better positioned to confront the economic challenges of globalisation
(vi) the full realisation of a 'critical mass' which individual states within CARICOM lack, as labour will be able to move freely across the region.

The end result of the implementation of the common market and economy would be an increase in a variety of goods, increase in employment, a reduction in the price of goods, protection of the regional market from international competition, the free movement of people, and the improvement of skills, which are necessary for the development of competitive firms. The free movement of people can also contribute to supplementing the local workforce and so prevent shortages where shortages are experienced.

However, there are also short-term disadvantages. Not only will liberalisation and greater harmonisation have diffused benefits, their implementation will also have concentrated costs, owing largely to the loss of protection of domestic markets. It is generally accepted in political trade theory that there will be losers and winners, and that countries with abundant factors will gain, while countries with scarce factors of production will lose their protection.

Given the lower level of economic development of member-states of the Eastern Caribbean, it is the member countries of the OECS who are likely to lose out initially when the Caribbean Single Market and Economy is implemented and this explains the reservations that have been expressed by OECS governments to certain of its measures. A gradualist or incremental approach to the establishment of the single market and economy will probably be the likely scenario.

Whatever the approach, policy concessions have to be made to the losers in order to neutralise their opposition, and to allow for democratically elected governments to appease groups bearing the costs of liberalisation within the national economy. In weighing the costs versus the benefits of the Caribbean Single Market and Economy, the following are important considerations:

1. Capital is likely to flow to countries that are perceived to be politically and economically stable resulting in the flight of capital from other countries
2. Loss of jobs in some industries as a consequence of the full weight of liberalised trade
3. Higher cost of living, which may have both social and political consequences
4. Social dislocation
5. Loss of national economic control and ownership of already limited resources, as a result of the free movement of capital.

The biggest political threat to national governments that the Caribbean Single Market and Economy and for that matter, any integration scheme will pose, is the impact on national sovereignty. It is an indisputable fact that irrespective of notions of interdependence and globalisation, the nation-state, while receding in importance as a social, economic and political category, is given overwhelming importance in countries which have recently emerged from centuries of colonialism. If a properly working integration as proposed under the framework of the Caribbean Single Market and Economy is to, therefore, be successful, it must not only have appropriate institutional structures of its own, but also it must be marked by legal arrangements of its own and the capacity to produce coherent policies. These are policies that will without doubt transfer certain elements of national sovereignty away from the nation-state towards the integration scheme. This in itself may be one of the biggest stumbling blocks against regional economic and political integration. Vere Bird Senior believed that Antigua's participation in the political unification of the OECS would result in a return to colonialism. Given current global developments, the persistence of an ideology of national sovereignty versus regional sovereignty will only result in continuing marginalisation and loss of sovereignty internationally.

The Association of Caribbean States

The establishment of the Association of Caribbean States (ACS) was proposed by the West Indian Commission in 1992. The view expressed by the commission was that the association could be seen as a means of creating within the wider Caribbean, special trading and functional cooperation arrangements. As such, the association should not be limited to the English-speaking Caribbean but would embrace, Spanish, French and Dutch-speaking Caribbean states.

It was further argued that the ACS could be used as a vehicle through which ACS countries could develop arrangements for regular consultation, thereby arriving at harmonised approaches to negotiations with third world countries. In this way ACS countries could attempt to achieve greater concessions from the international community.[10]

In July 1994, the constitution of the ACS was signed and it currently comprises 25 member- countries. The ACS marks an important juncture in the broadening of non-hegemonic and hemispheric relations. It is expected that the establishment of the ACS will lead to the development of a more liberal and expanded trade and investment area, greater cooperation and collaboration on issues pertaining to resources and assets and a geo-economic space enabling Caribbean countries to determine the conditions under which they enter into the economic system.

The Barbados-OECS Initiative

The call for a consideration of closer collaboration between Barbados and the OECS, came in the wake of the August 1995 signing of an 'Agreement for Economic Cooperation' which identified several areas of cooperation between Barbados and the OECS. The main areas of cooperation agreed under the agreement focused on the development of the services sector, particularly that of the financial and informatics sectors. Two other areas of cooperation were the participation of Barbados in the OECS single market and the negotiation of double taxation agreements and trade promotions.

The post-independence cooperative relationship between Barbados and the OECS was well-established. In 1982 for instance, at the height of security concerns in the region, members of the OECS signed a Memorandum of Understanding with Barbados which outlined a number of areas of cooperation. This new initiative, therefore, represents the culmination of a long series of agreements and cooperation between the islands since the collapse of the Federation.

William Demas and Dwight Venner argued that there was a pressing need to make suitable political arrangements in the OECS and then in the wider Commonwealth Caribbean. At the time, Venner argued that the only decision to be determined was the mechanics of the process.[11] For Venner:

> With respect to sequencing, the first step will have to be the taken by the OECS, which is furthest along the road to an effective union, followed by an association with Barbados and then the other states in the Eastern and Southern Caribbean.[12]

Prime Minister Kenny Anthony further argued, that in extending the current parameters of the OECS:

> . . . the first action should be the inclusion of Barbados into the OECS as quickly as possible. The inclusion of Barbados would signal the engagement of the OECS in a partnership and the preparedness to lay the foundation for a lasting relationship. This action will sound the clarion call for the other OECS countries to awake to the realities of a new dawn in the region.[13]

In 1998, the OECS governments and Barbados commissioned a joint task force, to advise on the establishment of a confederation between them. Prime Ministers Kenny Anthony of St Lucia and Owen Arthur of Barbados have articulated views on their ideal type of cooperation. In the view of Prime Minister Kenny Anthony:

> . . . the philosophy of integration has been compromised by a narrow, almost reductionist preoccupation with economic matters. We have tended to subordinate everything else to the simplistic notion that integration is only about economics and trade. Integration is not only about economic issues. It ought to be about people, how we live, our shared institutions and how we choose to manage and administer them.[14]

In terms of a concrete proposal coming from the leading proponents of the OECS-Barbados Initiative, Prime Minister Kenny Anthony called for a confederation, arguing that its attractiveness as a political model for Barbados and the OECS rests on the ease with which the participating countries could enter the alliance. According to him:

> What makes the Confederation particularly attractive, almost seductive . . . is the ease with which we can adapt, accommodate and refine existing structures already created by the OECS Treaty.[15]

Prime Minister Arthur also signalled his interest in political union of the Eastern Caribbean, arguing that the emphasis on economic as against political integration in the region was a 'massive mistake'.[16] He went on further to state that. . .Economic integration without political unity in the Caribbean will be shown increasingly to be a nonsense. . . (Sic).[17]

In concert with his St Lucian counterpart, Prime Minister Arthur argued that a confederation was a temporary, transitional stage towards the full political union of the sub-region. In his view, a higher level of political integration would only be possible when, '. . .people come to appreciate the value of intensive non-economic cooperation. . .'[18]

In their analysis of a national survey conducted in Barbados on public perceptions of the Barbados-OECS Initiative, Barrow-Giles and Farley sought to debunk the West Indian Commission Report's view that there is both governmental and popular resistance to the idea of political integration. Instead, they contend that in the case of Barbados there is '. . . significant strong support among committed respondents for both economic and political integration. . .'.[19] They conclude that there is no evidence to support the commission's view that there is 'popular resistance' to the idea of regional integration.

Regional security and the regional security system

The Eastern Caribbean constitutes an area which has experienced several attempted coups and acts of sabotage some with external support. In 1979 and 1981, coups plots were discovered against the government of Dominica, and from 1979–83, Grenada recorded many attempts at sabotage and destabilisation. Caribbean territories are also used as transshipment points for the drug trade between South and North America. Naturally, the activities of the traders in the territorial waters of the small islands are hazardous and call for the creation and maintenance of a security force which is adequate to deal with a minimum of threat, whether potential or real which confronts the island.

The vulnerability of small islands in the Eastern Caribbean to external threat is somewhat muted and given the geopolitical proximity of those islands to North America, there is a vested interest in the region's security by that continent.

The creation and maintenance of a competent security force is a costly one, therefore measures have to be taken to prevent serious jeopardy to the economic and social development of the states in the region. Prior to independence, the security needs of the Commonwealth Caribbean were overseen by the British Government, but with the realisation of independence, countries had to undertake their own needs for defense. However, finances dictated that the only way of achieving defensive capabilities was to act in concert with the other islands of the Eastern Caribbean experiencing similar difficulties. This led to the idea of a regional defence system being proposed.

A series of events including the internal disorder in Antigua in 1976,[20] as well as the Cubana Airline tragedy which took place off the coast of Barbados on October 6, 1975, highlighted the need for security in the region. The Cubana tragedy was preceded by the declaration of Barbados' prime minister, Tom Adams, that two American nationals were involved in a plan to overthrow his newly elected government.

It was not until 1979 that there was another move by the OECS to establish a regional defence force. Dion Phillips argues that the real catalyst to the militarisation of the Eastern Caribbean was the coming to power of the New JEWEL Movement in Grenada in March 1979 and the Nicaraguan revolution in July of that same year. Phillips further contends that the events in Afghanistan and Iran, in addition to Cuba's decision to send troops to crush a Somali invasion, which threatened the socialist regime in Ethiopia, added fuel to the fire which was already out of control.[21]

However, shortly after these events, general elections ushered in a more 'liberal' leadership in the Eastern Caribbean and Eastern Caribbean states did not contemplate the establishment of a system which would allow intervention in the affairs of other islands. It was in 1982 that momentum was given to the impetus to create a regional security system. Members of the OECS and Barbados signed a Memorandum of Understanding which outlined a number of areas of cooperation including the establishment of the Regional Security System. The initial signatories to the Memorandum were Antigua-Barbuda, Barbados, Dominica, St Lucia and St Vincent and the Grenadines. St Kitts-Nevis and Grenada acceded to the memorandum in February 1983 and January 1985 respectively.

Conclusion

Meaningful integration designed to maximise resources and take advantage of world developments, is the only real alternative for the individual small states of the Caribbean. However, it would be a mistake to assume that regional integration can be defined by a single set of actions. Rather, it is a dynamic process with a number of modalities which are clearly marked by membership, structures and objectives. Historically, Caribbean states have been primarily reactive in their external and domestic orientations but the present international conjuncture demands a positive response, which can only be in the direction of a deeper regional integration.

Key words and phrases

1	Interdependence
2	Cooperation
3	Integration
4	Customs union
5	Free trade area
6	Common market
7	Single market and economy
8	Association of Caribbean States
9	Economic integration
10	Political integration
11	Confederation
12	Federation
13	Unitary state
14	CARICOM
15	OECS
16	Barbados-OECS Initiative
17	Grand Anse Declaration
18	Manning Initiative
19	Incrementalism
20	Gradualism
21	Single currency
22	Common external tariff

Questions to Consider

- Assess the approaches to integration in the region and consider what have been the main failures and benefits of the movement. What else needs to be done and why?
- 'Recent global changes and the challenge to the nation-state posed by these changes, demand a regional approach as a survival mechanism'. Critically discuss this view with respect to the regional integration movement in the Commonwealth Caribbean.
- Critically examine the main problems of the regional integration movement in the region. How can these problems be alleviated? Critically discuss with relevant examples.
- Should Commonwealth Caribbean countries politically integrate?
- Is globalism incompatible with regionalism? Discuss in relation to efforts at Commonwealth Caribbean regional integration.
- 'Trends toward economic globalisation and neoliberalism in the Caribbean have been accompanied paradoxically by the region's economic and political marginalisation'. Critically comment on the above statement and show how regional integration can alleviate such marginalisation.
- 'Deepening the process of regionalism is the only way that Commonwealth Caribbean states will be able to cope with the pressures of the international environment'. Discuss.

Activities

* Consider the cultural, economic, political and social differences and similarities between member-countries of the Commonwealth Caribbean.
* On a separate sheet of paper list the most important differences.
* Compare any single Commonwealth Caribbean country with any developed society and assess the differences.
* List all the countries that you have visited.
* Honestly assess your attitude towards citizens of other Commonwealth Caribbean countries.
* Attempt to correlate your views on Caribbean people with that of your overseas visits.
* Discuss your findings with your group and assess the implications for the regional integration movement.

Readings

Caribbean Monetary Integration

Edited by Terrence Farrell and DeLisle Worrell

Introduction

Interest in monetary union or monetary integration has waxed in recent times owing largely to Europe's declared intention to create a monetary union in a specified time frame following on the creation of the Single Market. Understanding of the nature of monetary union and implications for particular participating countries has seemingly not kept pace with the movement toward it. Indeed this apparent gap between popular understanding and acceptance, and progress toward its implementation has caused the process to be set back in Europe as the ratification of the Maastricht Treaty has stumbled.

Part of the reason for this gap in understanding is no doubt the very different levels at which the discussion and debate on monetary union has taken place.

At the level of academics and professional economists, analysis is in terms of 'optimum currency areas', 'fiscal co-ordination', 'common currency', 'centralized management of monetary policy', 'exchange rate mechanism', etc. This terminology might leave economists somewhat perplexed if they are not trained in international or monetary economics. The layman is even more confused. He is mystified by the suggestion that one currency may be forged from currencies whose (nominal) exchange rates are so different, when there is a tendency to assume that the strength of a currency is directly proportional to its parity in terms of a numeraire such as the US dollar.[1]

Another source of discomfiture is the idea that acceptance of a 'common currency' means that the national community is giving up something, though what is being surrendered is often not well understood and articulated. There is perhaps the notion that sovereign countries must have their own currencies, much as they have a national flag, a coat-of-arms, and a national anthem. A national currency becomes one of the symbols of nationhood and sovereignty. However, there are several instances of sovereign countries happily sharing a common currency. In the Caribbean the OECS counties all use the EC dollar. The CFA franc zone in West Africa is another example.

Although they value the symbolism of a national currency, citizens have little compunction in protecting their real asset positions by fleeing the currency if its purchasing power is being continuously and rapidly eroded through inflation and devaluation. They want the symbolism of a national currency, but certainly not at the expense of their real wealth positions. Worrell's proposal for a common currency for CARICOM, seeks to resolve this ambiguity by proposing a Caribbean dollar so that the symbolism of a 'national' money is retained, but, goes on to suggest a structure which will ensure that the currency is stable and the real wealth positions of residents of the common currency area are preserved (Worrell, Ch. 3 below).

We have already introduced a number of complexities into the discussion which will be clarified as the discussion proceeds. The next section explains what constitutes monetary union, showing that a common currency is only one of several forms that a monetary union may take. Section 3 explains why countries might see it fit to enter a monetary union, i.e. what are the (net) benefits. Section 4 explores some of the implications of monetary union. Section 5 examines the various alternative paths or routes to monetary union. Section 6 summarizes and concludes the discussion and speaks to the CARICOM Initiative on monetary union.

What is Monetary Union?

A monetary union is a group of countries linked by a common currency or by permanently fixed nominal exchange rates, with guaranteed convertability.[2] The idea of a common currency is easily understood. One and only one currency (notes and coins) circulates in all the countries of the Union and all assets, liabilities and transactions are denominated in the common currency. Although there is only one currency, there may be separate central banks, economic policies may be pursued independently (subject to the constraint of the common currency), and capital flows among the countries may be restricted or free.

In the monetary union with irrevocably fixed nominal exchange rates, each country in the union has a separate national currency but the rate of exchange of that national currency in terms of some numeraire currency is fixed and cannot be changed. This means that the rates of exchange of the currencies of the countries will also be fixed and immutable, thus constituting a monetary union. It is in this sense that Caribbean countries had a monetary union when they were all under the Sterling Exchange Standard. Each country had its currency but this was fixed in terms of sterling and therefore the currencies were fixed in terms of each other. In this scenario, each country has its own central bank issuing the national currency. The countries may or may not pursue independent economic policies, and capital flows among them may or may not be restricted.

The preceding discussion provides four criteria or dimensions which would allow us to classify different types of monetary union. These are whether there is (i) one currency or multiple currencies; (ii) one central bank or multiple central banks; (iii) independent or coordinated economic – trade, fiscal, incomes, industrial – policies; (iv) freedom or restrictions on capital flows. It can readily be appreciated that in theory at least, there can be many combinations of these criteria which can be classified as monetary unions.

For the discussion here only three (3) types of monetary union are distinguished since these are more likely in the real world. First, we may define **weak monetary union**, where the countries elect to issue separate national currencies from separate central banks, to operate fixed nominal exchange rates among themselves, to conduct separate economic policies, and place institutional limits on capital flows. This model of monetary union is described as weak because monetary and fiscal policies are not coordinated. In addition, it would be easy for countries to defect from the union if it suited them since they continue to issue their own currencies.

Second, we may define **semi-strong monetary**, union. Here there is a common currency issued by a single central bank. However, economic policies are separately developed and managed, and there are institutional limitations on capital flows. In this model, monetary and fiscal policies are directly coordinated although the fact of a common currency engenders greater discipline over these policies. Moreover, the possibility of defection from the union is lower, since the costs of having to create a separate currency and central bank would be high. These costs are to be measured not in terms of the actual set up costs, but the costs of ensuring confidence and credibility in the new arrangements after the country has defected.

The third type may be characterized as **strong monetary union**. Here we have not only a common currency issued by a single central bank, but also the centralized management of monetary, fiscal and perhaps and trade and other policies. Capital movements are completely free as might be labour movements, i.e. there is a single market for goods and factors of production.

The foregoing discussion makes it clear that monetary of whatever type or form does imply (i) surrender of the exchange rate as an instrument of policy by participating countries; and (ii) constraint on the use of independent monetary policies by the participating countries. In evaluating the benefits and costs of monetary union therefore, the question arises as to what a participating country gives up in terms of the welfare of its nationals by foregoing the use of the exchange rate as an instrument of adjustment and by foregoing the exercise of an independent monetary policy.

The preceding discussion also makes it clear that a monetary union does not necessarily imply (i) a single central bank (ii) centralized management of economic policies, and (iii) diminution of political sovereignty. The last point has to be qualified however, in that any constraint on the exercise of policy may be viewed as some diminution of sovereignty. Moreover, in the case of strong monetary union, there is, in fact, little by way of discretionary (economic) policy left to the individual state. Hence the concern in some quarters that

strong monetary union is but a cloak to disguise what must eventually be political union.[3]

Why Monetary Union? The Benefits and Costs

All economic activity, i.e. the exchange of goods and services, takes place over a particular geographic space. When transactions among people in that space are sufficiently regular, it makes sense to innovate a medium of exchange, a money, to facilitate the transactions. In accepting the use of a medium of exchange over whose value the individual agent or household has no control, the benefits of participating in the circulation of the money are seen to outweigh the cost, which is that the individual agent or household is unable to establish a different rate of exchange for its money *vis-à-vis* the monies of its neighbours. It might wish to do this if for example, unemployment in the household or trade is unacceptably high. In such circumstances, the household or members of the trade would have to change their wage rates.[4]

The medium of exchange would usually evolve into a store of value and a unit of account. The 'store of value' concept means that once the value of the money in terms of command over goods and services is assured to be reasonably stable over time, people will comfortably hold the medium itself instead of or in addition to any real assets it can buy. If not, as in periods of high inflation, they will elect to flee from the money into real assets.

The size of a currency area would therefore seem to depend on (i) the volume and regularity of transactions within that domain, and (ii) the willingness of economic agents to accept the costs of not having their private money with its own rate of exchange. This latter condition actually translates into the ability of the household or the firm to move within the domain either from one place to another where employment prospects are better or to engage in a more profitable trade or business. It is in this sense that the optimum size of a currency area depends crucially on factor mobility, i.e. the ability of capital and labour to move within the domain.[5]

Governments enter the picture by defining a particular geographic space as the state, and by seeking to control and eventually monopolize the issue of money within the boundaries of the state. Control of the issue of money is important because the agent who controls the issue of money obtains the seignorage therefrom.[6] Governments have always taken the view that any seignorage should accrue to the state rather than private economic agents. On the other hand, with the issue of money in the hands of governments, it is possible that the volume at issue becomes detached from the volume of real transactions taking place in the geographic space, resulting in either inflation or deflation.

Consider then the case of two neighboring states, A and B, with separate currencies, but one of which, B, the smaller country, trades extensively with the other. We assume that B is so small that changes in demand and supply conditions in B have no effect whatsoever on economic activity in A. If B expands its supply of money to a degree not warranted by the volume of transactions, then it will incur a trade deficit with A, and B's currency would tend to depreciate relative to that of A. If the exchange rate between A and B is fixed, then adjustment in B will have to take the form of a reduction in output and employment and monetary correction.

The question then arises, under what conditions would it make sense for B to maintain a fixed exchange rate with A. If the government of B tends to be profligate and fails to maintain monetary discipline, periodic devaluations will most likely cause citizens to lose confidence in money which repeatedly loses value relative to the basket of goods they want to purchase. That basket contains, by assumption, a large proportion of imported goods and services. Fixing the exchange rate enforces a degree of monetary and fiscal discipline.

The argument for monetary union in the Caribbean turns largely on these premises. Each Caribbean state is very small with a high level of trade with the United States. It may, therefore, make good sense for these countries to peg to the US dollar, if there are tendencies to fiscal and monetary excesses arising from either internal shocks or external shocks. This would mean that each Caribbean state would have its own nominal rate of exchange with the US dollar. It may then make sense for these states to form a monetary union so as to promote factor mobility and trade among themselves, and derive the benefits of a single market and economy.

The foregoing discussion makes it clear that (i) the Caribbean itself does not constitute an optimum currency area since there is insufficient factor mobility and the level of interregional trade is relatively low; (ii) in small open economies, confidence in the currency and hence in the economy is strongly dependent on the stability of its external value; (iii) the case for monetary union in the Caribbean rests more on the need to promote a sound stable money, monetary and

fiscal discipline, and to provide some impetus for the formation of a single market and economy. The rationale for monetary union in the Caribbean therefore differs from that in Europe where the level of intra-regional trade is high, confidence in the external value of the currencies is less dependent on its (short-run) stability, and it is the formation of the single market and economy which is providing some of the impetus for creation of monetary union.[7]

Implications of Monetary Union

Monetary union carries certain implications for the participating countries, some of which were alluded to above, but which are discussed more fully in this section. First, a country entering a monetary union forgoes the use of the exchange rate as an instrument of policy which might be used to assist in the balance of payments adjustment process. In the previous section, it was suggested that in small highly open economies where the proportion of tradable good to non-tradables is very high, the exchange rate looms large in the consciousness of citizens because any change in the exchange rate ramifies a multiplicity of transactions in the domestic economy and changes the general price level. Fixing the exchange rate or the adoption of a common currency would help to eliminate or reduce the uncertainties arising from exchange rate changes.

Second, monetary union will reduce the transaction costs of doing business among participating countries by eliminating foreign exchange dealings and facilitating transactions in capital market instruments. Where there is a weak monetary union, the possibilities for arbitrage among the various currencies will be eliminated, and of course, would not arise at all in the context of a common currency arrangement.

A third implication of monetary union is that with the exchange rate removed as an instrument of policy, there will be necessarily more restraint in the fiscal policies of the participating countries. In semi-strong or strong arrangements with a common currency, fiscal expansion would not be accommodated by monetary expansion, since any such expansion would have to be agreed by all the other participating states, which is not likely to be forthcoming. The expanding country would have to borrow to finance its deficits and may find the markets exerting discipline with its borrowing costs rising. In a weak monetary union, the restraint on fiscal expansion is weaker and the smaller participating countries may expand at the expense of the others. It is for this reason that convergence criteria relating inter alia to the size and financing of fiscal deficits have to be agreed prior to monetary union.[8]

A fourth set of considerations relate to possible income and wealth distribution effects within the union. These may arise as follows. Suppose that the Caribbean constituted a monetary union and there was a decline in the price of bauxite. This would mean that economic activity in Jamaica and Guyana would decline and there would be higher unemployment in those 'regions'. Those 'regions' would not have the use of the exchange rate as an instrument of adjustment to enforce the decline in real incomes or to provide an incentive for the production of alternative exports.

In effect the only ways of relieving the situation would be (i) for labour to migrate from one 'region' to another where activity has not declined, thus putting downward pressure on wages there; and/or (ii) for the union to provide support for the depressed area through some kind of structural funds or stabilization fund mechanism.

Another source of polarization relates to the flow of investment. Particular parts of the region may be seen by investors as the best places to locate their activities, and this will be reinforced over time by agglomeration economies. For example, an investor in St. Vincent may find it better to locate his business in Bridgetown or Port of Spain because of the better infrastructure in these locations.

These effects would not be relieved unless the monetary union takes a proactive position by encouraging activity to locate in particular 'regions'. This has implications for tax policy across the region as well as for the opportunities for labour migration across regions.

Paths To Monetary Union

Monetary union is most often linked to the creation of a single market or economic union, i.e. an economic space comprising several countries but which, for all practical purposes, is one economy. One question which immediately arises in terms of timing and sequencing is whether monetary union should precede, follow or parallel economic union.

There is certainly a great deal of logic in the view that monetary union should follow or parallel economic union. This argument is based on the need to increase the intensity and regularity of transactions among the participating countries which would, in turn, justify the creation of a single currency. In this sequence the countries would move from a free trade area to customs union and then to a single market allowing uninhibited movement of factors of production. Only when this is achieved would they look to creating a single central bank issuing a common currency.

There is the alternative where a monetary union is instituted prior to the creation of a single market, and is in fact used to accelerate the creation of a single market and economy. This approach was argued in the previous section in relation to the Caribbean, where if the countries were to wait until the volume of intra-regional transactions warranted the institution of a monetary union, it would clearly be a long time coming.

A second question relates to the pace at which monetary union should proceed. On the European paradigm, progress toward monetary union would necessarily be gradual.[9] That process arguably began with the Treaty of Rome in 1959, was given further impetus with the Werner Report (1970), was derailed when the industrialized countries moved to generalized floating in 1973, and was put back on track with the 'snake' and the Exchange Rate Mechanism in the 1980s. The Maastricht Treaty (1991) envisages that monetary union will occur in Europe by the turn of the century as the participating countries cause their macro-economic policies to be coordinated and macro-economic conditions to converge to the norms established in the Treaty.

We may distinguish two paths to monetary union, although they are not mutually exclusive. The first is the Exchange Rate Mechanism path. Here the participating countries agree to maintain more or less fixed parities within specified bands. The bands are progressively tightened over time, and eventually the exchange rates are locked, at which point a common currency may be issued. On this approach the fixity of the exchange rates enforces the monetary and fiscal discipline needed to maintain a country's parity within the ERM and facilitates monetary and fiscal coordination. Recent developments in Europe have pointed up some of the limitations of this approach. If a country goes into the Mechanism at the 'wrong' rate, then its citizens may experience what may be for them, unacceptably high levels of unemployment and interest rates.

The second approach may be termed macro-economic convergence. Here a set of macro-economic conditions favouring monetary union are pre-specified. These may be in terms of inflation performance, the size of the fiscal deficit, the ratio of debt to GDP, etc. Participating countries work toward meeting those convergence conditions which, when met on a sustainable basis, allows the countries to enter monetary union.

In outlining these paths to monetary union, it is important to note that the process is often described in terms of 'stages' or 'phases'. These are intended to structure the move toward economic and monetary union by defining for each stage or phase a certain set of recognizable characteristics or milestones which would allow progress to be measured. Agreement on the stages also helps to extract the political commitment to a process that is not left open-ended and without measurable signposts of progress.

More recently a third path to monetary union has been broached, which may be described as the currency competition model. In this approach restrictions on the use of another country's currency would be lifted, thus allowing currencies to compete. Only currencies of countries with stable low inflation rates would remain. This was the essence of the British 'Hard Ecu' proposal, which however, has not found favour in Europe as a way forward to monetary union.

The CARICOM Initiative

Prior to the recent initiative of CARICOM Heads of Government, there had been little debate or discussion on the merits or otherwise of Caribbean monetary union. Indeed the possibility of strong monetary union seems to have been eschewed in the conceptualization of the Caribbean Community and Common Market, with the framers electing instead for a prescription for a form of weak monetary union. The Commonwealth Caribbean Regional Secretariat under William Demas noted:

> Provided that there is exchange rate stability among Member Countries and provided that these currencies all remain convertible with each other, it is not absolutely necessary to establish a common currency in order to promote effective economic integration-although this would be eminently desirable.[10]

The reasons for this careful avoidance of any notion of strong monetary union at that time seemed to have been essentially political.

William Demas noted:

> For a single independent currency entails a single set of economic, monetary, financial and fiscal policies designed to influence the balance of payments. Such a single set of ... policies is possible only with a high

degree of economic union tantamount to a political union.[11]

Sensitivities about the failed Federation were still raw in political, intellectual and popular circles. In addition, with independent central banks so recently established in newly independent countries, the technocrats of the region were not about to advocate strong monetary union, irrespective of what they might have thought otherwise.

Demas goes on to point out:

> ... in the absence of a political union and with each country having an autonomous monetary system, all that can be hoped for is a high degree of co-operation with respect to monetary and financial policies and policies with regard to exchange rates and exchange controls.[12]

Co-operation among the central banks of the region did begin and found its finest expression in the formation of the CARICOM Multilateral Clearing Facility (CMCF). Academics and researchers in the central banks focused on questions of reserves pooling, exchange rate harmonization and regional stabilization funds as mechanisms to further monetary cooperation.[13]

As the region plunged into difficulties and consequent structural adjustment, monetary cooperation lost ground. Experiments with special CARICOM exchange rates, floating against other CARICOM currencies, the tightening of exchange controls through licensing, and the eventual failure of the CMCF all contributed to the demise of monetary cooperation.

However, Europe's push toward a Single Market by 1992, President Bush's Enterprise for the Americas Initiative and the Canada/USA free trade agreement and the NAFTA negotiations impelled the CARICOM Heads to seek to accelerate the drive toward Caribbean Economic Integration. It was in this context that the Heads at their meeting in Grenada in 1989, broached the question of monetary union and a Single Market for CARICOM, and in 1990, commissioned the Governors of regional Central Banks to undertake a study on how the region might move to a monetary union. The current initiative therefore, does not have its roots in any internal regional dynamic, but it does have the not inconsiderable benefit that there had been some forms of regional monetary co-operation before, whose experiences could inform the construction of the current initiative.

How the current initiative will unfold remains to be seen. The Heads of Government have 'approved' the recommendations of the regional Central Bank Governors for a two-tier, stages approach to monetary integration to be activated in the first instance through a Council of Central Bank Governors who will prepare the ground as it were. There are many sceptics who would point to Caricom's poor record of implementation and conclude that this initiative too will be still born. Recent difficulties in Europe's progress toward monetary union, evidenced in the stumbles in the ratification of the Maastricht Treaty in Denmark and in the U.K, the failure to hold the pound sterling within the ERM and the strains on other currencies, are likely to have given some Caribbean leaders and technocrats pause. In addition, Courtney Blackman has argued that the Governors' Report is not likely to deliver since it required no commitment to immediate action on the part of the region's governments.

Another perceived difficulty is the floating exchange rate regimes in Jamaica, Guyana and Trinidad and Tobago. The Report of the Governors does not seek to institute an ERM but does indicate that these countries should manage their regimes to a point of stability, at which time it would be possible to join a common currency arrangement. The point is that the flexible regimes now operated by those countries were not viewed as insuperable obstacles to monetary integration, but it is recognized that **stability** of exchange rates is crucial to eventual monetary union. A tendency to stability has already been seen in Jamaica and Guyana, and it seems clear that both the monetary authorities and the general public prefer stable exchange rates as the 'nominal anchor' rather than exchange rates which are continually fluctuating.

The objective of Caribbean monetary integration has however been openly acknowledged as desirable and indeed feasible, and this is an advance on the situation 20 years ago. The notion of political union is still only raised in the most guarded tones, and even the West Indian Commission was careful not to put it squarely on the agenda. But some leaders in the Eastern Caribbean have raised this issue as well, and there has been endorsement for some form of closer association between Trinidad and Tobago. Barbados and Guyana. Progress in this matter will inevitably be slow, but the rest of the world is not waiting on the Caribbean to get its act together. The initiatives toward monetary integration as a catalyst for economic and eventual political integration must continue.

Notes

1   For example it is quite common in the Caribbean for people to say that the EC dollar is 'stronger' than the TT dollar or the Guyana dollar since OECS citizens exchange fewer EC dollars for one US dollar than do Trinidad and Tobago and Guyanese citizens. This 'exchange iiiusion' may be dispelled when one points to the high nominal exchange rates of the Japanese Yen or the Korean Won, although it is often not enough to convince many laypeople, for whom presumably, a 'dollar' has more than semantic meaning.

2   Convertibility means that residents of one country are assured that they are able to convert from one currency to another without restriction, for most purposes. The qualification 'for most purposes' is important since some kinds of transactions, particularly capital account transactions, may be restricted by exchange or other controls.

3   This is perhaps at the heart of the current difficulties facing European monetary integration efforts. The Delors Report and the Maastricht Treaty envisage strong monetary union. However, countries like Britain are resisting the political implications of the acceptance of this form of monetary union, especially given concerns that a united Europe might be dominated by Germany. For an analysis of the political dimension see Horst Ungerer, Political Aspects of European Monetary Integration, (unpublished lecture to European University Institute), November 1992.

4   At the level of the household or trade the effect is the same, at the national level however, there will be differential effects across households and industries of a change in the exchange rate.

5   The seminal article here is Robert Mundell (1961).

6   Seignorage is the difference between the face value of a money i.e. its command over goods and services in the economy of issue, and its intrinsic value. With a paper money, or today's coins, the intrinsic value is for all practical purposes zero, and is called a 'fiduciary' Issue, since having no recourse to real assets in the event of default, the value of the money is taken on trust by those who hold it.

7   See the paper by Italianer.

8   See Theodore in Ch. 8 for an extensive discussion of these issues.

9   See M. Fratiani, J. Von Hagen, and C. Waller, The Maastricht Way To EMU, Essays in International Finance, Princeton University, No. 187, June 1992 and Hilaire et al. Ch. 6.

10   From CARIFTA to Caribbean Community, Commonwealth Caribbean Regional Secretariat, Georgetown, 1972, p.95.

11   William Demas, 'Some Thoughts on Caribbean Community,' p. 54, in W. Demas, *West Indian Nationhood and Caribbean Integration*, CCC Publishing, Barbados, 1974.

12   Ibid.

13   See C.Y. Thomas, Reserve Adequacy and Regional Cooperation in Reserve and Payments Management, Regional Programme of Monetary Studies Conference, 1973, and Worrell, DeLisle, 'A Common Stabilization Fund for the Caricom region' Central Bank of Barbados, 1976.

Issues in the Government and Politics of the West Indies: A Reader Edited By John Gaffar Laguerre

Factors in the Integration and Disintegration of the Caribbean

Peter W. Wickham

Introduction

Integration can be defined as either a "process" toward, or "end product" of social, political or economic unification among separate national units within geographical proximity of one another,[1] while disintegration refers to the converse situation. Such a definition is appropriately wide since integration can take any of the above-mentioned forms. This essay will, however, pay special attention to the factors influencing political integration, since it is rigorously defined in the literature and has, until recently, been central to Caribbean efforts. Social and economic integration are comparatively new concepts which will be examined in light of more contemporary exercises.

Contemporary thinking has defined the Caribbean region as embracing all countries in the Caribbean basin, in addition to mainland American nations (Demas 1995, 95), however, the traditional concept of a Commonwealth Caribbean will be used throughout the essay. Hence, discussions will be confined largely to an examination of integration and disintegration among anglophone Caribbean countries with a wider orientation being reserved for discussions of future initiatives at integration.

Caribbean development is going through a phase where traditional prescriptions for development are unable to respond to current demands. Political integration has traditionally represented a model for Caribbean development which, like other models such as Industrialization by Invitation and the Non Capitalist Path, seems not to be working. It is therefore important that factors influencing the success or failure of integration be discussed in an effort to better understand its processes and potential benefits. The approach being utilized is, however, unusual since several writings on this subject adopt a historical perspective, which chronicles the events, instead of examining the factors influencing integration or disintegration. These factors are significant and can help explain why a particular initiative was successful or unsuccessful.

The discussion will be framed around two distinct historical epochs, namely the pre and post federal era. These historical periods, reflect two distinctively different approaches to integration among Caribbean countries and are also conveniently characterized by different stimuli. In each instance therefore, the integration exercise will be described and factors impacting on its existence and demise examined in some detail. Regarding more current initiatives described as integration, the discussion will attempt a synopsis of these efforts, as well as an examination of the contemporary efforts influencing such activity.

Pre-Federal Associations

The anglophone Caribbean has a history of formal association which dates back to the time of the first British settlement. Indeed there is even evidence to suggest the presence of an informal network for association among indigenous West Indian populations which predates formal exercises initiated by the British (Walker 1992; Burland 1970). The early British West Indian settlements could have represented the most integrated state of the region to date, since islands all shared one government, albeit the British government. Hence, a major inducement to integrate came from the British with their concern for administrative economy. Until 1671, the British established a governor in chief at Barbados with responsibility for the entire Lesser Antilles. During this period the governor in Chief exercised several powers in almost every sphere of government, hence the sharing of a governor was almost akin to the sharing of a government, the ultimate aim of integration efforts.

The interest in administrative economy gave way to a more pertinent concern, that of defense. Here, the administrative proximity required by defense concerns militated against shared governorship and separate governors were established. This situation represents possibly the first conflict of Caribbean integration. The logic of administrative amalgamation was juxtaposed to the need to react to current national demands, which in this instance were defense concerns.

Following this setback, the British attempted to unify areas of the administration in the colonies which they felt amenable to regional action, such as legislation within a uniform assembly. Hence there was an orientation toward disunion which continued until 1833, when the Secretary of state encouraged a reversion to the principle of consolidation. As a result, the Leeward Island act of 1871 was passed, due largely to the perceived administrative economy to be achieved by such an amalgamation. There was, however, a strong sentiment supporting disunion, that came from among the islands' ruling classes who saw union as substantially reducing their influence. Similarly strong resistance to integration was evident amongst the Windward islands, where the most successful initiative lasted until 1767 and united Grenada, St. Vincent, Dominica and Tobago. Anti regional sentiments were possibly strongest in Barbados, where opposition led to the Confederation Riots of 1876. While this did not fully exterminate efforts to include Barbados in future unions, it encouraged the efforts to continue with Barbados being treated somewhat differently.

The West Indies Federation

The association among Caribbean islands which ultimately became the 1958 West Indies Federation (WIF) was motivated by stimuli that were not dissimilar to those influencing pre federal associations. A survey of the documents preparatory to the establishment of the WIF demonstrates that various British commissions recommended closer association as a means of rationalizing British administration in the region. (Wickham 1993). Here, the commission carrying the most weight was the Closer Union Commission of 1933, which recommended that the Leeward and Windward Islands should form one colony under one governor. This recommendation would be the foundation of British policy toward the colonies for the next few decades.

The report of the Moyne Commission and the Second World War inadvertently introduced a new factor to this debate over the unification of Caribbean islands. It was during that period that the Self government idea crystallized significantly, hence any unification of the islands would need to have proceeded after consultation with local interests. As a result an important component in the integration process became the need to demonstrate tangible benefits to these local interests. The benefits being sought here were revealed as early as the meeting preparatory to the first conference on the Closer Association of British West Indian Colonies.[2] This conference, which drew representatives from throughout the West Indies, called for a mix of federation and full internal self government (Mordecai 1968), thus establishing self government as an important condition for unification. The Closer Association Conference produced a draft federal constitution and established a standing committee to guide the region toward unification. This agreed path received considerable support from sev-

eral studies commissioned around the same time. Among these were the reports of the Commission on the Unification of Public Services in the Caribbean Area, the report on the Unification of Customs Operations and Trade within the Caribbean Region and the report on the Regional Economic Committee. These documents all supported the closer integration of the islands and introduced new dimensions to the debate.

The next step in the path toward federation was the London Conference,[3] the first one in the integration experience where all delegates were truly democratically elected, as a result of the extension of the franchise in the colonies. Adjustment to the mode of selection for representatives was significant, since it would translate to a change in the directions given to representatives, where before representatives were responsible only to elite sections of the colonies. Representatives would have now wished to consider several social issues such as unemployment, poverty, malnutrition and housing which were major concerns at that time. Integration of these islands would therefore need to address such matters.

It is important to note here that there was a major difference between the reasons for supporting unification, when viewed from the perspective of the political leaders in the West Indies, as distinct from the populations of the colonies. The latter group was hopeful that federation would address the several social ills existing in the colonies (Seers 1957), while the former group had a more complex reason for support. James (1984) noted that several West Indian leaders at that time desired to ascend to positions they believed their talents and education levels entitled them, but were restricted by the limitations of their colonial status. Hence, if union could provide for greater self government, then the leadership of the region could have been expected to support it to the extent that it could increase their sphere of influence. These two factors, in fact, contained the seeds of disintegration in the first major unification experiment in the region.

Noteworthy is the position adopted by the commercial class in the West Indies which, unlike the labour movement, has often not been identified as a serious contributor to the federal initiative. Brathwaite (1957), notes that the Associated Chambers of Commerce in the West Indies saw benefits in the creation of free trade areas and the establishment of a Customs union. The associated chambers also supported the idea of pursuing what has now come to be known as functional cooperation by supporting the concept of joint representation and focusing attention on practical problems facing the WIC such as the non-existence of shipping facilities. There was, however, a certain territoriality in their positions based in the fact that they ultimately saw industrialization as a process that could occur in each country separately.

The constitution of the WIF which came into operation in 1958 provided for a bicameral parliamentary chamber with a lower house of representatives comprising elected representatives from the colonies numbered according to an arbitrary formula which, favored the larger units. Legislative powers were quite extensive, covering limited foreign affairs matters "as may from time to time be entrusted ... by her Majesty's government"[4] and allowed, as few colonial constitutions did, for a measure of real power and self respect (Lewis 1954). A far more significant feature of the constitution was the fact that it provided for a fixed budget for the initial period of the WIF's existence, a provision which arrested the creative ability of Parliament and facilitated their involvement in several idle and destructive exercises and debates (Wickham 1993).

The failure of the WIF can be viewed against the backdrop of what it possessed as well as what it lacked. In this regard K.C. Wheare (1967, 37) identifies inducements as well as predisposing characteristics which he suggested would either facilitate of militate against any federation. In consideration of these factors, Springer (1962) noted that while there was a strong desire to be independent among the WI islands, along with a hope of economic advantage to be derived, the absence of serious military threat reduced the influence of the predisposing characteristics identified by Wheare. Similarly, while political institutions in the territories were similar and there was a history of union, the remoteness of Jamaica meant that the inducement of geographical proximity was less strong. An analysis of these factors provides a theoretical insight into the reasons for the failure of the WIF.

Specifically, several disintegrative factors can be identified which were both structural and political. What appeared to be a most significant political issue was that of leadership. The constitution provided for a ceremonial governor, but executive leadership was to be drawn from the House of Representatives. The chosen PM therefore was Sir Grantley H. Adams, an accidental choice, inasmuch as he did not represent one of the larger islands (Mordecai 1968). The person expected to assume leadership of the party winning the federal elections, the West Indies Federal Labour Party (WIFLP), was Norman Manley, premier of Jamaica. He, however, opted to remain at home, in a

move which cast doubt on the importance, power and longevity of the WIF. Since the next logical person (Dr. Eric Williams of Trinidad and Tobago) was not affiliated to the WIFLP, the lot fell to Adams. The fact that these two key people were unable to assume leadership of the WIF was significant in destabalizing the union, since it suggested a lack of viability.

Lewis (1957) noted that the office of Prime Minister (PM) of the federation was not generously enough embellished with powers sufficient to ensure that he was master of his own house, indeed the structure suggested that the converse situation should have applied. He had no power to dissolve the House of Representatives or even appoint Senators, powers which are the basis of the power of the PM in the Westminster system. Hence any person assuming the office of PM of the WIF was immediately faced with the problem of governing without the necessary tools and Adams faced a handicap that was no different.

Adams' activities while in office, however, also destabilized the union (Mordecai 1968, 455). Possibly, the best known of his several blunders were his remarks which suggested that when given the power, he would tax the colonies retroactively. This statement did violence to the sense of security of the larger islands and encouraged talk of secession. Further, he developed a penchant for making jokes at the expense of other islands within and outside of Parliament.[5] Adams faced an almost insurmountable task as leader of the WIF, much was expected of him and his tools were very limited. Notwithstanding these difficulties, Adams conducted himself in a manner which did not endear him especially to the larger territories, a major ingredient in the destruction of the WIF. In addition he was unable to secure any necessary support from the WIFLP, since that party existed only in name, having been formed on the eve of the federal elections. It was therefore immature and unable to properly support the policy making role expected of a young federation (Ayearst 1957).

Earlier, it was noted that there was considerable distance between the aspirations of the WI population-and its leadership. Within these aspirations lay the seeds of the issue which ultimately led to the break up of the WIF. Several scholars (Mordecai 1968; Springer 1962; Lewis 1957; Ayearst 1957) have noted that by the time the WIF came into being, the major reason it was formerly desired ceased to be encouraging, or at least it became evident that more attractive means had become available. The reason herein referred to is sovereignty. West Indian leaders and by extension their electorate, desired sovereignty which they associated with federation from the inception of the debate. Hence, when the WIF constitution appeared unable to deliver this level of self government, it created a lack of confidence in the fledgling association. This apprehension was further exacerbated by the fact that even within the federal arrangements, colonies could achieve self government and later were promised independence by the colonial office, a status the WIF was unable to achieve. The WIF's inability to achieve self government was a point of criticism as early as 1954, when the London Conference Plan[6] was debated (Lewis 1957), that being the ultimate expression of independence within the British empire at the time. Since genuine independence was later offered, it was not surprising that some colonies, beginning with Jamaica left the federal arrangement and pursued it individually.

A less significant, but nevertheless important factor in the disintegration of the WIF was the clash of nationalisms within the leadership structure and among the people. Springer (1962) noted that a major factor in the break up of the WIF was the clash between West Indian and island nationalism. He suggested that Jamaican nationalism initiated the break up of the WIF. The strength and timing of this nationalism was identified with strong competent leadership and the improvement of the economy, born out of the bauxite industry. Such a strong economy and leadership contrasted with the poor economies of their regional counterparts (excluding Trinidad and Tobago) and the poor leadership being offered by the WIF. Several other problems were linked to the nationalism issue and have been discussed extensively by commentators such as Lewis (1957) and Ayearst (1957), who noted that concerns were often raised about the absence of immigration policies to prevent a feared influx of immigrants from less prosperous territories. Regarding several of these issues, the larger colonies faced conflict with the smaller territories. The conflict was resolved when Jamaica was offered a solution, independence of their territory, a move which facilitated the ultimate expression of Jamaican nationalism. This clash thus goes to the root of the failure of the WIF and speaks volumes about the problems that future initiatives would need to seek to avoid, as Ayearst (1957) notes, successful federations necessitate the cultivation of a dual loyalty to state and center.

The disintegration of the WIF was also the result of serious problems with the structure of its government (Wickham 1993). While the choice of the Westminster form of government was not surprising, since it was imposed in similar federations such as that existing in Canada, the variation did not allow for a delicate balance of power between local and federal units, as should have been the case with federal arrangements. Lewis (1957) suggests that the lower house was ably equipped to fulfill this mandate since members were elected to it on the basis of population, but in diminishing numbers so that no single territory could dominate the system. He was less optimistic about the Federal Senate, due partially to its nominative character, but mostly due to the manner in which nominations were to be made, bypassing the influence of the PM in favor of nomination by the Governor. Jointly, these two chambers did not guarantee the balance necessary for the success of the WIF.

In addition the WIF retained a system where the Prime Minister was placed as a virtual dictator among his ministers in a questionable arrangement known as *primus inter pares,* that contrast with what applies in the successful federation of the USA. Such an arrangement created friction at two levels firstly, it allowed the PM to identify ministers from his parliamentary party alone and secondly; it reserved elections to the chamber where persons were elected on the basis of population size. Since appointment to the other chamber, the Senate, did nothing to ensure balance between federal and local interest, or even to satisfy the innate desires of large and small territories to be equally represented, it was inevitable that the constitutional arrangement would create confusion among federal politicians who would be facing dual attractions to local and federal politics (Ayearst 1957). Such an arrangement also added the federal structure to a local one producing an indigestible plethora of politicians (Lewis 1968), the cost of which had to be borne by the West Indian tax payer.

The distribution of powers in the WIF was such that Federal Legislature prevailed over local legislatures in the event of conflict and the units held all residual powers not specifically defined. While this arrangement was not, in itself, a source of disequilibrium in the delicate federal balance, the arbitrary distribution of powers was (Lewis 1957). Confusion was therefore created where services such as the postal arrangements and aviation which required uniform regional action, were subject to the vagaries of both local and federal governments. Furthermore, the restrictions placed on the federal constitution during the first five years ensured that conflicts could not be resolved by the empowering of the center as happened in the US ar

rangement. Viewed against the backdrop of other constitutional provisions weakening the centre, this
division of powers would certainly have contributed
to the center-unit imbalance.

One final structural contributor to the disintegration of the federation was the choice of a center for
the union. One early study[7] had suggested that Trinidad
was unsuited for this purpose, it nevertheless became
the choice for political reasons. The problem created
here was that with the center so far south, an important player - Jamaica - was isolated from the heart of
the union. In addition as Lewis (1957) pointed out,
the capital debate was merely a manifestation of strong
island jealousies. Resentment could therefore be expected to follow therefrom and that was exactly the
state of affairs during the existence of the WIF,[8] which
created anti federal sentiments among Jamaicans.

The foregoing factors contributed to the destruction of the first genuine attempt at Caribbean
integration on the political level. It lasted a mere four
years, during which time it was considered irrelevant
to several units. Thereafter, regional politicians in the
LDCs discussed the possibility of establishing the federation of the "Little Eight", which included Barbados.
The "Little Eight" was intended to amalgamate the eight
smaller islands or LDCs in the Caribbean and was also
motivated by the urge to establish a higher level of
self-rule than was available to the individual sates
within the colonial empire. Efforts at establishing the
federation of the "Little Eight" received some support
from the Colonial office, but in the final analysis were
hinged on the involvement of Barbados who was at
the time considered the most progressive of the small
islands (Lewis 1962). Barbados soon capitulated to the
allure of independence in much the same way as her
regional counterparts and hence brought the discussions on the establishment of the Federation of the
"Little Eight" to a definitive close.

Other regional politicians soon turned their attention toward independence which they sought after
in a hurried frenzy. It is important to note that several of the issues which prompted union also
prompted independence. These were the several social ills in the colonies along with desires to achieve
greater self determination. Independence did not go
very far towards addressing many of these issues, indeed it created several new ones, such as high national
debt and the need to generate foreign exchange. These
and other factors prompted moves toward reintegration in the post federal era, based instead on
functional understandings.

Post Federal Associations

The role of the regional institutions surviving the WIF
suggests what factors were likely to influence post federal integration and moreover the shape such
integration would take. Here, the association was functional, as would be demonstrated in the cooperation
to be pursued later. Important ventures were the Regional Meteorological Service (RMS), the University
of the West Indies (UWI) and the Federal Shipping
Service. All these ventures were regional projects which
reflected a Caribbean integration that was functional
and not political in nature. These projects were chosen based on the need for a particular service in the
islands and the impractically of individual action, a
situation best exemplified with reference to the role
played by the RMS. This organization provides the
important weather forecasting service to the islands
which are all too small and too close together to make
individual forecasting feasible, but which nevertheless need such services. Due to this incontrovertible
relationship between demonstrable need and regional
action, these ventures recorded a high level of success
in their first few years of operation, prompting regional
heads to consider more formal arrangements.

The first of these post federal arrangements was
the Caribbean Free Trade Association (CARIFTA).
CARIFTA was initially a three-country association
among Barbados, Guyana and Antigua, which was later
widened to include Jamaica, Trinidad and the LDCS.
CARIFTA intended to remove barriers to trade among
Caribbean islands based on principles of reciprocity.
Such action would have the effect of increasing and
diversifying trade among Caribbean islands as well as
promoting the development of individual islands.

CARIFTA was a likely reaction to several realities
of independence identified earlier. The more significant of these would have been the necessity to create
foreign exchange and boost local industry. As early as
the immediate post independence period, Caribbean
islands would have found it necessary to identify new
markets for locally produced goods, since many traditional markets were locked into the colonial
arrangement from which now independent colonies
were no longer likely to benefit. Against this reality
was placed the impracticality of a full political union
based on past experiences. The idea of functional cooperation hence offered itself as a convenient half way
measure between full integration and separate arrangements. Such a direction was also likely to be influenced
by the increasing popularity, at that time, of this type
of approach to integration in Europe. Europe mani-

fested a similar cultural heterogeneity to the Caribbean, suggesting that both regions could receive similar treatment regarding integration. In addition, a large number of West Indian leaders received their tertiary education in Europe and were heavily influenced by this trend in regional development.

While fragile, due to its proximity to the failed federation, CARIFTA recorded some success regarding increased trade, at least among the MDCS. Among this group trade increased by some 65% (Payne 1980, 120) over the 4-year period 1967-1970. In addition, it was able to facilitate the establishment of a regional development bank, the Caribbean Development Bank (CDB), which would become pivotal in securing balanced development up to the present. While this success would become a factor in later integration of Caribbean islands, it also highlighted a major problem that could cause this fragile association to disintegrate. This was the longstanding disparity between the MDCs and the LDCs regarding benefits from trade associations. Briefly, such associations did and will continue to benefit the MDCs more significantly since that is where the major export centers are located. As a result, free trade area's merely provide a conduit via which goods can flow freely and cheaply from the MDCs to the LDCs often resulting in higher prices and loss of revenues for the LDCS.

CARIFTA manifested an ability to synthesize MDC trade advantages with LDC developmental concerns. Here, a component significant to the later integration of the Caribbean can be identified, the establishment of the CDB, a regional development bank based in Barbados. The CDB was intended to create a pool of funds to assist in the development of the LDCS, in the hope that they could be brought *en par* eventually, or at least that the deleterious effects of unequal development would be minimized. It would also act as a conduit to channel funds from the MDCs to the LDCs into specific projects aimed at boosting development. As a result of the establishment of the CDB, the disquiet created by the unequal benefits of CARIFTA were minimized and not allowed to be a contributor to the break up of this fragile association.

With the negative impacts of CARIFTA minimized, for the time being, the region was able to move toward the establishment of the Caribbean Community (CARICOM), the current focus of regional integration. CARICOM was the result of the convergence of several factors and a large amount of good fortune. CARICOM had its origins around 1971 with the release of a feasibility study on the Common External

Tariff (CET). The CET called for the elevation of the association to a significantly higher level, representing a closer form of integration. The success of this elevation, however faced several problems, including a less than cooperative Jamaica Labour Party (JLP) government, a problem resolved by the 1971 general elections in Jamaica. This election occurred shortly after Mr. William Demas assumed office as Secretary General of CARIFTA. Demas' commitment to the establishment of CARICOM was demonstrated by two publications *CARIFTA and the* New *Caribbean*[9] and *From CARIFTA to Caribbean Community,*[10] which together formed a blueprint for regional integration. Conveniently, the two documents were made available to the 7th Heads of Government Conference in October 1972 and impacted heavily on the outcome. The arguments articulated in these two documents coincided nicely with a softening of the LDC position and the new attitude displayed by Jamaica to Caribbean integration. The result was a decision to upgrade CARIFTA to CARICOM.

The CARICOM treaty[11] sought to establish a common market, which in addition to the free trade provisions of the CARIFTA treaty introduced a Common External Tariff (CET) and Common Protective Policy (CPP). In addition, it established the Caribbean Community as a larger entity, pursuing functional cooperation in areas such as health and foreign affairs. Significant also were the activities specifically ruled out in the treaty, including provisions for the freedom of movement, or monetary union. The intention of the latter stipulation was reversed in a subsequent declaration.[12]

It is important to note that the treaty of Chaguaramas in no way represented an integrated state for the Caribbean, instead it was the optimum unification manageable at that point in Caribbean development. Moreover, it outlined objectives and goals which turned out to be quite optimistic. The organization has, however, existed up to the present, notwithstanding frequent signs that dissolution was imminent. The issues surrounding CARICOM's instability are both internal to CARICOM, the region and external of the region.

Possibly the most significant intra CARICOM factor provoking disintegration is the organization's inability to deliver, a problem best illustrated with reference to the (CET) experience. The CET was identified closely with the establishment of CARICOM, as necessary to the fulfillment of its objectives. It is a requisite mechanism which ensures equally high, or low, tariffs throughout the country against external goods. This protects the integrity of the community and discourages practices such as re-exporting within the community. The CET had, however, not been implemented by some 10% of the population by 1993 (Wickham 1993), after having missed some three deadlines for implementation. The factors explaining the failure of implementation are basic and associated with the interests of CARICOM member states. Among the first countries to implement the CET was Trinidad and Tobago, no doubt due to the existence of a well developed local manufacturing sector which would benefit from high and secure external tariffs'. Conversely, the LDCs imported several items externally, hence, high import tariffs threatened to severely increase the cost of living. The tariff was therefore in the interest of some countries and not others, thus making consensus difficult. It is because of this way in which governments have behaved towards CARICOM that cracks in the organization have become more pronounced. Since so much was based on the CET, the fact that it has not been implemented has hampered the proper functioning of the community. The community is therefore unable to deliver what is promised and now appears obsolete.

The CET experience accurately mirrors the general situation within CARICOM, where several agreements are made to strengthen the organization, or merely pursue a particular policy. Upon reflection, however, these agreements are not implemented at the local level where action is required, thus constituting a major impediment to integration, or a contributor to disintegration. Recent evidence of this lies in the decision to allow freedom of movement to university graduates within the region by January 1996,[13] a decision requiring legislative action by all common market members, action which by that date had only been taken by Guyana and since then by CARICOM members including Barbados and Trinidad and Tobago, which restricted the categories of employees to Accountants, Dentists, Doctors, Lawyers and Engineers. Often, this reluctance to act has less to do with commitment to integration than practical, often political reasons why local leaders cannot act. Regarding the freedom of movement issue, the case of Barbados is easily the most illustrative. Barbados has a population density of 597 per sq. km (Marshall 1992), the highest in the Caribbean and one of the highest in the world. As a result Barbadian leaders are hesitant to engage in any legislative act which will exacerbate this critical situation that can have serious social fallout.

CARICOM has often been impeded by experiences which impacted negatively on a particular member state and left a "bitter taste" regarding future action in these areas. One such was the experience with the CARICOM Multilateral Clearing Facility (CMCF). This facility was alluded to in the Annex to the treaty of Chaguaramas[14] and was established on January 16, 1977. The CMCF was supervised by the Trinidad and Tobago Central Bank and established a line of credit to participants in US dollars, allowing for the settlement of payments between participating countries up to a maximum of US $40 million. It was used for CARICOM trade and covered the sale of CARICOM currencies in commercial banks in respect of these transactions, thereby conserving hard currency.

After a successful two year period, the facility was expanded and extended. A successful period, however, preceded the total collapse of the facility. This collapse arose out of indiscipline mainly on the part of Guyana which almost exhausted all of the facilities credit and caused its termination in 1982. It has left Guyana indebted to many of its CARICOM partners up to the present and has created a bogey which militates against any reintroduction of this necessary financial scheme. Furthermore, the millions of dollars owed, mainly by Guyana to her CARICOM partners is often cited as a reason to question the motives of regional partners, creating a serious sociopsychological impediment to integration.

The frequency with which these apparently insurmountable problems in the integration movement arose and the increasing international pressures, gave rise to the establishment of the Independent West Indian Commission (WIC) in 1989. The report of this body of eminent West Indians has become central to the future of Caribbean integration. It concluded, *inter alia*, that in light of changes taking place in the global political economy, Caribbean development would benefit from the pursuit of a unified community. In addition it also made suggestions concerning ways to overcome perennial problems within CARICOM such as implementation, as well as recommending complementary ventures like freedom of movement and a common currency. These, the WIC argued, were needed to ensure that CARICOM functioned as an effective community.

The significance of the WIC to the future of Caribbean integration lay in the fact that for its three-year existence it focused the region's attention on the problems associated with Caribbean integration and examined these in some detail. Their resulting report correctly identified several of the problems of Caribbean integration, however, their proposals were timid and in some cases unlikely to address the problem identified and as a result do not constitute a significant factor in the future of the Caribbean integration movement (Wickham 1994). The WIC's report did raise several social issues such as the role of women and cultural integration initiatives in addition to suggesting the establishment of a "CARICOM Commission." The latter proposal was not taken, but gave rise to the establishment of an "Implementation Bureau" comprising past and present chairmen of CARICOM and the Secretary General. The preoccupation of the members of this body with domestic matters is likely to ensure that it plays a very insignificant role in the future of integration of the Caribbean. Proposals likely to be of greater significance would be the proposal to establish the Association of Caribbean States (ACS), discussed later and the Assembly of Caribbean Parliamentarians (ACP) which had its inaugural session in 1996.

While integration has been pursued at the macro level, developments have been taking place within regional institutions which provide useful examples of integration and disintegration. The factors motivating these activities are instructive as to the currents affecting integration at the macro level. The UWI is one such regional institution. UWI's precursor, the University College of the West Indies (UCWI), predated the WIF by some 18 years and was driven by a desire to provide tertiary education to West Indians within the region (Sherlock and Nettleford 1990; Brathwaite 1954). The possibility of this being done at the local level was at the time not even the remotest possibility. During this period the Caribbean was a group of colonies, hence the significance of the British influence in the regional approach to education cannot be ignored.

However, even after the UWI gained full university status in 1963, it continued to be managed in a highly centralized manner from the headquarters in Mona Jamaica, notwithstanding the establishment of campuses in Trinidad and Barbados and several university centres throughout the entire eastern Caribbean non campus territories. Ironically, the UWI first pursued a decentralization programme in an effort to maintain a regional character. Hence campuses in Trinidad and Barbados were established with separate principals, administrations and even duplication of programmes in some instances. Here is an instance where apparent disintegration was effected to maintain regionalism. Such action was initiated by the desire to expand programmes into areas such as engineer-

ing, coupled with the ability of the Trinidad and Tobago government and no other to fund this expansion. Further decentralization of UWI took place in 1984 giving individual campuses greater powers of internal management. Most recently, the Chancellor's commission on governance recommended even further decentralization giving campuses the necessary power to ensure that relevant decisions are taken "closer to the scene of the activity involved" (UWI 1994, 12). These adjustments away from central governance, far from characterizing disintegration, act to regularize clumsy management arrangements and reduce cost which could ultimately threaten the existence of the institution. The regional fabric of the UWI is for the time being maintained by a common Chancellor, Vice Chancellor and central administration located in Jamaica. In this instance, economic reality and access demands have required that UWI be decentralized, but the institution remains regional in character.

Other examples of regional cooperation have not been as successful. Among them British West Indian Airways (BWIA) and Leeward Islands Air Transport (LIAT) provide useful examples. The latter is genuinely a regional airline, with an ownership which mirrors the membership of CARICOM, while BWIA's ownership has always been essentially Trinidadian. Both of these airlines have lost considerable sums of money and represent a financial burden on the region's taxpayers. At the same time, they provide a service which is necessary, especially to the LDCS. As the financial situation becomes more acute within the region, governments have pursued privatization programmes which threaten the regional character of the airlines. In addition the governments of Barbados and the Organization of Eastern Caribbean States (OECS) purchased interest in the now defunct CARIB EXPRESS, a private sector venture established to compete with and threaten the existence of LIAT, These acts appear to represent a move away from integrated activities and are motivated by economic realities facing individual governments.

Factors in the Future of Caribbean Integration

The foregoing has examined several factors contributing to apparent disintegration in the Caribbean. Hence, some of the issues likely to influence integration and disintegration in the future of the regional movement will now need to be examined. Initially, it was observed that Caribbean unity originated with administrative economy and it seems likely that such economy will continue to be sought after. Current evidence suggests that our governments are growing too large, compared with other countries (Dalrymple and Zephirin 1992). Barbados demonstrates this trend where the cost of government has risen approximately by 214% between 1980 and 1989 (IMF 1992), prompting the suggestion that sharing of certain government services would result in lower cost. However, as figure 1 demonstrates, the per capita cost of central government need not necessarily become lower within a political union, since both the federations of the USA and Canada have higher per capita cost than Barbados does. Therefore, the prospect of administrative economy is not likely to be a significant consideration in the future of the integration movement.

Stronger urges toward integration come from threats to the sovereignty of Caribbean islands and the likelihood that a united region could offer greater protection against these threats. In this regard economic threats are manifested in the role played by institutions such as the International Monetary Fund (IMF) in Caribbean countries. This role ensures that major decisions affecting Caribbean countries are made by agencies external to the countries in question. In the case of devaluations recommended for Jamaica, Guyana and Trinidad and Tobago, such decisions have had a negative impact on the quality of life of the citizens of these countries. Recently, the US ambassador to Barbados made an unusual reference to the significance of US influence when he suggested that Caribbean islands were not being "friendly" to the US by voting against them in the United Nations (UN) and at other international fora.[15] He encouraged a return to former friendliness.

Sovereignty in the Caribbean can therefore be, at best, described as dubious. Each island has the titular trappings of Prime Ministers. However, they are constrained in the execution of public policy by the preferred foreign policy programme of the US. The hope that a united Caribbean can reverse this trend acts as a strong inducement to integration within the Caribbean currently. This thinking has gained support following recent successful battles waged by CARICOM. One such was the decision to raise the head tax on cruise ships coming into the Caribbean. More striking, however, was the change in attitude of the Caribbean governments toward Cuba, for years alienated by the US and the Caribbean.[16] CARICOM made a surprise decision recently to send a trade mission to Cuba, in addition to inviting her to observe CARICOM's operations, a move that was in direct defiance of current US policy. This trend has continued more recently, as CARICOM has refused to tighten sanctions on Cuba in reaction to the shooting down of two Cuban/American planes. Such militant action on the part of CARICOM suggests that the sovereignty of Caribbean islands is more likely to be realized as a group, than individually.

FIGURE 1: CRUDE PER CAPITA COST OF CENTRAL GOVERNMENT

	Barbados	Canada	USA
Total Cost of Government			
1980 [1]	531,900,000	65,522,000,000	596,640,000,000
1989 [2]	1,136,800,000	148,962,000,000	1,429,050,000,000
Total population			
1980 [3]	249,000	24,067,000	227,757,000
1989 [4]	251,241	26,449,633	244,155,504
Per capita cost of Government			
1980	2,136.145	2,722.483	2,619.634
1989	4,524.739	5,631.912	5,853.032

Notes:

1. Source: Government Finance Statistics Yearbook 1992, International Monetary Fund 1992.
2. Source: Government Finance Statistics Yearbook 1992, International Monetary Fund 1992.
3. Source: 1992 PC Globe, Inc. Tempe, AZ USA/ National Government Statistics.
4. Estimate based on 1980 figures and population growth estimates. Source: 1992 PC Globe, Inc. Tempe, AZ USA/ Compilation of National Government Statistics

Current trends in the world economy form possibly the strongest inducement to reintegration among Caribbean countries. Increasingly, the world is becoming globalized, a feature which is having several impacts on the Caribbean. Globalization received a boost with the ending of the cold war and is characterized by increased world trade, reduced production and the emergence of mega trading blocs throughout the world (Demas 1989). The process has been triggered by technological developments which facilitate easy communication throughout the world.

Traditionally, countries sought to maximize their "comparative advantage" with regard to particular natural resources, to secure trade advantages. Global trends have, however, internationalized the production processes. As a result production is segmented and goods are often assembled where conditions are most favorable and advantages can be as transitory as a particular government's policy to which they are linked. This has been demonstrated in the highly successful East Asian countries. Among them, Singapore has few natural resources but has been able to secure economic growth averaging 9.4% in the 70's with a per capita GDP of US $5,196 in 1983 (Woronoff 1986). The challenge therefore is for a country to provide producers conditions which are attractive. Such conditions can often not be located in one country, but require community action from organizations such as CARICOM.

The recent strengthening of the General Agreement on Tariffs and Trade (GATT), now the World Trade Organization (WTO) has been indicative of a move toward greater trade liberalization in the world. Such activities are no longer highly regulated and any government interference is discouraged, ranging from subsidies to overt protectionism. This places producers in small islands in a position where they have to bring their production processes and marketing up to international standards of efficiency to allow them to compete. Such changes are aided by the existence of large home markets for the initial marketing of goods, as well as a pool from which skilled labour can be drawn. Such a market is unlikely to be available in any single Caribbean country.

The foregoing approach to production and trade has resulted in the increasing popularity of regionalism in world trade. The developing world is currently maximizing its advantages by establishing mega trading blocs such as the European Community (EU) and the North American Free Trade Area (NAFTA) which are both critical for the Caribbean. The effects of these blocs on the Caribbean are twofold; firstly as has already happened, these blocs can degenerate into large secure markets protected from outside influence by high external tariffs and countries outside of these blocs will thus have significant difficulty accessing these markets. The second consequence is less obvious, but more important to the Caribbean. These blocs have the potential to undermine a major premise of Caribbean Trade-the exploitation of protected markets guaranteed because of the historical exploitation of traditional linkages. Such traditional markets can no longer be justified since new protocols require concrete justifications instead of mere tradition. Unfortunately, these markets exist for export of agricultural products central to the economic survival of the LDCS. In this regard, the EU has already begun to impact on the Caribbean Banana trade in favour of the Latin American alternative, which is cheaper and similar in quality. In response to this world trend, CARICOM would find the establishment of a viable trading group an indispensable ingredient to its development.

The severity of regional imperatives favoring integration raises the issue of the appropriate size and membership for Caribbean cooperation. Current trends suggest that integration needs to embrace a body significantly larger than the English-speaking Caribbean. The WIC, referred to earlier, recommended that Caribbean integration be widened to include countries within the Caribbean that are non English-speaking such as Cuba, Venezuela and the Dominican Republic (WIC 1992, 447). Hence the idea of an ACS was introduced into Caribbean integration and has since become a reality. The fact that this association exists in addition to CARICOM can be viewed as a signal that CARICOM is being phased out, or as an attempt to widen the influence of CARICOM, while the core states continue their previous programme of integration. Regardless, the ACS has raised several issues which must be examined in the future of the integration movement.

One important concern is the fact that the ACS is numerically superior to CARICOM by some 97% (Demas 1995). It is therefore important that CARICOM's core states strengthen their production and general economies to ensure that they do not suffer some of the effects that the LDCs in CARICOM now suffer. In addition, there are some political concerns raised by virtue of the fact that CARICOM is now approaching quasi political dimensions by considering ventures such as the ACP, freedom of movement and the unification of currencies, after having overcome the difficulties created by considerable heterogeneity among members. The introduction of new territories, with even more diverse economies and cultures, therefore has the potential to hinder the CARICOM advance, in pursuit of a dubious advantage. In looking at this question, however, the real significance of these quasi political moves is likely to be seen as marginal considering the limited impact that such a small community can have in the first place. Furthermore, such activities may, upon reflection, not be central to a successful economic community. Regardless, the ACS has taken the Caribbean into a new dimension in integration and is likely to become an increasingly important player in the movement.

In the geopolitical arena, developments have taken place which encourage reintegration in the region. Two of these are important to this discussion the first being associated with the ending of the cold war. This has created an ideological homogeneity in the world that would no longer allow countries in the backyard of the US to "play off" West against the East. In addition, several eastern European countries are moving toward traditional market type practices and are competing for developmental assistance to which they are now entitled. Caribbean islands that have historically received heavy developmental assistance would now need to pay greater attention to generating revenue on their own.

The foregoing has examined the tangible factors in the integration and disintegration of the Caribbean. There are, however, several intangible factors worthy of examination. Among these are psychological, cultural and sociological factors, none of which have received the type of treatment here or in existing literature, that tangible factors have. The Caribbean shares a common historical experience, language and cricketing experience, along with involvement in several successful regional organizations discussed above (Demas 1995). This association has both positive and negative aspects, as it demonstrates both similarities and differences that divide the region. Certainly, however, this socio-cultural tradition needs to be further exploited to support integration efforts at other levels.

Conclusion

The foregoing has examined the various factors influencing moves, toward and away from Caribbean integration, that have been characteristic of three distinct historical epochs. These eras have reflected a momentum supporting integration, followed by failure, redirection and now increasing support. Several

distinctive trends can be identified in the factors influencing integration and these will be reviewed shortly. However, it is significant to note that after close to four hundred years of experimentation with Caribbean union, the forces influencing it have caused the objective of "political integration" to be altered. Hence, current efforts are directed at establishing a workable union which avoids political dimensions with all the attendant complications so that integration is increasingly becoming more functional.

Integration in the pre federal era was seen to have been motivated by factors largely external to the Caribbean, due to the islands colonial status. Here, the reduction of cost to the mother country was defined as the main motivating factor and was reflected in experiments which essentially established joint governorships. These structures were, however, soon dismantled because of the need to respond to the reality of warfare, a concern which could not be addressed within the clumsy joint management structures of the islands.

The federal experiment was initially motivated by stimuli similar to that of the pre federal era. However, to this was soon added local support. Such support was predicated on the belief that self government, greater sovereignty and less exploitation could be derived via this mechanism. The Caribbean people took the movement forward from that point and the British influence became less significant as independence was granted and their concern for high cost disappeared. These concerns for sovereignty later became the root of the demise of the WIF as the union appeared unable to deliver the level of sovereignty required of it. Hence the Caribbean leaders and by extension the people reacted accordingly.

The realities of independence have been the main motivation encouraging association following the failure of the WIF. It has caused the region to search for a development model which would yield the benefits demanded of the population. Often such development is constricted by the limitations of our size. Hence, integration has been considered once more. However, hindsight has suggested that the political component is omitted. This approach as been relatively successful, but has been hampered by minor conflicts such as the unequal benefits accruing to the states. The region has, as a consequence, established CARIFTA and more recently CARICOM, the organization that is now being developed. CARICOM too has problems, due to its inability to deliver on promises and again, the limitations of size. Concerns such as these have led to a deepening and widening of the organization to include other countries in the Caribbean region in a looser organization. This direction has not been characterized as damaging to the integration movement, but a redefinition of integration characteristic of trends in the International Political Economy. Similar forces that have shaped the EU and NAFTA are the need to establish large viable trading groups to maximize trading opportunities. The widening of CARICOM is a reaction to such forces to provide similar benefits to the regions' producers and traders, or alternatively to minimize the negative impacts of the existence of other trading blocs.

More recently social forces have been becoming more pronounced in the integration movement, a direction which is also characteristic of an era in which NGOs are gaining popularity and greater democratization is occurring. As with other eras, these factors are not only influencing decisions to integrate, but are also defining the level at which integration takes place and the dimensions of cooperative arrangements. The responsiveness of the regional movement to these factors should ensure that integration is both meaningful and successful.

Notes

1. This definition of regional integration was constructed using the opinions of Columbis & Wolfe 1990; Balassa 1961 and Plano & Olton 1988.
2. Montego Bay Jamaica, 11-19 Sept. 1947.
3. The Conference on the West Indian Federation, held in London England, April, 1953.
4. The West Indies (Federation) Order in Council 1957, Annex, Sec. 2(1).
5. Mordecai, 1968 p.126 discusses damaging extra parliamentary remarks, while Wickham, 1993, Appendix I details intra parliamentary remarks.
6. The London Plan arose from the Report of the Conference on the West Indian Federation.
7. The 1956 Report on the British Caribbean Federation Capital Commission.
8. One of the federal MPs Mr. Densham discussed this issue extensively in the course of federal debates. (Hansard Parliamentary Debates, 1960 Col. 2064).
9. Georgetown Guyana: Commonwealth Caribbean Regional Secretariat, 1971.
10. *Ibid*, 1972.
11. The Treaty Establishing the Caribbean Community, also known as the Treaty of Chaguaramas, signed initially on 4, July 1973 and coming into effect on 1, August 1973.
12. The Kingston Declaration, 1990.
13. The July, 1995 Heads of Government conference agreed to freedom of Movement for University Graduates and other skilled categories of workers, by January 1996.
14. Article 43, (3) (b).
15. Barbados Advocate, July II, 1992.

16. The WIC Report noted that the CARICOM should take/ play an active role in the process of ending the physical trade embargo against Cuba.

Additional Readings

Pre Federal Integration

Spackman, A. *Constitutional Development of the West Indies; 1922-1968*. London: Caribbean Universities Press in association with Bowker Publishing Company, 1975.

Wrong, Hume. *Government in the West Indies*. 1923. Reprint. New York: Negro University Press, 1969.

Wallace, Elisabeth. *The British Caribbean; from the Decline of Colonialism to the end of Federation*. Toronto: Toronto University Press.

The Rise and Fall of the West Indies Federation

Ayearst, Morley. "Political Aspects of Federation." *Social and Economic Studies* Vol. 6 No. 2 (June 1957) 247-195.

Brathwaite, Lloyd. "Federal Associations and Institutions in the British West Indies." *Social and Economic Studies* Vol. 6 No. 2 (June 1957) 247-195.

Lestrade, Swinburne. "Political Aspects of Integration in the Windward and Leeward Islands." *Caribbean Quarterly* Vol. 18 No. 2 (June 1972) 28-35.

Lewis, W. Arthur. "The Agony of the Eight." Bridgetown: Advocate, 1962.

Lewis, Gordon K. *The Growth of the Modern West Indies*. New York: Monthly Review Press, 1968.

"West Indian Federation: The Constitutional Aspects." *Social and Economic Studies* Vol.6 No. 2 (June 1957) 215-245.

Lewis, Vaughan. "Small States in the International Society: with special reference to the associated states." *Caribbean Quarterly* Vol. 18 No. 2 (June 1972) 36-47.

Lowenthal, David. "Two Federations." *Social and Economic Studies* Vol. 6 No. 2 (June 1957) 185-197.

Menon, P.K. "Regional Integration: A Case Study of the Caribbean Community [CARICOM]." *Caribbean Law Review* Vol. 5 No. I (June 1995) 81-143.

Mordecai, John. *The West Indies; the Federal Negotiations*. London: Allen & Unwin, 1968.

Roberts G.W. "Some Demographic Considerations of West Indian Federation." *Social and Economic Studies* Vol. 6 No. 2 (June 1957) 262-285.

Sires, Ronald V. "Government in the British West Indies: An Historical Outline." *Social and Economic Studies* Vol. 6 No. 2 (June 1957) 109-133.

Springer, Hugh. *Reflections on the Failure of the West Indies Federation*. Occasional Paper No. 4. Boston: Harvard Center for International Affairs, Harvard University 1962.

U.K. The West Indies (Federation) Order in Council, 1957, No. 1364.

U.K. *Report of Conference on the Closer Association of the British West Indian Colonies*. September 1947. Montego Bay, Jamaica. Parts I and II. London: H.M.S.O., 1947.

Wallace, Elisabeth. *The British Caribbean; from the Decline of Colonialism to the end of Federation*. Toronto: University of Toronto, 1977.

West Indies Federation *Hansard Parliamentary Debates*, (1958-62)

Wheare, K.C. *Federal Government*. Oxford: Oxford University Press, 1967.

Wickham, Peter. "Prospects for a United Caribbean: A Historico-Political Analysis of the Future of the Caribbean Integration

Movement." Master's thesis, University of the West Indies, 1993.

Post Federal Integration and CARICOM

Boxill, I. *Ideology and Caribbean Integration.* Kingston: Consortium Graduate School of Social Sciences, University of the West Indies 1993.

Brewster, H., and C.Y. Thomas. *The Dynamics of West Indian Economic Integration.* Kingston: Institute of Social and Economic Research, University of the West Indies, 1967.

Caribbean Community Secretariat. *The Caribbean Community in the 1980s;* Report by a group of Caribbean Experts. Georgetown: Caribbean Community Secretariat, 1981.

Commonwealth Caribbean Regional Secretariat. *CARIFTA and the New Caribbean.* Georgetown, Guyana: Commonwealth Caribbean Regional Secretariat, 1971.

_____. *From CARIFTA to Caribbean Community.* Georgetown: Guyana, Commonwealth Caribbean Regional Secretariat, 1972.

Demas, William G. *Essays on Caribbean Integration and Development.* Kingston: Institute of Social and Economic Research, University of the West Indies, 1976.

Lestrade, Swinburne. *CARICOM's Less Developed Countries: A Review of the Progress of the LDCs Under the CARICOM Arrangements.* Cave Hill: Institute of Social and Economic Research (Eastern Caribbean), University of the West Indies, 1981.

Mills, Gladstone E., Sir Carlisle Burton, and O'Neil J. Lewis. *Report on a Comprehensive Review of Programmes, Institutions and Organisations of the Caribbean Community.* Georgetown: Caribbean Community Secretariat, 1990.

Payne, Anthony. *The Politics of the Caribbean Community 1961-79, Regional Integration among New States.* Manchester: Manchester University Press, 1980.

Segal, Aaron. *The Politics of Caribbean-Economic Integration.* Rio Piedras, Puerto Rico: Institute of Caribbean Studies, University of Puerto Rico, 1968.

"Ten Years of CARICOM." Papers presented at a Seminar sponsored by the Inter-American Development Bank, Barbados, July 1983. Washington, D.C. 1984.

Wickham, Peter W. "More Shadow Than Substance." *Caribbean Affairs* Vol. 7 No.3 (July/August 1994) 38-61.

The Future of Caribbean Integration

Demas, William G. *Consolidating our Independence: The Major Challenge for the West Indies.* Distinguished Lecture Series. St. Augustine: Institute of International Relations, University of the West Indies, 1986.

_____. *Towards West Indian Survival.* Occasional Paper, No. 1. Black Rock, Barbados: The Independent West Indian Commission Secretariat, 1989.

_____. *West Indian Development and The Deepening and Widening of the Caribbean Community.* Kingston: Institute of Social and Economic Research, University of the West Indies, 1994.

Farrell, Terrence, and Delisle Worrell (eds). *Caribbean Monetary Integration.* Port of Spain: Caribbean Information Systems and Services Limited, 1994.

Independent West Indian Commission. *Time for Action; The Report of the West Indian Commission.* Black Rock, Barbados: The Independent West Indian Commission, 1992.

Robinson, Arthur N. R. "The West Indies Beyond 1992." Paper presented to the 1989 Heads of Government Conference of CARICOM, Grand Anse, Grenada, 1990.

Worrell, Delisle. *A Common Currency for the Caribbean.* Occasional Paper No.4. Black Rock, Barbados: The Independent West Indian Commission, 1992.

Wickham, Peter W. "Some Theoretical and Political Considerations on the Manning Initiative." *Bulletin of Eastern Caribbean Affairs* Vol. 19 No. 2 (June 1994) 25-37.

Select Bibliography

Ayearst, Morley. "Political Aspects of Federation." *Social and Economic Studies* Vol. 6 No. 2 (June 1957)247-195.

Boxil, I. *Ideology and Caribbean Integration.* Kingston: Consortium Graduate School of Social Sciences, University of the West Indies 1993.

Brathwaite, Lloyd. "Federal Associations and Institutions in the British West Indies." *Social and Economic Studies* Vol. 6 No. 2 (June 1957) 247-195.

Commonwealth Caribbean Regional Secretariat. *CARIFTA and the New Caribbean.* Georgetown, Guyana: Commonwealth Caribbean Regional Secretariat, 1971.

From CARIFTA to Caribbean Community. Georgetown: Guyana, Commonwealth Caribbean Regional Secretariat, 1972.

Dalrymple, Kelvin and Mary Zephirin. "The Role of the State." Paper prepared for presentation at the Central Bank of Barbados Research Department's Annual Review Seminar, Bridgetown Barbados, August 13-14,1992.

Demas, William G. *Towards West Indian Survival.* Occasional Paper, no. 1. Black Rock, Barbados: The Independent West Indian Commission Secretariat, 1989.

West Indian Development and The Deepening and Widening of the Caribbean Community. Kingston: Institute of Social and Economic Research, University of the West Indies, 1994.

Farrell, Terrence, and Delisle Worrell (eds). *Caribbean Monetary Integration.* Port of Spain: Caribbean Information Systems and Services Limited, 1994.

Government Finance Statistics Yearbook. (1980, 1981, 1990, 1991, 1992). Washington: International Monetary Fund.

Independent West Indian Commission. *Time for Action; The Report of the West Indian Commission.* Black Rock, Barbados: The Independent West Indian Commission, 1992.

Lestrade, Swinburne. *CARICOM's Less Developed Countries: A Review of the Progress of the LDCs Under the CARICOM Arrangements.* Cave Hill: Institute of Social and Economic Research (Eastern Caribbean), University of the West Indies, 1981.

"Political Aspects of Integration in the Windward and Leeward Islands." *Caribbean Quarterly* Vol. 18 No. 2 (June) 1972.

Lewis, W. Arthur. "Proposals for an Eastern Caribbean Federation Comprising the Territories of Antigua, Barbados, Dominica, Grenada, Montserrat, St. Kitts-Nevis-Anguilla, St. Lucia, and St. Vincent." Port of Spain: Government of the West Indies, 1962.

Lewis, Gordon K. "West Indian Federation: The Constitutional Aspects." Social and Economic Studies Vol. 6 No. 2 (June 1957) 215-245.

Lewis, Vaughan. "Small States in the International Society: with special reference to the Associated States." *Caribbean Quarterly* Vol. 18 No. 2 (June) 1972.

Marshall, lone. *Statistical Profile of the Caribbean Community.* Black Rock, Barbados: The Independent West Indian Commission, 1992.

Menon, P.K. "Regional Integration: A Case Study of the Caribbean Community [CARICOM]." *Caribbean Law Review* Vol. 5 No. I (June 1995) 81-143.

Mordecai, John. *The West Indies; the Federal Negotiations.* London: Allen & Unwin, 1968.

Payne, Anthony. *The Politics of the Caribbean Community 1961-79; Regional Integration among New States.* Manchester: Manchester University Press, 1980.

Plano, Jack C. and Roy Olton (eds). *The International Relations Dictionary.* 4th ed. Santa Barbara, California: Longman, 1988.

Roberts, G.W. "Some Demographic Considerations of West Indian Federation." *Social and Economic Studies* Vol. 6 No. 2 (June 1957) 262-285.

Seers, Dudley. "Federation of the British West Indies: The Economic and Financial Aspects." *Social and Economic Studies* Vol. 6 No. 2 (June 1957) 197-213.

Sherlock, Philip M. and Rex Nettleford. "The University of the West Indies: a Caribbean Response to the Challenge of Change." London: Macmillian Caribbean, 1990.

Sires, Ronald V. "Government in the British West Indies: An Historical Outline." *Social and Economic Studies* Vol. 6 No. 2 (June 1957) 109-133.

Springer, Hugh. *Reflections on the Failure of the West Indies Federation.* Occasional Paper No. 4. Boston: Harvard Center for International Affairs, Harvard University, 1962.

The University of the West Indies. *A New Structure; the Regional University in the 1990s and Beyond;* Report of the Chancellor's Commission on the Governance of UWI, July 1994.

U.K. Report of the Closer Union Commission, 1932-3, (Leeward Islands, Windward Islands, Trinidad & Tobago). London: H.M.S.O., 1933.

U.K. The West Indies (Federation) Order in Council, 1957, No. 1364.

U.K. Report of Conference on the Closer Association of the British West Indian Colonies. September 1947. Montego Bay, Jamaica. Parts I and II. London: H.M.S.O., 1947.

Walker, D. *Columbus and the Golden World of the Arawaks.* Kingston: Ian Randle Publishers, 1992.

Wheare, K.C. *Federal Government.* Oxford: Oxford University Press, 1967.

West Indies Federation *Hansard Parliamentary Debates,* (1958-62).

Wickham, Peter. "Prospects for a United Caribbean: A Historico-Political Analysis of the Future of the Caribbean Integration Movement." Master's thesis, University of the West Indies, 1993.

Wickham, Peter W. "More Shadow Than Substance." *Caribbean Affairs* Vol. 7 No. 3 (July/August 1994) 38-61.

Wrong, Hume. *Government in the West Indies.* 1923. Reprint. New York: Negro University Press, 1969.

Ideology And Caribbean Integration

Ian Boxill

Chapter 3
The Evolution of Regionalism in the Caribbean
The Early Development of the Federal Idea

Historically, regional integration in the Caribbean has always been seen as a means to an end and never as an end in its own right. Thus, a major weakness of the Federation and later attempts at economic integration

was the conceptual framework which was not concerned with the reproduction of integration as a system but used it as a route to ensure political and economic viability within the wider world system. Hence, when the need for regional integration ceased to be central to the achievement of certain goals of individual territories, it was eschewed.

An additional but related factor is that, given the historical evolution of the region which developed as a number of insular units, it was imperative that for any strong integration system to survive there would be the need to develop a regional identity and an ideology to guide the integration process. Unfortunately, this was not done by the integrationists.

The idea of regional integration has existed in the Caribbean for a considerable period of time. Since the seventeenth century, attempts at uniting territories of the region to rationalize administrative costs of running the colonies occupied the thinking of the British Government. Such attempts, however, met with little success.

It had been the practice under colonialism for countries in the region to share governors. This was especially the case with the Leeward Islands, Jamaica, the Cayman Islands and Turks and Caicos. The Leeward Islands had a federation dating from 1871 which surrendered to the West Indies Federation of 1958. There was also an attempt during the 1870s to join Barbados in a federal union which included the Windward Islands. Such an attempt was however greeted with violent local opposition which ended in the Confederation Riots (Springer 1962). These riots brought to a temporary halt, until the West Indies Federation, British attempts at federation in the region.

But the idea of federation continued to be attractive to the British colonial civil servants who, on various occasions, made suggestions for federal schemes in articles or through speeches. In each case, the major concern was with the provision of more effective government and the rationalization of administration costs in the colonies.

The Royal Commission of 1882-1883, which was sent to enquire into ways of rationalizing economic administration in the Leeward and Windward islands and Jamaica, recommended closer union, preferably of a federal type, as a solution. In 1894 a Royal Commission sent to Dominica to investigate conditions in the island suggested an administrative union of all the British Antilles under one governor general. The Royal Commission of 1896 and 1897 also suggested the unification of Barbados and the Windward Islands to make the management of these islands more efficient (Springer 1962).

However, the political agitation which began in the 1920s and the nationalist movement which consequently emerged added a new impetus to the federation idea. This movement of radical Caribbean leaders was led by Captain Andrew Cipriani (of Trinidad) and T. A. Marryshow (of Grenada) whose ideas and activities during the 1920s influenced leaders in other Eastern Caribbean countries (Mordecai 1963).

Cipriani, of upper-middle class stock, founded the Workingmen's Association in 1919. This organization, which had a considerable lower class following, was concerned with issues such as land settlement; slum clearance; educational reform; and representation by elections to the legislature. Marryshow, a journalist of humble origins, formed the Representative Government Association of Grenada in 1914. He engaged in similar activities to Cipriani with the ultimate goal of achieving constitutional self-government. Marryshow and Cipriani became two of the earliest and foremost advocates of federation.

It should be noted that neither Cipriani nor Marryshow started out with the idea of federation. As Mordecai quite rightly argues, federation came into the picture because of the commonly held view that it was only through a collective approach that constitutional reforms and self-government could be achieved in the region. This resulted from the view that the individual colonies were too small to be viable entities. Thus, from the outset, federation represented a means to an end, to achieve self-government.

Early support for a federation came from various interest groups in the territories. These groups included the Barbados Chamber of Commerce and the Trinidad Chamber of Commerce, joined by the Jamaica Imperial Association and the Associated West Indian Chambers by the 1920s. These groups supported federation on the basis of the economic efficiency afforded by the amalgamation of the government administrations. As a result, in 1922 Major E. F. Wood (later Lord Halifax) went on a three-month tour of the region to see if conditions allowed for federation. The Wood Report, which was the result of the visit, concluded that public opinion did not support a federation of the region. Another outcome of the Wood visit was a decision to allow for constitutional changes around 1924, resulting in elected membership to some of the legislatures of the region. Voting was, however, restricted to exclude the working classes. The result of this situation was the growth of frustrated political

leaders, in the legislatures in both Trinidad and the Windward Islands, continuously clamouring for political change and the greater autonomy of the region (Mordecai 1963).

In spite of the Wood Report, the Colonial Office continued to show interest in the closer union of the territories. In 1926, the Secretary of State organized a conference of legislative nominees which proposed a Standing Conference to promote co-operation in a number of areas. The Conference was to act simply in an advisory capacity. In the opinion of the political leaders of the region, the Conference only served to divert attention from the immediate concern of federation. By 1931 the Conference had ceased to exist because of the lack of local interest. Nevertheless, during this period a number of conferences were held dealing with ways to improve economic co-operation at the regional level.

The Great Depression of the 1930s gave some impetus to the development of the idea of federation. In the Caribbean, sugar prices had been falling dramatically and wages were slashed while unemployment increased. The result of this situation was a number of riots across the region, beginning in Saint Christopher/Nevis in 1935 (Mordecai 1963). In view of the impending turbulence, the Colonial Office sent out a Sugar Commission to investigate the sugar industry. Apart from suggesting a need for the increased preference of colonial sugar to the United Kingdom market, the commissioners recommended an association of the Windward and Leeward islands as a means of rationalizing the cost of government administration (Mordecai 1963).

As the economic and social crisis deepened and concern over the cost of political administration increased, both among the Colonial Office and the planters and merchants, it was announced in 1932 that a new commission, the Closer Union Commission, would be sent to the West Indies to examine the possibility of a closer union of the territories. Some political leaders within the region saw this as an opportunity to lobby their case for federation. In October 1932, at the invitation of the Dominica Tax-payers Reform Association, Caribbean leaders representing the Windward and Leeward Islands, along with Barbados and Trinidad, proceeded to draft a federal constitution along with a number of other proposals for the formation of a federation. Such proposals were subsequently rejected by the Closer Union Committee on the grounds that public opinion was against federation. The Committee, however, proposed that the Windward and Leeward Islands be brought together under one governor (Springer 1963). It should be noted that during the Roseau Conference participants were divided over whether full dominion status should accompany the federation or should come afterwards. Although a compromise was struck at the time, this issue continued to be a source of controversy to the very end of the federation.

The disturbances of the 1930s also brought about serious changes in the political power structure of the colonies which, in turn, had serious implications for the formation of the Federation. Out of the labour disturbances emerged staunch Caribbean nationalists such as Grantley Adams of Barbados, Norman Manley of Jamaica, Albertine Gomes of Trinidad, Hubert Critchlow of Guyana, among others, committed to the achievement of self-government. For them federation represented a means to self-government. By 1938, the political leaders of the Eastern Caribbean territories were unequivocally committed to federation.

In 1940 the Moyne Commission was sent to the colonies to look into the labour disturbances. Although admitting that sentiment among the leadership of the Eastern Caribbean was in favour of federation, it nevertheless suggested a federation of the Windward and Leeward Islands as a first step to full federation of the entire region. Mordecai argues that the main reason for this was because the Colonial Office preferred to have Jamaica included in its ideal federation (Mordecai 1963).

In 1945, Secretary of State Oliver Stanley sent a dispatch inviting the territories to meet and discuss the formation of a federation. The Caribbean Labour Congress (CLC) responded by bringing together most of the prominent labour leaders from the Caribbean. While the People's National Party, led by Norman Manley, was represented, the Jamaica Labour Party, led by Bustamante, who was chief minister at the time, was absent. Again, the issue of whether there should be full dominion status accompanying or after the federation resulted in a divided conference (Mordecai 1963). However, the final outcome called for a strongly centralized federation to be accompanied by full dominion status of the constituent countries.

In 1947 another dispatch was sent by the new secretary of state, Creech-Jones, inviting leaders to a meeting in Montego Bay to further discuss the formation of a federation. At this conference the CLC presented their proposals arrived at during their earlier meeting. The proposals were ultimately rejected by the conference. The fiercest objections came from Bustamante, who argued that the idea of full dominion status accompanying the federation was nonsense since the countries were too poor to be totally viable even in a federal union. Out of the conference arose the Standing Closer Association Committee (SCAC), which was responsible for drafting the federal constitution. Federation, it therefore seemed, would act as a type of tutelage for self-government. The constitution would be drafted so as to allow each country to achieve its own constitutional advance. Nevertheless, because there was a lack of consensus over the strength of the federal government and the status that should accompany the federated colonies, even after the drafting of the constitution, no final decision was taken on the type of federal structure.

In 1953 agreement for the commencement of the federation was secured at a conference held in London between the Colonial Office officials and Caribbean leaders. This was followed by another London conference in 1956, at which a decision was made to start the federation on 23 February of that year. The Federation was not inaugurated until 3 January 1958. It therefore proceeded without any final decision on the nature of the federal structure. As Mordecai puts it:

> What was decided in 1956 was to make a start with a federal structure which was really confederal rather than federal, postponing the problems of federal power for at least five years, in the hope that the passage of time, and experience of working together would make these problems easier to solve. But this decision did not stick ... all the problems were raised within the first year of the Federation's life; it was never allowed to cement (Mordecai 1963:61).

In 1962, the Federation came to an end as a result of the secession of Jamaica and, later, Trinidad. Attempts at a federation within the Eastern Caribbean all came to nought. The question which was to later haunt the analysts was: Why did the Federation fail? To such a perplexing question there has been no shortage of answers.

Millette (1969) argues that there have been three main approaches to the explanation of the failure of the Federation. First, there is the sociological explanation advanced by writers such as Etzioni (1965) and Bobb (1966). Secondly, there is the constitutional explanation advanced, for example, by Proctor (1964). Finally, there is the personality explanation offered by writers such as W.A. Lewis (1965), Mordecai (1963) and Springer (1962). Although Springer and Mordecai stress the personality factor, they, unlike Lewis, also pay some attention to sociological and constitutional factors.

Of these three approaches the constitutional explanation appears to be the least attractive since, as Thomas argues, such an analysis may lead "... to a study of form and not content. The relevance of the legal document must lie in the way it affects the integration ... the legal document ... should not be mistaken for reality itself" (Thomas 1979:286). For such a reason the sociological and personality explanations seem most productive here.

Both Mordecai and Lewis point to a conflict of interest between the leaders, namely Manley, Williams and Adams, as the fundamental cause for the failure of the Federation. This is moreso the case with Lewis who argues that for two years Williams and Manley were embroiled in a battle over the nature of the federal structure. Williams was in favour of a union with a strong centre, while Manley wanted the opposite. Manley was responding to a Jamaican populace which was seemingly apathetic towards a federation. According to Manley, a strong centre would pressure Jamaica into releasing scarce resources, something the country could ill afford in view of the mass poverty which existed. The conflict between Manley and Williams was exploited by Bustamante who, through his election rhetoric, undermined the Federation. Lewis argues that in addition to all of this the Leeward and Windward Islands became dissatisfied with the relations between Trinidad, Jamaica and themselves. This dissatisfaction ultimately led to suspicion when in 1960 the results of a secret meeting (held in Antigua between Trinidad and Jamaica) were withheld from the other countries including the federal prime minister, Grantley Adams. According to Lewis "... the eight now began to assemble under the banner of Sir Grantley Adams who became suspicious of the other two leaders who had nothing to lose by the growing hostilities" (W.A. Lewis 1965:8).

As a consequence, by 1961, at a conference held in Trinidad no mutual confidence existed among the territories. Jamaica fell out with Trinidad, and Trinidad fell out with the eight (the Leeward and Windward Islands and Barbados). Six of the eight countries were upset with Trinidad for backing down from a previous promise of assisting them economically after independence. Thus, Lewis contends: "So when in September 1961 Jamaicans voted by a small majority to leave the Federation, relations between the political leaders of Trinidad and those of the eight were at the lowest ebb" (Lewis 1965:9). Both Mordecai and Lewis conclude that the destruction of the Federation resulted from this perpetual conflict which ultimately reached its zenith

with the eruption of tempers. To quote Mordecai (1963:445), the "...West Indies Federation was finally destroyed by the eruption of anger". As far as Lewis was concerned, "if common sense were to prevail, the departure of Jamaica would have been hailed as a chance to build a strongly centralized federation .... But common sense does not flourish in an atmosphere where everybody is angry with everybody else" (W.A. Lewis 1965:10).

Springer, like Mordecai, while emphasizing differences of personality, also refers to the nationalist conflicts and the parochialism created by colonialism as contributing factors to the demise of the Federation. For Mordecai these factors formed part of the background from whence the personality conflicts arose. However, these factors could have been overcome only if the personalities of the actors had been different. For Springer these factors precipitated the ultimate collapse of the Federation.

He and Mordecai also highlight the prospects of increasing economic prosperity and viability as playing significant roles in determining the lack of commitment by Jamaica to federation. According to Mordecai, following the publication of a pamphlet in 1951 by W. A. Lewis, which argued that the West Indies could develop by inviting foreign investors to set up industries — thus providing the foreign capital, technology and entrepreneurial skills — the Jamaican government embarked on instituting the legal apparatus to encourage, such investment. Other positive developments were the expansion of bauxite production and the growth of the tourism industry. As a consequence, whereas Jamaican industrialists had formerly supported the Federation, by 1958 they had changed their position in favour of closer association with the United States as the most viable alternative for the country.

Another factor which underlay the weakness of the Federation, according to Springer, was the fact that the islands were more integrated with Britain than among themselves. Additionally, there was little contact between the Eastern Caribbean and Jamaica until after the advent of air travel.

Etzioni (1965), Bobb (1966) and Lowenthal (1984) are of the view that a critical shortcoming of the Federation was the appalling lack of communication among the countries. Etzioni writes "the poor communication conditions prevailing among the islands until World War Two seemed to have limited interaction among them and contributed to the development of separate identities" (Etzioni 1965:171). He further states that the Federation served the interest of certain ruling groups, had no mass base and depended on a number of charismatic leaders for its survival. Following a similar line of argument, Bobb states that the Federation failed for a number of reasons. First, the conditions for federation never existed. The lack of communication and contact between people allowed for the involvement of only a small section of the people in the process. People, he argues, must want to belong to a nation of multiple states in order for it to succeed. Second, the articulation of the federal idea was "propagandist" rather than "agitational". As a result, the federal idea was preached to people of "like mind", that is, people who already knew and supported the idea. The idea never really received full discussion among the ordinary working people. Third, the Federation was incapable of uniting the various conflicting classes and social groups which characterized the plural society of the region. There were three main conflicting interests: a White managerial class, a Brown bureaucratic class and the Black masses. The Black masses who saw little economic gain from federation were of the view that the Brown bureaucratic elite and the White managerial class were the movement's greatest beneficiaries. Bobb contends:

> ... for insofar as federation becomes a limiting device against disintegrative effects of pluralism for the same reason a federal state would become ineffectual unless it could harmonise and consolidate the society. The contradictory often grotesque social attitudes in the society delayed harmonization and weakened solidarity (Bobb 1966:257).

For Bobb, therefore, the personality conflicts and poor administration were expressions of these three basic problems. Any attempts at federation would have had to consider the unique geographical and historical nature of the region. These considerations, according to Bobb, were blatantly absent from the conceptual framework of the Federation.

There are a number of other studies on the Federation which use the sociological and personality approaches as outlined in this concise survey. Millette (1969), for example, holds the view that Grantley Adams was the wrong man for the Federation, that only Manley could have made the experiment successful since he was the "truest" Caribbean man. Additionally, the Federation was dominated by the small islands and administration was far from efficient.

In spite of their contribution to knowledge, these works suffer from a number of shortcomings. Lewis tends

to be too descriptive — not getting beyond the surface of the events; that is to say, he sees the manifestations of the problems as the cause of the problems. His analysis is divorced from the historical, social, political and economic reality of the region at the time. As a consequence, he arrives at the rather questionable conclusion that exploding tempers and a lack of commonsense prevented the formation of a stronger federation of the Eastern Caribbean after the secession of Jamaica.

Although Springer and Mordecai represent obvious improvements over Lewis in terms of analysis, they too occasionally fall prey to detail and description of personalities which ultimately reflect the social environment. Etzioni and Bobb, while trying to transcend the limitations of the personality approach, sometimes tend to be too general. The shortcomings of the writers are reflective of approaches which could have benefited from cross-fertilization. Perhaps the greatest failing of the writers is their lack of a clear theoretical framework, which could have generated general propositions explaining the failure of the federation, rather than having a multiplicity of apparently separate and oftentimes disconnected points.

Overall, there are two major issues which could account for the failure of the Federation. First, there is the historically insular development of the territories which militated against the creation of a common identity and, by implication, an ideology of regionalism; secondly, there is the conceptual framework of the federation — the idea of federation being used as a means of attaining constitutional self-government — which was not concerned with the reproduction of federation as an end in itself.

In relation to the first issue, it is important to note that all of the writers conceded the insular nature of the region before and after the federal experiment. This was due to the nature of the administration of the colonies of the region under British colonialism. As Gordon Lewis explains, "colonial rule in the West Indies has always been decentralized, separating island from island by means of separate administration" (G. Lewis 1968:89). Although the colonial era was characterized by the rise of West Indian nationalism, this was never strong enough to overcome the weaknesses of fragmentation. When conflicts emerged they always seemed to manifest parochial interests of the parties involved and were therefore incapable of being resolved in a collective spirit. Etzioni is correct when he states that the Federation did not develop "the ideological, economic or military power necessary to counter secessionist attempts" (Etzioni 1965:138).

The implications of this situation dictated that for any strong form of regional integration to succeed it would have to be conceived in such a way as to allow for institutional development aimed at overcoming these divisions. There would be need to develop a strong commitment to federation, which in turn would require that federation be seen both as a means to an end and also as an end in itself. This leads to the second point which is that the idea of federation arose, principally, as a means of achieving self-government and not as an end in itself. As Payne cogently puts it, federation had "always been seen in the West Indies as a means to an end, literally as a gateway to independence, and never, therefore, as an end and an ideal in its own right" (Payne 1980:19).

Manley made this point absolutely clear at the Montego Bay Conference. According to him:

> I say here we are all in a sea of world conditions, stormy and hazardous in the extreme, each huddled in some little craft of our own. Some hardly have oars and only a few have accomplished a rudimentary sail to take them along ... If we won't leave our little boats and get into a larger vessel which is able to carry us to the goal of our ambition then I say without hesitation we are doomed .... and history will condemn us (Manley 1948:57-62).

In 1956 Williams stated:

> Whether federation is more costly or less costly, whether federation is more efficient or less efficient, Federation is inescapable if the British Caribbean are to cease to parade themselves to the twentieth century as eighteenth century anachronisms. It is this point of view that I have frequently stated, that any federation is better than no federation (Williams 1956:11-12).

Federation got full British support as expressed in a British Colonial Office report of 1947 which expressed the view that it was impossible for the small and isolated island territories to achieve full self-government on their own (Springer 1962). But this was also a way for Britain to be rid of the now burdensome administration of the colonies. Thus, Thomas (1979:284) notes that federation was "... simply a way of getting around the so-called difficulties of dealing administratively with a large number of small communities" (Thomas 1979:284).

Conflict, however, existed over the nature of the federal structure. This lack of consensus reflected differences in both the perception of the region and commitment to federation. There were basically two opposing views of federation: one championed the need for a weak centre while the other favoured the opposite. These positions were most clearly articulated by Manley and Williams, respectively.

Williams held the view that the Federation should assume full dominion status which he suggested for 22 April 1960. In a publication entitled *Economics of Nationhood,* Williams set out the structure of the Federation. The Federation, he argued, should be based on a clear-cut comprehensive conception aimed at:

1. national independence and security
2. basic human freedoms including freedom of religious worship
3. the development of a national spirit
4. the economic development and integration of the area.

Williams further suggested increasing the powers of the federal government to intervene in the financial and policy areas of each country. In addition, the federal government would have the last say in the formulation of legislation and matters affecting planning and development of all kinds.

Manley adopted the opposite position, preferring to restrict federal powers. He suggested that issues of industrial development, power to levy income tax, excise duties and consumption be removed from the control of the federal government. He also argued that if the territories of the Eastern Caribbean so desired, a constitutional formula should be adopted to allow the federal government to have a greater say in the running of their affairs. Jamaica, he argued, was unequivocally opposed to such interventions.

These two conflicting approaches resulted in a split within the federal movement. Trinidad's proposals were in keeping with the original ones as advocated by the early nationalists such as Marryshow and Cipriani. They were supported by federalist stalwarts such as Grantley Adams who became the first federal prime minister. However, many thought that the Williams proposals were nothing more than naive idealism. Above all, the smaller territories saw the proposals outlined in the *Economics of Nationhood* as reducing them to nothing more than county councils (Williams 1959). The result of this was that leaders failed to agree on a formula for a federal structure.

The conflicting positions of Manley and Williams were the result of different perceptions of the region. Historically, Trinidad had been closely linked to the Eastern Caribbean and was involved in the federal debates from the outset. Jamaica, on the other hand, being geographically and politically isolated from the rest of the region, only became involved in the federation debates during the 1940s. While it is true that ultimately the Federation represented a means to an end, for Trinidad, as perhaps for most of the other countries of the Eastern Caribbean, it had a deeper emotional significance. Hence, Williams comments that: "only a powerful and centrally directed economic co-ordination and interdependence can create the true foundation of a *nation* (writer's emphasis)" (Williams 1959:11). The variations in support for these two positions indicated that the notion of a regional identity was not well developed during the federal era. Neither did the Federation follow any clear ideology of regionalism which would have acted as a base and guide to action.

Notwithstanding the support for federation, Lowenthal notes that by 1960, when Prime Minister Norman Manley became convinced that Jamaica could go it alone, the federalist idea became less of an attraction. Manley's change of heart had been, to a large degree, the result of Jamaica's increased economic prosperity and the prospects of independent economic viability (Lowenthal 1984). This idea of separate statehood, he continues, was further to influence Trinidad's decision to follow the Jamaican withdrawal. Trinidad, like Jamaica, had also been experiencing an economic boom as a result of increased earnings from oil. By the mid-1950s Trinidad had become one of the fastest growing economies in the world (Mordecai 1963). The notion of economic viability based on the concept of a particular size had been shattered. Hence, Trinidad's movement towards independence was followed by Guyana and Barbados. As Lowenthal notes, given this revolutionary departure from the past, "no theoretical justification remained to deny self-government to any Caribbean territory" (Lowenthal 1984:113-14).

Evidence of Manley's change of mood occurred in the inter-governmental conference of 1960 at which he made a speech which placed Jamaica's support for the Federation in doubt. Manley's views were also conditioned by the strong anti-federation campaigns of Bustamante who appealed to the nationalist sentiments of Jamaicans and suggested that a federation could not improve the living conditions of the people. The referendum of 1961 revealed the lack of zeal with which Manley approached federation. A considerably smaller number of supporters of Manley's People's National Party (PNP) than of Bustamante's Jamaica Labour Party (JLP) turned out to vote (Millette 1969). This was especially striking in the PNP's strongest constituencies.

According to Millette, Manley had shown a strange apathy for the campaign.

Although Trinidad had proposed a unitary state with the other eight countries after the Jamaican withdrawal, internal party sentiment of Williams's People's National Movement was against the idea because of the economic cost to be borne by Trinidad. Internal party conflicts and continuous controversy between Trinidad and the eight made further thoughts of federation less acceptable to Williams (Millette 1969). The prospects of independent economic development ultimately encouraged Trinidad to go to independence alone. As Coard puts it (1978:69), Trinidad had come to realize that "... the world's concept of the size required of an independent nation ... [had been] altered".

After the withdrawal of Trinidad from the ill-fated federation with the eight, a federation of the eight themselves was proposed. Initially, Barbados was reluctant to conclude constitutional arrangements for independence because: (i) it was not willing to make the establishment of federation a more difficult task; (ii) there was concern over the inability of the country to provide its own security; (iii) there was still the underlying view that a country so small could not be viable on its own. However, conflicts between Barbados and the other islands along with the perception that Barbados would have to bear the bulk of the economic cost of federation created some doubts in the mind of Errol Barrow, the then premier, about the idea. Given these tensions along with the possibility of independent viability, Barbados concluded constitutional arrangements to receive its independence on 30 November 1966. This action brought the curtain down on any further attempts at forming a regional federation.

From Federation to CARIFTA to CARICOM

Even though the Federation failed, efforts at bringing about integration within the region still continued. Such efforts were initially led by Williams who continuously championed the idea of an economic community. But it was only during the second half of the 1960s that actual steps were taken to realize such a goal. This was partly in response to a publication by William Demas entitled *The Economics of Development in Small Countries with Special Reference to the Caribbean* in which the argument was made that the countries of the region should pursue economic integration in order to overcome the development limitations imposed by their small size. In this publication, Demas recognized the existence of structural deficiencies in the countries as being the main cause of: high unemployment; a dual economy with a high-wage sector in the mineral and manufacturing economy, resulting in the flow of labour from agriculture to these areas; the poor use of local resources; an underdeveloped tourist industry because of a lack of linkages within the economies; and a situation where foreign investors were responding to investment incentives, created by the regional governments, by the setting up of screwdriver type industries. He concluded that failure to transform the economics of the region to make them become more viable entities was a direct result of their small size. As Payne puts it, the thrust of Demas's argument was:

> the smallness of the domestic market imposed sharp limits on the process of import substitution industrialization and thus removed the option of balanced growth, incorporating a roughly equal mixture of export stimulation and import substitution, a goal which could only be achieved by large continental countries (Payne 1980:58).

As a result of this situation, small countries were forced to produce a small number of manufactures for export to world markets, but this in itself was beset by a number of obstacles which lowered the competitiveness of the products. Demas therefore identified two options for the small countries to choose from if they were to achieve industrial development: (i) full economic integration with large countries, similar to Puerto Rico's relationship with the United States; (ii) integration with similar countries within the same geographical area. Demas chose the latter, arguing that by integrating the economics of the region there would be the elimination of excess capacity in the existing manufacturing industry and the stimulation of new industries which could become more viable given the expanded market (Payne 1980). In reality, Demas was calling for a collective approach to import substitution.

A point which is worth noting at this stage is that Demas's approach was vastly different from that advocated by the University of the West Indies economists who, in 1964, under the aegis of the Trinidadian and Jamaican governments, were commissioned to conduct studies on regional economic integration. The University team published a number of papers and books — the most celebrated being *The Dynamics of West Indian Integration* by C.Y. Thomas and Havelock Brewster, produced in 1967. The University team's proposals were rejected on the grounds that they were too naive and radical, although some effort was made to salvage some of the ideas by incorporating

aspects of production integration into the Caribbean Free Trade Association Agreement (CARIFTA) (Payne 1980). Thus, the signatories to the CARIFTA Agreement chose to pursue Demas's approach which followed the neoclassical economic perspective, not seeking to question or change the structure of the regional economics.

Although the CARIFTA Agreement came into effect in August 1968, events dating from 1965 led to its development. In 1965 the governments of Antigua, Barbados and Guyana responded to the idea of an economic community by agreeing to the creation of a Free Trade Association by 1966. In 1966, the Hunte Committee, named after a prominent Barbadian businessman, Kenneth Hunte, was appointed to tour the region to convince regional leaders to take action in order to start a free trade association (Payne 1980). In 1967, Forbes Burnham, prime minister of Guyana, met with Eric Williams to convince Trinidad to join the Free Trade Association. The announcement of a free trade association had caught the region by surprise — in particular Trinidad's Eric Williams, who had been one of the earliest and strongest advocates of post-federation economic integration. Williams must have been displeased by such reticence on the part of the three countries. In stressing the necessity for Trinidad to join the association, Burnham stated:

> Either we weld ourselves into a regional grouping serving primarily Caribbean needs, or lacking a common positive policy, have our various territories and nations drawn hither and thither into, and by, other large territories where the peculiar problems of the Caribbean are lost and where we become the objects of neo-colonialist exploitation, and achieve the pitiable status of international mendicants .... Either we integrate or we perish, unwept, unhonoured (Burnham 1970:246-47).

Here again history repeats itself, as these views are reminiscent of those articulated by Norman Manley during the Montego Bay Conference of 1947. In this quotation and in the works of Demas there exists a congruency in rationale for both the Federation and economic integration to overcome the limitations imposed by small size. Economic integration, like federation had been advocated as a means to an end and not as an end in itself. This point is even more vividly exemplified in the efforts to get the LDCs to join CARIFTA.

One of the central concerns of the LDCs has always been that of securing short and long term financing for development. Prospects for such financing would be used to convince the LDCs to join

CARIFTA. According to Payne "a Caribbean Development Bank financed chiefly by contributions from metropolitan countries and the larger Caribbean states but geared specifically to their needs was manifestly attractive bait to hold before the LDCs" (Payne 1980:95).

Thus in 1968 CARIFTA, comprising a group of countries pursuing pragmatic interests but holding the view that being in such an association made them more viable, was born. It was however for such reasons, economic pragmatism and continued individual interests, that for the four years of its existence CARIFTA became afflicted by perpetual conflict and intense rivalry. For instance, in 1968 both Barbados and Jamaica rejected a proposal by Trinidad to make British West Indian Airways (BWIA) the regional air carrier. BWIA had been purchased by the government of Trinidad from British Overseas Air Corporation (BOAC) when it ended operations in the Caribbean. Trinidad, which purchased the airline without consultation with other Caribbean counterparts, had started to incur extremely heavy losses from its operations. The formation of CARIFTA was therefore an opportunity for the Trinidad government to make the airline a regional one thereby reducing the costs of operation (Payne 1980). Although a working party set up at the Fourth Heads of Government Conference to examine the matter was unanimously in favour of making the airline regional, since above all it made economic sense, at the Ministerial Conference the idea was rejected. The main reason for the rejection was that Jamaica had already embarked on setting up its own airline, while Barbados was in the process of doing the same. In both cases the two countries were using national airlines to help in the development of their individual tourist industries (Payne 1980). Trinidad was displeased with the decision and even threatened to secede from the movement.

Another issue which caused much dissatisfaction within the movement was the growing trade polarization in favour of the MDCs. Between 1968 and 1970 the MDCs witnessed increases in exports from EC$96 million to EC$158 million, an increase of 65 per cent. Jamaica benefited most from such increases. In response to complaints by the LDCs about the need to address the imbalance, the MDCs blamed the LDCs for a lack of entrepreneurial drive. As a result of a perceived intransigence by the MDCs, the LDCs opposed suggestions by the MDCs for deepening the movement. As far as they were concerned, deepening the integration process would only worsen the already polarized

situation and work to the benefit of the MDCs. For example, deepening which meant the harmonization of fiscal incentives and the implementation of a common external tariff could cause the LDCs markets to be more open to the exports of the MDCs and also place them at a disadvantage in attracting foreign investment (Payne 1980). But neither was Jamaica interested in deepening the integration process. Prime Minister Shearer, who succeeded Bustamante, made this point very clear on numerous occasions and insisted that Jamaica was simply interested in economic co-operation. He proposed instead the widening of the movement to include non-English speaking territories, as this would widen the tariff free market size. Guyana, Trinidad and Barbados were, however, firmly in favour of the deepening process. As a result, CARIFTA became split along two conflicting viewpoints regarding its development.

Another issue which aggravated the existing tensions within the movement and served to reinforce the observation that the movement suffered from parochialism and lacked ideological cohesion was its failure to reach consensus on a common policy towards the European Economic Community (EEC). In 1969, regional governments realizing the imminence of Britain's entry into the European Economic Community, sent a delegation to Britain to lobby the case of the region for special consideration (Payne 1980). Although the Seventh Heads of Government Conference later agreed on the need for a collective approach to the matter, where a single form of relationship was to be negotiated, there was still dispute over which option would be most suitable. There were basically three options of association, Guyana and Trinidad preferring one type while Jamaica preferred another. In each case the choice of option was based on the perceived benefits that could be derived individually. In addition, there was also the case of the LDCs which, because of their associated status with Britain, were eligible for the most advantageous form of association within the group. They were subsequently persuaded to forego such an option in favour of the collective one. In the final analysis it was Britain which made the decision on the type of option for association. What was perhaps most startling about these series of events was the fact that Jamaica had been secretly negotiating with the European Economic Community for a new type of arrangement which suited their immediate economic needs (Payne 1980).

As a result of this perpetual conflict, by the 1970s, in spite of the progress made in the expansion of trade, the continued viability of CARIFTA had been threatened. Unlike the Federation though, this movement was not to fall into a state of disrepair.

In 1972 the integration movement got a fillip from the accession to power of the People's National Party (PNP) in Jamaica, under the leadership of Michael Manley. Michael, like his father Norman, made no secret of the fact that he was an unrepentant integrationist (Payne 1980). In 1970 Manley had published an article in *Foreign Affairs* which echoed strong sentiments in favour of regional economic integration. In this paper Manley emphasized the economic benefits that Jamaica and the region could achieve from closer regional integration. Manley's well articulated position and rhetoric became a morale booster for the integration movement. In 1972 Demas, who was then Secretary General of CARIFTA, published a booklet entitled *From CARIFTA to the Caribbean Community* in which he outlined a policy for the deepening of the integration process. These ideas would to a large degree influence the formation and structure of the new integration movement. He suggested increased economic co-operation through a common market and an extension to the areas of functional co-operation. The deepening of regional integration therefore rested on the same basic premise as CARIFTA: "CARIFTA and CARICOM have been designed in the first instance to overcome the constraints upon the economies of the region imposed by the small size" (Payne 1980:187).

CARICOM has three basic objectives: (i) economic co-operation through the Caribbean Common Market; (ii) co-ordination of foreign policy among independent member states; (iii) functional or non-functional co-operation in areas such as health, education, sea and air transport, culture, etc. The supreme organ of the community is the Conference of Heads of Government. It is made up of prime ministers, and in the case of Guyana and Montserrat, executive president and chief minister, respectively. The final authority on policy matters of the community rests with this Conference.

The principal organ of the Common Market is called the Common Market Council. It is responsible for the smooth running and development of the Common Market. There are several institutions of CARICOM responsible for formulating policies in relation to functional co-operation. Each member state is represented on each institution by a minister of government. The institutions are in the form of standing committees on health, education, science, technology, foreign affairs, agriculture, mines, energy and natural resources, transport, finance and labour. There are also associate institutions of the Community which form the main planks of functional co-operation. They include the Caribbean Examinations Council (CXC), Caribbean Meteorological Association (CMO), Council of Legal Education (CLE), University of the West Indies (UWI), University of Guyana (UG) and the West Indies Shipping Corporation (WISCO). The Community Secretariat is organized into five divisions, namely, trade and agriculture, economics and industry, functional co-operation, legal, and general services and administration.

There are thirteen countries in CARICOM. These are Saint Lucia, Saint Vincent, Grenada, Antigua and Barbuda, St. Christopher and Nevis, Montserrat, Belize and Dominica – classified as LDCs; Barbados, Trinidad and Tobago, Guyana and Jamaica – classified as MDCs. The Bahamas, which makes up the thirteenth member, has not been slotted into either of these categories.

In 1981 a sub-group comprising the LDCs from the Eastern Caribbean formed themselves into an association called the Organization of Eastern Caribbean States (OECS). The formation of this group was a response to the skewed level of economic development which had come to characterize the movement.

Unlike the Federation, CARICOM has managed to survive. However, like the Federation and CARIFTA, the movement has been characterized by tremendous conflict and instability. The following chapter attempts to examine some of the experiences of CARICOM with a view to offering an explanation as to why this conflict and instability persist.

The Union of East Caribbean States: Thoughts on a Form

by: Earl Huntley

Background Considerations

In designing a system of Government for an East Caribbean Union, one will have to consider, not only the objectives of Political Union, but the fact that the quest for Union is emerging from a particular integration experience, and will therefore have to take into account the nature of that experience. It is our contention that the OECS integration experience, has developed its own peculiar characteristic, and that this unique feature will have to be a dominant element in the shaping of the Union Government.

Theorists of political integrate on have been divided over, whether such integration can occur only after a well knit and successful economic integration movement has been established, or whether economic integration requires a deliberate political decision to take it to the higher stage of Political Union. The first approach – termed the functionalist approach – was the guiding principle behind the European Economic Community; the apparent success of the EEC experiment spawned attempts at economic integration throughout the developing world, including the Caribbean – hence the Caribbean Community whose engine was supposed to be its common market.

In the Eastern Caribbean, the approach was similar. A forum for meetings of the Heads of Government of the islands – The WISA Council of Ministers-set up in 1968, agreed to establish an East Caribbean Common Market later that year. In 1981, these two institutions were merged into the Organisation of East Caribbean States (OECS) – a stronger integrative institution than hitherto existed. Functional co-operation and economic integration proceeded in a number of areas – Civil Aviation, the Judiciary, Defence, Economic matters, External Representation, Currency, Education, Sports. While cohesion among the member-states grew, it developed not merely because of the effects of harmonisation or of the adoption of a common policy in those areas, but largely as a result of the system of decision-making which brought about that co-operation.

In economic integration schemes, the forces released from the creation of a common market, free trade area etc., are supposed to be the propellants for the growth of the scheme.

In the OECS integration experience however, the driving force for the development of an East Caribbean Community has been the Authority (the grouping of Heads of Government of the member-states). The focal point of the OECS since its existence, has been the Authority. The Heads of Government of the OECS, by meeting frequently, and taking decisions which successfully advanced the process of integration, have gradually developed a collective decision-making system, which has assumed a life of its own. The peculiar feature of the East Caribbean integration process therefore, is that it has evolved into a collective decision-making system in which the Heads of Government of the various member-states have virtually acted like a Cabinet of Ministers of a Government with respect to some of the matters which have come before them.

The focal point of the integration process has been the Authority and what it does. The regular meetings of the Authority which have given directions to the integration process have transformed the Authority into the primary integration institution of the sub-region. It is that collective decision-making institution which has been the engine of growth of the economic and functional community. If the Authority had failed to meet for any significant period of time, it would have adversely affected the integration movement. The success of the system has been the logic for its continuation; and when that logic is coupled with external pressures and demands, it means that the Heads of Government must further institutionalise the system in political terms if it is to meaningfully continue. Consequently, any new political system which locks those states into one new nation-state, must therefore give these Heads of Government a prominent role in the centre of that system. In other words, the collective decision-making system of the Heads of Government of the OECS, which has been partly responsible for the quest for political union, must now be transformed into an institution which will have a significant role in the new Union.

A number of decisions taken by the Authority illustrate how effective a collective decision-making institution it has become. The best known of these is the decision of the OECS to intervene in Grenada, in October 1983, along with the United States, following the assassination of Maurice Bishop by an extreme faction of his Government. That initiative was strongly condemned by the international community, and there have been varying views as to its legitimacy. Whatever those views are, the initiative by the Heads of Government was partly the result of a perception of the area as a single political community, and consequently the emergence of a disturbance or deviant behaviour in a part of that community, or family had to be corrected. Once the decision to mount the initiative had been taken, the Heads of Government did not waver or retreat from their position. On the contrary, the vociferous and sometimes virulent opposition and condemnation with which the international community greeted the intervention had the effect of binding the decision-making system into a firmer institution as it strengthened the perception of its decision-makers that the islands were indeed one entity. It confirmed their realisation that the territories could effectively respond to domestic and international pressures, only if they acted and remained together.

In the same vein, a decision by the Authority, to mount a concerted and co-ordinated approach to overturning a proposal by the IMF, to graduate OECS member countries from IDA concessionary financing, was successful in achieving a postponement of that proposal. In the field of education, when proposals to decentralise the University of the West Indies seemed likely to adversely affect the interests of the Governments and the students of the East Caribbean, a decision by the Heads of Government to challenge the proposals together, successfully steered the restructuring exercise in a direction which was more acceptable to the Eastern Caribbean.

In more recent times the Heads of Government have agreed to a full liberalisation of trade within the East Caribbean Common Market. There has been consensus on a revision of a scheme for allocation of industries among member countries. An East Caribbean Investment Promotion Service (ECIPS) has been established in Washington, with the aim of stimulating investment into the area. This was preceded by a decision to set up an East Caribbean Export Development Agency (ECSEDA) to co-ordinate the export of agro-industrial and industrial commodities. And in March of 1988, Heads of Government along with Ministers of Agriculture of the sub-region met and decided to adopt a joint approach to the diversification of agricultural production in the area.

While the circumstances of these islands have called for integrated approaches to their developmental thrusts, it is the Heads of Government through the collective decision-making system of the Organisation, that have provided the political direction needed to adopt the necessary measures. The Heads of Government, by acting as a collective entity, have managed the affairs of the region in areas where harmonised approaches have been necessary, and by so doing have developed a quasi-Governmental system for the regional integration movement. This, therefore, has been the unique characteristic of the East Caribbean integration experience; and it is this collective decision-making system which must be one of the influential forces in the formation of the political union which is emerging from the integration scheme.

The other factors that must be taken into account in determining the likely form of political union for the islands arise from the circumstances of the islands themselves. First, it must be realised that we are dealing with a group of islands, and the very nature of an island tends to breed a strong insular feeling among its people, no matter the strength of the bonds existing between them and the peoples of other adjacent islands. Secondly, and allied to this, is the fact that these islands have just become independent. Their people, and especially their politicians, have only recently begun to taste the heady wine of political freedom and enjoy the responsibility of managing their own affairs. For those in political office, and those seeking political office, the power of total control over an island, no matter how small that island is, no matter the difficulties encountered in delivering economic development to its people, is not going to be easy to part with. This is especially true in a situation where the Head of Government in each island is indeed a powerful figure. The fortunes of political parties, the outcome of general elections is more often than not, determined by the leaders of the parties. That prominent position of the party leader should be viewed in conjunction with the earlier observation of the role of the Heads of Government in the integration process.

To sum up therefore, from our point of view, the circumstances which should influence the form of a Union Government for the OECS are the following:

(1) The central role of the collective decision-making system of Heads of Government in the integration experience.
(2) The fact that the states concerned are islands with a background of strong insularity.
(3) The newly achieved independence of those islands.
(4) The desire of the political directorate to retain some form of power.
(5) The pre-eminence of the Head of Government and political leader in the domestic politics of those islands.

If a Political Union of the East Caribbean States does not build on these factors, they will sooner or later destroy the Union, regardless of the strength of the objective imperatives for union.

Classical Forms of Political Union and Their Relevance

The political union or the political integration of countries has always taken one of three general forms: Confederation, Federation, and a Unitary State. There are some commentators, who believe that there are in fact, only two general forms – Federal and Unitary, arguing that a confederal system is really a form of federation. Within each of these three classical moulds of government, there have been several variations of the general theme – variations dictated by the circumstances of the countries attempting the political union.

In this section we will define the characteristics of these classical forms of political union or government, and in the light of the background considerations for an East Caribbean political union which we examined earlier, we will seek to determine which of these three general forms is best suited to a political union of the member-states of the OECS

We are not arguing that an East Caribbean political union has to follow any of these forms in their classical context. We believe that in the same way, political unions in other parts of, the world, have produced variations of one of the general forms, conditions in the East Caribbean can result in a peculiar version of one of the general forms of union. What this section is attempting, is a determination of which of the three general forms is best suited for an adaptation to the needs of the East Caribbean.

Confederation

Confederation is a loose, usually temporary union of political or other territorial units, each of which retains the largest possible degree of independence. A confederation is usually formed by several sovereign states for certain common purposes – for example defence, foreign relations, or tariffs – in which the delegated powers of the central authority are strictly limited. More emphasis is laid upon the sovereignty of the members of the confederation, than on the confederation itself; and in some cases, some members may retain the right to secede. In fact a confederation is not a state. The internal sovereignty of each state remains unchanged and minimal limitation is placed on its external sovereignty.

Another feature of a confederation is that the central authority of the system is not directly elected by the people of the confederation. The confederal government is drawn from among members of the existing state governments and the members of the confederal parliament are nominees of the various parliaments of the member states.

The Federal State

In a political union which is a federal state, a number of independent states come together and agree to establish a central government which will take control of some of their affairs, while at the same time, individual governments in each of the co-ordinate states retain control of other matters. This division of powers between a central government, which undertakes the management of what concerns the nation as a whole, and the government of the separate states, who

undertake the management of what concerns each state individually, is the essential characteristic of the Federal State. A Federal State represents a sharing of sovereignty between the central government and the federating units, with each having full sovereignty in the areas allotted to them.

The division of powers between the federal government and the governments of the states which form the federation, is set out in the constitution of the federal state. The federal constitution either defines what powers the federal authority shall have and leaves the remainder to the federating units i.e. the individual states; or it states what powers the federating units – or states – shall possess and leaves the remainder to the central authority. The phrase "reserve of powers" is used to describe the remainder of powers not defined in the constitution. In the cases where the powers of the federal authority are defined, as in the U.S. constitution, the aim is to limit the powers of the federal government, and to yield to the individual states as much independence as possible. On the other hand in the cases where the constitution defines the powers of the federating units, as in Canada, the objective is to strengthen the federal authority at the expense of the member states of the federation.

Given the fact that in a federal state there must be a division of powers between the central and unit governments, all federal constitutions provide for an authority which will settle disputes between the central and state authorities over whether there has been any encroachment by either side on the powers of the other. In some countries, for example as in the Federal Republic of Germany, such an authority is a special constitutional court; in others, as in the United States of America, Canada, Australia, the Federal Supreme Court has the authority to arbitrate between the central and unit governments, and to interpret the constitution.

The three basic characteristics of a federal state, therefore, are the distribution of powers between governments of limited and co-ordinate authority, the supremacy of the constitution, and the authority of the courts to interpret the constitution. Examples of federal states in the world today are the United States of America, Canada, Australia, the Federal Republic of Germany, Switzerland, Mexico, the U.S.S.R. and St. Kitts/Nevis.

Unitary State

The form of government called a Unitary State is the one which will be familiar to most people in the region, since all the O.E.C.S. member states, except one, are unitary states. In a Unitary State there is a single central government with total control over all the affairs of the state, and a single central parliament. In contrast to a federation, there are no governments or parliaments within the various Territories that would compose the unitary state.

However, in a unitary state, a devolution of some power from the central government to a local government in each of the constituent units can take place. But even if there is devolution of some power to a locally elected unit administration, ultimate authority lies with the central government. The central government in a unitary state can over-rule acts passed by the local administrations; and in some cases, not only the character, but the life of local administrations, is determined by the central government. A unitary state, therefore represents almost a total integration of the sovereignty and governments of the participating units.

The main characteristics of a unitary state therefore are:-

The existence of a single central government and parliament with full and final authority over all matters pertaining to the state; the lack of other sovereign governments within the units making up the new state. Examples of unitary states comprising more than one territory or more than one nationality, are the United Kingdom (Scotland, England, Wales, Northern Ireland), Indonesia, Malaysia, The Bahamas, St. Vincent and the Grenadines, Trinidad and Tobago and The Phillipines.

Which of the Forms?

Given the background considerations which were examined in the first part of this paper, which of these three classical forms would be most suitable for a political union of the islands in the OECS?

A political union which was a confederation would represent just a slight advance on the current state of the integration system. In fact, in some respects, the present OECS is already a confederation. Any change in the present system which was of a confederal nature, would simply mean adding institutions like a regional parliament to the system, without giving the central authority the force of a government or the stronger political direction which the integration movement now requires. Such changes would have acknowledged that factors like the insularity, the independence of the islands, the desire by some to retain power, were too strong to overcome; and while these changes would have maintained the collective decision-making system of the integration experience, they would not have improved upon it.

On the other hand, while a unitary state would give the strong central control that would be desirable for the union, agreement on such a form would be difficult to achieve, since it would involve the relinquishing of so much by the unit territories, both in terms of the amount of power which local politicians wield, and in terms of people's sense of attachment to their island and their contact with their representatives. A unitary state would be an attempt to directly counter these background factors and those referred to earlier, but it is these very features which would render agreement on this type of union impossible.

It would seem therefore, that a federation would provide the union with the flexibility to deal with the background factors and to overcome them by building on them. A federal form of government would for example, satisfy the desire by the political and would-be political directorate in the islands to retain some measure of sovereign control over their islands; it would still give island residents the feeling that they had some contact with their local state administrations. It would be possible, with a federal form, to take care of those concerns and still maintain a strong central government. Based on the fact that there are several varieties of the federal form in the world today, it would also be possible under that form to devise a system which would address the main institutional lesson of the integration experience – viz: The emergence of a successful collective decision-making system among the heads of government of the member-states of the OECS Federal states have come into existence in other parts of the world because special historical circumstances at the time the new state was created, dictated the adoption of a more flexible arrangement of power than occurs in a unitary state.

It is therefore recommended that the Union of East Caribbean States should have a federal form of government which will absorb the unique characteristics of the East Caribbean integration process referred to earlier, as well as deal with the other peculiarities of Government and life in these islands. In this context, it would be important to note the comments by Sir Arthur Lewis in 1965 on the objective of a federation of these islands. Writing in "The Agony of the Eight," his analysis of the reasons for the collapse of the attempts in the mid 1960s to federate Barbados, the Windwards and the Leewards, he said: "The political leaders .... make a federation a question of customs unions, freedom of movement, exclusive lists, concurrent lists and the like. All this is secondary. The fundamental reason for federating these islands is that it is the only way that good government can be assured to their peoples."

As in all federal structures, in a federal union of the Eastern Caribbean, the powers of government would be divided between the central or union administration, which would have certain areas exclusively reserved to it, and state administrations which would have full control of those areas not allotted to the regional government.

The following areas would be the exclusive responsibility of the federal or union government:

(1) Foreign Affairs
(2) Defence, Security, Immigration, Citizenship, Police
(3) Finance – including currency, customs, ability to levy taxes
(4) Communications and Transport – including aviation, telecommunications, postal services
(5) The Economy – Planning, Industralisation, Trade
(6) Education (Tertiary)
(7) The Judiciary

There would also be areas of concurrent competence between the federal and state administrations – for example tourism promotion, agricultural marketing and diversification. However, in areas where there is overlapping, federal law would take precedence over state law.

There are two other principles that will be applied to the government of the union. The first is that there will be a separation of powers between the three departments of Government – Executive, Legislative, and Judicial. As in the American system of government, the three branches will be distinct and the powers of each will be balanced by the powers of the others, so that each branch acts as a check on the other. This system of checks and balances will be in further recognition of Sir Arthur Lewis' contention that the real need for federation of these islands is to ensure good government. The second principle would almost flow from the first. The new state will be Republican with an Executive Presidency.

The islands, except for one, currently operate under a monarchical parliamentary system of government. If political union is seen as a further step in the constitutional evolution of these states, then the creation of a new republic out of these states will be understandable. The concept of an Executive presidency stems from the application of the separation of powers.

The federal form of government envisaged for the union would also reflect, what was identified earlier as the major peculiarity of the East Caribbean integration experience i.e. the central role which the collective deci-

sion-making system of Heads of Government played in the growth of the integration movement. Given that experience, given also the pre-eminent position of Heads of Government/Political leaders in the Government and political life of the islands, the Heads of Government will have to play a significant role in the decision-making process of the government of the union. Consequently, in the model of the federal form of government being advocated, the Heads of Government of each state will collectively either (a) form the Executive of the new regional government or (b) form one of the other influential branches of the Government. The collective decision-making system of Heads of Government of the OECS would then have become the foundation of the new union government, and would have been transformed from an integrative institution to a mechanism of government.

In the following two sections we will put forward two models of a federal form of government for the union of East Caribbean States. In the first the Authority of the OECS (i.e. The Heads of government of the States) becomes the Executive of the Government of the Union; in the second, the Heads of Government of the states form part of the legislative branch of the federal government.

Conclusions

What we have attempted to show in these two models of a form of Union for the member-state of the O.E.C.S., is that like other political unions, the proposed Union of East Caribbean States, will have to be fashioned by the special historical circumstances surrounding the idea of political integration in the islands now. These special circumstances are for us mainly two strategic dictates:

(1) The peculiar nature of the integration experience of the member-states of the Union, in which a collective-decision-making system among Heads of Government has been the driving force of integration;
(2) The unique features of political life in these islands – viz; the dominant position of the Head of Government in the island, the newly achieved independence of the States concerned, traditional insularity among the islands.

The models therefore, incorporate those circumstances into the structure of the Union so as to give it strength; our belief is that any form of Government for the Union which fails to take these into account, will be putting tremendous stress on the Union.

However, there is another consideration that should be borne in mind in attempting to devise a form of political Union for the islands. It is that whatever form of Government that is agreed upon by the authorities, should not represent so drastic a change to what the people have been accustomed, that it renders the idea of political union unacceptable to them or makes it difficult for them to adapt to the Union Government. At the same time, the idea of political union, must be seen and must be represented as a revolutionary situation in the historical development of the islands, as a challenge to the creativity and strength of character of the peoples of the islands. The form of Government of the Union must therefore be something new and exciting, bold enough to fire their imagination into accepting this challenge of political evolution.

Finally, since two models of a form of Government have been presented in this paper, the question may be asked as to which of the two should be adopted. The answer is that it is really up to the people of the islands to choose the one they find more acceptable and more feasible.

We would wish to point out however, that the two models are not incompatible, and it is possible to see both as complementing each other. In that case, it is possible to implement both of them. If one accepts the political union of the East Caribbean States as a gradual evolution from the integrative experience of the O.E.C.S., and if it is accepted that naturally, the first few years of political union must necessarily be difficult ones by virtue of the fact of the novelty of union, then it would be useful to start the Union, with a form of Government as described under Model A – the collective Presidency.

After the first five years of operation of this Model – the collective Presidency of a Federal Executive Council – the second Model – Model B, the Unitary Presidency can be embarked upon. The Heads of Government would then move to become the upper house of the legislature of the union Government. During those five years, also, the members of the House of Representatives of the National Assembly, who would have to elect a President from among themselves, would have had the opportunity to assess the strengths and weaknesses of Presidential candidates. Of course, any of the Heads of Government who desired to be President would then have to seek the Presidency through the House of Representatives.

If this approach is used, of evolving from one form of Government to another, then the pattern would have been consistent with the historical development of integration efforts in the East Caribbean.

Suggestions for further reading

Cynthia Barrow-Giles, 'Political development and foreign Affairs of a Mini-state: A Case study of St Lucia: 1979–1987', master's thesis, (Kingston: Consortium Graduate School of Social Sciences, 1993).

Cynthia Barrow-Giles and Janice Farley, 'Barbadian Perception on Closer Collaboration with the Organisation of Eastern Caribbean States (OECS): The Barbados-OECS Initiative', *Journal of Eastern Caribbean Studies,* vol. 24, no. 2, June (1999), pp. 43–69.

Ian Boxill, *Ideology and Caribbean Integration* (Kingston: Consortium Graduate School of Social Sciences, 1993).

William G. Demas, *Critical Issues in Caribbean Development: West Indian Development and Widening of the Caribbean Community* (Kingston: Ian Randle Publishers, 1997).

William G. Demas, *Towards West Indian Survival,* Occasional Paper, no. 3, West Indian Commission Report

Patrick A. M. Emmanuel, *Approaches to Regional Political Integration,* Occasional Paper, no. 21 (Bridgetown: Institute of Social and Economic Research, 1987).

Peter Wickham, Prospects for a United Caribbean: A Historico-Political Analysis of the Future of the Caribbean, master's thesis, (Bridgetown: Cave Hill Campus, UWI).

West Indian Commission, *Time for Action Report* (Kingston: The UWI Press, 1992).

West Indian Commission Report, Occasional Paper, no. 6 (Bridgetown: West Indian Commission, 1992).

Notes

1. Foremost of these convulsions have been the breakdown of communism in Eastern Europe and the Soviet Union.
2. Kenneth Clinton Wheare, *Federal Government,* 4th edition (New York: Oxford University Press, 1963).
3. Ian Boxill, *Ideology and Caribbean Integration* (Kingston: Consortium Graduate School of Social Sciences, 1993).
4. Ronald Lampman Watts, *New Federations: Experiments in the Commonwealth* (Oxford: Clarendon Press, 1968) for an excellent discussion of the problems that contributed to the collapse of the 'federal' experiment.

5. Lewis Arthur, *The Agony of the Eight* (Bridgetown: Advocate Commercial Printery, 1965).

6. See Watts, *'New Federations'*.

7. Ian Boxill, *Ideology and Caribbean Integration,* p. 39.

8. Patrick A.M. Emmanuel, *Approaches to Caribbean Political Integration* (Bridgetown: Institute of Social and Economic Research, 1987), Occasional Paper no. 21.

9. See the *Barbados Advocate* and *Nation* newspapers, January 3rd– 8th for details on the discussion and resolution of disputes between governments and the airlines.

10. Michael Witter, 'Exchange Rate Policy in Jamaica: A Critical Assessment', in *Social and Economic Studies,* 32: 4, December (1983) pp. 1–50.

11. See *Time for Action Report of the West Indian Commission* (Kingston: The UWI Press, 1992).

12. Dwight Venner is the governor of the Eastern Caribbean Central Bank.

13. Dwight Venner, *'Prospects for a United Caribbean in the New International Economic Order'*, The Annual Lecture to the West India Committee (London, 1996).

14. Kenny D. Anthony, 'Caribbean Integration: The Future Relationship Between Barbados and the OECS', *Journal of Eastern Caribbean Studies,* 23:1 (1998) p. 44.

15. Anthony, 'Caribbean Integration. . .', p. 46.

16. Anthony, 'Caribbean Integration. . .', p. 48.

17. Owen S. Arthur, 'Prospects for Caribbean Political Unity', *Journal of Eastern Caribbean Studies,* 23:1 (1998) p. 31.

18. Arthur, 'Prospects for Caribbean Political Unity', p. 31.

19. Arthur, 'Prospects for Caribbean Political Unity', p. 31.

20. Cynthia Barrow-Giles and Janice Farley, 'Barbadian Perception on Closer Collaboration with the Organisation of Eastern Caribbean States (OECS): The Barbados-OECS Initiative', *Journal of Eastern Caribbean Studies,* 24:2 (1999), pp. 43–68.

21. This must be viewed against the backdrop of events in many developing third world countries, such as Nigeria between 1974 and 1975 when a number of military coups occurred. Other action of the military took place in Ghana, Niger, Cyprus, Pakistan, Bangladesh, Turkey, Peru, Ethiopia and nearer home in Trinidad and Tobago between 1970 and 1971.

22. Dion E. Phillip, 'The Increasing Emphasis on Security and Defence in the Eastern Caribbean', in Alma H. Young and Dion E. Phillip, eds., *Militarization in the Non-Hispanic Caribbean* (Boulder: Lynne Rienner Publishers Inc., 1988), pp. 42–64.

Appendices

Appendix 1
The Ship Rider Agreement

Ship Rider agreement taken from the *Nation* newspaper of October 23rd, 1996.

Following is the Ship Riders Agreement, which Barbados refused to sign with the United States, stating that it would be tantamount to sacrificing the island's sovereignty.

Preamble

The Government of the United States of America and the Government of Barbados (hereafter, 'the parties'); bearing in mind the special nature of the problem of illicit maritime drug traffic; having regard to the urgent need for international co-operation in suppressing illicit maritime drug traffic which is recognised in the 1961 Single Convention On Narcotic Drugs and its 1972 protocol, in the 1971 Convention on Psychotropic Substances, and in the 1988 United Nations Convention Against Illicit Traffic in Narcotic Drugs and Psychotropic Substances; and Barbados desire to promote greater co-operation between the parties in combating illicit maritime drug traffic; have agreed as follows:

Nature and Scope of agreement

1. The parties shall co-operate in combating illicit maritime drug traffic to the fullest extent possible, consistent with available law enforcement resources and related priorities.
2. Maritime counter-drug operations in Barbadian waters are the responsibility of, and subject to the authority of the Government of Barbados.
3. In the agreement, unless the context otherwise requires:
   a. Barbadian waters means the territorial sea and international waters of Barbados, and the airspace over such waters;
   b. Law enforcement vessels include any embarked aircraft.
4. The parties shall establish a joint law enforcement Ship Rider programme between the Barbados law enforcement authorities and the United States Coast Guard (hereafter 'Coast Guard'). Each party may designate a coordinator to organise it's programme activities and to identify the vessels and officials involved in the programme to the other party.
5. The government of Barbados may designate qualified law enforcement officials to act as law enforcement Ship Riders. Subject to Barbadian law these Ship Riders may, in appropriate circumstances.
   a. Embark on United States Coast Guard and Navy vessels with Coast Guard and Navy vessels with Coast guard enforcement detachments embarked (hereafter 'US vessels');
   b. Authorise the pursuit, by the US vessels on which they are embarked, of suspect vessels and aircraft fleeing into Barbadian waters;
   c. Authorise the US vessels on which they are embarked to conduct counter-drug patrols in Barbados' waters;
   d. Enforce the laws of Barbados in Barbadian waters or seaward there from in the exercise of the right of hot pursuit or otherwise in accordance with international law; and Barbados; and
   e. Authorise the Coast Guard to assist in the enforcement of Barbados;
6. The Government of the United States of America may designate qualified Coast Guard law enforcement officials to act as law enforcement Ship Riders. Subject to United States law, these Ship Riders may, in appropriate circumstances:
   a. Embark on Government of Barbados vessels
   b. Advise and assist Barbadian law enforcement officials in the conduct of boarding of vessels to enforce the laws of Barbados.
   c. Enforce, seaward the territorial sea of Barbados the laws of the United States where authorised to do so; and
   d. Authorise the Barbadian vessels on which they re-embarked to assist in the enforcement of the laws of the United States seaward of the territorial sea of Barbados.
7. When a Ship Rider is embarked on the other party's vessel, and the enforcement action being carried out is pursuant to the Ship Rider's authority, any search or seizure of property, any detention of a person, and any use of force pur-

suant to this Agreement whether or not involving weapons, shall be carried out by the Ship Rider except as follows:

a. Crew members of the other party's vessel may assist in any such action if expressly requested to do so by the Ship Rider and only to the extent and in the manner requested. Such request may only be made, agreed to and acted upon in accordance with the applicable laws and policies of both parties; and

b. Such crew members may use such force in self-defence in accordance with the applicable laws and policies of their government.

8. The Government of the United States of America shall not conduct counter-drug operations in waters without the permission of the Government of Barbados, granted by this agreement or otherwise. This agreement constitutes permission by the Government for the United States counter-drug operations in any of the circumstances:

a. An embarked Barbadian Ship Rider so authorises;

b. A suspect vessel or aircraft encountered seaward of the territorial sea of Barbados flees into Barbadian waters and is pursued therein by a US vessel without a Barbados Ship Rider embarked, in which case any vessel may be boarded and searched, and, if the evidence warrants detain any such vessel pending disposition instructions from Barbadian authorities. Nothing in this agreement precludes the Government or Barbados from otherwise expressly authorising United States counter drug operations in Barbadian waters or involving Barbadian flag vessels or aircraft suspect of illicit traffic.

Operations Seaward of the Territorial Sea

9. Except as expressly provided herein, this agreement does not apply to or to limit boarding of vessels conducted by either party seaward of any nation's 'territorial' waters; whether based on the right of the visit, the rendering of assistance to persons, vessels, and property in distress or peril, the consent of the vessel master, or an authorisation from the flag state to take law enforcement action.

10. Whenever Coast Guard officials encounter a Barbadian flag vessel bolted seaward of any nation's territorial sea and suspect of illicit traffic, this agreement constitutes the authorisation of the Government of Barbados for the boarding and search of the suspect vessel and the persons found on board by such officials. If evidence is found, Coast Guard officials may detain the vessel and persons on board pending disposition instructions from the Government of Barbados.

Jurisdiction over Detained Vessels

11. In all cases arising in Barbadian waters or concerning Barbados flag vessels seaward of any nation's territorial sea the Government of Barbados shall have the primary right to exercise jurisdiction and authorise the enforcement of the United States law against the vessel persons on board.

Implementation

12. Counter-drug operations pursuant to this Agreement shall be carried out only against vessels and aircraft used for the commercial or private purposes and suspect of illicit maritime drug traffic, including vessels and aircraft without nationality.

13. A party conducting a boarding and searching pursuant to this agreement shall notify the other party of the results thereof.

14. Each party shall ensure that its law enforcement officials, when conducting boarding and searches pursuant to this agreement, act in accordance with the applicable national laws and policies of their government and with international law and accepted international law and accepted international practices.

15. Boarding and searches pursuant to this agreement shall be carried out by uniformed officials from ships or aircraft clearly marked and identified as being on government service. The boarding and search teams may carry personal arms.

16. All use of force pursuant to this agreement shall be in strict accordance with applicable laws and policies of the respective government and shall in all cases be the minimum reasonably necessary under the circumstances. Nothing in this agreement shall impair the exercise of the inherent right of self-defence by the law enforcement or other officials of either party.

17. To facilitate implementation of this Agreement, each party shall ensure the other party is fully informed concerning its applicable laws and policies, particularly those pertaining to the use of force. Each party has the corresponding responsibility to ensure. . . of its officials engaging in law enforcement operations pursuant to this agreement

are knowledgeable concerning the applicable laws and policies of both parties.

18. Unless their status is specifically provided for on another agreement, all law enforcement and other officials of the government of the United States of America present in Barbados' water or territory or on Barbadian vessels in connection with this agreement shall be accorded the privileges and immunities equivalent to those of the administrative and technical of a diplomatic mission under the 1961 Vienna Convention on Diplomatic Relations.

19. Assets seized in consequences of any operation undertaken in Barbadian Waters pursuant to this agreement shall be disposed of in accordance with the laws of Barbados. Assets seized in consequence of any operation undertaken seaward of the Barbadian territorial sea of Barbados pursuant to this agreement shall be disposed of in accordance with the laws of the seizing party. To the extent permitted by its law and upon such terms as it deems appropriate, a party may, in any case, transfer forfeited assets proceeds of their sale to the other party.

20. In case a question arises in connection with implementation of this agreement either party may request a meeting to resolve the mailer. If any loss or injury is suffered as a result of any action taken by the law enforcement or other officials of one party in contravention of this agreement or any improper or unreasonable action is taken by a party pursuant thereto, the parties shall meet at the request of either party to resolve the matter and decide any questions relating to compensation.

21. Except as provided in paragraph 18, nothing in this agreement is intended to alter the rights and privileges due any individual in any legal proceeding. Entry Into Force and Duration

22. This agreement shall enter into force upon signature by both parties.

23. This agreement may be terminated at any time by either party upon written notification to the other party through the diplomatic channel, such termination to take effect one year from the date of notification.

24. This agreement shall continue to apply after termination with respect to any administrative or judicial proceedings arising out of actions taken pursuant to this agreement.

Appendix 2

Summary of Resolutions Passed By The British Guiana and West Indies Labour Congress, November, 1938

FEDERATION. (A draft bill embodying a constitution for the creation and governance of a Federated West Indies was agreed.)

CONSTITUTIONAL REFORM. This Conference calls upon the Royal Commission to recommend the granting of self-government with adult suffrage to the several West Indian colonies providing for:

(a) Purely elected legislatures.

(b) Qualifications of elected members to be solely on an educational basis.

(c) Executive Council to be elected by members of the Legislature and to be responsible to the Legislature.

(d) The Legislative Council to elect its own president.

(e) The constitutional position and relation of the Governor to the Legislature to be similar to that of the King to Parliament, that is, the Governor as representative of the King to exercise the King's prerogatives on the advice of the Executive Council.

LAND AND FACTORIES. This conference agrees with the principle of nationalisation of the sugar industry, and suggests to the Royal Commission a recommendation that legislation be enacted in the several West Indian colonies providing for:

(a) The purchase by government of large sugar estates for redistribution among peasants on easy terms of sale.

(b) The prohibition of the ownership by a single individual, firm or company, directly or indirectly, of a sugar estate of more than 50 acres in extent.

(c) The ownership by the Government alone of all sugar factories.

(d) The establishment of a single Government purchasing agency in each colony for sugar, such agency to be the sole exporters of sugar.

PREFERENTIAL TREATMENT. This conference further suggests to the Royal Commission to recommend that any increased preference on sugar granted to the sugar industry in the West Indies shall be granted by the Imperial Government on the condition that such preference be given as to 10 per cent to the employers and 90 per cent to the cane farmers and field and factory workers by way of increased wages and pay.

COOPERATIVE MARKETING. This conference asks the Royal Commission to recommend the establishment of cooperative marketing of cocoa, rice and other agricultural products.

LOCAL PRICES. This conference suggests to the Royal Commission to recommend that no sugar and oil manufactured and refined in the colonies should be sold to local consumers at more than the export value plus 5 per cent for distributors' profits.

PUBLIC UTILITIES. This conference recommends that all essential utility services, viz., railways, water, electricity, tramways and telephones should be owned by the state or municipality.

SOCIAL AND INDUSTRIAL LEGISLATION. This conference suggests to the Royal Commission to recommend that legislation be enacted in the several colonies providing for

i. Old age pensions.
ii. National health insurance.
iii. Unemployment insurance.
iv. An ordinance to penalise unfair labour practices, similar to the National Labour Relations Act of the USA.
v. A 44-hour week without reduction in pay.
vi. Minimum wages for all workers.
vii. Workmen's Compensation on the lines of Great Britain, including agricultural workers and domestic servants.
viii. Trade Union law, including the immunities and privileges enjoyed in Great Britain.

a) *CONCILIATION MACHINERY.* This conference is of the opinion that there should be uniform legislation throughout these colonies for the establishment of Wages Advisory Boards and of a Labour Officer (where there is none at present) to whom all disputes as to wages and other conditions of employment shall be referred, and that provision be made for representation on these Boards of Labour and Trade Unions in each particular trade and industry.

b) *FACTORY LEGISLATION.* This conference urges the enactment of legislation throughout these colonies to provide for factory inspection and other provisions of the Factory Law in Great Britain.

c) *MINIMUM WAGES.* While this conference accepts the principle that there should be a minimum wage for all workers (including shop assistants), it is of the opinion that in view of

the differences of supply and demand and otherwise in the separate colonies, each colony should accordingly prepare for submission what may be considered the minimum wages for workers in the different categories of trade and industry.

7. *COURTS.* This conference is of the opinion that the West Indian Court of Appeal should have its adjudication enlarged so as to permit of its hearing appeals in criminal cases.

The Conference deprecates the existing practice in certain colonies of the appointment of persons holding the dual position of Police Magistrate and Judge of the Supreme Court, and is of the opinion that all such posts should be held by separate individuals.

8. *POLITICAL OFFENCES.* This conference demands that the law relating to sedition in these colonies be given the same interpretation and be employed only as in the United Kingdom, and that the existing law whereby the Executive is empowered to declare what is a seditious publication be repealed.

This conference is of opinion that the practice of trial by special jury in the criminal courts be abolished.

This conference urges the early introduction of prison legislation similar to that which obtains in the United Kingdom for dealing with political offenders.

14. *POLICE.* This conference is appreciative of the fact that there is no statutory bar to men of the ranks attaining commissions in the police forces, but is aware that no facilities are in fact afforded for the promotion of men from the ranks beyond the grade of Sergeant Major or First Class Warrant Officer; and is of opinion that Sub-Inspectors and Assistant Superintendents of the police forces should be recruited as far as possible from the ranks; and further, the conference demands the cessation of the practice of racial discrimination in appointments to Commission rank.

15. *EDUCATION.* This conference regrets the neglect in the past by governments to provide technical schools for vocational training, and is of opinion that throughout these colonies institutions similar to the Tuskegee Institute of the USA, be established, that liberal bursary systems be introduced, and that special regard be paid to the establishment of agricultural farms.

In the case of secondary school this conference stresses the necessity for a more liberal grant than now exists of free exhibitions from the primary schools.

The Conference is emphatic in its demand for the introduction of free compulsory elementary education throughout the colonies up to the age of 15 years, with provision of free books, and a daily milk ration for those in need.

16. *HEALTH.* This conference is of opinion that the Imperial Government should send to the colonies a commission of water, sanitary and sewerage engineers to make a survey of conditions in each colony with a view to improvements; that the cost of all such improvements be met in the first instance by advances made by the Imperial Government, and repaid in due course from local revenues, free of interest. Further, that throughout these colonies the whole question of hospital administration be reviewed by a Medical Commission to be appointed by the Colonial Office.

The Conference is of opinion that there should be clinics to deal with ante-natal cases, child welfare, tuberculosis, cancer and venereal diseases.

17. *MINOR INDUSTRIES.* This conference is of opinion that the governments should extend the present help being given to the creation of new and minor industries in each colony, more especially in those colonies whose principal source of revenue is sugar.

18. *IMMIGRATION.* This conference is of opinion that, having regard to the deplorable conditions in the West Indies, though it is in full sympathy with the depressed minorities in certain states, it must deprecate the settlement of any aliens in these colonies, until such conditions shall have been materially improved for the well-being of the West Indian masses, and until suitable arrangements have been made for the settlement of surplus island populations. Further, that alien immigration of types of people who would lower the standard of living be fully restricted, both as to numbers and areas.

19. *POPULATION.* This conference suggests to the Royal Commission that an immediate census of the population be taken, and an economic survey made, with special reference to housing, dietary, and conditions of employment.

Arthur W. Lewis, Labour in the West Indies: The Birth of a Workers Movement.

Appendix 3
Barbados Constitutional Review Recommendation Report 1998
Summary
Chapter 15
Summary of recommendations

1. *The preamble*

The Commission recommends as the Preamble to the reformed Constitution the revised text which appears at pages 18 and 19 of this Report.

2. *The supreme law*

The Commission recommends that the Supreme Law Clause be retained. It should also be strengthened by expressly conferring on the courts the power to review legislation to ensure its conformity with the Constitution. Also citizens should be given the right to mount constitutional challenges concerning the validity of any legislation which they consider may be ultra vires the Constitution. Those recommendations were made in paragraphs 6 and 7 of the Cox Report. However, differing from the Cox Commission, we recommend that a citizen making such a challenge should have a relevant interest.

3. *Fundamental principles and responsibilities*

The Commission recommends that certain broad statements of principle defining the general policy framework within which the governance of Barbados is undertaken should be included in the reformed Constitution of Barbados. The application of the principles in the making of laws should be the responsibility of Parliament and should not be cognisable by any court under any of the provisions of the Constitution.

A. *Responsibilities of Persons.*

The Commission recommends that the reformed Constitution emphasise that it is the duty and responsibility of every person in Barbados to:

* obey the law and abide by the Constitution and respect the ideals which it enshrines and the institutions which it establishes;
* exercise that person's rights in a manner which respects the rights of others;
* cooperate with lawful agencies in the maintenance of law and order;
* respect the National Flag, the National Anthem, the National Pledge and all National Emblems;
* register for electoral and other lawful purposes;
* defend the country and render national service whenever necessary;

* value and preserve the rich heritage of Barbadian culture;
* create and maintain a clean and healthy environment and have compassion for its living creatures;
* participate in the economic, political and social life of Barbados;
* contribute to the well-being of Barbados to the best of that person's ability;
* strive towards excellence in all spheres of individual and collective activity, so that the nation constantly rises to higher levels of endeavour and achievement;
* promote harmony and a spirit of unity among all the people of Barbados,
* transcending religious, sectoral or racial diversities and abstain from practices derogatory to the dignity of the human person.

B. Responsibilities

The State shall:

* respect democratic principles and the fundamental rights and freedoms proclaimed in this Constitution, and encourage and facilitate the widest possible participation in all the processes and institutions of government;
* endeavour to operate the machinery of government, including the use and disposition of public finances, with the greatest degree of transparency consistent with good and the national interest, and in a manner that is in keeping with the democratic vocation of Barbados;
* endeavour to ensure the protection and promotion of the internationally recognised;
* economic and social rights of its People, including the right to work, the right to health, the right to education and the right to public assistance in cases of extreme need;
* endeavour to safeguard the economic interest of the weaker sections of the community and where required contribute to the support of the aged, the infirm, the disabled and children;
* endeavour to secure that private enterprise is so conducted as to ensure reasonable efficiency in the production and distribution of goods, the provision and delivery of services and to protect the public against unjust exploitation;
* direct its policies towards securing that the operation of free competition is not allowed to develop in such a manner as to result in the concentration of ownership or control of essential commodities

in a few individuals to the common detriment of the People;

* ensure that the beaches and public areas are accessible to all and do not become the exclusive preserve of any one sector of the community;
* fashion and direct its policies to ensure that land is not so owned and used as to result in a concentration of ownership and control in a few individuals to the common detriment of the People;
* give the highest priority in the planning and execution of government policy to the preservation and protection of the natural environment of Barbados, which it shall hold as a sacred trust for future generations;
* affirm its commitment to the idea of peace, friendly cooperation and security among all nations founded on international justice and morality and respect for human rights;
* in the conduct of state affairs, accept the generally recognised principles of international law and ensure that its Parliament and people respect and implement treaties and conventions which the State, through its Executive and Parliament, has negotiated and ratified.

4. Citizenship

The Commission recommends that:

(a) the Constitution be amended to recognise as citizens by birth the children born overseas to citizens of Barbados while serving in a diplomatic or consular capacity;

(b) children born in Barbados should be deemed citizens at birth only where at least one parent is a citizen of Barbados, a permanent resident, an immigrant of Barbados or is registered under the Immigration Act by the provision enacted in a l 996 enactment;

(c) a child aged not more than five years found in Barbados, whose parents are not known, shall be presumed to be a citizen of Barbados by birth;

(d) a child under the age of l8 years, neither of whose parents is a citizen of Barbados, who is adopted by a citizen of Barbados shall, on application, be registered as a citizen of Barbados;

(e) consequential amendments be made to other legislation to give full effect to the amended constitutional provisions;

(f) children born of Barbadian males and females should be equally treated subject to such exceptions and qualifications as may be prescribed in the Barbados Citizenship Act;

(g) the Constitution should be amended to make it absolutely clear that no child born outside Barbados may be recognised as a citizen by descent unless at least one parent is a citizen of Barbados by birth and holds Barbadian citizenship at the time of the child's birth;

(h) the present policy of recognising dual and multiple citizenship should be retained;

(i) the Constitution or related laws should make further provision prescribing the exceptions and qualifications to the grant of citizenship by virtue of marriage. This would prevent persons who would be considered prohibited persons in accordance with the First Schedule of the Immigration Act, Cap. 190, from being granted citizenship automatically;

(j) persons should not be deprived of citizenship without due process of law. The Commission recommends that the applicable law be amended to reflect this fundamental principle;

(k) existing legislation which provides for review of the cases of applicants who are denied citizenship or permanent resident or immigrant status under the appropriate laws should be strengthened. The Review Board should be obligated to report annually to the Minister. Reports should be laid in Parliament. This would achieve transparency and avoid opportunities for corruption, since Parliament would be in a position to monitor the system and debate the reports.

5. *The bill of rights*

The Commission recommends:

(a) Simplification of the language of the Chapters in order to make its meaning more accessible to non-specialists. For increased clarity of the text of the Chapter, the Commission proposes that the rights and freedoms protected should be presented in a clear and distinct manner; so too the exceptions and modifications which are a necessary and appropriate in a free and democratic society.

(b) The category of gender should be included in the definition of discriminatory in the revised Constitution.

(c) That the special care which society undoubtedly owes to persons with various physical and/or mental disabilities be dealt with by way of carefully crafted legislation as is, to some extent, already the case rather than in the broad sweep of constitutional provisions.

(d) Inclusion in the revised Constitution of declaratory language similar to that of the International Covenant on Economic, Social and Cultural Rights to meet concerns expressed by many who appeared before the Commission.

(e) That the right of every citizen to vote in an election of members of the House of Assembly and the right of every citizen to be qualified for membership therein be entrenched in the Constitution as fundamental rights, subject only to such exceptions and considerations as may be reasonable in a democratic society and as may be prescribed by law.

(f) That the emergency provisions in Chapter III of the Constitution should be included in a separate chapter.

(g) Deletion of section 15(2) which authorises the retention of certain punishments or treatments that were lawful before Independence.

(h) By a majority, deletion of section 26 which saves existing law and derogates from the supremacy of the Constitution.

6. *Private actions violating fundamental rights*

The Commission recommends that Parliament, as a matter of urgency, enact remedial legislation in all areas where the Constitution provides a remedy and redress against governmental or other state action, but where no law exists to provide an appropriate or adequate remedy against private action of the same character.

7. *The head of state: election and removal*

The Commission recommends that:

(a) The Head of State of Barbados should be a President, elected by an Electoral College constituted by the Senate and the House of Assembly meeting as a single body for the purpose of such an election.

(b) The system of government should be of a parliamentary democracy with substantive executive authority exercised by a Cabinet headed by a Prime Minister.

(c) The President should be a citizen of Barbados by birth or descent not less than 40 years of age and should have been resident in Barbados continuously for at least 5 years prior to election.

(d) The President should hold no other office of emolument or profit, whether in the public service or otherwise.

(e) The President should hold office for a fixed term of seven years.

(f) The salary and allowances of the President and the other terms of service should not be altered to the disadvantage of the President after assumption of office.

(g) The person holding the office of Governor General at the commencement of the reformed Constitution should hold office of President under the new Constitution until a President is elected under the provisions of the new Constitution.

(h) The Electoral College shall be convened by the Speaker of the House of Assembly, who shall preside as chairman over the proceedings of the Electoral College and shall have an original vote.

(i) Ten Senators, the Speaker, and fourteen other members of the House of Assembly shall constitute a quorum of the Electoral College.

(j) Whenever the office of the President is vacant, or within not more than 90 days nor less than 60 days before the term of office of the President will expire, the Prime Minister shall consult with the Leader of the Opposition with a view to their joint nomination of a suitable candidate for election as President.

(k) If the Prime Minister and the Leader of the Opposition submit to the Speaker in writing a joint nomination of a candidate for election as President, being a nomination to which the candidate has consented, the Speaker shall inform the Electoral College of the nomination and declare the candidate duly elected without a vote of the Electoral College for the election.

(l) If the Electoral College has been informed of the nomination of only one candidate the Speaker shall declare that candidate to have been duly elected without a vote of the Electoral College for the election.

(m) If the Prime Minister and the Leader of the Opposition are unable to agree a joint nomination of a candidate for election as President, the Prime Minister shall notify the Speaker to that effect and the Speaker shall inform the Electoral College accordingly.

(n) The Prime Minister or the Leader of the Opposition or any ten members of the House of Assembly, may, during the period expiring fourteen days after the day on which the Electoral College has been so informed, submit to the Speaker in writing a nomination of a candidate for election as President and the Speaker shall at the first meeting of the House after the expiration of that period and before the House proceeds to any other business inform the House of the nominations received to which the candidates named have consented.

(o) No candidate shall be elected President unless the person has secured the votes in secret ballot of not less than two-thirds of all members of the Electoral College.

(p) Whenever the question of the election of the President from among two or more candidates put to a vote, voting shall be by secret ballot, or in such manner as not to disclose the vote of any member of the Electoral College.

(q) The President may be removed from office if the President–

(i) wilfully violates any provision of the Constitution;

(ii) behaves in such a way as to bring the office into discredit, ridicule or contempt;

(iii) behaves in a way that endangers the security of the State;

(iv) because of physical or mental or other incapacity, is unable to perform the functions of the office.

(r) The President should be removed from office if–

(i) a motion is proposed in the House of Assembly that the removal of the President from office should be investigated by a tribunal;

(ii) the motion states with full particulars the grounds on which the removal from office is proposed, and is signed by not less than one-third of all members of the House of Assembly;

(iii) the motion for removal from office is approved by the vote of not less than two-thirds of all the members of the Senate and the House of Assembly assembled together;

(iv) a tribunal consisting of the Chief Justice and four other judges appointed by the Chief Justice (being as far as practicable the most senior judges of the Supreme Court of Judicature) investigates the complaint and reports on the facts to the Speaker;

(v) the Senate and the House of Assembly assembled together on the summons of the Speaker consider the report and by resolution supported by the votes of not less than two-thirds of all members of the Senate and the House of Assembly assembled together, declare that the President be removed from office.

(s) Where the office of President is vacant or the President is incapable of performing the functions of President by reason of absence from Barbados, or for any other reason, those functions should be performed by:

(i)   such person as the Prime Minister and the Leader of the Opposition may jointly designate;

(ii) where there is no person so designated within seven days of the vacancy, or as the case may be, the incapacity in question occurring, by the President of the Senate;

(iii) where the President of the Senate is unwilling or for whatever reason is unable to act, by such person as the Prime Minister may designate.

8. *The senate*

The Commission recommends:

(a) The number of Senators should remain at twenty-one. However the composition of the Senate should be modified, principally to provide for more representatives for those who do not support the Government of the day and also to give recognition to the fact that there are now more than two established political parties in Barbados and that the number of parties can increase. These objectives can be achieved by the following proposals:

Where there is a Leader of the Opposition, the appointment of Senators should be as follows:

(i)   twelve Senators shall be appointed by the President, acting in accordance with the advice of the Prime Minister;

(ii) four Senators shall be appointed by the President, acting in accordance with the advice of the Leader of the Opposition;

(iii) if there are members of a political party represented in the House of Assembly who do not support the Prime Minister or the Leader of the Opposition, two Senators shall be appointed by the President acting after consultation with the Leader of that political party or where there is more

than one such party, the leaders of those parties;

(iv) if there is represented in the House of Assembly no such political party as is described in sub-paragraph (iii) above, two Senators shall be appointed by the President acting in the President's discretion after consultation with (a) the leader of any political party which was supported in the election by the votes of at least ten per cent of all those who voted in the election and (b) such other persons as the President considers ought to be consulted;

(v)   three Senators shall be appointed by the President, acting in the President's discretion, after consultation with such persons as the President considers ought to be consulted, to represent such interests as the President considers ought to be represented in the Senate. Where there is no Leader of the Opposition by reason of the fact that the President, acting in the President's discretion, has determined that there is no person qualified under the Constitution for and willing to accept appointment to that office, the appointment of Senators should be as follows:

(i)   twelve Senators shall be appointed by the President, acting in accordance with the advice of the Prime Minister;

(ii) six Senators shall be appointed by the President, acting in the President's discretion after consultation with (a) the leader of any political party which was supported in the election by the votes of at least ten per cent of all those who voted in the election and (b) such other persons as the President considers ought to be consulted;

(iii) three Senators shall be appointed by the President acting in the President's discretion after consultation with such persons as the President considers ought to be consulted, to represent such interests as the President considers ought to be represented in the Senate.

(b) An appropriate amendment should be made to the Constitution to provide that the Senate can debate money resolutions before expenditure on such resolutions is authorised.

9. *Parliamentary committee system*

The Commission recommends that the Committee system in Parliament be expanded and that parliamentary committees be provided with adequate financial resources and appropriate staff so that they may be better able to ensure government accountability and to provide opportunities for concerned and interested persons to make representations to Parliament through its committees on issues that affect the community.

10. The electoral system

The Commission recommends that the present system of 'first-past-the-post' should be retained.

11. Integrity commission

The Commission recommends that a Parliamentary Integrity Commission should be established. The duty of the Commission would be to receive declarations of assets, liabilities and income of Members of Parliament with powers if necessary to investigate any declaration and generally to perform such other duties as may be prescribed by Parliament.

12. People's initiatives

The Commission recommends that, as soon as possible, Government should introduce into Parliament legislation creating a system of 'People's Initiatives' designed to accord to electors a measure of original law-making power without by-passing or distorting the fundamental authority of Parliament in this domain. It is recommended that, at the time when a general election is held, qualifying groups of electors should be empowered to present, for the approval or disapproval of the general electorate, simply-worded propositions for legislation by the incoming Parliament. It would be the responsibility of the Government, whenever any such proposition was approved by a qualifying proportion of the electorate, to present the relevant legislative measure to Parliament, where it would be the object of a free vote not subject to the discipline of the Party Whips.

13. Election disputes

The Commission recommends that:

(a)   There should be a right of appeal to the Court of Appeal on all questions of disputed membership of the Senate, and that section 39 of the Election Offences and By Act Cap. 3, should be amended to provide that the Election Court should be constituted by any three judges of the Court of Appeal, whose decision shall be

(b)   In relation to section 46(2) of the Constitution, Parliament should by law prescribe the authority or authorities responsible for determining certain questions concerning the membership of the House of Assembly, in particular whether any person has vacated a seat

or is required by section 45 (2) (a) to cease to function as a member.

14. The executive

The Commission recommends that:

(a)   The executive authority of Barbados shall be vested in the President who shall be Commander-in-Chief of the armed forces.

(b)   Section 66(2) of the Constitution should be amended to remove the power of the Minister to advise the President to dissolve Parliament when the House of Assembly has by a majority of all its members resolved that the appointment of the Prime Minister be revoked.

(c)   If, within seven days of a resolution to revoke the appointment of the Prime Minister, the President is unable to find anyone who can command the support of a majority of members of the House of Assembly, the President should be empowered to dissolve Parliament.

(d) Section 74(5) should be amended to provide that when the President is doubtful whether a person commands the support of a majority of those members of the House of Assembly who do not support the Government, the President should act in his own discretion, after consulting with the Speaker, in determining the question.

15. The privy council

The Commission recommends that the Privy Council should be renamed the 'Presidential Council', and that the tenure of its members be fixed at a maximum of seven years instead of the present maximum of fifteen years and that the age limit of seventy-five years for Presidential Councillors should be removed.

16. Director of public prosecutions

The Commission recommends:

(a)   By a majority, that section 79 A should be amended to remove the power of the Attorney General to give directions to the Director of Public Prosecutions in regard to the matters specified therein, and to provide that, in relation to those matters, the Director of Public Prosecutions should consult the Attorney General before exercising the relevant powers.

(b)   That the age of retirement for the Director of Public Prosecutions should be 65.

17. The judicature

The Commission recommends, by a majority, that sections 8 l and 89 of the Constitution should be amended to provide as follows:

(a)   That the Chief Justice be appointed by the Head of State on the joint recommendation of the

Prime Minister and the Leader of the Opposition after the latter have consulted with the Judicial and Legal Service Commission. If no joint recommendation is tendered the Head of State shall, in his own deliberate judgement, appoint a person from among those considered by the Prime Minister and the Leader of the Opposition.

(b) That the other judges of the Supreme Court be appointed by the Head of State acting on the recommendation of the Judicial and Legal Service Commission after that Commission has consulted with the Prime Minister and the Leader of the Opposition.

(c) That in appointing the members of the Judicial and Legal Service Commission (other than the Chief Justice and the Chairman of the Public Service Commission or nominee) the Head of State should act after consultation with the Prime Minister and the Leader of the Opposition, where, presently, the Governor General is required to act in accordance with the recommendation of the Prime Minister after the latter has consulted the Leader of the Opposition.

(d) That the retirement age for all judges of the Supreme Court, with the exception of the Chief Justice, should be fixed at 72.

(e) That the Head of State may, after consultation with the Prime Minister, the Leader of the Opposition, and the Judicial and Legal Service Commission, authorise the Chief Justice to continue in office until he has attained the age of 75 years.

(f) That the procedure for the removal of the Chief Justice should be initiated by referral to the Head of State by the Judicial and Legal Service Commission after consultation with the Prime Minister and the Leader of the Opposition; in the case of a judge the procedure should be initiated by referral to the Head of State by that Commission after consultation with the Prime Minister and the Chief Justice.

(g) That the Magistracy should be recognised in the Constitution as part of the judicial system of Barbados and that Government should, as a matter of urgency, undertake a detailed study of the status of the institution covering terms and conditions of service of magistrates, the appropriateness of establishing a career magistracy, the role of the Chief Magistrate in relation to the administration of the magistracy, and the scope of constitutional protection which should be afforded to its officers.

18. The public service

The Commission recommends that the relevant sections of the Constitution should be amended to provide for:

(a) Appointment of the Public Service Commission by the Head of State after consultation with the Prime Minister and the Leader of the Opposition and with such organisations as the Head of State sees fit to consult.

(b) The bringing into force of the existing constitutional provisions for the creation of a Teaching Service Commission.

(c) The creation of a Protective Services Commission to deal with matters relating to the appointment, removal and discipline of officers of the Police Force, the Prisons Service and the Fire Service, and the consequential abolition of the Police Service Commission.

(d) Inclusion in the revised Constitution of language similar to that of section 8 of the Police Act, Cap. 1 67 to the effect that the Commissioner of Police shall have the command and the superintendent of the Police Force and shall be responsible to the President for the efficient administration and government of the Force;

(e) The establishment of a Public Service Appeal Board comprising a Chairman and two other members, and appointed by the Head of State after consultation with the Prime Minister, the Leader of the Opposition, and the Chief Justice, to hear and determine appeals from any decisions of a Service Commission or from any person to whom powers of the Commission have been duly delegated.

(f) By a majority, the reversal of the 1974 constitutional amendments with respect to temporary and unestablished posts as well as to certain senior posts.

(g) A redefinition of 'public service' at section 1 17(7) so as to retain the meaning of the term in force before the 1 974 constitutional amendments.

(h) Inclusion of a definition of 'permanent secretary' to make it clear that the holder of such office has the principal responsibility for the management of the respective department of which the Minister has general direction and control.

(i) Removal of the posts of 'chief or deputy chief professional or technical adviser or officer' from the list of posts appointment to which requires that the respective Service Commission should consult the Prime Minister before tendering a recommendation to the Head of State.

19. Finance

The Commission recommends:

(a) that the Public Accounts Committee should be given greater constitutional importance by specifically providing for its establishment in the Constitution. Its membership should consist of not less than six nor more than ten members. The Chairman of the Public Accounts Committee should be a member of the Opposition in the House of Assembly, if any, and if willing to act. The Chairman and other members may comprise an equal number of members of the House of Assembly and the Senate as the House of Assembly may determine. Where no member of the Opposition in the House of Assembly is willing to act as Chairman of the Public Accounts Committee, a member of the Opposition in the Senate should be appointed, and where no member of the Opposition in the Senate is willing so to act, one of the Senators appointed by the President in his discretion should be appointed Chairman;

(b) that the Public Accounts Committee should consider and report to the House of Assembly on the examination of accounts showing the appropriation of the sums granted by Parliament to meet the public expenditure of Barbados; such other accounts as the Committee may think fit or such other accounts as the House of Assemrces. The Auditor General should also be authorised and given the necessary resources to employ auditors from the private sector to assist with audits within the purview of the Office of Auditor General;

(g) amendment of section 113(2) to permit the Auditor General to undertake comprehensive audits in order to provide an objective and constructive assessment of the extent to which financial, human and physical resources are managed with due regard to economy, efficiency and effectiveness. The audit should be an examination of both financial and management controls, including information systems and reporting;

(h) that the Auditor General should be empowered to carry out audits of the accounts, balance sheets and other financial statements of all state enterprises owned or controlled by the State;

(i) early completion and enactment of an updated and modern Financial Administration and Audit Act which would pay due regard to the independence necessary for the improvement in the performance of the functions of the Auditor General, permit the Auditor General to play a greater role in the appointment, transfer and retention of the staff of the Audit Office, and would also strengthen the Auditor General's relationship with Parliament to enable Parliament to be the real watchdog of the public purse;

(j) Provision for votes on account of annual appropriations and for an emergency draw-down by the Minister responsible for Finance from the Consolidated Fund.

20. Related laws and transitory provisions

The Commission recommends:

(a) The establishment of a special Task Force mandated to analyse urgently existing statutory provisions to ensure that they are in or are brought into conformity with the reformed Constitution and, in particular, with the fundamental rights provisions therein.

(b) That provision should be made for succession to the prerogatives which at present vest in the Crown by common law. A further detailed examination must also be undertaken to identify the contents of those prerogatives and which of them should be retained.

(c) That provision should be made in the Constitution to ensure succession to all property, assets, rights and liabilities which at present vest in the Crown in right of its government of Barbados.

(d) That legislation should be enacted urgently to make it obligatory for employers to recognise trade unions so as to buttress the constitutional right of freedom of association.

(e) That the Barbados National Honours system should be retained but appropriate changes made to reflect the change to a republican form of government and the new environment ensuing therefrom.

(f) That transitory provisions should be enacted to ensure continuity in the authority and effectiveness of the organs and institutions of State during the legal period and the process of transition from the existing Constitution to the reformed Constitution.

Appendix 4

RESULT OF THE GENERAL ELECTIONS IN THE COMMONWEALTH CARIBBEAN 1993–2000

Country	Election year	Political party	% vote	No. of seats	% seats	Proportio- nality seats
Barbados	1999	BLP	65.4	26	92.8	18
		DLP	34.6	2	7.1	10
Bahamas	1997	FNM	-	33	-	-
		PLP	-	6	-	-
Antigua & Barbuda	1994	ALP	54.5	11	64.7	9
		UPP	43.7	5	29.4	7\8
		BPM	2.04	1	5.88	0/1
Antigua & Barbuda	1999	ALP	52.9	12	70.58	9
		UPP	44.4	4	23.52	8
		BPM	1.3	1	5.88	0
Dominica	1995	DFP	35.8	5	23.8	8
		DUWP	34.4	11	52.38	7
		DLP	29.6	5	23.8	6
	2000	DFP	13.57	2	9.52	3
		DUWP	43.44	9	42.85	9
		DLP	42.91	10	47.61	9
Grenada	1999	NNP	62.4	15	100	9
		NDC	24.9	0	0	4
		GULP	12.1	0	0	2
Jamaica	1997	PNP	55.0	50	83.55	33
		JLP	40.0	9	15.0	24
Trinidad & Tobago	1995	PNM	48.3	17	47.2	17
		UNC	45.3	17	17.2	16
		NAR	7.7	2	5.5	3
St Lucia	1997	SLP	61.3	16	94.11	10
		UWP	36.6	1	5.88	7
St Vincent & the Grenadines	1998	ULP	54.2	7	46.66	8
		NDP	45.8	8	53.33	7
St Christopher & Nevis	1995	LP/WL	-	7	-	-
		CCM	-	2	-	-
		PAM	-	1	-	-
		NRP	-	1	-	-

Result of the General Elections in the Commonwealth Caribbean 1993–2000 Contd.

Country	Election year	Political party	% vote	No. of seats	% seats	Proportio-nality seats
St Christopher & Nevis	2000	LP/WL	-	8	-	-
		CCM	-	2	-	-
		PAM	-	0	-	-
		NRP	-	1	-	-
Guyana	1997	PPP/ CIVIC	55.3	29	54.71	-
		PNC	40.6	22	41.50	-
		U. F	1.5	1	1.88	-
		AFP	1.2	1	1.88	-

All Elections in the commonwealth Caribbean are based on the FPP electoral system with the exception of Guyana which operates under the proportionality system.

Self Assessment Test

1. The primary objective of the British Crown for expanding its empire through colonialism was:
   A. To spread its culture from Britain to the West Indian colonies.
   B. To exploit the colonies' resources for economic gain to the metropole.
   C. To spread their technologies, knowledge and skills.
   D. To diversify the economies of the West Indian colonies from sugar production to manufacturing and industry.

2. Imperialism is defined as:
   A. A symmetrical political, cultural and economic relationship between two or more nations.
   B. Interdependence of states.
   C. The conquest and settlement of a backward country by a more advanced nation.
   D. Any relationship of effective domination or control, whether political, economic or cultural.

3. Which of the following measures were *not* adopted by the local ruling class in the immediate post-emancipation period to govern the relationship between the various classes.
   i. The passing of vagrancy and coercive work laws.
   ii. Master and servant laws.
   iii. Reduction in the franchise qualifications.
   iv. Increased penalties on employers for violating worker's rights.

A. i only
B. i and ii only
C. i and iv only
D. iii only

4. The following basic elements make up the CCG political system, which replaced the ORS in the late nineteenth century.
   A. The Crown, Governor, Council Assembly.
   B. The Crown, Governor, Council.
   C. The Crown, Council, Assembly.
   D. The Crown, Governor, Assembly.

5. Which of the following contributed to the change over from ORS of Government to the Crown Colony system of Government.
   i. The events of the 1930s in the British West Indies.
   ii. The oligarchic nature of the existing governmental system.
   iii. The rise of the industrial revolution in Britain.
   iv. The intransigence of the local representative institution.
   v. Racism.

A. i, ii, iv, v only.
B. i, ii, iii, v only.
C. ii, iii, iv, v only.
D. i, iii, iv, v only.
E. All of the above

6. After 1865, CCG was *not* introduced in the British West Indies colony of:
   A. Jamaica

B. Barbados

C. St Lucia

D. British Guiana

7. Complete the statement with the appropriate response below.

Under the ORS. . .

    i. Members of the Assembly were elected by freeholders on a limited franchise

    ii. Senior administrative officials were nominated by the governor to be members of council

    iii. The Crown had the power to override all political opposition and dominated the colonial legislature

    iv. The unofficial members were nominated by the governor

A. i, ii, iii, and v

B. i iii, iv, only

C. ii, iii, iv and v.

8. Which of the following conditions spurred the 1930s labour revolts in the West Indies.

    i. The prices of West Indies exports had declined drastically between 1928 and 1933

    ii. The steady drift of unemployed workers from the plantations to towns

    iii. The Italian conquest of Abyssinia

    iv. No constitutional machinery for the redress of grievance

    v. Strict censorship on press

A. i, ii, iii and iv

B. i, ii, iii, and v only

C. i, and ii only

D. i, ii, and iv only

E. All of the above

9. According to Linden Lewis, race may be defined or is used to connote:

A. The rate/speed at which developing countries diversify their economy

B. The differential treatment of one group over another, based on the perceived superiority of one group over an inferior group

C. Socially defined characteristics that are based exclusively on physical characteristics

D. The use of physical characteristics to determine non-physical characteristics

10. During the epoch of classical colonialism, Caribbean societies were stratified on the basis of :

A. Income

B. Status

C. Class

D. Race

11. Kwamé Nkrumah defines neo-colonialism as a condition in which:

    i. A country which in theory is independent and has all the outward trappings of international sovereignty, but in reality its economic system and this its political policy is directed from outside

    ii. Those countries which practice it has power without responsibility.

    iii. Control of the world market by international capital.

    iv. A country which has a flag and a national anthem but the undivided masses still live in the middle ages.

A. i only

B. i, ii and iii.

C. iv only.

D. i and ii only.

12. The following measures typically constitute structural adjustment conditionalities imposed by the IMF on Caribbean countries seeking Balance of Payments assistance:

    i. Devaluation.

    Ii. Liberalisation of trade and foreign investment.

    iii. Reductions in public expenditure, particularly in social services such as health and education.

    iv. The sale and/or management of private sector enterprises to/by the government.

A. i, ii, iii.

B. i, ii, iii, iv.

C . i, iii, iv.

D. ii, iii, iv .

13. The IMF, one of the battering rams of the neo-liberal project was used effectively in attacking the socialist experiment in:

A. Barbados

B. Cuba

C. Jamaica

D. Grenada

14. The Structural Adjustment Project imposed by the IMF on Barbados in 1991 included all of the following *except*:

A. A reduction in wages of Civil Servants by 8 per cent

B. A devaluation of the local currency by 8 per cent

C. Privatisation of Government shares in hotels and Telecommunications companies

D. Reduction in subsidies and removal of concessions to industry

15. Raghavan is of the view that the spectre of re-colonialisation looms large for the nations of the economic south. Which of the definitions below best explain the phenomenon of re-colonialisation.
    A. Concert of capitalist nations and capitalist institutions seeking to compel all national governments to play the role of a metropolitan governor on behalf of metropolitan imperialism therefore frustrating the notion of self determination
    B. GATT
    C. Globalisation
    D. A phenomenon that became evident after the ending of the Cold War that is disadvantageous to the south

16. False decolonisation can be defined as:
    A. The grant of political independence to former colonies
    B. The presence of powerful financial institutions, foreign nations and other interests in the politics and economy of former colonies
    C. Insubstantial changes from colony to sovereign state
    D. The survival of the colonial economic system in spite of the formal recognition of political independence of former colonies

17. The following is NOT a major factor shaping economic and political relations and behaviour in this new era of globalisation.
    A. The spread of the TNC facilitated by technology and telecommunications.
    B. Evolution of trading blocs and economic communities
    C. Cold War politics
    D. Transformation of multilateral trading system and liberalisation of trade regimes.

18. Some of the economic, cultural and social consequences of colonialism in the Caribbean which have been perpetuated into the contemporary period are:
    i. A high import content of goods and services available in the economy.
    ii. Economies that focus mainly on the production of primary products with little diversification of the economy.
    iii. A preponderance of foreign programming in the electronic media.
    iv. A social structure that is characterised by the minority groups in society holding economic power.
    A. i, ii, iii, iv.
    B. ii, iii, iv only.

C. iv only
D. i, iii, iv only.

19. The most significant constitutional development to Caribbean people this century was:
    A. The legislation of trade unions.
    B. The creation of mass parties.
    C. Universal adult suffrage.
    D. The removal of the monarchy and the move toward a republican form of government.

20. Which political institution acted as an attack on CCG in the 20th century?
    A. Trade unions.
    B. Political Parties.
    C. Universal adult suffrage.
    D. Federation of the West Indies.

21. Union Busting is:
    A. Closing down of trade unions.
    B. Increase in the number of trade unions.
    C. Legislation to reduce the number of trade unions.
    D. Strategies aimed at reducing the overall effectiveness of trade unions.

22. It is becoming more apparent that the trade union movement globally is under severe stress. This can be attributed to:
    A. Political trade unionism.
    B. Collapse of Stalinism in the Soviet Union and Eastern Europe.
    C. Capitalist truimphalism and ascendant capital.
    D. Working classes becoming more fractured.

23. Political unionism can best be described as:
    A. The link between political parties and trade unions.
    B. The tendency of trade unions to become involved in politics.
    C. The tendency of political parties to infiltrate trade unions.
    D. Pork barrel politics.

24. Which of the following political parties in the region were not associated with trade unions?
    A. The Barbados Labour Party and the Jamaican Labour Party.
    B. The Jamaican Labour Party and the People's National Party.
    C. The People's National Movement and the Antigua Labour Party.
    D. The People's National Movement.

25. Which two Caribbean countries on March 06, 1997, lost leading political and trade union leaders?

A. Barbados and Guyana.

B. Trinidad and Tobago and Jamaica.

C. Jamaica and Guyana.

D. Antigua and Guyana.

26. The majority of the Caribbean countries accepted independence with a monarchical constitutional system fashioned after the Westminster model. However, one Caribbean territory did not follow this path and accepted independence as a Republic. Identify this territory.

A. Guyana.

B. Trinidad and Tobago.

C. Grenada.

D. Dominica.

27. Which of the following best describes the modifications which Caribbean Independent Constitutions adopted?

A. A written constitution.

B. Fusion of the branches of Government.

C. Proportional representation.

D. A partly elected Senate.

28. The Westminster model of Government in the Caribbean is one which is marked by:

A. Winner takes all.

B. Effective separation of power and check and balances.

C. Fusion of the legislative, executive and judicial arm of Government.

D. Excessive abuse and dictatorial tendencies.

29. The First-Past-the-Post electoral system is NOT a feature in the Commonwealth Caribbean territory of:

A. Trinidad and Tobago.

B. Brazil.

C. Cuba.

D. Guyana.

30. An electoral system determines:

A. The composition of a parliament and the representation of public interest.

B. How votes are translated into seats.

C. The number of political parties which are represented in a country.

D. The representational voids in a parliament.

31. According to Duverger, the difference between Majoritarian systems and proportional systems is that:

A. The majoritarian single ballot system tends to party pluralism, while proportional models tend to multipartisim.

B. The Majoritarian single ballot system in contrast to the proportional system focuses on producing equal allocation in representative institutions in proportion of votes to seats.

C. The Majoritarian System tends to cope badly with the governability requirement.

D. The Majoritarian System tends to favour weaker candidates and parties in contrast to proportional system.

32. Giovanni Sartori contends that all of the following *except*_____ are justifications for the support of Majoritarian systems.

A. They help to elect a governing majority and an effective government.

B. They reduce party fragmentation.

C. They create fairness in representation.

D. They create a more direct relationship between the electors and their representatives.

Questions 33 and 34 relate to Table 1.

TABLE 1: RESULTS OF THE 2000 GENERAL ELECTION IN A HYPOTHETICAL CARIBBEAN ISLAND

Party	MLP	NLP	PLM
Votes Cast	22 000	14 000	9 000
No. of Seats	14	8	6
% of Votes	49	31	20
% Seats	50	29	21

Assume a small Caribbean Island of an electorate of 45,000, had General Elections in which three political parties contested, vying for the 28 seats in Parliament. Assume also there is a 100 per cent voter turnout of the fully, eligible population. Percentage figures in Table 1 are rounded off for simplicity.

33. The statistics in Table 1 are a more accurate reflection of the:

A. First-Past-the-Post Electoral System.

B. Proportional Representation Electoral System.

C. Open list Electoral System.

D. Closed list Electoral System.

34. From an analysis of the data contained in Table 1, the following is an *INCORRECT* conclusion:

A. The system is democratic as the winning party is the one securing the plurality of all the votes cast.

B. The party with the minority of all votes will form the new government.

C. The percentage of seats gained by the losing parties is equal to that of the winning party.

D. The minority votes of the two losing parties combined constitute the majority vote.

35. In which Commonwealth Caribbean countries have the result of general elections in the last decade led to hung parliaments and coalition government.
A. St Vincent and the Grenadines and St Lucia.
B. Trinidad and Tobago and Guyana.
C. Trinidad and Tobago and St Kitts/Nevis.
D. Jamaica and Trinidad and Tobago.

36. The clearest and must dramatic recent manifestations of the main demerit of the Majoritarian single ballot system can be found in which of the following countries:
A. St Vincent & the Grenadines and Grenada.
B. Dominica and St Kitts-Nevis.
C. Barbados and Grenada.
D. St Lucia and St Vincent & the Grenadines.
E. Antigua and Barbuda, and Trinidad & Tobago.

37. In which three Commonwealth Caribbean countries in the 1990s have political leaders voluntarily resigned their post as Prime Ministers?
A. Jamaica, Trinidad and Tobago and Guyana.
B. St Lucia, St Vincent and the Grenadines and Grenada.
C. St Kitts/Nevis, Jamaica and Barbados.
D. St Lucia and Jamaica and St Vincent and the Grenadines.

38. The 'Executive Presidency' is a political office in which Commonwealth Caribbean country.
A. Trinidad and Tobago.
B. The Bahamas.
C. Guyana.
D. Dominica.
E. Jamaica.

39. The political system in the Commonwealth Caribbean can best be described as:
A. A parliamentary system.
B. A presidential system.
C. An authoritarian system.
D. A democratic system.

40. Which of the following is not a power of regional Prime Ministers?
A. To dissolve parliament.
B. To dismiss members of the opposition parliamentarians.
C. To appoint cabinet ministers.
D. To call general elections.

41. The following countries in the Commonwealth Caribbean attempted a non-capitalist path to development between the 1970s and 1980s:
A. Jamaica, Grenada and Guyana.
B. Guyana, Cuba and Grenada.
C. Grenada, Cuba and Jamaica.
D. Jamaica, Grenada and Trinidad and Tobago.

42. Presidentialism refers to_____ while parliamentarism refers to_____.
A. A constitutional structure which is marked by fusion of power and the direct or direct- like elections of the head of state; a constitutional system in which the head of Government depends on legislative confidence and the equal strength of its bicameral legislature.
B. A constitutional structure in which the head of Government is directly or direct- like elected to office, enjoys a fixed term of office and the perfectly symmetrical relationship between the two legislative arms of government; a constitutional structure in which the head of government is dependent on the support of the legislature, the head of government is selected by the legislature, and the bicameral legislature is of unequal strength.
C. A constitutional structure in which there is shared leadership and in which the president is popularly elected; a constitutional system in which the head of state checks the head of government, and in which there is a strong division of power and effective checks and balances.
D. An autocratic and rigid political system, a democratic and flexible political system.

43. The non-capitalist development philosophy experienced in Jamaica between the 1970s and early 1980s was called:
A. Socialist democracy experiment.
B. Cooperative Socialism.
C. Democratic Socialism.
D. Revolutionary Democracy.

44. The Non-capitalist development strategy pursued in the Caribbean did NOT consist of the:
A. Nationalisation of foreign enterprises.
B. Development of a tri-sectoral national economic structure of private, public and cooperative sectors.
C. Promotion of education and participation as a means of engendering a new political culture and attitudes.
D. Forging of closer imperialist ties in its foreign relations.

45. Which of the following provisions are included in the WTO's, MFN (Most Favoured Nation) principle.
    i. Preferential treatment granted in the context of regional agreements.
    ii. Non-discrimination in trade.
    iii. Cross border trade between Mexico, the US and Canada.
    iv. Parity with NAFTA.
    A. i only.
    B. i, iii and iv.
    C. iii only.
    D. i and ii.

46. The New Cuban Democratic Act provided for:
    A. Greater links between the Commonwealth Caribbean and Cuba.
    B. Cross border trading between Cuba and the United States.
    C. Increased restrictions on Cuba by the United States.
    D. The strengthening of international sanctions against Cuba.

47. The most politically relevant aspect of the Maritime and Drug Enforcement Agreement (Ship-riders Agreement) is the resultant:
    A. Protection of Caribbean countries from drug traffickers.
    B. Reduction in the sovereignty of Caribbean states.
    C. Empowerment of Caribbean Security Officers against drug traffickers.
    D. Limitation of the role of Caribbean nation-states to effectively patrol their own territorial waters.

48. All of the following except_____ contribute to an environment which is conducive to deepening and widening the regional integration Movement.
    A. Small geographical area, small population and otherwise closed systems with respect to natural resources.
    B. Unbalanced economies.
    C. Sweeping global market changes.
    D. Geopolitical vulnerability in light of international criminal activity.
    E. Fragmentation.

49. The establishment of a single currency is the goal of:
    A. Federal system of government
    B. A strong monetary union
    C. A customs trade area
    D. A free trade area
    E. None of the above.

50. The term widening regional integration refers to the process by which:

A. Commonwealth Caribbean countries increasingly place obstacles in the way of integration.
B. Commonwealth Caribbean countries deepen the regional integration agenda.
C. Non Commonwealth Caribbean states are included into the regional agenda.
D. The establishment of a CARICOM Single Market and Economy.

51. Which of the following is not an imperative of contemporary regional integration:
    A. Economic crisis of the 1990s.
    B. Excessive dependency on foreign aid, assistance and capital.
    C. Narco-trafficking and production.
    D. Defeating colonialism.

Bibliography

Alexis, Francis, *Changing Caribbean Constitutions* (Bridgetown: Carib Research Publishers Inc., 1995).

McHale, Andrew, 'The New International Economic Environment: The WTO and Implications for the OECS', *Journal Of Eastern Caribbean Studies*, vol. 24(2), June: 69–95, (1999).

Anthony, Kenny D., 'Caribbean Integration: The Future Relationship Between Barbados and the OECS', *Journal Of Eastern Caribbean Studies*, vol. 23(1), March: 35–50, (1998).

Lijphart, Arend, *Democracies: Patterns of Majoritarian and Consensus Government in Twenty-One Countries* (New Haven: Yale University Press, 1984).

Arthur, O., 'Prospects for Caribbean Political Unity', *Journal of Eastern Caribbean Studies*, vol. 23(1), March: 27–34, (1998).

Augier, R., '1865 Before and After', in H. Beckles and V. Shepherd, eds., *Caribbean Freedom: Economy and Society From Emancipation to the Present* (Kingston: Ian Randle Publishers, 1993).

Barrow, C., *Political Developments and Foreign Affairs of a Mini-State, A Case Study of St Lucia 1979–1987*, masters thesis (Jamaica: Mona Campus, Consortium Graduate School of Social Sciences, 1993).

Barrow-Giles, C., 'The 1997 Vote in St Lucia: The Beginning of a New Era?', *The Journal of Caribbean History*, vol. 32:1 and 2: 145–60, (1998).

Barrow-Giles, C. and Farley, J., 'Barbadian Perception on Closer Collaboration with the Organisation of Eastern Caribbean States (OECS): The Barbados-OECS Initiative', *Journal of Eastern Caribbean Studies*, vol. 24(2) June: 43–68, (1999).

Barry, T., B. Wood, and D. Preusch, *The Other Side of Paradise: Foreign Control in the Caribbean* (New York: Grove Press Inc., 1984).

Beckford, George and N. Girvan, *Development in Suspense* (Kingston: Friedrich, Ebert Stiftung, 1989).

Belle, George, A.V., 'Against Colonialism: Political Theory and Recolonisation in the Caribbean', paper presented at the conference on Caribbean culture, Jamaica, Mona Campus, March 3–5, (1996).

Berman, B., 'Clientelism and Neo-Colonialism: Centre-Periphery relations and Political Development in African States', *Studies in Comparative International Development*, vol. 15(1), (1974).

Bertsch, Gary K., et al., *Comparing Political Systems: Power and Policy in Three Worlds* (New York: Macmillan Publishing, 1991).

Blondel, Jean, ed., *Comparative Government: A Reader* (London: Macmillan Publishing, 1969).

Benn, D., *The Growth and Development of Political Ideas in the Caribbean* (Kingston: University of the West Indies, 1987).

Bolland, O. Nigel, *On the March: Labour Rebellions in the British Caribbean, 1934-39,* (Kingston: Ian Randle Publishers, 1995).

Bolland, O. Nigel, *The Politics of Labour in the British Caribbean* (Kingston: Ian Randle Publishers, 2001).

Boxill, I., *Ideology and Caribbean Integration* (Kingston: Consortium Graduate School of Social Sciences, 1993).

Bryan, Anthony T., ed., *The Caribbean New Dynamics in Trade and Political Economy* (Miami: North-South Center Press, 1995).

Castaneda, Jorge G., 'Democracy and Inequality in Latin America: A Tension of the Times', in Jorge I. Dominguez and Abraham F. Lowenthal, eds., *Constructing Democratic Governance: Latin America and the Caribbean in the 1990s – Themes and Issues,* (London: The John Hopkins University Press, 1996).

Castro, Fidel, *The World Crisis: Its Economic and Social Impact on the Underdeveloped Countries* (London: Zed Books Ltd., 1984).

Cox, Gary W., *Making Votes Count: Strategic Coordination in the World's Economic System* (Cambridge: Cambridge University Press, 1997).

Craig, S., *Smiles and Blood: The Ruling Class Response to Workers Rebellion in Trinidad and Tobago* (London: New Beacon Books, 1988).

Cutis, M. and J. Blondel, et al., *Introduction to Comparative Government: A Reader*, 2nd edition (New York: Harper Collins Publishers Inc., 1990).

Dahl, Robert A., *On Democracy* (London: Yale University Press, 1998).

Demas, William G., *Critical Issues in Caribbean Development: West Indian Development and the Deepening and Widening of the Caribbean Community* (Kingston: Ian Randle Publishers, 1997).

Desch, Michael C., Jorge I. Dominguez and Andres Serbin, eds., *From Pirates to Drug lords : The Post Cold-war Caribbean Security Environment* (New York: State University of New York Press, 1998).

Domhoff, G.W., *Who Rules America?* (New Jersey: Prentice Hall Inc., 1967).

Dominiguez, Jorge I., Robert A. Pastor and R. Deslisle Worrell, eds., *Democracy in the Caribbean: Political, Economic and Social Perspectives* (London: The Johns Hopkins University Press, 1993).

Duncan, N.C., ed., *Caribbean Integration: The OECS Experience Revisited* (Kingston: Friedrich, Ebert Stiftung 1995).

Duncan, N.C., ed., *Mechanisms of Impoverishment in Anglophone Caribbean: The Role of the Bretton Woods Institutions and the Recommendation of Caribbean NGOs,* (Kingston: FES, 1995).

Duncan, N.C., 'Barbados and the IMF – A Case Study', in John La Guerre, ed., *Structural Adjustment: Public Policy and Administration in the Caribbean* (Port of Spain: University of the West Indies, 1994).

Duncan, N.C., 'Barbados: Democracy at the Crossroads', in Carlene J. Edie, ed., *Democracy in the Caribbean: Myths and Realities* (London: Praeger, 1994).

Duncan, N.C., 'Changes in International Relations: Challenges and Options for the Caribbean', in L. Searwar, ed., *Diplomacy for Survival: CARICOM States in a World of Change* (Kingston: Friedrich, Ebert Stiftung, 1991).

Dunn, Hopeton S., ed., *Globalization, Communication and Caribbean Identity* (Kingston: Ian Randle Publishers, 1995).

Edie, C., *Democracy in the Caribbean: Myths and realities* (Westport: Praeger, 1994).

Emmanuel, P. A. M., ed., *The Ombudsman: Caribbean and International Perspectives* (Bridgetown: Institute of Social and Economic Research, 1993).

Emmanuel, P. A. M., *Governance and Democracy in the Commonwealth Caribbean,* (Bridgetown: Institute of Social and Economic Research, 1993).

Emmanuel, P. A. M., *Elections and Party Systems in the Commonwealth Caribbean 1944-1991* (Bridgetown: Caribbean Development Research Services, 1991).

Emmanuel, P. A. M., *Approaches to Caribbean Integration*, Occasional Paper (21), (Bridgetown: Institute of Social and Economic Research, 1987).

Fanon, F., *The Wretched of the Earth* (New York: Grove Press, 1968).

Farrell, Terrence and Worrell Delisle, eds., *Caribbean Monetary Integration* (Port of Spain: Caribbean Information Systems and Services Ltd., 1994).

Finer, S. E., *Comparative Government: An Introduction to the Study of Politics* (London: Penguin Books Press, 1970).

Gonsalves, Ralph E., *The Spectre of Imperialism: The Case of the Caribbean* (Mimeo).

Gonsalves, Ralph E., *History and the Future: A Caribbean Perspective* (Kingstown: Quick-Print, 1994).

Gonsalves, Ralph E., 'The Trade Union Movement in Jamaica: Its Growth and Some Resultant Problems', in Carl Stone and Aggrey Brown, eds., *Essays on Power and Change in Jamaica* (Kingston: Jamaica Publishing House, 1977).

Griffith, I.V., *Drugs and security in the Caribbean: Sovereignty Under siege*, (Pennsylvania: Pennsylvania State University Press, 1997).

Hall, Kenneth and Denis Benn, eds., *Contending with Destiny: The Caribbean in the 21ˢᵗ Century* (Kingston: Ian Randle Publishers, 2000).

Hamid, Ghany, 'Commonwealth Caribbean Presidencies: New Directions in the Exercise of State Power', in La Guerre John, ed., *Issues in the Government and Politics in the West Indies: A Reader* (St Augustine: School of Continuing Studies, 1997).

Heine, Jorge, ed., *A Revolution Aborted: The Lessons of Grenada* (Pittsburgh: The University of Pittsburgh Press, 1991).

Hoogvelt, Ankie, *Globalisation and the Postcolonial World: The New Political Economy of Development* (London: Macmillan Press, 1997).

Hoogvelt, Ankie, 'IMF Crime in Conditionality: An Open Letter to the Managing Director of the International Monetary Fund', *Monthly Review*, vol. 39, May, (1987).

Hufbauer, G.C. and J.J. Schott, *North American Free Trade: Issues and recommendations* (Washington: Institute for International Economics, 1992).

Huntington, Samuel P., *The Third Wave: Democratisation in the Late Twentieth Century*, (Oklahoma: University of Oklahoma Press, 1974).

Huntington, Samuel P., *Political Order in changing Societies* (London: Yale University Press, 1968).

Jamadhar, Peter A., *The Mechanics of Democracy: Proportional Representation vs First Past the Post* (Port of Spain: Inprint Caribbean Ltd., 1989).

James, C.L.R., *Party Politics in the West Indies* (Port of Spain: Inprint Caribbean Ltd., 1984).

James, R. and H. Lutchman, *Law and the Political Environment in Guyana* (Georgetown: Institute of Development Studies, 1984).

Kaufman, M., *Jamaica Under Manley: Dilemmas of Socialism and Democracy* (London: Zed Books Ltd., 1985).

Klak, Thomas, *Globalization and Neoliberalism: The Caribbean Context* (Boston: Rowman and Littlefield Publishers Inc., 1998).

Kwame, N., *Towards Colonial Freedom: Africa in the Struggle Against World Imperialism* (London: Panaf, 1973).

LaGuerre J.G., *Issues in the Government and Politics of the West Indies: A Reader* (St Augustine: School of Continuing Studies, 1997).

LaGuerre J.G., ed., *The General Elections of 1995 in Trinidad and Tobago* (St Augustine: School of Continuing Studies, 1997).

LaGuerre J.G., ed., *Structural Adjustment: Public Policy and Administration in the Caribbean* (St Augustine; School of Continuing Studies, 1994).

Lenin, V.I., *Imperialism: The Highest Stage of Capitalism a Popular Outline* (New York: International Publishers, 1939).

Levi, D.E., *Michael Manley: The Making of a Leader* (Heinemann Publishers [Caribbean] Ltd., 1989).

Lewis, A.W., 'The Agony of the Eight', *Journal of Eastern Caribbean Studies*, vol. 23(1), March: 6–26, (1998).

Lewis, A.W., *Labour in the West Indies: The Birth of Workers Movement*, (London: New Beacon Books 1977).

Lewis, A.W., 'The 1930s Social Revolution', in H. Beckles and V. Shepherd, eds., *Caribbean Freedom: Economy and Society from Emancipation to the Present* (Kingston: Ian Randle Publishers, 1993).

Lewis, G. K., *Grenada: The Jewel Despoiled* (London: The John Hopkins University Press, 1987).

Lewis, G. K., *The Growth of the Modern West Indies* (New York: Monthly Review Press, 1968).

Lewis, L., 'The Politics of Race in Barbados', *Bulletin of Eastern Caribbean Affairs*, vol. 16(6), Jan./Feb., (Bridgetown: Institute of Social and Economic Research, 1990).

Lewis, L. and L. Nurse, 'Caribbean Trade Unionism and Global Restructuring', in Hilbourne Watson, ed., *The Caribbean in the Global Political Economy* (Kingston: Ian Randle Publishers, 1994).

Lintz, Juan D., 'The Perils of Presidentialism', in Arend Lijphart, ed., *Parliamentary Versus Presidential Government* (London: Oxford University Press, 1992).

Lutchman, H. A., 'A The Westminster System in the Commonwealth Caribbean: Some Issues and Problems', *Transition*, issue 24, February:1–26, (1995).

Manley, M., *The Politics of Change: A Jamaican Testimony* (London: Andre Deutsch Ltd., 1994).

Manley, M., *Jamaica: Struggle in the Periphery* (Oxford: Third World Ltd., 1982).

Mainwaring, S., *Rethinking Party Systems in the Third Wave of Democratisation: The Case of Brazil* (Stanford: Stanford University Press, 1999).

Mason, Mike, *Development and Disorder: A History of the Third World since 1945* (Toronto: Between the Lines, 1997).

McAfee, K., *Storm Signals: Structural Adjustment and Development Alternatives in the Caribbean* (London: Zed Books Ltd., 1991).

Miliband, R., *The State in Capitalist Society: An Analysis of the Western System of Power* (London: Quartet, 1973).

Millett, J., *The Genesis of Crown Colony Government in Trinidad* (Port of Spain: Moko Enterprises, 1970).

Mills, Gladstone, *Westminster Style Democracy: The Jamaican Experience* (Kingston: Grace Kennedy Foundation, 1997).

Moonilal, Roodal, 'Structural Adjustment, Union Busting and the Future of Trade Unions', in J. La Guerre, ed., *Structural Adjustment: Public Policy and Administration in the Caribbean* (Port of Spain: University of the West Indies, 1997).

Mordecai, John, *The West Indies: The Federal Negotiations* (London: Allen & Unwin, 1968).

Munroe, T., *Renewing Democracy into the Millennium: The Jamaican Experience in Perspective* (Kingston: The UWI Press, 1999).

Munroe, T., *The Politics of Constitutional Decolonization – Jamaica 1944-62* (Kingston: Institute of Social and Economic Research, 1983).

Munroe, T. and R. Lewis, eds., *Readings in Government and Politics of the West Indies* (Kingston: Department of Government, Mona Campus, 1971).

Panton, David, *Jamaica's Michael Manley: The Great Transformation (1972-1992)*, (Kingston: Kingston Publishers, 1993).

Parenti, Michael, *Democracy For The Few* (New York: St Martin's Press Inc., 1988).

Payer, C., *The Debt Trap: The International Monetary Fund and the Third World* (New York: Monthly Review Press, 1974).

Phillip, D.E.A., 'The Increasing Emphasis on Security and Defense in the Eastern Caribbean', in A. Young and D. Phillips, eds., *Militarisation in the Non-Hispanic Caribbean* (Boulder: Lynne Rienner Publishers Inc., 1988).

Post, Ken, *Strike the Iron: A Colony at War Jamaica 1939–1945,* vol. 1&2 (New Jersey: Humanities Press Inc., 1981).

Raghavan, Chakravarthi, *Recolonialization: GATT, the Uruguay Round and the Third World* (London: Zed Books Ltd., 1980).

Report of the Commission to Enquire into the Disturbances (The Deane Commission Report, 1937).

Report of the Constitution Review Commission 1998 (Bridgetown: Barbados).

Report of the West Indies Royal Commission, 1938–1939 (The Royal Commission Report).

Rodney, Walter, *How Europe Underdeveloped Africa* (London: Bogle-L'Ouverture Publications, 1972).

Ryan, Selwyn, *Winner Takes All: The Westminster Experience in the Caribbean* (St Augustine: Institute of Social and Economic Research, 1999).

Ryan, Selwyn, *Race and Nationalism in Trinidad and Tobago: A Study of Decolonisation in a Multiracial Society* (Toronto: University of Toronto Press, 1972).

Sartori, Giovanni, *Comparing Constitutional Engineering: An Inquiry into Structures, Incentives and Outcomes,* 2nd edition (London: Macmillan Press Ltd., 1997).

Schumpeter, Joseph, *Capitalism, Socialism and Democracy* (New York: Harper, 1947).

Spackman, Ann, *Constitutional Development of the West Indies 1922-1968: A Selection from the Major Documents* (Bridgetown: Caribbean University Press, 1975).

Stone, Carl, 'Wither Caribbean Socialism? Grenada, Jamaica and Guyana in Perspective', in Jorge Heine, ed., *A Revolution Aborted: The Lessons of Grenada* (Pittsburgh: The University of Pittsburgh Press, 1990).

Stone, C. and A. Brown, eds., *Essays on Power and Change in Jamaica* (Kingston: Jamaica Publishing House, 1977).

Thomas, C.Y., *The Poor and the Powerless: Economic Policy and Change in the Caribbean* (London: Latin American Bureau, 1988).

Venner, D., 'Prospects for a United Caribbean in the New International Economic Order', A paper presented at the 1996 Annual Lecture to the West India Committee, London, (1996).

Walters, R.S. and D. H. Blake, *The Politics of Global Economic Relations*, 4th edition (London: Prentice Hall Inc., 1992).

Watson, H.A., *The Caribbean in the Global Political Economy* (Kingston: Ian Randle Publishers, 1994).

Watson, H.A., 'The Changing Structure of World Capital and Development Options in the Caribbean', in H. Watson and F. Fröbel, eds., *The Future of the Caribbean in the World System* (Kingston: University of the West Indies, 1988).

Watts, R.L., *New Federations: Experiments in the Commonwealth* (Oxford: Clarendon Press, 1968).

West Indian Commission, *Modern Constitutions* (New York: Oxford University Press, 1951).

West Indian Commission, *Time for Action Report* (Kingston: The UWI Press, 1992).

Wheare, K.C., *Federal Government*, 4th edition (New York: Oxford University Press, 1963).

Wickham, Peter, *Prospects for a United Caribbean: A Historico-Political Analysis of the Future of the Caribbean*, master's thesis, (Bridgetown: Cave Hill Campus, UWI, 1994).

Witter, M., 'Exchange Rate Policy in Jamaica: A Critical Assessment', *Social and Economic Studies*, vol. 32 (4) (1983).

Wooding Commission Report, 1974 – Trinidad and Tobago.